Physics
for the IB Diploma
Sixth Edition

K. A. Tsokos

Cambridge University Press's mission is to advance learning, knowledge and research worldwide.

Our IB Diploma resources aim to:
- encourage learners to explore concepts, ideas and topics that have local and global significance
- help students develop a positive attitude to learning in preparation for higher education
- assist students in approaching complex questions, applying critical-thinking skills and forming reasoned answers.

CAMBRIDGE
UNIVERSITY PRESS

University Printing House, Cambridge CB2 8BS, United Kingdom

One Liberty Plaza, 20th Floor, New York, NY 10006, USA

477 Williamstown Road, Port Melbourne, VIC 3207, Australia

314–321, 3rd Floor, Plot 3, Splendor Forum, Jasola District Centre, New Delhi – 110025, India

103 Penang Road, #05-06/07, Visioncrest Commercial, Singapore 238467

Cambridge University Press is part of the University of Cambridge.

It furthers the University's mission by disseminating knowledge in the pursuit of education, learning and research at the highest international levels of excellence.

www.cambridge.org
Information on this title: www.cambridge.org/9781107628199

First, second and third editions © K. A. Tsokos 1998, 1999, 2001
Fourth, fifth, fifth (full colour) and sixth editions © Cambridge University Press 2005, 2008, 2010, 2014

This publication is in copyright. Subject to statutory exception and to the provisions of relevant collective licensing agreements, no reproduction of any part may take place without the written permission of Cambridge University Press.

First published 1998
Second edition 1999
Third edition 2001
Fourth edition published by Cambridge University Press 2005
Fifth edition 2008
Fifth edition (full colour version) 2010
Sixth edition 2014

20 19 18 17 16 15

Printed in Poland by Opolgraf

A catalogue record for this publication is available from the British Library

ISBN 978-1-107-62819-9 Paperback
ISBN 978-1-107-53787-3 Cambridge Elevate enhanced edition (2 years)
ISBN 978-1-316-63777-7 Paperback + Cambridge Elevate enhanced edition (2 years)

Additional resources for this publication at cambridge.org/ibsciences

Cambridge University Press has no responsibility for the persistence or accuracy of URLs for external or third-party internet websites referred to in this publication, and does not guarantee that any content on such websites is, or will remain, accurate or appropriate. Information regarding prices, travel timetables, and other factual information given in this work is correct at the time of first printing but Cambridge University Press does not guarantee the accuracy of such information thereafter.

The material has been developed independently by the publisher and the content is in no way connected with nor endorsed by the International Baccalaureate Organization.

NOTICE TO TEACHERS IN THE UK
It is illegal to reproduce any part of this book in material form (including photocopying and electronic storage) except under the following circumstances:
(i) where you are abiding by a licence granted to your school or institution by the Copyright Licensing Agency;
(ii) where no such licence exists, or where you wish to exceed the terms of a licence, and you have gained the written permission of Cambridge University Press;
(iii) where you are allowed to reproduce without permission under the provisions of Chapter 3 of the Copyright, Designs and Patents Act 1988, which covers, for example, the reproduction of short passages within certain types of educational anthology and reproduction for the purposes of setting examination questions.

The website accompanying this book contains further resources to support your IB Physics studies.
Visit cambridge.org/ibsciences and register for access.

Separate website terms and conditions apply.

Contents

Introduction	**v**
Note from the author	vi

1 Measurements and uncertainties — 1
1.1 Measurement in physics — 1
1.2 Uncertainties and errors — 7
1.3 Vectors and scalars — 21
Exam-style questions — 32

2 Mechanics — 35
2.1 Motion — 35
2.2 Forces — 57
2.3 Work, energy and power — 78
2.4 Momentum and impulse — 98
Exam-style questions — 110

3 Thermal physics — 116
3.1 Thermal concepts — 116
3.2 Modelling a gas — 126
Exam-style questions — 142

4 Waves — 146
4.1 Oscillations — 146
4.2 Travelling waves — 153
4.3 Wave characteristics — 162
4.4 Wave behaviour — 172
4.5 Standing waves — 182
Exam-style questions — 190

5 Electricity and magnetism — 196
5.1 Electric fields — 196
5.2 Heating effect of electric currents — 207
5.3 Electric cells — 227
5.4 Magnetic fields — 232
Exam-style questions — 243

6 Circular motion and gravitation — 249
6.1 Circular motion — 249
6.2 The law of gravitation — 259
Exam-style questions — 265

7 Atomic, nuclear and particle physics — 270
7.1 Discrete energy and radioactivity — 270
7.2 Nuclear reactions — 285
7.3 The structure of matter — 295
Exam-style questions — 309

8 Energy production — 314
8.1 Energy sources — 314
8.2 Thermal energy transfer — 329
Exam-style questions — 340

9 Wave phenomena (HL) — 346
9.1 Simple harmonic motion — 346
9.2 Single-slit diffraction — 361
9.3 Interference — 365
9.4 Resolution — 376
9.5 The Doppler effect — 381
Exam-style questions — 390

10 Fields (HL) — 396
10.1 Describing fields — 396
10.2 Fields at work — 415
Exam-style questions — 428

11 Electromagnetic induction (HL) — 434
11.1 Electromagnetic induction — 434
11.2 Transmission of power — 444
11.3 Capacitance — 457
Exam-style questions — 473

12 Quantum and nuclear physics (HL) — 481
12.1 The interaction of matter with radiation — 481
12.2 Nuclear physics — 505
Exam-style questions — 517

Appendices   **524**
1 Physical constants   524
2 Masses of elements and selected isotopes   525
3 Some important mathematical results   527

Answers to Test yourself questions   **528**

Glossary   **544**

Index   **551**

Credits   **559**

Free online material

The website accompanying this book contains further resources to support your IB Physics studies. Visit **education.cambridge.org/ibsciences** and register to access these resources:

Options

Option A Relativity

Option B Engineering physics

Option C Imaging

Option D Astrophysics

Additional Topic questions to accompany coursebook

Detailed answers to all coursebook test yourself questions

Self-test questions

Assessment guidance

Model exam papers

Nature of Science

Answers to exam-style questions

Answers to Options questions

Answers to additional Topic questions

Options glossary

Appendices

A Astronomical data

B Nobel prize winners in physics

Introduction

This sixth edition of *Physics for the IB Diploma* is fully updated to cover the content of the IB Physics Diploma syllabus that will be examined in the years 2016–2022.

Physics may be studied at Standard Level (SL) or Higher Level (HL). Both share a common core, which is covered in Topics 1–8. At HL the core is extended to include Topics 9–12. In addition, at both levels, students then choose one Option to complete their studies. Each option consists of common core and additional Higher Level material. You can identify the HL content in this book by 'HL' included in the topic title (or section title in the Options), and by the red page border. The four Options are included in the free online material that is accessible using education.cambridge.org/ibsciences.

The structure of this book follows the structure of the IB Physics syllabus. Each topic in the book matches a syllabus topic, and the sections within each topic mirror the sections in the syllabus. Each section begins with learning objectives as starting and reference points. Worked examples are included in each section; understanding these examples is crucial to performing well in the exam. A large number of test yourself questions are included at the end of each section and each topic ends with exam-style questions. The reader is strongly encouraged to do as many of these questions as possible. Numerical answers to the test yourself questions are provided at the end of the book; detailed solutions to all questions are available on the website. Some topics have additional questions online; these are indicated with the online symbol, shown here.

Theory of Knowledge (TOK) provides a cross-curricular link between different subjects. It stimulates thought about critical thinking and how we can say we know what we claim to know. Throughout this book, TOK features highlight concepts in Physics that can be considered from a TOK perspective. These are indicated by the 'TOK' logo, shown here.

Science is a truly international endeavour, being practised across all continents, frequently in international or even global partnerships. Many problems that science aims to solve are international, and will require globally implemented solutions. Throughout this book, International-Mindedness features highlight international concerns in Physics. These are indicated by the 'International-Mindedness' logo, shown here.

Nature of science is an overarching theme of the Physics course. The theme examines the processes and concepts that are central to scientific endeavour, and how science serves and connects with the wider community. At the end of each section in this book, there is a 'Nature of science' paragraph that discusses a particular concept or discovery from the point of view of one or more aspects of Nature of science. A chapter giving a general introduction to the Nature of science theme is available in the free online material.

Free online material

Additional material to support the IB Physics Diploma course is available online. Visit education.cambridge.org/ibsciences and register to access these resources.

Besides the Options and Nature of science chapter, you will find a collection of resources to help with revision and exam preparation. This includes guidance on the assessments, additional Topic questions, interactive self-test questions and model examination papers and mark schemes. Additionally, answers to the exam-style questions in this book and to all the questions in the Options are available.

Note from the author

This book is dedicated to Alexios and Alkeos and to the memory of my parents.

I have received help from a number of students at ACS Athens in preparing some of the questions included in this book. These include Konstantinos Damianakis, Philip Minaretzis, George Nikolakoudis, Katayoon Khoshragham, Kyriakos Petrakos, Majdi Samad, Stavroula Stathopoulou, Constantine Tragakes and Rim Versteeg. I sincerely thank them all for the invaluable help.

I owe an enormous debt of gratitude to Anne Trevillion, the editor of the book, for her patience, her attention to detail and for the very many suggestions she made that have improved the book substantially. Her involvement with this book exceeded the duties one ordinarily expects from an editor of a book and I thank her from my heart. I also wish to thank her for her additional work of contributing to the Nature of science themes throughout the book.

Finally, I wish to thank my wife, Ellie Tragakes, for her patience with me during the completion of this book.

K. A. Tsokos

Measurement and uncertainties 1

1.1 Measurement in physics

Physics is an experimental science in which measurements made must be expressed in units. In the international system of units used throughout this book, the SI system, there are seven fundamental units, which are defined in this section. All quantities are expressed in terms of these units directly, or as a combination of them.

The SI system

The SI system (short for Système International d'Unités) has seven **fundamental units** (it is quite amazing that only seven are required). These are:

1. The **metre** (m). This is the unit of distance. It is the distance travelled by light in a vacuum in a time of $\frac{1}{299\,792\,458}$ seconds.
2. The **kilogram** (kg). This is the unit of mass. It is the mass of a certain quantity of a platinum–iridium alloy kept at the Bureau International des Poids et Mesures in France.
3. The **second** (s). This is the unit of time. A second is the duration of 9 192 631 770 full oscillations of the electromagnetic radiation emitted in a transition between the two hyperfine energy levels in the ground state of a caesium-133 atom.
4. The **ampere** (A). This is the unit of electric current. It is defined as that current which, when flowing in two parallel conductors 1 m apart, produces a force of 2×10^7 N on a length of 1 m of the conductors.
5. The **kelvin** (K). This is the unit of temperature. It is $\frac{1}{273.16}$ of the thermodynamic temperature of the triple point of water.
6. The **mole** (mol). One mole of a substance contains as many particles as there are atoms in 12 g of carbon-12. This special number of particles is called Avogadro's number and is approximately 6.02×10^{23}.
7. The **candela** (cd). This is a unit of luminous intensity. It is the intensity of a source of frequency 5.40×10^{14} Hz emitting $\frac{1}{683}$ W per steradian.

You do not need to memorise the details of these definitions.

In this book we will use all of the basic units except the last one. Physical quantities other than those above have units that are combinations of the seven fundamental units. They have **derived** units. For example, speed has units of distance over time, metres per second (i.e. m/s or, preferably, $m\,s^{-1}$). Acceleration has units of metres per second squared (i.e. m/s^2, which we write as $m\,s^{-2}$). Similarly, the unit of force is the newton (N). It equals the combination $kg\,m\,s^{-2}$. Energy, a very important quantity in physics, has the joule (J) as its unit. The joule is the combination N m and so equals $(kg\,m\,s^{-2}\,m)$, or $kg\,m^2\,s^{-2}$. The quantity

Learning objectives

- State the fundamental units of the SI system.
- Be able to express numbers in scientific notation.
- Appreciate the order of magnitude of various quantities.
- Perform simple order-of-magnitude calculations mentally.
- Express results of calculations to the correct number of significant figures.

power has units of energy per unit of time, and so is measured in Js^{-1}. This combination is called a watt. Thus:

$$1\,W = (1\,N\,m\,s^{-1}) = (1\,kg\,m\,s^{-2}\,m\,s^{-1}) = 1\,kg\,m^2\,s^{-3}$$

Metric multipliers

Small or large quantities can be expressed in terms of units that are related to the basic ones by powers of 10. Thus, a nanometre (nm) is 10^{-9} m, a microgram (µg) is 10^{-6} g = 10^{-9} kg, a gigaelectron volt (GeV) equals 10^9 eV, etc. The most common prefixes are given in Table **1.1**.

Power	Prefix	Symbol	Power	Prefix	Symbol
10^{-18}	atto-	A	10^1	deka-	da
10^{-15}	femto-	F	10^2	hecto-	h
10^{-12}	pico-	p	10^3	kilo-	k
10^{-9}	nano-	n	10^6	mega-	M
10^{-6}	micro-	µ	10^9	giga-	G
10^{-3}	milli-	m	10^{12}	tera-	T
10^{-2}	centi-	c	10^{15}	peta-	P
10^{-1}	deci-	d	10^{18}	exa-	E

Table 1.1 Common prefixes in the SI system.

Orders of magnitude and estimates

Expressing a quantity as a plain power of 10 gives what is called the **order of magnitude** of that quantity. Thus, the mass of the universe has an order of magnitude of 10^{53} kg and the mass of the Milky Way galaxy has an order of magnitude of 10^{41} kg. The ratio of the two masses is then simply 10^{12}.

Tables **1.2**, **1.3** and **1.4** give examples of distances, masses and times, given as orders of magnitude.

	Length / m
distance to edge of observable universe	10^{26}
distance to the Andromeda galaxy	10^{22}
diameter of the Milky Way galaxy	10^{21}
distance to nearest star	10^{16}
diameter of the solar system	10^{13}
distance to the Sun	10^{11}
radius of the Earth	10^7
size of a cell	10^{-5}
size of a hydrogen atom	10^{-10}
size of an $A=50$ nucleus	10^{-15}
size of a proton	10^{-15}
Planck length	10^{-35}

Table 1.2 Some interesting distances.

	Mass / kg
the universe	10^{53}
the Milky Way galaxy	10^{41}
the Sun	10^{30}
the Earth	10^{24}
Boeing 747 (empty)	10^{5}
an apple	0.2
a raindrop	10^{-6}
a bacterium	10^{-15}
smallest virus	10^{-21}
a hydrogen atom	10^{-27}
an electron	10^{-30}

Table 1.3 Some interesting masses.

	Time / s
age of the universe	10^{17}
age of the Earth	10^{17}
time of travel by light to nearby star	10^{8}
one year	10^{7}
one day	10^{5}
period of a heartbeat	1
lifetime of a pion	10^{-8}
lifetime of the omega particle	10^{-10}
time of passage of light across a proton	10^{-24}

Table 1.4 Some interesting times.

Worked examples

1.1 Estimate how many grains of sand are required to fill the volume of the Earth. (This is a classic problem that goes back to Aristotle. The radius of the Earth is about 6×10^6 m.)

The volume of the Earth is:

$$\tfrac{4}{3}\pi R^3 \approx \tfrac{4}{3} \times 3 \times (6 \times 10^6)^3 \approx 8 \times 10^{20} \approx 10^{21}\, \text{m}^3$$

The diameter of a grain of sand varies of course, but we will take 1 mm as a fair estimate. The volume of a grain of sand is about $(1 \times 10^{-3})^3$ m^3.

Then the number of grains of sand required to fill the Earth is:

$$\frac{10^{21}}{(1 \times 10^{-3})^3} \approx 10^{30}$$

1.2 Estimate the speed with which human hair grows.

I have my hair cut every two months and the barber cuts a length of about 2 cm. The speed is therefore:

$$\frac{2 \times 10^{-2}}{2 \times 30 \times 24 \times 60 \times 60}\, \text{m s}^{-1} \approx \frac{10^{-2}}{3 \times 2 \times 36 \times 10^4}$$

$$\approx \frac{10^{-6}}{6 \times 40} = \frac{10^{-6}}{240}$$

$$\approx 4 \times 10^{-9}\, \text{m s}^{-1}$$

1 MEASUREMENT AND UNCERTAINTIES

1.3 Estimate how long the line would be if all the people on Earth were to hold hands in a straight line. Calculate how many times it would wrap around the Earth at the equator. (The radius of the Earth is about 6×10^6 m.)

Assume that each person has his or her hands stretched out to a distance of 1.5 m and that the population of Earth is 7×10^9 people.

Then the length of the line of people would be $7 \times 10^9 \times 1.5 \, \text{m} = 10^{10}$ m.

The circumference of the Earth is $2\pi R \approx 6 \times 6 \times 10^6 \, \text{m} \approx 4 \times 10^7$ m.

So the line would wrap $\dfrac{10^{10}}{4 \times 10^7} \approx 250$ times around the equator.

1.4 Estimate how many apples it takes to have a combined mass equal to that of an ordinary family car.

Assume that an apple has a mass of 0.2 kg and a car has a mass of 1400 kg.

Then the number of apples is $\dfrac{1400}{0.2} = 7 \times 10^3$.

1.5 Estimate the time it takes light to arrive at Earth from the Sun. (The Earth–Sun distance is 1.5×10^{11} m.)

The time taken is $\dfrac{\text{distance}}{\text{speed}} = \dfrac{1.5 \times 10^{11}}{3 \times 10^8} \approx 0.5 \times 10^4 = 500 \, \text{s} \approx 8 \, \text{min}$

Significant figures

The **number** of digits used to express a number carries information about how precisely the number is known. A stopwatch reading of 3.2 s (two significant figures, s.f.) is less precise than a reading of 3.23 s (three s.f.). If you are told what your salary is going to be, you would like that number to be known as precisely as possible. It is less satisfying to be told that your salary will be 'about 1000' (1 s.f.) euro a month compared to a salary of 'about 1250' (3 s.f.) euro a month. Not because 1250 is larger than 1000 but because the number of 'about 1000' could mean anything from a low of 500 to a high of 1500. You could be lucky and get the 1500 but you cannot be sure. With a salary of 'about 1250' your actual salary could be anything from 1200 to 1300, so you have a pretty good idea of what it will be.

How to find the number of significant figures in a number is illustrated in Table **1.5**.

Number	Number of s.f.	Reason	Scientific notation
504	3	in an integer all digits count (if last digit is not zero)	5.04×10^2
608 000	3	zeros at the end of an integer do not count	6.08×10^5
200	1	zeros at the end of an integer do not count	2×10^2
0.000 305	3	zeros in front do not count	3.05×10^{-4}
0.005 900	4	zeros at the end of a decimal count, those in front do not	5.900×10^{-3}

Table 1.5 Rules for significant figures.

Scientific notation means writing a number in the form $a \times 10^b$, where a is decimal such that $1 \le a < 10$ and b is a positive or negative integer. The number of digits in a is the number of significant figures in the number.

In multiplication or division (or in raising a number to a power or taking a root), the result must have as many significant figures as the **least** precisely known number entering the calculation. So we have that:

$$\underbrace{23}_{2\text{ s.f.}} \times \underbrace{578}_{3\text{ s.f.}} = 13\,294 \approx \underbrace{1.3 \times 10^4}_{2\text{ s.f.}} \quad \text{(the least number of s.f. is shown in red)}$$

$$\frac{\underbrace{6.244}_{4\text{ s.f.}}}{\underbrace{1.25}_{3\text{ s.f.}}} = 4.9952\ldots \approx \underbrace{5.00 \times 10^0}_{3\text{ s.f.}} = 5.00$$

$$\underbrace{12.3^3}_{3\text{ s.f.}} = 1860.867\ldots \approx \underbrace{1.86 \times 10^3}_{3\text{ s.f.}}$$

$$\underbrace{\sqrt{58900}}_{3\text{ s.f.}} = 242.6932\ldots \approx \underbrace{2.43 \times 10^2}_{3\text{ s.f.}}$$

In adding and subtracting, the number of decimal digits in the answer must be equal to the least number of decimal places in the numbers added or subtracted. Thus:

$$\underbrace{3.21}_{2\text{ d.p.}} + \underbrace{4.1}_{1\text{ d.p.}} = 7.32 \approx \underbrace{7.3}_{1\text{ d.p.}} \quad \text{(the least number of d.p. is shown in red)}$$

$$\underbrace{12.367}_{3\text{ d.p.}} - \underbrace{3.15}_{2\text{ d.p.}} = 9.217 \approx \underbrace{9.22}_{2\text{ d.p.}}$$

Use the rules for rounding when writing values to the correct number of decimal places or significant figures. For example, the number $542.48 = 5.4248 \times 10^2$ rounded to 2, 3 and 4 s.f. becomes:

$5.4|248 \times 10^2 \approx 5.4 \times 10^2$ rounded to 2 s.f.
$5.42|48 \times 10^2 \approx 5.42 \times 10^2$ rounded to 3 s.f.
$5.424|8 \times 10^2 \approx 5.425 \times 10^2$ rounded to 4 s.f.

There is a special rule for rounding when the last digit to be dropped is 5 and it is followed only by zeros, or not followed by any other digit.

This is the odd–even rounding rule. For example, consider the number 3.250 000 0… where the zeros continue indefinitely. How does this number round to 2 s.f.? Because the digit before the 5 is **even** we do not round up, so 3.250 000 0… becomes 3.2. But 3.350 000 0… rounds up to 3.4 because the digit before the 5 is **odd**.

Nature of science

Early work on electricity and magnetism was hampered by the use of different systems of units in different parts of the world. Scientists realised they needed to have a common system of units in order to learn from each other's work and reproduce experimental results described by others. Following an international review of units that began in 1948, the SI system was introduced in 1960. At that time there were six base units. In 1971 the mole was added, bringing the number of base units to the seven in use today.

As the instruments used to measure quantities have developed, the definitions of standard units have been refined to reflect the greater precision possible. Using the transition of the caesium-133 atom to measure time has meant that smaller intervals of time can be measured accurately. The SI system continues to evolve to meet the demands of scientists across the world. Increasing precision in measurement allows scientists to notice smaller differences between results, but there is always uncertainty in any experimental result. There are no 'exact' answers.

? Test yourself

1 How long does light take to travel across a proton?
2 How many hydrogen atoms does it take to make up the mass of the Earth?
3 What is the age of the universe expressed in units of the Planck time?
4 How many heartbeats are there in the lifetime of a person (75 years)?
5 What is the mass of our galaxy in terms of a solar mass?
6 What is the diameter of our galaxy in terms of the astronomical unit, i.e. the distance between the Earth and the Sun (1 AU = 1.5×10^{11} m)?
7 The molar mass of water is 18 g mol^{-1}. How many molecules of water are there in a glass of water (mass of water 300 g)?
8 Assuming that the mass of a person is made up entirely of water, how many molecules are there in a human body (of mass 60 kg)?
9 Give an order-of-magnitude estimate of the density of a proton.
10 How long does light take to traverse the diameter of the solar system?
11 An electron volt (eV) is a unit of energy equal to 1.6×10^{-19} J. An electron has a kinetic energy of 2.5 eV.
   a How many joules is that?
   b What is the energy in eV of an electron that has an energy of 8.6×10^{-18} J?
12 What is the volume in cubic metres of a cube of side 2.8 cm?
13 What is the side in metres of a cube that has a volume of 588 cubic millimetres?
14 Give an order-of-magnitude estimate for the mass of:
   a an apple
   b this physics book
   c a soccer ball.

15 A white dwarf star has a mass about that of the Sun and a radius about that of the Earth. Give an order-of-magnitude estimate of the density of a white dwarf.

16 A sports car accelerates from rest to 100 km per hour in 4.0 s. What fraction of the acceleration due to gravity is the car's acceleration?

17 Give an order-of-magnitude estimate for the number of electrons in your body.

18 Give an order-of-magnitude estimate for the ratio of the electric force between two electrons 1 m apart to the gravitational force between the electrons.

19 The frequency f of oscillation (a quantity with units of inverse seconds) of a mass m attached to a spring of spring constant k (a quantity with units of force per length) is related to m and k. By writing $f = cm^x k^y$ and matching units on both sides, show that $f = c\sqrt{\frac{k}{m}}$, where c is a dimensionless constant.

20 A block of mass 1.2 kg is raised a vertical distance of 5.55 m in 2.450 s. Calculate the power delivered. ($P = \frac{mgh}{t}$ and $g = 9.81 \text{ m s}^{-2}$)

21 Find the kinetic energy ($E_K = \frac{1}{2}mv^2$) of a block of mass 5.00 kg moving at a speed of 12.5 m s^{-1}.

22 Without using a calculator, **estimate** the value of the following expressions. Then compare your estimate with the exact value found using a calculator.

a $\frac{243}{43}$

b 2.80×1.90

c $312 \times \frac{480}{160}$

d $\frac{8.99 \times 10^9 \times 7 \times 10^{-16} \times 7 \times 10^{-6}}{(8 \times 10^2)^2}$

e $\frac{6.6 \times 10^{-11} \times 6 \times 10^{24}}{(6.4 \times 10^6)^2}$

1.2 Uncertainties and errors

This section introduces the basic methods of dealing with experimental error and uncertainty in measured physical quantities. Physics is an experimental science and often the experimenter will perform an experiment to test the prediction of a given theory. No measurement will ever be completely accurate, however, and so the result of the experiment will be presented with an experimental error.

Types of uncertainty

There are two main types of uncertainty or error in a measurement. They can be grouped into **systematic** and **random**, although in many cases it is not possible to distinguish clearly between the two. We may say that random uncertainties are almost always the fault of the observer, whereas systematic errors are due to both the observer and the instrument being used. In practice, all uncertainties are a combination of the two.

Systematic errors

A **systematic error** biases measurements in the same direction; the measurements are always too large or too small. If you use a metal ruler to measure length on a very hot day, all your length measurements will be too small because the metal ruler expanded in the hot weather. If you use an ammeter that shows a current of 0.1 A even before it is connected to

Learning objectives

- Distinguish between random and systematic uncertainties.
- Work with absolute, fractional and percentage uncertainties.
- Use error bars in graphs.
- Calculate the uncertainty in a gradient or an intercept.

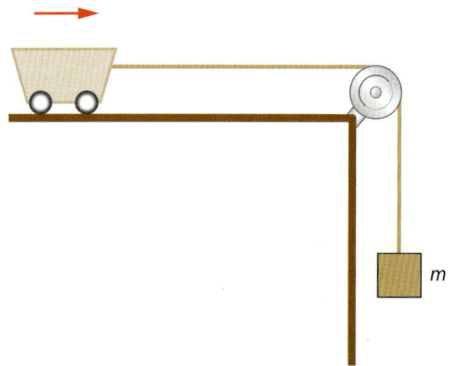

Figure 1.1 The falling block accelerates the cart.

a circuit, every measurement of current made with this ammeter will be larger than the true value of the current by 0.1 A.

Suppose you are investigating Newton's second law by measuring the acceleration of a cart as it is being pulled by a falling weight of mass m (Figure 1.1). Almost certainly there is a frictional force f between the cart and the table surface. If you forget to take this force into account, you would expect the cart's acceleration a to be:

$$a = \frac{mg}{M}$$

where M is the constant combined mass of the cart and the falling block.

The graph of the acceleration versus m would be a straight line through the origin, as shown by the red line in Figure 1.2. If you actually do the experiment, you will find that you do get a straight line, but not through the origin (blue line in Figure 1.2). There is a negative intercept on the vertical axis.

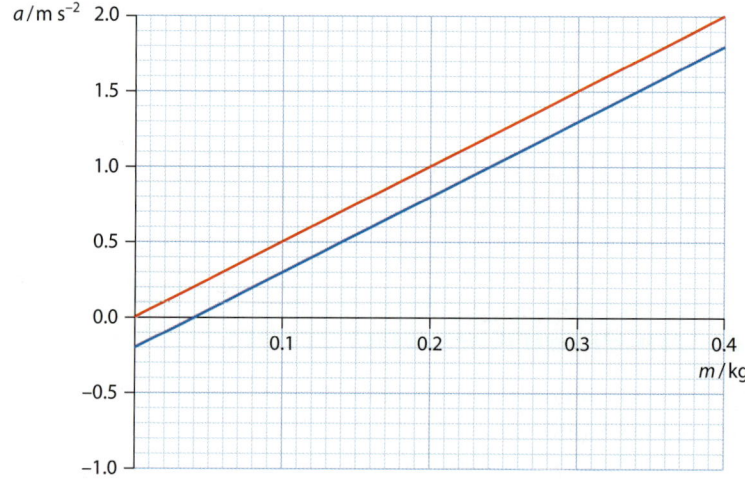

Figure 1.2 The variation of acceleration with falling mass with (blue) and without (red) frictional forces.

This is because with the frictional force present, Newton's second law predicts that:

$$a = \frac{mg}{M} - \frac{f}{M}$$

So a graph of acceleration a versus mass m would give a straight line with a negative intercept on the vertical axis.

Systematic errors can result from the technique used to make a measurement. There will be a systematic error in measuring the volume of a liquid inside a graduated cylinder if the tube is not exactly vertical. The measured values will always be larger or smaller than the true value, depending on which side of the cylinder you look at (Figure 1.3a). There will also be a systematic error if your eyes are not aligned with the liquid level in the cylinder (Figure 1.3b). Similarly, a systematic error will arise if you do not look at an analogue meter directly from above (Figure 1.3c).

Systematic errors are hard to detect and take into account.

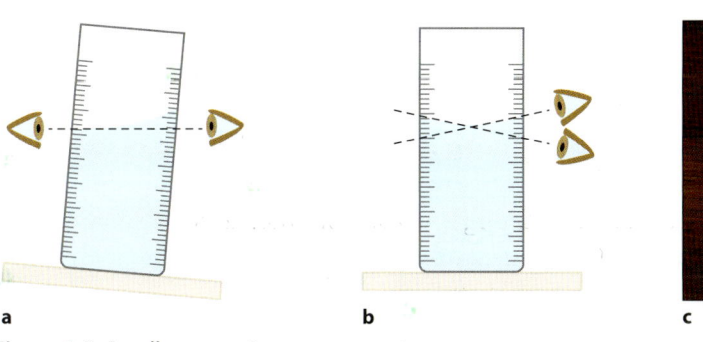

a b c

Figure 1.3 Parallax errors in measurements.

Random uncertainties

The presence of **random uncertainty** is revealed when repeated measurements of the same quantity show a spread of values, some too large some too small. Unlike systematic errors, which are always biased to be in the same direction, random uncertainties are unbiased. Suppose you ask ten people to use stopwatches to measure the time it takes an athlete to run a distance of 100 m. They stand by the finish line and start their stopwatches when the starting pistol fires. You will most likely get ten different values for the time. This is because some people will start/stop the stopwatches too early and some too late. You would expect that if you took an average of the ten times you would get a better **estimate** for the time than any of the individual measurements: the measurements **fluctuate** about some value. Averaging a large number of measurements gives a more **accurate** estimate of the result. (See the section on accuracy and precision, overleaf.)

We include within random uncertainties, **reading** uncertainties (which really is a different type of error altogether). These have to do with the precision with which we can read an instrument. Suppose we use a ruler to record the position of the right end of an object, Figure **1.4**.

The first ruler has graduations separated by 0.2 cm. We are confident that the position of the right end is greater than 23.2 cm and smaller than 23.4 cm. The true value is somewhere between these bounds. The average of the lower and upper bounds is 23.3 cm and so we quote the measurement as (23.3±0.1) cm. Notice that the uncertainty of ±0.1 cm **is half the smallest width** on the ruler. This is the conservative way of doing things and not everyone agrees with this. What if you scanned the diagram in Figure **1.4** on your computer, enlarged it and used your computer to draw further lines in between the graduations of the ruler. Then you could certainly read the position to better precision than the ±0.1 cm. Others might claim that they can do this even without a computer or a scanner! They might say that the right end is definitely short of the 23.3 cm point. We will not discuss this any further – it is an endless discussion and, at this level, pointless.

Now let us use a ruler with a finer scale. We are again confident that the position of the right end is greater than 32.3 cm and smaller than 32.4 cm. The true value is somewhere between these bounds. The average of the bounds is 32.35 cm so we quote a measurement of (32.35±0.05) cm. Notice

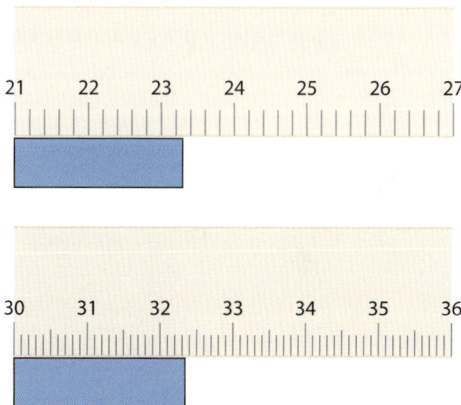

Figure 1.4 Two rulers with different graduations. The top has a width between graduations of 0.2 cm and the other 0.1 cm.

again that the uncertainty of ±0.05 cm is half the smallest width on the ruler. This gives the general rule for analogue instruments:

> The uncertainty in reading an instrument is ± half of the smallest width of the graduations on the instrument.

For digital instruments, we may take the reading error to be the smallest division that the instrument can read. So a stopwatch that reads time to two decimal places, e.g. 25.38 s, will have a reading error of ±0.01 s, and a weighing scale that records a mass as 184.5 g will have a reading error of ±0.1 g. Typical reading errors for some common instruments are listed in Table **1.6**.

Instrument	Reading error
ruler	±0.5 mm
vernier calipers	±0.05 mm
micrometer	±0.005 mm
electronic weighing scale	±0.1 g
stopwatch	±0.01 s

Table 1.6 Reading errors for some common instruments.

Accuracy and precision

In physics, a measurement is said to be **accurate** if the systematic error in the measurement is small. This means in practice that the measured value is very close to the accepted value for that quantity (assuming that this is known – it is not always). A measurement is said to be **precise** if the random uncertainty is small. This means in practice that when the measurement was repeated many times, the individual values were close to each other. We normally illustrate the concepts of accuracy and precision with the diagrams in Figure **1.5**: the red stars indicate individual measurements. The 'true' value is represented by the common centre of the three circles, the 'bull's-eye'. Measurements are precise if they are clustered together. They are accurate if they are close to the centre. The descriptions of three of the diagrams are obvious; the bottom right clearly shows results that are not precise because they are not clustered together. But they are accurate because their average value is roughly in the centre.

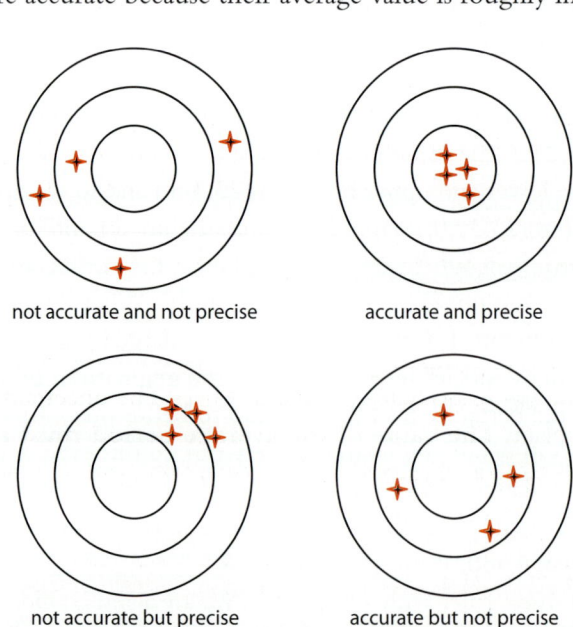

Figure 1.5 The meaning of accurate and precise measurements. Four different sets of four measurements each are shown.

Averages

In an experiment a measurement must be repeated many times, if at all possible. If it is repeated N times and the results of the measurements are $x_1, x_2, \ldots, x_N$, we calculate the **mean** or the **average** of these values ($\bar{x}$) using:

$$\bar{x} = \frac{x_1 + x_2 + \cdots + x_N}{N}$$

This average is the **best estimate** for the quantity x based on the N measurements. What about the uncertainty? The best way is to get the **standard deviation** of the N numbers using your calculator. Standard deviation will not be examined but you may need to use it for your Internal Assessment, so it is good idea to learn it – you will learn it in your mathematics class anyway. The standard deviation σ of the N measurements is given by the formula (the calculator finds this very easily):

$$\sigma = \sqrt{\frac{(x_1 - \bar{x})^2 + (x_2 - \bar{x})^2 + \cdots + (x_N - \bar{x})^2}{N - 1}}$$

A very simple rule (not entirely satisfactory but acceptable for this course) is to use as an **estimate of the uncertainty** the quantity:

$$\Delta x = \frac{x_{max} - x_{min}}{2}$$ ← *Random absolute uncertainty*

i.e. half of the difference between the largest and the smallest value.

For example, suppose we measure the period of a pendulum (in seconds) ten times:

1.20, 1.25, 1.30, 1.13, 1.25, 1.17, 1.41, 1.32, 1.29, 1.30

We calculate the mean:

$$\bar{t} = \frac{t_1 + t_2 + \cdots + t_{10}}{10} = 1.2620 \text{ s}$$

and the uncertainty:

$$\Delta t = \frac{t_{max} - t_{min}}{2} = \frac{1.41 - 1.13}{2} = 0.140 \text{ s}$$

How many significant figures do we use for uncertainties? The general rule is just one figure. So here we have $\Delta t = 0.1$ s. The uncertainty is in the first decimal place. **The value of the average period must also be expressed to the same precision as the uncertainty**, i.e. here to one decimal place, $\bar{t} = 1.3$ s. We then state that: *decimal places*

period = (1.3 ± 0.1) s

(Notice that each of the ten measurements of the period is subject to a reading error. Since these values were given to two decimal places, it is implied that the reading error is in the second decimal place, say ± 0.01 s.)

> **Exam tip**
> There is some case to be made for using **two** significant figures in the uncertainty when the first digit in the uncertainty is 1. So in this example, since $\Delta t = 0.140$ s does begin with the digit 1, we should state $\Delta t = 0.14$ s and quote the result for the period as 'period = (1.26 ± 0.14) s'.

1 MEASUREMENT AND UNCERTAINTIES

This is much smaller than the uncertainty found above so we ignore the reading error here. If instead the reading error were greater than the error due to the spread of values, we would have to include it instead. We will not deal with cases when the two errors are comparable.)

You will often see uncertainties with 2 s.f. in the scientific literature. For example, the charge of the electron is quoted as $e = (1.602\,176\,565 \pm 0.000\,000\,035) \times 10^{-19}$ C and the mass of the electron as $m_e = (9.109\,382\,91 \pm 0.000\,000\,40) \times 10^{-31}$ kg. This is perfectly all right and reflects the experimenter's **level of confidence** in his/her results. Expressing the uncertainty to 2 s.f. implies a more sophisticated statistical analysis of the data than what is normally done in a high school physics course. With a lot of data, the measured values of e form a normal distribution with a given mean ($1.602\,176\,565 \times 10^{-19}$ C) and standard deviation ($0.000\,000\,035 \times 10^{-19}$ C). The experimenter is then 68% confident that the measured value of e lies within the interval $[1.602\,176\,530 \times 10^{-19}$ C, $1.602\,176\,600 \times 10^{-19}$ C$]$.

Worked example

1.6 The diameter of a steel ball is to be measured using a micrometer caliper. The following are sources of error:
   1. The ball is not centred between the jaws of the caliper.
   2. The jaws of the caliper are tightened too much.
   3. The temperature of the ball may change during the measurement.
   4. The ball may not be perfectly round.

Determine which of these are random and which are systematic sources of error.

Sources 3 and 4 lead to unpredictable results, so they are random errors. Source 2 means that the measurement of diameter is always smaller since the calipers are tightened too much, so this is a systematic source of error. Source 1 certainly leads to unpredictable results depending on how the ball is centred, so it is a random source of error. But since the ball is not centred the 'diameter' measured is always smaller than the true diameter, so this is also a source of systematic error.

Propagation of uncertainties

A measurement of a length may be quoted as $L = (28.3 \pm 0.4)$ cm. The value 28.3 is called the **best estimate** or the **mean value** of the measurement and the 0.4 cm is called the **absolute uncertainty** in the measurement. The ratio of absolute uncertainty to mean value is called the **fractional uncertainty**. Multiplying the fractional uncertainty by 100% gives the **percentage uncertainty**. So, for $L = (28.3 \pm 0.4)$ cm we have that:

- absolute uncertainty = 0.4 cm
- fractional uncertainty = $\dfrac{0.4}{28.3} = 0.0141$
- percentage uncertainty = $0.0141 \times 100\% = 1.41\%$

In general, if $a = a_0 \pm \Delta a$, we have:
- absolute uncertainty = Δa
- fractional uncertainty = $\dfrac{\Delta a}{a_0}$
- percentage uncertainty = $\dfrac{\Delta a}{a_0} \times 100\%$

The subscript 0 indicates the mean value, so a_0 is the mean value of a.

Suppose that three quantities are measured in an experiment: $a = a_0 \pm \Delta a$, $b = b_0 \pm \Delta b$, $c = c_0 \pm \Delta c$. We now wish to calculate a quantity Q in terms of a, b, c. For example, if a, b, c are the sides of a rectangular block we may want to find $Q = ab$, which is the area of the base, or $Q = 2a + 2b$, which is the perimeter of the base, or $Q = abc$, which is the volume of the block. Because of the uncertainties in a, b, c there will be an uncertainty in the calculated quantities as well. How do we calculate this uncertainty?

There are three cases to consider. We will give the results without proof.

Addition and subtraction

The first case involves the operations of addition and/or subtraction. For example, we might have $Q = a + b$ or $Q = a - b$ or $Q = a + b - c$. Then, **in all cases** the absolute uncertainty in Q is the **sum** of the **absolute** uncertainties in a, b and c.

$Q = a + b \quad \Rightarrow \quad \Delta Q = \Delta a + \Delta b$
$Q = a - b \quad \Rightarrow \quad \Delta Q = \Delta a + \Delta b$
$Q = a + b - c \quad \Rightarrow \quad \Delta Q = \Delta a + \Delta b + \Delta c$

Exam tip
In addition and subtraction, we always add the absolute uncertainties, never subtract.

Worked examples

1.7 The side a of a square, is measured to be (12.4 ± 0.1) cm. Find the perimeter P of the square including the uncertainty.

Because $P = a + a + a + a$, the perimeter is 49.6 cm. The absolute uncertainty in P is:

$\Delta P = \Delta a + \Delta a + \Delta a + \Delta a$

$\Delta P = 4\Delta a$

$\Delta P = 0.4$ cm

Thus, $P = (49.6 \pm 0.4)$ cm.

1.8 Find the percentage uncertainty in the quantity $Q = a - b$, where $a = 538.7 \pm 0.3$ and $b = 537.3 \pm 0.5$. Comment on the answer.

The calculated value is 1.7 and the absolute uncertainty is $0.3 + 0.5 = 0.8$. So $Q = 1.4 \pm 0.8$. The fractional uncertainty is $\dfrac{0.8}{1.4} = 0.57$, so the percentage uncertainty is 57%.

The fractional uncertainty in the quantities a and b is quite small. But the numbers are close to each other so their difference is very small. This makes the fractional uncertainty in the difference unacceptably large.

1 MEASUREMENT AND UNCERTAINTIES   13

Multiplication and division

The second case involves the operations of multiplication and division. Here the **fractional uncertainty** of the result is the **sum** of the **fractional uncertainties** of the quantities involved:

$$Q = ab \quad \Rightarrow \quad \frac{\Delta Q}{Q_0} = \frac{\Delta a}{a_0} + \frac{\Delta b}{b_0}$$

$$Q = \frac{a}{b} \quad \Rightarrow \quad \frac{\Delta Q}{Q_0} = \frac{\Delta a}{a_0} + \frac{\Delta b}{b_0}$$

$$Q = \frac{ab}{c} \quad \Rightarrow \quad \frac{\Delta Q}{Q_0} = \frac{\Delta a}{a_0} + \frac{\Delta b}{b_0} + \frac{\Delta c}{c_0}$$

Powers and roots

The third case involves calculations where quantities are raised to powers or roots. Here the **fractional uncertainty** of the result is the **fractional uncertainty** of the quantity **multiplied** by the absolute value of the power:

$$Q = a^n \quad \Rightarrow \quad \frac{\Delta Q}{Q_0} = |n| \frac{\Delta a}{a_0}$$

$$Q = \sqrt[n]{a} \quad \Rightarrow \quad \frac{\Delta Q}{Q_0} = \frac{1}{n} \frac{\Delta a}{a_0}$$

Worked examples

1.9 The sides of a rectangle are measured to be $a = 2.5\,\text{cm} \pm 0.1\,\text{cm}$ and $b = 5.0\,\text{cm} \pm 0.1\,\text{cm}$. Find the area A of the rectangle.

The fractional uncertainty in a is:

$$\frac{\Delta a}{a} = \frac{0.1}{2.5} = 0.04 \text{ or } 4\%$$

The fractional uncertainty in b is:

$$\frac{\Delta b}{b} = \frac{0.1}{5.0} = 0.02 \text{ or } 2\%$$

Thus, the fractional uncertainty in the area is $0.04 + 0.02 = 0.06$ or 6%.

The area A_0 is:

$$A_0 = 2.5 \times 5.0 = 12.5\,\text{cm}^2$$

and $\dfrac{\Delta A}{A_0} = 0.06$

$\Rightarrow \quad \Delta A = 0.06 \times 12.5 = 0.75\,\text{cm}^2$

Hence $A = 12.5\,\text{cm}^2 \pm 0.8\,\text{cm}^2$ (the final absolute uncertainty is quoted to 1 s.f.).

1.10 A mass is measured to be $m = 4.4 \pm 0.2$ kg and its speed v is measured to be 18 ± 2 m s^{-1}. Find the kinetic energy of the mass.

The kinetic energy is $E = \frac{1}{2}mv^2$, so the mean value of the kinetic energy, E_0, is:

$E_0 = \frac{1}{2} \times 4.4 \times 18^2 = 712.8$ J

Using:

$$\frac{\Delta E}{E_0} = \frac{\Delta m}{m_0} + \underbrace{2\times}_{\text{because of the square}} \frac{\Delta v}{v_0}$$

we find:

$\frac{\Delta E}{712.8} = \frac{0.2}{4.4} = 2 \times \frac{2}{18} = 0.267$

So:

$\Delta E = 712.8 \times 0.2677 = 190.8$ J

To one significant figure, the uncertainty is $\Delta E = 200 = 2 \times 10^2$ J; that is $E = (7 \pm 2) \times 10^2$ J.

Exam tip
The final absolute uncertainty must be expressed to one significant figure. This limits the precision of the quoted value for energy.

1.11 The length of a simple pendulum is increased by 4%. What is the fractional increase in the pendulum's period?

The period T is related to the length L through $T = 2\pi\sqrt{\frac{L}{g}}$.

Because this relationship has a square root, the fractional uncertainties are related by:

$$\frac{\Delta T}{T_0} = \underbrace{\frac{1}{2}}_{\text{because of the square root}} \times \frac{\Delta L}{L_0}$$

We are told that $\frac{\Delta L}{L_0} = 4\%$. This means we have :

$\frac{\Delta T}{T_0} = \frac{1}{2} \times 4\% = 2\%$

1 MEASUREMENT AND UNCERTAINTIES

1.12 A quantity Q is measured to be $Q = 3.4 \pm 0.5$. Calculate the uncertainty in **a** $\frac{1}{Q}$ and **b** Q^2.

a $\quad \frac{1}{Q} = \frac{1}{3.4} = 0.294\,118$

$\frac{\Delta(1/Q)}{1/Q} = \frac{\Delta Q}{Q}$

$\Rightarrow \quad \Delta(1/Q) = \frac{\Delta Q}{Q^2} = \frac{0.5}{3.4^2} = 0.043\,25$

Hence: $\frac{1}{Q} = 0.29 \pm 0.04$

b $\quad Q^2 = 3.4^2 = 11.5600$

$\frac{\Delta(Q^2)}{Q^2} = 2 \times \frac{\Delta Q}{Q}$

$\Rightarrow \quad \Delta(Q^2) = 2Q \times \Delta Q = 2 \times 3.4 \times 0.5 = 3.4$

Hence: $Q^2 = 12 \pm 3$

1.13 The volume of a cylinder of base radius r and height h is given by $V = \pi r^2 h$. The volume is measured with an uncertainty of 4% and the height with with an uncertainty of 2%. Determine the uncertainty in the radius.

We must first solve for the radius to get $r = \sqrt{\frac{V}{\pi h}}$. The uncertainty is then:

$\frac{\Delta r}{r} \times 100\% = \frac{1}{2}\left(\frac{\Delta V}{V} + \frac{\Delta h}{h}\right) \times 100\% = \frac{1}{2}(4 + 2) \times 100\% = 3\%$

Best-fit lines

In mathematics, plotting a point on a set of axes is straightforward. In physics, it is slightly more involved because the point consists of measured or calculated values and so is subject to uncertainty. So the point $(x_0 \pm \Delta x, y_0 \pm \Delta y)$ is plotted as shown in Figure **1.6**. The uncertainties are

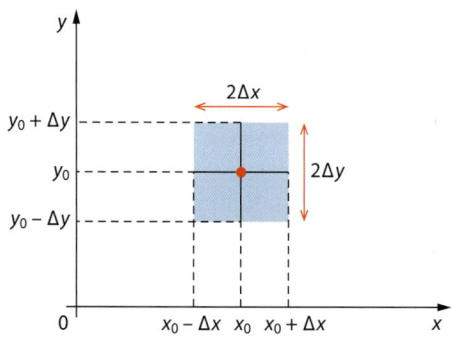

Figure 1.6 A point plotted along with its error bars.

represented by **error bars**. To 'go through the error bars' a best-fit line can go through the area shaded grey.

In a physics experiment we usually try to plot quantities that will give straight-line graphs. The graph in Figure **1.7** shows the variation with extension x of the tension T in a spring. The points and their error bars are plotted. The blue line is the best-fit line. It has been drawn by eye by trying to minimise the distance of the points from the line – this means that some points are above and some are below the best-fit line.

The **gradient (slope)** of the best-fit line is found by using two points **on the best-fit line** as far from each other as possible. We use (0, 0) and (0.0390, 7.88). The gradient is then:

$$\text{gradient} = \frac{\Delta F}{\Delta x}$$

$$\text{gradient} = \frac{7.88 - 0}{0.0390 - 0}$$

$$\text{gradient} = 202 \, \text{N m}^{-1}$$

The best-fit line has equation $F = 202x$. (The vertical intercept is essentially zero; in this equation x is in metres and F in newtons.)

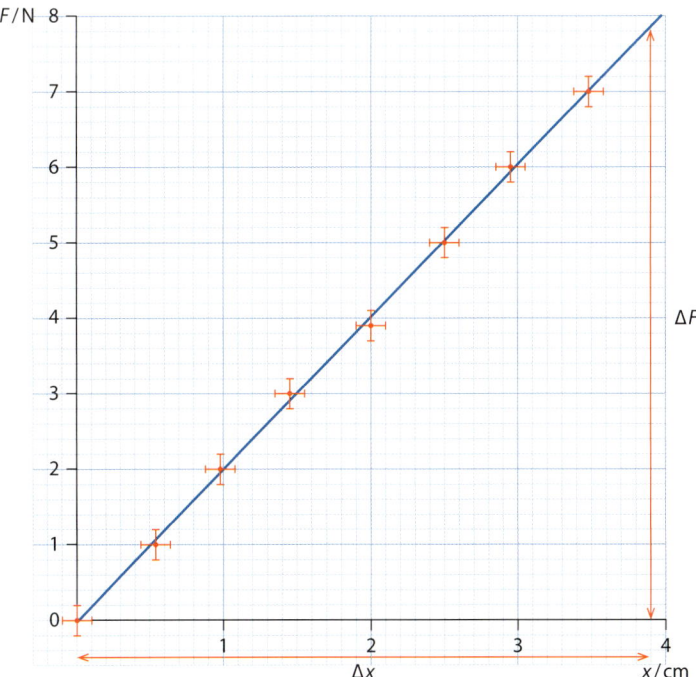

Figure 1.7 Data points plotted together with uncertainties in the values for the tension. To find the gradient, use two points on the best-fit line far apart from each other.

1 MEASUREMENT AND UNCERTAINTIES 17

On the other hand it is perfectly possible to obtain data that cannot be easily manipulated to give a straight line. In that case a smooth curve passing through all the error bars is the best-fit line (Figure **1.8**).

From the graph the maximum power is 4.1 W, and it occurs when $R = 2.2\,\Omega$. The estimated uncertainty in R is about the length of a square, i.e. $\pm 0.1\,\Omega$. Similarly, for the power the estimated uncertainty is ± 0.1 W.

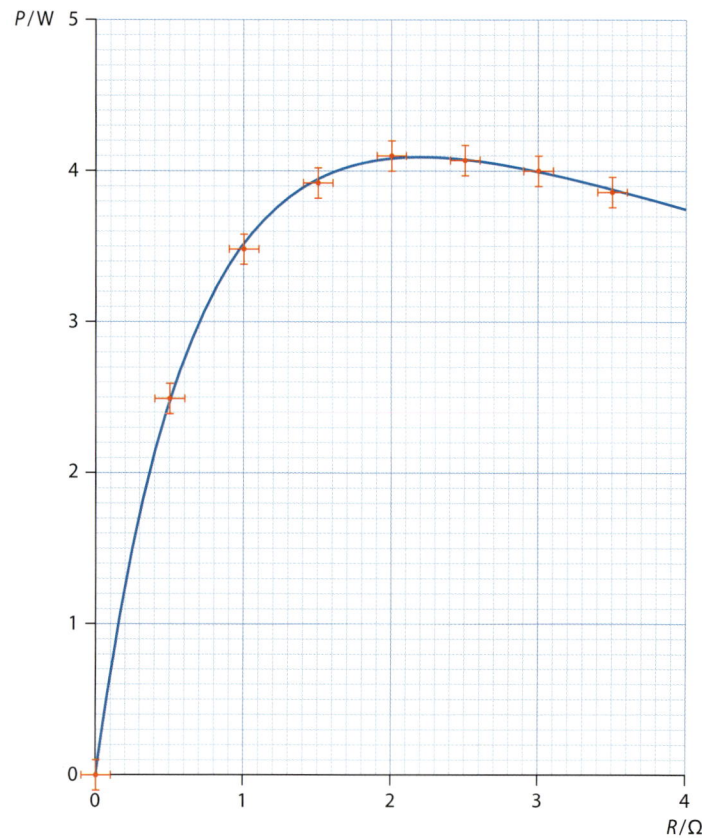

Figure 1.8 The best-fit line can be a curve.

Uncertainties in the gradient and intercept

When the best-fit line is a straight line we can easily obtain uncertainties in the gradient and the vertical intercept. The idea is to draw lines of maximum and minimum gradient in such a way that they go through all the **error bars** (not just the 'first' and the 'last' points). Figure **1.9** shows the best-fit line (in blue) and the lines of maximum and minimum gradient. The green line is the line through all error bars of greatest gradient. The red line is the line through all error bars with smallest gradient. All lines are drawn by eye.

The green line has gradient $k_{max} = 210\,\text{N m}^{-1}$ and intercept -0.18 N. The red line has gradient $k_{min} = 193\,\text{N m}^{-1}$ and intercept $+0.13$ N. So we can find the uncertainty in the gradient as:

$$\Delta k = \frac{k_{max} - k_{min}}{2} = \frac{210 - 193}{2} = 8.5 \approx 8\,\text{N m}^{-1}$$

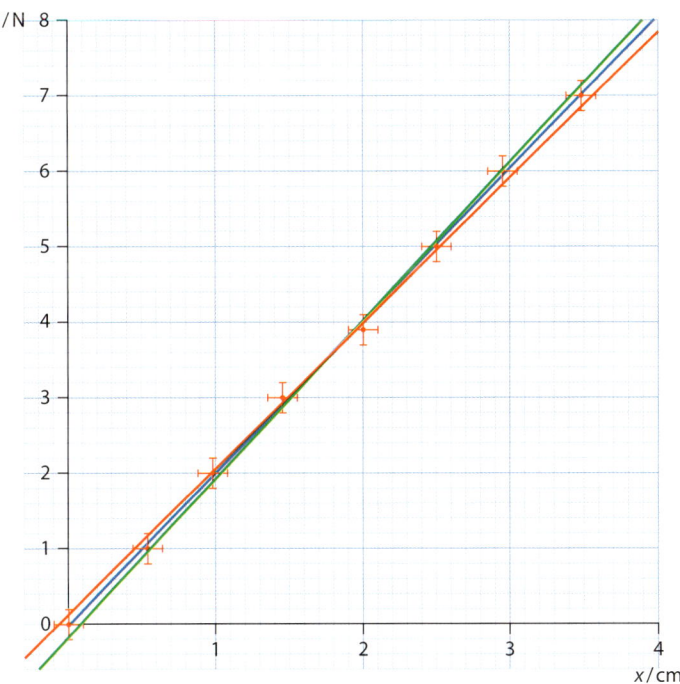

Figure 1.9 The best-fit line, along with lines of maximum and minimum gradient.

The uncertainty in the vertical intercept is similarly:

$$\Delta_{\text{intercept}} = \frac{0.13 - (-0.18)}{2} = 0.155 \approx 0.2 \, \text{N}$$

We saw earlier that the line of best fit has gradient $202 \, \text{N m}^{-1}$ and zero intercept. So we quote the results as $k = (2.02 \pm 0.08) \times 10^2$ and intercept $= 0.0 \pm 0.2 \, \text{N}$.

Nature of science

A key part of the scientific method is recognising the errors that are present in the experimental technique being used, and working to reduce these as much as possible. In this section you have learned how to calculate errors in quantities that are combined in different ways and how to estimate errors from graphs. You have also learned how to recognise systematic and random errors.

No matter how much care is taken, scientists know that their results are uncertain. But they need to distinguish between inaccuracy and uncertainty, and to know how confident they can be about the validity of their results. The search to gain more accurate results pushes scientists to try new ideas and refine their techniques. There is always the possibility that a new result may confirm a hypothesis for the present, or it may overturn current theory and open a new area of research. Being aware of doubt and uncertainty are key to driving science forward.

Test yourself

23 The magnitudes of two forces are measured to be 120 ± 5 N and 60 ± 3 N. Find the sum and difference of the two magnitudes, giving the uncertainty in each case.

24 The quantity Q depends on the measured values a and b in the following ways:
  a $Q = \frac{a}{b}$, $a = 20 \pm 1$, $b = 10 \pm 1$
  b $Q = 2a + 3b$, $a = 20 \pm 2$, $b = 15 \pm 3$
  c $Q = a - 2b$, $a = 50 \pm 1$, $b = 24 \pm 1$
  d $Q = a^2$, $a = 10.0 \pm 0.3$
  e $Q = \frac{a^2}{b^2}$, $a = 100 \pm 5$, $b = 20 \pm 2$

  In each case, find the value of Q and its uncertainty.

25 The centripetal force is given by $F = \frac{mv^2}{r}$. The mass is measured to be 2.8 ± 0.1 kg, the velocity 14 ± 2 m s^{-1} and the radius 8.0 ± 0.2 m; find the force on the mass, including the uncertainty.

26 The radius r of a circle is measured to be 2.4 cm ± 0.1 cm. Find the uncertainty in:
  a the area of the circle
  b the circumference of the circle.

27 The sides of a rectangle are measured as 4.4 ± 0.2 cm and 8.5 ± 0.3 cm. Find the area and perimeter of the rectangle.

28 The length L of a pendulum is increased by 2%. Find the percentage increase in the period T.
  $\left(T = 2\pi \sqrt{\frac{L}{g}} \right)$

29 The volume of a cone of base radius R and height h is given by $V = \frac{\pi R^2 h}{3}$. The uncertainty in the radius and in the height is 4%. Find the percentage uncertainty in the volume.

30 In an experiment to measure current and voltage across a device, the following data was collected: $(V, I) = \{(0.1, 26), (0.2, 48), (0.3, 65), (0.4, 90)\}$. The current was measured in mA and the voltage in mV. The uncertainty in the current was ± 4 mA. Plot the current versus the voltage and draw the best-fit line through the points. Suggest whether the current is proportional to the voltage.

31 In a similar experiment to that in question 30, the following data was collected for current and voltage: $(V, I) = \{(0.1, 27), (0.2, 44), (0.3, 60), (0.4, 78)\}$ with an uncertainty of ± 4 mA in the current. Plot the current versus the voltage and draw the best-fit line. Suggest whether the current is proportional to the voltage.

32 A circle and a square have the same perimeter. Which shape has the larger area?

33 The graph shows the natural logarithm of the voltage across a capacitor of capacitance $C = 5.0\,\mu\text{F}$ as a function of time. The voltage is given by the equation $V = V_0 e^{-t/RC}$, where R is the resistance of the circuit. Find:
  a the initial voltage
  b the time for the voltage to be reduced to half its initial value
  c the resistance of the circuit.

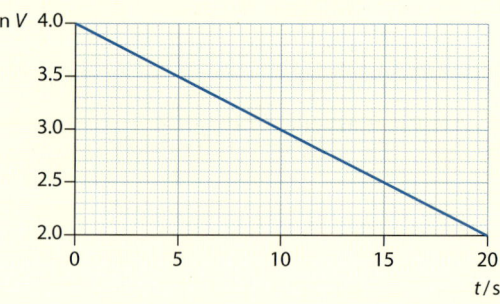

34 The table shows the mass M of several stars and their corresponding luminosity L (power emitted).
  a Plot L against M and draw the best-fit line.
  b Plot the logarithm of L against the logarithm of M. Use your graph to find the relationship between these quantities, assuming a power law of the kind $L = kM^\alpha$. Give the numerical value of the parameter α.

Mass M (in solar masses)	Luminosity L (in terms of the Sun's luminosity)
1.0 ± 0.1	1 ± 0
3.0 ± 0.3	42 ± 4
5.0 ± 0.5	230 ± 20
12 ± 1	4700 ± 50
20 ± 2	$26\,500 \pm 300$

1.3 Vectors and scalars

Quantities in physics are either scalars (i.e. they just have magnitude) or vectors (i.e. they have magnitude and direction). This section provides the tools you need for dealing with vectors.

Vectors

Some quantities in physics, such as time, distance, mass, speed and temperature, just need one number to specify them. These are called scalar quantities. For example, it is sufficient to say that the mass of a body is 64 kg or that the temperature is −5.0 °C. On the other hand, many quantities are fully specified only if, in addition to a number, a direction is needed. Saying that you will leave Paris now, in a train moving at 220 km/h, does not tell us where you will be in 30 minutes because we do not know the **direction** in which you will travel. Quantities that need a direction in addition to magnitude are called **vector** quantities. Table 1.7 gives some examples of vector and scalars.

A vector is represented by a straight arrow, as shown in Figure **1.10a**. The direction of the arrow represents the direction of the vector and the length of the arrow represents the **magnitude** of the vector. To say that two vectors are the same means that **both** magnitude and direction are the same. The vectors in Figure **1.10b** are all equal to each other. In other words, vectors do not have to start from the same point to be equal.

We write vectors as italic boldface *a*. The magnitude is written as $|a|$ or just a.

Learning objectives

- Distinguish between vector and scalar quantities.
- Resolve a vector into its components.
- Reconstruct a vector from its components.
- Carry out operations with vectors.

Vectors	Scalars
displacement	distance
velocity	speed
acceleration	mass
force	time
weight	density
electric field	electric potential
magnetic field	electric charge
gravitational field	gravitational potential
momentum	temperature
area	volume
angular velocity	work/energy/power

Table 1.7 Examples of vectors and scalars.

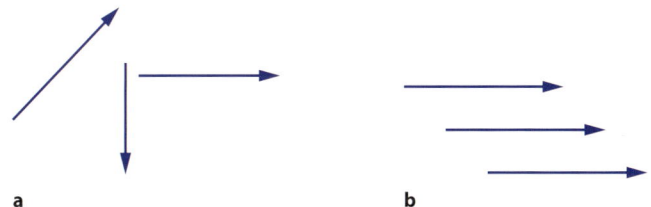

Figure 1.10 a Representation of vectors by arrows. **b** These three vectors are equal to each other.

Multiplication of a vector by a scalar

A vector can be multiplied by a number. The vector *a* multiplied by the number 2 gives a vector in the same direction as *a* but 2 times longer. The vector *a* multiplied by −0.5 is opposite to *a* in direction and half as long (Figure **1.11**). The vector −*a* has the same magnitude as *a* but is opposite in direction.

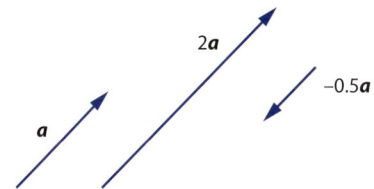

Figure 1.11 Multiplication of vectors by a scalar.

1 MEASUREMENT AND UNCERTAINTIES

Addition of vectors

Figure **1.12a** shows vectors *d* and *e*. We want to find the vector that equals *d* + *e*. Figure **1.12b** shows one method of adding two vectors.

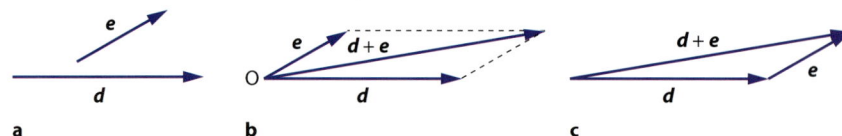

Figure 1.12 **a** Vectors *d* and *e*. **b** Adding two vectors involves shifting one of them parallel to itself so as to form a parallelogram with the two vectors as the two sides. The diagonal represents the sum. **c** An equivalent way to add vectors.

To add two vectors:
1 Draw them so they start at a common point O.
2 Complete the parallelogram whose sides are *d* and *e*.
3 Draw the diagonal of this parallelogram starting at O. This is the vector *d* + *e*.

Equivalently, you can draw the vector *e* so that it starts where the vector *d* stops and then join the beginning of *d* to the end of *e*, as shown in Figure 1.12c.

Exam tip

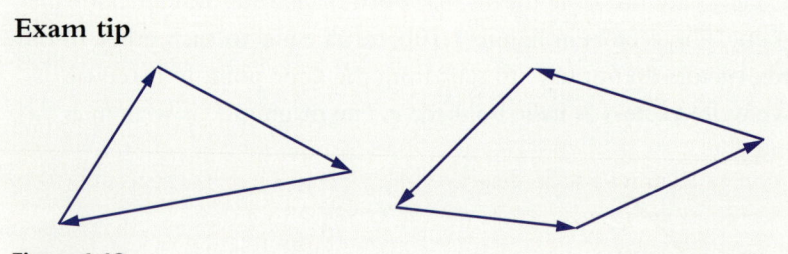

Figure 1.13

Vectors (with arrows pointing in the same sense) forming closed polygons add up to zero.

Subtraction of vectors

Figure **1.14** shows vectors *d* and *e*. We want to find the vector that equals *d* − *e*.

To subtract two vectors:
1 Draw them so they start at a common point O.
2 The vector from the tip of *e* to the tip of *d* is the vector *d* − *e*. (Notice that is equivalent to adding *d* to −*e*.)

Exam tip
The change in a quantity, and in particular the change in a vector quantity, will follow us through this entire course. You need to learn this well.

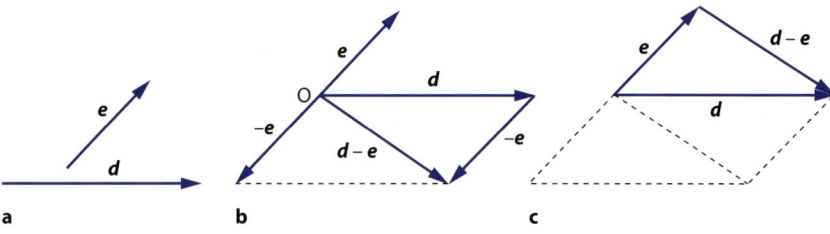

Figure 1.14 Subtraction of vectors.

Worked examples

1.14 Copy the diagram in Figure **1.15a**. Use the diagram to draw the third force that will keep the point P in equilibrium.

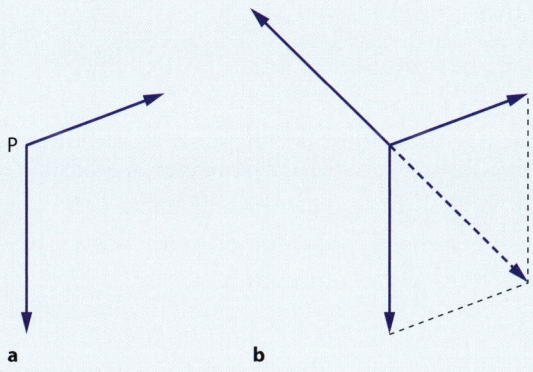

Figure 1.15

We find the sum of the two given forces using the parallelogram rule and then draw the opposite of that vector, as shown in Figure **1.15b**.

1.15 A velocity vector of magnitude $1.2\,\text{m s}^{-1}$ is horizontal. A second velocity vector of magnitude $2.0\,\text{m s}^{-1}$ must be added to the first so that the sum is vertical in direction. Find the direction of the second vector and the magnitude of the sum of the two vectors.

We need to draw a scale diagram, as shown in Figure **1.16**. Representing $1.0\,\text{m s}^{-1}$ by 2.0 cm, we see that the $1.2\,\text{m s}^{-1}$ corresponds to 2.4 cm and $2.0\,\text{m s}^{-1}$ to 4.0 cm.

First draw the horizontal vector. Then mark the vertical direction from O. Using a compass (or a ruler), mark a distance of 4.0 cm from A, which intersects the vertical line at B. AB must be one of the sides of the parallelogram we are looking for.

Now measure a distance of 2.4 cm horizontally from B to C and join O to C. This is the direction in which the second velocity vector must be pointing. Measuring the diagonal OB (i.e. the vector representing the sum), we find 3.2 cm, which represents $1.6\,\text{m s}^{-1}$. Using a protractor, we find that the $2.0\,\text{m s}^{-1}$ velocity vector makes an angle of about 37° with the vertical.

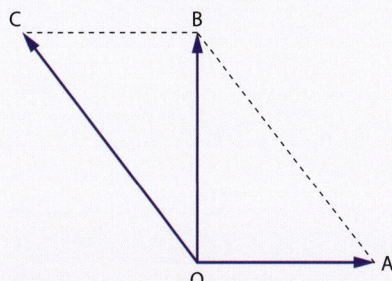

Figure 1.16 Using a scale diagram to solve a vector problem.

1 MEASUREMENT AND UNCERTAINTIES   **23**

1.16 A person walks 5.0 km east, followed by 3.0 km north and then another 4.0 km east. Find their final position.

The walk consists of three steps. We may represent each one by a vector (Figure **1.17**).
- The first step is a vector of magnitude 5.0 km directed east (**OA**).
- The second is a vector of magnitude 3.0 km directed north (**AB**).
- The last step is represented by a vector of 4.0 km directed east (**BC**).

The person will end up at a place that is given by the vector sum of these three vectors, that is **OA** + **AB** + **BC**, which equals the vector **OC**. By measurement from a scale drawing, or by simple geometry, the distance from O to C is 9.5 km and the angle to the horizontal is 18.4°.

Vectors corresponding to line segments are shown as bold capital letters, for example **OA**. The magnitude of the vector is the length OA and the direction is from O towards A.

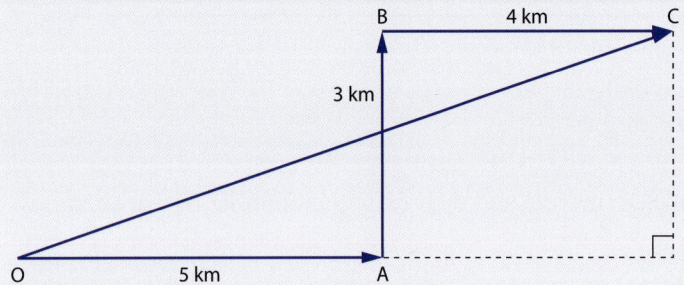

Figure 1.17 Scale drawing using 1 cm = 1 km.

1.17 A body moves in a circle of radius 3.0 m with a constant speed of 6.0 m s^{-1}. The velocity vector is at all times tangent to the circle. The body starts at A, proceeds to B and then to C. Find the change in the velocity vector between A and B and between B and C (Figure **1.18**).

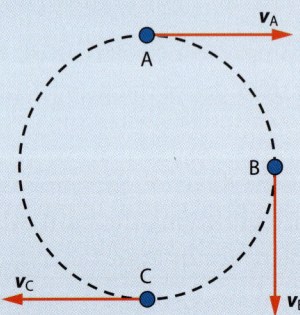

Figure 1.18

For the velocity change from A to B we have to find the difference $v_B - v_A$. and for the velocity change from B to C we need to find $v_C - v_B$. The vectors are shown in Figure **1.19**.

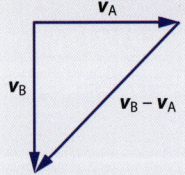 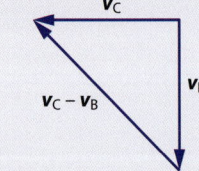

Figure 1.19

The vector $v_B - v_A$ is directed south-west and its magnitude is (by the Pythagorean theorem):

$$\sqrt{v_A^2 + v_B^2} = \sqrt{6^2 + 6^2}$$
$$= \sqrt{72}$$
$$= 8.49 \, m\,s^{-1}$$

The vector $v_C - v_B$ has the same magnitude as $v_B - v_A$ but is directed north-west.

Components of a vector

Suppose that we use perpendicular axes x and y and draw vectors on this x–y plane. We take the origin of the axes as the starting point of the vector. (Other vectors whose beginning points are not at the origin can be shifted parallel to themselves until they, too, begin at the origin.) Given a vector **a** we define its **components along the axes** as follows. From the tip of the vector draw lines parallel to the axes and mark the point on each axis where the lines intersect the axes (Figure **1.20**).

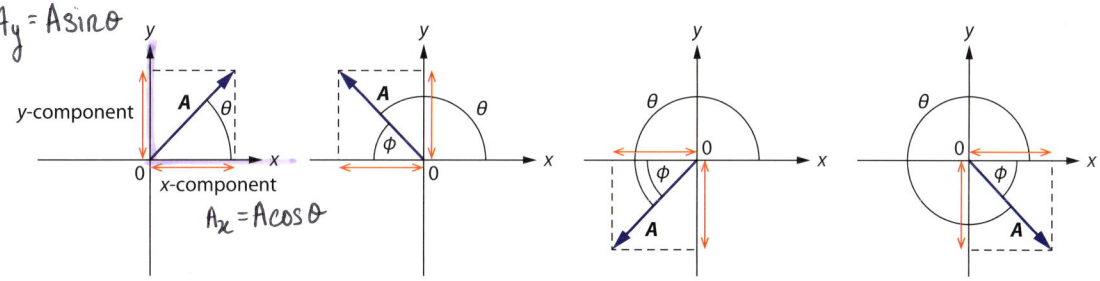

Figure 1.20 The components of a vector **A** and the angle needed to calculate the components. The angle θ is measured counter-clockwise from the positive x-axis.

The x- and y-components of **A** are called A_x and A_y. They are given by:

$A_x = A \cos \theta$

$A_y = A \sin \theta$

where A is the magnitude of the vector and θ is the angle between the vector and the **positive** x-axis. These formulas and the angle θ defined as shown in Figure **1.20** always give the correct components with the correct signs. But the angle θ is not always the most convenient. A more convenient angle to work with is φ, but when using this angle the signs have to be put in by hand. This is shown in Worked example **1.18**.

Exam tip
The formulas given for the components of a vector can **always** be used, but the angle must be the one defined in Figure **1.20**, which is sometimes awkward. You can use other more convenient angles, but then the formulas for the components may change.

1 MEASUREMENT AND UNCERTAINTIES 25

Worked examples

1.18 Find the components of the vectors in Figure **1.21**. The magnitude of *a* is 12.0 units and that of *b* is 24.0 units.

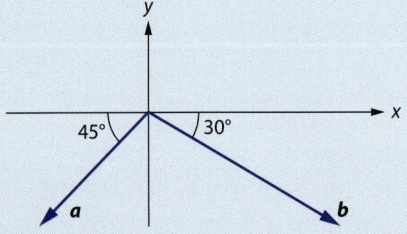

Figure 1.21

Taking the angle from the positive *x*-axis, the angle for *a* is $\theta = 180° + 45° = 225°$ and that for *b* is $\theta = 270° + 60° = 330°$. Thus:

$a_x = 12.0 \cos 225°$ $\qquad b_x = 24.0 \cos 330°$

$a_x = -8.49$ $\qquad\qquad b_x = 20.8$

$a_y = 12.0 \sin 225°$ $\qquad b_y = 24.0 \sin 330°$

$a_y = -8.49$ $\qquad\qquad b_y = -12.0$

But we do not have to use the awkward angles of 225° and 330°. For vector *a* it is better to use the angle of $\varphi = 45°$. In that case simple trigonometry gives:

$a_x = \underset{\underset{\text{put in by hand}}{\uparrow}}{-}12.0 \cos 45° = -8.49$ and $a_y = \underset{\underset{\text{put in by hand}}{\uparrow}}{-}12.0 \sin 45° = -8.49$

For vector *b* it is convenient to use the angle of $\varphi = 30°$, which is the angle the vector makes with the *x*-axis. But in this case:

$b_x = 24.0 \cos 30° = 20.8$ and $b_y = \underset{\underset{\text{put in by hand}}{\uparrow}}{-}24.0 \sin 30° = -12.0$

1.19 Find the components of the vector **W** along the axes shown in Figure 1.22.

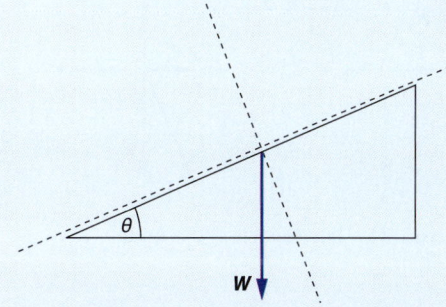

Figure 1.22

See Figure 1.23. Notice that the angle between the vector **W** and the negative *y*-axis is θ.

Then by simple trigonometry

$W_x = -W\sin\theta$ (W_x is opposite the angle θ so the sine is used)

$W_y = -W\cos\theta$ (W_y is adjacent to the angle θ so the cosine is used)

(Both components are along the negative axes, so a minus sign has been put in by hand.)

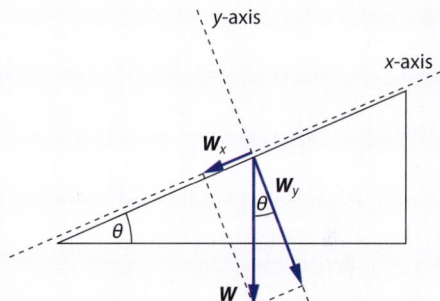

Figure 1.23

Reconstructing a vector from its components

Knowing the components of a vector allows us to reconstruct it (i.e. to find the magnitude and direction of the vector). Suppose that we are given that the *x*- and *y*-components of a vector are F_x and F_y. We need to find the magnitude of the vector *F* and the angle (θ) it makes with the *x*-axis (Figure 1.24). The magnitude is found by using the Pythagorean theorem and the angle by using the definition of tangent.

$F = \sqrt{F_x^2 + F_y^2}, \quad \theta = \arctan\dfrac{F_y}{F_x}$

As an example, consider the vector whose components are $F_x = 4.0$ and $F_y = 3.0$. The magnitude of **F** is:

$F = \sqrt{F_x^2 + F_y^2} = \sqrt{4.0^2 + 3.0^2} = \sqrt{25} = 5.0$

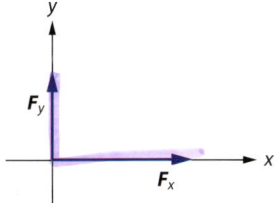 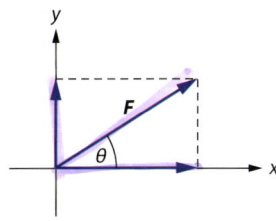

Figure 1.24 Given the components of a vector we can find its magnitude and direction.

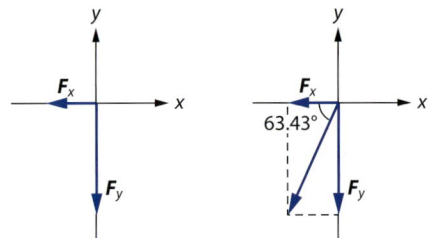

Figure 1.25 The vector is in the third quadrant.

and the direction is found from:

$$\theta = \arctan\frac{F_y}{F_x} = \arctan\frac{3}{4} = 36.87° \approx 37°$$

Here is another example. We need to find the magnitude and direction of the vector with components $F_x = -2.0$ and $F_y = -4.0$. The vector lies in the third quadrant, as shown in Figure 1.25.

The magnitude is:

$$F = \sqrt{F_x^2 + F_y^2} = \sqrt{(-2.0)^2 + (-4.0)^2}$$
$$= \sqrt{20} = 4.47 \approx 4.5$$

The direction is found from:

$$\varphi = \arctan\frac{F_y}{F_x} = \arctan\frac{-4}{-2} = \arctan 2$$

The calculator gives $\theta = \tan^{-1} 2 = 63°$. This angle is the one shown in Figure 1.25.

In general, the simplest procedure to find the angle without getting stuck in trigonometry is to evaluate $\varphi = \arctan\left|\frac{F_y}{F_x}\right|$ i.e. **ignore the signs** in the components. The calculator will then give you the angle between the vector and the x-axis, as shown in Figure 1.26.

Adding or subtracting vectors is very easy when we have the components, as Worked example 1.20 shows.

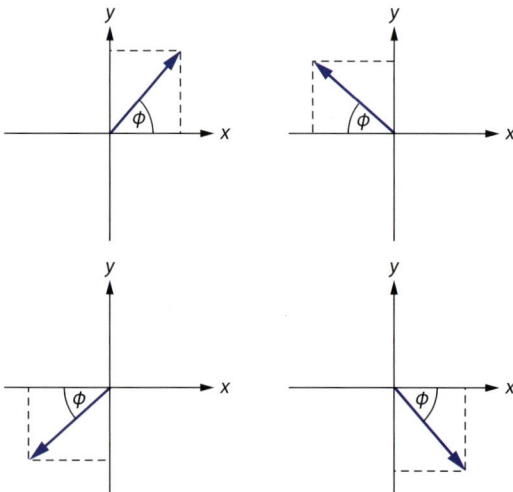

Figure 1.26 The angle φ is given by $\varphi = \arctan\left|\frac{F_y}{F_x}\right|$

Worked example

1.20 Find the sum of the vectors shown in Figure **1.27**. F_1 has magnitude 8.0 units and F_2 has magnitude 12 units. Their directions are as shown in the diagram.

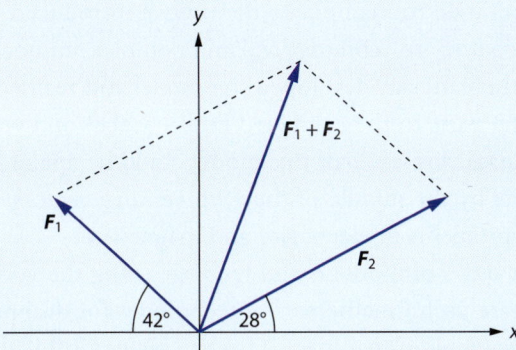

Figure 1.27 The sum of vectors F_1 and F_2 (not to scale).

Find the components of the two vectors:
$F_{1x} = -F_1 \cos 42°$
$F_{1x} = -5.945$

$F_{1y} = F_1 \sin 42°$
$F_{1y} = 5.353$

$F_{2x} = F_2 \cos 28°$
$F_{2x} = 10.595$

$F_{2y} = F_2 \sin 28°$
$F_{2y} = 5.634$

The sum $F = F_1 + F_2$ then has components:

$F_x = F_{1x} + F_{2x} = 4.650$
$F_y = F_{1y} + F_{2y} = 10.987$

The magnitude of the sum is therefore:

$F = \sqrt{4.650^2 + 10.987^2}$

$F = 11.9 \approx 12$

and its direction is:

$\varphi = \arctan\left(\dfrac{10.987}{4.65}\right)$

$\varphi = 67.1 \approx 67°$

Nature of science

For thousands of years, people across the world have used maps to navigate from one place to another, making use of the ideas of distance and direction to show the relative positions of places. The concept of vectors and the algebra used to manipulate them were introduced in the first half of the 19th century to represent real and complex numbers in a geometrical way. Mathematicians developed the model and realised that there were two distinct parts to their directed lines – scalars and vectors. Scientists and mathematicians saw that this model could be applied to theoretical physics, and by the middle of the 19th century vectors were being used to model problems in electricity and magnetism.

Resolving a vector into components and reconstructing the vector from its components are useful mathematical techniques for dealing with measurements in three-dimensional space. These mathematical techniques are invaluable when dealing with physical quantities that have both magnitude and direction, such as calculating the effect of multiple forces on an object. In this section you have done this in two dimensions, but vector algebra can be applied to three dimensions and more.

Test yourself

35 A body is acted upon by the two forces shown in the diagram. In each case draw the one force whose effect on the body is the same as the two together.

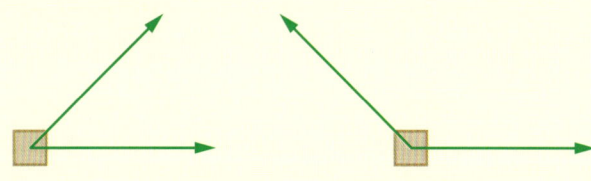

36 Vector A has a magnitude of 12.0 units and makes an angle of 30° with the positive x-axis. Vector B has a magnitude of 8.00 units and makes an angle of 80° with the positive x-axis. Using a graphical method, find the magnitude and direction of the vectors:
  a $A + B$ b $A - B$ c $A - 2B$

37 Repeat the previous problem, this time using components.

38 Find the magnitude and direction of the vectors with components:
  a $A_x = -4.0\,\text{cm}$, $A_y = -4.0\,\text{cm}$
  b $A_x = 124\,\text{km}$, $A_y = -158\,\text{km}$
  c $A_x = 0$, $A_y = -5.0\,\text{m}$
  d $A_x = 8.0\,\text{N}$, $A_y = 0$

39 The components of vectors A and B are as follows: ($A_x = 2.00$, $A_y = 3.00$), ($B_x = -2.00$, $B_y = 5.00$). Find the magnitude and direction of the vectors:
  a A b B c $A + B$
  d $A - B$ e $2A - B$

40 The position vector of a moving object has components ($r_x = 2$, $r_y = 2$) initially. After a certain time the position vector has components ($r_x = 4$, $r_y = 8$). Find the displacement vector.

41 The diagram shows the velocity vector of a particle moving in a circle with speed $10\,\text{m s}^{-1}$ at two separate points. The velocity vector is tangential to the circle. Find the vector representing the **change** in the velocity vector.

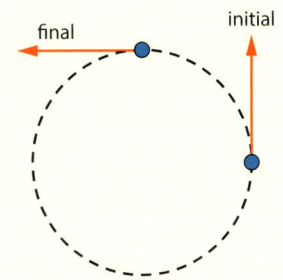

42 In a certain collision, the momentum vector of a particle changes direction but not magnitude. Let p be the momentum vector of a particle suffering an elastic collision and changing direction by 30°. Find, in terms of $p\ (=|p|)$, the magnitude of the vector representing the change in the momentum vector.

43 The velocity vector of an object moving on a circular path has a direction that is tangent to the path (see diagram).

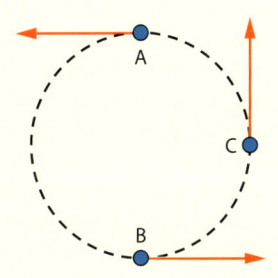

If the speed (magnitude of velocity) is constant at $4.0\,\text{m s}^{-1}$, find the change in the velocity vector as the object moves:
 a from A to B
 b from B to C.
 c What is the change in the velocity vector from A to C? How is this related to your answers to **a** and **b**?

44 For each diagram, find the components of the vectors along the axes shown. Take the magnitude of each vector to be 10.0 units.

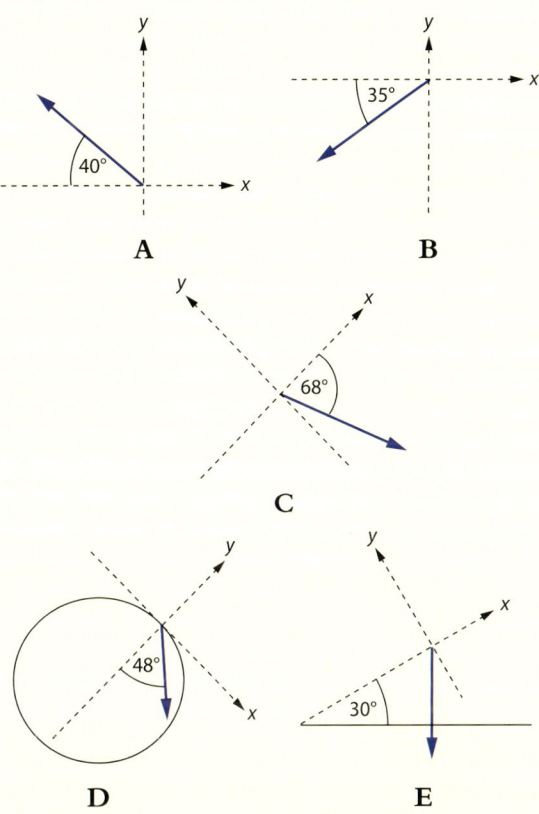

45 Vector **A** has a magnitude of 6.00 units and is directed at 60° to the positive x-axis. Vector **B** has a magnitude of 6.00 units and is directed at 120° to the positive x-axis. Find the magnitude and direction of vector **C** such that $A + B + C = 0$. Place the three vectors so that one begins where the previous ends. What do you observe?

46 Plot the following pairs of vectors on a set of x- and y-axes. The angles given are measured counter-clockwise from the positive x-axis. Then, using the algebraic component method, find their sum in magnitude and direction.
 a 12.0 N at 20° and 14.0 N at 50°
 b 15.0 N at 15° and 18.0 N at 105°
 c 20.0 N at 40° and 15.0 N at 310° (i.e. −50°)

1 MEASUREMENT AND UNCERTAINTIES   31

Exam-style questions

1. What is the equivalent of 80 years in seconds?

   A 10^7 **B** 10^9 **C** 10^{11} **D** 10^{13}

2. A book has 500 pages (printed on both sides). The width of the book excluding the covers is 2.5 cm. What is the approximate width in mm of one sheet of paper?

   A 0.01   **B** 0.1   **C** 0.5   **D** 1.0

3. The speed of sound is approximately $330\,\text{m s}^{-1}$. A storm is 3 km away. Approximately how much later after seeing lightning will thunder be heard?

   A 0.1 s   **B** 1 s   **C** 3 s   **D** 10 s

4. In which of the following diagrams do the three forces add up to zero?

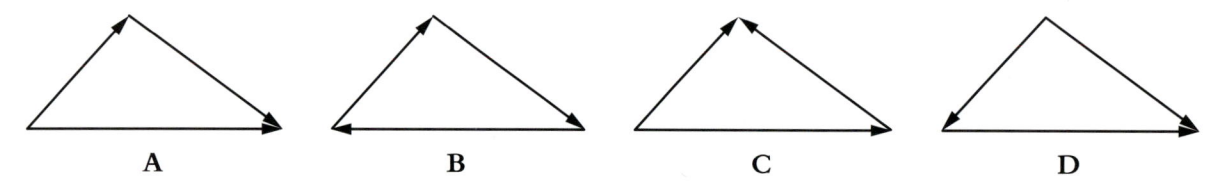

5. Three forces act on a body as shown.

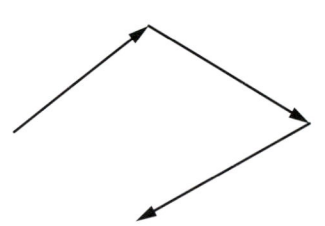

   Which fourth force is required so that the four forces add up to zero?

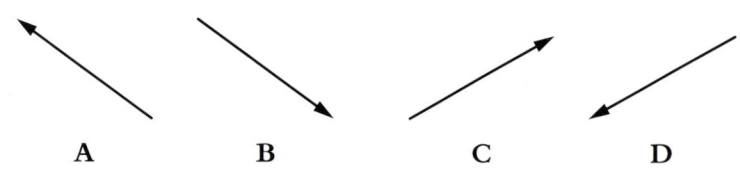

6. A force of 25 N acts normally on a surface of area $5.0\,\text{cm}^2$. What is the pressure on the surface in N m^{-2}?

   A 5   **B** 5×10^4 **C** 5.0   **D** 5.0×10^4

7. The side of a cube is measured with an uncertainty of 2%. What is the uncertainty in the volume of the cube?

   A 2%   **B** 4%   **C** 6%   **D** 8%

8 The flow rate Q through a tube of length L and radius r whose ends are kept at a pressure difference ΔP is given by $Q = \dfrac{cr^4 \Delta P}{L}$, where c is a constant. The percentage uncertainty of which quantity has the largest effect on the percentage uncertainty in Q?

    A r
    B ΔP
    C L
    D r, L and ΔP each give the same contribution

9 The force of air resistance F on a car depends on speed v through the formula $F = av^2 + bv$, where a and b are constants. Which of the following graphs will result in a straight-line graph?

    A F against v
    B F against v^2
    C $\dfrac{F}{v}$ against v
    D $\dfrac{F}{v}$ against $\dfrac{1}{v}$

10 The diagram shows the temperature of a liquid before and after heating.

```
20   25   30   35        60   65   70
++++|++++|++++|         ++++|++++|++
```

What is the best estimate for the temperature increase of the liquid?

    A (44.0 ± 0.5) degrees
    B (44 ± 1.0) degrees
    C (44 ± 1) degrees
    D (44.0 ± 2.0) degrees

11 A student wishes to measure the acceleration of free fall by letting a ping pong ball drop from one fixed height from the floor. He measures the height. Using a stopwatch, he measures the time for the ball to drop to the floor. He then uses the equation $h = \tfrac{1}{2}gt^2$ to calculate g.

State and discuss **three** improvements to the student's lab experiment. [6]

12 A man wants to cross a river with a motorboat. The speed of the motorboat in still water is $4.0\,\text{m s}^{-1}$. The river is 30 m wide. There is a current in the river whose speed with respect to the shore is $3.0\,\text{m s}^{-1}$.

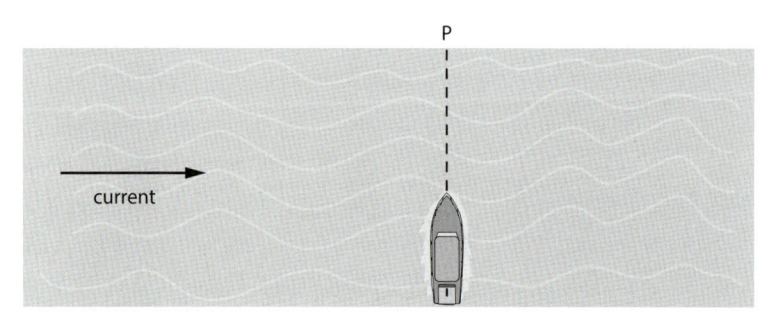

- **a** The man aims the boat towards P. Determine the distance from P at which he will reach the shore. [2]
- **b** A woman in an identical boat leaves from the same spot as the man but wants to land at P. Determine the direction in which she has to turn her boat to do this. [3]
- **c** Determine which person reaches the shore in the least time. [2]

13 A student investigated the oscillation period, T, of a clamped rod for various loads F applied to the rod. She graphed the following results.

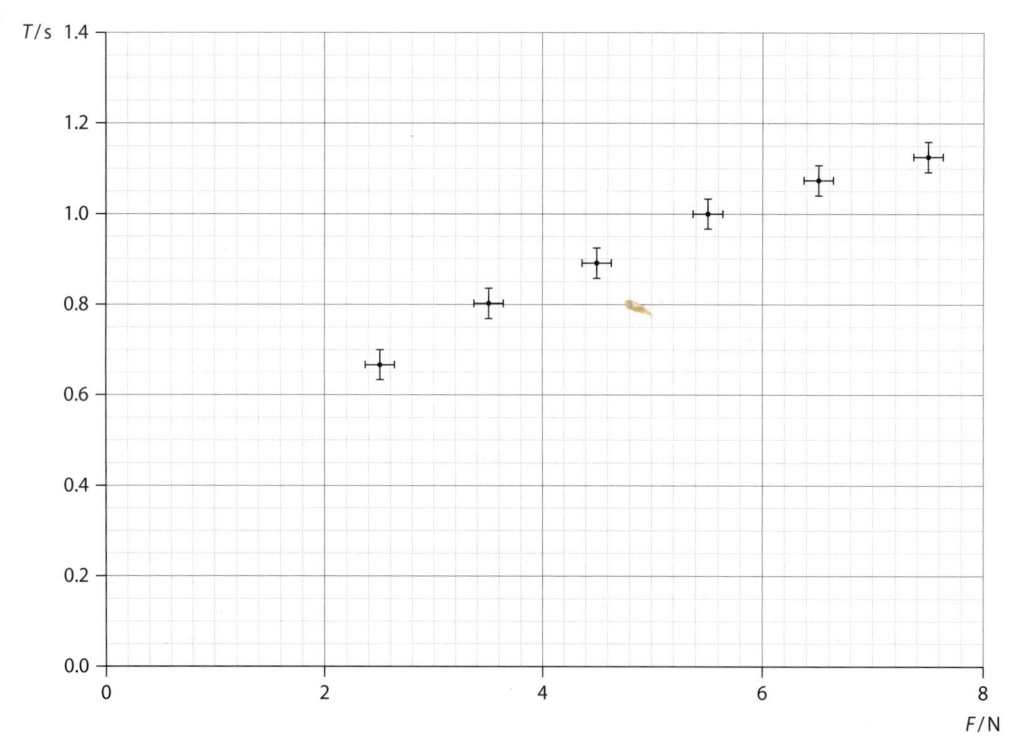

- **a** Copy the graph and draw the best-fit line for these data. [2]
- **b** Predict the period of oscillation of the rod when no load is applied to it. [1]
- **c** The student claims that T is proportional to F. Explain to the student how the results show she is not correct. [2]
- **d** Determine the absolute uncertainty in T^2 for the data point corresponding to $F = 5.5\,\text{N}$. [2]
- **e** Another student suspects that T^2 is proportional to F. By drawing a graph of T^2 against F discuss whether this student's claim is correct. [4]
- **f** Calculate the slope of the graph drawn in **e**, including its uncertainty. [3]

Mechanics 2

2.1 Motion

This section is an introduction to the basic concepts used in describing motion. We will begin with motion in a straight line with constant velocity and then constant acceleration. Knowledge of uniformly accelerated motion allows analysis of more complicated motions, such as the motion of projectiles.

Kinematical quantities

We will begin our discussion of motion with straight line motion in one dimension. This means that the particle that moves is constrained to move along a straight line. The **position** of the particle is then described by its coordinate on the straight line (Figure **2.1a**). If the line is horizontal, we may use the symbol x to represent the coordinate and hence the position. If the line is vertical, the symbol y is more convenient. In general, for an arbitrary line we may use a generic name, s, for position. So in Figure **2.1**, $x = 6\,\text{m}$, $y = -4\,\text{m}$ and $s = 0$.

Learning objectives

- Understand the difference between distance and displacement.
- Understand the difference between speed and velocity.
- Understand the concept of acceleration.
- Analyse graphs describing motion.
- Solve motion problems using the equations for constant acceleration.
- Discuss the motion of a projectile.
- Show a qualitative understanding of the effects of a fluid resistance force on motion.
- Understand the concept of terminal speed.

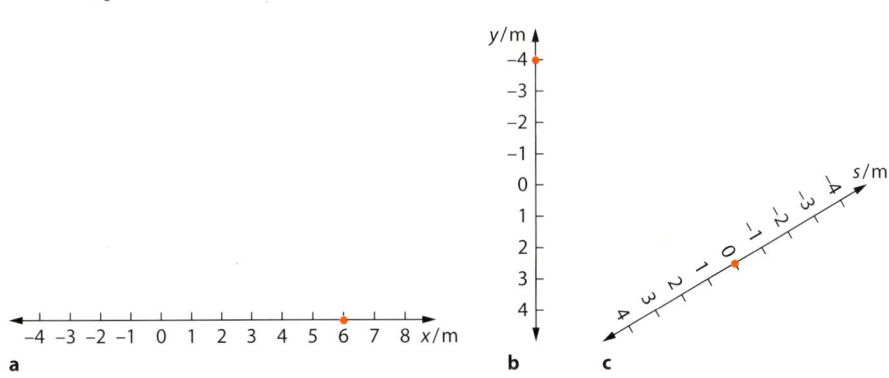

Figure 2.1 The position of a particle is determined by the coordinate on the number line.

As the particle moves on the straight line its position changes. In **uniform motion** the graph of position against time is a straight line (Figure **2.2**). In equal intervals of time, the position changes by the same amount. This means that the slope of the position–time graph is constant. This slope is defined to be the **average velocity** of the particle:

$$v = \frac{\Delta s}{\Delta t}$$

where Δs is the change in position.

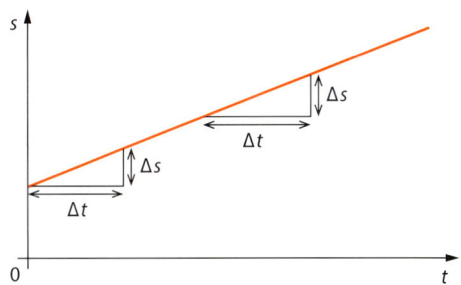

Figure 2.2 In uniform motion the graph of position versus time is a straight line.

> The average velocity during an interval of time Δt is the ratio of the change in position Δs during that time interval to Δt.

2 MECHANICS 35

(In uniform motion velocity is constant so the term 'average' is unnecessary. The velocity is the same at all times.)

Positive velocity means that the coordinate s that gives the position is increasing. Negative velocity means that s is decreasing.

Suppose we choose a time interval from $t = 0$ to some arbitrary time t later. Let the position at $t = 0$ (the initial position) be s_i and the position at time t be s. Then:

$$v = \frac{s - s_i}{t - 0}$$

which can be re-arranged to give:

$$s = s_i + vt$$

This formula gives, in uniform motion, the position s of the moving object t seconds after time zero, given that the velocity is v and the initial position is s_i.

Worked example

2.1 Two cyclists, A and B, start moving at the same time. The initial position of A is 0 m and her velocity is $+20 \,\text{km h}^{-1}$. The initial position of B is 150 km and he cycles at a velocity of $-30 \,\text{km h}^{-1}$. Determine the time and position at which they will meet.

The position of A is given by the formula: $\quad s_A = 0 + 20t$

The position of B is given by the formula: $\quad s_B = 150 - 30t$

They will meet when they are the same position, i.e. when $s_A = s_B$. This implies:

$20t = 150 - 30t$

$50t = 150$

$t = 3.0$ hours

The common position is found from either $s_A = 20 \times 3.0 = 60 \,\text{km}$ or $s_B = 150 - 30 \times 3.0 = 60 \,\text{km}$.

Consider two motions shown in Figure 2.3. In the first, the particle leaves its initial position s_i at -4 m and continues to its final position at 16 m. The change in position is called **displacement** and in this case equals $16 - (-4) = 20$ m. The **distance** travelled is the actual length of the path followed and in this case is also 20 m.

Displacement = change in position
Distance = length of path followed

In the second motion, the particle leaves its initial position at 12 m, arrives at position 20 m and then comes back to its final position at 4.0 m.

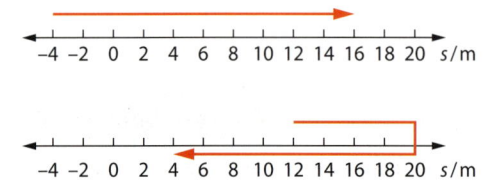

Figure 2.3 A motion in which the particle changes direction.

The second motion is an example of motion with changing direction. The change in the position of this particle, i.e. the displacement is $\Delta s = s_f - s_i = 4.0 - 12 = -8.0$ m. But the distance travelled by the particle (the length of the path) is 8.0 m in the outward trip and 16 m on the return trip, making a total distance of 24 m. So we must be careful to distinguish distance from displacement. Distance is a scalar but displacement is a vector. Numerically, they are different if there is a change of direction, as in this example.

For constant velocity, the graph of velocity versus time gives a horizontal straight line (Figure **2.4a**). An example of this type of motion is coasting in a straight line on a bicycle on level ground (Figure **2.4b**).

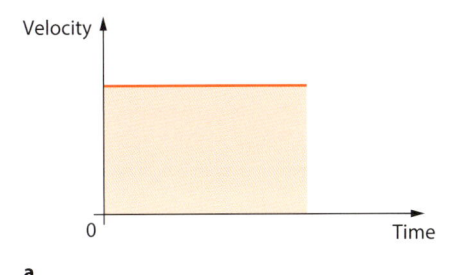

Figure 2.4 a In uniform motion the graph of velocity versus time is a horizontal straight line. **b** This motion is a good approximation to uniform motion.

But we now observe that the area under the graph from $t = 0$ to time t is vt. From $s = s_i + vt$ we deduce that this area is the change in position or the displacement.

Uniformly accelerated motion

In the last section we discussed uniform motion. This means motion in a straight line with **constant velocity**. In such motion the graph of position versus time is a straight line.

In most motions velocity is not constant. In **uniformly accelerated motion** the graph of velocity versus time is a non-horizontal straight line (Figure **2.5**).

In equal intervals of time the velocity changes by the same amount. The slope of the velocity–time graph is constant. This slope is defined to be the acceleration of the particle:

$$a = \frac{\Delta v}{\Delta t}$$

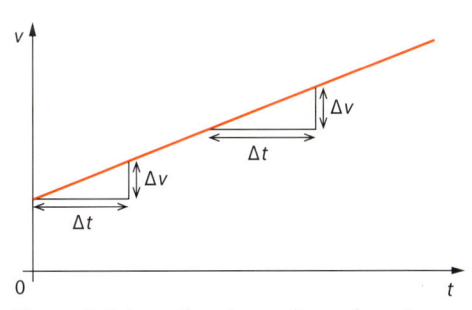

Figure 2.5 In uniformly accelerated motion the graph of velocity versus time is a straight line with non-zero slope.

> **Acceleration** is the rate of change of velocity.

When the acceleration is positive, the velocity is increasing (Figure **2.6**). Negative acceleration means that v is decreasing. The plane reaches a take-off speed of 260 km h^{-1} (about 72 m s^{-1}) in about 2 seconds, implying an average acceleration of about 36 m s^{-2}. The distance travelled until take-off is about 72 m.

Figure 2.6 This F/A-18C is accelerating!

2 MECHANICS 37

Suppose we choose a time interval from $t=0$ to some arbitrary time t later. Let the velocity at $t=0$ (the initial velocity) be u and the velocity at time t be v. Then:

$$a = \frac{v-u}{t-0}$$

which can be re-arranged to:

$$v = u + at$$

For uniformly accelerated motion, this formula gives the velocity v of the moving object t seconds after time zero, given that the initial velocity is u and the acceleration is a.

Worked example

2.2 A particle has initial velocity $12\,\text{m s}^{-1}$ and moves with a constant acceleration of $-3.0\,\text{m s}^{-2}$. Determine the time at which the particle stops instantaneously.

The particle is getting slower. At some point it will stop instantaneously, i.e. its velocity v will be zero.

We know that $v = u + at$. Just substituting values gives:

$0 = 12 + (-3.0) \times t$

$3.0t = 12$

Hence $t = 4.0\,\text{s}$.

Defining velocity in non-uniform motion

But how is velocity defined now that it is not constant? We define the average velocity as before:

$$\bar{v} = \frac{\Delta s}{\Delta t}$$

But since the velocity changes, it has different values at different times. We would like to have a concept of the velocity at an instant of time, the **instantaneous velocity**. We need to make the time interval Δt very small. The instantaneous velocity is then defined as:

$$v = \lim_{\Delta t \to 0} \frac{\Delta s}{\Delta t}$$

In other words, instantaneous velocity is the average velocity obtained during an interval of time that is very, very small. In calculus, we learn that $\lim_{\Delta t \to 0} \frac{\Delta s}{\Delta t}$ has the following meaning: look at the graph of position s versus time t shown in Figure **2.7a**. As there is uniform acceleration, the graph is a curve. Choose a point on this curve. Draw the tangent line to the curve at the point. The slope of the tangent line is the meaning of $\lim_{\Delta t \to 0} \frac{\Delta s}{\Delta t}$ and therefore also of velocity.

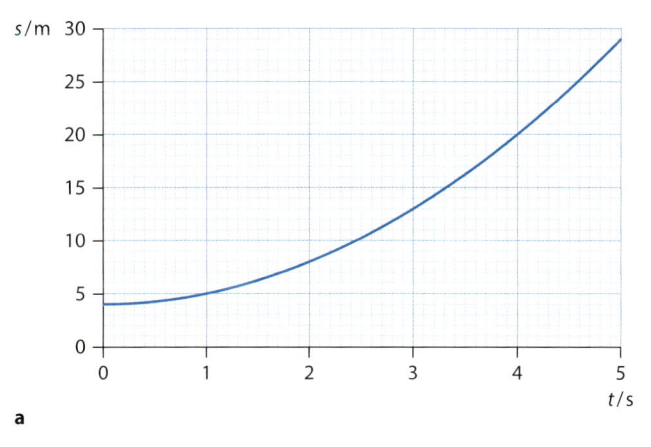

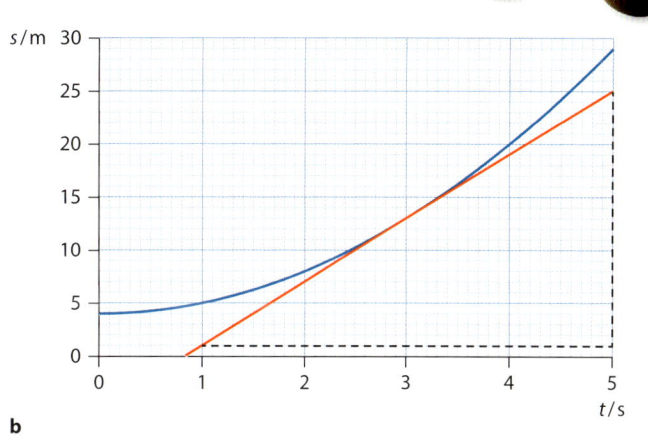

Figure 2.7 a In uniformly accelerated motion the graph of position versus time is a curve. **b** The slope of the tangent at a particular point gives the velocity at that point.

In Figure **2.7b** the tangent is drawn at $t = 3.0\,\text{s}$. We can use this to find the instantaneous velocity at $t = 3.0\,\text{s}$. The slope of this tangent line is:

$$\frac{25 - 1.0}{5.0 - 1.0} = 6.0\,\text{m s}^{-1}$$

To find the instantaneous velocity at some other instant of time we must take another tangent and we will find a different instantaneous velocity. At the point at $t = 0$ it is particularly easy to find the velocity: the tangent is horizontal and so the velocity is zero.

Instantaneous velocity can be positive or negative. The magnitude of the instantaneous velocity is known as the **instantaneous speed**.

We define the **average speed** to be the total distance travelled divided by the total time taken. The **average velocity** is defined as the change in position (i.e. the displacement) divided by the time taken:

$$\text{average speed} = \frac{\text{total distance travelled}}{\text{total time taken}}$$

$$\text{average velocity} = \frac{\text{displacement}}{\text{total time taken}}$$

> The slope of the tangent to the graph of position versus time is velocity

Consider the graph of velocity versus time in Figure **2.8**. Imagine approximating the straight line with a staircase. The area under the staircase is the change in position since at each step the velocity is constant. If we make the steps of the staircase smaller and smaller, the area under the line and the area under the staircase will be indistinguishable and so we have the general result that:

> The area under the curve in a velocity versus time graph is the change in position.

From Figure **2.8** this area is (the shape is a trapezoid):

$$\Delta s = \left(\frac{u + v}{2}\right)t$$

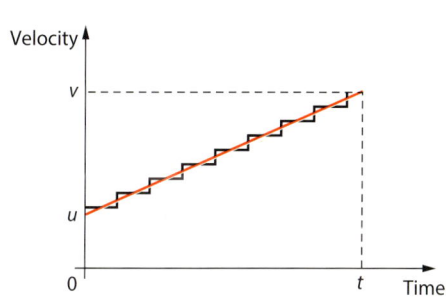

Figure 2.8 The straight-line graph may be approximated by a staircase.

2 MECHANICS 39

But $v = u + at$, so this becomes:

$$\Delta s = \left(\frac{u + u + at}{2}\right)t = ut + \frac{1}{2}at^2$$

So we have two formulas for position in the case of uniformly accelerated motion (recall that $\Delta s = s - s_i$):

$$s = s_i + \left(\frac{u + v}{2}\right)t$$

$$s = s_i + ut + \frac{1}{2}at^2$$

We get a final formula if we combine $s = s_i + ut + \frac{1}{2}at^2$ with $v = u + at$. From the second equation write $t = \frac{v - u}{a}$ and substitute in the first equation to get:

$$s - s_i = u\frac{v - u}{a} + \frac{1}{2}\left(\frac{v - u}{a}\right)^2$$

After a bit of uninteresting algebra this becomes:

$$v^2 = u^2 + 2a(s - s_i)$$

This is useful in problems in which no information on time is given.

Graphs of position versus time for uniformly accelerated motion are parabolas (Figure 2.9). If the parabola 'holds water' the acceleration is positive. If not, the acceleration is negative.

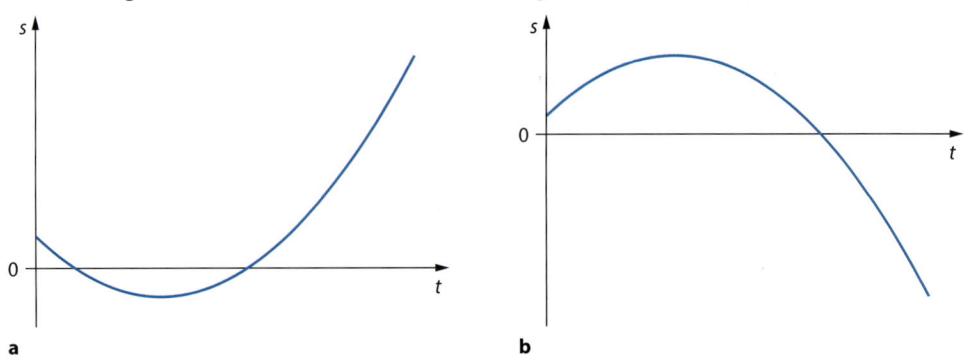

Figure 2.9 Graphs of position s against time t for uniformly accelerated motion. **a** Positive acceleration. **b** Negative acceleration.

Exam tip
The table summarises the meaning of the slope and area for the different motion graphs.

Graph of …	Slope	Area
position against time	velocity	
velocity against time	acceleration	change in position
acceleration against time		change in velocity

These formulas can be used for constant acceleration only (if the initial position is zero, Δs may be replaced by just s).

$$v = u + at \qquad \Delta s = ut + \frac{1}{2}at^2 \qquad \Delta s = \left(\frac{u + v}{2}\right)t \qquad v^2 = u^2 + 2a\Delta s$$

Worked examples

2.3 A particle has initial velocity $2.00\,\mathrm{m\,s^{-1}}$ and acceleration $a = 4.00\,\mathrm{m\,s^{-2}}$. Find its displacement after $10.0\,\mathrm{s}$.

Displacement is the change of position, i.e. $\Delta s = s - s_i$. We use the equation:

$\Delta s = ut + \frac{1}{2}at^2$

$\Delta s = 2.00 \times 10.0 + \frac{1}{2} \times 4.00 \times 10.0^2$

$\Delta s = 220\,\mathrm{m}$

2.4 A car has an initial velocity of $u = 5.0\,\mathrm{m\,s^{-1}}$. After a displacement of $20\,\mathrm{m}$, its velocity becomes $7.0\,\mathrm{m\,s^{-1}}$. Find the acceleration of the car.

Here, $\Delta s = s - s_i = 20\,\mathrm{m}$. So use $v^2 = u^2 + 2a\Delta s$ to find a.

$7.0^2 = 5.0^2 + 2a \times 20$

$24 = 40a$

Therefore $a = 0.60\,\mathrm{m\,s^{-2}}$.

2.5 A body has initial velocity $4.0\,\mathrm{m\,s^{-1}}$. After $6.0\,\mathrm{s}$ the velocity is $12\,\mathrm{m\,s^{-1}}$. Determine the displacement of the body in the $6.0\,\mathrm{s}$.

We know u, v and t. We can use:

$\Delta s = \left(\dfrac{v+u}{2}\right)t$

to get:

$\Delta s = \left(\dfrac{12 + 4.0}{2}\right) \times 6.0$

$\Delta s = 48\,\mathrm{m}$

A slower method would be to use $v = u + at$ to find the acceleration:

$12 = 4.0 + 6.0a$

$\Rightarrow\quad a = 1.333\,\mathrm{m\,s^{-2}}$

Then use the value of a to find Δs:

$\Delta s = ut + \frac{1}{2}at^2$

$\Delta s = 4.0 \times 6.0 + \frac{1}{2} \times 1.333 \times 36$

$\Delta s = 48\,\mathrm{m}$

2.6 Two balls start out moving to the right with constant velocities of $5.0\,\text{m}\,\text{s}^{-1}$ and $4.0\,\text{m}\,\text{s}^{-1}$. The slow ball starts first and the other 4.0 s later. Determine the position of the balls when they meet.

Let the two balls meet t s after the first ball starts moving.

The position of the slow ball is: $s = 4t$

The position of the fast ball is: $5(t-4)$

(The factor $t-4$ is there because after t s the fast ball has actually been moving for only $t-4$ seconds.)

These two positions are equal when the two balls meet, and so:

$4t = 5t - 20$

$\Rightarrow\ t = 20\,\text{s}$

Substituting into the equation for the position of the slow ball, the position where the balls meet is 80 m to the right of the start.

2.7 A particle starts out from the origin with velocity $10\,\text{m}\,\text{s}^{-1}$ and continues moving at this velocity for 5 s. The velocity is then abruptly reversed to $-5\,\text{m}\,\text{s}^{-1}$ and the object moves at this velocity for 10 s. For this motion find:
  a the change in position, i.e. the displacement
  b the total distance travelled
  c the average speed
  d the average velocity.

The problem is best solved using the velocity–time graph, which is shown in Figure **2.10**.

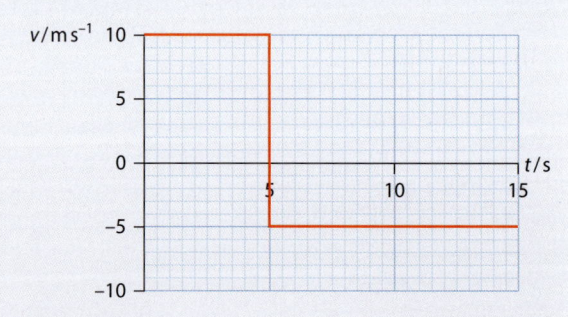

Figure 2.10

a The initial position is zero. Thus, after 5.0 s the position is $10 \times 5.0\,\text{m} = 50\,\text{m}$ (the area under the first part of the graph). In the next 10 s the displacement changes by $-5.0 \times 10 = -50\,\text{m}$ (the area under the second part of the graph). The change in position, i.e. the displacement, is thus $50 - 50 = 0\,\text{m}$.

b Take the initial velocity as moving to the right. The object moved toward the right, stopped and returned to its starting position (we know this because the displacement was 0). The distance travelled is 50 m in moving to the right and 50 m coming back, giving a total distance travelled of 100 m.

c The average speed is $\dfrac{100\,\text{m}}{15\,\text{s}} = 6.7\,\text{m}\,\text{s}^{-1}$.

d The average velocity is zero, since the displacement is zero.

2.8 An object with initial velocity $20\,\text{m s}^{-1}$ and initial position of $-75\,\text{m}$ experiences a constant acceleration of $-2\,\text{m s}^{-2}$. Sketch the position–time graph for this motion for the first $20\,\text{s}$.

Use the equation $s = ut + \frac{1}{2}at^2$. Substituting the values we know, the displacement is given by $s = -75 + 20t - t^2$. This is the function we must graph. The result is shown in Figure 2.11.

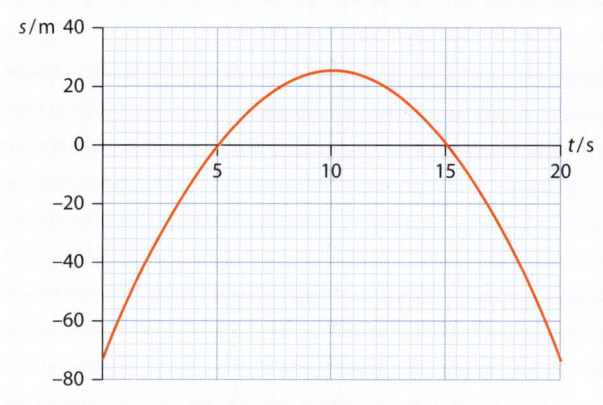

Figure 2.11

At $5\,\text{s}$ the object reaches the origin and overshoots it. It returns to the origin $10\,\text{s}$ later ($t = 15\,\text{s}$). The furthest it gets from the origin is $25\,\text{m}$. The velocity at $5\,\text{s}$ is $10\,\text{m s}^{-1}$ and at $15\,\text{s}$ it is $-10\,\text{m s}^{-1}$. At $10\,\text{s}$ the velocity is zero.

A special acceleration

Assuming that we can neglect air resistance and other frictional forces, an object thrown into the air will experience the **acceleration of free fall** while in the air. This is an acceleration caused by the attraction between the Earth and the body. The magnitude of this acceleration is denoted by g. Near the surface of the Earth $g = 9.8\,\text{m s}^{-2}$. The direction of this acceleration is always vertically downward. (We will sometimes approximate g by $10\,\text{m s}^{-2}$.)

Worked example

2.9 An object is thrown vertically upwards with an initial velocity of $20\,\text{m s}^{-1}$ from the edge of a cliff that is $30\,\text{m}$ from the sea below, as shown in Figure 2.12.

Determine:
  a the ball's maximum height
  b the time taken for the ball to reach its maximum height
  c the time to hit the sea
  d the speed with which it hits the sea.
(You may approximate g by $10\,\text{m s}^{-2}$.)

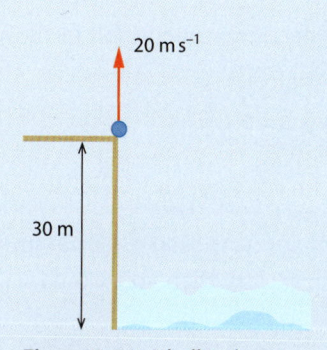

Figure 2.12 A ball is thrown upwards from the edge of a cliff.

We have motion on a vertical line so we will use the symbol y for position (Figure **2.13a**). We make the vertical line point upwards. The zero for displacement is the ball's initial position.

a The quickest way to get the answer to this part is to use $v^2 = u^2 - 2gy$. (The acceleration is $a = -g$.) At the highest point $v = 0$, and so:

$$0 = 20^2 - 2 \times 10y$$

$$\Rightarrow y = 20\,\text{m}$$

b At the highest point the object's velocity is zero. Using $v = 0$ in $v = u - gt$ gives:

$$0 = 20 - 10 \times t$$

$$t = \frac{20}{10} = 2.0\,\text{s}$$

c There are many ways to do this. One is to use the displacement arrow shown in blue in Figure **2.13a**. Then when the ball hits the sea, $y = -30\,\text{m}$. Now use the formula $y = ut - \frac{1}{2}gt^2$ to find an equation that only has the variable t:

$$-30 = 20 \times t - 5 \times t^2$$

$$t^2 - 4t - 6 = 0$$

This is a quadratic equation. Using your calculator you can find the two roots as $-1.2\,\text{s}$ and $5.2\,\text{s}$. Choose the positive root to find the answer $t = 5.2\,\text{s}$.

Another way of looking at this is shown in Figure **2.13b**. Here we start at the highest point and make the line along which the ball moves point downwards. Then, at the top $y = 0$, at the sea $y = +50$ and $g = +10\,\text{m s}^{-2}$. Now, the initial velocity is zero because we take our initial point to be at the top.

Using $y = ut + \frac{1}{2}gt^2$ with $u = 0$, we find:

$$50 = 5t^2$$

$$\Rightarrow t = 3.2\,\text{s}$$

This is the time to fall to the sea. It took $2.0\,\text{s}$ to reach the highest point, so the total time from launch to hitting the sea is:

$2.0 + 3.2 = 5.2\,\text{s}$.

d Use $v = u - gt$ and $t = 5.2\,\text{s}$ to get $v = 20 - 10 \times 5.2 = -32\,\text{m s}^{-1}$. The speed is then $32\,\text{m s}^{-1}$.

(If you preferred the diagram in Figure **2.13b** for working out part **c** and you want to continue this method for part **d**, then you would write $v = u + gt$ with $t = 3.2\,\text{s}$ and $u = 0$ to get $v = 10 \times 3.2 = +32\,\text{m s}^{-1}$.)

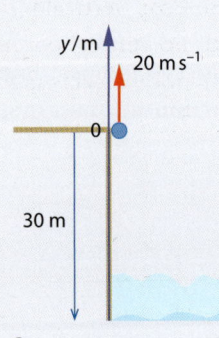

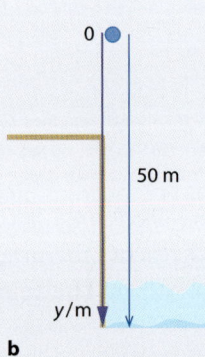

Figure 2.13 Diagrams for solving the ball's motion. **a** Displacement upwards is positive. **b** The highest point is the zero of displacement.

Projectile motion

Figure **2.14** shows the positions of two objects every 0.2 s: the first was simply allowed to drop vertically from rest, the other was launched horizontally with no vertical component of velocity. We see that in the vertical direction, both objects fall the **same distance** in the **same time**.

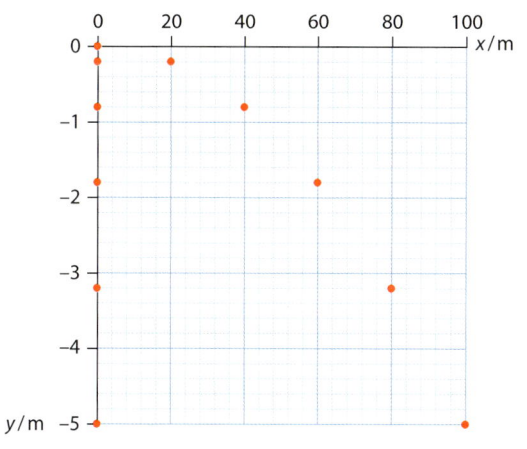

Figure 2.14 A body dropped from rest and one launched horizontally cover the same vertical displacement in the same time.

How do we understand this fact? Consider Figure **2.15**, in which a black ball is projected horizontally with velocity v. A blue ball is allowed to drop vertically from the same height. Figure **2.15a** shows the situation when the balls are released as seen by an observer X at rest on the ground. But suppose there is an observer Y, who moves to the right with velocity $\frac{v}{2}$ with respect to the ground. What does Y see? Observer Y sees the black ball moving to the right with velocity $\frac{v}{2}$ and the blue ball approaching with velocity $-\frac{v}{2}$ (Figure **2.15b**) The motions of the two balls are therefore **identical** (except for direction). So this observer will determine that the two bodies reach the ground at the **same time**. Since time is absolute in Newtonian physics, the two bodies must reach the ground at the same time as far as any other observer is concerned as well.

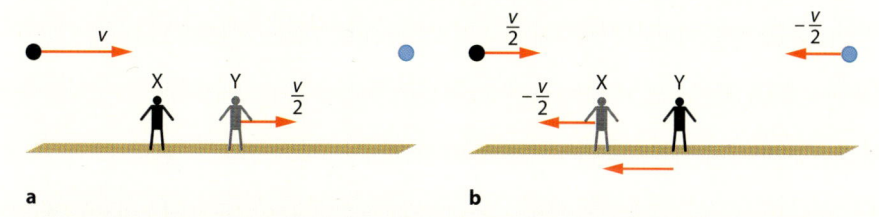

Figure 2.15 a A ball projected horizontally and one simply dropped from rest from the point of view of observer X. Observer Y is moving to the right with velocity $\frac{v}{2}$ with respect to the ground. **b** From the point of view of observer Y, the black and the blue balls have identical motions.

2 MECHANICS 45

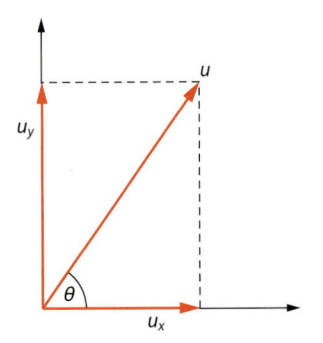

Figure 2.16 A projectile is launched at an angle θ to the horizontal with speed u.

The discussion shows that the motion of a ball that is projected at some angle can be analysed by separately looking at the horizontal and the vertical directions. All we have to do is consider two motions, one in the horizontal direction in which there is no acceleration, and another in the vertical direction in which we have an acceleration, g.

Consider Figure 2.16, where a projectile is launched at an angle θ to the horizontal with speed u. The components of the *initial* velocity vector are $u_x = u\cos\theta$ and $u_y = u\sin\theta$. At some later time t the components of velocity are v_x and v_y. In the x-direction we do not have any acceleration and so:

$$v_x = u_x$$

$$v_x = u\cos\theta$$

In the y-direction the acceleration is $-g$ and so:

$$v_y = u_y - gt$$

$$v_y = u\sin\theta - gt$$

The green vector in Figure 2.17a shows the position of the projectile t seconds after launch. The red arrows in Figure 2.17b show the velocity vectors.

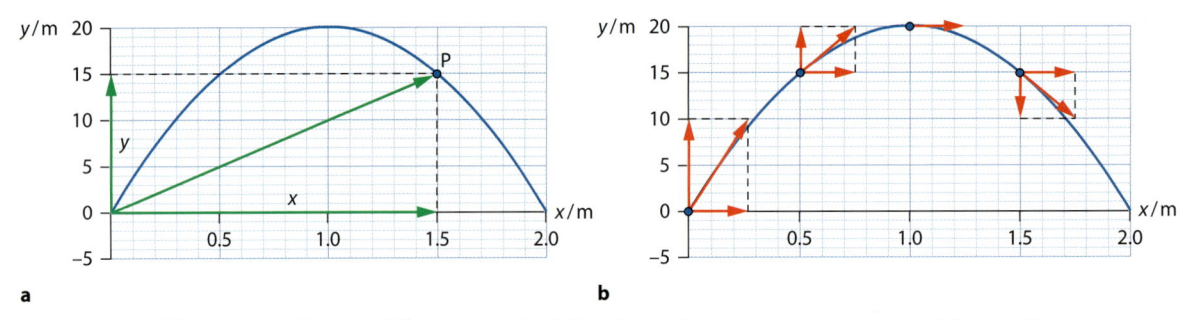

Figure 2.17 a The position of the particle is determined if we know the x- and y-components of the position vector. **b** The velocity vectors for projectile motion are tangents to the parabolic path.

Exam tip
All that we are doing is using the formulas from the previous section for velocity and position $v = u + at$ and $s = ut + \frac{1}{2}at^2$ and rewriting them **separately** for each direction x and y.

In the x-direction there is zero acceleration and in the y-direction there is an acceleration $-g$.

We would like to know the x- and y-components of the position vector. We now use the formula for position. In the x-direction:

$$x = u_x t$$

$$x = ut\cos\theta$$

And in the y-direction:

$$y = u_y t - \frac{1}{2}gt^2$$

$$y = ut\sin\theta - \frac{1}{2}gt^2$$

Let us collect what we have derived so far. We have four equations with which we can solve any problem with projectiles, as we will soon see:

$$\underbrace{v_x = u\cos\theta}_{x\text{-velocity}}, \qquad \underbrace{v_y = u\sin\theta - gt}_{y\text{-velocity}}$$

$$\underbrace{x = ut\cos\theta}_{x\text{-displacement}}, \qquad \underbrace{y = ut\sin\theta - \frac{1}{2}gt^2}_{y\text{-displacement}}$$

The equation with 'squares of speeds' is a bit trickier (carefully review the following steps). It is:

$$v^2 = u^2 - 2gy$$

Since $v^2 = v_x^2 + v_y^2$ and $u^2 = u_x^2 + u_y^2$, and in addition $v_x^2 = u_x^2$, this is also equivalent to:

$$v_y^2 = u_y^2 - 2gy$$

Exam tip
Always choose your x- and y-axes so that the origin is the point where the launch takes place.

Worked examples

2.10 A body is launched with a speed of $18.0\,\text{m s}^{-1}$ at the following angles:
  a 30° to the horizontal
  b 0° to the horizontal
  c 90° to the horizontal.
  Find the x- and y-components of the initial velocity in each case.

a $v_x = u\cos\theta$ $\qquad$ $v_y = u\sin\theta$
$v_x = 18.0 \times \cos 30°$ $\qquad$ $v_y = 18.0 \times \sin 30°$
$v_x = 15.6\,\text{m s}^{-1}$ $\qquad$ $v_y = 9.00\,\text{m s}^{-1}$

b $v_x = 18.0\,\text{m s}^{-1}$ $\qquad$ $v_y = 0\,\text{m s}^{-1}$

c $v_x = 0$ $\qquad$ $v_y = 18.0\,\text{m s}^{-1}$

2.11 Sketch graphs to show the variation with time of the horizontal and vertical components of velocity for a projectile launched at some angle above the horizontal.

The graphs are shown in Figure **2.18**.

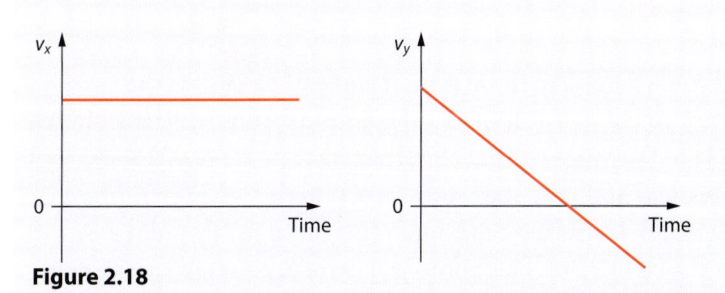

Figure 2.18

2 MECHANICS 47

2.12 An object is launched horizontally from a height of 20 m above the ground with speed 15 m s^{-1}. Determine:
  a the time at which it will hit the ground
  b the horizontal distance travelled
  c the speed with which it hits the ground.
  (Take $g = 10$ m s^{-2}.)

a The launch is horizontal, i.e. $\theta = 0°$, and so the formula for vertical displacement is just $y = -\frac{1}{2}gt^2$.

The object will hit the ground when $y = -20$ m.

Substituting the values, we find:

$-20 = -5t^2$

$\Rightarrow \quad t = 2.0$ s

Exam tip
This is a basic problem – you must know how to do this!

b The horizontal distance is found from $x = ut$. Substituting values:

$x = 15 \times 2.0 = 30$ m

(Remember that $\theta = 0°$).

c Use $v^2 = u^2 - 2gy$ to get:

$v^2 = 15^2 - 2 \times 10 \times (-20)$

$v = 25$ m s^{-1}

2.13 An object is launched horizontally with a velocity of 12 m s^{-1}. Determine:
  a the vertical component of velocity after 4.0 s
  b the x- and y-components of the position vector of the object after 4.0 s.

a The launch is again horizontal, i.e. $\theta = 0°$, so substitute this value in the formulas. The horizontal component of velocity is 12 m s^{-1} at all times.

From $v_y = -gt$, the vertical component after 4.0 s is $v_y = -20$ m s^{-1}.

b The coordinates after time t are:

$x = ut$ and $y = -\frac{1}{2}gt^2$

$x = 12.0 \times 4.0$ $\quad y = -5 \times 16$

$x = 48$ m $\quad y = -80$ m

Figure **2.19** shows an object thrown at an angle of $\theta = 30°$ to the horizontal with initial speed 20 m s^{-1}. The position of the object is shown every 0.2 s. Note how the dots get closer together as the object rises (the speed is decreasing) and how they move apart on the way down (the speed is increasing). It reaches a maximum height of 5.1 m and travels a horizontal distance of 35 m. The photo in Figure **2.20** show an example of projectile motion.

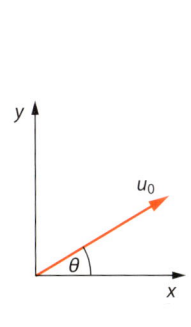

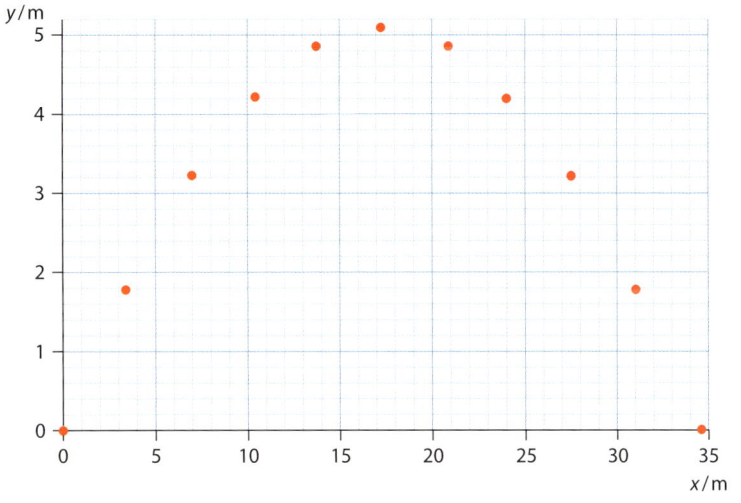

Figure 2.19 A launch at of $\theta = 30°$ to the horizontal with initial speed $20\,\text{m s}^{-1}$.

At what point in time does the vertical velocity component become zero? Setting $v_y = 0$ we find:

$$0 = u\sin\theta - gt$$

$$\Rightarrow \quad t = \frac{u\sin\theta}{g}$$

The time when the vertical velocity becomes zero is, of course, the time when the object attains its maximum height. What is this height? Going back to the equation for the vertical component of displacement, we find that when:

$$t = \frac{u\sin\theta}{g}$$

y is given by:

$$y_{\text{max}} = u\frac{u\sin\theta}{g}\sin\theta - \frac{1}{2}g\left(\frac{u\sin\theta}{g}\right)^2$$

$$y_{\text{max}} = \frac{u^2\sin^2\theta}{2g}$$

Figure 2.20 A real example of projectile motion!

Exam tip
You should not remember these formulas by heart. You should be able to derive them quickly.

What about the maximum displacement in the horizontal direction (sometimes called the range)? At this point the vertical component of displacement y is zero. Setting $y = 0$ in the formula for y gives:

$$0 = ut\sin\theta - \tfrac{1}{2}gt^2$$

$$0 = t(u\sin\theta - \tfrac{1}{2}gt)$$

and so:

$$t = 0 \quad \text{and} \quad t = \frac{2u\sin\theta}{g}$$

2 MECHANICS 49

The first time $t = 0$ is, of course, when the object first starts out. The second time is what we want – the time in which the range is covered. Therefore the range is:

$$x = \frac{2u^2 \sin\theta \cos\theta}{g}$$

A bit of trigonometry allows us to rewrite this as:

$$x = \frac{u^2 \sin(2\theta)}{g}$$

> One of the identities in trigonometry is $2\sin\theta\cos\theta = \sin 2\theta$

The maximum value of $\sin 2\theta$ is 1, and this happens when $2\theta = 90°$ (i.e. $\theta = 45°$); in other words, we obtain the maximum range with a launch angle of 45°. This equation also says that there are two different angles of launch that give the same range for the same initial speed. These two angles add up to a right angle (can you see why?).

Worked examples

2.14 A projectile is launched at 32.0° to the horizontal with initial speed 25.0 m s^{-1}. Determine the maximum height reached. (Take $g = 9.81$ m s^{-2}.)

The vertical velocity is given by $v_y = u\sin\theta - gt$ and becomes zero at the highest point. Thus:

$$t = \frac{u\sin\theta}{g}$$

$$t = \frac{25.0 \times \sin 32.0°}{9.81}$$

$$t = 1.35 \text{ s}$$

Substituting in the formula for y, $y = ut\sin\theta - \frac{1}{2}gt^2$, we get:

$$y = 25 \times \sin 32.0° \times 1.35 - \frac{1}{2} \times 9.81 \times 1.35^2$$

$$y = 8.95 \text{ m}$$

2.15 A projectile is launched horizontally from a height of 42 m above the ground. As it hits the ground, the velocity makes an angle of 55° to the horizontal. Find the initial velocity of launch. (Take $g = 9.8 \text{ m s}^{-2}$.)

The time it takes to hit the ground is found from $y = \frac{1}{2}gt^2$ (here $\theta = 0°$ since the launch is horizontal).

The ground is at $y = -42$ m and so:

$-42 = -\frac{1}{2} \times 9.8 t^2$

$\Rightarrow \quad t = 2.928 \text{ s}$

Using $v = u - at$, when the projectile hits the ground:

$v_y = 0 - 9.8 \times 2.928$

$v_y = -28.69 \text{ m s}^{-1}$

We know the angle the final velocity makes with the ground (Figure 2.21). Hence:

$\tan 55° = \left| \dfrac{v_y}{v_x} \right|$

$\Rightarrow \quad v_x = \dfrac{28.69}{\tan 55°}$

$v_x = 20.03 \approx 20 \text{ m s}^{-1}$

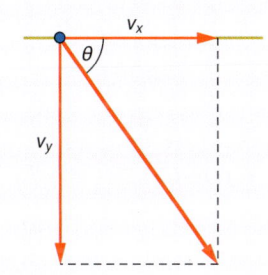

Figure 2.21

$\tan \theta = \left| \dfrac{v_y}{v_x} \right|$

Fluid resistance

The discussion of the previous sections has neglected air resistance forces. In general, whenever a body moves through a fluid (gas or liquid) it experiences a **fluid resistance force** that is directed opposite to the velocity. Typically $F = kv$ for low speeds and $F = kv^2$ for high speeds (where k is a constant). The magnitude of this force increases with increasing speed.

Imagine dropping a body of mass m from some height. Assume that the force of air resistance on this body is $F = kv$. Initially, the only force on the body is its weight, which accelerates it downward. As the speed increases, the force of air resistance also increases. Eventually, this force will become equal to the weight and so the acceleration will become zero: the body will then move at constant speed, called **terminal speed**, v_T. This speed can be found from:

$mg = kv_T$

which leads to:

$v_T = \dfrac{mg}{k}$

2 MECHANICS

Figure **2.22** shows how the speed and acceleration vary for motion with an air resistance force that is proportional to speed. The speed eventually becomes the terminal speed and the acceleration becomes zero. The initial acceleration is g.

The effect of air resistance forces on projectiles is very pronounced. Figure **2.23** shows the positions of a projectile with (red) and without (blue) air resistance forces. With air resistance forces the range and maximum height are smaller and the shape is no longer symmetrical. The projectile hits the ground with a steeper angle.

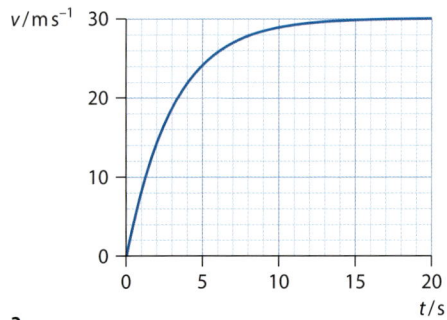

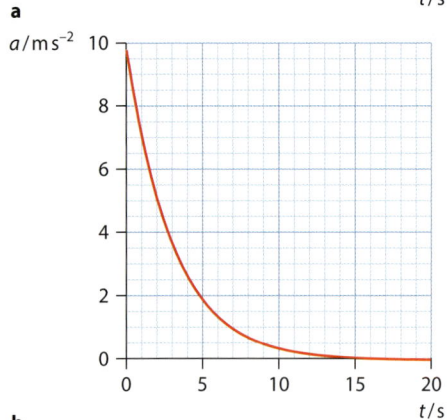

Figure 2.22 The variation with time of **a** speed and **b** acceleration in motion with an air resistance force proportional to speed.

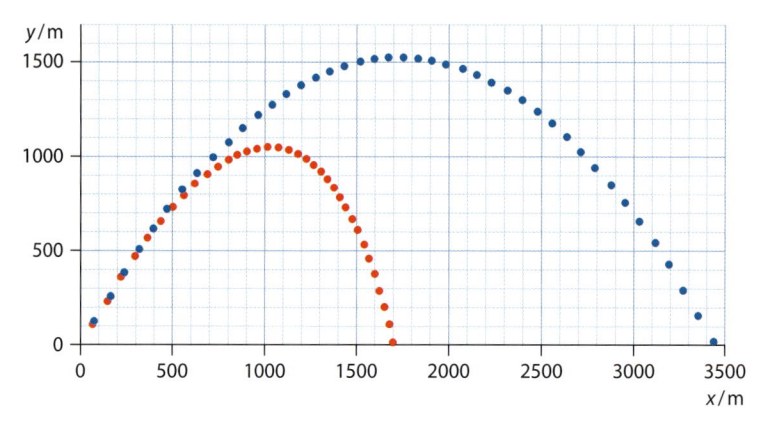

Figure 2.23 The effect of air resistance on projectile motion.

Worked example

2.16 The force of air resistance in the motion described by Figure **2.22** is given by $F = 0.653v$. Determine the mass of the projectile.

The particle is getting slower. At some point it will stop instantaneously, i.e. its velocity v will be zero.

We know that $v = u + at$. Just substituting values gives:

$0 = 12 + (-3.0) \times t$

$3.0t = 12$

Hence $t = 4.0\,\text{s}$.

The terminal speed is $30\,\text{m s}^{-1}$ and is given by $v_T = \dfrac{mg}{k}$. Hence:

$m = \dfrac{kv_T}{g}$

$m = \dfrac{0.653 \times 30}{9.8}$

$m \approx 2.0\,\text{kg}$

Nature of science

The simple and the complex

Careful observation of motion in the natural world led to the equations for motion with uniform acceleration along a straight line that we have used in this section. Thinking about what causes an object to move links to the idea of forces. However, although the material in this section is perhaps some of the 'easiest' material in your physics course, it does not enable one to understand the falling of a leaf off a tree. The falling leaf is complicated because it is acted upon by several forces: its weight, but also by air resistance forces that constantly vary as the orientation and speed of the leaf change. In addition, there is wind to consider as well as the fact that turbulence in air greatly affects the motion of the leaf. So the physics of the falling leaf is far away from the physics of motion along a straight line at constant acceleration. But learning the principles of physics in a simpler context allows its application in more involved situations.

? Test yourself

Uniform motion

1. A car must be driven a distance of 120 km in 2.5 h. During the first 1.5 h the average speed was 70 km h^{-1}. Calculate the average speed for the remainder of the journey.

2. Draw the position–time graph for an object moving in a straight line with a velocity–time graph as shown below. The initial position is zero. You do not have to put any numbers on the axes.

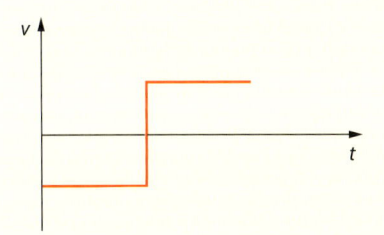

3. Two cyclists, **A** and **B**, have displacements 0 km and 70 km, respectively. At $t=0$ they begin to cycle towards each other with velocities 15 km h^{-1} and 20 km h^{-1}, respectively. At the same time, a fly that was sitting on **A** starts flying towards **B** with a velocity of 30 km h^{-1}. As soon as the fly reaches **B** it immediately turns around and flies towards **A**, and so on until **A** and **B** meet.
   a. Find the position of the two cyclists and the fly when all three meet.
   b. Determine the distance travelled by the fly.

4. An object moving in a straight line has the displacement–time graph shown.
   a. Find the average speed for the trip.
   b. Find the average velocity for the trip.

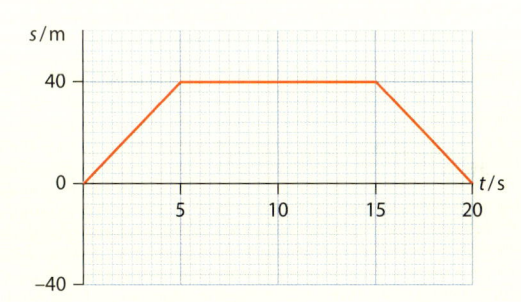

Accelerated motion

5. The initial velocity of a car moving on a straight road is 2.0 m s^{-1}. It becomes 8.0 m s^{-1} after travelling for 2.0 s under constant acceleration. Find the acceleration.

6. A car accelerates from rest to 28 m s^{-1} in 9.0 s. Find the distance it travels.

7. A particle has an initial velocity of 12 m s^{-1} and is brought to rest over a distance of 45 m. Find the acceleration of the particle.

8. A particle at the origin has an initial velocity of −6.0 m s^{-1} and moves with an acceleration of 2.0 m s^{-2}. Determine when its position will become 16 m.

2 MECHANICS 53

9 A plane starting from rest takes 15.0 s to take off after speeding over a distance of 450 m on the runway with constant acceleration. Find the take-off velocity.

10 A car is travelling at 40.0 m s^{-1}. The driver sees an emergency ahead and 0.50 s later slams on the brakes. The deceleration of the car is 4.0 m s^{-2}.
   a Find the distance travelled before the car stops.
   b Calculate the stopping distance if the driver could apply the brakes instantaneously without a reaction time.
   c Calculate the difference in your answers to **a** and **b**.
   d Assume now that the car was travelling at 30.0 m s^{-1} instead. Without performing any calculations, state whether the answer to **c** would now be less than, equal to or larger than before. Explain your answer.

11 Two balls are dropped from rest from the same height. One of the balls is dropped 1.00 s after the other.
   a Find the distance that separates the two balls 2.00 s after the second ball is dropped.
   b State what happens to the distance separating the balls as time goes on.

12 A particle moves in a straight line with an acceleration that varies with time as shown in the diagram. Initially the velocity of the object is 2.00 m s^{-1}.
   a Find the maximum velocity reached in the first 6.00 s of this motion.
   b Draw a graph of the velocity versus time.

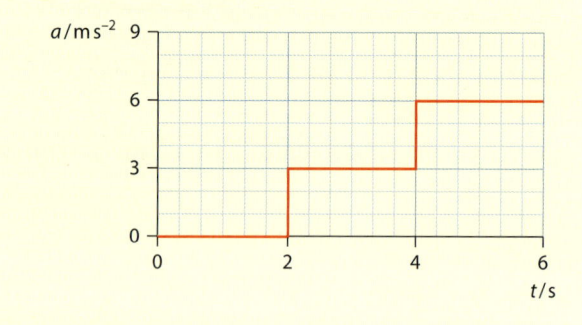

13 The graph shows the variation of velocity with time of an object. Find the acceleration at 2.0 s.

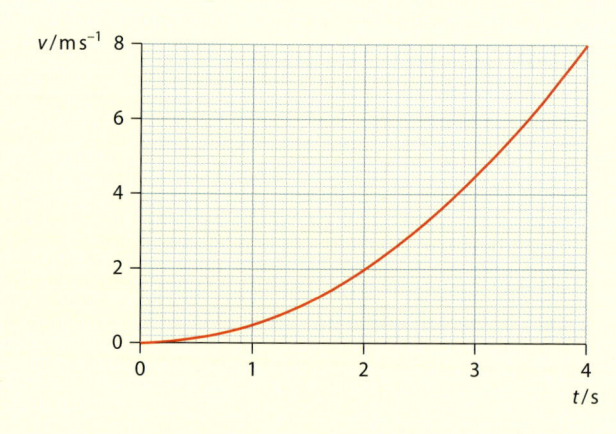

14 The graph shows the variation of the position of a moving object with time. Draw the graph showing the variation of the velocity of the object with time.

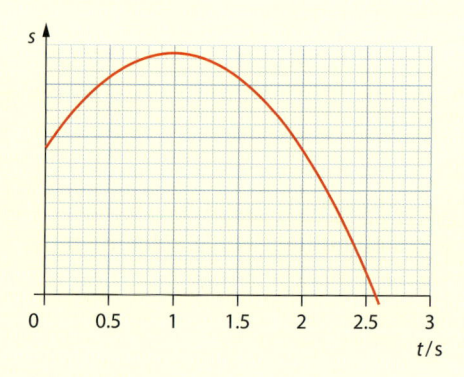

15 The graph shows the variation of the position of a moving object with time. Draw the graph showing the variation of the velocity of the object with time.

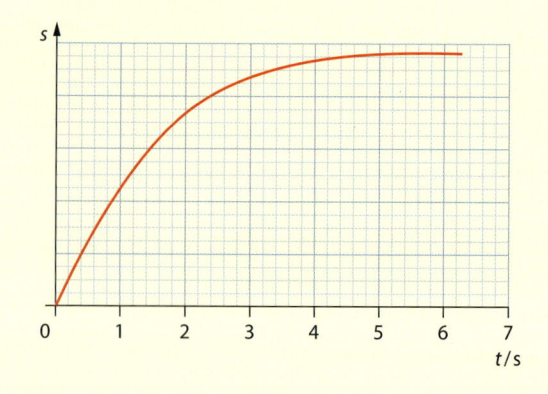

16 The graph shows the variation of the position of a moving object with time. Draw the graph showing the variation of the velocity of the object with time.

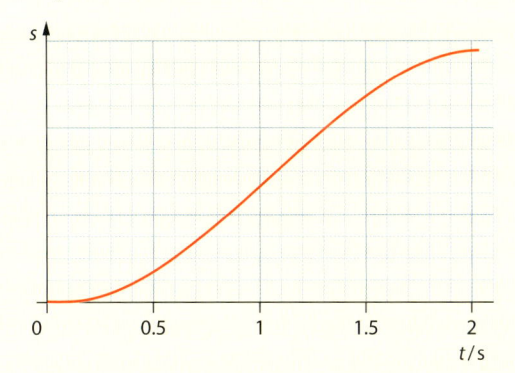

17 The graph shows the variation of the velocity of a moving object with time. Draw the graph showing the variation of the position of the object with time.

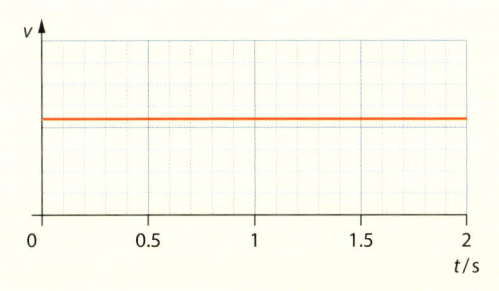

18 The graph shows the variation of the velocity of a moving object with time. Draw the graph showing the variation of the position of the object with time (assuming a zero initial position).

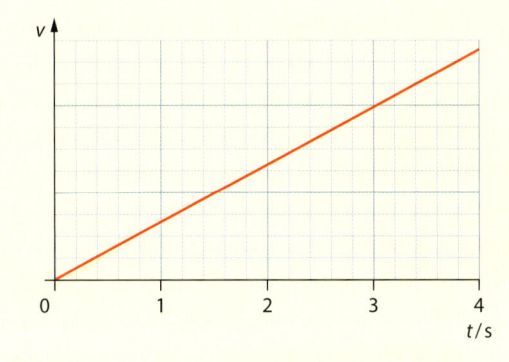

19 The graph shows the variation of the velocity of a moving object with time. Draw the graph showing the variation of the acceleration of the object with time.

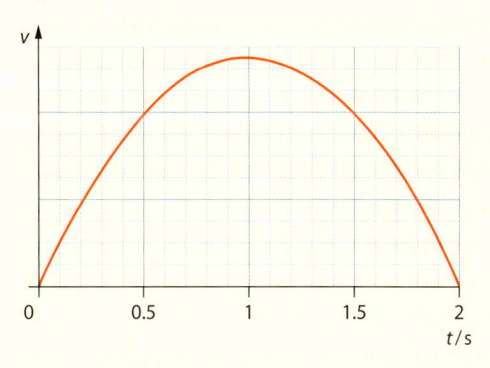

20 Your brand new convertible Ferrari is parked 15 m from its garage when it begins to rain. You do not have time to get the keys, so you begin to push the car towards the garage. The maximum acceleration you can give the car is $2.0\,\text{m s}^{-2}$ by pushing and $3.0\,\text{m s}^{-2}$ by pulling back on the car. Find the least time it takes to put the car in the garage. (Assume that the car, as well as the garage, are point objects.)

21 The graph shows the displacement versus time of an object moving in a straight line. Four points on this graph have been selected.

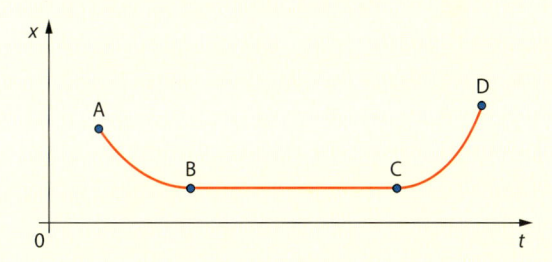

a Is the velocity between **A** and **B** positive, zero or negative?
b What can you say about the velocity between **B** and **C**?
c Is the acceleration between **A** and **B** positive, zero or negative?
d Is the acceleration between **C** and **D** positive, zero or negative?

2 MECHANICS 55

22 Sketch velocity–time sketches (no numbers are necessary on the axes) for the following motions.
 a A ball is dropped from a certain height and bounces off a hard floor. The speed just before each impact with the floor is the same as the speed just after impact. Assume that the time of contact with the floor is negligibly small.
 b A cart slides with negligible friction along a horizontal air track. When the cart hits the ends of the air track it reverses direction with the same speed it had right before impact. Assume the time of contact of the cart and the ends of the air track is negligibly small.
 c A person jumps from a hovering helicopter. After a few seconds she opens a parachute. Eventually she will reach a terminal speed and will then land.

23 A stone is thrown vertically up from the edge of a cliff 35.0 m from the sea. The initial velocity of the stone is 8.00 m s^{-1}.

$v = 8.00$ m s^{-1}

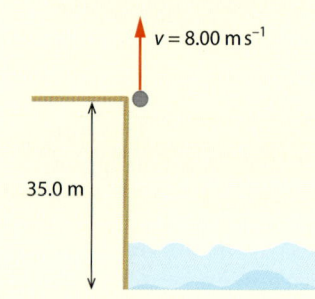

35.0 m

 Determine:
 a the maximum height of the stone
 b the time when it hits the sea
 c the velocity just before hitting the sea
 d the distance the stone covers
 e the average speed and the average velocity for this motion.

24 A ball is thrown upward from the edge of a cliff with velocity 20.0 m s^{-1}. It reaches the bottom of the cliff 6.0 s later.
 a Determine the height of the cliff.
 b Calculate the speed of the ball as it hits the ground.

Projectile motion

25 A ball rolls off a table with a horizontal speed of 2.0 m s^{-1}. The table is 1.3 m high. Calculate how far from the table the ball will land.

26 Two particles are on the same vertical line. They are thrown horizontally with the same speed, 4.0 m s^{-1}, from heights of 4.0 m and 8.0 m.
 a Calculate the distance that will separate the two objects when both land on the ground.
 b The particle at the 4.0 m height is now launched with horizontal speed u such that it lands at the same place as the particle launched from 8.0 m. Calculate u.

27 For an object thrown at an angle of 40° to the horizontal at a speed of 20 m s^{-1}, draw graphs of:
 a horizontal velocity against time
 b vertical velocity against time
 c acceleration against time.

28 Determine the maximum height reached by an object thrown with speed 24 m s^{-1} at 40° to the horizontal.

29 An object is thrown with speed 20.0 m s^{-1} at an angle of 50° to the horizontal. Draw graphs to show the variation with time of:
 a the horizontal position
 b the vertical position.

30 A cruel hunter takes aim horizontally at a chimp that is hanging from the branch of a tree, as shown in the diagram. The chimp lets go of the branch as soon as the hunter pulls the trigger. Treating the chimp and the bullet as point particles, determine if the bullet will hit the chimp.

31 A ball is launched from the surface of a planet. Air resistance and other frictional forces are neglected. The graph shows the position of the ball every 0.20 s.

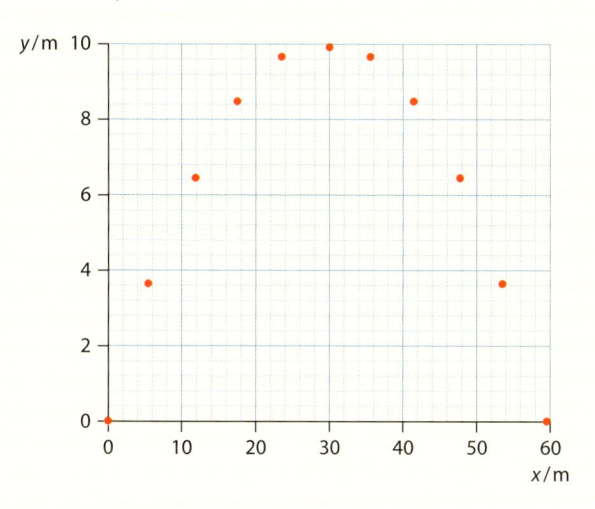

a Use this graph to determine:
  i the components of the initial velocity of the ball
  ii the angle to the horizontal the ball was launched at
  iii the acceleration of free fall on this planet.

b Make a copy of the graph and draw two arrows to represent the velocity and the acceleration vectors of the ball at $t = 1.0$ s.

c The ball is now launched under identical conditions from the surface of a **different** planet where the acceleration due to gravity is twice as large. Draw the path of the ball on your graph.

32 A stone is thrown with a speed of $20.0 \, \text{m s}^{-1}$ at an angle of 48° to the horizontal from the edge of a cliff 60.0 m above the surface of the sea.

a Calculate the velocity with which the stone hits the sea.

b Discuss qualitatively the effect of air resistance on your answer to **a**.

33 a State what is meant by **terminal speed**.

b A ball is dropped from rest. The force of air resistance in the ball is proportional to the ball's speed. Explain why the ball will reach terminal speed.

2.2 Forces

This section is an introduction to Newton's laws of motion. Classical physics is based to a great extent on these laws. It was once thought that knowledge of the present state of a system and all forces acting on it would enable the complete prediction of the state of that system in the future. This classical version of determinism has been modified partly due to quantum theory and partly due to chaos theory.

Forces and their direction

A **force** is a vector quantity. It is important that we are able to correctly identify the **direction** of forces. In this section we will deal with the following forces.

Learning objectives

- Treat bodies as point particles.
- Construct and interpret free-body force diagrams.
- Apply the equilibrium condition, $\Sigma F = 0$.
- Understand and apply Newton's three laws of motion.
- Solve problems involving solid friction.

Weight

This force is the result of the gravitational attraction between the mass m of a body and the mass of the planet on which the body is placed. The **weight** of a body is given by the formula:

$$W = mg$$

where m is the mass of the body and g is gravitational field strength of the planet (Subtopic **6.2**). The unit of g is newton per kilogram, $N\,kg^{-1}$. The gravitational field strength is also known as 'the acceleration due to gravity' or the 'acceleration of free fall'. Therefore the unit of g is also $m\,s^{-2}$.

If m is in kg and g in $N\,kg^{-1}$ or $m\,s^{-2}$ then W is in newtons, N. On the **surface** of the Earth, $g = 9.81\,N\,kg^{-1}$ – a number that we will often approximate by the more convenient $10\,N\,kg^{-1}$. This force is always directed vertically downward, as shown in Figure **2.24**.

The mass of an object is the same everywhere in the universe, but its weight depends on the **location** of the body. For example, a mass of 70 kg has a weight of 687 N on the surface of the Earth ($g = 9.81\,N\,kg^{-1}$) and a weight of 635 N at a height of 250 km from the Earth's surface (where $g = 9.07\,N\,kg^{-1}$). However, on the surface of Venus, where the gravitational field strength is only $8.9\,N\,kg^{-1}$, the weight is 623 N.

Figure 2.24 The weight of an object is always directed vertically downward.

Tension

The force that arises in any body when it is stretched is called **tension**. A string that is taut is said to be under tension. The tension force is the result of electromagnetic interactions between the molecules of the material making up the string. A tension force in a string is created when two forces are applied in opposite directions at the ends of the string (Figure **2.25**).

Figure 2.25 A tension force in a string.

To say that there is tension in a string means that an arbitrary point on the string is acted upon by two forces (the tension T) as shown in Figure **2.26**. If the string hangs from a ceiling and a mass m is tied at the other end, tension develops in the string. At the point of support at the ceiling, the tension force pulls down on the ceiling and at the point where the mass is tied the tension acts upwards on the mass.

In most cases we will idealise the string by assuming it is massless. This does not mean that the string really is massless, but rather that its mass is so small compared with any other masses in the problem that we can neglect it. In that case, the tension T is the same at all points on the string. The direction of the tension force is along the string. Further examples of tension forces in a string are given in Figure **2.27**. A string or rope that is not taut has zero tension in it.

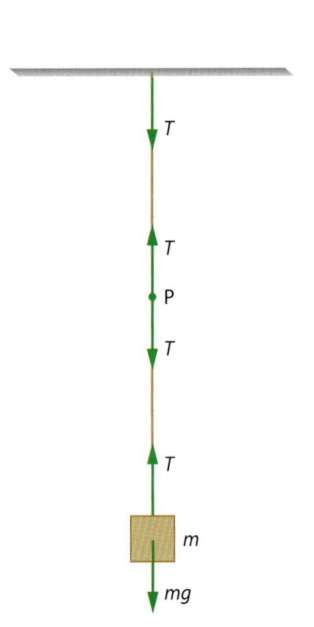

Figure 2.26 The tension is directed along the string.

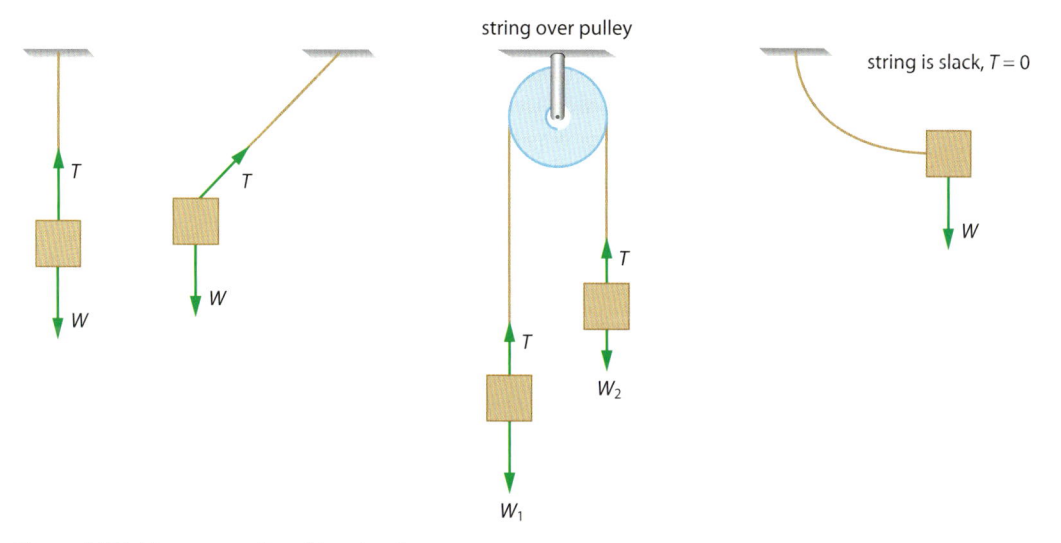

Figure 2.27 More examples of tension forces.

Forces in springs

A spring that is pulled so that its length increases will develop a tension force inside the spring that will tend to bring the length back to its original value. Similarly, if it is compressed a tension force will again try to restore the length of the spring, Figure 2.28. Experiments show that for a range of extensions of the spring, the tension force is proportional to the extension, $T = kx$, where k is known as the spring constant. This relation between tension and extension is known as **Hooke's law**.

Normal reaction contact forces

If a body touches another body, there is a **force of reaction** or **contact force** between the two bodies. This force is perpendicular to the surface of the body exerting the force. Like tension, the origin of this force is also electromagnetic. In Figure 2.29 we show the reaction force on several bodies.

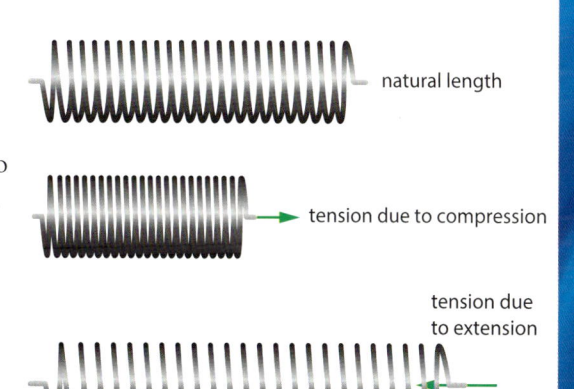

Figure 2.28 Tension forces in a spring.

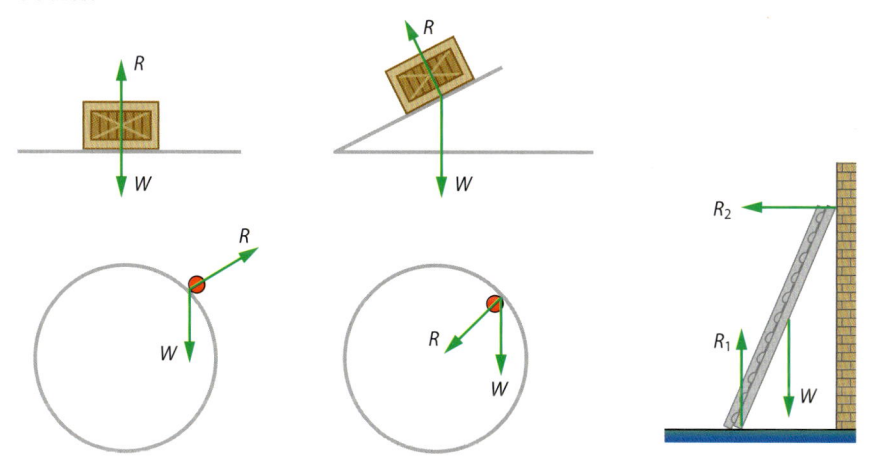

Figure 2.29 Examples of reaction forces, R.

2 MECHANICS 59

We can understand the existence of contact reaction forces in a simple model in which atoms are connected by springs. The block pushes down on the atoms of the table, compressing the springs under the block (Figure **2.30**). This creates the normal reaction force on the block.

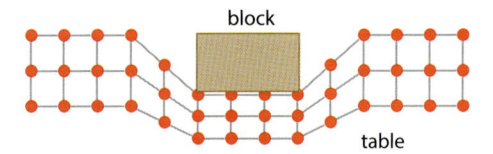

Figure 2.30 A simple model of contact forces.

Drag forces

Drag forces are forces that oppose the motion of a body through a fluid (a gas or a liquid). Typical examples are the air resistance force experienced by a car (Figure **2.31**) or plane, or the resistance force experienced by a steel marble dropped into a jar of honey. Drag forces are directed opposite to the velocity of the body and in general depend on the speed and shape of the body. The higher the speed, the higher the drag force.

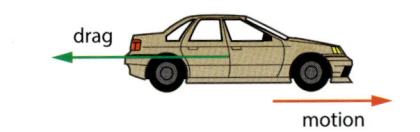

Figure 2.31 The drag force on a moving car.

Upthrust

Any object placed in a fluid experiences an upward force called **upthrust** (Figure **2.32**). If the upthrust force equals the weight of the body, the body will float in the fluid. If the upthrust is less than the weight, the body will sink. Upthrust is caused by the pressure that the fluid exerts on the body.

Frictional forces

Frictional forces generally oppose the motion of a body (Figure **2.33**). These forces are also electromagnetic in origin.

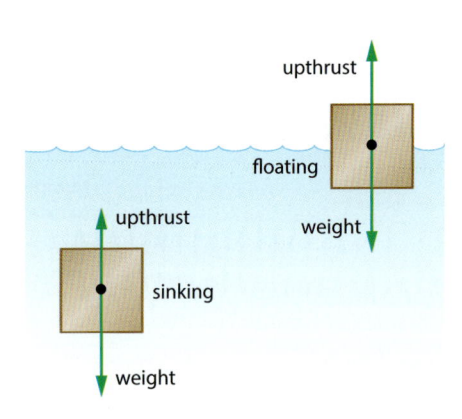

Figure 2.32 Upthrust.

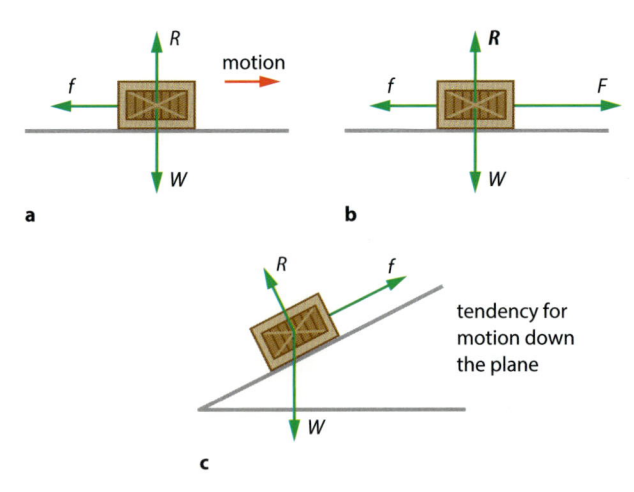

Figure 2.33 Examples of frictional forces, f. In **a** there is motion to the right, which is opposed by a single frictional force that will eventually stop the body. In **b** the force accelerating the body is opposed by a frictional force. In **c** the body does not move; but it does have a tendency to move down the plane and so a frictional force directed up the plane opposes this tendency, keeping the body in equilibrium.

Friction arises whenever one body slides over another. In this case we have **dynamic or kinetic friction**. Friction also arises whenever there is a tendency for motion, not necessarily motion itself. For example a block that rests on an inclined plane has a tendency to slide down the plane, so there is a force of friction up the plane. Similarly, if you pull on a block on a level rough road with a small force the block will not move. This is because a force of friction develops that is equal and opposite to the pulling force. In this case we have **static friction**.

In the simple model of matter consisting of atoms connected by springs, pushing the block to the right results in springs stretching and compressing. The net result is a force opposing the motion: friction (Figure 2.34).

A more realistic model involves irregularities (called **asperities**) in the surfaces which interlock, opposing sliding, as shown in Figure 2.35.

Frictional forces are still not very well understood and there is no theory of friction that follows directly from the fundamental laws of physics. However, a number of simple, empirical 'laws' of friction have been discovered. These are not always applicable and are only approximately true, but they are useful in describing frictional forces in general terms.

These so-called **friction laws** may be summarised as follows:

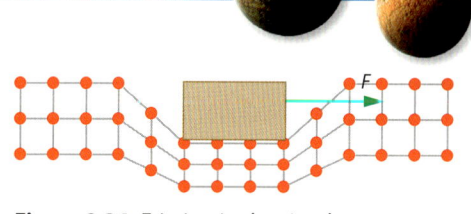

Figure 2.34 Friction in the simple atoms-and-springs model of matter.

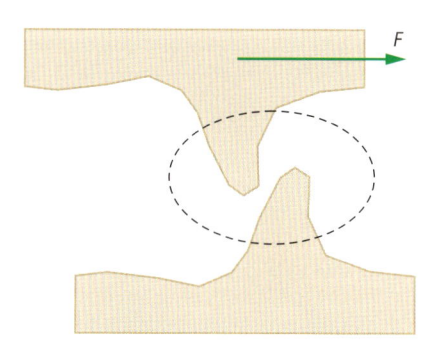

Figure 2.35 Exaggerated view of how asperities oppose the sliding of one surface over the other.

- The area of contact between the two surfaces does not affect the frictional force.
- The force of dynamic friction is equal to:
  $$f_d = \mu_d R$$
  where R is the normal reaction force between the surfaces and μ_d is the **coefficient of dynamic friction**.
- The force of dynamic friction does not depend on the speed of sliding.
- The **maximum** force of static friction that can develop between two surfaces is given by:
  $$f_s = \mu_s R$$
  where R is the normal reaction force between the surfaces and μ_s is the **coefficient of static friction**, with $\mu_s > \mu_d$.

Exam tip
One of the most common mistakes is to think that $\mu_s R$ is the formula that gives the static friction force. This is not correct. This formula gives the maximum possible static friction force that can develop between two surfaces.

Figure 2.36 shows how the frictional force f varies with a pulling force F. The force F pulls on a body on a horizontal rough surface. Initially the static frictional force matches the pulling force and we have no motion, $f_s = F$. When the pulling force exceeds the maximum possible static friction force, $\mu_s R$, the frictional force drops abruptly to the dynamic value of $\mu_d R$ and stays at that constant value as the object accelerates. This is a well-known phenomenon of everyday life: it takes a lot of force to get a heavy piece of furniture to start moving (you must exceed the maximum value of the static friction force), but once you get it moving, pushing it along becomes easier (you are now opposed by the smaller dynamic friction force).

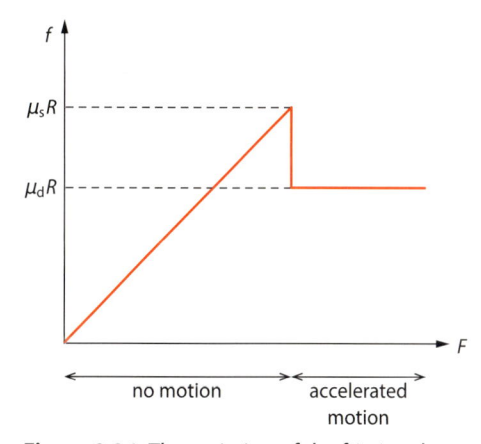

Figure 2.36 The variation of the frictional force f between surfaces with the pulling force F.

2 MECHANICS 61

Worked example

2.17 A brick of weight 50 N rests on a horizontal surface. The coefficient of static friction between the brick and the surface is 0.60 and the coefficient of dynamic friction is 0.20. A horizontal force F is applied to the brick, its magnitude increasing uniformly from zero. Once the brick starts moving the pulling force no longer increases. Estimate the net force on the moving brick.

The maximum frictional force that can develop between the brick and the surface is:

$f_s = \mu_s R$

which evaluates to:

$0.60 \times 50 = 30$ N

So motion takes place when the pulling force is just barely larger than 30 N.

Once motion starts the frictional force will be equal to $\mu_d R$, i.e.

$0.20 \times 50 = 10$ N

The net force on the brick in that case will be just larger than $30 - 10 = 20$ N.

Free-body diagrams

A **free-body diagram** is a diagram showing the magnitude and direction of all the forces acting on a chosen body. The body is shown on its own, free of its surroundings and of any other bodies it may be in contact with. We treat the body as a **point particle**, so that all forces act through the same point. In Figure 2.37 we show three situations in which forces are acting; below each is the corresponding free-body diagram for the coloured bodies.

In any mechanics problem, it is important to be able to draw correctly the free-body diagrams for all the bodies of interest. It is also important that the length of the arrow representing a given force is proportional to the magnitude of the force.

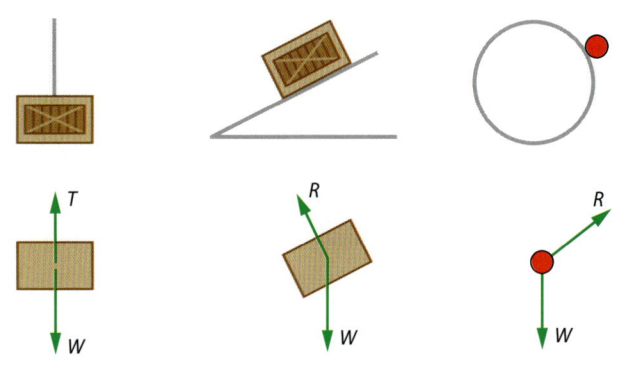

Figure 2.37 Free-body diagrams for the coloured bodies.

Newton's first law of motion

Suppose you have two identical train carriages. Both are equipped with all the apparatus you need to do physics experiments. One train carriage is at rest at the train station. The other moves in a straight line with constant speed – the ride is perfectly smooth, there are no bumps, there is no noise and there are no windows to look outside. Every physics experiment conducted in the train at rest will give identical results to similar experiments made in the moving train. We have no way of determining whether a carriage is 'really at rest' or 'really moving'. We find it perfectly natural to believe, correctly, that no net force is present in the case of the carriage at rest. Therefore no net force is required in the case of the carriage moving in a straight line with constant speed.

Newton's first law (with a big help from Galileo) states that:

> When the net force on a body is zero, the body will move with constant velocity (which may be zero).

In effect, Newton's first law defines what a force is. A force is what changes a body's velocity. A force is *not* what is required to keep something moving, as Aristotle thought.

Using the law in reverse allows us to conclude that if a body is not moving with constant velocity (which may mean not moving in a straight line, or not moving with constant speed, or both) then a force must be acting on the body. So, since the Earth revolves around the Sun we know that a force must be acting on the Earth.

Newton's first law is also called the law of **inertia**. Inertia is what keeps the body in the same state of motion when no forces act on the body. When a car accelerates forward, the passengers are thrown back into their seats because their original state of motion was motion with low speed. If a car brakes abruptly, the passengers are thrown forward (Figure **2.38**). This implies that a mass tends to stay in the state of motion it was in before the force acted on it. The reaction of a body to a change in its state of motion (acceleration) is inertia.

Figure 2.38 The car was originally travelling at high speed. When it hits the wall the car stops but the passenger stays in the original high speed state of motion. This results in the crash dummy hitting the steering wheel and the windshield (which is why it is a good idea to have safety belts and air bags).

Newton's third law of motion

Newton's third law states that if body A exerts a force on body B, then body B will exert an equal and opposite force on body A. These forces are known as **force pairs**. Make sure you understand that these equal and opposite forces act on different bodies. Thus, you cannot use this law to claim that it is impossible to ever have a net force on a body because for every force on it there is also an equal and opposite force. Here are a few examples of this law:

- You stand on roller skates facing a wall. You push on the wall and you move away from it. This is because you exerted a force on the wall and in turn the wall exerted an equal and opposite force on you, making you move away (Figure **2.39**).

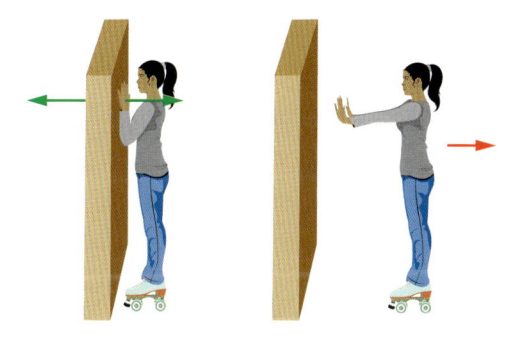

Figure 2.39 The girl pushes on the wall so the wall pushes on her in the opposite direction.

2 MECHANICS 63

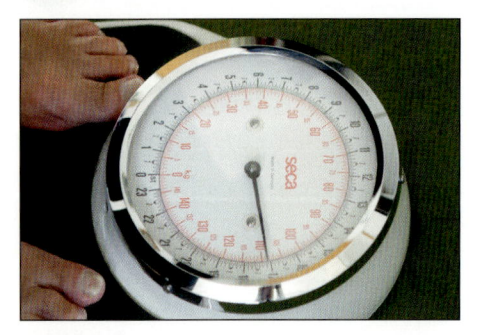

Figure 2.40 The familiar bathroom scales do not measure mass. They measure the force that you exert on the scales. This force is equal to the weight only when the scales are at rest.

Figure 2.41 The upward force on the rotor is due to the force the rotor exerts on the air downward.

- You step on the bathroom scales. The scales exert an upward force on you and so you exert a downward force on the scales. This is the force shown on the scales (Figure **2.40**).
- A helicopter hovers in air (Figure **2.41**). Its rotors exert a force downward on the air. Thus, the air exerts the upward force on the helicopter that keeps it from falling.
- A book of mass 2 kg is allowed to fall feely. The Earth exerts a force on the book, namely the weight of the book of about 20 N. Thus, the book exerts an equal and opposite force on the Earth – a force upward equal to 20 N.

You must be careful with situations in which two forces are equal and opposite; they do not always have to do with the third law. For example, a block of mass 3 kg resting on a horizontal table has two forces acting on it – its weight of about 30 N and the normal reaction force from the table that is also 30 N. These two forces are equal and opposite, but they are acting on the same body and so have nothing to do with Newton's third law. (We have seen in the last bullet point above the force that pairs with the weight of the block. The force that pairs with the reaction force is a downward force on the table.)

Newton's third law also applies to cases where there is no contact between the bodies. Examples are the **electric** force between two electrically charged particles or the **gravitational** force between any two massive particles. These forces must be equal and opposite (Figure **2.42**).

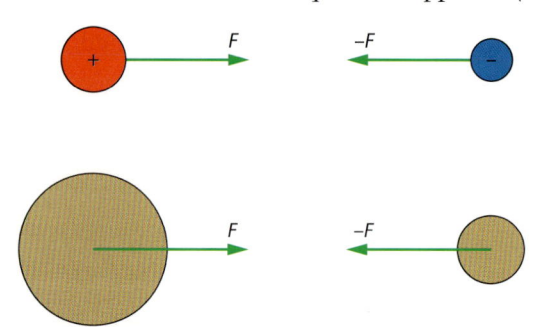

Figure 2.42 The two charges and the two masses are different, but the forces are equal and opposite.

Equilibrium

Equilibrium of a point particle means that the **net force** on the particle is zero. The net force on a particle is the one single force whose effect is the same as the combined effect of individual forces acting on the particle. We denote it by ΣF. Finding the net force is easy when the forces are in the same or opposite directions (Figure **2.43**).

In Figure **2.43a**, the net force is (if we take the direction to the right to be positive) $\Sigma F = 12 + 6.0 - 8.0 = 10$ N. This is positive, indicating a direction to the right.

In Figure **2.43b**, the net force is (we take the direction upward to be positive) $\Sigma F = 5.0 + 6.0 - 4.0 - 8.0 = -1.0$ N. The negative sign indicates a direction vertically down.

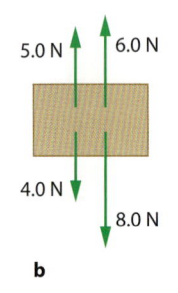

Figure 2.43 The net force is found by plain addition and/or subtraction when the forces are in the same or opposite direction.

Worked example

2.18 Determine the magnitude of the force F in Figure **2.44**, given that the block is in equilibrium.

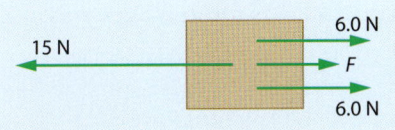

Figure 2.44

For equilibrium, $\Sigma F = 0$, and so:

$6.0 + F + 6.0 - 15 = 0$

This gives $F = 3.0\,\text{N}$.

Solving equilibrium problems

When there are angles between the various forces, solving equilibrium problems will involve finding components of forces using vector methods. We choose a set of axes whose origin is the body in question and find the components of all the forces on the body. Figure **2.45** shows three forces acting at the same point. We have equilibrium, which means the net force acting at the point is zero. We need to find the unknown magnitude and direction of force F_1. This situation could represent three people pulling on three ropes that are tied at a point.

Finding components along the horizontal (x) and vertical (y) directions for the known forces F_2 and F_3, we have:

$F_{2x} = 0$
$F_{2y} = -22.0\,\text{N}$ (add minus sign to show the direction)
$F_{3x} = -29.0\cos 37° = -23.16\,\text{N}$ (add minus sign to show the direction)
$F_{3y} = 29.0\sin 37° = 17.45\,\text{N}$

Equilibrium demands that $\Sigma F_x = 0$ and $\Sigma F_y = 0$.

$\Sigma F_x = 0$ implies:

$F_{1x} + 0 - 23.16 = 0 \Rightarrow F_{1x} = 23.16\,\text{N}$

$\Sigma F_y = 0$ implies:

$F_{1y} - 22.0 + 17.45 = 0 \Rightarrow F_{1y} = 4.55\,\text{N}$

Therefore, $F_1 = \sqrt{23.16^2 + 4.55^2} = 23.6\,\text{N}$

The angle is found from $\tan\theta = \dfrac{F_{1y}}{F_{1x}} \Rightarrow \theta = \tan^{-1}\left(\dfrac{4.55}{23.16}\right) = 11.1°$

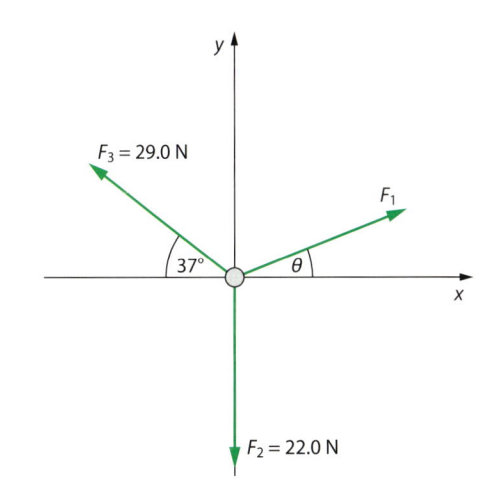

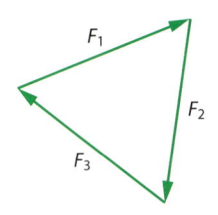

Figure 2.45 Force diagram of three forces in equilibrium pulling a common point. Notice that the three vectors representing the three forces form a triangle.

Exam tip
If we know the x- and y-components of a force we can find the magnitude of the force from $F = \sqrt{F_x^2 + F_y^2}$.

2 MECHANICS

Worked example

2.19 A body of weight 98.0 N hangs from two strings that are attached to the ceiling as shown in Figure **2.46**. Determine the tension in each string.

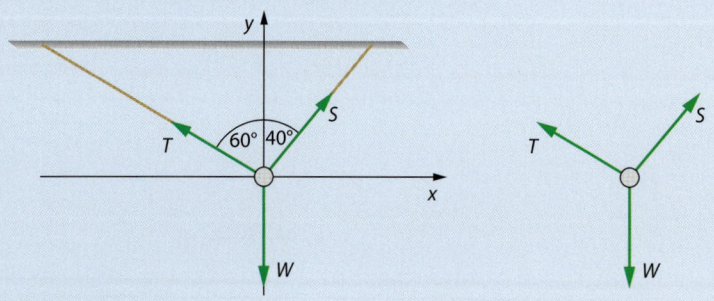

Figure 2.46

The three forces acting on the body are as shown, with T and S being the tensions in the two strings and W its weight. Taking components about horizontal and vertical axes through the body we find:

$T_x = -T\cos 30°$ (add minus sign to show the direction) $S_x = S\cos 50°$ $W_x = 0$

$T_y = T\sin 30°$ $S_y = S\sin 50°$ $W_y = -98.0$ N

Equilibrium thus demands $\Sigma F_x = 0$ and $\Sigma F_y = 0$.

$\Sigma F_x = 0$ implies:

$-T\cos 30° + S\cos 50° = 0$

$\Sigma F_y = 0$ implies:

$T\sin 30° + S\sin 50° - 98.0 = 0$

From the first equation we find that:

$S = T\dfrac{\cos 30°}{\cos 50°} = 1.3473 \times T$

Substituting this in the second equation gives:

$T(\sin 30° + 1.3473 \sin 50°) = 98$

which solves to give:

$T = 63.96 \approx 64.0$ N

Hence $S = 1.3473 \times 63.96 = 86.17 \approx 86.2$ N.

> **2.20** A mass of 125 g is attached to a spring of spring constant $k = 58\,\text{N}\,\text{m}^{-1}$ that is hanging vertically.
> **a** Find the extension of the spring.
> **b** If the mass and the spring are placed on the Moon, will there be any change in the extension of the spring?

a The forces on the hanging mass are its weight and the tension in the spring. By Hooke's law, the tension in the spring is kx, where x is the extension and k the spring constant. Since we have equilibrium, the two forces are equal in magnitude. Therefore:

$kx = mg$

$x = \dfrac{mg}{k}$

$x = \dfrac{0.125 \times 10}{58}$ (taking $g = 10\,\text{N}\,\text{kg}^{-1}$)

$x = 0.022\,\text{m}$

The extension is 2.2 cm.

b The extension will be less, since the acceleration of gravity is less.

Newton's second law of motion

Newton's second law states that:

> The net force on a body of constant mass is proportional to that body's acceleration and is in the same direction as the acceleration.

Mathematically:

$F = ma$

where the constant of proportionality, m, is the *mass* of the body.

Figure 2.47 shows the net force on a freely falling body, which happens to be its weight, $W = mg$. By Newton's second law, the net force equals the mass times the acceleration, and so:

$mg = ma$

$a = g$

That is, the acceleration of the freely falling body is exactly g. Experiments going back to Galileo show that indeed all bodies fall with the same acceleration in a vacuum (the acceleration of free fall) irrespective of their density, their mass, their shape and the material from which they are made. Look for David Scott's demonstration dropping a hammer and feather on the Moon in Apollo 15's mission in 1971. You can do the same demonstration without going to the Moon by placing a hammer and a

Figure 2.47 A mass falling to the ground acted upon by gravity.

Exam tip
To solve an '$F = ma$' problem:
- Make a diagram.
- Identify the forces on the body of interest.
- Find the net force on each body, taking the direction of acceleration to be the positive direction.
- Apply $F_{net} = ma$ to each body.

feather on a book and dropping the book. If the heavy and the light object fell with different accelerations the one with the smaller acceleration would lift off the book – but it doesn't.

The equation $F = ma$ defines the unit of force, the newton (N). One newton is the force required to accelerate a mass of 1 kg by $1\,\mathrm{m\,s^{-2}}$ in the direction of the force.

It is important to realise that the force in the second law is the net force ΣF on the body.

Worked examples

2.21 A man of mass $m = 70\,\mathrm{kg}$ stands on the floor of an elevator. Find the force of reaction he experiences from the elevator floor when the elevator:
   a is standing still
   b moves up at constant speed $3.0\,\mathrm{m\,s^{-1}}$
   c moves up with acceleration $4.0\,\mathrm{m\,s^{-2}}$
   d moves down with acceleration $4.0\,\mathrm{m\,s^{-2}}$
   e moves down, slowing down with deceleration $4.0\,\mathrm{m\,s^{-2}}$.

Take $g = 10\,\mathrm{m\,s^{-2}}$.

Two forces act on the man: his weight mg vertically down and the reaction force R from the floor vertically up.

a There is no acceleration and so by Newton's second law the net force on the man must be zero. Hence:

$R = mg$
$R = 7.0 \times 10^2\,\mathrm{N}$

b There is no acceleration and so again:

$R = mg$
$R = 7.0 \times 10^2\,\mathrm{N}$

c There is acceleration upwards. The net force in the direction of the acceleration is given by:

$\Sigma F = R - mg$
So: $ma = R - mg$
$\Rightarrow R = mg + ma$
$R = 700\,\mathrm{N} + 280\,\mathrm{N}$
$R = 9.8 \times 10^2\,\mathrm{N}$

d We again have acceleration, but this time in the downward direction. We need to find the net force in the direction of the acceleration:

$\Sigma F = mg - R$
So: $ma = mg - R$
$\Rightarrow R = mg - ma$
$R = 700\,\mathrm{N} - 280\,\mathrm{N}$
$R = 4.2 \times 10^2\,\mathrm{N}$

e The deceleration is equivalent to an upward acceleration, so this case is identical to part **c**.

2.22 A man of mass 70 kg is standing in an elevator. The elevator is moving **upward** at a speed of $3.0\,\mathrm{m\,s^{-1}}$. The elevator comes to rest in a time of 2.0 s. Determine the reaction force on the man from the elevator floor during the period of deceleration.

Use $a = v - \dfrac{u}{t}$ to find the acceleration experienced by the man:

$$a = -\dfrac{3.0}{2.0} = -1.5\,\mathrm{m\,s^{-2}}$$

The minus sign shows that this acceleration is directed in the **downward** direction. So we must find the net force in the down direction, which is $\Sigma F = mg - R$. (We then use the **magnitude** of the accelerations, as the form of the equation takes care of the direction.)

$ma = mg - R$

$\Rightarrow\ R = mg - ma$

$R = 700 - 105$

$R = 595 \approx 6.0 \times 10^2\,\mathrm{N}$

If, instead, the man was moving **downward** and then decelerated to rest, the acceleration is directed upward and $\Sigma F = R - mg$.

So: $ma = R - mg$

$\Rightarrow\ R = mg + ma$

$R = 700 + 105$

$R = 805 \approx 8.0 \times 10^2\,\mathrm{N}$

Both cases are easily experienced in daily life. When the elevator goes up and then stops we feel 'lighter' during the deceleration period. When going down and about to stop, we feel 'heavier' during the deceleration period. The feeling of 'lightness' or 'heaviness' has to do with the reaction force we feel from the floor.

2.23 **a** Two blocks of mass 4.0 kg and 6.0 kg are joined by a string and rest on a frictionless horizontal table (Figure 2.48). A force of 100 N is applied horizontally on one of the blocks. Find the acceleration of each block and the tension in the string.

b The 4.0 kg block is now placed on top of the other block. The coefficient of static friction between the two blocks is 0.45. The bottom block is pulled with a horizontal force F. Calculate the magnitude of the maximum force F that will result in both blocks moving together without slipping.

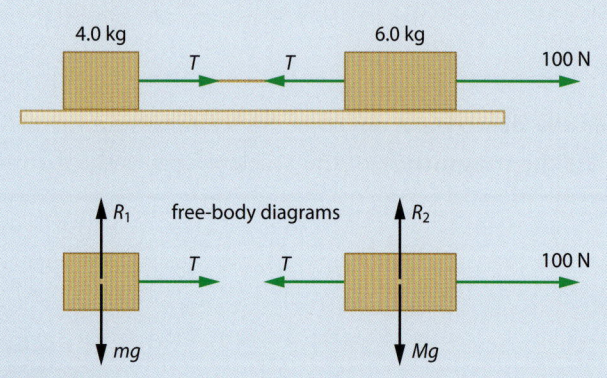

Figure 2.48

a This can be done in **two** ways.

Method 1

Let the acceleration of the system be a. The net horizontal force on the 6.0 kg mass is $100 - T$ and the net horizontal force on the 4.0 kg mass is just T. Thus, applying Newton's second law separately on each mass:

$100 - T = 6.0a$

$T = 4.0a$

Solving for a (by adding the two equations) gives:

$100 = 10a$

$\Rightarrow \quad a = 10\,\mathrm{m\,s^{-2}}$

The tension in the string is therefore:

$T = 4.0 \times 10$

$T = 40\,\mathrm{N}$

Note: The free-body diagram makes it clear that the 100 N force acts only on the body to the right. It is a common mistake to say that the body to the left is also acted upon by the 100 N force.

Method 2

We may consider the two bodies as one of mass 10 kg. The net force on the body is 100 N. Note that the tensions are irrelevant now since they cancel out. (They did not in Method 1, as they acted on different bodies. Now they act on the same body. They are now **internal** forces and these are irrelevant.)

Applying Newton's second law on the single body we have:

$$100 = 10a$$

$$\Rightarrow \quad a = 10 \, \text{m s}^{-2}$$

But to find the tension we must break up the combined body into the original two bodies. Newton's second law on the 4.0 kg body gives:

$$T = 4a = 40 \, \text{N}$$

(the tension on this block is the net force on the block). If we used the other block, we would see that the net force on it is $100 - T$ and so:

$$100 - T = 6 \times 10 = 60 \, \text{N}$$

This gives $T = 40$ N, as before.

b If the blocks move together they must have the same acceleration. Treating the two blocks as one (of mass 10 kg), the acceleration will be $a = \dfrac{F}{10}$ (Figure **2.49a**).

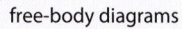

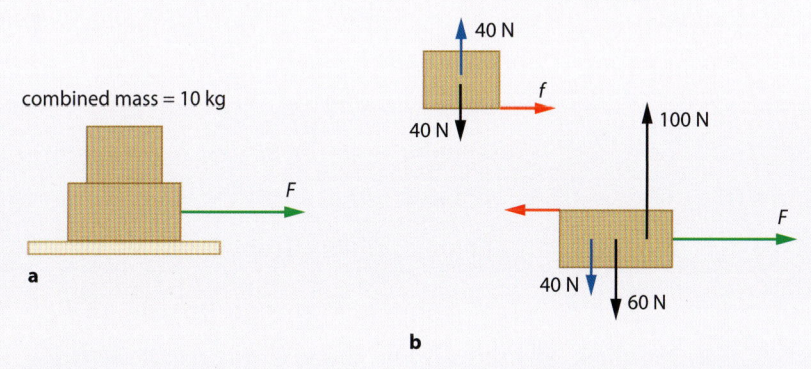

Figure 2.49 a Treating the blocks as one. **b** The free-body diagram for each block.

The forces on each block are shown in Figure **2.49b**. The force pushing the smaller block forward is the frictional force f that develops between the blocks. The **maximum** value f can take is:

$$f = \mu_s R = 0.45 \times 40 = 18 \, \text{N}$$

So the acceleration of the small block is:

$$a = \frac{18}{4.0} = 4.5 \, \text{m s}^{-2}$$

But $a = \dfrac{F}{10}$, so:

$$\frac{F}{10} = 4.5 \, \text{m s}^{-2}$$

$$\Rightarrow \quad F = 45 \, \text{N}$$

2 MECHANICS

2.24 Two masses of $m = 4.0$ kg and $M = 6.0$ kg are joined together by a string that passes over a pulley (this arrangement is known as Atwood's machine). The masses are held stationary and suddenly released. Determine the acceleration of each mass.

Intuition tells us that the larger mass will start moving downward and the small mass will go up. So if we say that the larger mass's acceleration is a, then the other mass's acceleration will also be a in magnitude but, of course, in the opposite direction. The two accelerations are the same because the string cannot be extended.

Method 1
The forces on each mass are weight mg and tension T on m and weight Mg and tension T on M (Figure **2.50**).

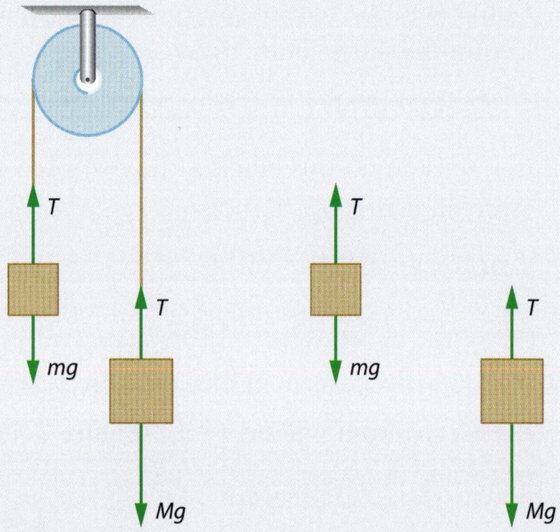

Newton's second law applied to each mass gives:

$T - mg = ma$ (1)

$Mg - T = Ma$ (2)

Note these equations carefully. Each says that the net force on the mass in question is equal to that mass times that mass's acceleration. In the first equation, we find the net force in the upward direction, because that is the direction of acceleration. In the second, we find the net force in downward direction, since that is the direction of acceleration in that case. We want to find the acceleration, so we simply add these two equations to find:

$Mg - mg = (m + M)a$

Figure 2.50

Hence:

$$a = \frac{M - m}{M + m}g$$

(Note that if $M \gg m$ the acceleration tends to g. Can you think why this is?) This shows clearly that if the two masses are equal, then there is no acceleration. This is a convenient method for measuring g. Atwood's machine effectively 'slows down' g so the falling mass has a much smaller acceleration from which g can then be determined. Putting in the numbers for our example we find $a = 2.0 \, \text{m s}^{-2}$.

Having found the acceleration we may, if we wish, also find the tension in the string, T. Putting the value for a in formula (1) we find:

$$T = m\left(\frac{M - m}{M + m}\right)g + mg$$

$$T = 2\left(\frac{Mm}{M + m}\right)g$$

(If $M \gg m$ the tension tends to $2mg$. Can you see why?)

Method 2

We treat the two masses as one body and apply Newton's second law on this body (but this is trickier than in the previous example) – see Figure **2.51**.

In this case the net force is $Mg - mg$ and, since this force acts on a body of mass $M + m$, the acceleration is found as before from $F = $ mass $\times$ acceleration. Note that the tension T does not appear, as it is now an internal force.

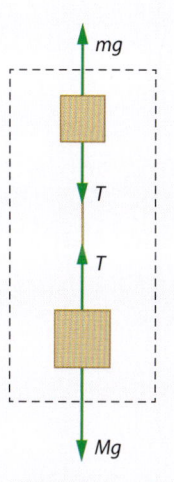

Figure 2.51

2.25 In Figure **2.52**, a block of mass M is connected to a smaller mass m through a string that goes over a pulley. Ignoring friction, find the acceleration of each mass and the tension in the string.

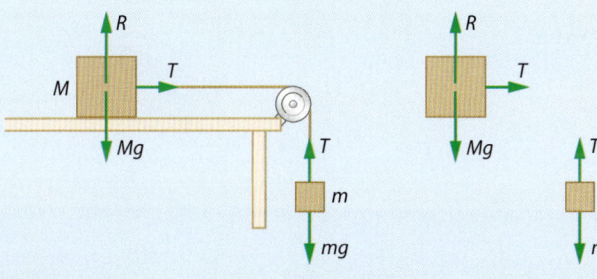

Figure 2.52

Method 1

The forces are shown in Figure **2.52**. The acceleration must be the same magnitude for both masses, but the larger mass accelerates horizontally and the smaller mass accelerates vertically downwards. The free-body diagrams on the right show the forces on the individual masses. Taking each mass separately:

$mg - T = ma$ (small mass accelerating downwards)

$T = Ma$ (large mass accelerating horizontally to the right)

Adding the two equations, we get:

$mg = ma + Ma$

$\Rightarrow \quad a = \dfrac{mg}{M + m}$

(If $M \gg m$ the acceleration tends to zero. Why?)

From the expression for T for the larger mass, we have:

$T = Ma = \dfrac{Mmg}{M + m}$

2 MECHANICS

Method 2

Treating the two bodies as one results in the situation shown in Figure **2.53**.

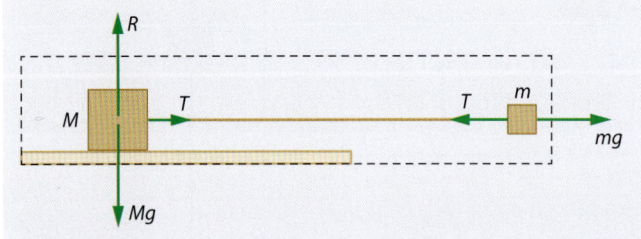

Figure 2.53

The net horizontal force on the combined mass $M+m$ is mg. Hence:

$$mg = (M+m)a$$

$$\Rightarrow a = \frac{mg}{M+m}$$

The tension can then be found as before.

2.26 A block of mass 2.5 kg is held on a rough inclined plane, as shown in Figure **2.54**. When released, the block stays in place. The angle of the incline is slowly increased and when the angle becomes slightly larger than 38° the block begins to slip down the plane.

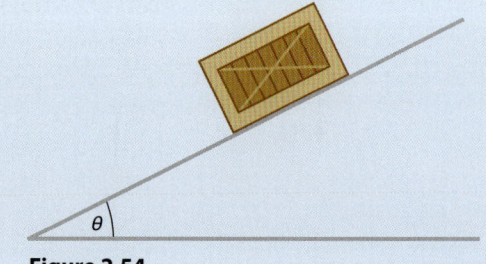

Figure 2.54

  a Calculate the coefficient of static friction between the block and the inclined plane.

  b The angle of the incline is increased to 49°. The coefficient of dynamic friction between the block and the incline is 0.26. Calculate the force that must be applied to the block along the plane so it moves up the plane with an acceleration of $1.2\,\text{m s}^{-2}$.

---

  a The forces on the block just before slipping are shown in Figure **2.55**. The frictional force is f and the normal reaction is R. The components of the weight are $mg\sin\theta$ down the plane and $mg\cos\theta$ at right angles to the plane.

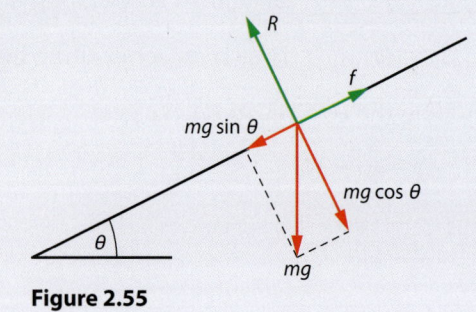

Figure 2.55

Because the block is about to slip, the frictional force is the maximum possible static frictional force and so $f = \mu_s R$. Equilibrium demands that:

$$mg\sin\theta = f$$

$$mg\cos\theta = R$$

Divide the first equation by the second to get:

$$\tan\theta = \frac{f}{R}$$

Now use the fact that $f = \mu_s R$ to find:

$$\tan\theta = \frac{\mu_s R}{R}$$

$$\tan\theta = \mu_s$$

Hence $\mu_s = \tan\theta = \tan 38° = 0.78$

b Let F be the required force up the plane. The net force up the plane is $F - mg\sin 49° - f_d$, since the force of friction now opposes F.

We have that:

$$f_d = \mu_s R = \mu_s mg\cos 49°$$

Therefore:

$$F - mg\sin 49° - \mu_s mg\cos 49° = ma$$

$$F = ma + mg\sin 49° + \mu_s mg\cos 49°$$

Substituting values:

$$F = 2.5 \times 1.2 + 2.5 \times 9.8 \times \sin 49° + 0.26 \times 2.5 \times 9.8 \cos 49°$$

$$F = 25.67 \approx 26\,\text{N}$$

Exam tip
Notice that for a block on a frictionless inclined plane the net force down the plane is $mg\sin\theta$, leading to an acceleration of $g\sin\theta$, independent of the mass.

Nature of science

Physics and mathematics

In formulating his laws of motion, published in 1687 in *Philosophiæ Naturalis Principia Mathematica*, Newton used mathematics to show how the work of earlier scientists could be applied to forces and motion in the real world. Newton's second law (for particle of constant mass) is written as $F = ma$. In this form, this equation does not seem particularly powerful. However, using calculus, Newton showed that acceleration is given by:

$$a = \frac{dv}{dt} = \frac{d^2x}{dt^2}$$

The second law then becomes:

$$\frac{d^2x}{dt^2} - \frac{F}{m} = 0$$

This is a differential equation that can be solved to give the actual path that the particle will move on under the action of the force. Newton showed that if the force depends on position as $F \propto \frac{1}{x^2}$, then the motion has to be along a conic section (ellipse, circle, etc.).

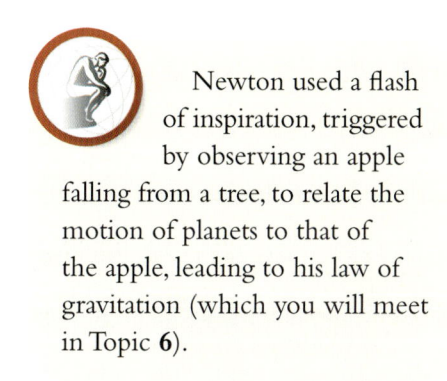

Newton used a flash of inspiration, triggered by observing an apple falling from a tree, to relate the motion of planets to that of the apple, leading to his law of gravitation (which you will meet in Topic **6**).

Test yourself

Equilibrium

34 A block rests on a rough table and is connected by a string that goes over a pulley to a second hanging block, as shown in the diagram. Draw the forces on each body.

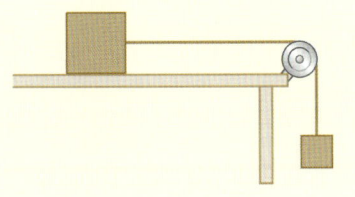

35 A bead rolls on the surface of a sphere, having started from the top, as shown in the diagram. On a copy of the diagram, draw the forces on the bead:
 a at the top
 b at the point where it is about to leave the surface of the sphere.

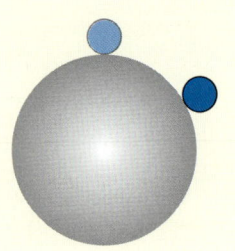

36 Look at the diagram. State in which case the tension in the string is largest.

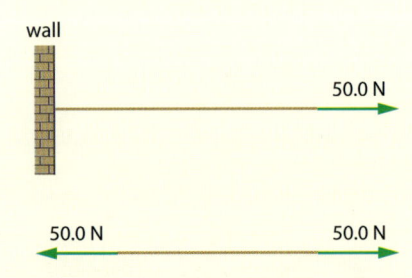

37 A spring is compressed by a certain distance and a mass is attached to its right end, as shown in the diagram. The mass rests on a rough table. On a copy of the diagram, draw the forces acting on the mass.

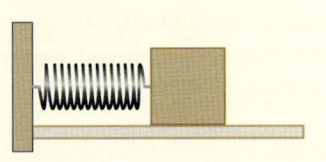

38 A mass hangs attached to three strings, as shown in the diagram. On a copy of the diagram, draw the forces on:
 a the hanging mass
 b the point where the strings join.

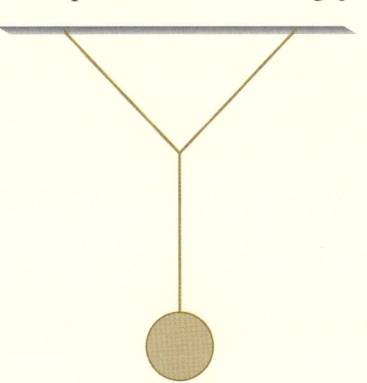

39 Find the net force on each of the bodies shown in the diagrams. The only forces acting are the ones shown. Indicate direction by 'right', 'left', 'up' and 'down'.

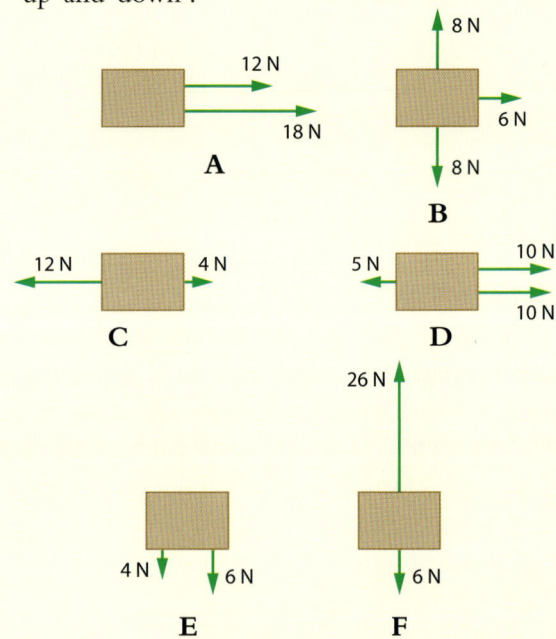

A: 12 N, 18 N
B: 8 N, 6 N, 8 N
C: 12 N, 4 N
D: 5 N, 10 N, 10 N
E: 4 N, 6 N
F: 26 N, 6 N

40 Find the magnitude and direction of the net force in the diagram.

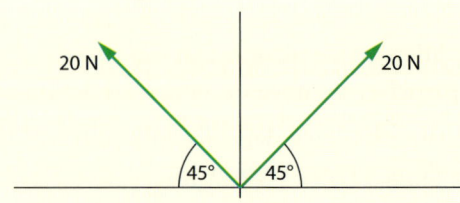

20 N, 20 N, 45°, 45°

41 Explain why is it impossible for a mass to hang attached to two horizontal strings as shown in the diagram.

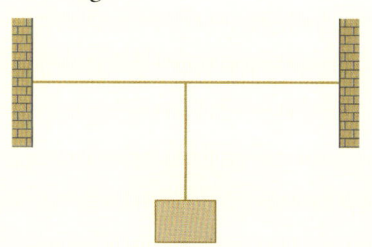

42 A mass is hanging from a string that is attached to the ceiling. A second piece of string (identical to the first) hangs from the lower end of the mass (see diagram).

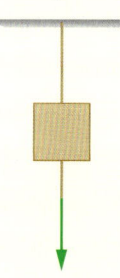

State and explain which string will break if:
a the bottom string is slowly pulled with ever increasing force
b the bottom string is very abruptly pulled down.

43 A mass of 2.00 kg rests on a rough horizontal table. The coefficient of static friction between the block and the table is 0.60. The block is attached to a hanging mass by a string that goes over a smooth pulley, as shown in the diagram. Determine the largest mass that can hang in this way without forcing the block to slide.

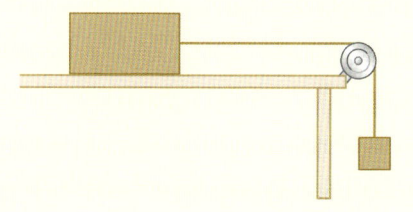

44 A girl tries to lift a suitcase of weight 220 N by pulling upwards on it with a force of 140 N. The suitcase does not move. Calculate the reaction force from the floor on the suitcase.

45 A block of mass 15.0 kg rests on a horizontal table. A force of 50.0 N is applied vertically downward on the block. Calculate the force that the block exerts on the table.

46 A block of mass M is connected with a string to a smaller block of mass m. The big block is resting on a smooth inclined plane as shown in the diagram. Determine the angle of the plane in terms of M and m in order to have equilibrium.

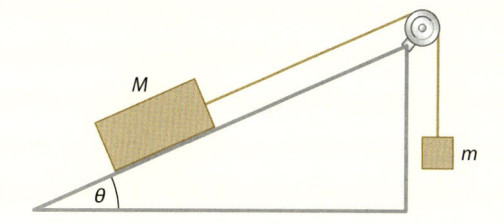

Accelerated motion

47 Describe under what circumstances a constant force would result in **a** an increasing and **b** a decreasing acceleration on a body.

48 A car of mass 1400 kg is on a muddy road. If the force from the engine pushing the car forward exceeds 600 N, the wheels slip (i.e. they rotate without rolling). Estimate the car's maximum acceleration on this road.

49 A man of mass m stands in an elevator.
  a Find the reaction force from the elevator floor on the man when:
   i the elevator is standing still
   ii the elevator moves up at constant speed v
   iii the elevator accelerates down with acceleration a
   iv the elevator accelerates down with acceleration $a = g$.
  b What happens when $a > g$?

50 Get in an elevator and stretch out your arm holding your heavy physics book. Press the button to go up. Describe and explain what is happening to your stretched arm. Repeat as the elevator comes to a stop at the top floor. What happens when you press the button to go down and what happens when the elevator again stops? Explain your observations carefully using the second law of motion.

2 MECHANICS   77

51 The diagram shows a person in an elevator pulling on a rope that goes over a pulley and is attached to the top of the elevator. The mass of the elevator is 30.0 kg and that of the person is 70 kg.
   a On a copy of the diagram, draw the forces on the person.
   b Draw the forces on the elevator.
   c The elevator accelerates upwards at $0.50\,\mathrm{m\,s^{-2}}$. Find the reaction force on the person from the elevator floor.
   d The force the person exerts on the elevator floor is 300 N. Find the acceleration of the elevator ($g = 10\,\mathrm{m\,s^{-2}}$).

52 A massless string has the same tension throughout its length. Suggest why.

53 a Calculate the tension in the string joining the two masses in the diagram.
   b If the position of the masses is interchanged, will the tension change?

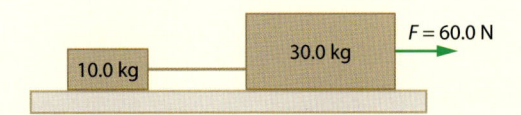

54 A mass of 3.0 kg is acted upon by three forces of 4.0 N, 6.0 N and 9.0 N and is in equilibrium. Convince yourself that these forces can indeed be in equilibrium. The 9.0 N force is suddenly removed. Determine the acceleration of the mass.

Learning objectives

- Understand the concepts of kinetic, gravitational potential and elastic potential energy.
- Understand work done as energy transferred.
- Understand power as the rate of energy transfer.
- Understand and apply the principle of energy conservation.
- Calculate the efficiency in energy transfers.

2.3 Work, energy and power

This section deals with energy, one of the most basic concepts in physics. We introduce the principle of energy conservation and learn how to apply it to various situations. We define kinetic and potential energy, work done and power developed.

Energy

Energy is a concept that we all have an intuitive understanding of. Chemical energy derived from food keeps us alive. Chemical energy from gasoline powers our cars. Electrical energy keeps our computers going. Nuclear fusion energy produces light and heat in the Sun that sustains life on Earth. And so on. Very many experiments, from the subatomic to the cosmic scale, appear to be consistent with the principle of **conservation of energy** that states that energy is not created or destroyed but is only transformed from one form into another. This means that any change in the energy of a system must be accompanied by a change in the energy of the surroundings of the system such that:

$$\Delta E_{\text{system}} + \Delta E_{\text{surroundings}} = 0$$

In other words, if the system's energy increases, the energy of the surroundings must decrease by the same amount and vice-versa.

The energy of the system may change as a result of **interactions** with its surroundings (Figure **2.56**). These interactions mainly involve **work done** W by the surroundings and/or the **transfer of thermal energy** (heat) Q, to or from the surroundings. But there are many other interactions between a system and its surroundings. For example, waves of many kinds may transfer energy to the system (the Sun heats the Earth); gasoline, a chemical fuel, may be added to the system, increasing its energy; wind incident on the blades of a windmill will generate electrical energy as a generator is made to turn, etc. So:

$\Delta E_{system} = W + Q +$ other transfers

But in this section we will deal with $Q = 0$ and no other transfers so we must understand and use the relation:

$\Delta E = W$

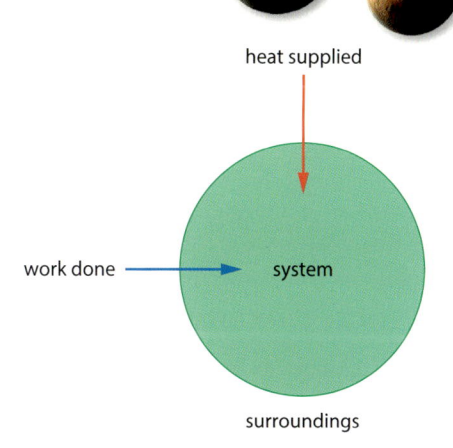

Figure 2.56 The total energy of a system may change as a result of interactions with its surroundings.

(we dropped the subscript in E_{system}). To do so, we need to define what we mean by work done and what exactly we mean by E, the total energy of the system.

Work done by a force

We first consider the definition of **work done** by a constant force for motion in a straight line. By constant force we mean a force that is constant in magnitude as well as in direction. Figure **2.57** shows a block that is displaced along a straight line. The distance travelled by the body is s. The force makes an angle θ with the displacement.

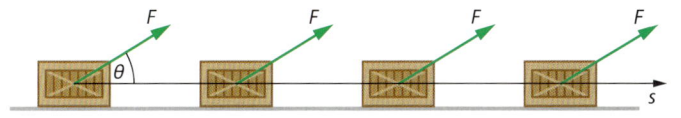

Figure 2.57 A force moving its point of application performs work.

The force acts on the body all the time as it moves. The work done by the force is defined as:

$W = Fs \cos \theta$

But $F \cos \theta$ is the component of the force in the direction of the displacement and so:

> The work done by a force is the product of the force in the direction of the displacement times the distance travelled.

(Equivalently, since $s \cos \theta$ is the distance travelled in the direction of the force, work may also be defined as the product of the force time, the distance travelled in the direction of the force.)

2 MECHANICS

The cosine here can be positive, negative or zero; thus work can be positive, negative or zero. We will see what that means shortly.

The unit of work is the joule. One joule is the work done by a force of 1 N when it moves a body a distance of 1 m in the direction of the force. 1 J = 1 N m.

Worked examples

2.27 A mass is being pulled along a level road by a rope attached to it in such a way that the rope makes an angle of 34° with the horizontal. The force in the rope is 24 N. Calculate the work done by this force in moving the mass a distance of 8.0 m along the level road.

We just have to apply the formula for work done:

$W = Fs \cos\theta$

Substituting the values from the question:

$W = 24 \times 8.0 \times \cos 34°$

$W = 160$ J

2.28 A car with its engine off moves on a horizontal level road. A constant force of 620 N opposes the motion of the car. The car comes to rest after 84 m. Calculate the work done on the car by the opposing force.

We again apply the formula for work done, but now we have to realise that $\theta = 180°$. So:

$W = 620 \times 84 \times \cos 180°$

$W = -52$ kJ

2.29 You stand on roller skates facing a wall. You push against the wall and you move away. Discuss whether the force exerted by the wall on you performed any work.

No work was done because there is no displacement. You moved but the point where the force is applied never moved.

Varying force and curved path

You will meet situations where the force is not constant in magnitude or direction and the path is not a straight line. To find the work done we must break up the curved path into very many small straight segments in a way that approximates the curved path (Figure **2.58**). Think of these segments as the dashes that make up the curve when it is drawn as a dashed line. The large arrowed segments at the bottom of Figure **2.58** show this more clearly. The total work done is the sum of the work done on each segment of the path.

We assume that along each segment the force is constant. The work done on the *k*th segment is just $F_k s_k \cos \theta_k$. So the work done on all the segments is found by adding up the work done on individual segments, i.e.

$$W = \sum_{k=1}^{N} F_k s_k \cos \theta_k$$

Do not be too worried about this formula. You will not be asked to use it, but it can help you to understand one very special and important case: the work done in circular motion. We will learn in Topic **6** that in circular motion there must be a force directed towards the centre of the circle. This is called the **centripetal force**.

Figure **2.59** shows the forces pointing towards the centre of the circular path. When we break the circular path into straight segments the angle between the force and the segment is always a right angle. This means that work done along each segment is zero because $\cos 90° = 0$. So for circular motion the total work done by the centripetal force is zero.

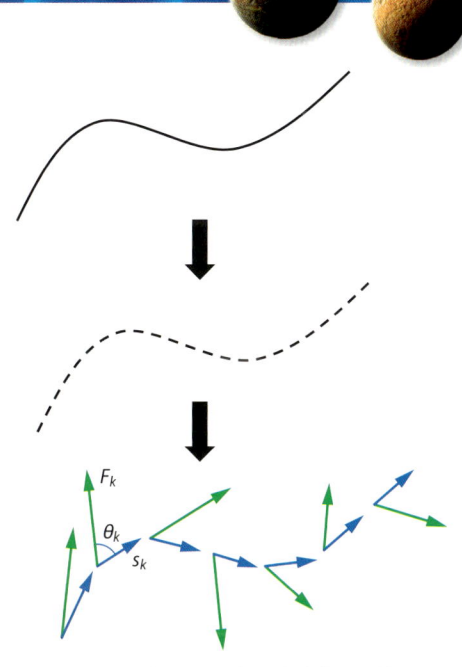

Figure 2.58 The curved path followed by a particle is shown as a dashed line, and then as larger segments, s_k. The green arrows show the varying size and direction of the force acting on the particle as it moves.

forces point towards the centre   forces are perpendicular to each segment

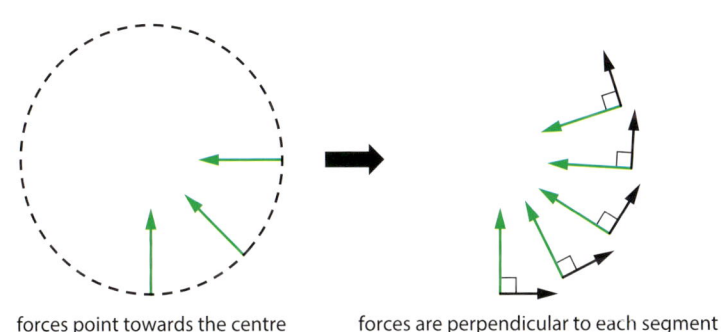

Figure 2.59 The work done by the centripetal force is zero.

In practice, when the force varies in magnitude but is constant in direction, we will be given a graph of how the force varies with distance travelled. The work done can be found from the area under the graph. For the motion shown in Figure **2.60**, the work done in moving a distance of 4.0 m is given by the area of the shaded trapezoid:

$$W = \frac{2.0 + 10}{2} \times 4.0 = 24 \, \text{J}$$

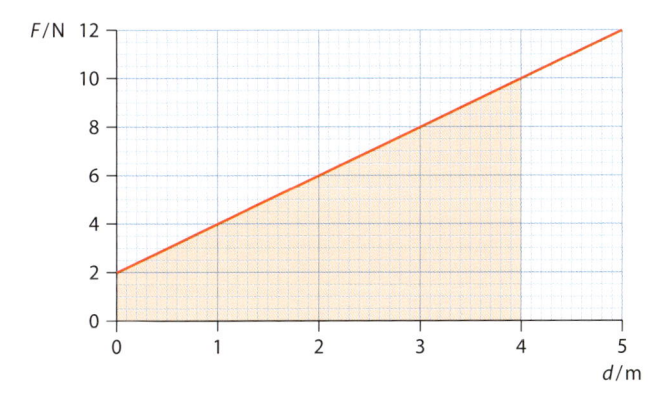

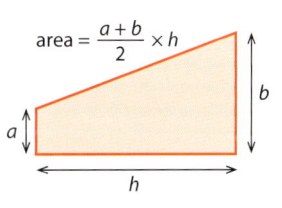

area $= \dfrac{a+b}{2} \times h$

Figure 2.60 The work done is the area under the graph. The area of a trapezoid is half the sum of the parallel sides multiplied by the perpendicular distance between them.

2 MECHANICS 81

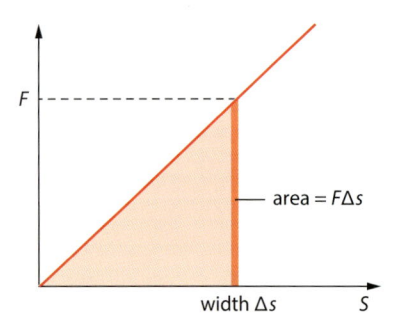

Figure 2.61 The area under the graph is the sum of all the rectangles $F\Delta s$.

The work done by a force is the area under the graph that shows the variation of the magnitude of the force with distance travelled.

How do we know that the area is the work done? For a varying force, consider a very small distance Δs (Figure 2.61). Because Δs is so small we may assume that the force does not vary during this distance. The work done is then $F\Delta s$ and is the area of the rectangle shown. For the total work we have to add the area of many rectangles under the curve. The sum is the area under the curve.

Work done by a force on a particle

Imagine a net force F that acts on a particle of mass m. The force produces an acceleration a given by:

$$a = \frac{F}{m}$$

Let the initial speed of the particle be u. Because we have acceleration, the speed will change. Let the speed be v after travelling a distance s. We know from kinematics that:

$$v^2 = u^2 + 2as$$

Substituting for the acceleration, this becomes:

$$v^2 = u^2 + 2\frac{F}{m}s$$

We can rewrite this as:

$$Fs = \tfrac{1}{2}mv^2 - \tfrac{1}{2}mu^2$$

We interpret this as follows: Fs is the work done on the particle by the net force. The quantity $\tfrac{1}{2} \times$ mass $\times$ speed^2 is the energy the particle has due to its motion, called kinetic energy. For speed v, **kinetic energy** E_K is defined as:

$$E_K = \tfrac{1}{2}mv^2$$

In our example, the initial kinetic energy of the particle is $\tfrac{1}{2}mu^2$ and the kinetic energy after travelling distance s is $\tfrac{1}{2}mv^2$. The result says that the work done has gone into the change in the kinetic energy of the particle.

We can write this as:

$$W_{net} = \Delta E_K$$

where W_{net} is the net work done and ΔE_K is the change in kinetic energy. This is known as the **work–kinetic energy relation**.

We can think of the work done as energy transferred. In this example, the work done has transferred energy to the particle by increasing its kinetic energy.

Worked example

2.30 A block of mass 2.5 kg slides on a rough horizontal surface. The initial speed of the block is 8.6 m s^{-1}. It is brought to rest after travelling a distance of 16 m. Determine the magnitude of the frictional force.

We will use the work–kinetic energy relation, $W_{net} = \Delta E_K$.

The only force doing work is the frictional force, f, which acts in the opposite direction to the motion.

$$W_{net} = f \times 16 \times (-1)$$

The angle between the force and the direction of motion is 180°, so we need to multiply by cos 180°, which is −1.

The change in kinetic energy is:

$$\Delta E_K = \tfrac{1}{2}mv^2 - \tfrac{1}{2}mu^2 = -92.45\,\text{J}$$

So: $-16f = -92.45$

$$f = 5.8\,\text{N}$$

The magnitude of the frictional force is 5.8 N.

Work done in stretching a spring

Consider a horizontal spring whose left end is attached to a vertical wall. If we apply a force F to the other end we will stretch the spring by some amount, x. Experiments show that the force F and the extension x are directly proportional to each other, i.e. $F = kx$ (this is known as **Hooke's law**). How much work does the stretching force F do in stretching the spring from its natural length (i.e. from zero extension) to a length where the extension is x_1, as shown in Figure 2.62.

Since the force F and the extension x are directly proportional, the graph of force versus extension is a straight line through the origin and work done is the area under the curve (Figure 2.63).

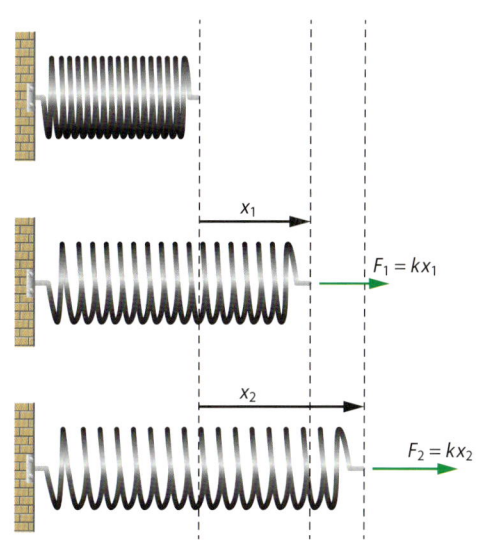

Figure 2.62 Stretching a spring requires work to be done.

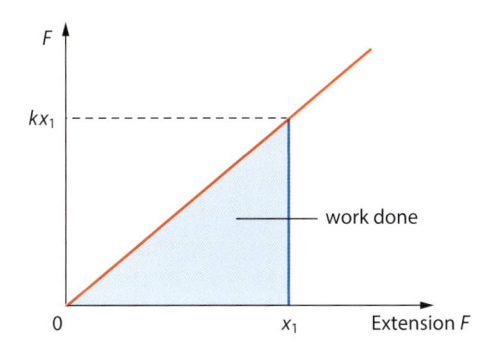

Figure 2.63 The force F stretches the spring. Notice that as the extension increases the force increases as well.

2 MECHANICS 83

To find the work done in extending the spring from its natural length ($x=0$) to extension x_1, we need to calculate the area of the triangle of base x_1 and height kx_1. Thus:

$$\text{area} = \tfrac{1}{2}kx_1 \times x_1$$

$$\text{area} = \tfrac{1}{2}kx_1^2$$

The work to extend a spring from its natural length by an amount x_1 is thus:

$$W = \tfrac{1}{2}kx_1^2$$

It follows that the work done when extending a spring from an extension x_1 to an extension x_2 (so $x_2 > x_1$) is:

$$W = \tfrac{1}{2}k(x_2^2 - x_1^2)$$

The work done by the force extending the spring goes into elastic potential energy stored in the spring. The elastic potential energy of a spring whose extension is x is $E_{el} = \tfrac{1}{2}kx^2$.

Exam tip
In discussing work done it is always important to keep a clear picture of the force whose work we are calculating.

Worked example

2.31 A mass of 8.4 kg rests on top of a vertical spring whose base is attached to the floor. The spring compresses by 5.2 cm.
  a Calculate the spring constant of the spring.
  b Determine the energy stored in the spring.

a The mass is at equilibrium so $mg = kx$. So:

$$k = \frac{mg}{x}$$

$$k = \frac{8.4 \times 9.8}{5.2 \times 10^{-2}}$$

$$k = 1583 \approx 1600 \, \text{N m}^{-1}$$

b The stored energy E_{el} is:

$$E_{el} = \tfrac{1}{2}kx^2$$

$$E_{el} = \tfrac{1}{2} \times 1583 \times (5.2 \times 10^{-2})^2$$

$$E_{el} = 2.1 \, \text{J}$$

Work done by gravity

We will now concentrate on the work done by a very special force, namely the weight of a body. Remember that weight is mass times acceleration of free fall and is directed vertically down. Thus, if a body is displaced horizontally, the work done by mg is zero. In this case the angle between the force and the direction of motion is 90° (Figure **2.64**), so:

$W = mgs \cos 90° = 0$

Exam tip
When a body is displaced such that its final position is at the same vertical height as the original position, the work done by the weight is zero.

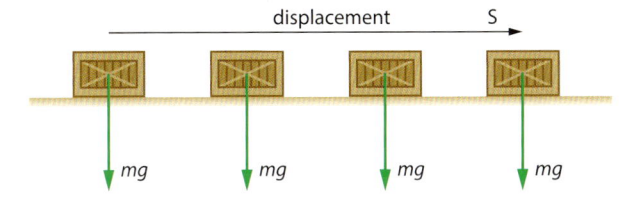

Figure 2.64 The force of gravity is normal to this horizontal displacement, so no work is being done.

We are not implying that it is the weight that is forcing the body to move along the table. We are calculating the work done by a particular force (the weight) if the body (somehow) moves in a particular way.

If the body falls a vertical distance h, then the work done by the weight is $+mgh$. The force of gravity is parallel to the displacement, as in Figure **2.65a**.

If the body moves vertically upwards to a height h from the launch point, then the work done by the weight is $-mgh$ since now the angle between direction of force (vertically down) and displacement (vertically up) is 180°. The force of gravity is parallel to the displacement but opposite in direction, as in Figure **2.65b**.

Suppose now that instead of just letting the body fall or throwing it upwards, we use a rope to either lower it or raise it, at constant speed, by a height h (Figure **2.66**). The work done by the weight is the same as before, so nothing changes. But we now ask about the work done by the force F that lowers or raises the body. Since F is equal and opposite to the weight, the work done by F is $-mgh$ as the body is lowered and $+mgh$ as it is being raised.

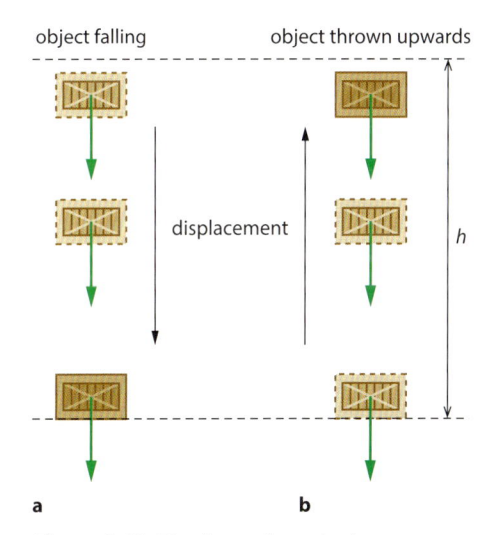

Figure 2.65 The force of gravity (green arrows) is parallel to the displacement in **a** and opposite in **b**.

You should be able to see how this is similar to the work done by the stretching and tension forces in a spring.

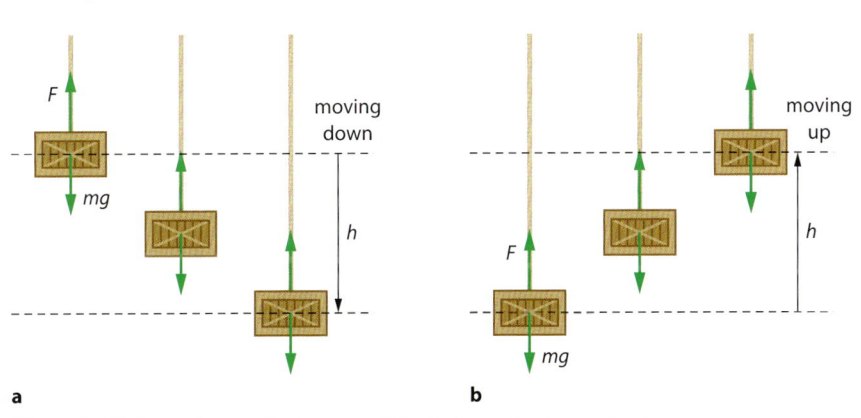

Figure 2.66 Lowering and raising an object at constant speed using a rope.

2 MECHANICS 85

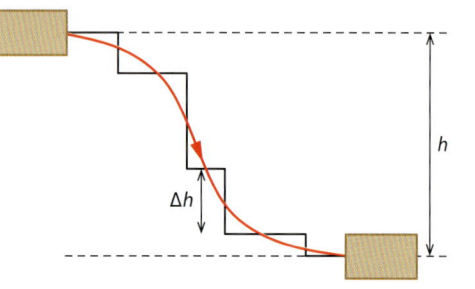

Figure 2.67 The work done by gravity is independent of the path followed.

Consider now the case where a body moves along some arbitrary path, as shown by the red line in Figure **2.67**. The work done by the weight of the body as the body descends along the curve is still mgh. You can prove this amazing result easily by approximating the curved path with a 'staircase' of vertical and horizontal steps. Along the horizontal steps the work done is zero, $\cos 90° = 0$. Along the vertical steps the work is $mg\Delta h$, where Δh is the step height. Adding up all the vertical steps gives mgh. This means that:

> The work done by gravity is independent of the path followed and depends only on the vertical distance separating the initial and final positions.

The independence of the work done on the path followed is a property of a class of forces (of which weight is a prominent member) called **conservative forces**.

Mechanical energy

In the previous two sections we discussed the work done when a body is moved when attached to a spring and in a gravitational field. We derived two main results.

In the case of the spring, we showed that the work done by the stretching force in extending the spring a distance x away from the natural length of the spring is $W = \frac{1}{2}x^2$.

In the case of motion within a gravitational field the work done by the force moving the body, is $W = mgh$ to raise the body a height h from its initial position.

We use these results to define two different kinds of **potential energy**, E_P.

For the mass–spring system we define the **elastic potential energy** to be the work done by the pulling force in stretching the spring by an amount x, that is:

$$E_P = \frac{1}{2}kx^2$$

For the Earth–mass system we define the **gravitational potential energy** to be the work done by the moving force in placing a body a height h above its initial position, that is:

$$E_P = mgh$$

Notice that potential energy is the property of a system, not of an individual particle.

So we are now in a position to go back to the first part of Subtopic **2.3** and answer some of the questions posed there. We said that:

$$\Delta E = W + Q$$

Exam tip
Potential energy is the energy of a system due to its position or shape and represents the work done by an external agent in bringing the system to that position or shape.

Exam tip
Notice that in the data booklet the formula uses Δx in place of our x.

If the system is in contact with surroundings at a different temperature there will be a transfer of heat, Q. If there is no contact and no temperature difference, then $Q = 0$.

If no work is done on the system from outside, then $W = 0$. When $Q + W = 0$, the system is called **isolated** and in that case $\Delta E = 0$. The total energy of the system does not change. We have **conservation of the total energy** of the system.

What does the total energy E consist of? It includes chemical energy, **internal energy** (due to the translational, rotational energy and vibrational energy of the molecules of the substance), nuclear energy, kinetic energy, elastic potential energy, gravitational potential energy and any other form of potential energy such as electrical potential energy.

But in this section, dealing with mechanics, the total energy E will be just the sum of the kinetic, the elastic and the gravitational potential energies.

So for a single particle of mass m, the energy is:

$E = \frac{1}{2}mv^2 + mgh + \frac{1}{2}kx^2$

This is also called the **total mechanical energy** of the system consisting of the particle, the spring and the Earth. W stands for work done by forces outside the system. So this does not include work due to spring tension forces or the weight since the work of these forces is already included as potential energy in E.

Exam tip
You must make sure that you do not confuse the work–kinetic energy relation $W_{net} = \Delta E_K$ with $\Delta E = W$. The work–kinetic energy relation relates the net work on a system to the change in the system's kinetic energy. The other relates the work done by outside forces to the change of the total energy.

Worked examples

2.32 You hold a ball of mass 0.25 kg in your hand and throw it so that it leaves your hand with a speed of $12\,\text{m s}^{-1}$. Calculate the work done by your hand on the ball.

The question asks for work done but here we do not know the forces that acted on the ball nor the distance by which we moved it before releasing it. But using $\Delta E = W$, we find:

$W = \frac{1}{2}mv^2$

$W = \frac{1}{2} \times 0.25 \times 12^2 = 36\,\text{J}$

Notice that here we have no springs and we may take $h = 0$.

2.33 Suppose that in the previous example your hand moved a distance of 0.90 m in throwing the ball. Estimate the average net force that acted on the ball.

The work done was 36 J and so $Fs = 36\,\text{J}$ with $s = 0.90\,\text{m}$. This gives $F = 40\,\text{N}$.

2 MECHANICS

2.34 A body of mass 4.2 kg with initial speed 5.6 m s^{-1} begins to move up an incline, as shown in Figure **2.68**.

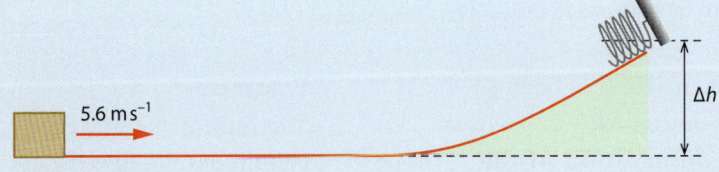

Figure 2.68

The body will be momentarily brought to rest after colliding with a spring of spring constant 220 N m^{-1}. The body stops a vertical distance 0.85 m above its initial position. Determine the amount by which the spring has been compressed. There are no frictional forces.

There are no external forces doing work and so $W=0$. The system is isolated and we have conservation of total energy.

Initially we have just kinetic energy, so:

$E_{\text{initial}} = \frac{1}{2}mv^2 + mgh + \frac{1}{2}kx^2 = \frac{1}{2} \times 4.2 \times 5.6^2 + 0 + 0 = 65.856 \text{ J}$

When the body stops we have:

$E_{\text{final}} = \frac{1}{2}mv^2 + mgh + \frac{1}{2}kx^2 = 0 + 4.2 \times 9.8 \times 0.85 + \frac{1}{2} \times 220 \times x^2 = 34.99 + 110x^2$

Thus, equating E_{initial} to E_{final} we find:

$34.99 + 110x^2 = 65.856$
$110x^2 = 30.866$
$x^2 = 0.2806$
$x = 0.53 \text{ m}$

2.35 We repeat the previous example question but now there is constant frictional force opposing the motion along the uphill part of the path. The length of this path is 1.2 m and the frictional force is 15 N.

We have $\Delta E = W$. The work done is:

$Fs \cos\theta = 15 \times 1.2 \times (-1) = -18 \text{ J}$

As in the previous example, we have:

$E_{\text{initial}} = 65.856 \text{ J}$
$E_{\text{final}} = 34.99 + 110x^2$

leading to:

$110x^2 = 12.866$
$x^2 = \frac{12.866}{110}$
$x = 0.34 \text{ m}$

The 'work done by friction' of -18 J is energy that is dissipated as thermal energy inside the body *and* its surroundings. It is in general very difficult to estimate how much of this thermal energy stays within the body and how much goes into the surroundings.

2.36 A mass of 5.00 kg moving with an initial velocity of 2.0 m s^{-1} is acted upon by a force 55 N in the direction of the velocity. The motion is opposed by a frictional force. After travelling a distance of 12 m the velocity of the body becomes 15 m s^{-1}. Determine the magnitude of the frictional force.

Here $Q = 0$ so that $\Delta E = W$.

The change in total energy ΔE is the change in kinetic energy (we have no springs and no change of height):

$\Delta E = \frac{1}{2} \times 5.00 \times 15^2 - \frac{1}{2} \times 5.00 \times 2.0^2 = 552.5$ J

Let the frictional force be f. The work done on the mass is $(55 - f) \times 12$, and so:

$(55 - f) \times 12 = 552.5$

$55 - f = \frac{552.5}{12}$

$55 - f = 46.0$

$f = 9.0$ N

The 'work done by friction' of $-9.0 \times 12 = -108$ J is energy that is dissipated as thermal energy inside the body *and* its surroundings.

2.37 A mass m hangs from two strings attached to the ceiling such that they make the same angle with the vertical (as shown in Figure 2.69). The strings are shortened very slowly so that the mass is raised a distance Δh above its original position. Determine the work done by the tension in each string as the mass is raised.

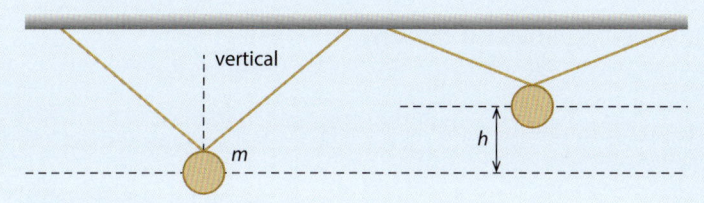

Figure 2.69

The net work done is zero since the net force on the mass is zero. The work done by gravity is $-mg\Delta h$ and thus the work done by the two equal tension forces is $+mg\Delta h$. The work done by each is thus $\frac{mg\Delta h}{2}$.

2.38 A pendulum of length 1.0 m is released from rest with the string at an angle of 10° to the vertical. Find the speed of the mass on the end of the pendulum when it passes through its lowest position.

Let us take as the reference level the lowest point of the pendulum (Figure **2.70**). The total energy at that point is just kinetic, $E_K = \frac{1}{2}mv^2$, where v is the unknown speed.

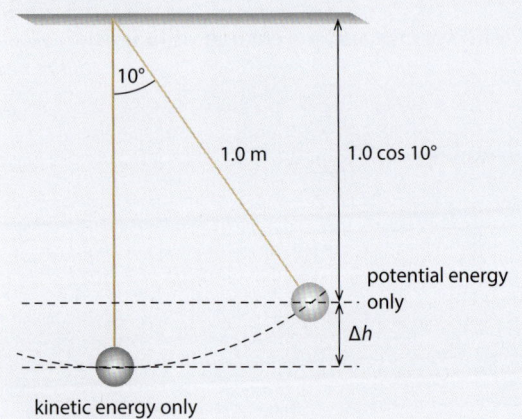

Figure 2.70

At the initial point, the total energy is just potential, $E_P = mg\Delta h$, where Δh is the vertical difference in height between the two positions. From the diagram:

$\Delta h = 1.00 - 1.00 \cos 10°$

$\Delta h = 0.015$ m

Equating the expressions for the total energy at the lowest point and at the start:

$\frac{1}{2}mv^2 = mg\Delta h$

$v = \sqrt{2g\Delta h}$

$v = 0.55$ m s^{-1}

Note how the mass has dropped out of the problem. (At positions other than the two shown, the mass has both kinetic and potential energy.)

2.39 Determine the minimum speed of the mass in Figure **2.71** at the initial point such that the mass makes it over the barrier of height h.

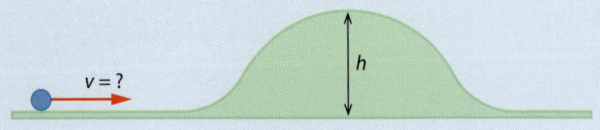

Figure 2.71

To make it over the barrier the mass must be able to reach the highest point. Any speed it has at the top will mean it can carry on to the other side. Therefore, at the very least, we must be able to get the ball to the highest point with zero speed.

With zero speed at the top, the total energy at the top of the barrier is $E = mgh$.

The total energy at the starting position is $\frac{1}{2}mv^2$.

Equating the initial and final energy:

$\frac{1}{2}mv^2 = mgh$

$\Rightarrow v = \sqrt{2gh}$

Thus, the initial speed must be bigger than $v = \sqrt{2gh}$.

Note that if the initial speed u of the mass is larger than $v = \sqrt{2gh}$, then when the mass makes it to the original level on the other side of the barrier, its speed will be the same as the starting speed u.

2.40 A ball rolls off a 1.0 m high table with a speed of 4.0 m s^{-1}, as shown in Figure 2.72. Calculate the speed as the ball strikes the floor.

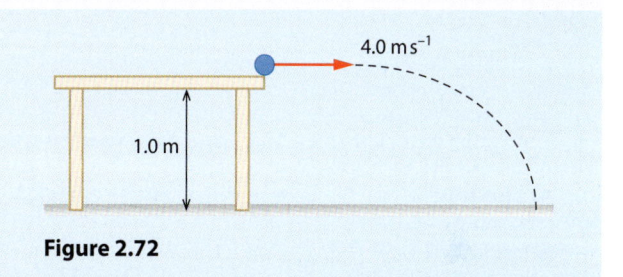

Figure 2.72

The total energy of the mass is conserved. As it leaves the table with speed u it has total energy given by $E_{initial} = \frac{1}{2}mu^2 + mgh$ and as it lands with speed v the total energy is $E_{final} = \frac{1}{2}mv^2$ (v is the speed we are looking for).

Equating the two energies gives:

$\frac{1}{2}mv^2 = \frac{1}{2}mu^2 + mgh$

$\Rightarrow v^2 = u^2 + 2gh$

$v^2 = 16 + 20 = 36$

$\Rightarrow v = 6.0 \text{ m s}^{-1}$

2.41 Two identical balls are launched from a table with the same speed u (Figure 2.73). One ball is thrown vertically up and the other vertically down. The height of the table from the floor is h. Predict which of the two balls will hit the floor with the greater speed.

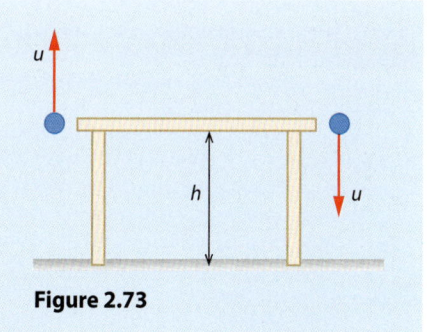

Figure 2.73

At launch both balls have the same kinetic energy and the same potential energy. When they hit the floor their energy will be only kinetic. Hence the speeds will be identical and equal to v, where:

$\frac{1}{2}mv^2 = \frac{1}{2}mu^2 + mgh$

$\Rightarrow v^2 = u^2 + 2gh$

$\Rightarrow v = \sqrt{u^2 + 2gh}$

2 MECHANICS

2.42 A body of mass 2.0 kg (initially at rest) slides down a curved path of total length 22 m, as shown in Figure 2.74. The body starts from a vertical height of 5.0 m from the bottom. When it reaches the bottom, its speed is measured and found to equal 6.0 m s^{-1}.

a Show that there is a force resisting the motion.
b Assuming the force to have constant magnitude, determine the magnitude of the force.

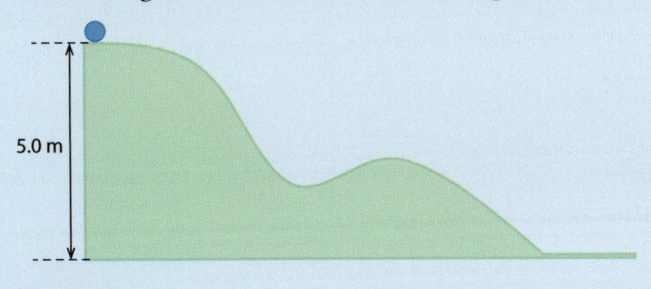

Figure 2.74

a The only external force that could do work is a frictional force.

At the top: $E_{initial} = \frac{1}{2}mv^2 + mgh = 0 + 2.0 \times 9.8 \times 5.0 = 98\,J$

At the bottom: $E_{final} = \frac{1}{2}mv^2 + mgh = \frac{1}{2} \times 2.0 \times 6.0^2 + 0 = 36\,J$

The total energy has reduced, which shows the presence of a frictional force resisting the motion.

b From $\Delta E = W$ we deduce that $W = -62\,J$. This is the work done by the frictional force, magnitude f.

The force acts in the opposite direction to the motion, so:

$fs \times (-1) = -62\,J$

$\Rightarrow f = \dfrac{62}{22}$

$f = 2.8\,N$

Power

When a machine performs work, it is important to know not only how much work is being done but also how much work is performed within a given time interval. A cyclist will perform a lot of work in a lifetime of cycling, but the same work can be performed by a powerful car engine in a much shorter time. **Power** is the rate at which work is being performed or the rate at which energy is being transferred.

> When a quantity of work ΔW is performed within a time interval Δt the power developed is given by the ratio:
>
> $$P = \frac{\Delta W}{\Delta t}$$
>
> is called the power developed. Its unit is joule per second and this is given the name watt (W): $1\,W = 1\,J\,s^{-1}$.

Consider a constant force F, which acts on a body of mass m. The force does an amount of work $F\Delta x$ in moving the body a small distance Δx along its direction. If this work is performed in time Δt, then:

$$P = \frac{\Delta W}{\Delta t}$$

$$P = F\frac{\Delta x}{\Delta t}$$

$$P = Fv$$

where v is the instantaneous speed of the body. This is the power produced in making the body move at speed v. As the speed increases, the power necessarily increases as well.

Consider an aeroplane moving at constant speed on a straight-line path. If the power produced by its engines is P, and the force pushing it forward is F, then P, F and v are related by the equation above. But since the plane moves with no acceleration, the total force of air resistance must equal F. Hence the force of air resistance can be found simply from the power of the plane's engines and the constant speed with which it coasts.

Worked example

2.43 Estimate the minimum power required to lift a mass of 50.0 kg up a vertical distance of 12 m in 5.0 s.

The work done in lifting the mass is mgh:

$$W = mgh = 50.0 \times 10 \times 12$$

$$W = 6.0 \times 10^3 \text{ J}$$

The power is therefore:

$$P = \frac{W}{\Delta t}$$

$$P = \frac{6.0 \times 10^3}{5.0} = 1200 \text{ W}$$

This is the minimum power required. In practice, the mass has to be accelerated from rest, which will require additional work and hence more power. There will also be frictional forces to overcome.

Efficiency

If a machine, such as an electric motor, is used to raise a load, electrical energy must be provided to the motor. This is the input energy to the motor. The motor uses some of this energy to do the useful work of raising the load. But some of the input energy is used to overcome frictional forces and therefore gets converted to thermal energy. So the ratio:

$$\frac{\text{useful energy out}}{\text{actual energy in}} \quad \text{or} \quad \frac{\text{useful power out}}{\text{actual power in}}$$

is less than one. We call this ratio the **efficiency** of the machine.

2 MECHANICS

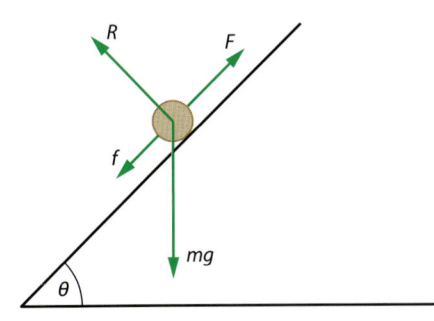

Figure 2.75 Forces on a body on an inclined plane: pulling force F, frictional force f, reaction R and weight mg.

Suppose that a body is being pulled up along a rough inclined plane with constant speed. The mass is 15 kg and the angle of the incline is 45°. There is a constant frictional force of 42 N opposing the motion.

The forces on the body are shown in Figure 2.75. Since the body has no acceleration, we know that:

$$R = mg\cos\theta = 106.1\,\text{N}$$

$$F = mg\sin\theta + f = 106.1 + 42 = 148.1\,\text{N} \approx 150\,\text{N}$$

Let the force raise the mass a distance of 20 m along the plane. The work done by the force F is:

$$W = 148.1 \times 20$$

$$W = 2960\,\text{J} \approx 3.0 \times 10^3\,\text{J}$$

The force effectively raised the 15 kg a vertical height of 14.1 m and so increased the potential energy of the mass by $mgh = 2121\,\text{J}$. The efficiency with which the force raised the mass is thus:

$$\text{efficiency} = \frac{2121}{2960}$$

$$\text{efficiency} = 0.72$$

Worked example

2.44 A 0.50 kg battery-operated toy train moves with constant velocity 0.30 m s^{-1} along a level track. The power of the motor in the train is 2.0 W and the total force opposing the motion of the train is 5.0 N.
  a Determine the efficiency of the train's motor.
  b Assuming the efficiency and the opposing force stay the same, calculate the speed of the train as it climbs an incline of 10.0° to the horizontal.

a The power delivered by the motor is 2.0 W. Since the speed is constant, the force developed by the motor is also 5.0 N.

The power used in moving the train is $Fv = 5.0 \times 0.30 = 1.5\,\text{W}$.

Hence the efficiency is:

$$\frac{\text{total power out}}{\text{total power in}} = \frac{1.5\,\text{W}}{2.0\,\text{W}}$$

$$\frac{\text{total power out}}{\text{total power in}} = 0.75$$

The efficiency of the train's motor is 0.75 (or 75%).

b The component of the train's weight acting down the plane is $mg\sin\theta$ and the force opposing motion is 5.0 N. Since there is no acceleration (constant velocity), the net force F pushing the train up the incline is:

$$F = mg\sin\theta + 5.0$$

$$F = 0.50 \times 10 \times \sin 10° + 5.0$$

$$F = 5.89\,\text{N} \approx 5.9\,\text{N}$$

Thus:

$$\text{efficiency} = \frac{5.89 \times v}{2.0}$$

But from part **a** the efficiency is 0.75, so:

$$0.75 = \frac{5.89 \times v}{2.0}$$

$$\Rightarrow v = \frac{2.0 \times 0.75}{5.89}$$

$$v = 0.26\,\text{m s}^{-1}$$

Nature of science

The origin of conservation principles

Understanding of what energy is has evolved over time, with Einstein showing that there is a direct relationship between mass and energy in his famous equation $E = mc^2$. In this section we have seen how the principle of conservation of energy can be applied to different situations to predict and explain what will happen. Scientists have been able to use the theory to predict the outcome of previously unknown interactions in particle physics.

The principle of conservation of energy is perhaps the best known example of a conservation principle. But where does it come from? It turns out that all conservation principles are consequences of symmetry. In the case of energy, the symmetry is that of 'time translation invariance'. This means that when describing motion (or anything else) it does not matter when you started the stopwatch. So a block of mass 1 kg on a table 1 m above the floor will have a potential energy of 10 J according to both an observer who starts his stopwatch 'now' and another who started it 10 seconds ago. The principle of conservation of momentum, which is discussed in Subtopic **2.4**, is also the result of a symmetry. The symmetry this time is 'space translation invariance', which means that in measuring the position of events it does not matter where you place the origin of your ruler.

Test yourself

55 A horizontal force of 24 N pulls a body a distance of 5.0 m along its direction. Calculate the work done by the force.

56 A block slides along a rough table and is brought to rest after travelling a distance of 2.4 m. A force of 3.2 N opposes the motion. Calculate the work done by the opposing force.

57 A block is pulled as shown in the diagram by a force making an angle of 20° to the horizontal. Find the work done by the pulling force when its point of application has moved 15 m.

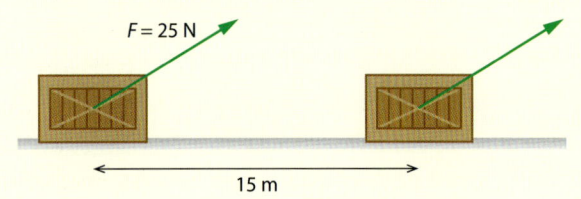

F = 25 N

15 m

58 A block of mass 2.0 kg and an initial speed of 5.4 m s^{-1} slides on a rough horizontal surface and is eventually brought to rest after travelling a distance of 4.0 m. Calculate the frictional force between the block and the surface.

59 A spring of spring constant $k = 200$ N m^{-1} is slowly extended from an extension of 3.0 cm to an extension of 5.0 cm. Calculate the work done by the extending force.

60 Look at the diagram.
   a i Calculate the minimum speed v the ball must have in order to make it to position **B**.
      ii What speed will the mass have at **B**?
   b Given that $v = 12.0$ m s^{-1}, calculate the speed at **A** and **B**.

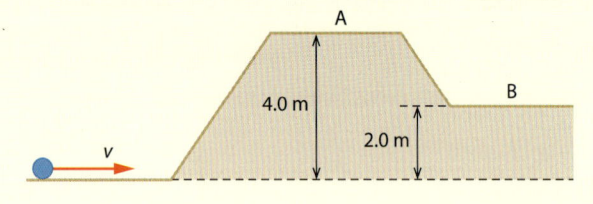

61 The speed of the 8.0 kg mass in position **A** in the diagram is 6.0 m s^{-1}. By the time it gets to **B** the speed is measured to be 12.0 m s^{-1}.

h = 12.0 m

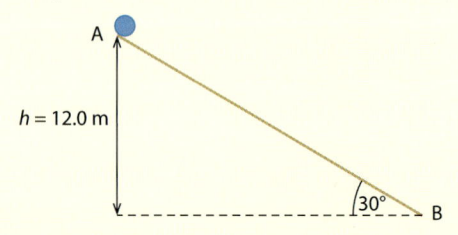

30°

Estimate the frictional force opposing the motion. (The frictional force is acting along the plane.)

62 A force F acts on a body of mass $m = 2.0$ kg initially at rest. The graph shows how the force varies with distance travelled (along a straight line).

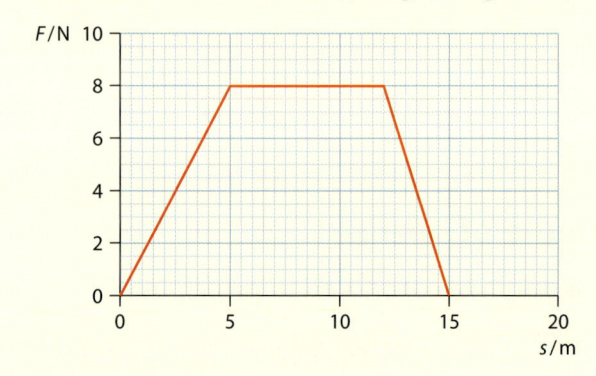

F/N

   a Find the work done by this force.
   b Calculate the final speed of the body.

63 A body of mass 12 kg is dropped vertically from rest from a height of 80 m.
   a Ignoring any resistance forces during the motion of this body, draw graphs to represent the variation with distance fallen of:
      i the potential energy
      ii the kinetic energy.
   b For the same motion draw graphs to represent the variation with time of:
      i the potential energy
      ii the kinetic energy.
   c Describe qualitatively the effect of a constant resistance force on each of the four graphs you drew.

64 The engine of a car is developing a power of 90 kW when it is moving on a horizontal road at a constant speed of 100 km h^{-1}. Estimate the total horizontal force opposing the motion of the car.

65 The motor of an elevator develops power at a rate of 2500 W.
  a Calculate the speed that a 1200 kg load is being raised at.
  b In practice it is found that the load is lifted more slowly than indicated by your answer to a. Suggest reasons why this is so.

66 A load of 50 kg is raised a vertical distance of 15 m in 125 s by a motor.
  a Estimate the power necessary for this.
  b The power supplied by the motor is in fact 80 W. Calculate the efficiency of the motor.
  c The same motor is now used to raise a load of 100 kg the same distance. The efficiency remains the same. Estimate how long this would take.

67 The top speed of a car whose engine is delivering 250 kW of power is 240 km h^{-1}. Calculate the value of the resistance force on the car when it is travelling at its top speed on a level road.

68 An elevator starts on the ground floor and stops on the 10th floor of a high-rise building. The elevator reaches a constant speed by the time it reaches the 1st floor and decelerates to rest between the 9th and 10th floors. Describe the energy transformations taking place between the 1st and 9th floors.

69 A mass m of 4.0 kg slides down a frictionless incline of $\theta = 30°$ to the horizontal. The mass starts from rest from a height of 20 m.
  a Sketch a graph of the kinetic and potential energies of the mass as a function of time.
  b Sketch a graph of the kinetic and potential energies of the mass as a function of distance travelled along the incline.
  c On each graph, sketch the sum of the potential and kinetic energies.

70 A mass m is being pulled up an inclined plane of angle θ by a rope along the plane.
  a Find the tension in the rope if the mass moves up at constant speed v.
  b Calculate is the work done by the tension when the mass moves up a distance of d m along the plane.
  c Find the work done by the weight of the mass.
  d Find the work done by the normal reaction force on the mass.
  e What is the net work done on the mass?

71 A battery toy car of mass 0.250 kg is made to move up an inclined plane that makes an angle of 30° with the horizontal. The car starts from rest and its motor provides a constant acceleration of 4.0 m s^{-2} for 5.0 s. The motor is then turned off.
  a Find the distance travelled in the first 5 s.
  b Find the furthest the car gets on the inclined plane.
  c Calculate when the car returns to its starting position.
  d Sketch a graph of the velocity as a function of time.
  e On the same axes, sketch a graph of the kinetic energy and potential energy of the car as a function of the distance travelled.
  f State the periods in the car's motion in which its mechanical energy is conserved.
  g Estimate the average power developed by the car's motor.
  h Determine the maximum power developed by the motor.

2 MECHANICS

Learning objectives

- Be able to re-formulate Newton's second law when the mass is variable.
- Understand the concept of impulse and be able to analyse force–time graphs.
- Be able to derive and apply the law of conservation of momentum.
- Analyse elastic and inelastic collisions and explosions.

2.4 Momentum and impulse

This section introduces the concept of linear momentum, which is a very useful and powerful concept in physics. Newton's second law is expressed in terms of momentum. The law of conservation of linear momentum makes it possible to predict the outcomes in very many physical situations.

Newton's second law in terms of momentum

We saw earlier that Newton's second law was expressed as $F_{net} = ma$. In fact, this equation is only valid when the mass of the system remains constant. But there are plenty of situations where the mass does *not* remain constant. In cases where the mass changes, a different version of the second law must be used. Examples include:

- the motion of a rocket, where the mass decreases due to burnt fuel ejected away from the rocket
- sand falling on a conveyor belt so the mass increases
- a droplet of water falling through mist and increasing in mass as more water condenses.

We define a new concept, **linear momentum**, p, to be the product of the mass of a body times its velocity:

$$p = mv$$

Momentum is a vector and has the direction of the velocity. Its unit is $kg\,m\,s^{-1}$ or the equivalent $N\,s$.

In terms of momentum, Newton's second law is:

$$F_{net} = \frac{\Delta p}{\Delta t}$$

The average net force on a system is equal to the rate of change of the momentum of the system.

It is easy to see that if the mass stays constant, then this version reduces to the usual ma:

$$F_{net} = \frac{\Delta p}{\Delta t} = \frac{p_{final} - p_{initial}}{\Delta t}$$

$$= \frac{mv_{final} - mv_{initial}}{\Delta t}$$

$$= m\left(\frac{v_{final} - v_{initial}}{\Delta t}\right)$$

$$= \frac{m\Delta v}{\Delta t}$$

$$F_{net} = ma$$

Worked examples

2.45 A cart moves in a horizontal line with constant speed v. Rain starts to fall and the cart fills with water at a rate of $\sigma\,\text{kg s}^{-1}$. (This means that in one second, $\sigma\,\text{kg}$ have fallen on the cart.) The cart must keep moving at constant speed. Determine the force that must be applied on the cart.

Exam tip
Worked example **2.45** should alert you right away that you must be careful when mass changes. Zero acceleration does not imply zero net force in this case.

Notice right away that if $F_{\text{net}} = ma$ (we drop the bold italic of the vector notation) were valid, the force would have to be zero since the car is not accelerating. But we do need a force to act on the cart because the momentum of the cart is increasing (because the mass is increasing). This force is:

$$F_{\text{net}} = \frac{\Delta p}{\Delta t} = \frac{\Delta(mv)}{\Delta t} = \frac{v\Delta m}{\Delta t} = v\sigma$$

Putting some real values in, if $\sigma = 0.20\,\text{kg s}^{-1}$ and $v = 3.5\,\text{m s}^{-1}$, the force would have to be $0.70\,\text{N}$.

2.46 Gravel falls vertically on a conveyor belt at a rate of $\sigma\,\text{kg s}^{-1}$, as shown in Figure 2.76.

This very popular exam question is similar to Worked example **2.45**, but is worth doing again.

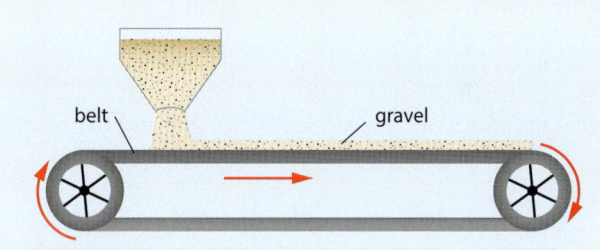

Figure 2.76

a Determine:
  i the force that must be applied on the belt to keep it moving at constant speed v
  ii the power that must be supplied by the motor turning the belt
  iii the rate at which the kinetic energy of the gravel is changing.
b Explain why the answers to **a ii** and **a iii** are different.

a i The force is:

$$F_{\text{net}} = \frac{\Delta p}{\Delta t} = \frac{\Delta(mv)}{\Delta t} = \frac{v\Delta m}{\Delta t} = v\sigma$$

ii The power is found from $P = Fv$. Substituting for F:

$P = (v\sigma)v = \sigma v^2$

iii In 1 second the mass on the belt increases by $\sigma\,\text{kg}$. The kinetic energy of this mass is:

$E_K = \tfrac{1}{2}\sigma v^2$

This is the increase in kinetic energy in a time of 1 s, so the rate of kinetic energy increase is $\tfrac{1}{2}\sigma v^2$.

b The rate of increase in kinetic energy is less than the power supplied. This is because the power supplied by the motor goes to increase the kinetic energy of the gravel and also to provide the energy needed to accelerate the gravel from 0 to speed v in the short interval of time when the gravel slides on the belt before achieving the constant final speed v.

2 MECHANICS

2.47 A 0.50 kg ball is dropped from rest above a hard floor. When it reaches the floor it has a velocity of $4.0\,\text{m}\,\text{s}^{-1}$. The ball then bounces vertically upwards. Figure **2.77** is the graph of velocity against time for the ball. The positive direction for velocity is upwards.
  a Find the magnitude of the momentum change of the ball during the bounce.
  b The ball stayed in contact with the floor for 0.15 s. What average force did the floor exert on the ball?

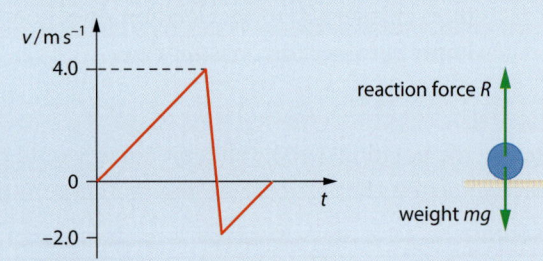

Figure 2.77

a The momentum when the ball hits the floor is: $0.50 \times 4.0 = 2.0\,\text{N}\,\text{s}$

The momentum when the ball rebounds from the floor is: $0.50 \times (-2.0) = -1.0\,\text{N}\,\text{s}$

The magnitude of the momentum change is therefore 3.0 N s.

b The forces on the ball are its weight and the reaction from the floor, R.

$F_{net} = R - mg$

This is also the force that produces the change in momentum:

$F_{net} = \dfrac{\Delta p}{\Delta t}$

Substituting in this equation:

$F_{net} = \dfrac{3.0}{0.15} = 20\,\text{N}$

We need to find R, so:

$R = 20 + 5.0 = 25\,\text{N}$.

The average force exerted on the ball by the floor is 25 N.

> **Exam tip**
> This is a very tricky problem with lots of possibilities for error. A lot of people forget to include the minus sign in the rebound velocity and also forget the weight, so they answer incorrectly that $R = 20\,\text{N}$.

Impulse and force–time graphs

We may rearrange the equation:

$$F_{net} = \frac{\Delta p}{\Delta t}$$

to get:

$$\Delta p = F_{net}\Delta t$$

The quantity $F_{net}\Delta t$ is called the **impulse** of the force, and is usually denoted by J. It is the product of the average force times the time for which the force acts. The impulse is also equal to the change in momentum. Notice that impulse is a vector whose direction is the same as that of the force (or the change in momentum).

When you jump from a height of, say, 1 m, you will land on the ground with a speed of about $4.5\,\text{m s}^{-1}$. Assuming your mass is 60 kg, your momentum just before landing will be 270 N s and will become zero after you land. From $F_{net} = \frac{\Delta p}{\Delta t}$, this can be achieved with a small force acting for a long time or large force acting for a short time. You will experience the large force if you do not bend your knees upon landing – keeping your knees stiff means that you will come to rest in a short time. This means Δt will be very small and the force large (which may damage your knees).

The three graphs of Figure **2.78** show three different force–time graphs. Figure **2.78a** shows a (non-constant) force that increases from zero, reaches a maximum value and then drops to zero again. The force acted for a time interval of about 2 ms. The impulse is the area under the curve. Without calculus we can only estimate this area by tediously counting squares: each small square has area $0.1\,\text{ms} \times 0.2\,\text{N} = 2 \times 10^{-5}\,\text{N s}$. There are about 160 full squares under the curve and so the impulse is $3 \times 10^{-3}\,\text{N s}$. (In this case it is not a bad approximation to consider the shape under the curve to be a triangle but with a base of 1.3 ms so that the area is then $\frac{1}{2} \times 1.3 \times 10^{-3} \times 4 \approx 3 \times 10^{-3}\,\text{N s}$.)

In the second graph, the force is constant (Figure **2.78b**). The impulse of the force is $6.0 \times (8.0 - 2.0) = 36\,\text{N s}$. Suppose this force acts on a body of mass 12 kg, initially at rest. Then the speed v of the body after the force stops acting can be found from:

$$\Delta p = 36\,\text{N s}$$

$$mv - 0 = 36\,\text{N s}$$

$$v = \frac{36}{12} = 3.0\,\text{m s}^{-1}$$

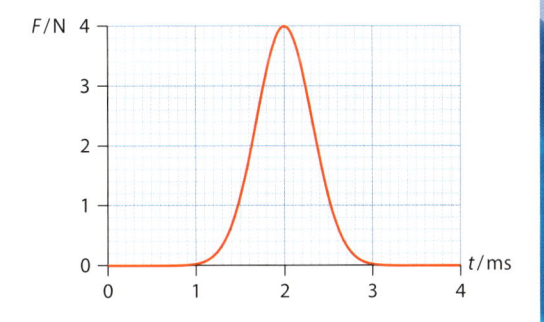

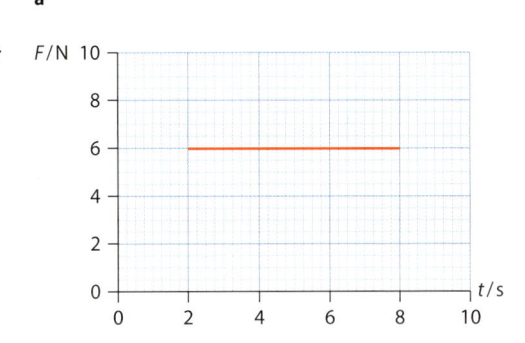

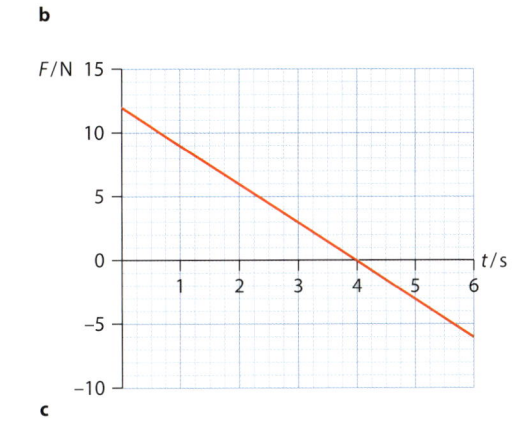

Figure 2.78 Three different force–time graphs: **a** non-constant force, **b** constant force; **c** force that varies linearly with time.

Worked examples

2.48 Consider the graph of Figure **2.78c**. The force acts on a body of mass 3.0 kg initially at rest. Calculate:
  a the initial acceleration of the body
  b the speed at 4.0 s
  c the speed at 6.0 s.

a The initial acceleration a is at $t = 0$, when $F = 12$ N.

$$a = \frac{F}{m} = \frac{12}{3.0} = 4.0 \text{ m s}^{-2}$$

b The impulse from 0 s to 4.0 s is the area under this part of the graph:

$$\tfrac{1}{2} \times 4.0 \times 12 = 24 \text{ N s}$$

This is equal to the change in momentum.

Let v be the speed at 4.0 s. As the body is initially at rest, the momentum change is:

$$mv - 0 = 24$$

So $v = \dfrac{24}{m} = \dfrac{24}{3.0} = 8.0 \text{ m s}^{-1}$

c The impulse from 0 s to 6.0 s is the area under the graph, which includes part above the axis and part below the axis. The part under the axis is negative, as the force is negative here, so the impulse is:

$$\tfrac{1}{2} \times 4.0 \times 12 - \tfrac{1}{2} \times 2.0 \times 6.0 = 18 \text{ N s}$$

Hence the speed at 6.0 s is $v = \dfrac{18}{3.0} = 6.0 \text{ m s}^{-1}$.

2.49 A ball of mass 0.20 kg moving at 3.6 m s^{-1} on a horizontal floor collides with a vertical wall. The ball rebounds with a speed of 3.2 m s^{-1}. The ball was in contact with the wall for 12 ms. Determine the maximum force exerted on the ball, assuming that the force depends on time according to Figure **2.79**.

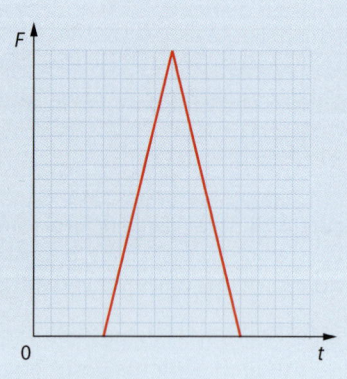

Figure 2.79

Let the initial velocity be positive. The rebound velocity is then negative.

Initial momentum: $0.20 \times 3.6 = 0.72 \, \text{N s}$

Final momentum: $0.20 \times (-3.2) = -0.64 \, \text{N s}$

The change in momentum of the ball is:

$-0.64 - 0.72 = -1.36 \, \text{N s}$

The magnitude of the change in momentum is equal to the area under the force–time graph.

The area is $\frac{1}{2} \times 12 \times 10^{-3} \times F_{max}$ and so:

$\frac{1}{2} \times 12 \times 10^{-3} \times F_{max} = 1.36 \, \text{N s}$

$\Rightarrow F_{max} = 0.227 \times 10^3 \approx 2.3 \times 10^2 \, \text{N}$

Conservation of momentum

Consider a system with momentum p. The net force on the system is:

$$F_{net} = \frac{\Delta p}{\Delta t}$$

and so if $F_{net} = 0$ it follows that $\Delta p = 0$. There is no change in momentum. This is expressed as the law of **conservation of momentum**:

> When the net force on a system is zero the momentum does not change, i.e. it stays the same. We say it is conserved.

Notice that 'system' may refer to a single body or a collection of many different bodies.

Let us consider the blue block of mass 4.0 kg moving at speed 6.0 m s^{-1} to the right shown in Figure **2.80**. The blue block collides with the red block of mass 8.0 kg that is initially at rest. After the collision the two blocks move off together.

As the blocks collide, each will exert a force on the other. By Newton's third law, the magnitude of the force on each block is the same. There are no forces that come from outside the system, i.e. no external forces. You might say that the weights of the blocks are forces that come from the outside. That is correct, but the weights are cancelled by the normal reaction forces from the table. So the net external force on the system is zero. Hence we expect that the total momentum will stay the same.

The total momentum before the collision is:

$4.0 \times 6.0 + 8.0 \times 0 = 24 \, \text{N s}$

The total momentum after the collision is:

$(4.0 + 8.0) \times v = 12v$

where v is the common speed of the two blocks.

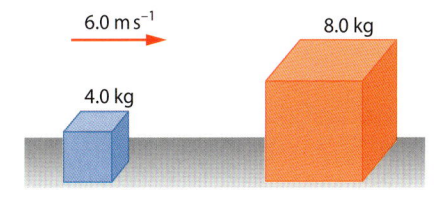

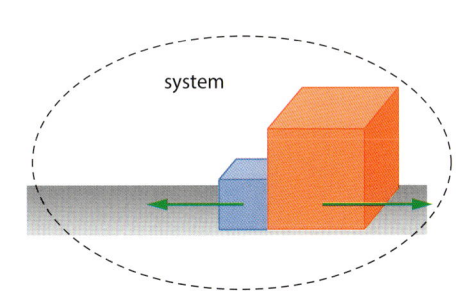

Figure 2.80 In a collision with no external forces acting, the total momentum of the system stays the same.

Equating the momentum after the collision and the momentum before the collision:

$$12v = 24$$
$$\Rightarrow \quad v = 2.0 \, \text{m s}^{-1}$$

The kinetic energy before the collision is:

$$\tfrac{1}{2} \times 4.0 \times 6.0^2 = 72 \, \text{J}$$

After the collision the kinetic energy is:

$$\tfrac{1}{2} \times 12 \times 2.0^2 = 24 \, \text{J}$$

It appears that 48 J has been 'lost' (into other forms of energy, e.g. thermal energy in the blocks themselves and the surrounding air or energy to deform the bodies during the collision and some to sound generated in the collision).

But consider now the outcome of the collision of these two blocks in which the blue block rebounds with speed $2.0 \, \text{m s}^{-1}$, as shown in Figure 2.81. The red block moves off in the original direction with speed v.

What is the speed of the red block? As before, the total momentum before the collision is 24 N s. The total momentum after the collision is (watch the minus sign):

$$(4.0 \times -2.0) + (8.0 \times v)$$
$$\text{blue block} \quad \text{red block}$$

Figure 2.81 An outcome of the collision in which total kinetic energy stays the same.

Equating the total momentum before and after the collision we find:

$$-8.0 + 8.0 \times v = 24$$

This gives $v = 4.0 \, \text{m s}^{-1}$.

The total kinetic energy after the collision is then:

$$\tfrac{1}{2} \times 4.0 \times (-2.0)^2 + \tfrac{1}{2} \times 8.0 \times 4.0^2 = 72 \, \text{J}$$
$$\text{blue block} \qquad \text{red block}$$

This is the same as the initial kinetic energy.

So, in a collision the momentum is always conserved but kinetic energy may or may not be conserved. You will find out more about this in the next section.

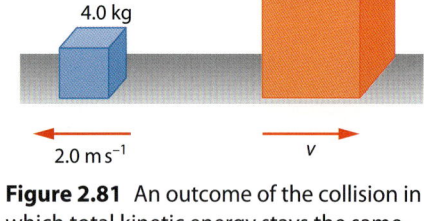

Predicting outcomes

Physics is supposed to be able to predict outcomes. So why is there more than one outcome in the collision of Figure 2.80? Physics does predict what happens, but more information about the nature of the colliding bodies is needed. We need to know if they are soft or hard, deformable or not, sticky or breakable, etc. If this information is given physics will uniquely predict what will happen.

Kinetic energy and momentum

We have seen that, in a collision or explosion where no external forces are present, the total momentum of the system is conserved. You can easily convince yourself that in the three collisions illustrated in Figure **2.82** momentum is conserved. The incoming body has mass 8.0 kg and the other a mass of 12 kg.

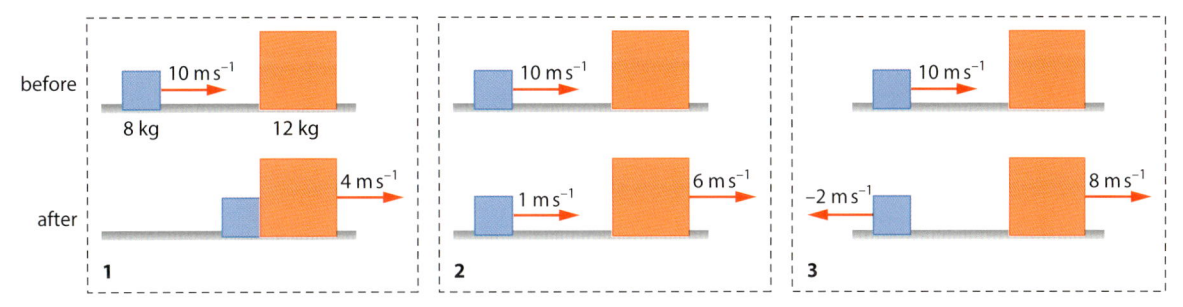

Figure 2.82 Momentum is conserved in these three collisions.

Let us examine these collisions from the point of view of energy. In all cases the total kinetic energy before the collision is:

$$E_K = \tfrac{1}{2} \times 8.0 \times 10^2 = 400\,\text{J}$$

The total kinetic energy after the collision in each case is:

case 1: $E_K = \tfrac{1}{2} \times 20 \times 4^2 = 160\,\text{J}$

case 2: $E_K = \tfrac{1}{2} \times 8.0 \times 1^2 + \tfrac{1}{2} \times 12 \times 6^2 = 220\,\text{J}$

case 3: $E_K = \tfrac{1}{2} \times 8.0 \times 2^2 + \tfrac{1}{2} \times 12 \times 8^2 = 400\,\text{J}$

We thus observe that whereas momentum is conserved in all cases, kinetic energy is not. When kinetic energy is conserved (case 3), the collision is said to be **elastic**. When it is not (cases 1 and 2), the collision is *inelastic*. In an inelastic collision, kinetic energy is lost. When the bodies stick together after a collision (case 1), the collision is said to be **totally inelastic** (or **plastic**), and in this case the maximum possible kinetic energy is lost.

The lost kinetic energy is transformed into other forms of energy, such as thermal energy, deformation energy (if the bodies are permanently deformed as a result of the collision) and sound energy.

Notice that using momentum, we can obtain a useful additional formula for kinetic energy:

$$E_K = \tfrac{1}{2}mv^2 = \frac{m^2 v^2}{2m}$$

$$E_K = \frac{p^2}{2m}$$

Worked examples

2.50 A moving body of mass m collides with a stationary body of double the mass and sticks to it. Calculate the fraction of the original kinetic energy that is lost.

The original kinetic energy is $\frac{1}{2}mv^2$ where v is the speed of the incoming mass. After the collision the two bodies move as one with speed u that can be found from momentum conservation:

$$mv = (m + 2m)u$$

$$\Rightarrow u = \frac{v}{3}$$

The total kinetic energy after the collision is therefore:

$$\frac{1}{2}(3m) \times \left(\frac{v}{3}\right)^2 = \frac{mv^2}{6}$$

and so the lost kinetic energy is

$$\frac{mv^2}{2} - \frac{mv^2}{6} = \frac{mv^2}{3}$$

The fraction of the original energy that is lost is thus

$$\frac{mv^2/3}{mv^2/2} = \frac{2}{3}$$

2.51 A body at rest of mass M explodes into two pieces of masses $M/4$ and $3M/4$. Calculate the ratio of the kinetic energies of the two fragments.

Here it pays to use the formula for kinetic energy in terms of momentum: $E_K = \frac{p^2}{2m}$. The total momentum before the explosion is zero, so it is zero after as well. Thus, the two fragments must have equal and opposite momenta. Hence:

$$\frac{E_{light}}{E_{heavy}} = \frac{p^2/(2M_{light})}{(-p)^2/(2M_{heavy})}$$

$$\frac{E_{light}}{E_{heavy}} = \frac{M_{heavy}}{M_{light}}$$

$$\frac{E_{light}}{E_{heavy}} = \frac{3M/4}{M/4}$$

$$\frac{E_{light}}{E_{heavy}} = 3$$

It all depends on the system!

Consider a ball that you drop from rest from a certain height. As the ball falls, its speed and hence its momentum increases so momentum does not stay the same (Figure **2.83**).

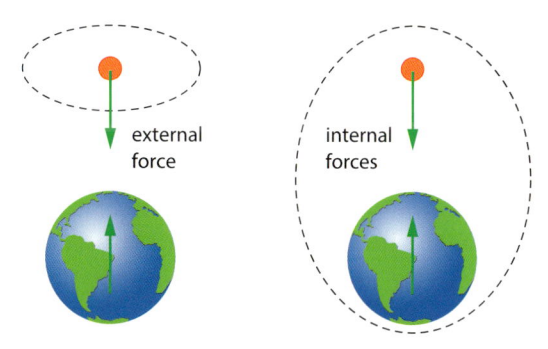

Figure 2.83 As the ball falls, an external force acts on it (its weight), increasing its momentum.

This is to be expected – there is an external force on the ball, namely its weight. So the momentum of the system that consists of just the falling ball is not conserved. If we include the Earth as part of the system then there are no external forces and the total momentum will be conserved. This means that the Earth moves up a bit as the ball falls!

The rocket equation

The best example of motion with varying mass is, of course, the rocket (Figure **2.84**).

This is quite a complex topic and is included here only as supplementary material. The rocket moves with speed v. The engine is turned on and gases leave the rocket with speed u relative to the rocket. The initial mass of the rocket including the fuel is M. After a short time δt the rocket has ejected fuel of mass δm. The mass of the rocket is therefore reduced to $M - \delta m$ and its speed increased to $v + \delta v$ (Figure **2.85**).

Figure 2.84 Exhaust gases from the booster rockets propel this space shuttle during its launch.

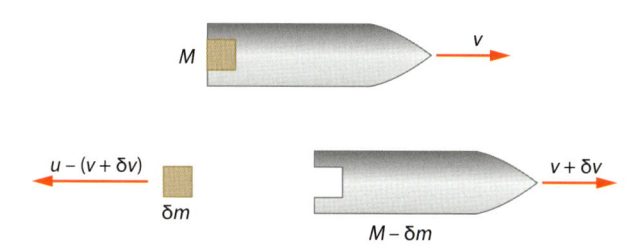

Figure 2.85 Diagram for deriving the rocket equation. The velocities are relative to an observer 'at rest on the ground'.

2 MECHANICS 107

Applying the law of conservation of momentum gives (in the equation below terms shaded the same colour cancel out):

$$Mv = (M - \delta m)(v + \delta v) - \delta m \underbrace{(u - v - \delta v)}_{\text{speed relative to ground}}$$

$$Mv = Mv + M\delta v - v\delta m - \delta m\delta v - u\delta m + v\delta m + \delta m\delta v$$

$$M\delta v = u\delta m$$

$$\delta v = \frac{\delta m}{Mu}$$

This gives the change in speed of the rocket as a result of gases leaving with speed u relative to the rocket. At time t the mass of the rocket is M. Dividing by δt and taking the limit as δt goes to zero gives the rocket differential equation:

$$M\frac{dv}{dt} = \mu u$$

where μ is the rate at which mass is being ejected.

Nature of science

General principles such as the conservation of momentum allow for simple and quick solutions to problems that may otherwise look complex. Consider, for example, a man of mass m who stands on a plank also of mass m. There is no friction between the floor and the plank. A man starts walking on the plank until he get gets to the other end, at which point he stops. What happens to the plank?

The centre of mass must remain in the same place since there is no external force. So the final position of the plank will be as shown in Figure 2.86: the plank moves half its length to the left and stops.

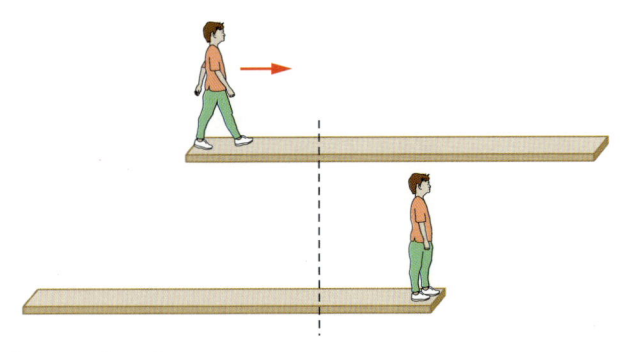

Figure 2.86 Conservation of momentum.

The same principles can be extended to analyse and predict the outcomes of a wide range of physical interactions, from large-scale motion to microscopic collisions.

Test yourself

72 The momentum of a ball increased by 12.0 N s as a result of a force that acted on the ball for 2.00 s. Find the average force on the ball.

73 A 0.150 kg ball moving horizontally at 3.00 m s^{-1} collides normally with a vertical wall and bounces back with the same speed.
  a Calculate the impulse delivered to the ball.
  b The ball was in contact with the wall for 0.125 s. Find the average force exerted by the ball on the wall.

74 The bodies in the diagram suffer a head-on collision and stick to each other afterwards. Find their common velocity.

75 A ball of mass 250 g rolling on a horizontal floor with a speed 4.00 m s^{-1} hits a wall and bounces with the same speed, as shown in the diagram.

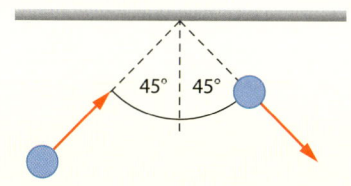

  a What is the magnitude and direction of the momentum change of the ball?
  b Is momentum conserved here? Why or why not?

76 Two masses moving in a straight line towards each other collide as shown in the diagram. Find the velocity (magnitude and direction) of the heavier mass after the collision.

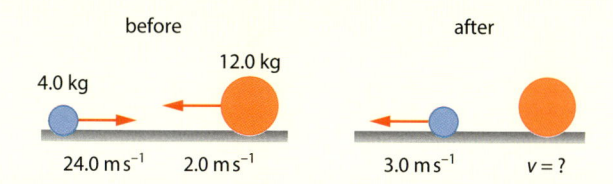

77 A time-varying force varies with time as shown in the graph. The force acts on a body of mass 4.0 kg.
  a Find the impulse of the force from $t = 0$ to $t = 15$ s.
  b Find the speed of the mass at 15 s, assuming the initial velocity was zero.
  c State the initial velocity of the body such that it is brought to rest at 15 s.

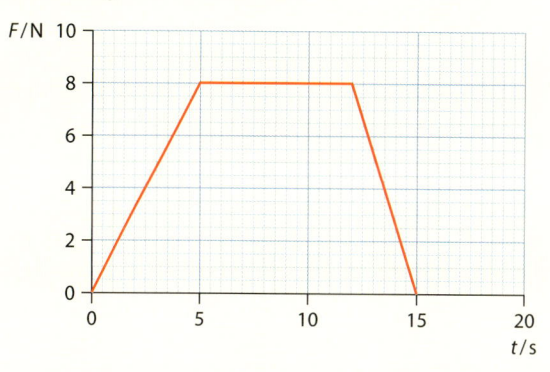

78 A boy rides on a scooter pushing on the road with one foot with a horizontal force that depends on time, as shown in the graph. While the scooter rolls, a constant force of 25 N opposes the motion. The combined mass of the boy and scooter is 25 kg.
  a Find the speed of the boy after 4.0 s, assuming he started from rest.
  b Draw a graph to represent the variation of the boy's speed with time.

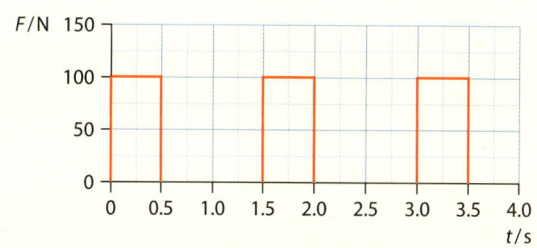

79 A ball of mass m is dropped from a height of h_1 and rebounds to a height of h_2. The ball is in contact with the floor for a time interval of t.
  a Show that the average net force on the ball is given by:
  $$F = m\frac{\sqrt{2gh_1} + \sqrt{2gh_2}}{t}$$
  b If $h_1 = 8.0$ m, $h_2 = 6.0$ m, $t = 0.125$ s and $m = 0.250$ kg, calculate the average force exerted by the ball on the floor.

2 MECHANICS 109

80 A ball of mass m moving vertically, hits a horizontal floor normally with speed v_1 and rebounds with speed v_2. The ball was in contact with the floor for a time t.
   a Show that the average force F on the ball from the floor during the collision is given by:
   $$F = \frac{m(v_1 + v_2)}{t} + mg$$
   b Find an expression for the average net force on the ball.

81 The diagram shows the variation with time of the force exerted on a ball as the ball came into contact with a spring.

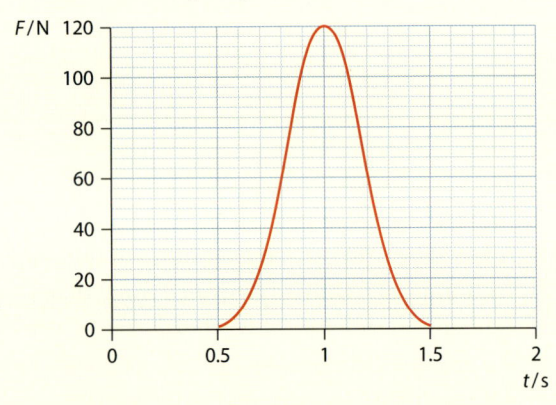

   a For how long was the spring in contact with the ball?
   b Estimate the magnitude of the change in momentum of the ball.
   c What was the average force that was exerted on the ball?

82 Two masses of 2.0 kg and 4.0 kg are held in place, compressing a spring between them. When they are released, the 2.0 kg moves away with a speed of $3.0\,\text{m s}^{-1}$. What was the energy stored in the spring?

83 A rocket in space where gravity is negligible has a mass (including fuel) of 5000 kg. It is desired to give the rocket an average acceleration of $15.0\,\text{m s}^{-2}$ during the first second of firing the engine. The gases leave the rocket at a speed of $1500\,\text{m s}^{-1}$ (relative to the rocket). Estimate how much fuel must be burnt in that second.

Exam-style questions

1 Four cars race along a given race track starting at the same time. The car that will reach the finishing line first is the one with the largest

       A maximum speed
       B acceleration
       C power
       D average speed

2. A body that started from rest moves with constant acceleration in a straight line. After travelling a distance d the speed of the car is v. What is the distance travelled when the speed of the car was $\frac{v}{2}$?

   A $\frac{d}{2}$ **B** $\frac{d}{\sqrt{2}}$ **C** $\frac{d}{4}$ **D** $\frac{d}{2\sqrt{2}}$

3. A sphere falls trough a liquid and eventually reaches terminal speed. Which graph shows the variation with time of the distance travelled by the sphere?

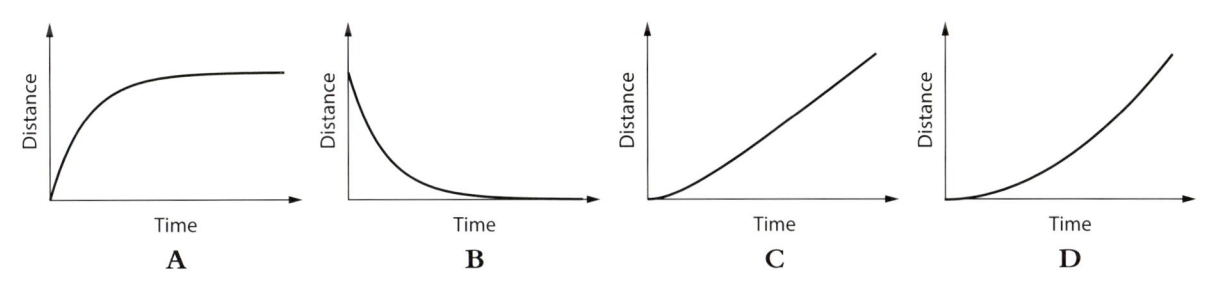

4. A steel ball of mass m is thrown vertically downwards with initial speed u near the Earth's surface. The rate of change of the momentum of the ball as it falls is:

   A 0   **B** mu **C** $m(u+gt)$ **D** mg

5. A lunar module is descending vertically above the lunar surface. The speed of the module is decreasing. Which is a free-body diagram of the forces on the landing module?

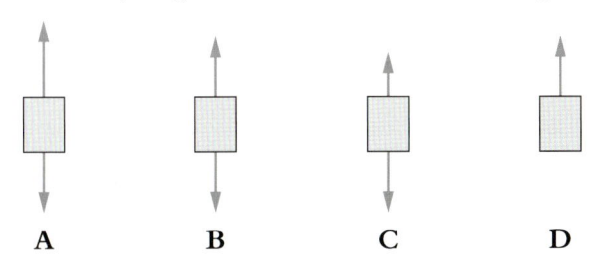

6. A person of mass m stands on weighing scales in an elevator. The elevator is accelerating upwards with acceleration a. The reaction force from the scales on the person is R. What is the reading on the scales?

   A mg **B** $R+ma$ **C** $R-ma$ **D** R

7. A body of mass $3M$ at rest explodes into two pieces of mass M and $2M$. What is the ratio of the kinetic energy of M to that of $2M$?

   A $\frac{1}{4}$ **B** $\frac{1}{2}$ **C** 4   **D** 2

2 MECHANICS

8 The power delivered by a car engine is constant. A car starts from rest. Resistance forces are negligible. Which graph shows the variation with time of the speed of the car?

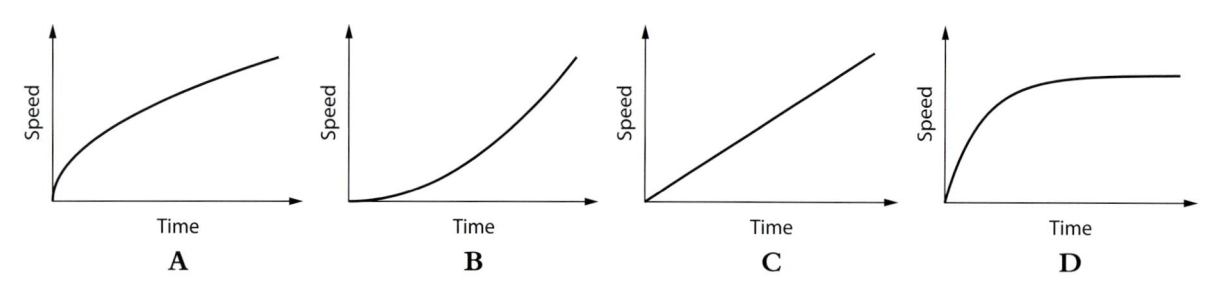

A   B   C   D

9 The diagram shows two identical containers, X and Y, that are connected by a thin tube of negligible volume. Initially container X is filled with water of mass m up to a height h and Y is empty.

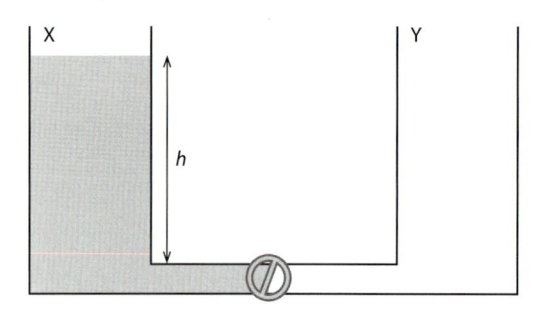

The valve is then opened and both containers contain equal quantities of water. The loss of gravitational potential energy of the water is:

A 0 **B** $\frac{mgh}{8}$ **C** $\frac{mgh}{4}$ **D** $\frac{mgh}{2}$

10 A person of mass m stands on roller skates facing a wall. After pushing against the wall with a constant force F he moves away, reaching speed v after a distance d. What is the work done by F?

A zero **B** mv^2 **C** $\frac{1}{2}mv^2$ **D** Fd

11 In a factory blocks of ice slide down a smooth curved path AB and then on to a rough horizontal path starting at B.

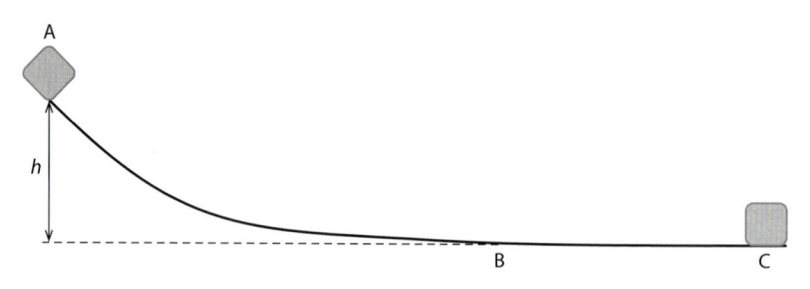

The length of the curved path AB is s; the block of ice takes time t to move from A to B.

a Explain why, for the motion of the block from A to B:
   i the formula $s = \frac{1}{2}gt^2$ does not apply. [1]
   ii the formula $v = \sqrt{2gh}$ does apply. [1]

b A block of ice of mass 25 kg slides from A to B. The speed of the block at B is $v_B = 4.8\,\text{m s}^{-1}$. Calculate the height h. [3]

c **i** The coefficient of dynamic friction between the block of ice and the rough surface BC is 0.45. Show that the distance BC at which the block of ice is brought to rest is 0.26 m. [2]

ii Calculate the time it takes the block of ice to cover the distance BC. [2]

d The factory also produces blocks of ice of mass 50 kg that slide down the same path starting at A. Predict, for this heavier block of ice, the speed at B and the stopping distance BC. (The coefficient of friction stays the same.) [3]

12 A stone of mass 0.20 kg is thrown with speed $22\,\text{m s}^{-1}$ from the edge of a cliff that is 32 m above the sea. The initial velocity of the stone makes an angle of 35° with the horizontal. Air resistance is neglected.

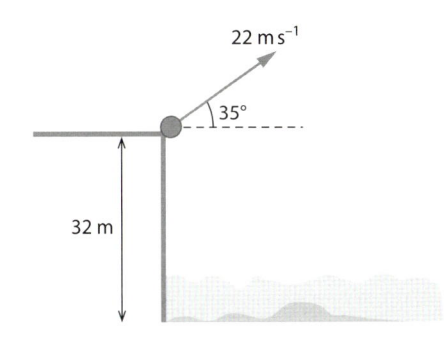

a **i** Determine the horizontal and vertical components of the initial velocity. [2]
ii Sketch graphs showing the variation with time of the horizontal and vertical components of velocity. [2]
b **i** Calculate the maximum height above the cliff reached by the stone. [3]
ii State the net force on the stone at the highest point in its path. [1]
c **i** Using conservation of energy, determine the speed of the stone as it hits the sea. [2]
ii Hence or otherwise, determine the time it took the stone to reach the surface of the sea. [2]

The graph shows the path followed by this stone, until just before hitting the sea, in the absence of air resistance.

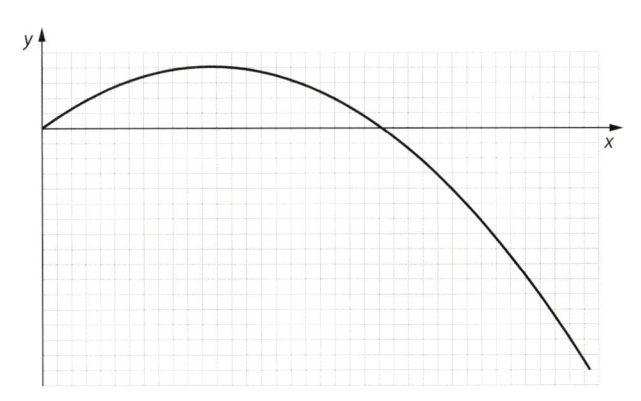

d **i** On a copy of the axes above, draw the path of the stone in the presence of an air resistance force opposite to the velocity and proportional to the speed. [3]
ii State and explain one difference between your graph and the graph above. [2]

2 MECHANICS 113

13 A toy helicopter has mass $m = 0.30\,\text{kg}$ and blade rotors of radius $R = 0.25\,\text{m}$. It may be assumed that as the blades turn, the air exactly under the blades is pushed downwards with speed v. The density of air is $\rho = 1.2\,\text{kg}\,\text{m}^{-3}$.

    a i Show that the force that the rotor blades exert on the air is $\rho \pi R^2 v^2$. [3]
        ii Hence estimate the speed v when the helicopter just hovers. [2]
    b Determine the power generated by the helicopter's motor when it just hovers as in **a**. [2]
    c The rotor blades now move faster pushing air downwards at a speed double that found in **a**. The helicopter is raised vertically a distance of 12 m.
      Estimate:
        i the time needed to raise the helicopter. [2]
        ii the speed of the helicopter after it is raised 12 m. [2]
        iii the work done by the rotor in raising the helicopter. [1]

14 It is proposed to launch projectiles of mass 8.0 kg from satellites in space in order to destroy incoming ballistic missiles. The launcher exerts a force on the projectile that varies with time according to the graph.

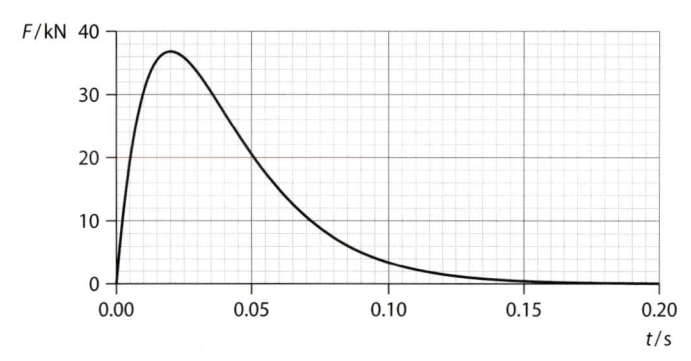

The impulse delivered to the projectile is $2.0 \times 10^3\,\text{N s}$. The projectile leaves the launcher in 0.20 s.

    a Estimate:
        i the area under the curve [1]
        ii the average acceleration of the projectile [3]
        iii the average speed of the projectile [2]
        iv the length of the launcher. [2]
    b Calculate, for the projectile as it leaves the launcher:
        i the speed [2]
        ii the kinetic energy. [2]
    c Estimate the power delivered to the projectile by the launcher. [2]

15 A car of weight $1.4 \times 10^4\,\text{N}$ is moving up an incline at a constant speed of $6.2\,\text{m s}^{-1}$. The incline makes an angle of $5.0°$ to the horizontal. A frictional force of 600 N acts on the car in a direction opposite to the velocity.

    a i State the net force on the car. [1]
        ii Calculate the force F pushing the car up the incline. [3]
    b The power supplied by the car is 15 kW. Determine the efficiency of the car engine in pushing the car uphill. [3]

c The car is now allowed to roll down the incline from rest with the engine off. The only resistance force on the car is assumed to be proportional to speed. On a copy of the axes below, draw sketch graphs to show the variation with time of:

  i the speed of the car [2]
  ii the acceleration of the car. [2]

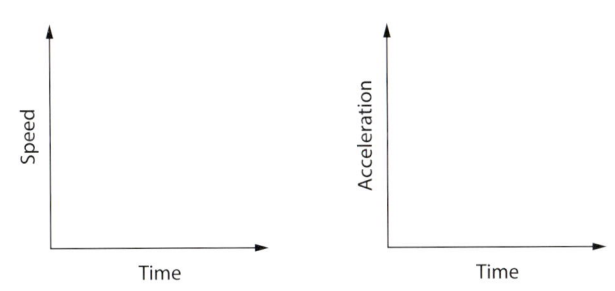

16 A bullet of mass 0.090 kg is shot at a wooden block of mass 1.20 kg that is hanging vertically at the end of a string.

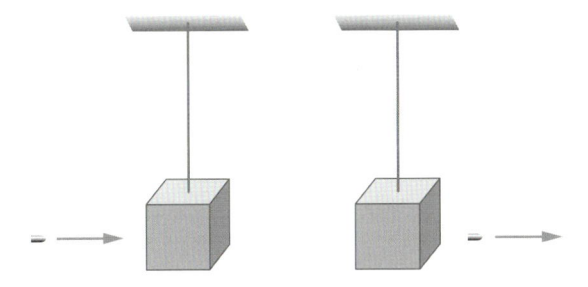

The bullet enters the block with speed 130 m s^{-1} and leaves it with speed 90 m s^{-1}. The mass of the block does not change appreciably as a result of the hole made by the bullet.

a **i** Calculate the change in the momentum of the bullet. [2]
  ii Show that the initial velocity of the block is 3.0 m s^{-1}. [1]
  iii Estimate the loss of kinetic energy in the bullet–block system. [2]

As a result of the impact, the block is displaced. The maximum angle that the string makes with the vertical is θ. The length of the string is 0.80 m.

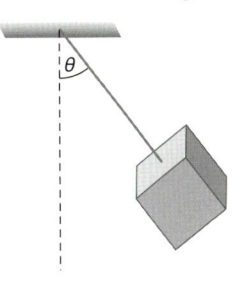

b Show that $\theta \approx 65°$. [3]
c **i** State and explain whether the block in **b** is in equilibrium. [2]
  ii Calculate the tension in the string in **b**. [3]

2 MECHANICS 115

3 Thermal physics

Learning objectives

- Describe solids, liquids and gases in terms of atoms and molecules.
- Use the concept of temperature and the relation of absolute temperature to the average kinetic energy of molecules.
- Understand and use the concept of internal energy.
- Solve problems in calorimetry using the specific heat capacities.
- Describe phase change and performing calculations using the concept of specific latent heat.

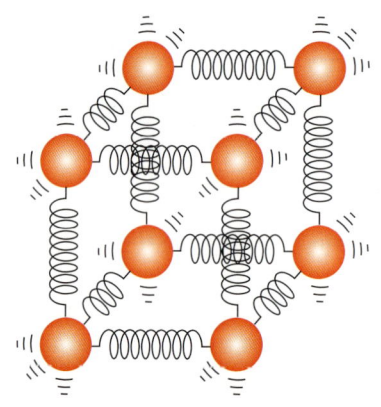

Figure 3.1 Particles in the solid phase oscillate about fixed positions but are not free to move inside the solid.

3.1 Thermal concepts

This section is devoted to the connections and the differences between the basic concepts of temperature, internal energy and heat. This section also deals with thermal equilibrium, phase changes and basic calorimetry problems.

The particle model of matter

As we look closer and closer into matter we discover smaller and smaller **structures**. We find that compounds are made out of molecules, molecules are made out of atoms and atoms contain nuclei and electrons. Nuclei, in turn, contain protons and neutrons. Today it is believed that electrons do not have any substructure but the nucleons (i.e. protons and neutrons) are known to be made out of quarks. It is not known if the quarks themselves are made out of smaller particles. In thermal physics we are mostly interested in molecules, atoms and electrons – we do not need to consider any smaller structures.

In a solid there are forces between the particles that can be **modelled** by springs joining neighbouring particles (Figure 3.1). The springs then represent the **bonds** between the particles. In liquids the forces between the particles are weaker. The particles are able to move around the volume of the liquid and the liquid will take the shape of the container in which it is placed. However, the inter-particle forces between the particles in a liquid are sufficiently strong that the particles cannot move far from each other. In gases the inter-particle forces are very weak so as to be almost negligible. The only time significant forces exist between the particles is during collisions.

Temperature

We have an intuitive concept of **temperature** as the 'coldness' or 'hotness' of a body, but it wasn't until the 19th century that one of the greatest discoveries in physics related the concept of temperature to the random motion of molecules. This connection, which will be explored in greater detail in Subtopic **3.2**, is that temperature is proportional to the average random kinetic energy of the molecules.

This direct proportionality between temperature and the average random kinetic energy is only true for the absolute or kelvin temperature scale. In this scale zero is the lowest possible temperature, the **absolute zero** of temperature. There has to be an absolute zero in temperature since there is a lowest possible value of the average kinetic energy of molecules, namely zero kinetic energy. Since temperature is proportional to the average kinetic energy, the temperature must be zero when the kinetic energy is zero.

Many other temperature scales exist. In 1742, Anders Celsius (1701–1744) created the temperature scale that is still commonly used today and is known by his name. On the Celsius scale a value of zero degrees is assigned to the freezing point of water (Figure 3.2) and a value of 100 degrees is assigned to the boiling point of water. The connection between the Celsius and Kelvin scales is:

T (in kelvin, K) = T (in degrees Celsius, °C) + 273

The magnitude of a kelvin is the same as that of a degree Celsius.

The lowest possible temperature on the absolute scale is zero kelvin, 0 K. On the Celsius scale the lowest possible temperature is, therefore, −273 °C. (Notice that we never say degrees kelvin, just kelvin.)

Temperature has varied a lot in the life of the Universe: at the time of the Big Bang, some 13.8 billion years ago, the temperature of the universe was about 10^{32} K. The Universe has been expanding ever since and so the temperature has been dropping. In the emptiness of space, far from stars and galaxies, its value today is only 2.7 K.

Exam tip
The magnitude of a kelvin is the same as that of a degree Celsius.

The need to agree on internationally accepted units, among them those for temperature, is a good example of international collaboration to establish international systems of measurement.

Worked example

3.1 The temperature of a body increases from 320 K to 340 K. State the temperature increase in degrees Celsius.

The temperature increase in kelvin is 340 − 320 = 20 K.

Since the magnitude of a kelvin is the same as that of a degree Celsius, the temperature increase is 20 °C.

(Another way to look at this is to convert both temperatures to kelvin. 320 K corresponds to 320 − 273 = 47 °C and 340 K corresponds to 340 − 273 = 67 °C, giving a change of 20 °C.)

Measuring temperature

Temperature can be measured with a thermometer, which is simply a device that has one property that changes in a predictable way as temperature changes. That property is volume in liquid-in-glass thermometers: the liquid column changes its volume and hence its length since the cross-sectional area stays the same when the temperature changes and so can be used to measure temperature if we first **calibrate** the thermometer. But properties other than volume can be used, for example, electrical resistance.

When a thermometer is used to measure the temperature of a body it has to come into contact with the body. A **thermal interaction** takes place and energy is transferred until the thermometer and the body are at the same temperature. When this happens we say that we have **thermal equilibrium**. The reading on the thermometer is then the temperature of the body. (For thermometers such as infrared thermometers thermal contact is not necessary – the thermometer absorbs radiation emitted by the body whose temperature is to be measured.) The average temperature on Earth is different at different locations. Figure 3.3 shows the temperature distribution in January.

Figure 3.2 A Celsius thermometer shows zero when immersed in melting ice.

3 THERMAL PHYSICS 117

Heat was once thought to be a fluid (called 'caloric') that moved from body to body. The more caloric a body contained the hotter it was, and as caloric left a body the body became colder. This idea was rejected when it was realised that you could warm your hands by rubbing them together. If caloric entered your hands it must have come from another body, making it colder. But this does not happen. In the 19th century heat was shown to just another form of energy.

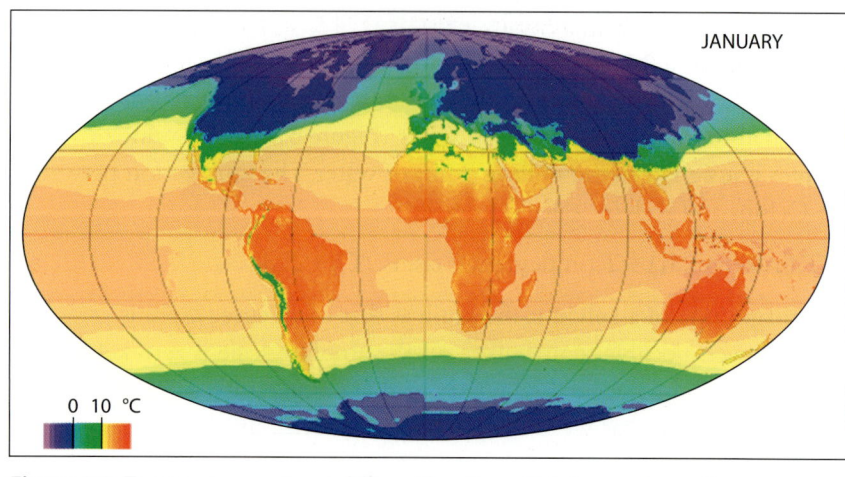

Figure 3.3 Temperature varies at different locations. This image shows the average surface temperature of the Earth in January for the period 1961–1990.

Heat

We have already mentioned that two bodies that are in thermal contact and have different temperatures will have a thermal interaction. So when a glass of cold water is placed in a warm room, **heat** flows from the room into the colder water until the temperature of the water becomes equal to that of its surroundings. We say that the colder body has been 'heated'.

> **Heat** is energy that is transferred from one body to another as a result of a difference in temperature.

Now, all substances consist of particles and, whether in the solid, liquid or gas phase, the particles are in constant motion. They therefore have kinetic energy. In a gas, the particles move randomly throughout the entire volume of the gas. In a solid the motion of the particles is on a very much smaller scale – the particles simply vibrate about their equilibrium positions. But this also requires kinetic energy.

In addition, there are forces between particles. For gases, these forces are very small – under reasonable conditions they are almost negligible (see ideal gases in Subtopic **3.2**). But forces between particles are substantial for solids. Increasing the average separation of two particles of a solid requires work to be done. This work goes into increasing the potential energy associated with inter-particle forces. Figure **3.4** shows the potential energy E_P of one pair of particles as a function of the distance r separating the two particles.

So, to describe the total energy in a substance we need to consider both the kinetic energy and the potential energy. We define the internal energy of a substance as follows:

> **Internal energy** is the total random kinetic energy of the particles of a substance, plus the total inter-particle potential energy of the particles.

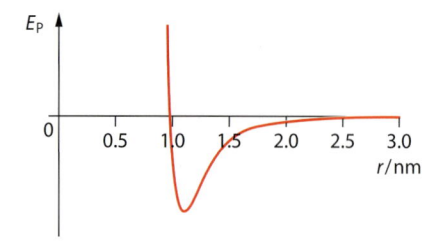

Figure 3.4 The average separation of the two particles is the separation at the minimum of the curve, i.e. at approximately 1.1 nm.

Energy transferred from a hot to a cold body by **heating** increases the internal energy of the cold body (and decreases the internal energy of the hot body by the same amount). **Work** done on the particles of a substance increases the potential energy of the particles, and so increases the internal energy.

> The internal energy of a system can change as a result of heat added or taken out and as a result of work performed.

Internal energy, heat and work are thus three different concepts. What they have in common is that they are all measured in joules. Temperature is a measure of the random kinetic energy of a substance – not its internal energy.

We define the **specific heat capacity** c of a body to be the energy required to increase the temperature of a unit mass of the body by one kelvin. So, to increase the temperature of a body of mass m by ΔT degrees the heat Q required is:

> $Q = mc\Delta T$

Exam tip
The term 'capacity' implies somehow that the body contains a certain amount of heat just as a water bottle contains water. This is incorrect. Heat is energy 'in transit' that moves from one body into another; it is not energy contained in any one body.

Worked examples

3.2 A quantity of heat equal to 9800 J is absorbed by a piece of iron of mass 1.8 kg and specific heat capacity 450 J kg^{-1} K^{-1}.
  a Calculate the temperature increase of the iron.
  b The heat of 9800 J was removed from 3.2 kg of water initially at 48 °C. The specific heat capacity of water is 4200 J kg^{-1} K^{-1}. Calculate the final temperature of the water.

Substance	c / J kg^{-1} K^{-1}
aluminium	900
lead	128
iron	450
copper	385
silver	240
water	4200
ice	2200
ethanol	2430
marble	880

Table 3.1 Specific heat capacities for several substances.

a We need to use $Q = mc\Delta T$. This gives:

$9800 = 1.8 \times 450 \times \Delta T$

Solving for the change in temperature gives:

$\Delta T = \dfrac{9800}{1.8 \times 450} = 12.1 \approx 12\,\text{K}$

(Notice that we do not need to know the initial temperature of the iron to answer this question.)

3 THERMAL PHYSICS

b We use $Q = mc\Delta T$ to get:

$$9800 = 3.2 \times 4200 \times \Delta T$$

Solving for the change in temperature gives:

$$\Delta T = \frac{9800}{3.2 \times 4200} = 0.729 \approx 0.73 \, \text{K}$$

So the final temperature of the water is:

$$48 - 0.73 \approx 47 \, °C$$

(Notice that the temperature changes of the iron and the water are very different. Notice also that it is unnecessary to convert between kelvin and °C since the temperature changes are the same in both scales.)

3.3 A piece of iron of mass 200 g and temperature 300 °C is dropped into 1.00 kg of water of temperature 20 °C. Predict the final equilibrium temperature of the water.

(Take c for iron as $450 \, \text{J kg}^{-1} \text{K}^{-1}$ and for water as $4200 \, \text{J kg}^{-1} \text{K}^{-1}$.)

Let T be the final unknown temperature. The iron will also be at this temperature, so:

amount of thermal energy lost by the iron = $m_{iron} c_{iron} (300 - T)$

and

amount of thermal energy gained by the water = $m_{water} c_{water} (T - 20)$

Conservation of energy demands that thermal energy lost = thermal energy gained, so:

$$m_{iron} c_{iron} (300 - T) = m_{water} c_{water} (T - 20)$$

$$0.200 \times 450 \times (300 - T) = 1.0 \times 4200 \times (T - 20)$$

$$\Rightarrow T = 25.9 \, °C \approx 26 \, °C$$

(Note how the large specific heat capacity of water results in a small increase in the temperature of the water compared with the huge drop in the temperature of the iron.)

Figure 3.5 Hot lava turns into a solid upon contact with water. The cold water takes heat away from the hot lava.

Change of phase

When heat is provided to a body or removed from it, the body may not necessarily change its temperature. The body may change **phase** instead. Changes of phase happen at constant temperature (Figure 3.5) and include:

- **melting** – when a solid changes to a liquid (heat must be provided to the solid)
- **freezing** – when a liquid changes into a solid (heat must be taken out of the liquid)
- **vaporisation** (or **boiling**) – when a liquid changes into vapour (by giving heat to the liquid)
- **condensation** – when a vapour changes into a liquid (by taking heat out of the vapour).

Why does the heat absorbed or removed not result in a temperature change? Consider the process of melting. At the melting temperature, changing from solid to liquid means that the average distance between the molecules increases. But increasing the separation of the molecules requires work (because there are attractive forces between the molecules that need to be overcome). This is where heat supplied goes – it is used to 'break the bonds'. What the supplied heat does not do is to increase the kinetic energy of the molecules – hence the temperature stays the same.

We define the specific latent heat L to be the amount of energy required to change the phase of a unit mass at constant temperature. So the energy required to change the phase of a mass m is $Q = mL$. If the change is melting or freezing, we call it the **specific latent heat of fusion**, L_F. If the change is vaporisation or condensing then we call it **specific latent heat of vaporisation**, L_V.

Substance	Specific latent heat of fusion / kJ kg^{-1}	Melting temperature / °C	Specific latent heat of vaporisation / kJ kg^{-1}	Boiling temperature / °C
water	334	0	2260	100
ethanol	109	−114	840	78
aluminium	395	660	10550	2467
lead	23	327	850	1740
copper	205	1078	2600	5190
iron	275	1540	6300	2800

Table 3.2 Specific latent heats of fusion and vaporisation together with the melting and boiling temperatures.

Notice from Table 3.2 that the specific latent heat for vaporisation is greater than that for melting. This is because the increase in separation of the molecules is much larger when going from the liquid to the vapour phase than when going from the solid to the liquid phase. More work is needed to achieve the greater separation, and so more energy is required.

Worked examples

3.4 An ice cube of mass 25.0 g and temperature −10.0 °C is dropped into a glass of water of mass 300.0 g and temperature 20.0 °C. Calculate the final temperature.

(Specific heat capacity of ice = 2200 J kg^{-1} K^{-1}; specific latent heat of fusion of ice = 334 kJ kg^{-1}, specific heat capacity of water = 4200 kJ kg^{-1}.)

Let the final temperature be T. Ignoring any thermal energy lost by the glass itself, the water will cool down by losing thermal energy.

Using $Q = mc\Delta T$, the thermal energy lost by the water is:

$0.3 \times 4200 \times (20 - T)$

3 THERMAL PHYSICS 121

This thermal energy will be taken up by the ice to:
- increase its temperature from $-10\,°C$ to $0\,°C$: the thermal energy required is $25 \times 10^{-3} \times 2200 \times 10\,\text{J}$
- melt the ice cube into water at $0\,°C$: the thermal energy required is $25 \times 10^{-3} \times 334 \times 10^3\,\text{J}$
- increase the temperature of the former ice cube from $0\,°C$ to the final temperature T: the thermal energy required is $25 \times 10^{-3} \times 4200 \times T$.

Thus:

$$0.3 \times 4200 \times (20 - T) = (25 \times 10^{-3} \times 2200 \times 10) + (25 \times 10^{-3} \times 334 \times 10^3) + (25 \times 10^{-3} \times 4200 \times T)$$

> **Exam tip**
> You can save yourself time and possible errors if you write this equation, as is, in the equation solver of your graphic display calculator (GDC) and ask the GDC to solve it for you.

Solving for T gives $T = 11.9\,°C$.

3.5 A sample of 120 g of a solid initially at $20\,°C$ is heated by a heater of constant power. The specific heat capacity of the solid is $2500\,\text{J}\,\text{kg}^{-1}\,\text{K}^{-1}$. The temperature of the sample varies with time as shown in Figure **3.6**.

Use the graph to determine:
a the power of the heater
b the melting temperature of the sample
c the specific latent heat of fusion of the sample
d the specific heat capacity of the sample in the liquid phase.

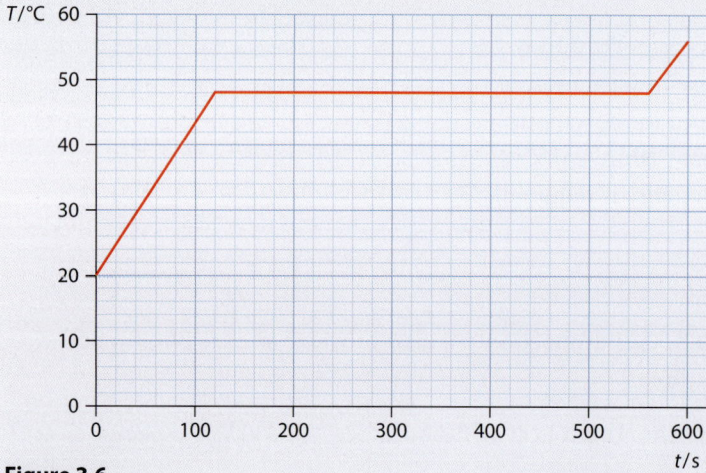

Figure 3.6

a It takes 120 s to raise the temperature of the solid sample from $20\,°C$ to $48\,°C$.

Using $Q = mc\Delta T$, the heat required is:

$0.120 \times 2500 \times (48 - 20) = 8400\,\text{J}$

So the power is:

$$P = \frac{Q}{t} = \frac{8400}{120} = 70\,\text{W}$$

b The temperature is constant at melting, shown by the flat part of the graph, so the melting temperature is 48 °C.

c The sample is melting from 120 s to 560 s, i.e. for 440 s. The heat supplied during this time is therefore:

$$Q = Pt = 70 \times 440 = 30\,800\,\text{J}$$

So the specific latent heat of fusion is:

$$L_F = \frac{Q}{m} = \frac{30\,800}{0.120} = 2.6 \times 10^5 \,\text{J}\,\text{kg}^{-1}$$

d The liquid increases its temperature from 48 °C to 56 °C in 40 s. In these 40 s the heat provided is:

$$Q = Pt = 70 \times 40 = 2800\,\text{J}$$

Using $Q = mc\Delta T$:

$$0.120 \times c \times (56 - 48) = 2800\,\text{J}$$

$$\Rightarrow c = 2.9 \times 10^3 \,\text{J}\,\text{kg}^{-1}\,\text{K}^{-1}$$

The method of mixtures

The electrical method described in Worked example **3.5** is one method for measuring specific heat capacity and latent heat. Another method, the **method of mixtures**, measures the specific heat capacity of a solid as follows. A solid is put in a container of hot water and allowed time to reach a constant temperature. The temperature of the solid is thus that of the water and is recorded. The solid is then transferred into a calorimeter of known specific heat capacity and initial temperature, which contains a liquid such as water (Figure **3.7**). The calorimeter is insulated. The final temperature of the water is recorded after thermal equilibrium has been reached.

For example, consider a mass of 0.400 kg of a solid at 80 °C that is put in a 100 g copper calorimeter containing 800 g of water at 20 °C. The final temperature of the water is measured to be 22 °C. From these values, we may deduce the specific heat capacity of the solid as follows.

Using $Q = mc\Delta T$, the amount of thermal energy (in joules) lost by the solid is:

$$0.400 \times c \times (80 - 22) = 23.2c$$

Exam tip
It is likely that the solid lost heat to the surrounding air while it was being transferred. This means that the actual temperature of the solid is less than we supposed. The actual specific heat capacity is therefore larger than the calculated value.

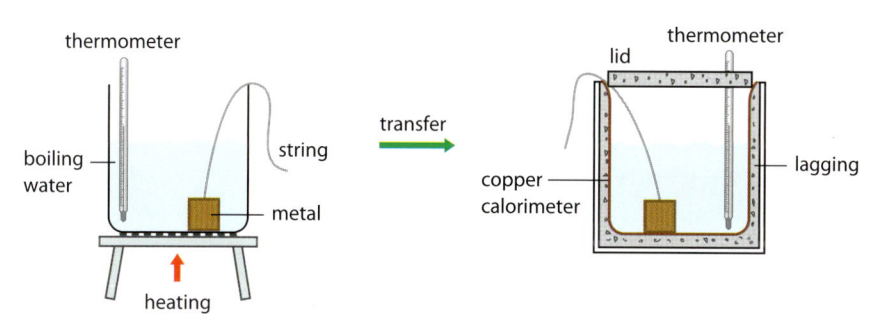

Figure 3.7 The hot metal is placed in the cold water in the calorimeter. The hot metal is removed from the container of boiling water and is quickly placed inside an insulated calorimeter containing cold water.

3 THERMAL PHYSICS 123

The amount of thermal energy gained by the calorimeter (see Table **3.1** for the value of c for copper) and the water is:

$$\underbrace{0.100 \times 385 \times (22-20)}_{\text{calorimeter}} + \underbrace{0.800 \times 4200 \times (22-20)}_{\text{water}} = 6797\,\text{J}$$

Equating the two we find that $c = 293\,\text{J}\,\text{kg}^{-1}\,\text{K}^{-1}$.

The same method can be applied to measure the specific latent heat of fusion of ice. To do this, place a quantity of ice at $0\,°\text{C}$ (the ice must therefore come from a mixture with water at $0\,°\text{C}$) into a calorimeter containing water at a few degrees above room temperature. Blot the ice dry before putting it into the calorimeter. The mass of the ice can be determined by weighing the calorimeter at the end of the experiment.

For example, suppose that $25.0\,\text{g}$ of ice at $0.00\,°\text{C}$ is placed in an aluminium calorimeter of mass $250\,\text{g}$ containing $300\,\text{g}$ of water at $24.0\,°\text{C}$. The temperature of the water is measured at regular intervals of time until the temperature reaches a minimum value of $17.0\,°\text{C}$. The calorimeter and water lost heat, which the ice received.

Heat lost by calorimeter and water:

$$0.250 \times 900 \times (24-17) + 0.300 \times 4200 \times (24-17) = 10\,395\,\text{J}$$

Heat received by ice:

$$0.025 \times L_F + 0.025 \times 4200 \times 17 = 0.025 \times L_F + 1785$$

Equating the two gives:

$$1785 + 0.025 \times L_F = 10\,395 \Rightarrow L \approx 344\,\text{kJ}\,\text{kg}^{-1}$$

Nature of science

Models change

As already mentioned, heat was once thought to be a fluid (caloric). Conservation of energy was a natural consequence of this model of heat: a body lost a certain amount of fluid and another gained it. Energy was conserved. So the concept of heat as a fluid seemed natural. But there are phenomena that cannot be explained with this simple picture. For one thing, if heat is a fluid it must have mass. So when heat leaves a body, the body must lose mass. This is not observed, so the caloric theory must be wrong. The theory has many other failings and was abandoned in the 19th century. A major problem is that it does not take account the atomic theory of matter. The theory we use now is based on statistical mechanics, which uses probability theory to predict the average behaviour of very large numbers of particles.

Test yourself

1. A hot body is brought into contact with a colder body until their temperatures are the same. Assume that no other bodies are nearby.
   a. Discuss whether the energy lost by one body is equal to the energy gained by the other.
   b. Discuss whether the temperature drop of one body is equal to the temperature rise of the other.

2. a. A body of mass 0.150 kg has its temperature increased by 5.00 °C when 385 J of energy is provided to it. Calculate the body's specific heat capacity.
   b. Another body of mass 0.150 kg has its temperature increased by 5.00 K when 385 J of energy is provided to it. Calculate this body's specific heat capacity.

3. A calorimeter of mass 90 g and specific heat capacity 420 J kg^{-1} K^{-1} contains 310 g of a liquid at 15.0 °C. An electric heater rated at 20.0 W warms the liquid to 19.0 °C in 3.0 min. Assuming there are no energy losses to the surroundings, estimate the specific heat capacity of the liquid.

4. A calorimeter for which mc = 25 J K^{-1} contains 140 g of a liquid. An immersion heater is used to provide energy at a rate of 40 W for a total time of 4.0 min. The temperature of the liquid increases by 15.8 °C. Calculate the specific heat capacity of the liquid. State an assumption made in reaching this result.

5. A car of mass 1360 kg descends from a hill of height 86 m at a constant speed. Assuming that all of the gravitational potential energy lost by the car goes into heating the brakes, estimate the rise in the temperature of the brakes. (It takes 16 kJ of energy to increase the temperature of the brake drums by 1 K; ignore any energy losses to the surroundings.)

6. A radiator made out of iron of specific heat capacity 450 J kg^{-1} K^{-1} has a mass of 45.0 kg and is filled with 23.0 kg of water of specific heat capacity 4200 J kg^{-1} K^{-1}.
   a. Determine the energy required to raise the temperature of the radiator–water system by 1 K.
   b. If energy is provided to the radiator at the rate of 450 W, calculate how long it will take for the temperature to increase by 20.0 °C.

7. How much ice at −10 °C must be dropped into a cup containing 300 g of water at 20 °C in order for the temperature of the water to be reduced to 10 °C? The cup itself has a mass of 150 g and is made out of aluminium. Assume that no energy is lost to the surroundings.

8. The surface of a pond of area 20 m^2 is covered by ice of uniform thickness 6 cm. The temperature of the ice is −5 °C. Calculate how much energy is required to melt this amount of ice into water at 0 °C. (Take the density of ice to be 900 kg m^{-3}.)

9. Radiation from the Sun falls on the frozen surface of a pond at a rate of 600 W m^{-2}. The ice temperature is 0 °C.
   a. Calculate how long it will take to melt a 1.0 cm thick layer of ice. (Take the density of ice to be 900 kg m^{-3}.)
   b. Suggest why the actual mass of ices that melts is less than your answer to **a**.

10. a. Calculate how much energy is required to warm 1.0 kg ice initially at −10 °C to ice at 0 °C.
    b. Calculate how much energy is required to melt the ice at 0 °C.
    c. Calculate how much energy is required to further increase the temperature of the water from 0 °C to 10 °C.
    d. State in which stage (warming the ice, melting the ice, warming the water) the energy requirement is largest.

11. Ice at 0 °C is added to 1.0 kg of water at 20 °C, cooling it down to 10 °C. Determine how much ice was added.

12. A quantity of 100 g of ice at 0 °C and 50 g steam at 100 °C are added to a container that has 150 g water at 30 °C. Determine the final temperature in the container. Ignore the container itself in your calculations.

3 THERMAL PHYSICS

Learning objectives

- Use the concept of pressure.
- Solve problems using the equation of state of an ideal gas.
- Understand the assumptions behind the kinetic model of an ideal gas.
- Solve problems using moles, molar masses and the Avogadro constant.
- Describe differences between ideal and real gases.

3.2 Modelling a gas

This section introduces the equation of state of an ideal gas, which is the equation that relates the pressure, volume, absolute temperature and number of moles of an ideal gas. The connection between the average random kinetic energy of the molecules and the kelvin temperature is derived.

The Avogadro constant

By definition, one **mole** of any substance contains as many **particles** as there are atoms in 12 g of carbon-12. What we mean by 'particle' depends on the substance; it can be a single atom or a molecule. For example, in carbon the particles are single **atoms**, the particles in hydrogen gas (H_2) are diatomic **molecules**, in carbon dioxide gas (CO_2) they are triatomic molecules, and in methane gas (CH_4) they are molecules with five atoms.

Experiments show that the number of particles in a mole is $N_A = 6.02 \times 10^{23}$ mol^{-1}, a number known as the **Avogadro constant** and one of the basic constants of physics. So one mole of carbon, one mole of H_2, one mole of CO_2 and one mole of CH_4 all contain 6.02×10^{23} particles. This means 6.02×10^{23} atoms for carbon, $2 \times 6.02 \times 10^{23}$ atoms for H_2, $3 \times 6.02 \times 10^{23}$ atoms for CO_2 and $5 \times 6.02 \times 10^{23}$ atoms for CH_4. Figure 3.8 shows one mole of different substances.

If a substance contains N particles (atoms or molecules, as discussed above) then the number of moles n is:

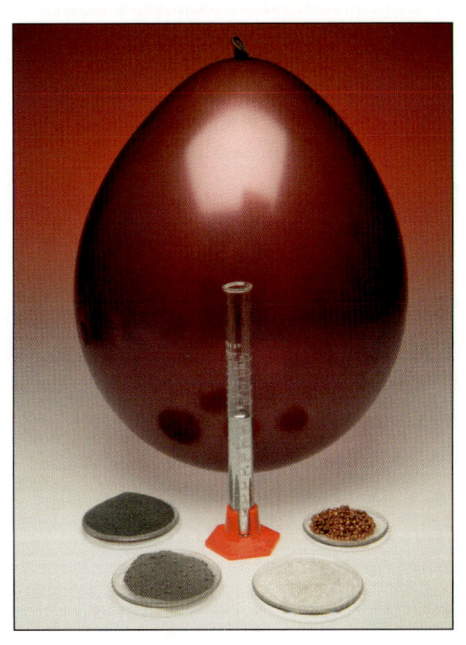

$$n = \frac{N}{N_A}$$

Figure 3.8 One mole of different substances.

The atomic mass scale defines one **atomic mass unit** (1 u) as $\frac{1}{12}$ of the mass of one atom of carbon-12, $^{12}_{6}C$. The mass of one atom of $^{12}_{6}C$ is therefore exactly 12 u. The notation $^{12}_{6}C$ means that the carbon atom has six protons and the number of protons and neutrons combined is 12 (i.e. six neutrons). The neutral atom also has six electrons. Neglecting the mass of the six electrons, the mass of the six protons and six neutrons is about 12 u. The proton and the neutron are approximately equal in mass and so approximately the mass of one proton and that of one neutron is 1 u. So an atom of helium ($^{4}_{2}He$) has a mass that is (approximately) 4 u and the mass of one atom of $^{56}_{26}Fe$ is (approximately) 56 u.

Now, remember that the mole is defined as the number of atoms in 12 g of $^{12}_{6}C$. We also defined the mass of one atom of $^{12}_{6}C$ to be 12 u. This means that:

$$\underbrace{N_A}_{\text{number of particles in 1 mol}} \times \underbrace{12u}_{\text{mass of 1 atom}} = \underbrace{12g}_{\text{mass in g of 1 mol}}$$

and so the u (in grams) is given by:

$$u = \frac{1\,g}{N_A} \quad (\approx 1.66 \times 10^{-24}\,g \approx 1.66 \times 10^{-27}\,kg)$$

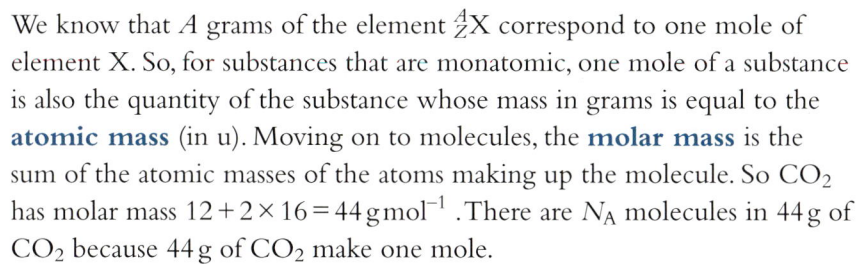

We know that A grams of the element $^A_Z X$ correspond to one mole of element X. So, for substances that are monatomic, one mole of a substance is also the quantity of the substance whose mass in grams is equal to the **atomic mass** (in u). Moving on to molecules, the **molar mass** is the sum of the atomic masses of the atoms making up the molecule. So CO_2 has molar mass $12 + 2 \times 16 = 44\,g\,mol^{-1}$. There are N_A molecules in 44 g of CO_2 because 44 g of CO_2 make one mole.

So, it is important to know that:

> One mole of a substance is a quantity of the substance that contains a number of particles equal to the Avogadro constant and whose mass in grams is equal to the molar mass of the substance.

The number of moles in a quantity of m grams of a substance with molar mass μ is then $n = \frac{m}{\mu}$.

Worked examples

3.6 Estimate the number of atoms of gold in 1.0 kg of gold ($^{197}_{79}Au$).

The molar mass of gold is $197\,g\,mol^{-1}$. So 1000 g of gold (= 1 kg) contains $\frac{1000}{197} \approx 5.1$ mol of atoms.

Each mole contains 6.02×10^{23} atoms, so the number of atoms in 1 kg of gold is $6.02 \times 10^{23} \times 5.1 = 3 \times 10^{24}$.

3.7 Calculate how many grams of scandium, $^{45}_{21}Sc$, contain the same number of molecules as 8.0 g of argon, $^{40}_{18}Ar$.

The molar mass of argon is $40\,g\,mol^{-1}$, so a quantity of 8.0 g of argon corresponds to $\frac{8.0}{40} = 0.20$ mol.

Thus, we need 0.20 mol of scandium. This corresponds to $0.20 \times 45 = 9.0$ g.

3.8 Estimate the number of water molecules in an ordinary glass of water.

A glass contains about $200\,cm^3$ of water, which has a mass of 200 g.

Since the molar mass of water is $18\,g\,mol^{-1}$, the glass contains $\frac{200}{18} \approx 10$ mol or $6 \times 10^{23} \times 10 \approx 10^{25}$ molecules of water.

Pressure

Pressure is defined as the normal force applied per unit area. In Figure **3.9a** the force is normal to the area A, so the pressure is:

$$p = \frac{F}{A}$$

3 THERMAL PHYSICS

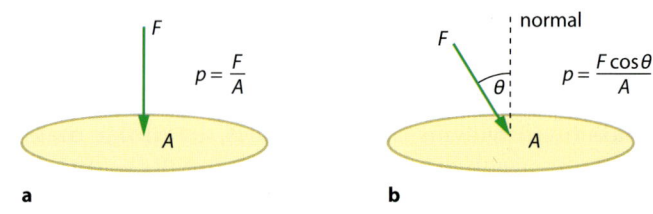

Figure 3.9 Pressure is the normal force per unit area.

The force in Figure **3.9b** acts at an angle θ, so the pressure on the area A is given by the expression:

$$p = \frac{F \cos \theta}{A}$$

The unit of pressure is newton per square metre, $N\,m^{-2}$, also known as the pascal, Pa. Another commonly used non-SI unit is the **atmosphere**, atm, which is equal to 1.013×10^5 Pa.

Worked example

3.9 Two hollow cubes of side 25 cm with one face missing are placed together at the missing face (Figure **3.10**). The air inside the solid formed is pumped out. Determine the force that is necessary to separate the cubes.

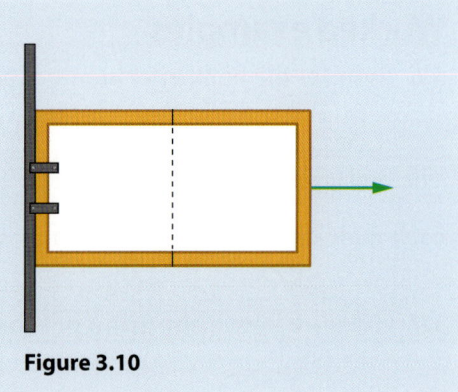

Figure 3.10

The pressure inside the solid is zero and outside it equals atmospheric pressure, 1.01×10^5 Pa.

Thus, the force is given by:

$F = pA = 1.01 \times 10^5 \times (0.25)^2 = 6.3 \times 10^3$ N

Ideal gases

An **ideal gas** is a theoretical model of a gas. It helps us to understand the behaviour of real, actual gases. We assume that an ideal gas obeys the following:
- The molecules are point particles, each with negligible volume.
- The molecules obey the laws of mechanics.
- There are no forces between the molecules except when the molecules collide.
- The duration of a collision is negligible compared to the time between collisions.
- The collisions of the molecules with each other and with the container walls are elastic.
- Molecules have a range of speeds and move randomly.

Exam tip
You must be able to recall and describe a few of these assumptions in an exam

An ideal gas (unlike real gases) cannot be liquefied or solidified. You should be able to see how some of these assumptions may not be obeyed by a **real gas**. For example, there will always be forces between molecules of a real gas, not just when the molecules are in contact. In general, we expect that a real gas will behave like an ideal gas when the density is low (so that molecules are not close to each other and hence the forces between them are negligible). We do not expect ideal gas behaviour at high densities (molecules will be too close to each other and will exert forces on each other). Similarly, we do not expect ideal gas behaviour from a real gas at very low temperature, because the gas will then become a liquid or even a solid!

> A real gas may be approximated by an ideal gas when the density is low.

Figure **3.11** shows a molecule that collides with a container wall. The momentum normal to the wall before the collision is $mv\cos\theta$. After the collision momentum normal to the wall is $-mv\cos\theta$. So the change in momentum has magnitude $2mv\cos\theta$. The fact that the momentum of the molecule has changed means that a force acted on the molecule (from the wall). By Newton's third law, therefore, the molecule exerted on the wall an equal and opposite force. Taking into account the forces due to all the molecules colliding with the walls results in a force, and hence pressure, on the walls.

The **state of a gas** is determined when we know the values of the pressure, the volume, the temperature and the number of moles present. The parameters p, V, T and n are related to each other. The equation relating them is called the **equation of state**. Our objective is to discover the equation of state for a gas. To do this a number of simple experiments can be performed, as described in the following sections.

The pressure–volume law

The equipment shown in Figure **3.12** can be used to investigate the relationship between pressure and volume of a fixed quantity of gas that is kept at constant temperature.

The pump forces oil to move higher, decreasing the volume of the air trapped in the tube above the oil. A pressure gauge reads the pressure of the trapped air and so the relationship between pressure and volume may investigated. The changes in pressure and volume must take place slowly so that the temperature stays the same.

Exam tip
You must be able to describe the conditions under which a real gas may be approximated by that of an ideal gas. The main idea is that the density must be low. For a fixed quantity of gas, density will be low at low pressure and high temperature.

Exam tip
You must be able to give an explanation of pressure in terms of molecules colliding with their container walls.

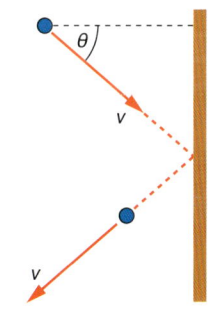

Figure 3.11 A molecule has its momentum changed when it collides with a wall. A force is exerted on the molecule and so the molecule exerts an equal and opposite force on the wall.

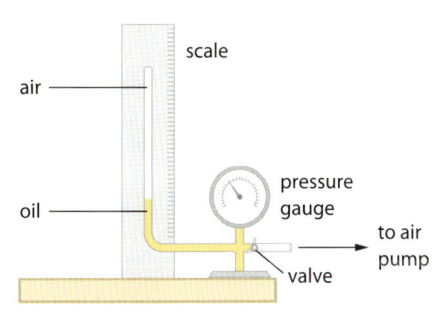

Figure 3.12 Apparatus for investigating the pressure–volume law. The pump forces oil to move up the tube, decreasing the volume of air.

3 THERMAL PHYSICS 129

The results of a typical experiment are shown in Figure 3.13. We have plotted pressure against the inverse of the volume and obtained a straight line.

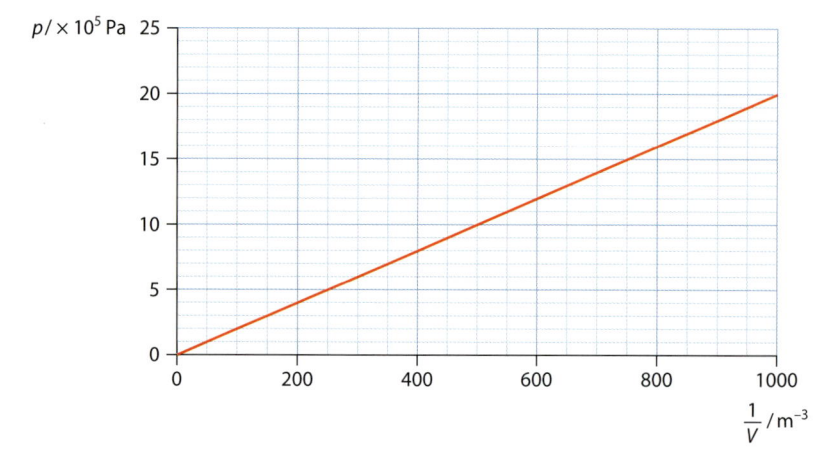

Figure 3.13 Graph of pressure against inverse volume at constant temperature.

This implies that:

> At constant temperature and with a fixed quantity of gas, pressure is inversely proportional to volume, that is:
> $$p \propto \frac{1}{V} \quad \text{or} \quad pV = \text{constant}$$

This relationship is known as the **Boyle's law**.

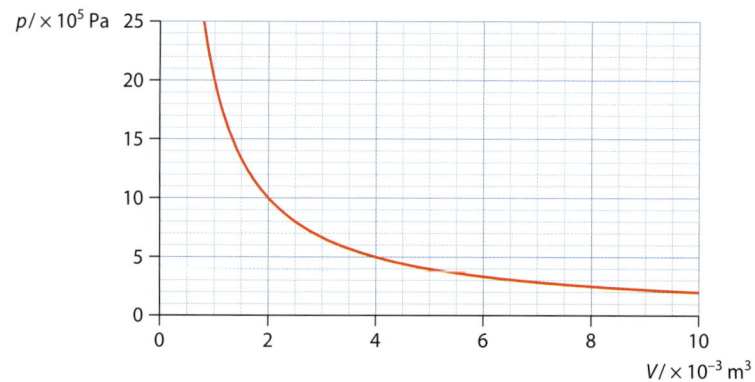

Figure 3.14 The relationship between pressure and volume at constant temperature for a fixed quantity of a gas. The product pV is the same for all points on the curve.

Figure 3.14 shows the same data now plotted as pressure against volume.
The curve in the pressure–volume diagram is a hyperbola and in physics it is known as an **isothermal** curve or **isotherm**: the temperature at all points on the curve is the same.

Exam tip
In practice we use the relation $pV = $ constant in the equivalent form $p_1 V_1 = p_2 V_2$ when the initial pressure and volume (p_1, V_1) change to a new pressure and volume (p_2, V_2) at constant temperature.

Exam tip
If you are asked to confirm the relationship $pV = $ constant, take three points from a pressure–volume graph and show that their product is the same.

Worked example

3.10 The pressure of a fixed quantity of gas is 2.0 atm and its volume 0.90 dm³. The pressure is increased to 6.0 atm at constant temperature. Determine the new volume.

Use $p_1V_1 = p_2V_2$. Substituting the known values we have:

$$2.0 \times 0.90 = 6.0 \times V$$

$\Rightarrow \qquad V = 0.30$

The new volume is 0.30 dm³.

Remember that 1 dm³ = 1000 cm³ = 1 litre.

(Notice that since this problem compares the pressure at two different volumes we do not have to change units to SI units.)

The volume–temperature law

The dependence of volume on temperature of a fixed quantity of gas kept at constant pressure can be investigated with the apparatus shown in Figure 3.15. Air is trapped in a thin capillary tube that is immersed in heated water. The air is trapped by a thin thread of very concentrated sulfuric acid. The thread is exposed to the atmosphere and so the pressure of the trapped air is constant.

It is found that the volume increases uniformly with temperature. The striking fact is that when the straight line is extended backwards it always crosses the temperature axis at −273 °C, as in Figure 3.16. This suggests that there exists a minimum possible temperature, namely −273 °C. (With a real gas the experiment cannot be conducted at very low temperatures since the gas would liquefy – hence the dotted line. With an ideal gas there would be no such restriction.)

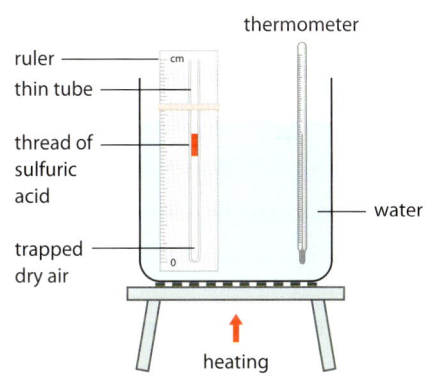

Figure 3.15 Apparatus for verifying the volume–temperature law.

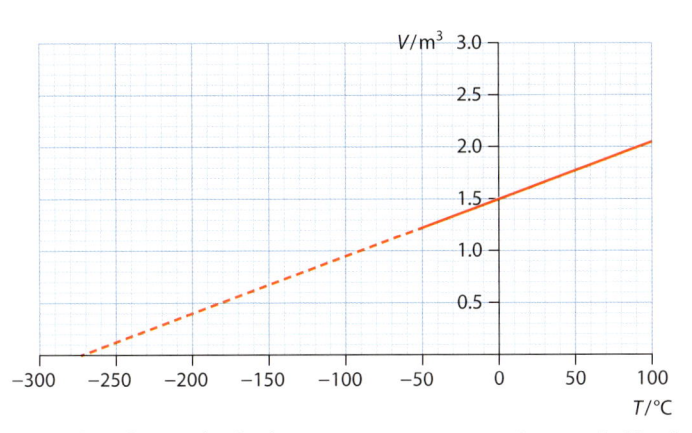

Figure 3.16 When the graph of volume versus temperature is extended backwards the line intersects the temperature axis at −273 °C.

3 THERMAL PHYSICS 131

If this same experiment is repeated with a different quantity of gas, or a gas at a different constant pressure, the result is the same. In each case, the straight-line graph of volume versus temperature crosses the temperature axis at −273 °C (Figure **3.17**). In Figure **3.18**, the same graphs are drawn using the Kelvin temperature scale.

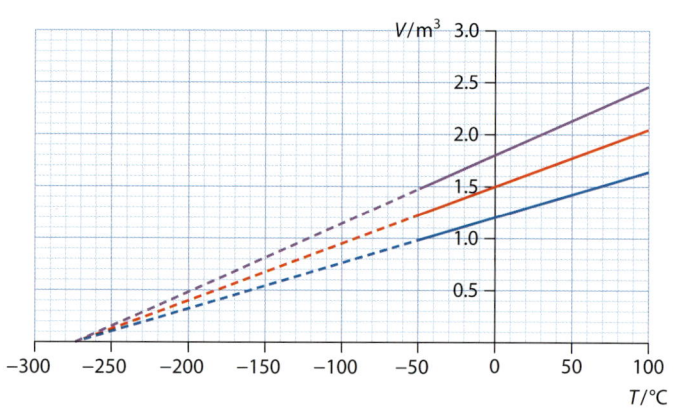

Figure 3.17 When the graph of volume versus temperature is extended backwards, all the lines intersect the temperature axis at the same point.

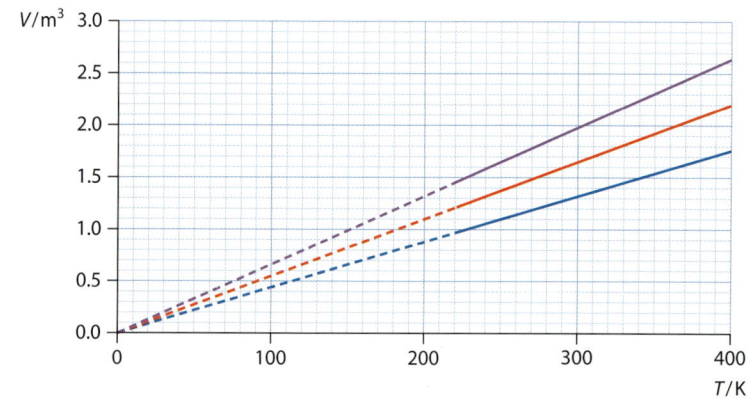

Figure 3.18 When temperature is expressed in kelvin, the lines start at zero temperature.

When the temperature is expressed in kelvin, this experiment implies that at constant pressure:

$$\frac{V}{T} = \text{constant}$$

This relationship is know as **Charles' law**.

Exam tip
In practice we use the relation $\frac{V}{T}$ = constant in the equivalent form as $\frac{V_1}{T_1} = \frac{V_2}{T_2}$ where the initial volume and temperature of the gas (V_1, T_1) change to a new volume and temperature (V_2, T_2) at constant pressure.

Worked example

3.11 A gas expands at constant pressure from an original volume of 2.0 dm³ at 22 °C to a volume of 4.0 dm³. Calculate the new temperature.

Substituting in $\dfrac{V_2}{T_1} = \dfrac{V_2}{T_2}$ it follows that:

$$\dfrac{2.0}{295} = \dfrac{4.0}{T}$$

$\Rightarrow \quad T = 590\,\text{K}$ or $317\,°C$

Note that we converted the original temperature into kelvin. (It is very easy to forget this conversion and get the incorrect answer of 44 °C.)

The pressure–temperature law

What remains now is to investigate the dependence of pressure on temperature of a fixed quantity of gas in a fixed volume. This can be done with the apparatus shown in Figure 3.19. The gas container is surrounded by water whose temperature can be changed. A pressure gauge measures the pressure of the gas. We find that pressure increases uniformly with increasing temperature, as shown by the graph in Figure 3.20.

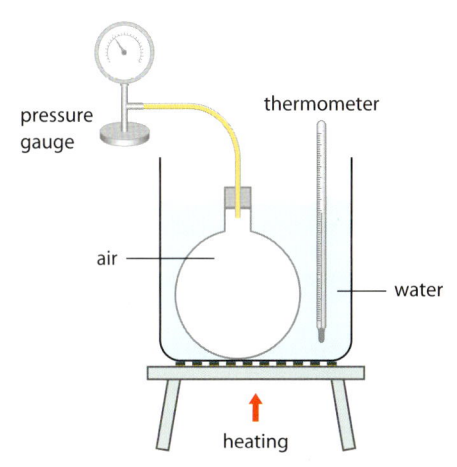

Figure 3.19 Investigating the pressure–temperature law.

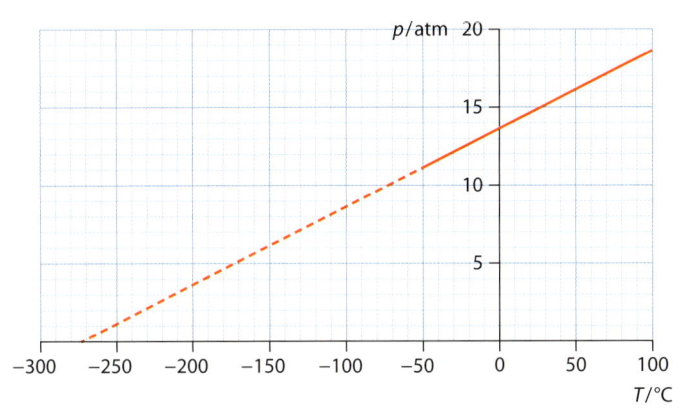

Figure 3.20 The graph of pressure versus temperature is a straight line that, when extended backwards, again intersects the temperature axis at −273 °C.

3 THERMAL PHYSICS 133

For quantities of gases containing different numbers of moles at different volumes the results are the same, as shown in Figure **3.21**. When the temperature is expressed in kelvin, the straight lines all pass through the origin (Figure **3.22**).

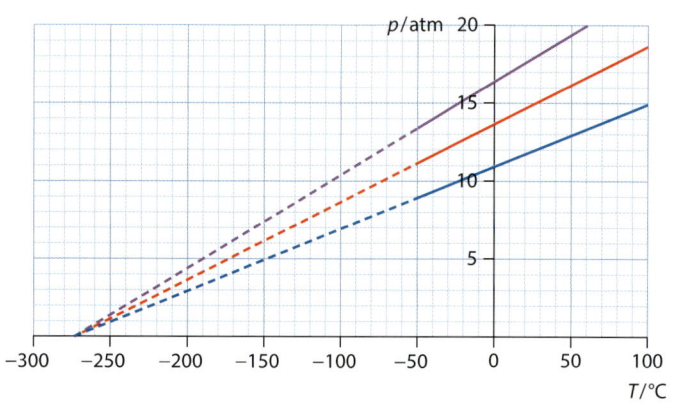

Figure 3.21 When extended backwards, the graphs of pressure versus temperature for three different quantities of gas all intersect the temperature axis at the same point.

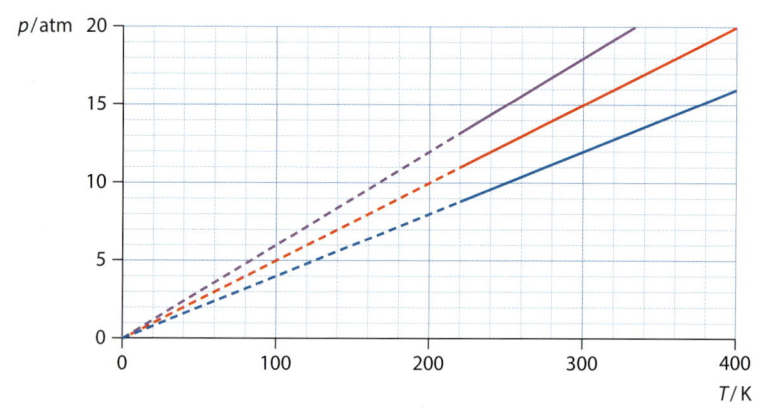

Figure 3.22 If temperature is expressed in kelvin, the lines start at zero temperature.

When the temperature is expressed in kelvin, this experiment implies that at constant volume:

$$\frac{p}{T} = \text{constant}$$

This relationship is known as **Gay-Lussac's law** or **Amontons' law**.

Exam tip
In practice we use the relation $\frac{p}{T}$ = constant in the equivalent form as $\frac{p_1}{T_1} = \frac{p_2}{T_2}$ where the initial pressure and temperature of the gas (p_1, T_1) change to a new pressure and temperature (p_2, T_2) at constant volume. (Remember, T is in kelvin.)

Worked example

3.12 A gas in a container of fixed volume is heated from a temperature of 37 °C and pressure 3.0×10^5 Pa to a temperature of 87 °C. Calculate the new pressure.

Substituting in $\frac{p_1}{T_1} = \frac{p_2}{T_2}$ we have:

$$\frac{3.0 \times 10^5}{310} = \frac{p}{360}$$

$$\Rightarrow p = 3.5 \times 10^5 \text{ Pa}$$

(Notice that we had to change the temperature into kelvin.)

The equation of state of an ideal gas

If we combine the results of the three preceding experiments, we find that:

$$\frac{pV}{T} = \text{constant}$$

What is the value of the constant? To determine that, we repeat all of the preceding experiments, this time using different quantities of the gas. We discover that the constant in the last equation is proportional to the number of moles n of the gas in question:

$$\frac{pV}{T} = n \times \text{constant}$$

We can now measure the pressure, temperature, volume and number of moles for a large number of different gases and calculate the value of $\frac{pV}{nT}$. We find that this constant has the same value for all gases – it is a universal constant. We call this the gas constant R. It has the numerical value:

$$R = 8.31 \text{ J K}^{-1} \text{ mol}^{-1}$$

Thus, finally, the equation of state is:

$$pV = RnT$$

(Remember that temperature must always be in kelvin.)

Exam tip
In practice we use this in the form $\frac{p_1 V_1}{T_1} = \frac{p_2 V_2}{T_2}$ when a gas changes from values (p_1, V_1, T_1) to (p_2, V_2, T_2). Cancel out any quantities that stay the same.

3 THERMAL PHYSICS

Worked examples

3.13 Estimate how many molecules there are in a gas of temperature 320 K, volume 0.025 m³ and pressure 4.8×10^5 Pa.

First we find the number of moles:

$$n = \frac{pV}{RT}$$

$$n = \frac{4.8 \times 10^5 \times 0.025}{8.31 \times 320} = 4.51 \text{ mol}$$

Each mole contains the Avogadro number of molecules, so the number of molecules is:

$$4.51 \times 6.02 \times 10^{23} \approx 2.7 \times 10^{24}$$

3.14 A container of hydrogen of volume 0.10 m³ and temperature 25 °C contains 3.2×10^{23} molecules. Calculate the pressure in the container.

The number of moles present is:

$$n = \frac{3.2 \times 10^{23}}{6.02 \times 10^{23}} = 0.53$$

So: $p = \dfrac{RnT}{V} = \dfrac{8.31 \times 0.53 \times 298}{0.10} = 1.3 \times 10^4$ Pa

3.15 A fixed quantity of gas of volume 3.0×10^{-3} m³, pressure 3.0×10^5 Pa and temperature 300 K expands to a volume of 4.0×10^{-3} m³ and a pressure of 6.0×10^5 Pa. Calculate the new temperature of the gas.

Use $\dfrac{p_1 V_1}{n_1 T_1} = \dfrac{p_2 V_2}{n_2 T_2}$ to get:

$$\frac{3.0 \times 10^5 \times 3.0 \times 10^{-3}}{300} = \frac{6.0 \times 10^5 \times 4.0 \times 10^{-3}}{T}$$

Solving for T gives: $T = 800$ K

3.16 Figure 3.23 shows two isothermal curves for equal quantities of two ideal gases. State and explain which gas is at the higher temperature.

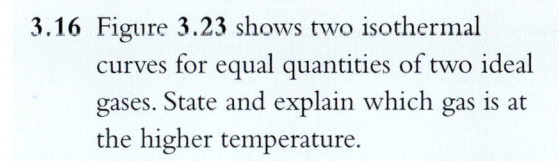

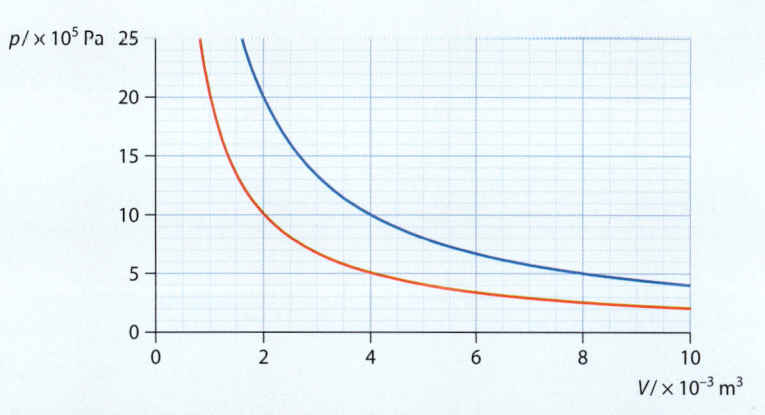

Figure 3.23 Two isothermal curves for equal quantities of two gases.

Draw a vertical line that intersects the two isotherms at two points. At these points both gases have the same volume, and as the quantities of gas are equal n is the same. So for these points $\frac{p}{T}$ is constant. The point on the blue curve has higher pressure, so it must have the higher temperature.

The Boltzmann equation

The molecules of a gas move about randomly with a range of speeds. The graph in Figure 3.24 shows the distribution of speeds for oxygen molecules kept at two different temperatures: the blue curve is at 100 K and the red curve at 300 K. The vertical axis shows the fraction of molecules having a given speed v. You will not be examined on this graph but knowing a few of its features helps a lot in understanding how gases behave.

We see that there is a speed that corresponds to the peak of the curve. For the blue curve this is about $225\,\mathrm{m\,s^{-1}}$ and for the red curve at $400\,\mathrm{m\,s^{-1}}$. The speed at the peak represents the most probable speed that would be found if you picked a molecule at random. Two other speeds are important:
- the average speed of the molecules, $\bar{v} = \dfrac{v_1 + v_2 + v_3 + \cdots + v_N}{N}$
- the r.m.s. speed or root mean square speed c, which is the square root of the average of the squares of the speeds of the molecules, i.e.

$$c = \sqrt{\dfrac{v_1^2 + v_2^2 + v_3^2 + \cdots + v_N^2}{N}}$$

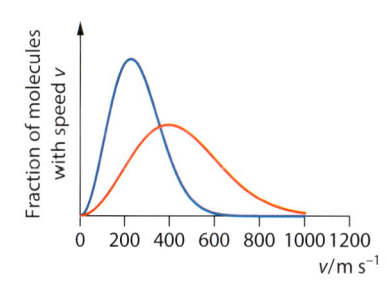

Figure 3.24 The distribution of speeds at two different temperatures.

Why do we bother to work with an r.m.s. speed? Consider the *average kinetic energy* for the N molecules, which is given by:

$$\bar{E}_\mathrm{K} = \dfrac{\tfrac{1}{2}mv_1^2 + \tfrac{1}{2}mv_2^2 + \tfrac{1}{2}mv_3^2 + \cdots + \tfrac{1}{2}mv_N^2}{N}$$

$$= \tfrac{1}{2}m\left(\dfrac{v_1^2 + v_2^2 + v_3^2 + \cdots + v_N^2}{N}\right)$$

$$= \tfrac{1}{2}mc^2$$

So we see that the average kinetic energy involves the r.m.s. speed. These three speeds (most probable, average and r.m.s. speed) are all different but numerically close to each other. So, even though it is not technically correct, we may assume that all three speeds mean the same thing and we will use the symbol c for all of them.

Now, it can be proven that the pressure of a gas is $p = \frac{1}{3}\rho c^2$, where the quantity c stands for the r.m.s. speed and ρ is the density of the gas. (You will not need to know this equation for the exam.) We get a very interesting result if we combine this equation with the equation of state for an ideal gas, i.e. the equation $pV = nRT$. There are many steps in the derivation in the box below. N stands for the number of molecules and m for the mass of one molecule.

> Since $\frac{1}{2}mc^2$ is equal to E, the average random kinetic energy of the molecules, we can write:
>
> $pV = nRT$
>
> $(\frac{1}{3}\rho c^2)V = nRT$ replacing the pressure with $p = \frac{1}{3}\rho c^2$
>
> $\frac{1}{3}\frac{Mc^2 V}{V} = nRT$ replacing the density by mass ÷ volume
>
> $\frac{1}{3}Mc^2 = nRT$ cancelling the volume
>
> $\frac{1}{3}Nmc^2 = \frac{N}{N_A}RT$ writing $M = Nm$ and $n = \frac{N}{N_A}$
>
> $\frac{1}{2}Nmc^2 = \frac{3}{2}\frac{R}{N_A}T$ multiplying both sides by $\frac{3}{2}$

The product of all this algebra is the very important result that relates the average random kinetic energy to the absolute temperature.

$$\bar{E}_K = \frac{3}{2}\frac{R}{N_A}T$$

The ratio $\frac{R}{N_A}$ is called the Boltzmann constant, k_B. So the final result is that the average random kinetic energy of the particles is directly proportional to the kelvin temperature:

$$\bar{E}_K = \frac{3}{2}k_B T$$

Using this equation we can find an expression for the internal energy of an ideal gas. Remember that the internal energy of an ideal gas consists only of the random kinetic energy of its molecules and no potential energy. Suppose that the gas has N molecules. Then, since the average

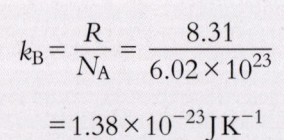

$$k_B = \frac{R}{N_A} = \frac{8.31}{6.02 \times 10^{23}}$$
$$= 1.38 \times 10^{-23} \, J\,K^{-1}$$

kinetic energy is $\frac{3}{2}k_B T$, the **total** random kinetic energy, i.e. the internal energy U, is:

$$U = \frac{3}{2}Nk_B T$$

But recall that $k_B = \frac{R}{N_A}$, so that another expression is:

$$U = \frac{3}{2}nRT$$

Yet another expression comes from using the equation of state, $pV = nRT$, which gives:

$$U = \frac{3}{2}pV$$

Exam tip
You must be able to obtain an expression for the internal energy of an ideal gas even though this formula is not in the IB data booklet.

Worked examples

3.17 The kelvin temperature of a gas is doubled. By what factor does the average speed increase?

From $\frac{1}{2}mc^2 = \frac{3}{2}k_B T$ we find that when T is doubled then c^2 will double, so c itself will increase by a factor of $\sqrt{2}$.

3.18 Calculate the ratio of the average speed of oxygen (O_2) to carbon dioxide (CO_2) molecules when both gases are at the same temperature.

Since the temperature is the same for both gases, using $\frac{1}{2}mc^2 = \frac{3}{2}k_B T$ we find that:

$$\frac{1}{2}m_O c_O^2 = \frac{1}{2}m_{CO_2} c_{CO_2}^2 \quad \text{and so} \quad \frac{c_O^2}{c_{CO_2}^2} = \frac{m_{CO_2}}{m_O}$$

So we need to find the ratio of the masses of the molecules. One mole of oxygen has a mass of 32 g so one molecule has a mass (in grams) of $\frac{32}{N_A}$. Similarly, the mass in grams of a carbon dioxide molecule is $\frac{44}{N_A}$. So:

$$\frac{c_O^2}{c_{CO_2}^2} = \frac{44/N_A}{32/N_A} = \frac{44}{32} = 1.375 \Rightarrow \frac{c_O}{c_{CO_2}} = \sqrt{1.375} = 1.17 \approx 1.2$$

3.19 Calculate the average speed of helium ($^4_2 He$) molecules at a temperature of $-15\,°C$.

We use $\frac{1}{2}mc^2 = \frac{3}{2}k_B T$. First we need to find the mass m of a helium atom. One mole of helium has a mass of 4.0 g so the mass of one molecule is given by:

$$m = \frac{4.0}{N_A} = \frac{4.0}{6.02 \times 10^{23}} = 6.64 \times 10^{-24}\,g = 6.64 \times 10^{-27}\,kg$$

Now remember to convert the temperature into kelvin: $273 - 15 = 258\,K$. So we have:

$$\tfrac{1}{2} \times 6.64 \times 10^{-27} \times c^2 = \tfrac{3}{2} \times 1.38 \times 10^{-23} \times 258$$

This gives $c^2 = 1.61 \times 10^6$ and so $c = 1.3 \times 10^3\,m\,s^{-1}$.

Nature of science

Models must be correct but also simple

Boyle thought that a gas consists of particles joined by springs. Newton thought that a gas consists of particles that exert repulsive forces on each other. Bernoulli thought that a gas is a collection of a very large number of particles that exert forces on each other only when they collide. All three could explain why a gas exerts a pressure on its container but it is Bernoulli's picture that is the simplest. We assume that the ordinary laws of mechanics apply to the individual particles making up the gas. Even though the laws apply to each individual particle we cannot observe or analyse each particle individually since there are so many of them. By concentrating on average behaviours of the whole gas and using probability and statistics, physicists developed a new field of physics known as statistical mechanics. This has had enormous success in advancing our understanding of gases and other systems, including where the approximation to an ideal gas breaks down.

Test yourself

13 Calculate the number of molecules in 28 g of hydrogen gas (molar mass $2 \, \text{g mol}^{-1}$).

14 Calculate the number of moles in 6.0 g of helium gas (molar mass $4 \, \text{g mol}^{-1}$).

15 Determine the number of moles in a sample of a gas that contains 2.0×10^{24} molecules.

16 Determine the mass in grams of carbon (molar mass $12 \, \text{g mol}^{-1}$) that contains as many molecules as 21 g of krypton (molar mass $84 \, \text{g mol}^{-1}$).

17 A sealed bottle contains air at 22.0 °C and a pressure of 12.0×10^5 Pa. The temperature is raised to 120.0 °C. Calculate the new pressure.

18 A gas has pressure 8.2×10^6 Pa and volume 2.3×10^{-3} m³. The pressure is reduced to 4.5×10^6 Pa at constant temperature. Calculate the new volume of the gas.

19 A mass of 12.0 kg of helium is required to fill a bottle of volume 5.00×10^{-3} m³ at a temperature of 20.0 °C. Determine the pressure in helium.

20 Determine the mass of carbon dioxide required to fill a tank of volume 12.0×10^{-3} m³ at a temperature of 20.0 °C and a pressure of 4.00 atm.

21 A flask of volume 300.0×10^{-6} m³ contains air at a pressure of 5.00×10^5 Pa and a temperature of 27.0 °C. The flask loses molecules at a rate of 3.00×10^{19} per second. Estimate how long it takes for the pressure in the flask to fall to half its original value. (Assume that the temperature of the air remains constant during this time.)

22 The point marked in the diagram represents the state of a fixed quantity of ideal gas in a container with a movable piston. The temperature of the gas in the state shown is 600 K. Copy the diagram. Indicate on the diagram the point representing the new state of the gas after the following separate changes.
   a The volume doubles at constant temperature.
   b The volume doubles at constant pressure.
   c The pressure halves at constant volume.

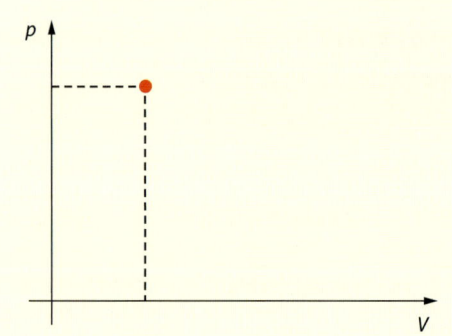

23 Two ideal gases are kept at the same temperature in two containers separated by a valve, as shown in the diagram. Estimate the pressure when the valve is opened. (The temperature stays the same.)

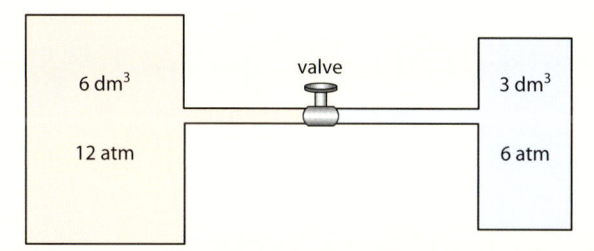

[Diagram: 6 dm³ at 12 atm connected via valve to 3 dm³ at 6 atm]

24 The diagram shows a cylinder in a vacuum, which has a movable, frictionless piston at the top. An ideal gas is kept in the cylinder. The piston is at a distance of 0.500 m from the bottom of the cylinder and the volume of the cylinder is 0.050 m³. The weight on top of the cylinder has a mass of 10.0 kg. The temperature of the gas is 19.0 °C.

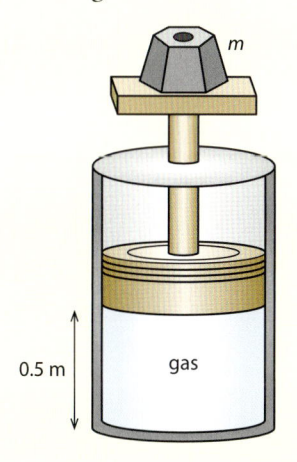

[Diagram: cylinder with gas, piston at 0.5 m, mass m on top]

  a Calculate the pressure of the gas.
  b Determine how many molecules there are in the gas.
  c The temperature is increased to 152 °C. Calculate the new volume of the gas.

25 The molar mass of a gas is $28\,\text{g}\,\text{mol}^{-1}$. A container holds 2.00 mol of this gas at 0.00 °C and a pressure of 1.00×10^5 Pa. Determine the mass and volume of the gas.

26 A balloon has a volume of 404 m³ and is filled with helium of mass 70.0 kg. The temperature inside the balloon is 17.0 °C. Determine the pressure inside the balloon.

27 A flask has a volume of 5.0×10^{-4} m³ and contains air at a temperature of 300 K and a pressure of 150 kPa.
  a Calculate the number of moles of air in the flask.
  b Determine the number of molecules in the flask.
  c Estimate the mass of air in the flask. You may take the molar mass of air to be $29\,\text{g}\,\text{mol}^{-1}$.

28 The molar mass of helium is $4.00\,\text{g}\,\text{mol}^{-1}$.
  a Calculate the volume of 1.0 mol of helium at standard temperature and pressure (stp) i.e. at $T = 273$ K, $p = 1.0 \times 10^5$ Pa.
  b Determine the density of helium at stp.
  c Estimate the density of oxygen gas at stp (the molar mass of, oxygen gas is $32\,\text{g}\,\text{mol}^{-1}$).

29 The density of an ideal gas is $1.35\,\text{kg}\,\text{m}^{-3}$. The temperature in kelvin and the pressure are both doubled. Calculate the new density of the gas.

30 Calculate the average speed (r.m.s.) of helium atoms at a temperature of 850 K. The molar mass of helium is $4.0\,\text{g}\,\text{mol}^{-1}$.

31 Show that the average (r.m.s.) speed of molecules of a gas of molar mass M (in $\text{kg}\,\text{mol}^{-1}$) kept at a temperature T is given by $c = \sqrt{\dfrac{3RT}{M}}$.

32 a Calculate the average random kinetic energy of a gas kept at a temperature of 300 K.
  b Determine the ratio of the average speeds (r.m.s. speeds) of two ideal gases of molar mass $4.0\,\text{g}\,\text{mol}^{-1}$ and $32\,\text{g}\,\text{mol}^{-1}$, which are kept at the same temperature.

3 THERMAL PHYSICS

Exam-style questions

1 Body X whose temperature is 0 °C is brought into thermal contact with body Y of equal mass and temperature 100 C. The only exchanges of heat that take place are between X and Y. The specific heat capacity of X is greater than that of Y. Which statement about the final equilibrium temperature T of the two bodies is correct?

    A $T = 50\,°C$
    B $0 < T < 50\,°C$
    C $100\,°C > T > 50\,°C$
    D Answer depends on value of mass

2 Energy is provided to a liquid at its boiling point at a rate of P joules per second. The rate at which mass is boiling away is μ kg per second. The specific latent heat of vaporisation of the liquid is

    A μP **B** $\dfrac{P}{\mu}$ **C** $\dfrac{\mu}{P}$ **D** $\dfrac{1}{\mu P}$

3 The following are all assumptions of the kinetic theory of gases, except which one?

    A The duration of a collision is very small compared to the time in between collisions.
    B The collisions are elastic.
    C The average kinetic energy of molecules is proportional to temperature.
    D The volume of molecules is negligible compared to the volume of the gas.

4 In the context of a fixed mass of an ideal gas, the graph could represent the variation of:

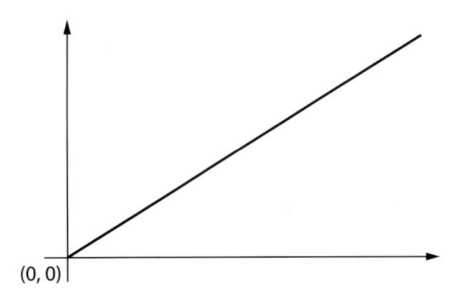

    A pressure with volume at constant temperature
    B volume with Celsius temperature at constant pressure
    C pressure with Celsius temperature at constant volume
    D pressure with inverse volume at constant temperature

5 The temperature of an ideal gas of pressure 200 kPa is increased from 27 °C to 54 °C at constant volume. Which is the best estimate for the new pressure of the gas?

    A 400 kPa   **B** 220 kPa   **C** 180 kPa   **D** 100 kPa

6 A container of an ideal gas that is isolated from its surroundings is divided into two parts. One part has double the volume of the other. The pressure in each part is p and the temperature is the same. The partition is removed. What is the pressure in the container now?

   A p **B** $2p$ **C** $\dfrac{3p}{2}$ **D** $4p$

7 Different quantities of two ideal gases X and Y are kept at the same temperature. Which of the following is a correct comparison of the average kinetic energy and internal energy of the two gases?

	Average kinetic energy	Internal energy
A	same	same
B	same	different
C	different	same
D	different	different

8 The temperature of an ideal gas is doubled. The average speed of the molecules increases by a factor of

   A $\sqrt{2}$ **B** 2   **C** $2\sqrt{2}$ **D** 4

9 Two ideal gases X and Y are kept at the same temperature and have equal moles. Gas X has molar mass μ_X and gas Y has molar mass μ_Y. The ratio of average speeds of the molecules of gas X to that of gas Y is

   A $\dfrac{\mu_X}{\mu_Y}$ **B** $\dfrac{\mu_Y}{\mu_X}$ **C** $\sqrt{\dfrac{\mu_X}{\mu_Y}}$ **D** $\sqrt{\dfrac{\mu_Y}{\mu_X}}$

10 The pressure of a fixed quantity of ideal gas is doubled. The average speed of the molecules is also doubled. The original density of the gas is ρ. Which is the new density of the gas?

   A $\dfrac{\rho}{2}$ **B** ρ **C** 2ρ **D** 4ρ

11 **a** Calculate the volume of 1 mol of helium gas (molar mass $4\,\text{g}\,\text{mol}^{-1}$) at temperature 273 K and pressure $1.0 \times 10^5\,\text{Pa}$. [2]

   b **i** Find out how much volume corresponds to each molecule of helium. [2]
   ii The diameter of an atom of helium is about 31 pm. Discuss whether or not the ideal gas is a good approximation to the helium gas in **a**. [2]

   c Consider now 1 mol of lead (molar mass $207\,\text{g}\,\text{mol}^{-1}$, density $11.3 \times 10^3\,\text{kg}\,\text{m}^{-3}$). How much volume corresponds to each atom of lead? [3]

   d Find the ratio of these volumes (helium to lead) and hence determine the order of magnitude of the ratio: separation of helium atoms to separation of lead atoms. [2]

12 a Define what is meant by **specific heat capacity** of a substance. [1]

b Consider two metals that have different specific heat capacities. The energies required to increase the temperature of 1 mol of aluminium and 1 mol of copper by the same amount are about the same. Yet the specific heat capacities of the two metals are very different. Suggest a reason for this. [2]

A hair dryer consists of a coil that warms air and a fan that blows the warm air out. The coil generates thermal energy at a rate of 600 W. Take the density of air to be $1.25\,\text{kg}\,\text{m}^{-3}$ and its specific heat capacity to be $990\,\text{J}\,\text{kg}^{-1}\,\text{K}^{-1}$. The dryer takes air from a room at 20 °C and delivers it at a temperature of 40 °C.

c What mass of air flows through the dryer per second? [2]

d What volume of air flows per second? [1]

e The warm air makes water in the hair evaporate. If the mass of the hair is 180 g, calculate how long it will take to dry the hair assuming that heat extracted at a rate of 750 W. (The heat required to evaporate 1 g of water at 40 °C is 2200 J.) [2]

13 The graph shows the variation with time of the speed of an object of mass 8.0 kg that has been dropped (from rest) from a certain height.

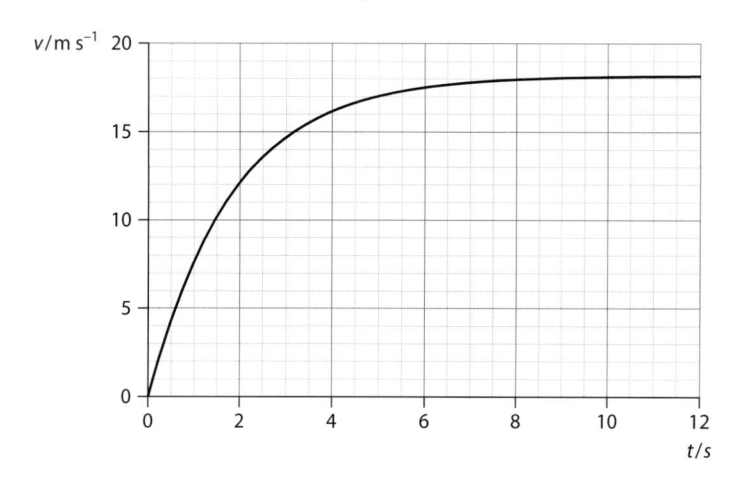

The body hits the ground 12 seconds later. The specific heat capacity of the object is $320\,\text{J}\,\text{kg}^{-1}\,\text{K}^{-1}$.

a i Explain how we may deduce that there must be air resistance forces acting on the object. [2]
   ii Estimate the height from which the object was dropped. [2]
   iii Calculate the speed the object would have had if there were no air resistance forces. [2]

b Estimate the change in temperature of the body from the instant it was dropped to just before impact. List any assumptions you make. [4]

14 A piece of tungsten of mass 50 g is placed over a flame for some time. The metal is then quickly transferred to a well-insulated aluminium calorimeter of mass 120 g containing 300 g of water at 22 °C. After some time the temperature of the water reaches a maximum value of 31 °C.

  a State what is meant by the internal energy of a piece of tungsten. [1]

  b Calculate the temperature of the flame. You may use these specific heat capacities: water 4.2×10^3 J kg^{-1} K^{-1}, tungsten 1.3×10^2 J kg^{-1} K^{-1} and aluminum 9.0×10^2 J kg^{-1} K^{-1}. [3]

  c State and explain whether the actual flame temperature is higher or lower than your answer to **b**. [2]

15 a Describe what is meant by the internal energy of a substance. [1]

  b A student claims that the kelvin temperature of a body is a measure of its internal energy. Explain why this statement is not correct by reference to a solid melting. [2]

  c In an experiment, a heater of power 35 W is used to warm 0.240 kg of a liquid in an uninsulated container. The graph shows the variation with time of the temperature of the liquid.

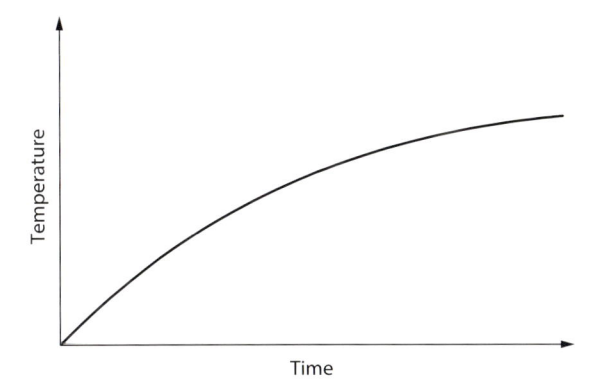

The liquid never reaches its boiling point.

Suggest why the temperature of the liquid approaches a constant value. [2]

  d After the liquid reaches a constant temperature the heater is switched off. The temperature of the liquid decreases at a rate of 3.1 K min^{-1}.

  Use this information to estimate the specific heat capacity of the liquid. [3]

16 The volume of air in a car tyre is about 1.50×10^{-2} m^3 at a temperature of 0.0 °C and pressure 250 kPa.

  a Calculate the number of molecules in the tyre. [2]

  b Explain why, after the car is driven for a while, the pressure of the air in the tyre will increase. [3]

  c Calculate the new pressure of the tyre when the temperature increases to 35 °C and the volume expands to 1.60×10^{-2} m^3. [1]

  d The car is parked for the night and the volume, pressure and temperature of the air in the tyre return to their initial values. A small leak in the tyre reduces the pressure from 250 kPa to 230 kPa in the course of 8 h. Estimate (stating any assumptions you make):
  i the average rate of loss of molecules (in molecules per second) [3]
  ii the total mass of air lost (take the molar mass of air to be 29 g mol^{-1}). [2]

3 THERMAL PHYSICS

4 Waves

Learning objectives

- Understand the conditions under which simple harmonic oscillations take place.
- Identify and use the concepts of period, frequency, amplitude, displacement and phase difference.
- Describe simple harmonic oscillations graphically.
- Describe the energy transformations taking place in oscillations.

4.1 Oscillations

This section deals with one of the most common phenomena in physics, that of oscillations. Airplane wings, suspension bridges, skyscrapers, tree branches and car suspension systems all oscillate. These diverse phenomena can be analysed by similar methods. Understanding oscillations is the first step in understanding the behaviour of waves.

Simple harmonic oscillations

Oscillations refer to back and forth motion. A typical example of an oscillation is provided by the simple pendulum, i.e. a mass attached to a vertical string. When the mass is displaced slightly sideways and then released, the mass begins to oscillate. In an oscillation the motion is repetitive, i.e. **periodic**, and the body moves back and forth around an equilibrium position.

A characteristic of oscillatory motion is the time taken to complete one full oscillation. This is called the **period**, T (Figure **4.1**). The **amplitude** of the oscillation is the maximum displacement from the equilibrium position.

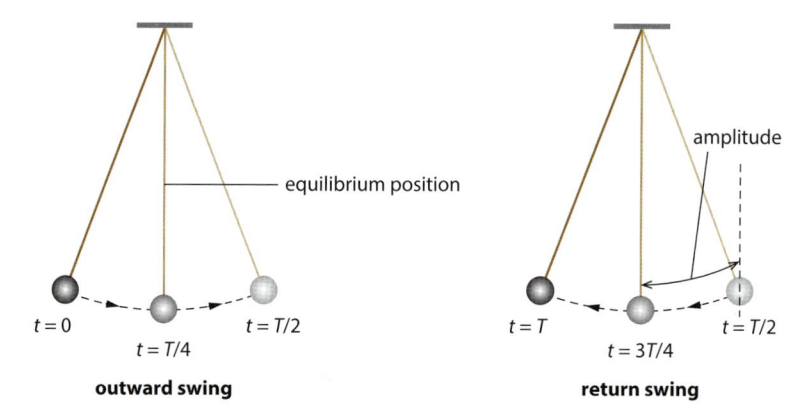

Figure 4.1 A full oscillation lasts for one period. At the end of a time interval equal to one period T, the system is in the same state as at the beginning of that time interval.

Examples of oscillations include:
- the motion of a mass at the end of a horizontal or vertical spring after the mass is displaced away from its equilibrium position
- the motion of a ball inside a round-bottomed bowl after it has been displaced away from its equilibrium position at the bottom of the bowl
- the vertical motion of a body floating in a liquid under the action of wind and waves (e.g. an iceberg)
- a tight guitar string that is set in motion by plucking the string
- the motion of a diving board as a diver prepares to dive
- the oscillation of an airplane wing
- the motion of a tree branch or a skyscraper under the action of the wind.

For a system to oscillate it is necessary to have a **restoring force**, i.e. a force that brings the system back towards its equilibrium position when the system is displaced away from equilibrium.

A very special periodic oscillation is called **simple harmonic motion (SHM)** and is the main topic of this section. The defining property of all simple harmonic oscillations is that the magnitude of the acceleration of the body that has been displaced away from equilibrium is proportional to the displacement and the direction of the acceleration is towards the equilibrium position. Mathematically these two conditions can be stated as:

$$a \propto -x$$

(Since $F = ma$, this is equivalent to saying that the restoring force is proportional to and opposite to the displacement.)

> The main characteristics of SHM are:
> - the period and amplitude are constant
> - the period is independent of the amplitude
> - the displacement, velocity and acceleration are sine or cosine functions of time.

Consider a block of mass m placed at the end of a horizontal spring. If we displace the block to the right and then release it, it will perform oscillations about its equilibrium position (the vertical dotted line) between the extreme positions of the second and last diagrams in Figure 4.2. The oscillations have amplitude A.

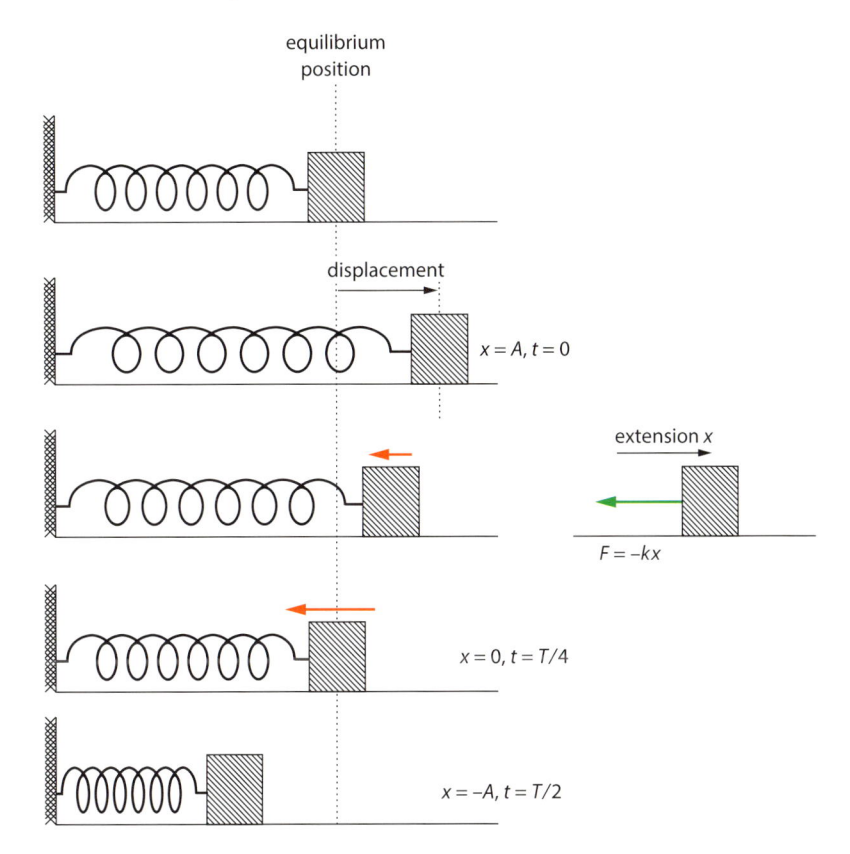

Oscillations in which the period is independent of the amplitude are called **isochronous**. Such oscillations are essential for accurate time-keeping. The oscillations of a simple pendulum are approximately isochronous, which means that the period is independent of the amplitude as long as the amplitude is small. While he was attempting to solve the non-isochronous aspect of the simple pendulum, the great Dutch scientist Christiaan Huygens (1629–1695) discovered important mathematical and physical aspects of the cycloid curve. The cycloid is the curve that is traced by a point on the rim of a wheel as the wheel turns.

Figure 4.2 The mass–spring system. The net force on the body is proportional to the displacement and opposite in direction.

4 WAVES

Consider the block when it is in an arbitrary position, as in the third diagram in Figure **4.2** on the previous page. At that position the extension of the spring is x. The magnitude of the tension F in the spring is therefore (by Hooke's law) equal to $F = kx$, where k is the spring constant. The tension force is directed to the left.

Taking **displacement** to the right of the equilibrium position as positive, then $ma = -kx$ since the tension force is directed to the left, and so is taken as negative. We can rewrite this equation as:

$$a = -\frac{k}{m} x$$

This tells us that the acceleration has a direction which is opposite to and a magnitude that is proportional to the displacement from equilibrium, so the oscillations will be simple harmonic (assuming there are no frictional forces). A graph of acceleration versus displacement gives a straight line through the origin with a negative slope, as shown in Figure **4.3**.

Therefore, in general, to check whether SHM will take place, we must check that:

1 there is a fixed equilibrium position
2 when the particle is moved away from equilibrium, the acceleration of the particle is both proportional to the amount of displacement and in the opposite direction to it.

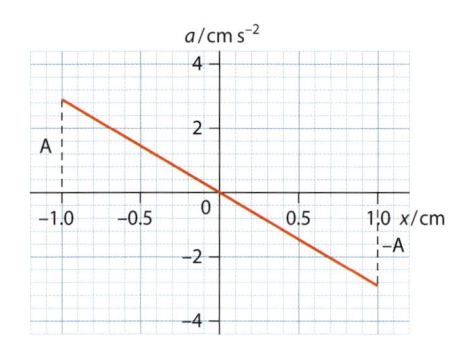

Figure 4.3 The graph of acceleration a versus displacement x is a straight line through the origin with a negative slope.

Let us have a look at Figure **4.4**. A body has been displaced from equilibrium and is then released. The figure shows how the displacement x varies with time t. We can extract lots of information from this graph. To begin with we see that the maximum displacement is 5.0 cm and so this is the amplitude of the motion: $x_0 = 5.0$ cm.

Next we see that the period is 2.0 s: we obtain this by looking at the time from one peak to the next. What about the velocity in this oscillation? We know that velocity is the gradient of a displacement–time graph. So we can say something about velocity by looking at the gradient of this graph at each point. At $t = 0$ the gradient is zero, so the velocity is also zero. As t increases the gradient becomes negative and at $t = 1.0$ s it becomes zero again. The gradient has its largest magnitude at $t = 0.5$ s. From $t = 1.0$ s to $t = 2.0$ s the gradient is positive. Its magnitude is largest at $t = 1.5$ s. Figure **4.5** shows the actual velocity plotted against time, which agrees with our qualitative analysis.

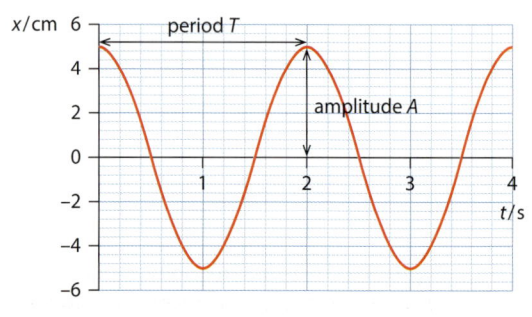

Figure 4.4 The variation of displacement x with time t in SHM.

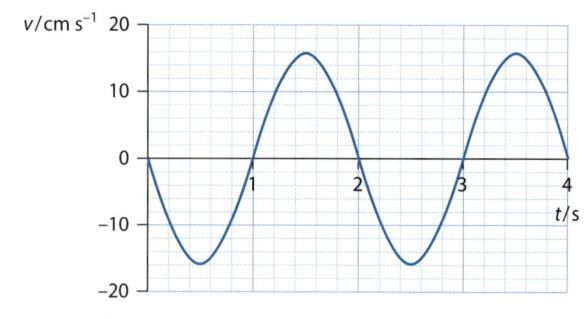

Figure 4.5 The variation of velocity v with time t in SHM.

In the same way, we can get information about acceleration by looking at the gradient of the velocity–time graph. But it is much simpler to recall that $a \propto -x$. This means that the acceleration–time graph has the opposite shape to the displacement–time graph – the peaks on the displacement–time graph become troughs on the acceleration–time graph (of course the scale on the vertical axis will be different). The actual acceleration–time graph is shown in Figure **4.6**. Figure **4.7** shows all three graphs together.

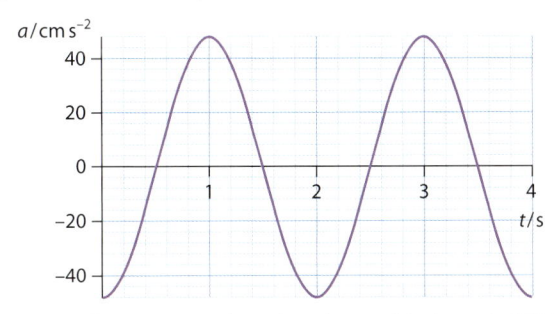

Figure 4.6 The variation of acceleration *a* with time *t* in SHM.

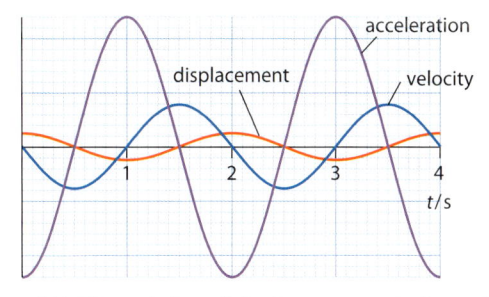

Figure 4.7 The variation of displacement, velocity and acceleration in SHM on the same axes.

We define the **frequency** *f* of the oscillations as the number of full oscillations per second. Since we have one oscillation in a time equal to the period *T*, the number of oscillations per second is $\frac{1}{T}$ and so:

$$f = \frac{1}{T}$$

The three curves in Figure **4.7** all have the same period, so all three curves also have the same frequency.

In Figure **4.4** the maximum displacement is at $t = 0$, so the displacement is a cosine function of time. However, the graph of displacement versus time does not have to be a cosine function. The three graphs of Figure **4.8** all show simple harmonic oscillations with the same amplitude and period (and hence frequency). There is however a **phase difference** between them. The blue curve is the red curve shifted forward by some amount. And the purple curve is the red curve shifted forward by an even greater amount. The amount by which one curve is shifted forward relative to another curve is called the phase difference between the two curves. Technically, the phase difference is described in terms of an angle φ, where:

$$\varphi = \frac{\text{shift}}{T} \times 360°$$

The unit of frequency is the inverse second, s^{-1}, which is called the hertz (Hz).

Relative to the red curve, the blue curve is shifted by 0.125 s and the period is 1.00 s, so the phase difference is:

$$\varphi = \frac{0.125}{1.00} \times 360° = 45° \text{ (or } \frac{\pi}{4} \text{ radians)}$$

Relative to the purple curve, the purple curve is shifted by 0.250 s and the period is again 1.00 s, so the phase difference is:

$$\varphi = \frac{0.250}{1.00} \times 360° = 90° \text{ (or } \frac{\pi}{2} \text{ radians)}$$

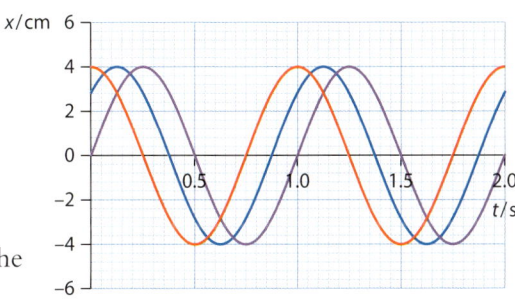

Figure 4.8 Three graphs of simple harmonic oscillations with a phase difference between them.

4 WAVES

Worked examples

4.1 State and explain whether graphs I, II and III in Figure 4.9 represent simple harmonic oscillations.

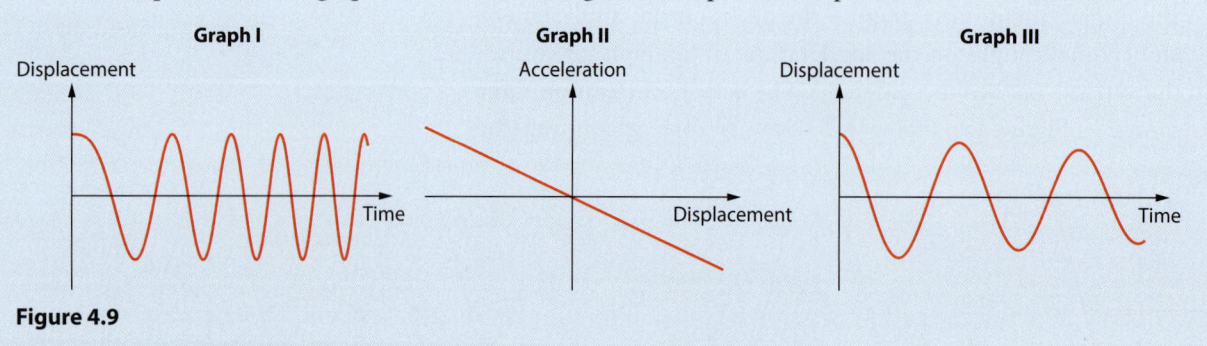

Figure 4.9

Graph I does not show SHM, since the period does not stay constant as time goes on. Graph II does, since the acceleration is proportional and opposite to displacement (straight-line graph through origin with negative slope). Graph III does not, since the amplitude does not stay constant.

4.2 The graph in Figure 4.10 shows the displacement of a particle from a fixed equilibrium position.

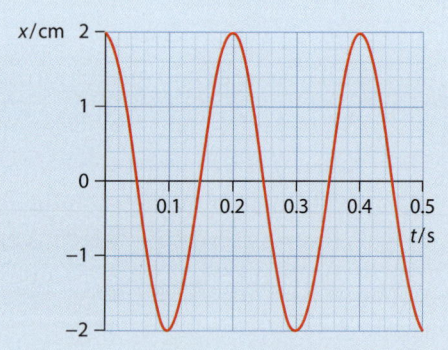

Figure 4.10 Graph showing the variation with time of the displacement of a particle performing SHM.

  a Use the graph to determine the period of the motion.
  b On a copy of the graph, mark:
   i a point where the velocity is zero (label this with the letter Z)
   ii a point where the velocity is positive and has the largest magnitude (label this with the letter V)
   iii a point where the acceleration is positive and has the largest magnitude (label this with the letter A).

a The period is read off the graph as $T = 0.20$ s.

b i The velocity is zero at any point where the displacement is at a maximum or a minimum.
  ii For example at $t = 0.15$ s.
  iii For example at $t = 0.10$ s or $t = 0.30$ s.

Energy in simple harmonic motion

Consider again a particle at the end of a horizontal spring. Let the extension of the spring be x at a particular instant of time, and let the velocity of the particle be v at that time. The system has elastic potential energy and kinetic energy, Figure **4.11**.

The total energy of the system is then:

$$E = E_P + E_K$$

In the absence of frictional and other resistance forces, this total energy is conserved, and so E = constant.

The maximum velocity is achieved when $x = 0$, i.e. as the mass moves past its equilibrium position. Here there is no extension, so the elastic potential energy is zero. At the extremes of the motion, $x = \pm A$ and $v = 0$, so the kinetic energy is zero. Thus at $x = \pm A$ the system has elastic potential energy only, and at $x = 0$ it has kinetic energy only. At intermediate points the system has both forms of energy: elastic potential energy and kinetic energy. During an oscillation, we therefore have **transformations** from one form of energy into another. This allows us to write:

$$E = E_P + E_K = (E_K)_{max} = (E_P)_{max}$$

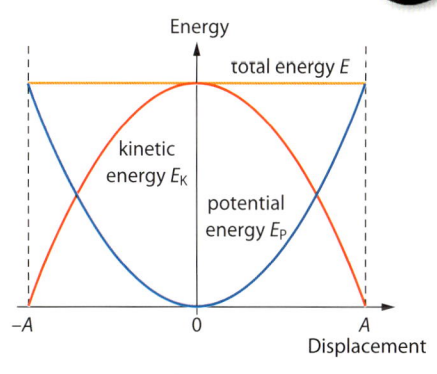

Figure 4.11 Graphs showing the variation with displacement of the potential energy and kinetic energy of a particle on a spring. The total energy is a horizontal straight line.

Worked example

4.3 The graph in Figure **4.12** shows the variation with displacement of the kinetic energy of a particle of mass 0.40 kg performing SHM at the end of a spring.
  a Use the graph to determine:
   i the total energy of the particle
   ii the maximum speed of the particle
   iii the amplitude of the motion
   iv the potential energy when the displacement is 2.0 cm.
  b On a copy of the axes, draw the variation with displacement of the potential energy of the particle.

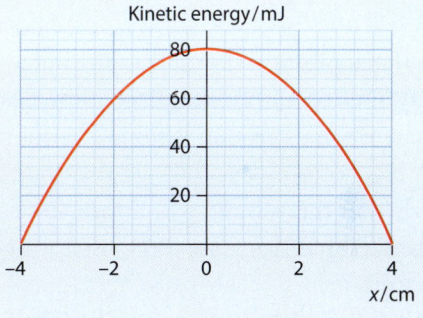

Figure 4.12 Graph showing the variation with displacement of the kinetic energy of a particle.

a i The total energy is equal to the maximum kinetic energy, i.e. 80 mJ.
 ii The maximum speed is found from:

$$\tfrac{1}{2} m v_{max}^2 = E_{max}$$

$$v_{max}^2 = \frac{2 E_{max}}{m}$$

$$v_{max} = \sqrt{\frac{2 \times 80 \times 10^{-3}}{0.40}}$$

$$v_{max} = 0.63 \text{ m s}^{-1}$$

 iii The amplitude is 4.0 cm.
 iv When $x = 2.0$ cm, the kinetic energy is 60 mJ and so the potential energy is 20 mJ.

b The graph is an inverted parabola as the blue curve in Figure **4.11**.

Oscillations and time

The measurement of time depends on regular oscillations. In early time-keeping devices the oscillations were mechanical, for example the swinging of a simple pendulum in a clock. Now they are electrical oscillations in electronic circuits. The need for internationally accepted measures of time is essential for communications, travel, electricity supply and practically all other aspects of modern life.

Nature of science

In real life we observe many oscillations for which the period is not independent of amplitude, for example the waving of a branch in the wind or the bouncing of a ball released above the ground. These do not obey the simple SHM equations in this section. But the general principles of physics we have met in this section govern many oscillations in the world about us, from water waves in the deep ocean to the vibration of a car's suspension system. The idea of the simple harmonic oscillator and the mathematics of SHM give physicists powerful tools to describe all periodic oscillations.

Test yourself

1 State what is meant by: **a** oscillation and **b** simple harmonic oscillation.
2 A ball goes back and forth along a horizontal floor, bouncing off two vertical walls. Suggest whether this motion is an example of an oscillation. If yes, state if the oscillation is simple harmonic.
3 A ball bounces vertically off the floor. Suggest whether this motion is an example of an oscillation. If yes, state if the oscillation is simple harmonic.
4 The graph shows the variation with displacement of the acceleration of a particle that is performing oscillations.

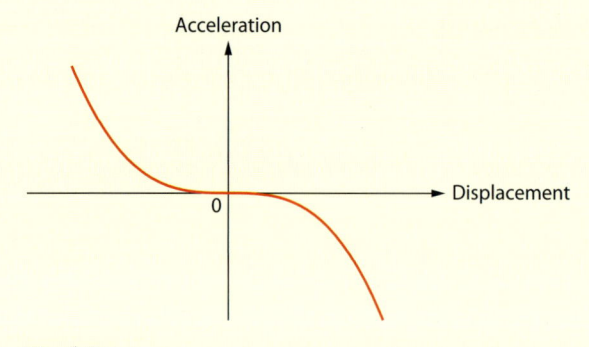

Explain:
a how it is known that the particle is performing oscillations
b why the oscillations are not simple harmonic.

5 The graph shows the variation with time of kinetic energy of a particle that is undergoing simple harmonic oscillations.

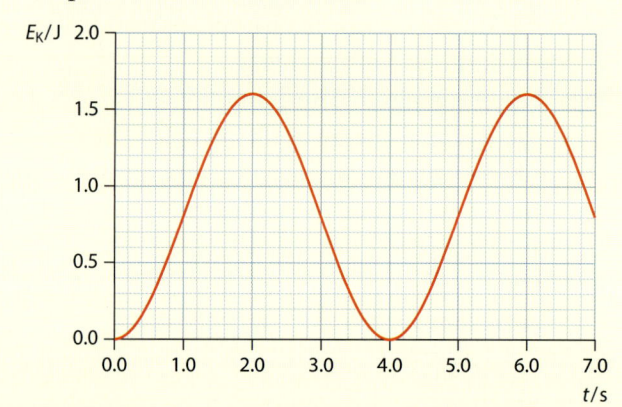

a Use the graph to calculate the period of oscillation.
b Draw a graph to show the variation with time of the potential energy.

4.2 Travelling waves

This section introduces waves and wave motion. All music (and all noise), the heating of the Earth by the Sun and the motion of electrons inside atoms can be analysed in the same way using the language and physics of waves. There are three large classes of wave: mechanical waves (e.g. sound), electromagnetic waves (e.g. light) and matter waves (e.g. electron motion in atoms).

Learning objectives

- Describe waves and wave motion.
- Identify wavelength, frequency and period from graphs of displacement against distance or time.
- Solve problems with wavelength, frequency, period and wave speed.
- Describe the motion of a particle in a medium through which a wave travels.
- Classify waves as transverse and longitudinal.
- Describe the nature of electromagnetic waves.
- Describe the nature of sound waves.

What is a wave?

If we take the free end of a taut, horizontal rope and we give it a sudden up and down jerk, a **pulse** will be produced that will travel down the length of the rope at a certain speed (Figure 4.13).

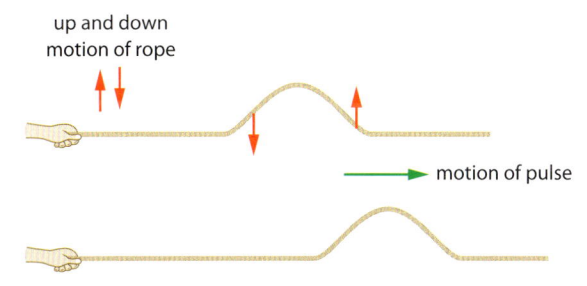

Figure 4.13 A pulse on a taut rope. The rope itself moves up and down. What moves to the right is the pulse.

The upward force, due to the hand, forces a section of the rope to move up. Because of the tension in the rope, this section pulls the section in front of it upwards. In this way the pulse moves forward. In the meantime the hand has moved down, forcing sections of the rope to return to their horizontal equilibrium position. Neighbouring sections again do the same because of the tension in the rope. If the motion of the hand holding the free end is continuous then a **wave** is established on the rope. Figure 4.14 shows two complete oscillations travelling down the length of the rope.

Now if the right end of the rope is attached to a body that is free to move, the body will move when the wave gets to it. This means that the wave transfers energy and momentum. So we can define a wave as follows:

> A wave is a disturbance that travels in a medium (which can be a vacuum in the case of electromagnetic waves) transferring energy and momentum from one place to another. The direction of propagation of the wave is the direction of energy transfer. There is no large-scale motion of the medium itself as the wave passes through it.

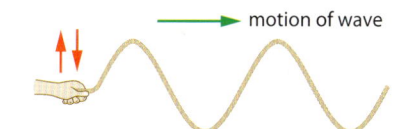

Figure 4.14 A continuous wave travelling along the rope.

The length of a complete oscillation is known as the **wavelength** of the wave. The symbol for wavelength is λ. It is also the distance from **crest** to crest or **trough** to trough (Figure 4.15). (A crest is the highest point on the wave and a trough the lowest.)

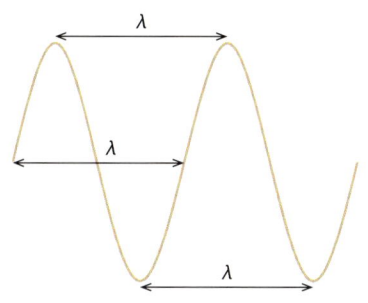

Figure 4.15 Three distances that all give the wavelength.

4 WAVES 153

Notice that the concepts of frequency and period are the same as those we met in Subtopic **4.1** on oscillations.

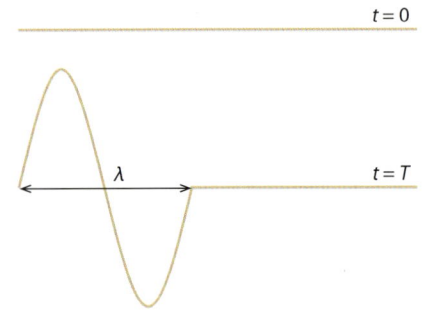

Figure 4.16 In a time of one period the wave has moved forward a distance of one wavelength.

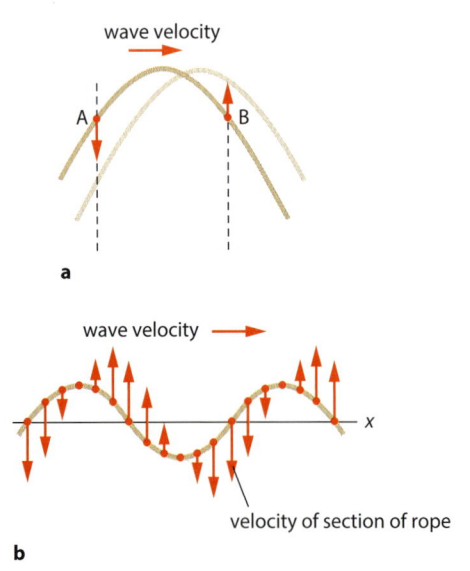

Figure 4.17 a The shape of the rope at two slightly different times. **b** Velocity vectors for various points on the rope at a given instant of time. You should be able to verify this diagram by drawing an identical wave on top of this one, but displaced slightly to the right.

The time to create one complete oscillation is known as the **period** of the wave. The symbol for period is T. If the period of wave is $T = 0.25\,\text{s}$, for example, then the number of oscillations produced in one second is 4. The number of oscillations per second is called the **frequency** f of the wave. In general if the period is T then the frequency is the inverse:

$$f = \frac{1}{T}$$

The unit of frequency is the inverse second, which is given the name hertz (Hz).

So suppose we have a wave on a rope, of wavelength λ, period T and frequency f. Figure **4.16** shows the rope at time zero when we have not yet produced any oscillations, and at time T where we have produced one oscillation. The wave has moved a distance equal to one wavelength in a time equal to one period and the speed of the wave is:

$$v = \frac{\text{distance for one oscillation}}{\text{time for one oscillation}} = \frac{\lambda}{T}$$

Since $f = \frac{1}{T}$ we also have that:

$$v = f\lambda$$

> The speed of the wave depends only on the properties of the medium and not on how it is produced.

Transverse waves

How do the particles of the medium in which a wave travels move? We have already seen that in the case of the wave on the rope the motion of the rope itself is at right angles to the direction of energy transfer. This is a typical example of a **transverse wave**. (Electromagnetic waves are also transverse – there is more on this in the section Electromagnetic waves.)

> We call a wave transverse if the displacement is at **right angles** to the direction of energy transfer.

Figure **4.17a** shows a snapshot of a rope with a wave travelling along its length. A very short time later the rope looks like the faint outline on the right: the wave has moved forward. Points on the rope move vertically up and down (along the dotted lines for the two points shown). Comparing the two snapshots allows us to find out how the points on the rope move. Figure **4.17b** shows the velocity vectors of various points on the rope at the instant of time the snapshot was taken. Notice that the arrows have different lengths. This is because every point on the rope performs simple harmonic oscillations and, as we learned in Subtopic **4.1**, the velocities in SHM are not constant.

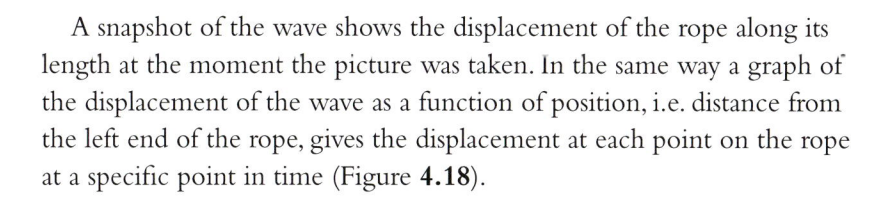

A snapshot of the wave shows the displacement of the rope along its length at the moment the picture was taken. In the same way a graph of the displacement of the wave as a function of position, i.e. distance from the left end of the rope, gives the displacement at each point on the rope at a specific point in time (Figure **4.18**).

> We get two important pieces of information from a displacement–distance graph: the first is the **amplitude** of the wave, i.e. the largest displacement, and the second is the **wavelength**.

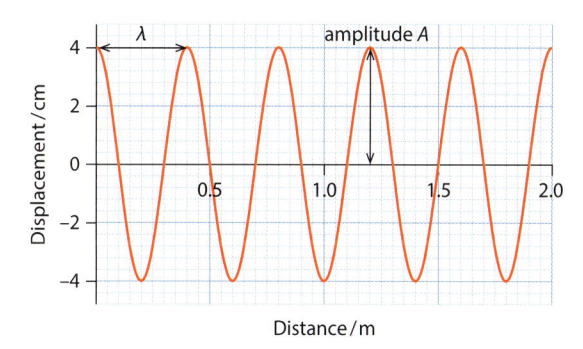

Figure 4.18 A graph of displacement versus position tells us the disturbance of any point on the rope at a specific moment in time.

For the wave of Figure **4.18** the amplitude is 4.0 cm. The wavelength is 0.40 m. This graph also tells us that at the point on the string that is 0.10 m from the rope's left end the displacement is zero at that specific instant of time. At that same instant of time at a point 1.0 m from the left end the displacement is −4.0 cm, etc. Thus, a graph of displacement versus position is like a photograph or a snapshot of the string taken at a particular time. If we take a second photograph of the string some time later, the string will look different because the wave has moved in the meantime.

There is a second type of graph that we may use to describe waves. This is a graph of displacement versus time: we imagine looking at one specific point on the rope and observe how the displacement of that point varies with time. So, for example, Figure **4.19** shows the variation with time of some point on a rope as the same wave as that in Figure **4.18** travels down the length of the rope.

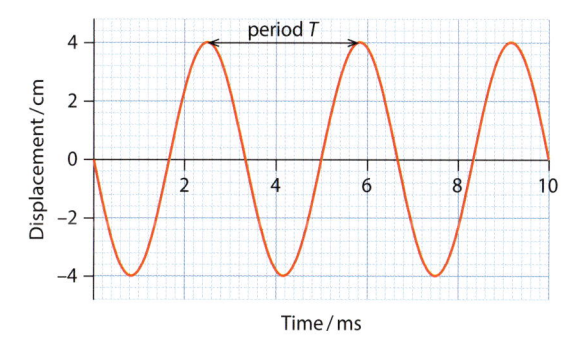

Exam tip
It is a common mistake to think that the amplitude is the crest to trough distance.

Figure 4.19 The same wave as in Figure **4.18** now showing the variation of the displacement of a specific point with time.

4 WAVES 155

We get two important pieces of information from a displacement–time graph: the first is the **amplitude** of the wave, i.e. the largest displacement, and the second is the **period**.

Exam tip
It is easier here to count three loops so that 3 periods are 10 ms. Also, make sure to check carefully the units on the axes – in this example time is in 'ms', not seconds.

We already know the amplitude: it is 4.0 cm from Figure **4.18**. The period is 3.33 ms. So the frequency is:

$$\frac{1}{3.33 \times 10^{-3}} = 300\,\text{Hz}$$

The speed of this wave is therefore $v = f\lambda = 0.40 \times 300 = 120\,\text{m s}^{-1}$.

Now suppose that we are told that Figure **4.19** shows the displacement of the point at $x = 0.10$ m (call it P). And suppose that the graph of Figure **4.18** is a snapshot of the wave at 0.0 ms. Which way is the wave travelling? Go to Figure **4.18** and find $x = 0.10$ m: this is point P. If you shift the wave slightly to the left (i.e. if the wave moves left) P gets a negative displacement. If you shift it to the right (i.e. if the wave moves right) P gets a positive displacement. Which is correct? Go to Figure **4.19**: a short time after $t = 0.0$ ms the displacement becomes negative. So the wave is travelling to the left.

Figure **4.20** (opposite) shows a sequence of pictures taken every 0.5 ms of a wave on a rope. As time passes the point Q moves at right angles to the direction of the wave. By joining the crests of the waves it is easy to see that they move forward with time. This is what is meant by the term **travelling wave**.

Longitudinal waves

Imagine that you push the left end of a slinky in and out as in Figure **4.21**. The coils of the slinky move in a direction that is parallel to that of the wave. As the hand moves to the right it forces coils to move forward, causing a **compression** (coils crowd together). As the hand moves to the left, coils right in front of it also move left, causing an **expansion** or **rarefaction** (coils move apart). All **longitudinal waves** require a medium in which the wave travels.

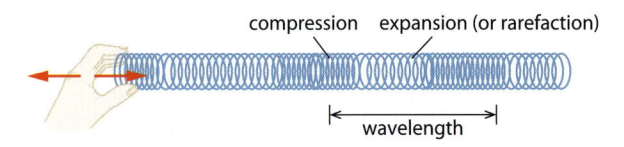

Figure 4.21 A longitudinal wave in which the medium moves parallel to the direction of energy transfer.

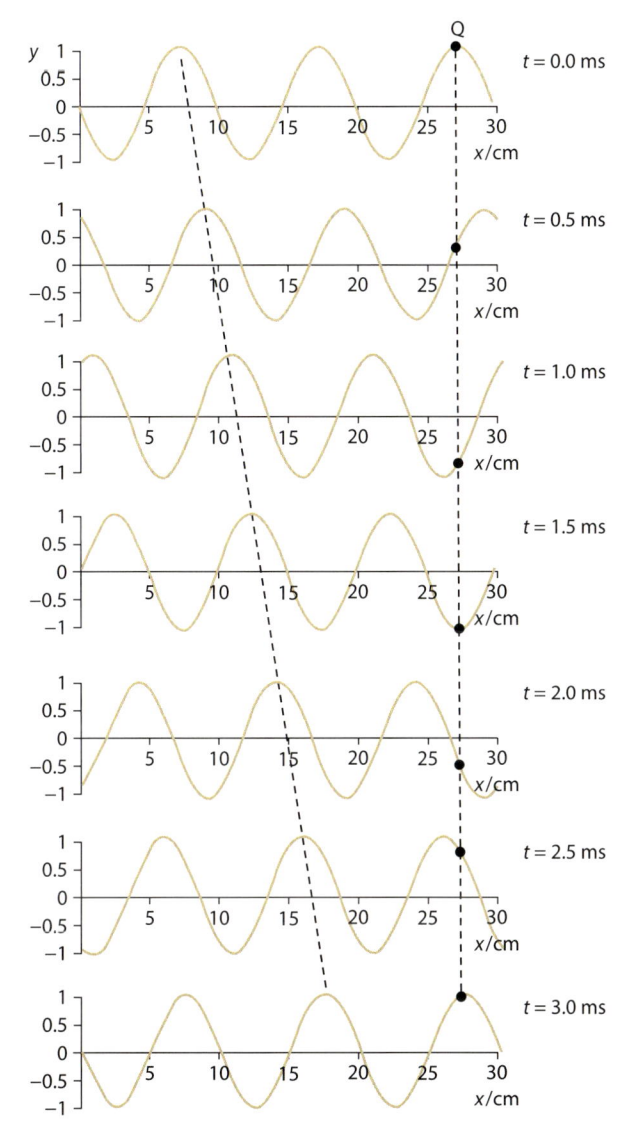

Figure 4.20 A travelling wave. At 3.0 ms the rope looks as it did at the beginning ($t=0$), so the period of the wave is 3.0 ms. The speed of the wave is 33.3 m s^{-1} (found by dividing the wavelength by the period) and the frequency is 333 Hz.

Sound waves are longitudinal waves that can travel in gases and liquids as well as solids. A sound wave consists of a series of compressions and rarefactions in the medium in which it is travelling. Figure **4.22** shows the compressions and rarefactions produced in the air by a loudspeaker.

> In a **longitudinal** wave the displacement is parallel to the direction of energy transfer.

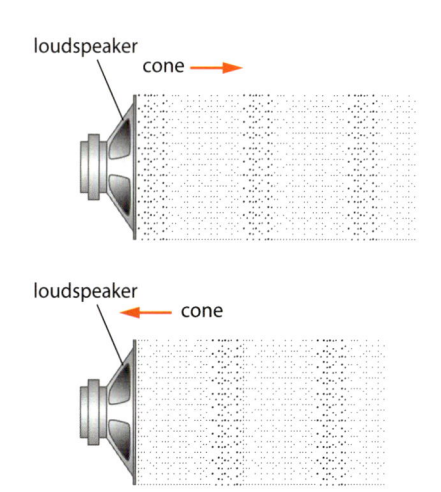

Figure 4.22 A vibrating loudspeaker produces compressions when the cone moves to the right and expansions when it moves to the left. These compressions and expansions move through air as a wave called sound.

4 WAVES 157

As with transverse waves, we can plot a graph of displacement versus distance along the wave. Figure **4.23** shows a row of air molecules equally spaced in the equilibrium position. The row below shows their displacement at a particular instant in time. The graph in Figure **4.23** shows the displacement y of the molecules against distance x at the same instant in time. The red arrows represent the displacement of the molecules. Molecules at $x = 0$, 2.0 and 4.0 cm have not moved ($y = 0$); those between $x = 0$ and 2.0 cm and between $x = 4.0$ and 5.0 cm have moved to the right ($y > 0$); and those between $x = 2.0$ and 4.0 cm have moved to the left ($y < 0$). The molecule at $x = 2.0$ cm is therefore at the centre of a **compression** (a region of higher than normal density), while that at $x = 4.0$ cm is at the centre of a **rarefaction** (a region of lower than normal density).

Exam tip
You cannot tell whether a wave is transverse or longitudinal by looking at displacement–distance graphs. The graphs look the same for both.

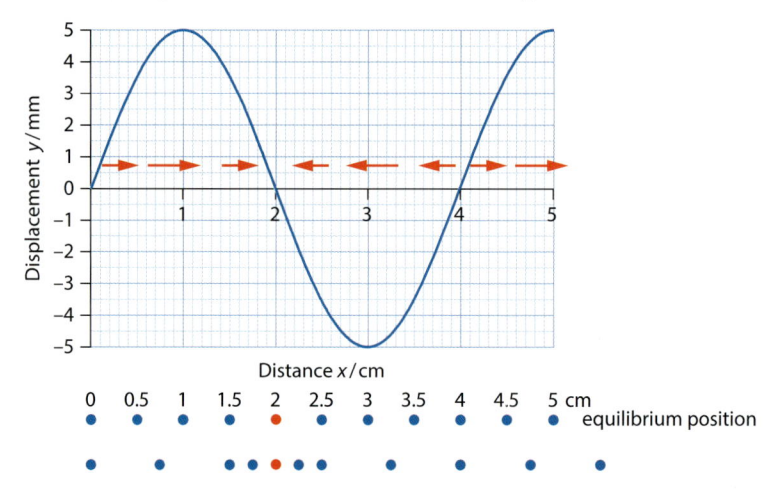

Figure 4.23 Molecules to the left of that at $x = 2.0$ cm move to the right, while the neighbours to the right move left. This means that the region at $x = 2.0$ is the centre of a compression.

Since a compression is a region where molecules crowd together, the pressure and density of the medium in a compression is higher than normal. To give an idea of the differences in pressure involved, a sound of frequency 1000 Hz can be heard by the human ear when the pressure of air at the eardrum exceeds atmospheric pressure by just 20 µPa. (Normal atmospheric pressure is 10^5 Pa.) The amplitude of oscillations for air molecules under these conditions is about 10^{-11} m, or a tenth of the diameter of the hydrogen atom! In a rarefaction the reverse is true, with the molecules moving farther apart so that the density and pressure are a bit less than normal.

Electromagnetic waves

Each and every one of us is irradiated by **electromagnetic waves** (EM waves) from a myriad of sources: radio and TV stations, mobile phone and base station antennas, from doctors' and dentists' X-ray machines, the Sun, computer screens, light bulbs, etc. It was the towering achievement of J.C. Maxwell (Figure **4.24**) in the mid-1800s to predict the existence of a new, special kind of wave – EM waves – of which visible light is a very small, but important, part. What Maxwell showed is that an oscillating electric

Figure 4.24 A young Maxwell at Trinity College, Cambridge.

field (see Topic 6) produces an oscillating magnetic field (see Topic 5) such that the two are at right angles to each other and both propagate in space at the speed of light (Figure 4.25).

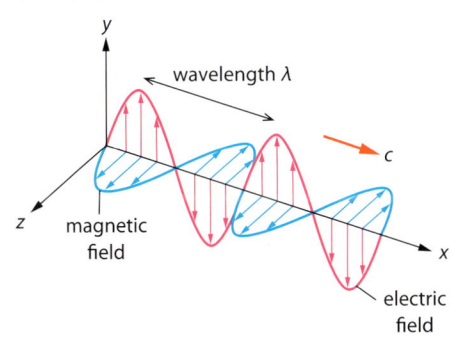

Figure 4.25 An EM wave propagating along the direction of the x-axis. The electric and magnetic fields are in phase, i.e. they have matching crests, troughs and zeroes. The two fields are at right angles to each other at all times.

The huge family of EM waves consists of many waves of different wavelength (and hence also frequency), as shown in Figure **4.26**.

What all EM waves have in common is that they move at the speed of light in a **vacuum**. That speed is (exactly) $c = 299\,792\,458\,\text{m s}^{-1}$ or approximately $3.00 \times 10^8\,\text{m s}^{-1}$. According to Einstein's relativity theory this is the limiting speed for anything moving through space. Maxwell's theory predicts that the speed of light is not affected by the speed of its source – a most curious fact. Einstein used this fact as one of the building blocks of his theory of relativity.

Since both the electric and the magnetic field making up the EM wave are at right angles to the direction of energy transfer of the wave, EM waves are transverse.

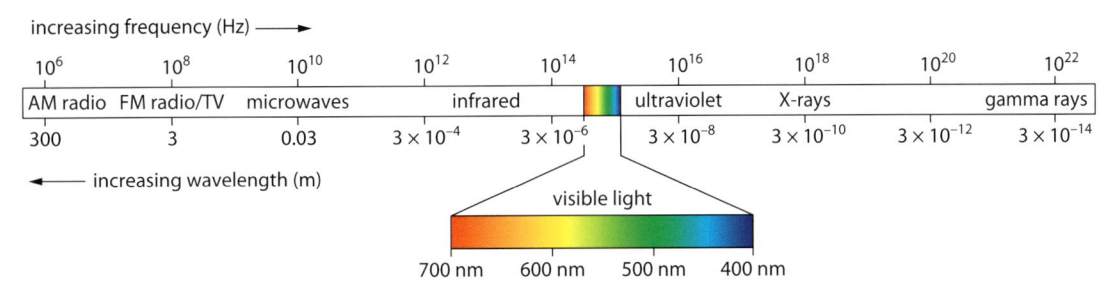

Figure 4.26 The electromagnetic spectrum

Maxwell's equations

$$\oint \boldsymbol{E} \cdot d\boldsymbol{A} = \frac{q}{\varepsilon_0}$$

$$\oint \boldsymbol{E} \cdot d\boldsymbol{l} = -\frac{d\Phi_m}{dt}$$

$$\oint \boldsymbol{B} \cdot d\boldsymbol{A} = 0$$

$$\oint \boldsymbol{B} \cdot d\boldsymbol{l} = \mu_0 I + \mu_0 \varepsilon_0 \frac{d\Phi_e}{dt}$$

4 WAVES

Worked examples

4.4 A radio station emits at a frequency of 90.8 MHz. What is the wavelength of the waves emitted?

The waves emitted are electromagnetic waves and move at the speed of light ($3 \times 10^8 \, m\,s^{-1}$). Therefore, from $c = f\lambda$ we find $\lambda = 3.3 \, m$.

4.5 A sound wave of frequency 450 Hz is emitted from **A** and travels towards **B**, a distance of 150 m away. How many wavelengths fit in the distance from **A** to **B**?

(Take the speed of sound to be $341 \, m\,s^{-1}$.)

The wavelength is:

$$\lambda = \frac{341}{450}$$

$$\lambda = 0.758 \, m$$

Thus the number of wavelengths that fit in the distance 150 m is:

$$N = \frac{150}{0.758}$$

$N = 198$ wavelengths (approximately)

4.6 The noise of thunder is heard 3 s after the flash of lightning. How far away is the place where lightning struck?

(Take the speed of sound to be $340 \, m\,s^{-1}$.)

Light travels so fast that we can assume that lightning struck exactly when we see the flash of light. If thunder is heard 3 s later, it means that it took 3 s for sound to cover the unknown distance, d. Thus:

$$d = vt$$

$$d = 340 \times 3$$

$$d = 1020 \, m$$

4.7 Water wave crests in a lake are 5.0 m apart and pass by an anchored boat every 2.0 s. What is the speed of the water waves?

Use $v = f\lambda$. The wavelength is 5.0 m and the period is 2 s. So:

$$v = \frac{5.0}{2.0}$$

$$v = 2.5 \, m\,s^{-1}$$

Nature of science

Careful observations of the vibrations of a plucked violin string led the Swiss mathematician Bernoulli to find a way to describe the oscillation using mathematics. This was a simple setting – a single string fixed at both ends – and led to a simple solution. Scientists found similar patterns in more complex oscillations and waves in the natural world, but also differences in the way that waves propagated. By looking for trends and discrepancies in their models for different waves produced under different conditions, scientists developed wave equations that apply across many areas of physics.

? Test yourself

6 In football stadiums fans often create a 'wave' by standing up and sitting down again. Suggest factors that determine the speed of the 'wave'.

7 A number of dominoes are stood next to each other along a straight line. A small push is given to the first domino, and one by one the dominoes fall over.
   a Outline how this is an example of wave motion.
   b Suggest how the speed of the wave pulse could be increased.
   c Design an experiment in which this problem can be investigated.

8 By making suitably labelled diagrams explain the terms:
   a wavelength
   b period
   c amplitude
   d crest
   e trough.

9 a Explain, in the context of wave motion, what you understand by the term **displacement**.
   b Using your answer in **a**, explain the difference between longitudinal and transverse waves.
   c A rock thrown onto the still surface of a pond creates circular ripples moving away from the point of impact. Suggest why more than one ripple is created.
   d Why does the amplitude decrease as the ripple moves away from the centre?

10 The diagram shows three points on a string on which a transverse wave propagates to the right.

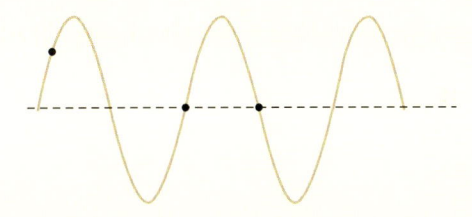

   a Indicate how these three points will move in the next instant of time.
   b How would your answers change if the wave were moving to the left?

11 The diagram shows a piece of cork floating on the surface of water when a wave travels through the water to the right. Copy the diagram, and add to it the position of the cork half a wave period later.

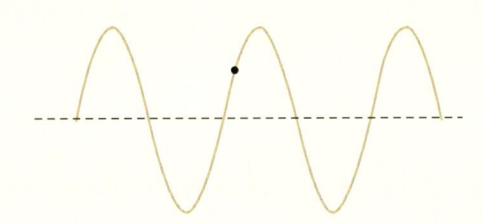

12 Calculate the wavelength that corresponds to a sound frequency of:
   a 256 Hz
   b 25 kHz.
   (Take the speed of sound to be 330 m s^{-1}.)

13 The graph shows the displacement y of the particles in a medium against position x when a longitudinal wave pulse travels through the medium from left to right with speed $1.0\,\mathrm{cm\,s^{-1}}$. This is the displacement at $t=0$.

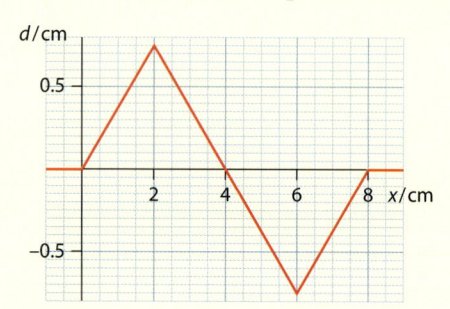

a State what is meant by a **longitudinal** wave pulse.

The diagram shows a line of nine molecules separated by 1.0 cm. The positions shown are the equilibrium positions of the molecules when no wave travels in the medium.

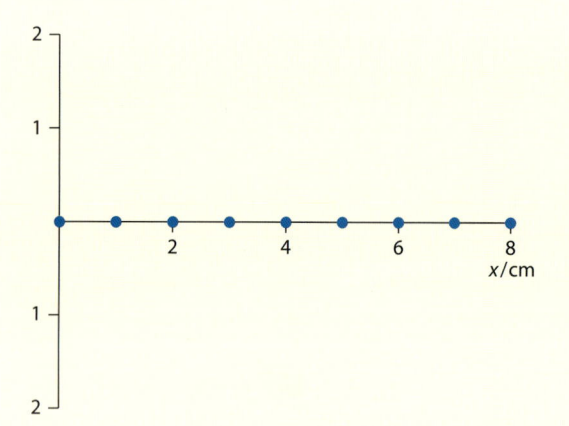

b i Copy the diagram. Immediately below the copied line draw another line to show the position of these molecules when the pulse travels through the medium at $t=0$.
  ii Indicate on the diagram the position of a compression.
c i Repeat b i to show the position of these molecules at $t=1.0\,\mathrm{s}$.
  ii Comment on the position of the compression at 1.0 s.

14 The graph shows the variation with distance x of the displacement y of air molecules as a sound wave travels to the right through air. Positive displacement means motion to the right. The speed of sound in air is $340\,\mathrm{m\,s^{-1}}$.

a Determine the frequency of the sound wave.
b State a distance x at which i a compression and ii a rarefaction occurs.

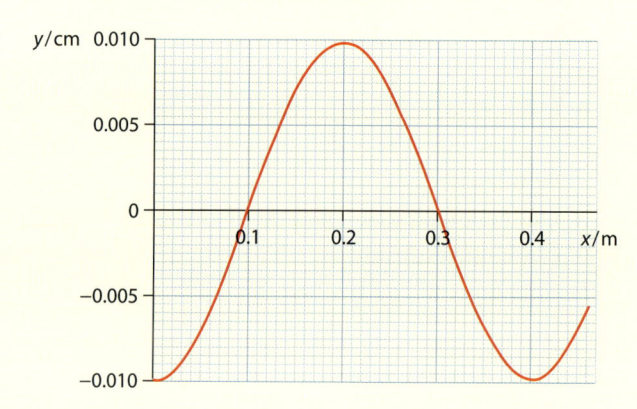

4.3 Wave characteristics

This section deals with ways to describe waves and the important principle of superposition. When two tennis balls collide they bounce off each other, but waves are different: they can go through each other without any 'memory' of a collision. Polarisation is a phenomenon that applies to transverse waves only. Light can be polarised, and so light is a transverse wave.

Learning objectives

- Describe waves in terms of wavefronts and rays.
- Solve problems using the concepts of intensity and amplitude and the inverse square law.
- Apply the principle of superposition to pulses and waves.
- Interpret diagrams of incident, reflected and transmitted beams in terms of polarisation.
- Solve problems with Malus' law.

Wavefronts and rays

Imagine waves on the surface of water approaching the shore (Figure 4.27). These waves are propagating in a horizontal direction. If we imagine vertical planes going through the crests of the waves, the planes will be normal to the direction of the wave. These planes are called **wavefronts**. Lines at right angles to the wavefronts show the direction of wave propagation – these are called **rays** (Figure 4.28).

> A **wavefront** is a surface through crests and normal to the direction of energy transfer of the wave. Lines in the direction of energy transfer of the wave (and hence normal to the wavefronts) are called **rays**.

(A wavefront is properly defined through the concept of phase difference: all points on a wavefront have zero phase difference.)

Now imagine the waves on the surface of water caused by a stone dropped in a pool of water. These waves radiate out across the water surface from the point of impact. In this case the wavefronts are cylindrical surfaces (Figure 4.29a).

A source that emits waves in all directions is called a point source. The wavefronts from a point source are spherical (Figure 4.29b).

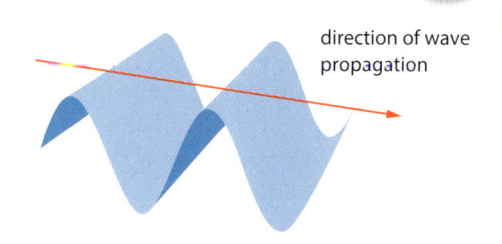

Figure 4.27 A two-dimensional wave.

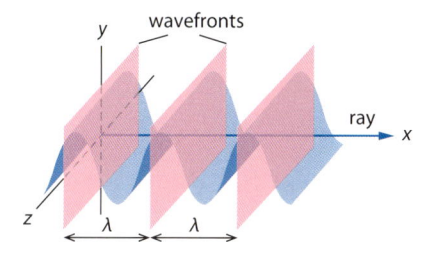

Figure 4.28 Surfaces through crests and normal to the direction of energy propagation of the wave are called wavefronts. Rays are mathematical lines perpendicular to the wavefronts and give the direction of energy transfer.

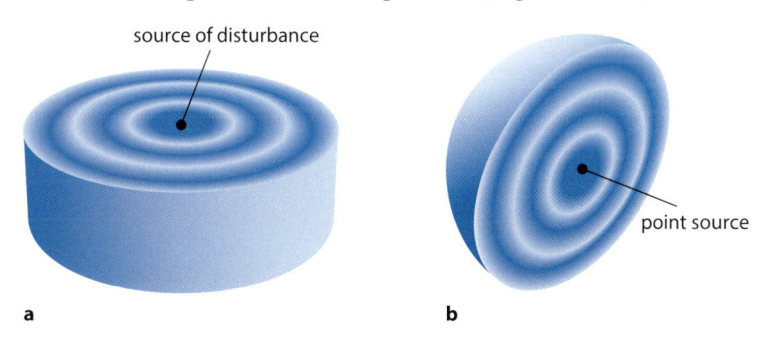

Figure 4.29 Example of cylindrical and spherical wavefronts. **a** The cylinders go through the crests and are normal to the plane of the paper. **b** The wavefronts from a point source radiate in all directions. For clarity, only half of each spherical wavefront is shown.

Amplitude and intensity

A wave carries energy and the rate at which the energy is carried is the power P of the wave. Thus a 60 W light bulb radiates energy in all directions such that 60 J of energy are emitted every second. When some of this power is incident on an area a we define the **intensity** to be $I = \dfrac{P}{a}$. The unit of intensity is $W\,m^{-2}$.

4 WAVES 163

If a point source of power P radiates equally in all directions, then the intensity at a distance x from the source is given by:

$$I = \frac{P}{4\pi x^2}$$

since the power is distributed over the surface area of a sphere of radius x, which is $4\pi x^2$. This can also be expressed as an **inverse square law** relationship:

$$I \propto x^{-2}$$

The intensity at a particular point is related to the amplitude A of the wave at that point. Since the energy of a wave is proportional to the square of the amplitude, we can write:

$$I \propto A^2$$

So, doubling the amplitude of a wave increases the energy carried by a factor of $2^2 = 4$.

Worked examples

4.8 The power radiated by the Sun is 3.9×10^{26} W. The distance between the Sun and the Earth is 1.5×10^{11} m.
  a Calculate the intensity of the Sun's radiation at the upper atmosphere of the Earth.
  b On a clear summer day 70% of this amount arrives at the surface of the Earth. Calculate how much energy is received by an area of $0.50\,m^2$ in 1 hour.

Applying the formula for intensity gives:

$$I = \frac{3.9 \times 10^{26}}{4\pi \times (1.5 \times 10^{11})^2} = 1379 \approx 1.4\,kW\,m^{-2}$$

$P = IA$ and so:

$P = 0.70 \times 1379 \times 0.50 = 482.65$ W

The energy in 1 hour is therefore $E = 482.65 \times 60 \times 60 = 1.7 \times 10^6$ J

4.9 A stone dropped in still water creates circular ripples that move away from the point of impact, Z. The height of the ripple at point P is 2.8 cm and at point Q it is 1.5 cm. Calculate the ratio of the energy carried by the wave at P to that at Q.

Let E_P be the energy carried by the wave at point P and E_Q be the energy carried by the wave at point Q.

The energy carried by the wave is proportional to the square of the amplitude. Hence:

$$\frac{E_P}{E_Q} = \left(\frac{2.8}{1.5}\right)^2 \approx 3.5$$

Imagine a white ball moving to the right colliding elastically with a heavier stationary black ball. The white ball will bounce back and the black ball will start moving to the right. If you try to solve this problem in mechanics by applying the laws of conservation of energy and momentum to the problem you will find that there is another solution. The equations say that the black ball stays where it is and the white ball goes straight through unaffected. In mechanics we reject this solution as unphysical but this is exactly what happens when pulses collide. The laws of physics apply equally to particles as they do to waves and do not distinguish between the two!

The principle of superposition

Suppose that two pulses are produced in the same rope and are travelling towards each other from opposite ends. Something truly amazing happens when the two pulses meet. Figure **4.30** shows what happens in a sequence of pictures. For simplicity we have drawn idealised square pulses.

The disturbance gets bigger when the two pulses meet but subsequently the two pulses simply 'go through each other' with no 'memory' of what happened. You should contrast this with what happens in the motion of material particles: when two balls collide they bounce off each other.

What happens when two (or more) pulses meet at some point in space is described by the principle of **superposition**, which states that:

> When two or more waves of the same type arrive at a given point in space at the same time, the displacement of the medium at that point is the algebraic sum of the individual displacements. So if y_1 and y_2 are individual displacements, then at the point where the two meet the total displacement has the value:
> $y = y_1 + y_2$

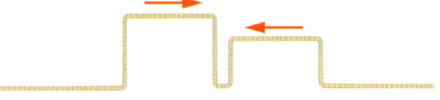

Note the word 'algebraic'. This means that if one pulse is 'up' and the other is 'down', then the resulting displacement is the difference of the individual ones.

Let us look at Figure **4.30b** in detail. In Figure **4.30b** the two pulses are partially overlapping – Figure **4.31** shows both of them separately (the pulse moving toward the right is drawn in dark blue and the one moving to the left in pale blue). There are five regions to consider. In region **a**, both pulses are zero. In region **b**, the dark blue pulse is non-zero and the

a The pulses are approaching each other.

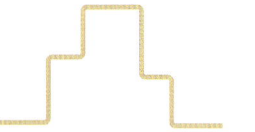

b The pulses are beginning to overlap.

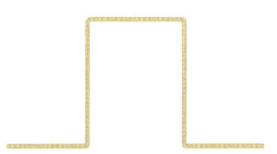

c The overlap is complete; the pulses are on top of each other.

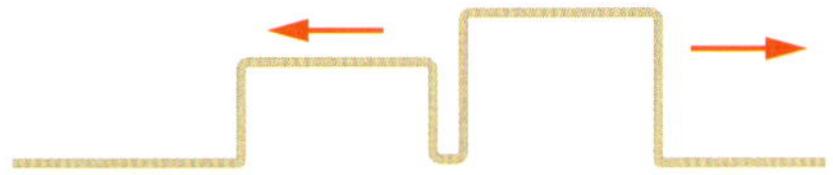

d The pulses move through each other.

Figure 4.30 The superposition of two positive pulses.

Figure 4.31 The situation in Figure **4.30b** analysed.

4 WAVES 165

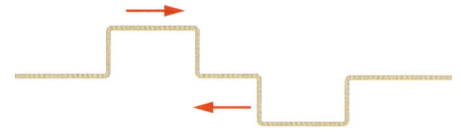

a Positive and negative pulses are approaching each other.

b The positive and negative pulses momentarily cancel each other out when they totally overlap.

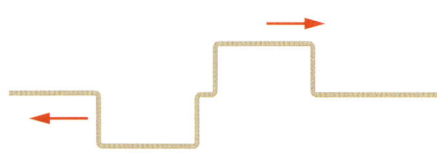

c The positive and negative pulses move through each other.

Figure 4.32 The superposition of a positive and a negative pulse.

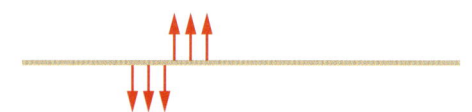

Figure 4.33 Parts of the rope are moving when the two pulses cancel each other out.

pale blue is zero. In region **c**, both are non-zero. In region **d**, the dark blue is zero and the pale blue is not. In region **e**, both are zero. The shape of the resulting pulse is simply the sum of the two pulses. Thus, in region **a**, we get zero. In region **b**, we get the height of just the dark blue pulse. In region **c**, we get a pulse whose height is the sum of the heights of the dark blue and pale blue pulses. In region **d**, the height equals the height of just the grey pulse. In region **e**, we get zero.

Figure 4.32 shows the superposition of a positive and a negative pulse on the same rope. In Figure 4.32a the positive and negative pulses are approaching each other. In Figure 4.32b the positive and negative pulses momentarily cancel each other out when they totally overlap. The pulses move through each other, and Figure 4.32c shows the positive and negative pulses continuing along the rope.

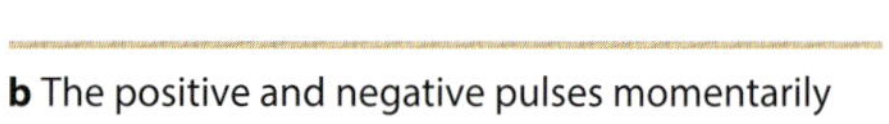

At that instant when there is complete cancellation of the two pulses, the rope looks flat but it is moving as shown in Figure 4.33.

Reflection of pulses

What happens when a pulse created in a rope with one end fixed approaches that fixed end? Consider the pulse of Figure 4.34a. The instant the pulse hits the fixed end, the rope attempts to move the fixed end upward: that is, it exerts an upward force on the fixed end. By Newton's third law, the wall will then exert an equal but opposite force on the rope. This means that a displacement will be created in the rope that will be negative and will start moving towards the left.

The pulse has been reflected by the wall and has been inverted. This is the same as saying that the wave experiences a phase change of 180° when reflected.

If the end of the rope is not fixed but free to move (imagine that the end of the rope is now tied to a ring that can slide up and down a vertical pole), the situation is different (Figure 4.34b). As the pulse arrives at the ring it pulls it upwards. Eventually the ring falls back down and in so doing creates a pulse moving to the left that is not inverted, i.e. there is no phase change.

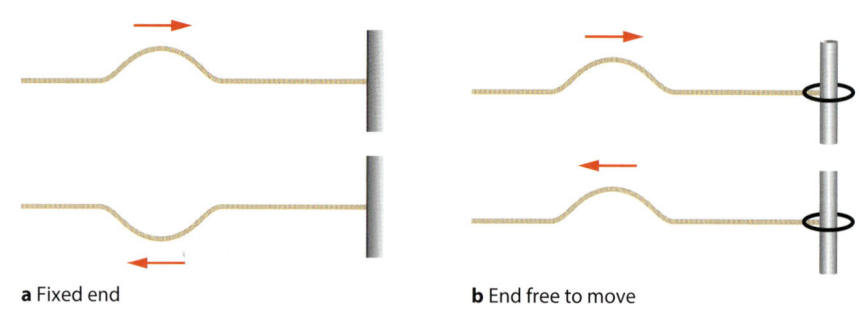

a Fixed end   **b** End free to move

Figure 4.34 Reflection of a pulse from **a** a fixed end and **b** a free end. Notice the inversion in the case of the fixed end.

Worked example

4.10 Use the results about pulses reflecting from fixed and free ends to predict what happens when:
  a a pulse in a heavy rope encounters a light rope (Figure **4.35a**)
  b a pulse in a light rope encounters a heavy rope (Figure **4.35b**).

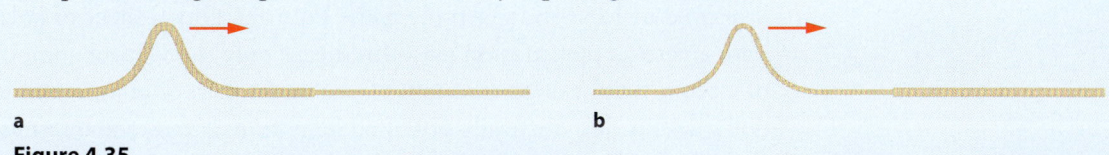

Figure 4.35

a With the light rope to the right, the situation is similar to a pulse in a rope approaching a free end. So the reflected pulse will not be inverted.

b With the heavy rope to the right, the situation is similar to a pulse in a rope approaching a fixed end. So the reflected pulse will be inverted.

Notice that in both cases, there will a pulse **transmitted** into the rope to the right.

Polarisation

Like all other electromagnetic waves, visible light is a transverse wave in which an electric field and a magnetic field at right angles to each other propagate along a direction that is normal to both fields.

Figure **4.36a** shows light in which the electric field oscillates on a vertical plane. We say that the light is vertically polarised. In Figure **4.36b** the electric field oscillates on a horizontal plane and we have horizontally polarised light.

> An electromagnetic wave is said to be **plane polarised** if the electric field oscillates on the **same** plane.

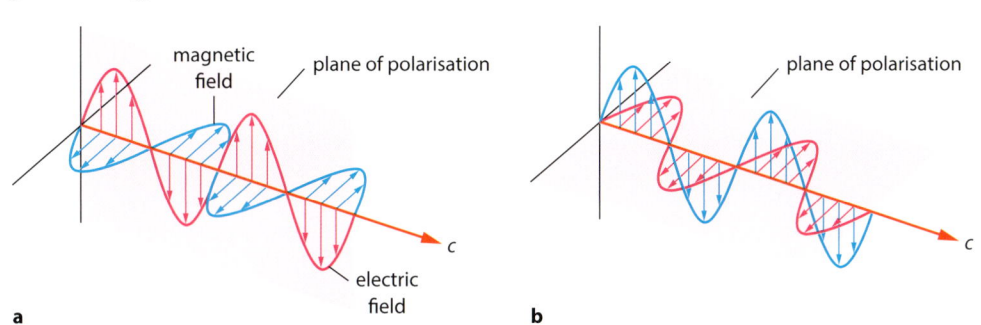

Figure 4.36 An EM wave that is **a** vertically polarised and **b** horizontally polarised.

Individual emitters of light emit polarised light waves. But in a large collection of individual emitters the plane of polarisation of one emitter is different from that of another. The result is that a given ray of light may consist of a huge number of differently polarised waves and so we call this light **unpolarised**. Most of the light around us, for example light from the Sun or from a light bulb, is unpolarised light. We show polarised and unpolarised light as in Figure **4.37**.

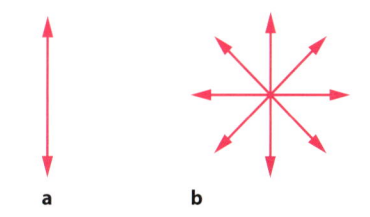

Figure 4.37 Electric field vectors of **a** polarised and **b** unpolarised light. Both waves are propagating at right angles to the electric field, i.e. into the page.

4 WAVES 167

Unpolarised light can be polarised by passing it through a **polariser**. A polariser is a sheet of material with a molecular structure that only allows a specific orientation of the electric field to go through (Figure **4.38**). The most common polariser is a plastic invented by Edwin Land in 1928, when he was a 19-year-old undergraduate at Harvard. The material was improved in 1938 and given the name Polaroid. Thus a sheet of Polaroid with a vertical transmission axis (this means only the vertical components of electric fields can go through) placed in the path of unpolarised light will transmit only vertically polarised light. In diagrams, the transmission axis of the polariser is indicated with a line.

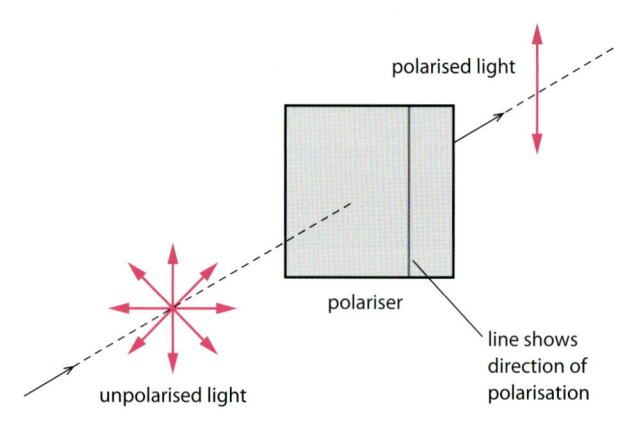

Figure 4.38 This polariser only allows components of electric fields parallel to the vertical transmission axis to go through. The light transmitted by this polariser is vertically polarised light.

Malus's law

Consider an electromagnetic wave whose electric field E_0 makes an angle θ with the transmission axis of a polariser. Since electric field strength is a vector quantity, we may resolve the electric field into a component along the transmission axis and a component at right angles to it. Only the component along the axis will go through (Figure **4.39**).

This component of the electric field along the transmission axis is:

$E = E_0 \cos \theta$

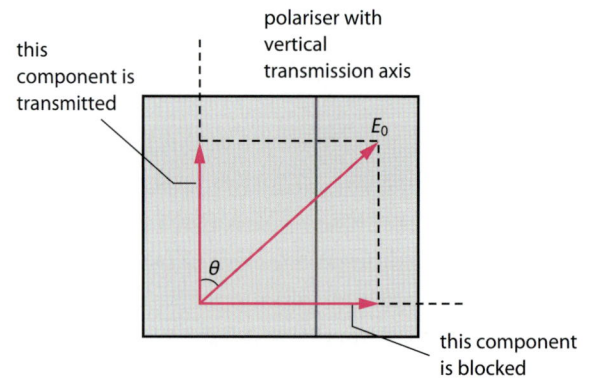

Figure 4.39 This polariser has a vertical transmission axis. Therefore, only the component of the electric field along the vertical axis will be transmitted.

The transmitted intensity I is proportional to the square of the amplitude of the electric field, i.e. $I = kE^2$ where k is a constant. So we have that:

$$I = k(E_0 \cos\theta)^2 = (kE_0^2)\cos^2\theta = I_0 \cos^2\theta$$

where I_0 is the incident intensity.

This relationship is known as **Malus's law**, named after the Frenchman Etienne Malus (1775–1812), who studied this effect in 1808. Depending on the angle between the electric field vector and the transmission axis, the polariser reduces the intensity of the transmitted light. When the electric field is along the transmission axis ($\theta = 0$), then $I = I_0$. When the electric field is at right angles to the transmission axis ($\theta = 90°$), then $I = 0$. This is illustrated in Figure **4.40**. When unpolarised light is incident on a polariser, very many angles of θ are involved and so we need to take the average of $\cos^2\theta$. This is $\frac{1}{2}$, and so the transmitted intensity is half of the incident intensity.

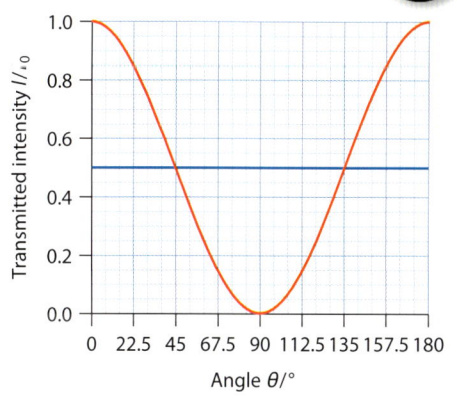

Figure 4.40 The variation of the transmitted intensity I through a polariser as the angle θ between the transmission axis and the electric field is varied. The red curve applies to polarised incident light. The blue line applies to unpolarised incident light.

Worked example

4.11 Vertically polarised light of intensity I_0 is incident on a polariser that has its transmission axis at $\theta = 30°$ to the vertical. The transmitted light is then incident on a second polariser whose axis is at $\theta = 60°$ to the vertical, as shown in Figure **4.41**.

Calculate the factor by which the transmitted intensity is reduced.

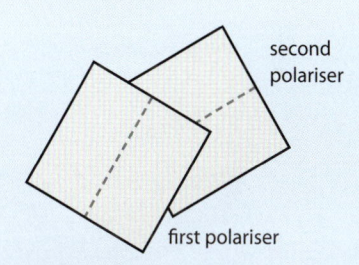

Figure 4.41

After passing through the first polariser the intensity of light is:

$$I_1 = I_0 \cos^2\theta = I_0 \cos^2 30° = \frac{3I_0}{4}$$

The second polariser has its transmission axis at $\theta = 30°$ to the first polariser, and so the final transmitted light has intensity:

$$I_2 = \frac{3I_0}{4}\cos^2 30° = \frac{9I_0}{16}$$

The intensity is thus reduced by a factor of $\frac{9}{16}$.

Figure **4.42** shows two polarisers with their transmission axes at right angles. Only the vertical components of the electric field are transmitted through the first polariser. The axis of the second polariser is horizontal, so no light emerges.

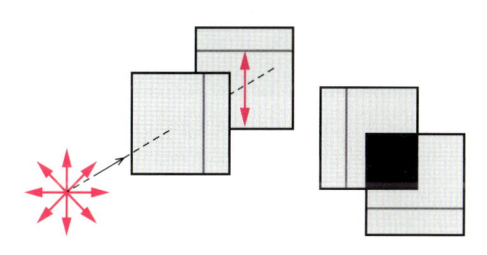

Figure 4.42 Crossed polarisers transmit no light, so where they overlap appears black.

4 WAVES 169

Polarisation by reflection

Polarised light can be obtained not only by passing light through a polariser, but also by reflection from a non-metallic surface. When unpolarised light reflects off a non-metallic surface, the reflected ray is **partially** polarised (Figure 4.43). Partially polarised light means that the reflected light has various components of electric field of unequal magnitude. The component with the greatest magnitude is found in the plane parallel to the surface, and so the light is said to be partially polarised in this plane. The plane of polarisation is parallel to the reflecting surface.

The 'glare' from reflections from the surface of water, such as from lakes or the sea, is partially horizontally polarised. The glare can be reduced by wearing Polaroid sunglasses (which have vertical transmission axes), which makes it possible to see what lies beneath the water surface (Figure 4.44).

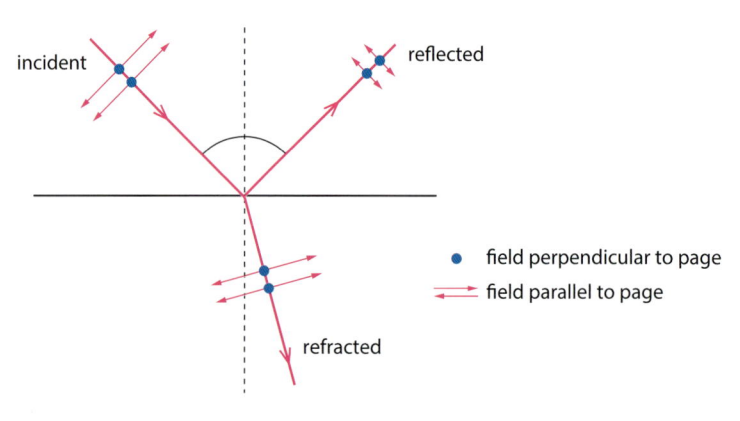

Figure 4.43 Partial polarisation by reflection. The reflected ray has a small electric field component in the plane of incidence and a larger electric field component in the plane parallel to the reflecting surface.

Figure 4.44 The reflected light from the water is reduced when observed through a vertical polariser. This allows detail inside the water (the vegetation and pebbles) to be seen more clearly.

Nature of science

Particles or a wave?

The early 19th century saw a revival of the wave approach to light, mainly due to the work of Young and Fresnel. In the 18th century, the Newtonian view of a particle nature of light prevailed, making research in directions that Newton would not 'approve' almost impossible. So the early researchers of the 19th century had to be brave as well as ingenious! It is interesting to note, however, that light waves were first thought to be longitudinal waves, like sound. The discovery of polarisation created enormous difficulties for the supporters of the wave theory because it could not be understood in terms of a longitudinal wave theory of light. It was Young who finally suggested that light was a transverse wave (an idea which Maxwell took much further when he proposed that light was an electromagnetic wave). So the phenomenon of polarisation that helps Monarch butterflies, bees and ants navigate (it may even have helped the Vikings reach Vinland, i.e. North America) is the phenomenon that for the first time introduced light as a transverse wave in physics.

Test yourself

15 The diagram shows two pulses of equal width and height travelling in opposite directions on the same string. Draw the shape of the string when the pulses completely overlap.

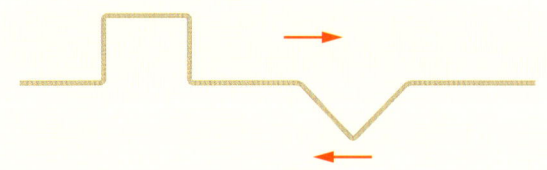

16 The diagram shows two pulses of equal width and height travelling in opposite directions on the same string. Draw the shape of the string when the pulses completely overlap.

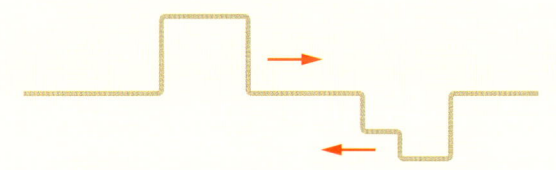

17 The wave pulses shown in the diagram travel at $1\,\text{cm}\,\text{s}^{-1}$ and both have width $2\,\text{cm}$. The heights are indicated on the diagram. In each case, draw the shape of the resulting pulse according to the principle of superposition at times $t = 0.5\,\text{s}$, $t = 1.0\,\text{s}$ and $t = 1.5\,\text{s}$. Take $t = 0\,\text{s}$ to be the time when the pulses are about to meet each other.

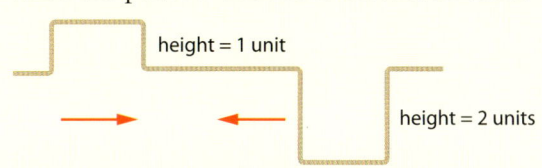

18 Two waves are simultaneously generated on a string. The graph shows the variation of displacement y with distance x. Draw the actual shape of the string.

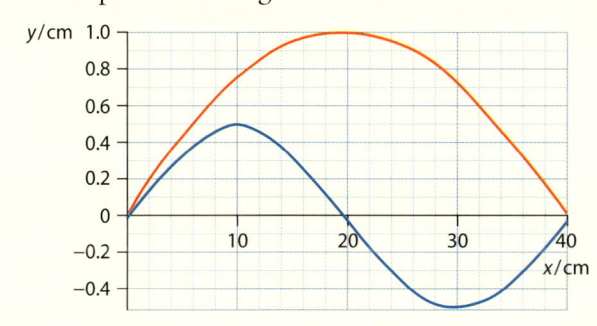

19 In the context of wave motion explain, with the aid of a diagram, the terms:
   a **wavefront**
   b **ray**.

20 a State what is meant by **polarised light**.
   b State **two** methods by which light can be polarised.

21 Suggest why only transverse waves can be polarised.

22 Light is incident on a polariser. The transmitted intensity is measured as the orientation of the polariser is changed. In each of the following **three** outcomes, determine whether the incident light is polarised, partially polarised or completely unpolarised, explaining your answers.
   a The intensity of the transmitted light is the same no matter what the orientation of the polariser.
   b The intensity of the transmitted light varies depending on the orientation of the polariser. At a particular orientation, the transmitted intensity is zero.
   c The transmitted intensity varies as the orientation varies, but it never becomes zero.

23 a State Malus's law.
   b Polarised light is incident on a polariser whose transmission axis makes an angle of 25° with the direction of the electric field of the incident light. Calculate the fraction of the incident light intensity that is transmitted through the polariser.

24 Two polarisers have their transmission axes at right angles to each other.
   a Explain why no light will get transmitted through the second polariser.
   b A third polariser is inserted in between the first two. Its transmission axis is at 45° to the other two. Determine whether any light will be transmitted by this arrangement of three polarisers.
   c If the third polariser were placed in front of the first rather than in between the two, would your answer to **b** change?

4 WAVES 171

Learning objectives

- Interpret incident, reflected and refracted waves at boundaries between media.
- Solve problems using Snell's law, the critical angle and total internal reflection.
- Qualitatively describe diffraction through a single slit and around objects.
- Describe interference from two sources.
- Describe double-slit interference patterns.

4.4 Wave behaviour

This section deals with the wave phenomena of reflection and refraction as they apply to waves, especially light. The study of light has played a crucial role in the history of science. Newton discovered that ordinary white light is composed of different colours when he let sunlight go through a prism and saw the colours of the rainbow emerging from the other side. The wave nature of light was put forward by the Dutch physicist Christiaan Huygens in his book *Treatise on Light* published in 1690. A bitter controversy between Huygens and Newton (Newton had postulated a particle theory of light) ended in Huygens' favour.

Reflection

Reflection is an everyday phenomenon: you can see your reflection in a mirror and the reflection of the blue sky in sea water makes the water look blue. The law of reflection states that:

> The angle of incidence i (angle between the ray and the normal to the reflecting surface at the point of incidence) is equal to the angle of reflection r (angle between the normal and the reflected ray). The reflected and incident rays and the normal to the surface lie on the same plane, called the plane of incidence.

The ray diagrams in Figure 4.45 illustrate reflection from a plane surface.

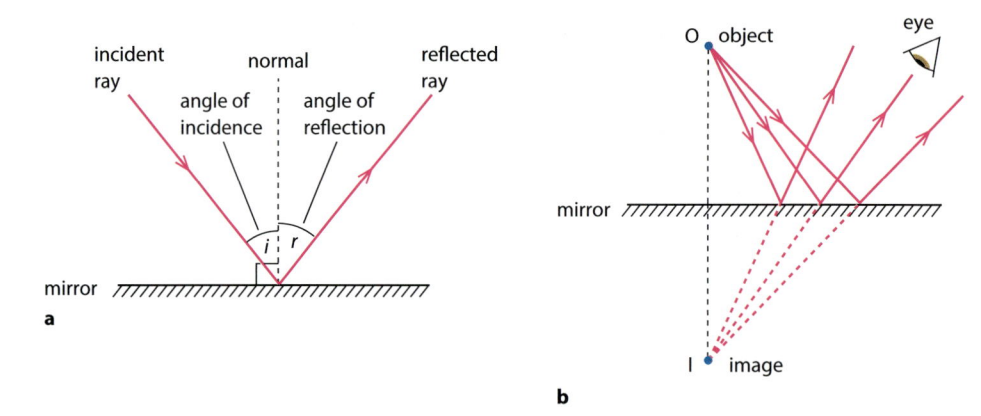

Figure 4.45 a Reflection at a plane (flat) surface. **b** The position of an image seen in a plane mirror.

Reflection takes place when the reflecting surface is sufficiently smooth. This means that the wavelength of the incident wave has to be larger than the size of any irregularities of the surface. The wavelength of the reflected waves is the same as that of the incident wave.

Refraction and Snell's law

Light travels with a velocity of (approximately) $3.0 \times 10^8 \, \text{m s}^{-1}$ in a vacuum. In all other media, the velocity of light is smaller. **Refraction** is the travel of light from one medium into another where it has a different speed. Refraction changes the direction of the incident ray (unless the incident ray is normal to the boundary of the two media).

Usually, when a ray of light strikes an interface between two media, there is both reflection and refraction (Figure **4.46**).

Experiments (and theory) show that:

$$\frac{\sin\theta_2}{\sin\theta_1} = \frac{c_2}{c_1}$$

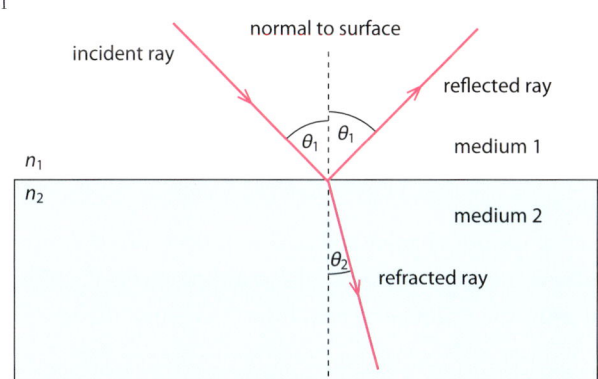

Figure 4.46 A ray of light incident on the interface of two media partly reflects and partly refracts.

where θ_1 is the angle of incidence, θ_2 is the angle of refraction, and c_1 and c_2 are the speeds of the wave in the two media (Figure **4.46**). This relationship is known as **Snell's law**. This law relates the sines of the angles of incidence and refraction to the wave speeds in the two media. This form of the law applies to all waves.

In the case of light only, we usually define a quantity called the **refractive index** of a given medium n_m as:

$$n_m = \frac{c}{c_m}$$

where c is the speed of light in vacuum and c_m is the speed of light in the medium in question.

So for *light*, Snell's law may be rewritten as:

$$\frac{\sin\theta_2}{\sin\theta_1} = \frac{c/c_1}{c/c_2}$$

$$\frac{\sin\theta_2}{\sin\theta_1} = \frac{n_1}{n_2}$$

(This is sometimes better remembered as $n_1 \sin\theta_1 = n_2 \sin\theta_2$.)

So for light we have the equivalent forms:

$$\frac{n_1}{n_2} = \frac{\sin\theta_2}{\sin\theta_1} = \frac{c_2}{c_1}$$

Since the speed of light is always greatest in a vacuum, the refractive index of any medium other than a vacuum is always larger than 1. By definition,

4 WAVES

Medium	Refractive index
vacuum	1
water	1.33
acetone	1.36
quartz	1.46
crown glass	1.52
sapphire	1.77
diamond	2.42

Table 4.1 Values of refractive index for different media.

the refractive index of a vacuum (and approximately of air) is 1. Table **4.1** lists some values of refractive index. Media with high values of refractive index are called optically dense. Thus, if we are given the refractive index of a medium we can find the speed of light in that medium. For example, in a glass with $n = 1.5$, the speed of light is:

$$c_{glass} = \frac{c}{n_{glass}} = \frac{3.0 \times 10^8}{1.5} = 2.0 \times 10^8 \, m\,s^{-1}$$

The refractive index depends slightly on wavelength, so rays with the same angle of incidence but of different wavelength are refracted by different angles. This phenomenon is called **dispersion**. White light that is transmitted through a prism will, because of dispersion, split up into the colours of the rainbow.

The frequency cannot change as the wave moves into the second medium: imagine an observer right at the boundary of the two media. The frequency can be found from the number of wavefronts that cross the interface per second. This number is the same for both media. So since the frequency does not change but the speed does, it follows that in refraction the wavelength also changes as the medium changes (see Worked example **4.12**).

Worked examples

4.12 Light of wavelength 686 nm in air enters water, making an angle of 40.4° with the normal.

Determine **a** the angle of refraction and **b** the wavelength of light in water. Explain your working.

(The refractive index of water is 1.33.)

a By straightforward application of Snell's law we find:

$1 \times \sin 40.4° = 1.33 \times \sin \theta$

$\Rightarrow \theta = 29.2°$

b The wavelength in air is 680 nm, so the frequency in air is:

$$f = \frac{3.00 \times 10^8}{686 \times 10^{-9}} \approx 4.37 \times 10^{14} \, Hz$$

The frequency cannot change as the wave moves into the second medium. Since the speed of light in water is:

$$c_w = \frac{3.00 \times 10^8}{1.33}$$

$c_w = 2.26 \times 10^8 \, m\,s^{-1}$

It follows that the wavelength in water is:

$$\lambda = \frac{2.26 \times 10^8}{4.37 \times 10^{14}}$$

$\lambda = 517 \, nm$

1.13 The paths of rays of red and violet light passing through a glass prism are as shown in Figure 4.47. Discuss what can be deduced about the refractive index of glass for red and violet light.

Figure 4.47 Dispersion of white light passing through a prism.

Considering the first refraction when the rays first enter the glass, we see that blue makes a smaller angle of refraction (draw the normal at the point of incidence to see that this is so). Hence its index of refraction must be larger.

Total internal reflection

An interesting phenomenon occurs when a wave moving in an optically dense medium arrives at the interface with a less dense medium, for example light in water reaching the boundary with air. Some light is reflected at the boundary and some light is refracted. As shown in Figure 4.48a, the angle of refraction is greater than the angle of incidence. As the angle of incidence increases the angle of refraction eventually reaches 90°, as shown in Figure 4.48b. The angle of incidence for which the angle of refraction is 90° is called the **critical angle**.

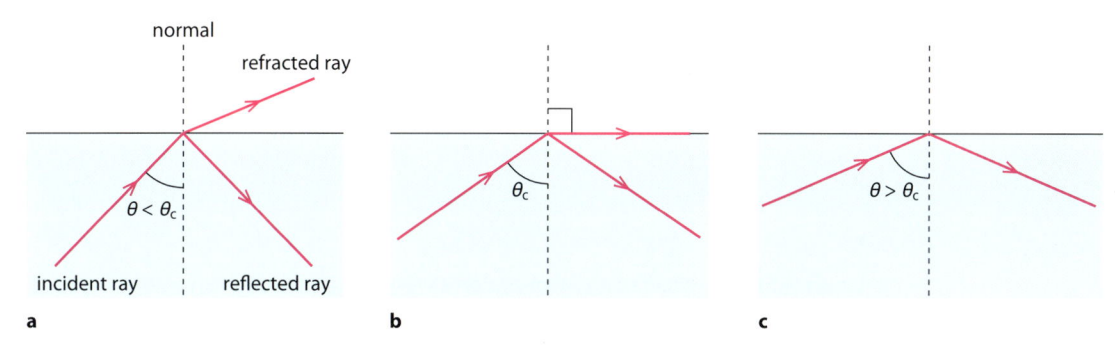

Figure 4.48 Total internal reflection occurs when the angle of incidence is greater than the critical angle.

The critical angle for light passing between two media can be found using Snell's law. For example, for light moving from a medium with refractive index 1.60 into a medium with refractive index 1.20, the critical angle can be found using the relationship $n_1 \sin \theta_1 = n_2 \sin \theta_2$:

$1.60 \sin \theta_c = 1.20 \sin 90°$

This gives:

$$\sin\theta_c = \frac{1.20 \times 1}{1.60} = 0.75$$

$$\Rightarrow \theta_c = \sin^{-1}(0.75) = 48.6°$$

Now, let the angle of incidence exceed the critical angle, say $\theta_1 = 52°$. If we now try to find the angle of refraction we get:

$$1.60 \sin 52° = 1.20 \sin\theta_2$$

$$\Rightarrow \sin\theta_2 = 1.05$$

which is impossible. There is no refracted ray when the angle of incidence is greater than the critical angle; there is just the reflected ray and so we call this phenomenon **total internal reflection**.

One of the great modern applications of total internal reflection is the propagation of digital signals, carrying information, in optical fibres. The signal stays within the core, as shown in Figure **4.49**.

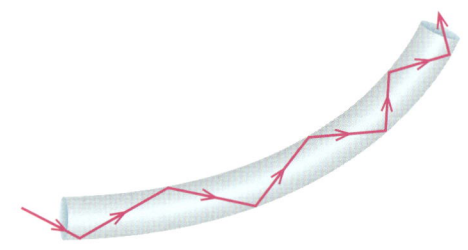

Figure 4.49 Laser light carrying coded information travels down the length of the optical fibre in a sequence of total internal reflections.

Diffraction

The spreading of a wave as it goes past an obstacle or through an aperture is called **diffraction**. Let us consider a plane wave of wavelength λ moving towards an aperture of size a (Figure **4.50**). What will the wavefronts look like after the wave has gone through the aperture? The answer depends on the size of the wavelength compared with the size of the aperture.

Exam tip
When you draw diffraction diagrams, make sure that you do not change the distance between the wavefronts.

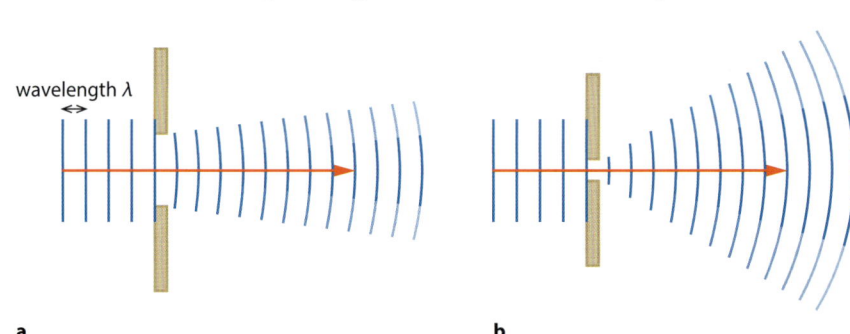

Figure 4.50 The effect of aperture size on a wave passing through an aperture. **a** Wavelength small compared to gap so little diffraction. **b** Wavelength comparable to gap so lots of diffraction

In Figure **4.50a** the wavelength is small compared with a. There is little diffraction. In Figure **4.50b** the wavelength is comparable to a and the diffraction is greater. The width of the diffracted wavefronts is proportional to the intensity of the wave. In the diagrams, the paler colour at the edges of the wavefronts shows that the intensity decreases as we move to the sides.

Figure 4.51 shows diffraction around obstacles, and Figure 4.52 shows a real-life example of diffraction of water waves.

> Diffraction takes place when a wave with wavelength comparable to or larger than the size of an aperture or an obstacle moves through or past the aperture or obstacle. In general, the larger the wavelength, the greater the effect.

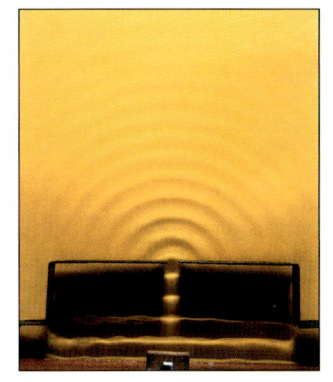

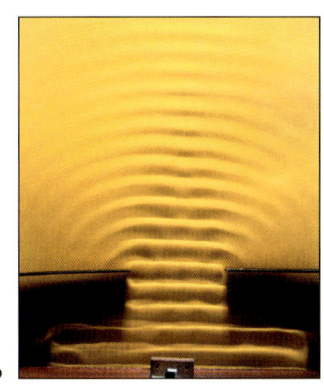

Figure 4.52 Waves in a ripple tank passing through an aperture, demonstrating the principle of diffraction. **a** When these waves pass through a large aperture they change shape and form flattened concentric waves centred on the aperture. The amount by which the waves change shape depends on the size of the aperture. Diffraction is greatest when the aperture size is similar to the wavelength. This is seen in **b**, where waves of the same wavelength are passing through a smaller aperture.

Interference effects in a single slit create a complicated pattern, Figure 4.53. Diffraction explains why we can hear, but not see, around corners. For example, a person talking in the next room can be heard through the open door because sound diffracts around the opening of the door – the wavelength of sound for speech is roughly the same as the door size. On the other hand, light does not diffract around the door since its wavelength is much smaller than the door size. Hence we can hear through the open door, even though we cannot see the speaker.

Double-source interference

When two waves meet at the same point in space the principle of superposition states that the resulting wave has a displacement that is the sum of the individual displacements. The resulting pattern when two (or more) waves meet is called interference. All waves show interference.

Consider two identical sources S_1 and S_2 (Figure 4.54). Wavefronts from the two sources meet at various points. The waves from both sources have the same speed, wavelength, frequency and amplitude. Let us focus on point P. Point P is a distance from source S_1 equal to 2λ and a distance of 3λ from S_2. The **path difference** is the difference in distance of the point from the two sources, $\Delta r = |S_1 P - S_2 P|$. For point P the path difference is equal to λ. All the points marked red in Figure 4.54 have a path difference that is one wavelength, λ. At point P the waves from both sources arrive as crests. At point Q (the path difference is still λ) the waves arrive as troughs.

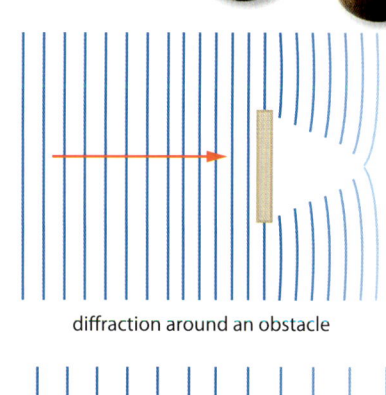

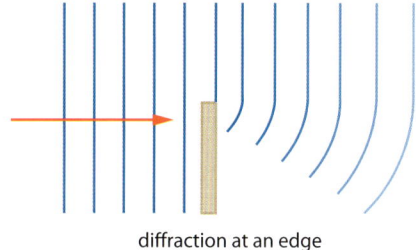

Figure 4.51 Diffraction around obstacles.

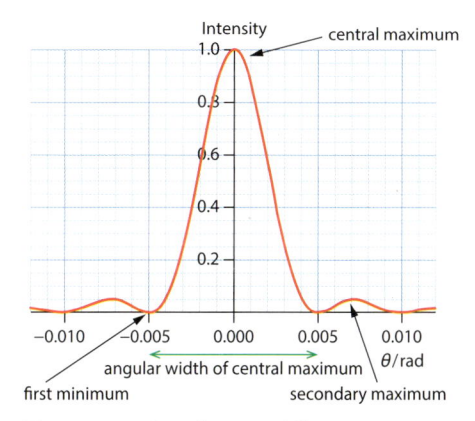

Figure 4.53 Rays leaving different parts of the slit interfere creating complicated intensity patterns, see Subtopic 9.2.

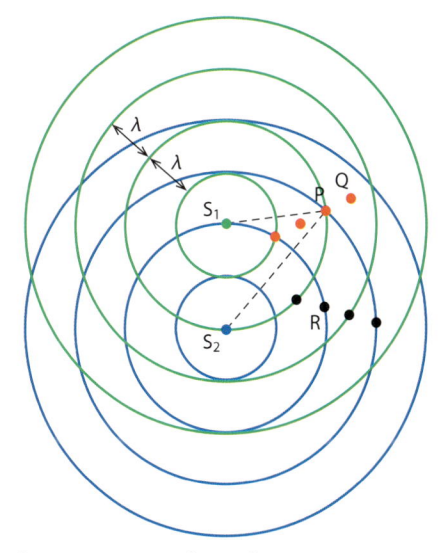

Figure 4.54 Wavefronts from two sources meet and interfere.

4 WAVES 177

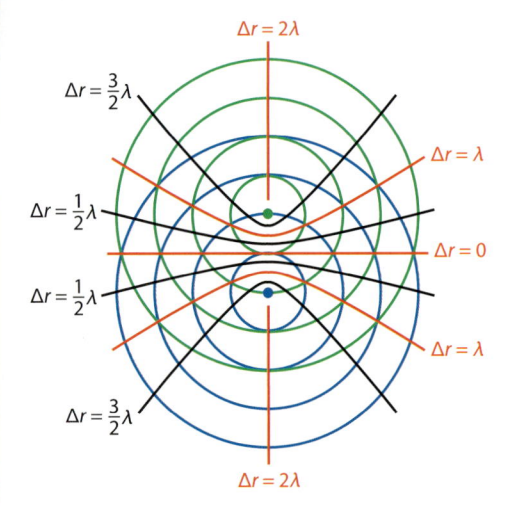

Figure 4.55 Curves in red join points where the path difference is an integral multiple of the wavelength. Curves in black join points with a path difference that is a half integral multiple of the wavelength. (The curves are hyperbolas.)

In either case when the individual waves are added (as the principle of superposition says) the resulting wave will have the same wavelength, frequency and speed as the individual waves but double the amplitude. This is true for all the points in red.

Now look at the points marked in black on Figure 4.54. The path difference for all of these points is $\Delta r = \frac{\lambda}{2}$. At point R, the wave from source S_2 arrives as a crest but the wave from S_1 arrives as a trough. When the two waves are added the resulting wave has amplitude zero – the waves cancel each other out and vanish! This is true for all the points in black. We say there is **constructive interference** for the points in red and **destructive interference** for those in black.

We can imagine joining points with the same path difference with a smooth curve. Figure 4.55 shows this. Red curves go through points whose path difference is $0, \lambda, 2\lambda$. Black curves go through points whose path difference is $\frac{\lambda}{2}$ and $\frac{3\lambda}{2}$. (If the diagram showed more wavefronts from the two sources, we would be able to find points with larger path differences.)

From this we can make the general observation that points in red have a path difference that is an integer times the wavelength, whereas points in black have a path difference that is a half-integer times the wavelength. So we conclude that:

> Constructive interference occurs when the path difference
> $|S_1P - S_2P| = n\lambda$ with $n = 0, 1, 2, 3, \ldots$
> Destructive interference occurs when the path difference is
> $|S_1P - S_2P| = (n + \frac{1}{2})\lambda$ with $n = 0, 1, 2, 3, \ldots$

Thus constructive interference occurs when the waves are in phase (so waves meet crest to crest and trough to trough), and destructive interference occurs when they are exactly out of phase (so they meet crest to trough) (Figure 4.56).

(Note that the discussion above applies to sources that emit waves in phase, and this will be the case in most exam questions. If the sources have a phase difference φ, then an amount of $\frac{\varphi\lambda}{2\pi}$ must be added to the path difference.)

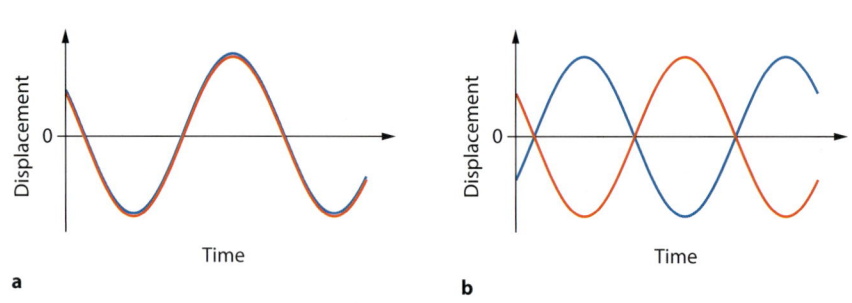

Figure 4.56 Displacement–time curves for waves that interfere **a** constructively and **b** destructively.

178

Worked example

4.14 Identical waves leaving two sources arrive at point P. Point P is 12 m from the first source and 16.5 m from the second. The waves from both sources have a wavelength of 3 m. State and explain what is observed at P.

The path difference is $16.5 - 12 = 4.5$ m.

Dividing by the wavelength, the path difference is equal to $(1 + \frac{1}{2}) \times 3$ m, i.e. it is a half-integral multiple of the wavelength. We thus have destructive interference.

If the path difference is anything other than an integral or half-integral multiple of the wavelength, then the resultant amplitude of the wave at P will be some value between zero and $2A$, where A is the amplitude of one of the waves (we are again assuming that the two waves have equal amplitudes).

When sound waves from two sources interfere, points of constructive interference are points of high intensity of sound. Points of destructive interference are points of no sound at all. If the waves involved are light waves, constructive interference produces points of bright light, and destructive interference results in points of darkness. Complete destructive interference takes place only when the two waves have equal amplitudes.

Double-slit interference

Interference for light was first demonstrated in 1801 by Thomas Young. Figure **4.57** shows plane wavefronts of light approaching two extremely thin, parallel, vertical slits. Because of diffraction the wavefronts spread out from each slit. Wavefronts from the slits arrive on a screen and so interfere. At those points on the screen where the path difference is an integral multiple of the wavelength of light constructive interference takes place. The screen looks bright at those points, marked on the diagram as $n = 0$, $n = \pm 1$, … . The value of n indicates that the path difference is $n\lambda$. At other points where the path difference is a half-integral multiple of λ, the screen looks dark: we have destructive interference.

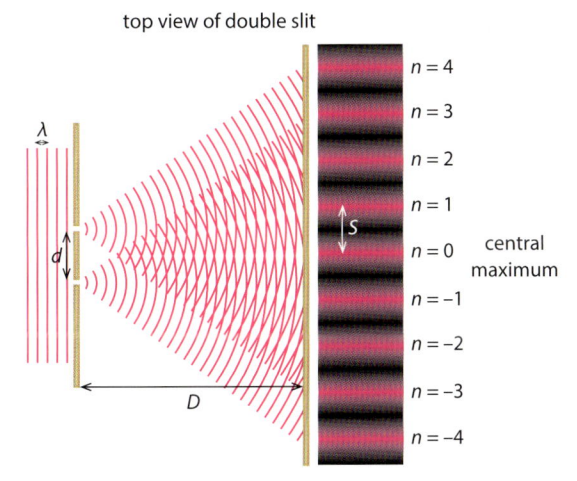

Figure 4.57 Double-slit interference for light.

4 WAVES

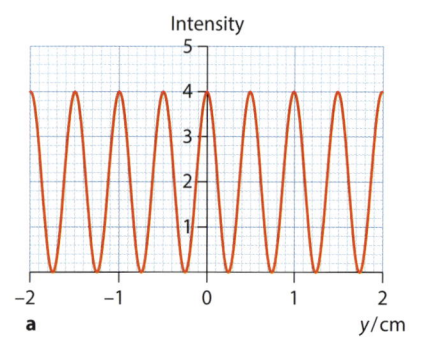

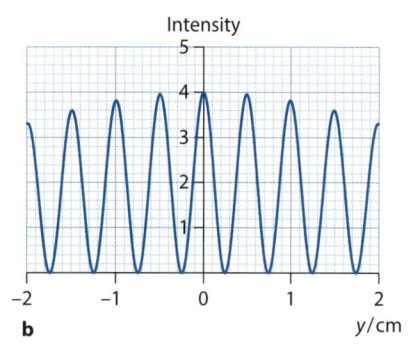

Figure 4.58 The intensity pattern for two slits **a** of negligible width and **b** with a slit width that is not negligible. The horizontal axis label *y* refers to the distance from the centre of the screen.

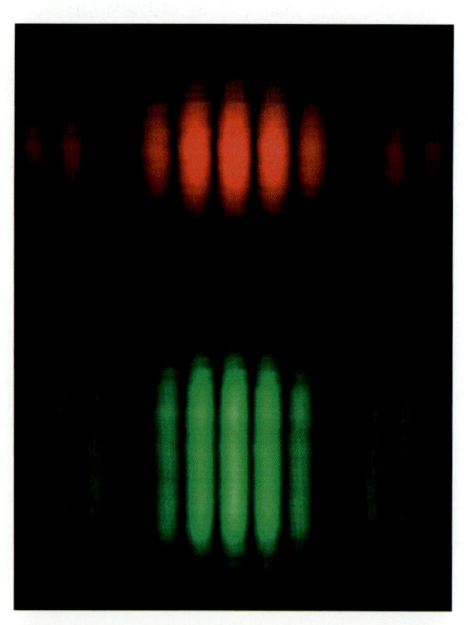

Figure 4.59 Slit patterns for two slits of finite width with two different wavelengths. Notice that the largest separation of the fringes is obtained with the longest wavelength i.e. red light.

The distance on the screen between the middle of a bright spot and the middle of the next bright spot is called the 'fringe spacing' and is denoted by *s*. It can be shown that:

$$s = \frac{\lambda D}{d}$$

where *D* is the distance between the slits and the screen and *d* is the distance between the slits.

The graphs in Figure **4.58** show how the intensity of the waves on the screen varies with distance from the middle of the screen. The graph in Figure **4.58a** applies if the slit width is negligible. In this case successive peaks in intensity (corresponding to points of constructive interference) have the same intensity and are separated by a distance equal to *s*. The graph in Figure **4.58b** shows the intensity when the slit width cannot be neglected. In this case the width is about 45 times the wavelength.

In Figure **4.58**, the units on the vertical axis are arbitrary. An intensity of one unit corresponds to the intensity from only one slit. At points of constructive interference the amplitude is double that of just one wave. Since intensity is proportional to the square of the amplitude, the intensity is four times as large. Figure **4.59** shows actual interference patterns with two slits and two different wavelengths.

Worked example

4.15 Use the graph in Figure **4.58a** for this question. In a double-slit interference experiment the two slits are separated by a distance of 4.2×10^{-4} m and the screen is 3.8 m from the slits.
   a Determine the wavelength of light used in this experiment.
   b Suggest the effect on the separation of the fringes of decreasing the wavelength of light.
   c State the feature of the graph that enables you to deduce that the slit width is negligible.

a Reading from the graph, the separation of the bright fringes is 0.50 cm. Applying $s = \frac{\lambda D}{d}$ gives:

$$\lambda = \frac{ds}{D} = \frac{4.2 \times 10^{-4} \times 0.50 \times 10^{-2}}{3.8}$$

$$\lambda = 5.5 \times 10^{-7} \text{ m}$$

Exam tip
Watch the units!

b From the separation formula we see that if we decrease the wavelength the separation decreases.

c The intensity of the side fringes is equal to the intensity of the central fringe.

Nature of science

Competing theories and progress in science

At the start of this section we mentioned the conflict between Newton and Huygens over the nature of light. In 1817 Augustin-Jean Fresnel published a new wave theory of light. The mathematician Siméon Poisson favoured the particle theory of light, and worked out that Fresnel's theory predicted the presence of a bright spot in the shadow of a circular object, which he believed was impossible. François Arago, a supporter of Fresnel, was able to show there was indeed a bright spot in the centre of the shadow. In further support of his theory, Fresnel was able to show that the polarisation of light could only be explained if light was a transverse wave. The wave theory then took precedence, until new evidence showed that light could behave as both a wave and a particle.

Test yourself

25 Red light of wavelength 6.8×10^{-7} m in air enters glass with a refractive index of 1.583, with an angle of incidence of 38°. Calculate:
 a the angle of refraction
 b the speed of light in the glass
 c the wavelength of light in the glass.

26 Light of frequency 6.0×10^{14} Hz is emitted from point **A** and is directed toward point **B** a distance of 3.0 m away.
 a Determine how long will it take light to get to **B**.
 b Calculate how many waves fit in the space between **A** and **B**.

27 A ray of light is incident on a rectangular block of glass of refractive index 1.450 at an angle of 40°, as shown in the diagram. The thickness of the block is 4.00 cm. Calculate the amount d by which the ray is deviated.

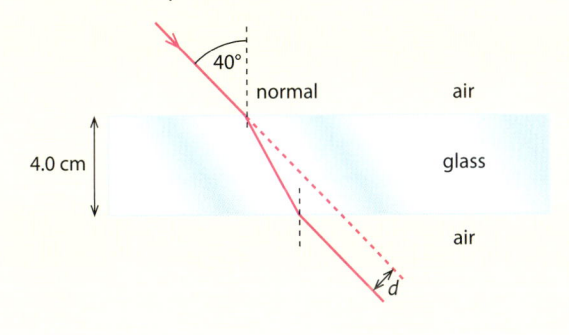

28 The speed of sound in air is 340 m s^{-1} and in water it is 1500 m s^{-1}. Determine the angle at which a beam of sound waves must hit the air–water boundary so that no sound is transmitted into the water.

29 Planar waves of wavelength 1.0 cm approach an aperture whose opening is also 1.0 cm. Draw the wavefronts of this wave as they emerge through the aperture.

30 Repeat question **29** for waves of wavelength 1 mm approaching an aperture of size 20 cm.

31 A radio station, R, emits radio waves of wavelength 1600 m which reach a house, H, directly and after reflecting from a mountain, M, behind the house (see diagram). The reception at the house is very poor. Estimate the shortest possible distance between the house and the mountain. (Pay attention to phase changes.)

4 WAVES

Learning objectives

- Explain the formation of standing waves using superposition.
- Discuss the differences between standing waves and travelling waves.
- Describe nodes and antinodes.
- Work with standing waves on strings and in pipes.
- Solve problems with standing waves on strings and pipes.

4.5 Standing waves

A special wave is formed when two identical waves travelling in opposite directions meet and interfere. The result is a standing (or stationary) wave: a wave in which the crests stay in the same place. The theory of wind and string musical instruments is based on the theory of standing waves.

Standing waves on strings and tubes

When two waves of the same speed, wavelength and amplitude travelling in opposite directions meet, a **standing wave** is formed. According to the principle of superposition, the resulting wave has a displacement that is the sum of the displacements of the two travelling waves.

Figure **4.60** shows a red travelling wave moving to the left and an identical blue travelling wave travelling to the right. Both waves travel on the same string. The graphs show the displacement due to each wave every one-tenth of a period. The purple wave is the sum of the two and therefore shows the actual shape of the string. In the top graph, at $t = 0$, the two travelling waves are on top of each other and so the resultant wave has its maximum displacement at this time. In the next graphs the waves are moving apart and the amplitude decreases. In the last graph, half a period later, the two waves are opposite and the resulting wave is zero: the entire string is flat at that particular instant of time.

We can make the following observations that apply to standing waves but not to travelling waves.

- The crests of the standing wave (i.e. the purple peaks) stay at the same place – they do not move right or left as they do in the case of travelling waves. Thus the shape of the wave does not move in a standing wave.
- There are some points on the string where, as a result of destructive interference between the two waves, the displacement is always zero. We call these points **nodes**. The distance between two consecutive nodes is half a wavelength.
- Half-way between nodes are points where, as a result of constructive interference, the displacement gets as large as possible. These points are called **antinodes**. Note that the nodes always have zero displacement whereas the antinodes are at maximum displacement for an instant of time only.
- Points between consecutive nodes are in phase. This implies that such points have a velocity in the same direction.
- Points in-between the next pair of consecutive nodes have a velocity direction that is opposite (Figure **4.63**).
- The amplitude of oscillation is different at different points on the string.
- A standing wave does not transfer energy: it consists of two travelling waves that transfer energy in opposite directions so the standing wave itself transfers no energy.
- The ends of a standing wave are either nodes or antinodes. These 'end or boundary conditions' determine the possible shape of the wave.

How do we create standing waves in practice? We will examine just two cases: standing waves on strings and in pipes.

Exam tip
You must be able to explain the formation of a standing waves in terms of the superposition of two oppositely moving travelling waves.

Standing waves on strings

Take a string of length L, tighten it and keep both ends fixed by attaching one end to a clamp and the other end to an oscillator. In this case the end conditions are node–node. The oscillator creates travelling waves that move towards the fixed end of the string. The waves **reflect** at the fixed end and so at any one time there are two identical travelling waves on the string travelling in opposite directions. As we saw, this is the condition for a standing wave to form. Depending on the frequency of the oscillator, different standing wave patterns will be established on the string. Figure **4.61** shows four possibilities. In the top diagram we see one loop, with two nodes and one antinode. This is the standing wave with the longest wavelength (and the lowest frequency): it is called the **first harmonic**. The higher harmonics have more loops and the wavelength decreases, as shown in the lower part of Figure **4.61**. These harmonics appear as the frequency of the oscillator increases. In the figure, the symbol n stands for the number of the harmonic, so that, for example, $n = 3$ indicates the third harmonic.

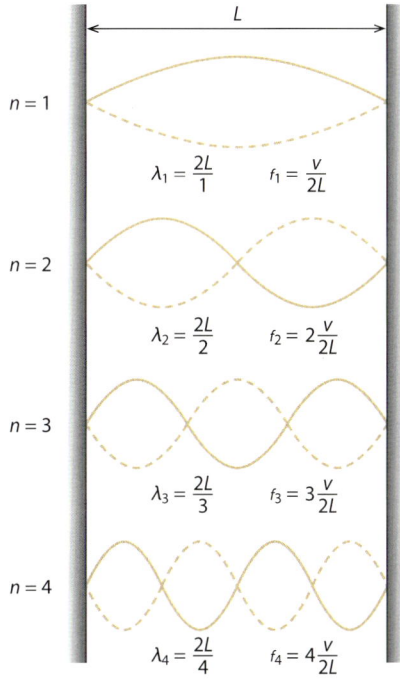

$n = 1$ $\lambda_1 = \frac{2L}{1}$ $f_1 = \frac{v}{2L}$

$n = 2$ $\lambda_2 = \frac{2L}{2}$ $f_2 = 2\frac{v}{2L}$

$n = 3$ $\lambda_3 = \frac{2L}{3}$ $f_3 = 3\frac{v}{2L}$

$n = 4$ $\lambda_4 = \frac{2L}{4}$ $f_4 = 4\frac{v}{2L}$

Figure 4.61 Standing waves on a string with both ends fixed. The first four harmonics are shown.

It is important to realise that for each harmonic there is a definite relationship between the wavelength and the length of the string. Remember that the distance between two consecutive nodes is half a wavelength.

So for the first harmonic we have:

$$\frac{\lambda_1}{2} = L$$

$$\Rightarrow \quad \lambda_1 = 2L = \frac{2L}{1}$$

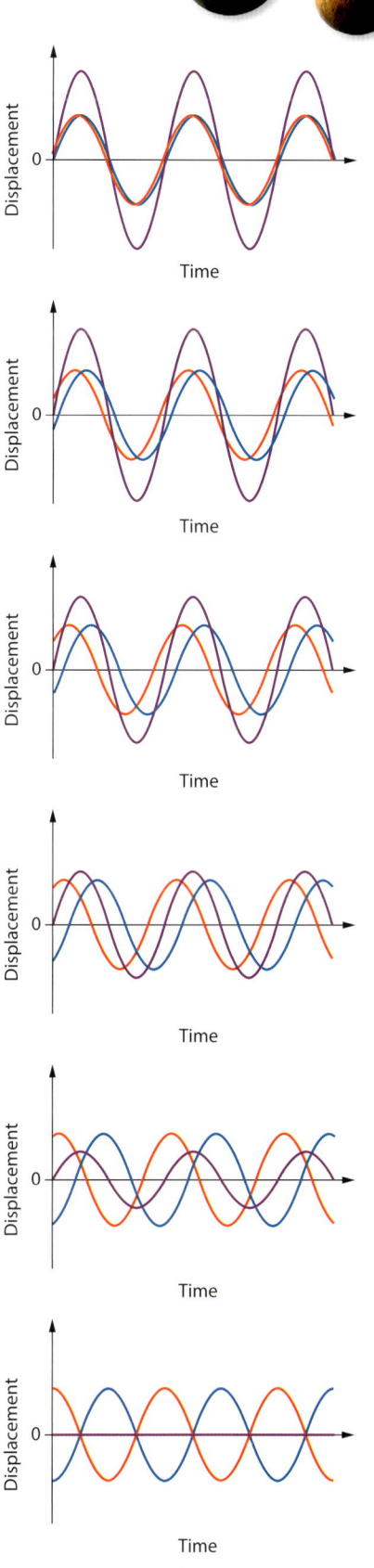

Figure 4.60 A series of graphs showing two travelling waves and their superposition.

For the second harmonic:

$$2 \times \frac{\lambda_2}{2} = L$$

$$\Rightarrow \quad \lambda_2 = L = \frac{2L}{2}$$

For the third harmonic:

$$3 \times \frac{\lambda_3}{2} = L$$

$$\Rightarrow \quad \lambda_3 = \frac{2L}{3}$$

In general, we find that the wavelengths satisfy:

$$\lambda_n = \frac{2L}{n}, \quad n = 1, 2, 3, 4, \ldots$$

Figure **4.60** also gives the frequencies of the harmonics using the equation $f = \frac{v}{\lambda}$, where v is the speed of the travelling waves making up the standing wave and λ the wavelength of the harmonic. The first harmonic has the lowest frequency, called the **fundamental frequency**.

Notice the important fact that:

> All harmonics have frequencies that are integral multiples of the fundamental frequency, i.e. of the first harmonic.

The diagrams in Figure **4.61** show the extreme positions of the string as the string oscillates in a standing wave pattern. Successive positions of the string for the first harmonic are shown in Figure **4.62**. This diagram shows that different points on the standing wave oscillate with different amplitudes. Figures **4.63** and **4.64** shows how the string oscillates in its second harmonic. The arrows represent the velocity vectors of points on the string. Notice how the direction changes as we move from one loop and into the next.

The standing waves discussed in this section apply to string musical instruments such as guitars and violins.

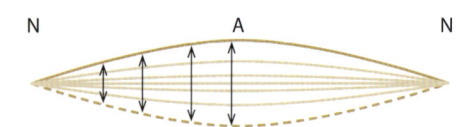

Figure 4.62 Different points on the string have different amplitudes.

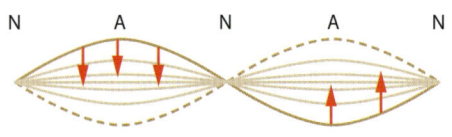

Figure 4.63 Points within consecutive nodes have velocity in the same direction. Points in the next loop have opposite velocity directions.

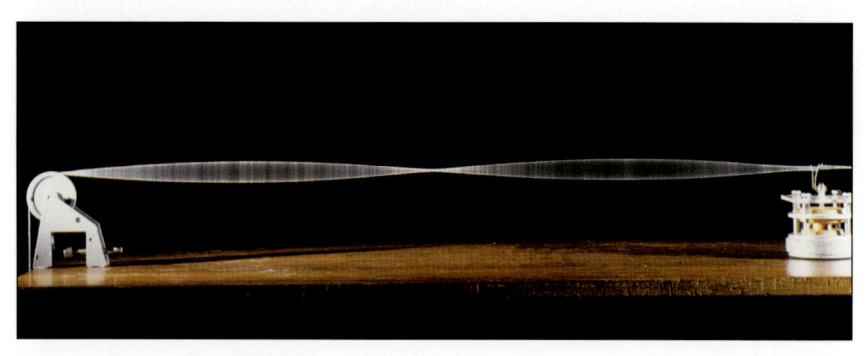

Figure 4.64 A string vibrating.

Standing waves in pipes

Standing waves can also be produced within pipes which can have open or closed ends. Consider first a pipe of length L that is open at both ends, i.e. the end conditions are **antinode**–antinode (Figure **4.65**). A flute is an example of this. A travelling wave sent down the pipe will reflect from the ends (even though they are open) and we again have the condition for the formation of a standing wave.

The top diagram in Figure **4.65a** represents the first harmonic in a pipe with open ends. The dots represent molecules of air in the pipe. The double-headed arrows show how far these molecules oscillate back and forth (the amplitude of the oscillations). We see that the molecules at the ends oscillate the most: they are at antinodes. The molecules in the middle of the pipe do not oscillate at all: they are at a node. We have antinodes at the open ends and there is a node in the middle. The lower diagram is how we normally represent the standing wave in the pipe – you must understand that it represents what the top diagram shows. Figure **4.65b** represents the second harmonic.

Exam tip
You must be able to explain how molecules move in a longitudinal standing wave such as those in pipes.

Note that these diagrams also give the harmonics for the unrealistic case of a string with both ends free.

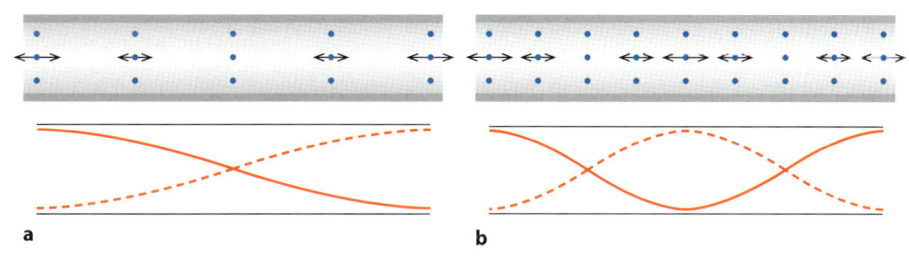

Figure 4.65 a A pipe with both ends open has two antinodes at the open ends and a node in the middle. **b** The second harmonic in an open pipe.

The case of a pipe with both ends closed (which is not very useful) is similar to that of a string with ends fixed: Figure **4.66** shows the first and second harmonics.

The wavelength for pipes with both ends closed or both ends open is:

$$\lambda_n = \frac{2L}{n}, \quad n = 1, 2, 3, 4, \ldots$$

We consider finally the case of a pipe with one closed and one open end (i.e. end conditions node–antinode). This could apply to some organ pipes. The closed end will be a node and the open end an antinode.

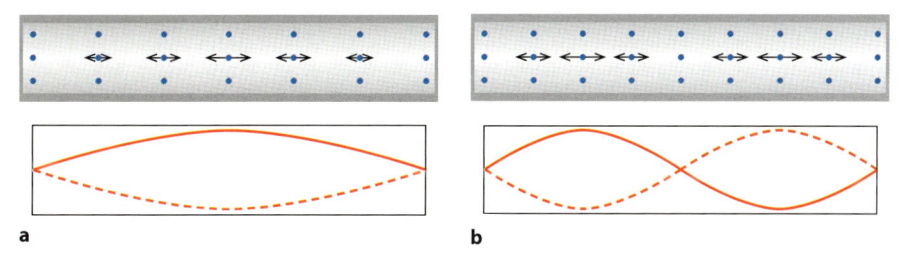

Figure 4.66 The first and second harmonics for a pipe with both ends closed.

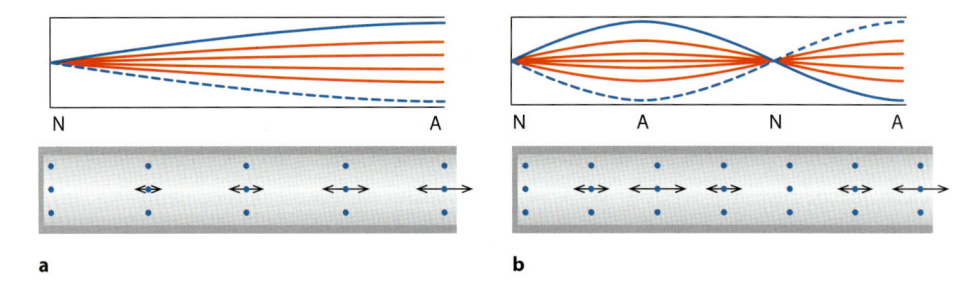

Figure 4.67 The first two harmonics in a pipe with one open and one closed end.

Figure 4.67 shows the first two harmonics. The distance between a node and an antinode is a quarter of a wavelength and so the wavelength of first harmonic (the fundamental wavelength) is given by:

$$1 \times \frac{\lambda_1}{4} = L$$

$$\Rightarrow \lambda_1 = 4L = \frac{4L}{1}$$

The wavelength of the next harmonic is:

$$3 \times \frac{\lambda_3}{4} = L$$

$$\Rightarrow \lambda_3 = \frac{4L}{3}$$

Notice that there only 'odd' harmonics present. In general, the allowed wavelengths are:

$$\lambda_n = \frac{4L}{n}, \quad n = 1, 3, 5, \ldots$$

This formula also gives the wavelength in the unrealistic case of a string with one fixed and one free end.

Table 4.2 summarises the relationships for standing waves in strings and pipes.

String of length L	Both ends fixed or both free: $\lambda_n = \frac{2L}{n}$	$n = 1, 2, 3, 4, \ldots$
	One end fixed, the other free: $\lambda_n = \frac{4L}{n}$	$n = 1, 3, 5, \ldots$
Pipe of length L	Both ends open or both closed: $\lambda_n = \frac{2L}{n}$	$n = 1, 2, 3, 4, \ldots$
	One end closed, the other open: $\lambda_n = \frac{4L}{n}$	$n = 1, 3, 5, \ldots$

Table 4.2 Wavelengths for allowed harmonics for standing waves in strings and pipes.

Worked examples

4.16 A standing wave is set up on a string with both ends fixed. The frequency of the first harmonic is 150 Hz. Calculate:
  a the length of the string
  b the wavelength of the sound produced.
  (The speed of the wave on the string is 240 m s^{-1} and the speed of sound in air is 340 m s^{-1}.)

a The wavelength is given by:

$$\lambda_1 = \frac{240}{150} = 1.6 \, \text{m}$$

The wavelength of the first harmonic is $2L$ and so $L = 0.80$ m.

b The sound will have the same frequency as that of the standing wave, i.e. 150 Hz. The wavelength of the sound is thus:

$$\lambda = \frac{340}{150} \approx 2.3 \, \text{m}$$

4.17 A pipe has one open and one closed end. Determine the ratio of the frequency of the first harmonic to that of the next harmonic.

The first harmonic has wavelength $\lambda_1 = 4L$ and the next harmonic has wavelength $\lambda_3 = \frac{4L}{3}$. Hence:

$$\frac{f_1}{f_3} = \frac{4L/3}{4L} = \frac{1}{3}$$

4.18 A source of sound of frequency 2100 Hz is placed at the open end of a tube. The other end of the tube is closed. Powder is sprinkled inside the tube. When the source is turned on it is observed that the powder collects in heaps a distance of 8.0 cm apart.
  a Explain this observation.
  b Use this information to estimate the speed of sound.

a A standing wave is established inside the tube since the travelling waves from the source superpose with the reflected waves from the closed end. At the antinodes air oscillates the most and pushes the powder right and left. The powder collects at the nodes where the air does not move.

b The heaps collect at the nodes and the distance between nodes is half a wavelength. So the wavelength is 16 cm. The speed of sound is then:

$$v = f\lambda = 2100 \times 0.16 = 336 \approx 340 \, \text{m s}^{-1}$$

4 WAVES

4.19 A tube with both ends open is placed inside a container of water. When a tuning fork above the tube is sounded a loud sound comes out of the tube. The shortest length of the column of air for which this happens is L. The frequency of the tuning fork is 486 Hz and the speed of sound is 340 m s^{-1}.
  a Determine the length L.
  b Predict the least distance by which the tube must be raised for another loud sound to be heard from the tube when the same tuning fork is sounding.

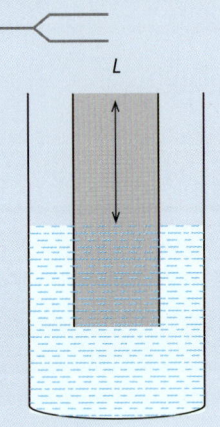

Figure 4.68

> **Exam tip**
> Draw the standing wave in part **a**. It is the first harmonic. Now raise the tube and draw the next harmonic. What is the connection between the distance the tube was raised and the wavelength?

a The wave in the tube must be the first harmonic whose wavelength is $4L$. The wavelength is given by:

$$\lambda = \frac{340}{486} = 0.6996 \approx 0.70 \, \text{m}$$

and so:

$$L = \frac{0.6996}{4} = 0.1749 \approx 0.17 \, \text{m}$$

b The length of the air column in the tube must be increased so that the next harmonic can fit. This means that the distance by which the tube must be raised is a half wavelength, i.e. 0.35 m.

Nature of science

Physics is universal

The universality of physics is evident almost everywhere including in the theory of standing waves. From the time of Pythagoras onwards philosophers and scientists have used mathematics to model the formation of standing waves on strings and in pipes. The theory that we have developed here applies to simple vibrating strings and air columns, but it can be used to give detailed accounts of the formation of musical sound in instruments as well as the stability of buildings shaken by earthquakes.

? Test yourself

32 Describe what is meant by a standing wave. List the ways in which a standing wave differs from a travelling wave.

33 Outline how a standing wave is formed.

34 In the context of standing waves describe what is meant by:
   a node
   b antinode
   c wave speed.

35 a Describe how you would arrange for a string that is kept under tension, with both ends fixed, to vibrate in its second harmonic mode.
   b Draw the shape of the string when it is vibrating in its second harmonic mode.

36 A string is held under tension, with both ends fixed, and has a first harmonic frequency of 250 Hz. The tension in the string is changed so that the speed increases by $\sqrt{2}$. Predict the new frequency of the first harmonic.

37 A string has both ends fixed. Determine the ratio of the frequency of the second to that of the first harmonic.

38 The wave velocity of a transverse wave on a string of length 0.500 m is 225 m s^{-1}.
   a Determine the frequency of the first harmonic of a standing wave on this string when both ends are kept fixed.
   b Calculate the wavelength of the sound produced in air by the oscillating string in a. (Take the speed of sound in air to be 340 m s^{-1}.)

39 Draw the standing wave representing the third harmonic standing wave in a tube with one closed and one open end.

40 A glass tube is closed at one end. The air column it contains has a length that can be varied between 0.50 m and 1.50 m. A tuning fork of frequency 306 Hz is sounded at the top of the tube. Predict the lengths of the air column at which loud sounds would be heard from the tube. (Take the speed of sound to be 340 m s^{-1}.)

41 A glass tube with one end open and the other closed is used in an experiment to determine the speed of sound. A tuning fork of frequency 427 Hz is used and a loud sound is heard when the air column has length equal to 20.0 cm.
   a Calculate the speed of sound.
   b Predict the next length of air column when a loud sound will again be heard.

42 A pipe with both ends open has two consecutive harmonics of frequency 300 Hz and 360 Hz.
   a Suggest which harmonics are excited in the pipe.
   b Determine the length of the pipe. (Take the speed of sound to be 340 m s^{-1}.)

43 A pipe X with both ends open and a pipe Y with one open and one closed end have the same frequency in the first harmonic. Calculate the ratio of the length of pipe X to that of pipe Y.

44 If you walk at one step a second holding a cup of water (diameter 8 cm) the water will spill out of the cup. Use this information to **estimate** the speed of the waves in water.

45 Consider a string with both ends fixed. A standing wave in the second harmonic mode is established on the string, as shown in the diagram. The speed of the wave is 180 m s^{-1}.

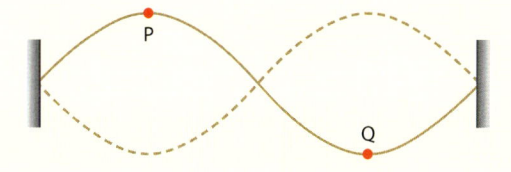

   a Explain the meaning of **wave speed** in the context of standing waves.
   b Consider the vibrations of two points on the string, P and Q. The displacement of point P is given by the equation $y = 5.0 \cos(45\pi t)$, where y is in mm and t is in seconds. Calculate the length of the string.
   c State the phase difference between the oscillation of point P and that of point Q. Hence write down the equation giving the displacement of point Q.

46 A horizontal aluminium rod of length 1.2 m is hit sharply with a hammer. The hammer rebounds from the rod 0.18 ms later.
   a Explain why the hammer rebounds.
   b Calculate the speed of sound in aluminium.
   c The hammer created a longitudinal standing wave in the rod. Estimate the frequency of the sound wave by assuming that the rod vibrates in the first harmonic.

Exam-style questions

1 The diagram shows a point P on a string at a particular instant of time. A transverse wave is travelling along the string from left to right.

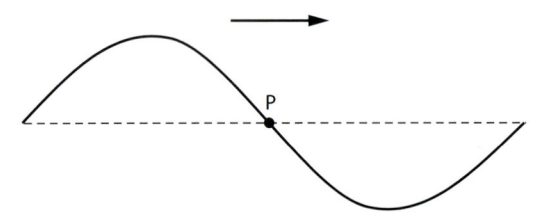

Which is correct about the direction and the magnitude of the velocity of point P at this instant?

	Direction	Magnitude
A	up	maximum
B	up	minimum
C	down	maximum
D	down	minimum

2 A tight horizontal rope with one end tied to a vertical wall is shaken with frequency f so that a travelling wave of wavelength λ is created on the rope. The rope is now shaken with a frequency $2f$. Which gives the new wavelength and speed of the wave?

	Wavelength	Speed
A	λ	$f\lambda$
B	λ	$2f\lambda$
C	$\dfrac{\lambda}{2}$	$f\lambda$
D	$\dfrac{\lambda}{2}$	$2f\lambda$

3 The graph shows the displacement of a medium when a longitudinal wave travels through the medium from left to right. Positive displacements correspond to motion to the right. Which point corresponds to the centre of a compression?

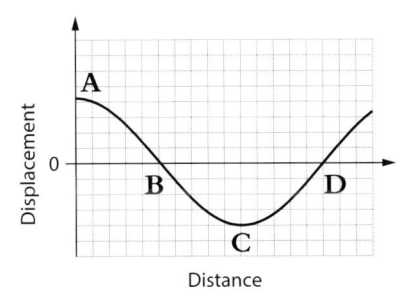

4 The diagram shows wavefronts of a wave entering a medium in which the wave speed decreases. Which diagram is correct?

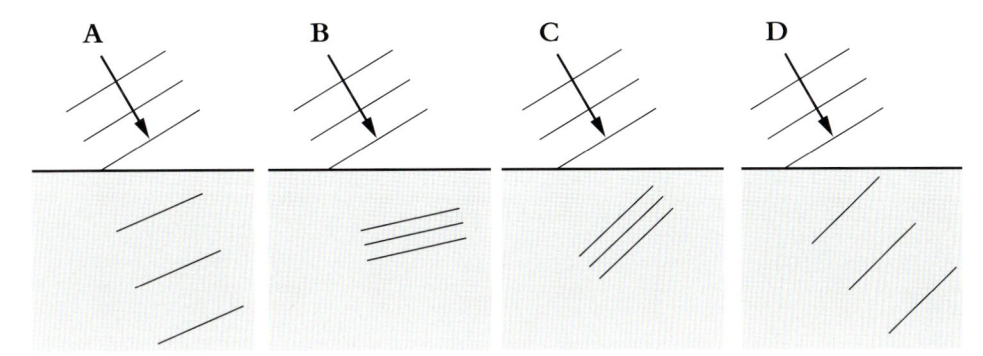

5 The graph shows the variation with time of the displacement of a particle in a medium when a wave of intensity I travels through the medium.

The intensity of the wave is halved. Which graph now represents the variation of displacement with time? (The scale on all graphs is the same.)

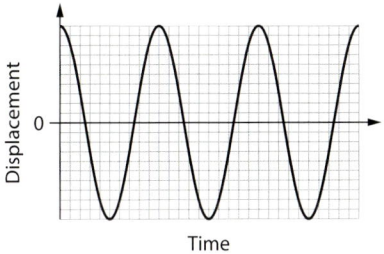

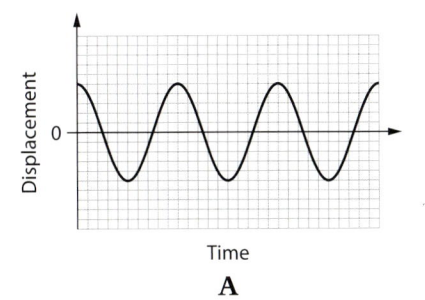

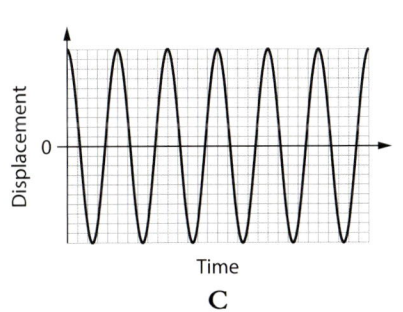

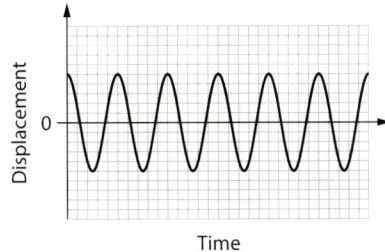

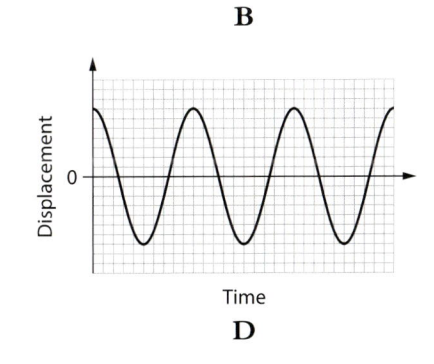

6 Which of the following does **not** apply to longitudinal waves?

    A superposition
    B formation of standing waves
    C interference
    D polarisation

7 Interference is observed with two identical coherent sources. The intensity of the waves at a point of constructive interference is I. What is the intensity when one source is removed?

    A 0   **B** I **C** $\dfrac{I}{2}$ **D** $\dfrac{I}{4}$

8 Unpolarised light of intensity I_0 is incident on two polarisers, one behind the other, with parallel transmission axes. The first polariser is rotated by 30° clockwise and the second 30° counter-clockwise. What is the intensity transmitted?

    A $\dfrac{I_0}{2}$ **B** $\dfrac{I_0}{4}$ **C** $\dfrac{I_0}{8}$ **D** $\dfrac{I_0}{16}$

9 A pipe of length 8.0 m is open at one end and closed at the other. The speed of sound is 320 m s^{-1}. Which is the lowest frequency of a standing wave that can be established within this pipe?

    A 5.0 Hz   **B** 10 Hz   **C** 15 Hz   **D** 30 Hz

10 Travelling waves of wavelength 32 cm are created in a closed–open pipe X of length 40 cm and an open–open pipe Y of length 50 cm.

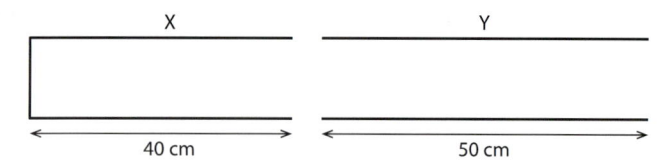

In which pipe or pipes will a standing wave be formed?

    A X only   **B** Y only   **C** neither X nor Y   **D** both X and Y

11 A longitudinal wave is travelling through a medium. The displacement of the wave at $t = 10$ s is shown below. Positive displacements are directed to the right.

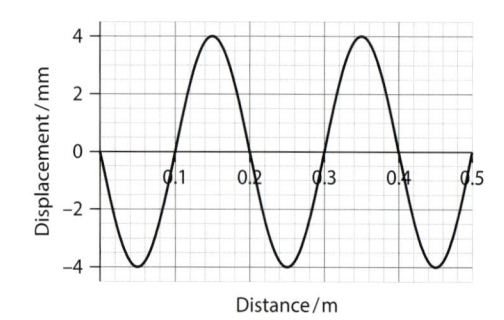

Point P is at a distance of 20 cm from the origin. The graph shows the variation with time of the displacement of point P.

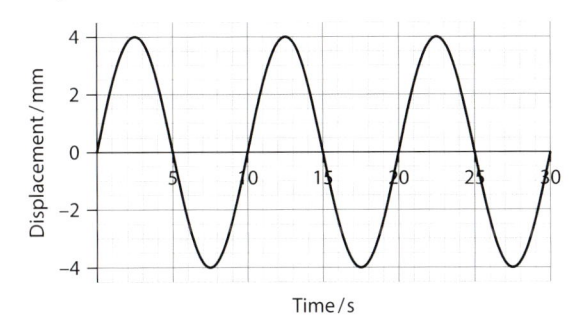

a Distinguish a longitudinal from a transverse wave. [2]

b State, for this wave:
  i the amplitude [1]
  ii the wavelength [1]
  iii the frequency. [1]

c Calculate the speed of the wave. [2]

d Suggest whether the wave is travelling to the right or to the left. [3]

e Point Q is a distance of 15 cm to the right of P. Draw the variation of the displacement of Q with time. [2]

f The travelling wave in parts **a–d** is directed towards a pipe that has one end closed and the other open.
  i State and explain the length of the pipe so that a standing wave in its first harmonic is established within the pipe. [2]
  ii State **two** differences between a standing wave and a travelling wave. [2]
  iii In the context of a standing wave state the meaning of the term **wave speed**. [2]

12 Two pulses travel towards each other on the same taut rope. The two graphs show the pulses before and after the collision. The speed of the black pulse is 15 m s^{-1}. The left diagram shows the pulses at $t = 0$.

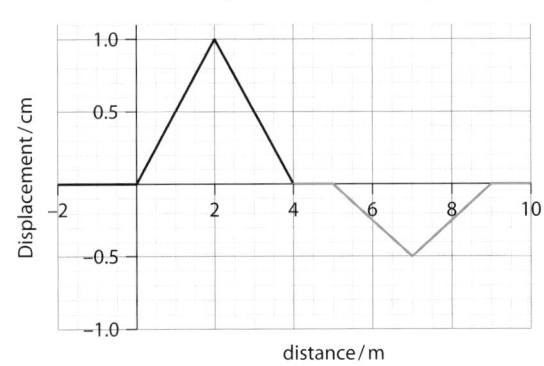

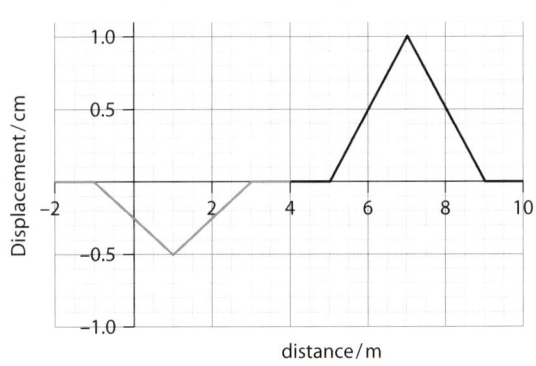

a State the principle of superposition. [2]

b State the speed of the grey pulse. [1]

c **i** Determine the time after which the two pulses completely overlap. [1]
  ii Draw the shape of the rope at the time of complete overlap. [2]

d **i** Suggest whether any energy was lost during the collision of the two pulses. [2]
  ii Comment on the shape of the rope in **c ii** by reference to your answer in **d i**. [3]

4 WAVES   193

13 A man is swimming underwater at a depth of 2.0 m. The man looks upwards.

   a Explain why he can see the world outside the water only through a circle on the surface of the water. [2]
   b Calculate the radius of this circle given that the refractive index of water is 1.33. [2]
   c Discuss how the answer to **b** changes (if at all) if he looks up from a greater depth. [2]
   d Sound waves travelling in air approach an air–water boundary. The speed of sound in air is 340 m s^{-1} and in water it is 1500 m s^{-1}. The wavefronts make an angle of 12° with the boundary.

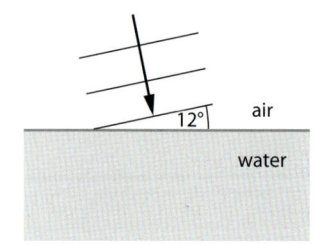

   i   Calculate the angle the wavefronts in the water make with the boundary. [2]
   ii Draw three wavefronts in the water. [2]
   iii Use your answer to **ii** to suggest why a person swimming underwater near a noisy beach does not hear much noise. [2]

14 a Describe what is meant by **polarised light**. [1]
   b Unpolarised light of intensity 320 W m^{-2} is incident on the first of three polarisers that are one behind the other. The first and third polarisers have vertical transmission axes. The middle polariser's transmission axis is rotated by an angle θ to the vertical. The transmitted intensity is 10 W m^{-2}. Determine θ. [3]
   c Partially polarised light is a combination of completely unpolarised light and light that is polarised. Partially polarised light is transmitted through a polariser. As the polariser is rotated by 360° the ratio of the maximum to the minimum transmitted intensity is 7.

   Determine the fraction of the beam's intensity that is due to the polarised light. [3]

   d A person is sitting behind a vertical glass wall. The person cannot be clearly seen because of the glare of reflections from the glass wall. Suggest how the use of a polariser makes it easier to see the person more clearly. [3]

15 In a two-slit experiment, red light is incident on two parallel slits. The light is observed on a screen far from the slits. The graph shows how the intensity of the light on the screen varies with distance y from M.

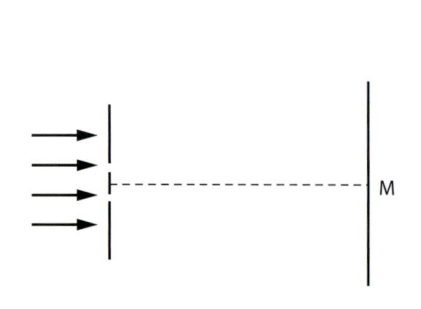

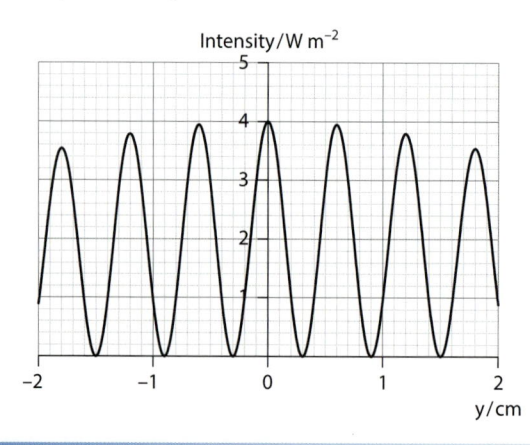

a Explain why light is able to reach the middle of the screen. [2]

b One of the slits is covered. State and explain the intensity of the light at M. [3]

c State the feature of this graph that shows that the slit width is not negligibly small. [1]

The distance to the screen is 3.2 m and the separation of the slits is 0.39 mm.

d Determine the wavelength of the light. [2]

e The red light is replaced by blue light. Predict what (if anything) will happen to the separation of the bright fringes on the screen. [2]

16 a Outline how a standing wave may be formed. [2]

A source of sound is placed above a tube containing water. The longest length of the air column above the water for which a strong sound is heard from the tube is 66 cm. The next length of the air column for which another strong sound is heard is 54 cm.

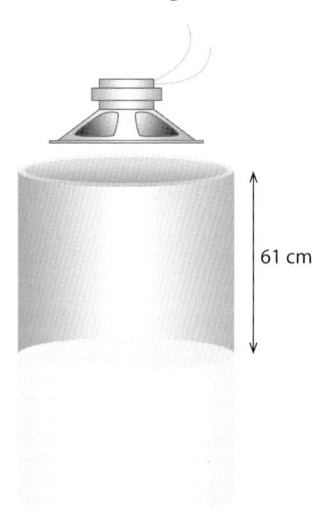

b **i** Explain the origin of the loud sound from the tube. [2]
  ii Suggest why a strong sound is heard for specific lengths of the air column. [2]
  iii Predict the next length of the air column for which a loud sound will be heard. [1]
  iv The frequency of the source is 1400 Hz. Estimate the speed of sound in the tube. [2]

5 Electricity and magnetism

Learning objectives

- Understand the concept and properties of electric charge.
- Apply Coulomb's law.
- Understand the concept of electric field.
- Work with electric current and direct current (dc).
- Understand the concept of electric potential difference.

5.1 Electric fields

This section examines the properties of electric charge and the phenomena that take place when charge is allowed to move so as to create an electric current. The concept of electric field is crucial to understanding electric current, as it is the electric field inside a conductor that forces electric charge to move.

Electric charge

Electric charge is a property of matter. Ordinarily, matter appears electrically neutral but if, for example, we take two plastic rods and rub each with a piece of wool, we find that the two rods repel each other. If we now rub two glass rods with silk, we find that the glass rods again repel each other, but the charged glass rod attracts the charged plastic rod. We can understand these observations (Figure 5.1) by assuming that:

- charge can be positive or negative, and the process of rubbing involves the transfer of charge from one body to the other
- there is a force between charged bodies that can be attractive or repulsive.

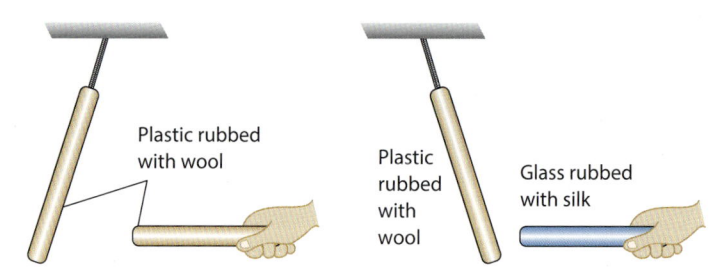

Figure 5.1 Two simple experiments to investigate properties of electric charge.

Benjamin Franklin (1706–1790) decided to call the sign of the charge on the glass rubbed with silk 'positive'. Much later, when electrons were discovered, it was found that electrons were attracted to the charged glass rod. This means that electrons must have negative charge. But if Franklin had called the charge on the glass rod negative, we would now be calling the electron's charge positive!

From experiments with charged objects, we learn that there is a force of attraction between charges of opposite sign and a force of repulsion between charges of the same sign. The magnitude of the force becomes smaller as the distance between the charged bodies increases.

Properties of electric charge

In ordinary matter, negative charge is a property of particles called electrons. Positive charge is a property of protons, which exist in the nuclei of atoms. (There are many other particles that have charge but they do not appear in ordinary matter – see Topic **7**.)

The second important property of electric charge is that it is **quantised**; this means the amount of electric charge on a body is always an integral multiple of a basic unit. The basic unit is the magnitude of the charge on the proton, an amount equal to 1.6×10^{-19} C, where C stands for coulomb, the SI unit of charge. This amount of charge is symbolised by e. The charge on an electron is $-e$. (If we take quarks into account, see Topic **7**, then the basic unit of charge is $\frac{e}{3}$.)

The third property is that charge is **conserved**. Like total energy, electric charge cannot be created or destroyed. In any process the total charge cannot change (see Worked example **5.1**).

In solid metals the atoms are fixed in position in a lattice but there are many 'free' electrons that do not belong to a particular atom. These electrons can move, carrying charge through the metal (see the section on the Tolman–Stewart experiment below). In liquids, and especially in gases, positive ions can also transport charge.

Materials that have many 'free' electrons (Figure **5.2**) are called **conductors**. As we will see, when these electrons are exposed to an electric field they begin to drift in the same direction, creating electric current.

Materials that do not have many 'free' electrons, so charge cannot move freely, are called **insulators**.

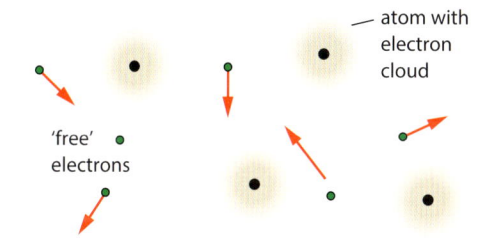

Figure 5.2 In a conductor there are many 'free' electrons that move around much like molecules of a gas.

Worked example

5.1 Two separated, identical conducting spheres are charged with charges of $4.0\,\mu C$ and $-12\,\mu C$, respectively. The spheres are allowed to touch and then are separated again. Determine the charge on each sphere.

The net charge on the two spheres is $4.0 - 12 = -8.0\,\mu C$. By symmetry, when the spheres are allowed to touch they will end up with the same charge, since they are identical.

The total amount of charge on the two spheres after separation must be $-8.0\,\mu C$ by charge conservation.

When they separate, each will therefore have a charge of $-4.0\,\mu C$.

The Tolman–Stewart experiment

Conclusive proof that the **charge carriers** in metals are electrons came in 1916 in an amazing experiment by R.C. Tolman (1881–1948) and T.D. Stewart (1890–1958). The idea behind the experiment was that if the charge carriers in a piece of metal were negative electrons, then these would be 'floating' inside the metal and would be free to move, whereas the positive charges would be anchored to fixed positions. Therefore, if the metal was very suddenly accelerated with a very large acceleration (Figure **5.3**), the electrons would be 'thrown back', creating an excess negative charge at the back of the metal and leaving an excess positive charge at the front – a great example of inertia! This excess charge was measured by Tolman and Stewart and found to be consistent with negative charge carriers inside metals. (More evidence is provided by the Hall effect – see Exam-style question **14** at the end of this topic.)

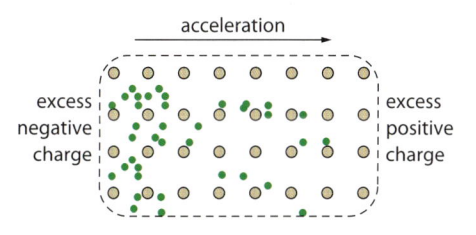

Figure 5.3 Redistribution of charge in a conductor accelerated to the right.

5 ELECTRICITY AND MAGNETISM 197

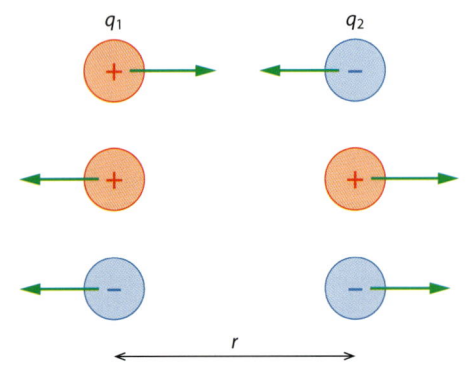

Figure 5.4 The force between two point electric charges is given by Coulomb's law and can be attractive or repulsive.

Coulomb's law for the electric force

The electric force between two electric charges, q_1 and q_2, was investigated in 1785 by Charles Augustin Coulomb (1736–1806). Coulomb discovered that this force is inversely proportional to the square of the separation of the charges and is proportional to the product of the two charges. It is attractive for charges of opposite sign and repulsive for charges of the same sign.

> In equation form, **Coulomb's law** states that the electric force F between two *point* charges q_1 and q_2 is given by:
> $$F = k\frac{q_1 q_2}{r^2}$$
> where r is the separation of the two charges (Figure 5.4).

The constant k is also written as $\dfrac{1}{4\pi\varepsilon_0}$, so that Coulomb's law reads:

$$F = \frac{1}{4\pi\varepsilon_0}\frac{q_1 q_2}{r^2}$$

The numerical value of the factor $\dfrac{1}{4\pi\varepsilon_0}$ or k is $8.99 \times 10^9 \, \text{N}\,\text{m}^2\,\text{C}^{-2}$ in a vacuum. The constant ε_0 is called the electric **permittivity of vacuum** and $\varepsilon_0 = 8.85 \times 10^{-12} \, \text{C}^2\,\text{N}^{-1}\,\text{m}^{-2}$. If the charges are in a medium, such as plastic or water, then we must use the value of ε appropriate to that medium. Air has roughly the same value of ε as a vacuum.

Worked examples

5.2 The electric permittivity of graphite is 12 times larger than that of a vacuum. The force between two point charges in a vacuum is F. The two charges are embedded in graphite and their separation is doubled. Predict the new force between the charges in terms of F.

The force F in a vacuum is given by:

$$F = \frac{1}{4\pi\varepsilon_0}\frac{q_1 q_2}{r^2}$$

The new value of ε is $12\varepsilon_0$ and the separation of the charges is $2r$. Force F' in graphite is therefore:

$$F' = \frac{1}{4\pi(12\varepsilon_0)}\frac{q_1 q_2}{(2r)^2} = \frac{1}{12 \times 4}\frac{1}{4\pi\varepsilon_0}\frac{q_1 q_2}{r^2} = \frac{1}{48} \times F$$

The new force is $\dfrac{F}{48}$.

5.3 Two charges, $q_1 = 2.0\,\mu C$ and $q_2 = 8.0\,\mu C$, are placed along a straight line separated by a distance of 3.0 cm.
    a Calculate the force exerted on each charge.
    b The charge q_1 is increased to $4.0\,\mu C$. Determine the force on each charge now.

a This is a straightforward application of the formula $F = k\dfrac{q_1 q_2}{r^2}$. We find that:

$$F = \dfrac{9 \times 10^9 \times 2.0 \times 8.0 \times 10^{-12}}{9.0 \times 10^{-4}}$$

$$F = 160\,\text{N}$$

This is the force that q_1 exerts on q_2, and vice versa.

b Since the charge doubles the force doubles to $F = 320\,\text{N}$ on both charges.

Exam tip
It is a common mistake to double the force on one charge, but not the other.

5.4 A positive charge q is placed on the line joining q_1 and q_2 in Worked example **5.3**. Determine the distance from q_1 where this third positive charge experiences zero net force.

Let that distance be x. A positive charge q at that point would experience a force from q_1 equal to $F_1 = k\dfrac{q_1 q}{x^2}$ and a force in the opposite direction from q_2 equal to $F_2 = k\dfrac{q_2 q}{(d-x)^2}$
where $d = 3.0\,\text{cm}$ is the distance between q_1 and q_2 (Figure **5.5**).

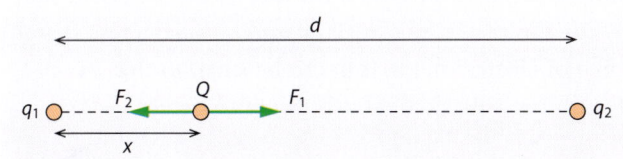

Figure 5.5

Charge q will experience no net force when $F_1 = F_2$, so:

$$k\dfrac{q_1 q}{x^2} = k\dfrac{q_2 q}{(d-x)^2}$$

Dividing both sides by kq and substituting $q_1 = 2.0\,\mu C$ and $q_2 = 8.0\,\mu C$ gives:

$$\dfrac{2.0}{x^2} = \dfrac{8.0}{(d-x)^2}$$

$$(d-x)^2 = 4x^2$$

$$(d-x) = 2x$$

$$x = \dfrac{d}{3} = 1.0\,\text{cm}$$

Exam tip
We do not have to change units to C. The units on both sides of the equation are the same (μC) and cancel out.

5 ELECTRICITY AND MAGNETISM

> ### Action at a distance and fields
>
> These are some of the words of the Scottish theoretical physicist James Clerk Maxwell (1831–1879). Maxwell was one of the scientists who created the concept of the field.
>
> I have preferred to seek an explanation [of electricity and magnetism] by supposing them to be produced by actions which go on in the surrounding medium as well as in the excited bodies, and endeavouring to explain the action between distant bodies without assuming the existence of forces capable of acting directly … The theory I propose may therefore be called a theory of the Electromagnetic field because it has to do with the space in the neighbourhood of the electric and magnetic bodies.
>
> J.C. Maxwell, 1865

Electric field

The space around a charge or an arrangement of charges is different from space in which no charges are present. It contains an **electric field**. We can test whether a space has an electric field by bringing a small, point, positive charge q into the space. If q experiences an electric force, then there is an electric field. If no force is experienced, then there is no electric field (the electric field is zero). For this reason the small charge is called a test charge: it tests for the existence of electric fields. It has to be small so that its presence does not disturb the electric field it is trying to detect.

> The **electric field strength** is defined as the electric force per unit charge experienced by a small, positive point charge q:
> $$E = \frac{F}{q}$$
> Note that electric field is a vector quantity. The direction of the electric field is the same as the direction of the force experienced by a positive charge at the given point (Figure 5.6). The unit of electric field is N C^{-1}.

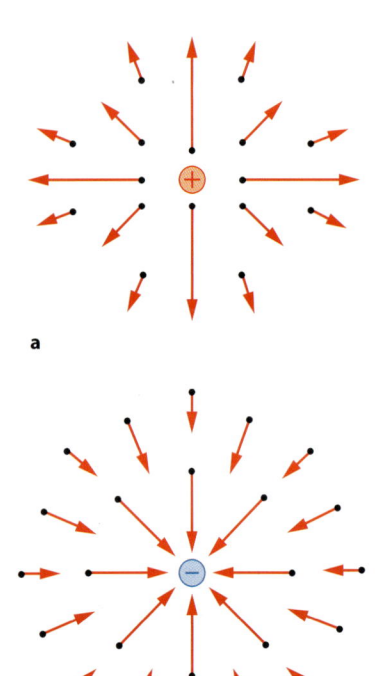

Figure 5.6 The electric field at various positions near **a** a positive and **b** a negative point charge.

The force experienced by a test charge q placed a distance r from a point charge Q is (by Coulomb's law):

$$F = k\frac{Qq}{r^2}$$

and so from the definition $E = \frac{F}{q}$ the magnitude of the electric field is:

$$E = k\frac{(Qq/r^2)}{q}$$

$$E = k\frac{Q}{r^2}$$

This formula also applies outside a conducting sphere that has charge Q on its surface. (Inside the sphere the field is zero; the net charge on the sphere is distributed on the surface.)

Electric current

In a conductor the 'free' electrons move randomly, much like gas molecules in a container. They do so with high speeds, of the order of $10^5\,\mathrm{m\,s^{-1}}$. This random motion, however, does not result in electric current – as many electrons move in one direction as in another (Figure **5.7**) and so no charge is transferred.

As we just mentioned, the electric field inside a conductor is zero in static situations, i.e. when there is no current.

If an electric field is applied across the conductor, the free electrons experience a force that pushes them in the opposite direction to the direction of the field (the direction is opposite because the charge of the electron is negative). This motion of electrons in the *same direction* is a **direct current** (dc). This topic deals with direct current and we will refer to this as, simply, current. (Alternating current (ac) will be dealt with in Topic **11**.)

We define electric current I in a conductor as the rate of flow of charge through its cross-section:

$$I = \frac{\Delta q}{\Delta t}.$$

The unit of electric current is the ampere (A), which is a flow of one coulomb of charge per second ($1\,\mathrm{A} = 1\,\mathrm{C\,s^{-1}}$). The ampere is one of the fundamental units of the SI system.

(The definition of the ampere is in terms of the magnetic force between two parallel conductors; we will look at this in Subtopic **5.4**.)

Figure **5.8** shows the electric field inside a conductor. The field follows the shape of the conductor, forcing electrons to move in the opposite direction along the conductor.

In Figure **5.9**, electrons are moving in a metallic wire. The average speed with which the electrons move in the direction opposite to the electric field is called the drift speed, v. How many electrons will move through the cross-sectional area of the wire (coloured orange) within

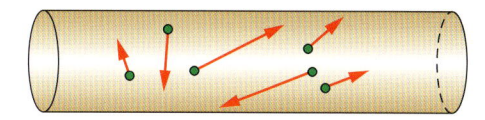

Figure 5.7 The random electron velocities do not carry net charge in any direction.

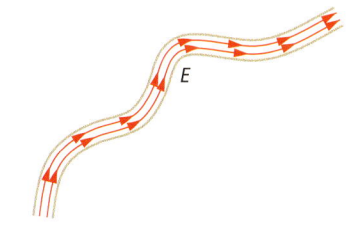

Figure 5.8 The electric field inside a conductor follows the shape of the conductor.

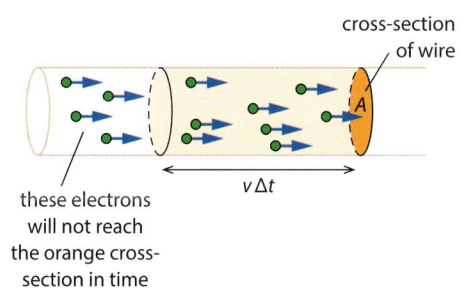

Figure 5.9 Only the electrons within the shaded volume will manage to go through the marked cross-sectional area in time Δt.

5 ELECTRICITY AND MAGNETISM

time Δt? Those electrons that are far away from the orange cross-section will not travel far enough. The distance covered by electrons in a time interval Δt is $v\Delta t$, and so only those electrons within the volume of the wire shaded pale orange will reach the cross-section in time. How many electrons are there in this volume? The shaded volume is $Av\Delta t$, where A is the cross-sectional area of the wire. If there are n electrons per unit volume, the number of electrons within the shaded volume is $nAv\Delta t$. If each electron carries charge q, then the charge that passes through the cross-section is $nAvq\Delta t$. So:

$$I = \frac{\Delta q}{\Delta t}$$

$$I = \frac{nAvq\Delta t}{\Delta t}$$

$$I = nAvq$$

(For charge carriers other than electrons, q is the charge on that carrier.)

Worked examples

5.5 Estimate the magnitude of the drift speed in a wire that carries a current of 1 A. The wire has radius 2 mm and the number of electrons per unit volume (the number density) of free electrons is $n = 10^{28}\,\text{m}^{-3}$.

The cross-sectional area of the wire is $A = \pi(2\,\text{mm})^2 \approx 1.3 \times 10^{-5}\,\text{m}^2$.

Substituting in $I = nAvq$, we have:

$1 = 10^{28} \times 1.3 \times 10^{-5} \times v \times 1.6 \times 10^{-19}$

Collecting powers of 10 and rearranging:

$$v = \frac{1}{1.3 \times 1.6 \times 10^4}$$

$v \approx 5 \times 10^{-5}\,\text{m s}^{-1}$

So v is about $0.05\,\text{mm s}^{-1}$. This is quite a low speed, perhaps surprisingly so.

5.6 In view of the very low drift speed of electrons, discuss why lights turn on essentially without delay after the switch is turned on.

Lights come on immediately because when the switch is turned on, an electric field is established within the wire at a speed close to the speed of light. As soon as the field is established, every free electron in the wire starts moving no matter where it is, and this includes the electrons in the lamp filament itself.

5.7 Figure **5.10** shows electric current that flows in a conductor of variable cross-sectional area. State and explain whether the electron drift speed at **B** is smaller than, equal to, or greater than that at **A**.

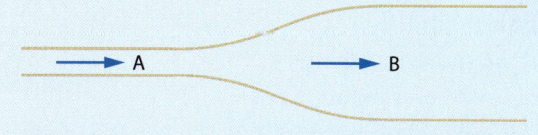

Figure 5.10

The current at A and B is the same (because of conservation of charge). Since the current is given by $I = nAvq$, and n and q are constant, the drift speed at B is smaller than that at A because the area is greater.

Electric potential difference

When charge q moves near other charges it will, in general, experience forces. So in moving the charge, work must be done. If the work done in moving a charge q from A to B is W, the ratio W/q is defined to be the potential difference between points A and B (Figure **5.11**).

> The **potential difference** V between two points is the work done per unit charge to move a point charge from one point to the other:
> $$V = \frac{W}{q}$$
> The unit of potential is the volt, V, and $1\,\text{V} = 1\,\text{J}\,\text{C}^{-1}$.

Therefore the work required to move a charge q between two points with potential difference V is $W = qV$.

> It is very important to realise that whenever there is a potential difference there has to be an electric field.

The actual path taken does not affect the amount of work that has to be done on the charge, as shown in Figure **5.12**.

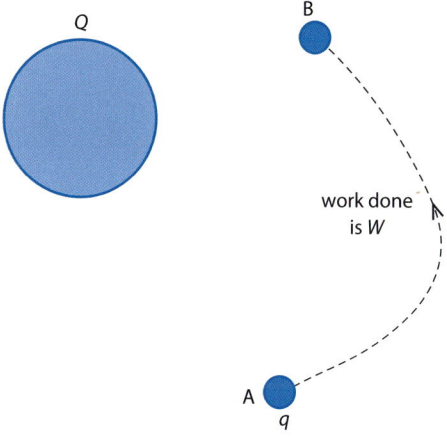

Figure 5.11 The potential difference between points A and B is the work done to move the charge from A to B divided by q.

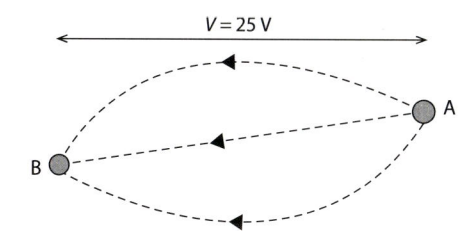

Figure 5.12 The work done in moving a charge q from A to B is the same no matter what path is followed. If $q = 2\,\mu\text{C}$, the work done is 50 μJ for all three paths.

Worked example

5.8 The work done in moving a charge of $2.0\,\mu\text{C}$ between two points in an electric field is $1.50 \times 10^{-4}\,\text{J}$. Determine the potential difference between the two points.

From the definition, the potential difference is:

$$V = \frac{W}{q}$$

$$V = \frac{1.50 \times 10^{-4}}{2.0 \times 10^{-6}}$$

$$V = 75\,\text{V}$$

5 ELECTRICITY AND MAGNETISM

Exam tip
If we move the charge q between two points whose potential difference is V, we will have to do work qV. We are assuming that the charge is moved slowly and with constant speed from one point to the other. If, on the other hand, the charge is left alone in the electric field, the electric forces will do work qV on the charge; this work will go into changing the kinetic energy of the charge. The kinetic energy may increase or decrease – see Worked example 5.9.

The electronvolt

The joule is too large a unit of energy for the microscopic world. A more convenient unit (but not part of the SI system) is the electronvolt, eV.

> We define the electronvolt as the work done when a charge equal to one electron charge is taken across a potential difference of one volt.

Thus, using $W = qV$:

$$1\,\text{eV} = 1.6 \times 10^{-19}\,\text{C} \times 1\,\text{V}$$
$$= 1.6 \times 10^{-19}\,\text{J}$$

When a charge equal to two electron charges is taken across a potential difference of 1 V, the work done is 2 eV; moving a charge equal to three electron charges across a potential difference of 5 V results in work of 15 eV, and so on.

Worked example

5.9 a Determine the speed of a proton ($m = 1.67 \times 10^{-27}$ kg) that is accelerated from rest by a potential difference of 5.0×10^3 V.

b A proton with speed $4.4 \times 10^5\,\text{m s}^{-1}$ enters a region of electric field directed in such a way that the proton is slowed down. Determine the potential difference required to slow the proton down to half its initial speed.

a The work done by the electric forces in accelerating the proton is $W = qV$, so:

$$W = 5.0 \times 10^3\,\text{eV}$$

In joules this is:

$$W = 1.6 \times 10^{-19} \times 5.0 \times 10^3 = 8.0 \times 10^{-16}\,\text{J}$$

The work done goes into increasing the kinetic energy of the proton. Thus:

$$E_K = \tfrac{1}{2} m v^2$$

$$\Rightarrow v = \sqrt{\frac{2 E_K}{m}}$$

$$v = \sqrt{\frac{2 \times 8.0 \times 10^{-16}}{1.67 \times 10^{-27}}}$$

$$v = 9.8 \times 10^5\,\text{m s}^{-1}$$

Exam tip
In **a** it is clear that the proton is being accelerated and so qV goes towards increasing the kinetic energy. In **b** it is equally clear that the kinetic energy is decreasing.
In calculations, the unit eV must be changed to joules, the SI unit of energy.

$$W(\text{J}) = W(\text{eV}) \times e$$

b The magnitude of the decrease in kinetic energy of the proton is:

$\Delta E_K = \frac{1}{2} \times 1.67 \times 10^{-27} [(4.4 \times 10^5)^2 - (2.2 \times 10^5)^2]$

$\Delta E_K = 1.2 \times 10^{-16}$ J

Converting to electronvolts:

$\Delta E_K = \dfrac{1.2 \times 10^{-16} \text{ J}}{1.6 \times 10^{-19} \text{ J eV}^{-1}}$

$= 750$ eV

Hence $qV = 750$ eV, implying $V = 750$ volts.

Nature of science

The microscopic–macroscopic connection

If you are plumber, do you need to know the molecular structure of water? The flow of water in pipes is a macroscopic phenomenon whereas the detailed molecular structure of water is microscopic. We have a vast difference in scales of length in the two cases. In very many phenomena the presence of two different scales means that the detailed physics operating at one scale does not affect the physics at the other. This is also the case with current: it was possible to give detailed descriptions of the behaviour of current in circuits long before it was discovered that current is electrons moving in the same direction. (However, the most complicated problems in physics are those in which the physics at one length scale does affect the physics at the other scale.)

? Test yourself

1 a Calculate the force between two charges q_1 of $2.0\,\mu$C and q_2 $4.0\,\mu$C separated by $r = 5.0$ cm.
  b Let the force calculated in a be F. In terms of F and without further calculations, state the force between these charges when:
    i the separation r of the charges is doubled
    ii q_1 and r are both doubled
    iii q_1, q_2 and r are all doubled.
2 Three charges are placed on a straight line as shown in the diagram. Calculate the net force on the middle charge.

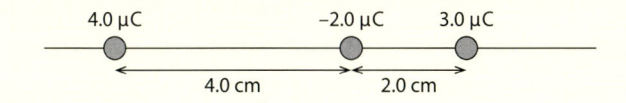

4.0 µC   −2.0 µC   3.0 µC
  ●──────────────●────────●
       4.0 cm   2.0 cm

3 In the previous question, determine the position of the middle charge so that it is in equilibrium.
4 Calculate the force (magnitude and direction) on the charge q in the diagram where $q = 3.0\,\mu$C.

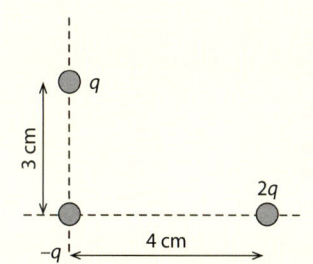

```
            ● q
            |
         3 cm
            |
  -q ●------+------● 2q
            4 cm
```

5 ELECTRICITY AND MAGNETISM

5 Two plastic spheres each of mass 100.0 mg are suspended from very fine insulating strings of length 85.0 cm. When equal charges are placed on the spheres, the spheres repel and are in equilibrium when 10.0 cm apart.
   a Determine the charge on each sphere.
   b Estimate how many electron charges this corresponds to.

6 Consider two people, each of mass 60 kg, a distance of 10 m apart.
   a Assuming that all the mass in each person is made out of water, estimate how many electrons there are in each person.
   b Hence, estimate the electrostatic force of repulsion between the two people due to the electrons.
   c List any other simplifying assumptions you have made to make your estimate possible.
   d No such force is observed in practice. Suggest why this is so.

7 A charge of magnitude $+5.0\,\mu C$ experiences an electric force of magnitude $3.0 \times 10^{-5}\,N$ when placed at a point in space. Determine the electric field at that point.

8 The electric field is a vector and so two electric fields at the same point in space must be added according to the laws of vector addition. Consider two equal positive charges q, each $2.00\,\mu C$, separated by $a = 10.0\,cm$ and a point P a distance of $d = 30.0\,cm$, as shown in the diagram. The diagram shows the directions of the electric fields produced at P by each charge. Determine the magnitude and direction of the net electric field at P.

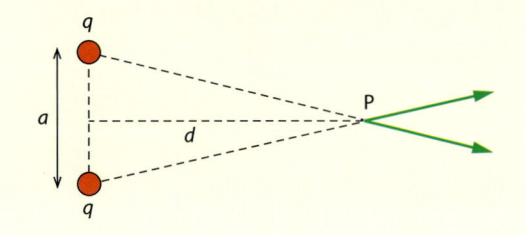

9 Repeat the calculation of question 8 where the top charge is $+2.00\,\mu C$ and the bottom charge is $-2.00\,\mu C$.

10 The electron drift speed in a copper wire of diameter 1.8 mm is $3.6 \times 10^{-4}\,m\,s^{-1}$. The number of free electrons per unit volume for copper is $8.5 \times 10^{28}\,m^{-3}$. Estimate the current in the wire.

11 In the diagram, the current through the 1.0 mm diameter part of the wire is 1.2 A and the drift speed is $2.2 \times 10^{-4}\,m\,s^{-1}$.

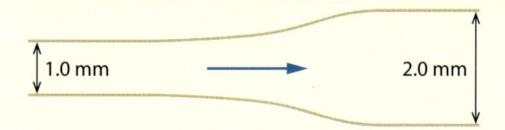

Calculate a the current and b the drift speed in the part of the wire with 2.0 mm diameter.

12 Silver has 5.8×10^{28} free electrons per m^3. If the current in a 2 mm radius silver wire is 5.0 A, find the velocity with which the electrons drift in the wire.

13 a If a current of 10.0 A flows through a heater, how much charge passes through the heater in 1 h?
   b How many electrons does this charge correspond to?

14 A conducting sphere of radius 15.0 cm has a positive charge of $4.0\,\mu C$ deposited on its surface. Calculate the magnitude of the electric field produced by the charge at distances from the centre of the sphere of:
   a 0.0 cm
   b 5.0 cm
   c 15.0 cm
   d 20.0 cm.

5.2 Heating effect of electric currents

This section will introduce the main ideas behind electric circuits. We begin by discussing how the movement of electrons inside conductors (i.e. electric current) results in heating of the conductor.

Collisions of electrons with lattice atoms

The effect of an electric field within a conductor, for example in a metal wire, is to accelerate the free electrons. The electrons therefore gain kinetic energy as they move through the metal. The electrons suffer **inelastic** collisions with the metal atoms, which means they lose energy to the atoms of the wire. The electric field will again accelerate the electrons until the next collision, and this process repeats. In this way, the electrons keep providing energy to the atoms of the wire. The atoms in the wire vibrate about their equilibrium positions with increased kinetic energy. This shows up **macroscopically** as an increase in the temperature of the wire.

Electric resistance

In Subtopic **5.1** we stressed that whenever there is a potential difference there must also be an electric field. So when a potential difference is established at the ends of a conductor, an electric field is established within the conductor that forces electrons to move, i.e. creating an electric current (Figure **5.13a**). Now, when the same potential difference is established at the ends of different conductors, the size of the current is different in the different conductors. What determines how much current will flow for a given potential difference is a property of the conductor called its **electric resistance**.

> The electric resistance R of a conductor is defined as the potential difference V across its ends divided by the current I passing through it:
>
> $$R = \frac{V}{I}$$
>
> The unit of electric resistance is the volt per ampere. This is defined to be the ohm, symbol Ω.

The electric resistance of conducting wires is very small so it is a good approximation to ignore this resistance. Conducting wires are represented by thin line segments in diagrams. Conductors whose resistance cannot be neglected are denoted by boxes; they are called **resistors** (Figure **5.13b**).

In 1826, the German scientist Georg Ohm (1789–1854) discovered that, when the temperature of most metallic conductors is kept constant, the current through the conductor is proportional to the potential difference across it:

$$I \propto V$$

This statement is known as **Ohm's law**.

Learning objectives

- Understand how current in a circuit component generates thermal energy.
- Find current, potential difference and power dissipated in circuit components.
- Define and understand electric resistance.
- Describe Ohm's law.
- Investigate factors that affect resistance.
- Apply Kirchhoff's laws to more complicated circuits.

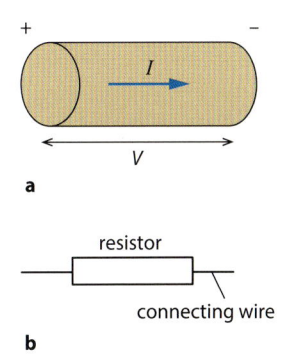

Figure 5.13 a The potential difference V across the ends of the conductor creates an electric field within the conductor that forces a current I through the conductor. **b** How we represent a resistor and connecting wires in a circuit diagram.

Materials that obey Ohm's law have a constant resistance at constant temperature. For these ohmic materials, a graph of I versus V gives a straight line through the origin (Figure **5.14a**).

A filament light bulb will obey Ohm's law as long as the current through it is small. As the current is increased, the temperature of the filament increases and so does the resistance. Other devices, such as the **diode** or a **thermistor**, also deviate from Ohm's law. Graphs of current versus potential difference for these devices are shown in Figure **5.14**.

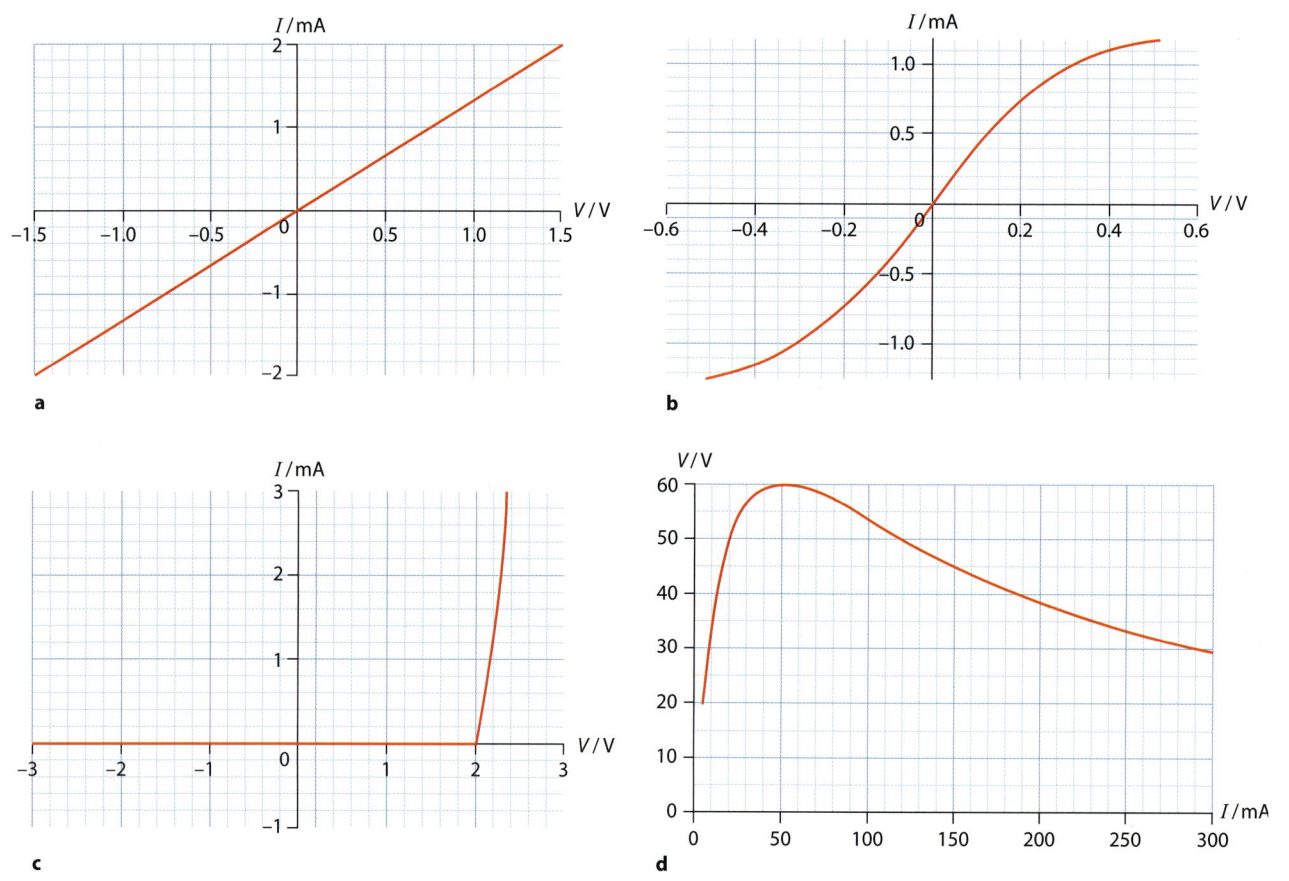

Figure 5.14 Graph **a** shows the current–potential difference graph for a material that obeys Ohm's law. The graphs for **b** a lamp filament, **c** a diode and **d** a thermistor show that these devices do not obey this law. (Notice that for the thermistor we plot voltage versus current.)

In the first graph for the ohmic material, no matter which point on the graph we choose (say the one with voltage 1.2 V and current 1.6 mA), the resistance is always the same:

$$R = \frac{1.2}{1.6 \times 10^{-3}} = 750\,\Omega$$

However, looking at the graph in Figure **5.14b** (the lamp filament), we see that at a voltage of 0.2 V the current is 0.8 mA and so the resistance is:

$$R = \frac{0.2}{0.8 \times 10^{-3}} = 250\,\Omega$$

208

At a voltage of 0.3 V the current is 1.0 mA and the resistance is:

$$R = \frac{0.3}{1.0 \times 10^{-3}} = 300\,\Omega$$

We see that as the current in the filament increases the resistance increases, so Ohm's law is not obeyed. This is a **non-ohmic** device.

Experiments show that three factors affect the resistance of a wire kept at constant temperature. They are:
- the nature of the material
- the length of the wire
- the cross-sectional area of the wire.

For most metallic materials, an increase in the temperature results in an increase in the resistance.

> It is found from experiment that the electric resistance R of a wire (at fixed temperature) is proportional to its length L and inversely proportional to the cross-sectional area A:
>
> $$R = \rho \frac{L}{A}$$
>
> The constant ρ is called **resistivity** and depends on the material of the conductor and the temperature. The unit of resistivity is $\Omega\,m$.

The formula for resistance shows that if we double the cross-sectional area of the conductor the resistance halves; and if we double the length, the resistance doubles. How do we understand these results? Figure **5.15** shows that if we double the cross-sectional area A of a wire, the current in the metal for the same potential difference will double as well (recall that $I = nAvq$). Since $R = \frac{V}{I}$, the resistance R halves. What if we double the length L of the wire? The work done to move a charge q can be calculated two ways: one is through $W = qV$. The other is through $W = FL = qEL$. So, if L doubles the potential difference must also double. The current stays the same and so the resistance R doubles.

For most metallic conductors, increasing the temperature increases the resistance. With an increased temperature the atoms of the conductor vibrate more and this increases the number of collisions per second. This in turn means that the average distance travelled by the electrons between collisions is reduced, i.e. the drift speed is reduced. This means the current is reduced and so resistance increases.

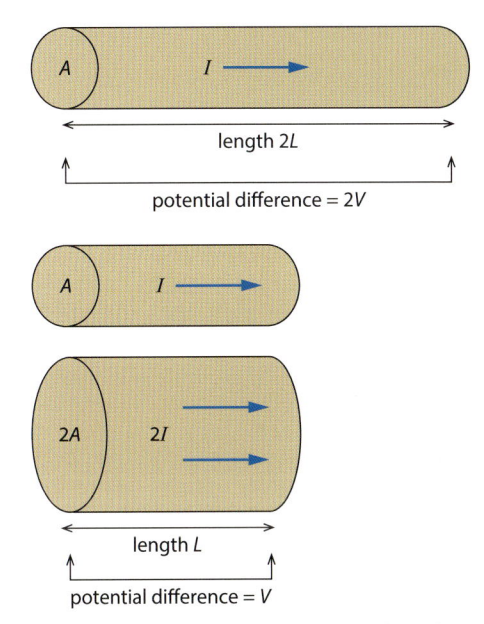

Figure 5.15 The effect of change in length L and cross-sectional area A on the current flowing in a wire.

5 ELECTRICITY AND MAGNETISM

Worked example

5.10 The resistivity of copper is $1.68 \times 10^{-8}\,\Omega\,m$. Calculate the length of a copper wire of diameter 4.00 mm that has a resistance of 5.00 Ω.

We use $R = \rho \dfrac{L}{A}$ to get $L = \dfrac{RA}{\rho}$ and so:

$$L = \dfrac{5.00 \times \pi \times (2.00 \times 10^{-3})^2}{1.68 \times 10^{-8}}$$

$$L = 3739\,m$$

The length of copper wire is about 3.74 km.

Exam tip
Do not confuse diameter with radius.

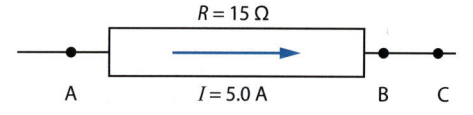

Figure 5.16 There is a voltage across points A and B and zero voltage across B and C.

Voltage

The defining equation for resistance, $R = \dfrac{V}{I}$, can be rearranged in terms of the potential difference V:

$$V = IR$$

This says that if there is a current through a conductor that has resistance, i.e. a resistor, then there must be a potential difference across the ends of that resistor. The term **voltage** is commonly used for the potential difference at the ends of a resistor.

Figure 5.16 shows part of a circuit. The current is 5.0 A and the resistance is 15 Ω. The voltage across the resistor is given by $V = IR = 5.0 \times 15 = 75\,V$. The resistance between B and C is zero, so the voltage across B and C is zero.

Electric power

We saw earlier that whenever an electric charge q is moved from one point to another when there is a potential difference V between these points, work is done. This work is given by $W = qV$.

Consider a resistor with a potential difference V across its ends. Since power is the rate of doing work, the power P dissipated in the resistor in moving a charge q across it in time t is:

$$P = \dfrac{\text{work done}}{\text{time taken}}$$

$$P = \dfrac{qV}{t}$$

But $\dfrac{q}{t}$ is the current I in the resistor, so the **power** is given by:

$$P = IV$$

This power manifests itself in thermal energy and/or work performed by an electrical device (Figure **5.17**). We can use $R = \frac{V}{I}$ to rewrite the formula for power in equivalent ways:

$$P = IV = RI^2 = \frac{V^2}{R}$$

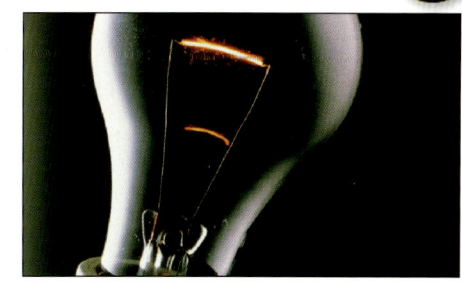

Figure 5.17 The metal filament in a light bulb glows as the current passes through it. It is also very hot. This shows that electrical energy is converted into both thermal energy and light.

Worked examples

5.11 A resistor of resistance 12 Ω has a current of 2.0 A flowing through it. How much energy is generated in the resistor in one minute?

The power generated in the resistor is:

$P = RI^2$

$P = 12 \times 4 = 48$ W

Thus, in one minute (60 s) the energy E generated is:

$E = 48 \times 60 \text{ J} = 2.9 \times 10^3 \text{ J}$

Electrical devices are usually rated according to the power they use. A light bulb rated as 60 W at 220 V means that it will dissipate 60 W when a potential difference of 220 V is applied across its ends. If the potential difference across its ends is anything other than 220 V, the power dissipated will be different from 60 W.

5.12 A light bulb rated as 60 W at 220 V has a potential difference of 110 V across its ends. Find the power dissipated in this light bulb.

Exam tip
The power of the light bulb is 60 W only when the voltage across it is 220 V. If we change the voltage we will change the power.

Let R be the resistance of the light bulb and P the power we want to find. Assuming R stays constant (so that it is the same when 220 V and 110 V are applied to its ends), we have:

$P = \frac{110^2}{R}$ and $60 = \frac{220^2}{R}$

Dividing the first equation by the second, we find:

$\frac{P}{60} = \frac{110^2}{220^2}$

This gives:

$P = 15$ W

5 ELECTRICITY AND MAGNETISM

Exam tip
You must understand the ideas that keep coming up in this topic: to make charges move in the same direction we need an electric field to exert forces on the charges. To have an electric field means there must be a potential difference. So something must provide that potential difference.

Electromotive force (emf)

The concept of emf will be discussed in detail in Subtopic 5.3. Here we need a first look at emf in order to start discussing circuits. Charges need to be pushed in order to drift in the same direction inside a conductor. To do this we need an electric field. To have an electric field requires a source of potential difference. Cells use the energy from chemical reactions to provide potential difference. Figure 5.18 shows a simple circuit in which the potential difference is supplied by a battery – a battery is a collection of cells. The symbols for cells and batteries are shown in Table 5.1.

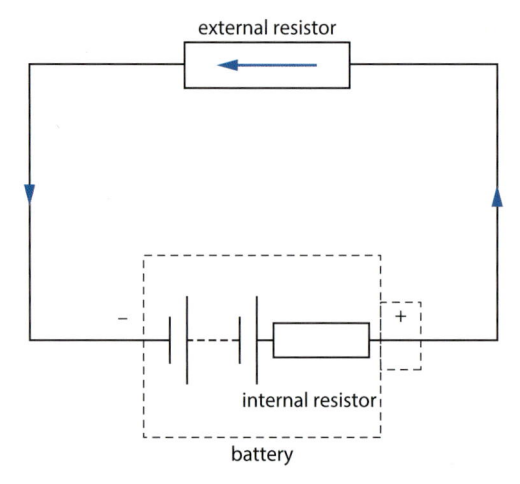

Figure 5.18 A simple circuit consisting of a battery, connecting wires and a resistor. Note that the battery has internal resistance. The current enters the circuit from the positive pole of the battery.

We define **emf** as the work done per unit charge in moving charge across the battery terminals. As we will see in Subtopic 5.3, emf is the potential difference across the battery terminals when the battery has no internal resistance. Emf is measured in volts. Emf is also the power provided by the battery per unit current:

$$\varepsilon = \mathrm{emf} = \frac{W}{q} = \frac{P}{I}$$

This definition is very useful when discussing circuits.

Simple circuits

We have so far defined emf, voltage, resistance, current and power dissipated in a resistor. This means that we are now ready to put all these ideas together to start discussing the main topic of this chapter, electric circuits. The circuits we will study at Standard Level will include cells and batteries, connecting wires, ammeters (to measure current) and voltmeters (to measure voltage). The symbols used for these circuit components are shown in Table 5.1. In Topic 11 we will extend things so as to include another type of circuit element, the capacitor.

Symbol	Component name
	connection lead
	cell
	battery of cells
	resistor
	dc power supply
	ac power supply
	junction of conductors
	crossing conductors (no connection)
	lamp
	voltmeter
	ammeter
	switch
	galvanometer
	potentiometer
	variable resistor
	heating element

Table 5.1 Names of electrical components and their circuit symbols.

We start with the simplest type of circuit – a single-loop circuit, as shown in Figure 5.19. The current enters the circuit from the positive terminal of the cell. The direction of the current is shown by the blue arrow. The terminals of the cell are directly connected to the ends of the resistor (there is no intervening internal resistor). Therefore the potential difference at the ends of the resistor is 12 V. Using the definition of resistance we write $R = \frac{V}{I}$, i.e. $24 = \frac{12}{I}$, giving the current in the circuit to be $I = 0.5$ A.

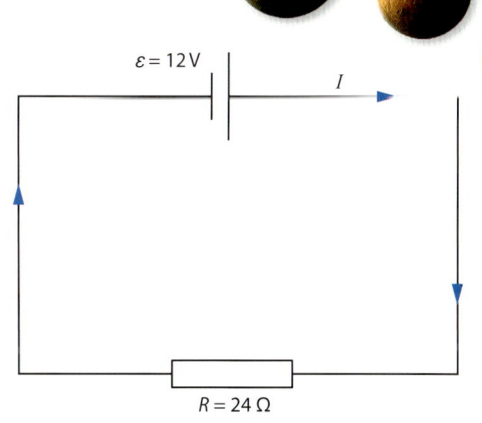

Figure 5.19 A simple one-loop circuit with one cell with negligible internal resistance and one resistor.

Resistors in series

Figure 5.20 shows part of a simple circuit, but now there are three resistors connected in series. Connecting resistors in **series** means that there are no junctions in the wire connecting any two resistors and so the current through all of them is the same. Let I be the common current in the three resistors.

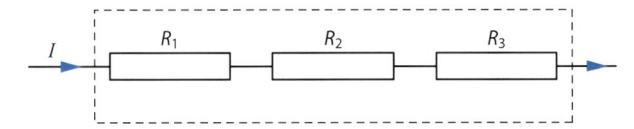

Figure 5.20 Three resistors in series.

The potential difference across each of the resistors is:

$V_1 = IR_1$, $V_2 = IR_2$ and $V_3 = IR_3$

The sum of the potential differences is thus:

$V = IR_1 + IR_2 + IR_3 = I(R_1 + R_2 + R_3)$

If we were to replace the three resistors by a single resistor of value $R_1 + R_2 + R_3$ (in other words, if we were to replace the contents of the dotted box in Figure 5.20 with a single resistor, as in the circuit shown in Figure 5.21), we would not be able to tell the difference. The same current comes into the dotted box and the same potential difference exists across its ends.

We thus define the equivalent or total resistance of the three resistors of Figure 5.21 by:

$R_{total} = R_1 + R_2 + R_3$

If more than three were present, we would simply add all of them. Adding resistors in series increases the total resistance.

In a circuit, a combination of resistors like those in Figure 5.21 is equivalent to the single total or equivalent resistor. Suppose we now connect the three resistors to a battery of negligible internal resistance and emf equal to 24 V. Suppose that $R_1 = 2.0\,\Omega$, $R_2 = 6.0\,\Omega$ and $R_3 = 4.0\,\Omega$. We replace the three resistors by the equivalent resistor of $R_{total} = 2.0 + 6.0 + 4.0 = 12\,\Omega$. We now observe that the potential difference

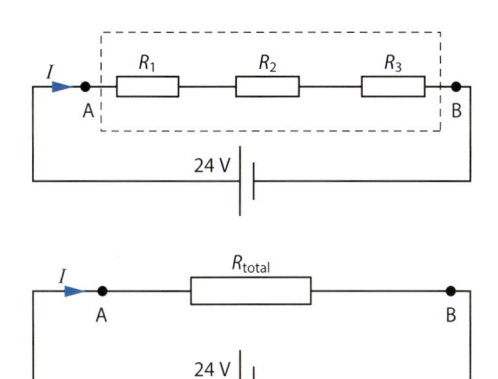

Figure 5.21 The top circuit is replaced by the equivalent circuit containing just one resistor.

5 ELECTRICITY AND MAGNETISM

across the equivalent resistor is known. It is simply 24 V and hence the current through the equivalent resistor is found as follows:

$$R = \frac{V}{I}$$

$$\Rightarrow I = \frac{V}{R} = \frac{24}{12} = 2.0 \text{ A}$$

This current, therefore, is also the current that enters the dotted box: that is, it is the current in each of the three resistors of the original circuit. We may thus deduce that the potential differences across the three resistors are:

$$V_1 = IR_1 = 4.0 \text{ V}$$

$$V_2 = IR_2 = 12 \text{ V}$$

$$V_3 = IR_3 = 8.0 \text{ V}$$

Resistors in parallel

Consider now part of another circuit, in which the current splits into three other currents that flow in three resistors, as shown in Figure **5.22**. The current that enters the junction at A must equal the current that leaves the junction at B, by the law of conservation of charge. The left ends of the three resistors are connected at the same point and the same is true for the right ends. This means that three resistors have the same potential difference across them. This is called a **parallel connection**.

We must then have that:

$$I = I_1 + I_2 + I_3$$

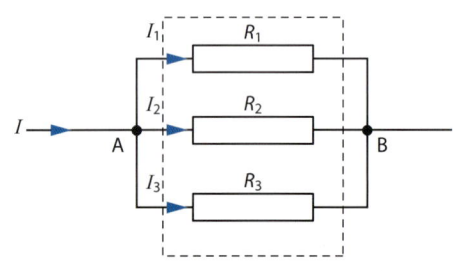

Figure 5.22 Three resistors connected in parallel.

This is a consequence of charge conservation. The current entering the junction is I and the currents leaving the junction are I_1, I_2 and I_3. Whatever charge enters the junction must exit the junction and so the sum of the currents into a junction equals the sum of the currents leaving the junction. This is known as **Kirchhoff's current law**.

> Kirchhoff's current law (Kirchhoff's first law) states that:
>
> $$\Sigma I_{in} = \Sigma I_{out}$$

Let V be the common potential difference across the resistors. Then:

$$I_1 = \frac{V}{R_1}, \quad I_2 = \frac{V}{R_2} \quad \text{and} \quad I_3 = \frac{V}{R_3}$$

and so:

$$I = \frac{V}{R_1} + \frac{V}{R_2} + \frac{V}{R_3}$$

$$I = V\left(\frac{1}{R_1} + \frac{1}{R_2} + \frac{1}{R_3}\right)$$

214

If we replace the three resistors in the dotted box with a single resistor, the potential difference across it would be V and the current through it would be I. Thus:

$$I = \frac{V}{R_{\text{total}}}$$

Comparing with the last equation, we find:

$$\frac{1}{R_{\text{total}}} = \frac{1}{R_1} + \frac{1}{R_2} + \frac{1}{R_3}$$

The formula shows that the total resistance is **smaller** than any of the individual resistances being added.

We have thus learned how to replace resistors that are connected in series or parallel by a single resistor in each case, thus greatly simplifying the circuit.

Exam tip
Adding resistors in series increases the total resistance of a circuit (and so decreases the current leaving the battery). Adding resistors in parallel decreases the total resistance of the circuit (and so increases the current leaving the battery).

More complex circuits

A typical circuit will contain both parallel and **series connections**.
In Figure 5.23, the two top resistors are in series. They are equivalent to a single resistor of $8.0\,\Omega$. This resistor and the $24\,\Omega$ resistor are in parallel, so together they are equivalent to a single resistor of:

$$\frac{1}{R_{\text{total}}} = \frac{1}{8.0} + \frac{1}{24} = \frac{1}{6}$$

$$\Rightarrow R_{\text{total}} = 6.0\,\Omega$$

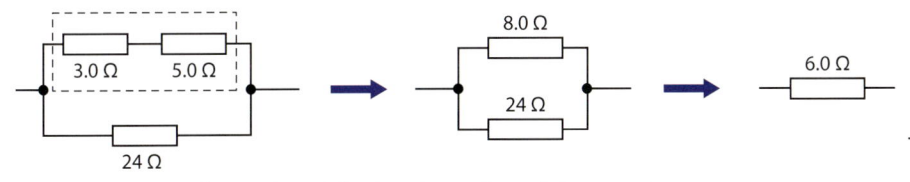

Figure 5.23 Part of a circuit with both series and parallel connections.

Consider now Figure 5.24. The two top $6.0\,\Omega$ resistors are in series, so they are equivalent to a $12\,\Omega$ resistor. This, in turn, is in parallel with the other $6.0\,\Omega$ resistor, so the left block is equivalent to:

$$\frac{1}{R_{\text{total}}} = \frac{1}{12} + \frac{1}{6.0} = \frac{1}{4}$$

$$\Rightarrow R_{\text{total}} = 4.0\,\Omega$$

Let us go to the right block. The $12\,\Omega$ and the $24\,\Omega$ resistors are in series, so they are equivalent to $36\,\Omega$. This is in parallel with the top $12\,\Omega$, so the equivalent resistor of the right block is:

$$\frac{1}{R_{\text{total}}} = \frac{1}{36} + \frac{1}{12} = \frac{1}{9}$$

$$\Rightarrow R_{\text{total}} = 9.0\,\Omega$$

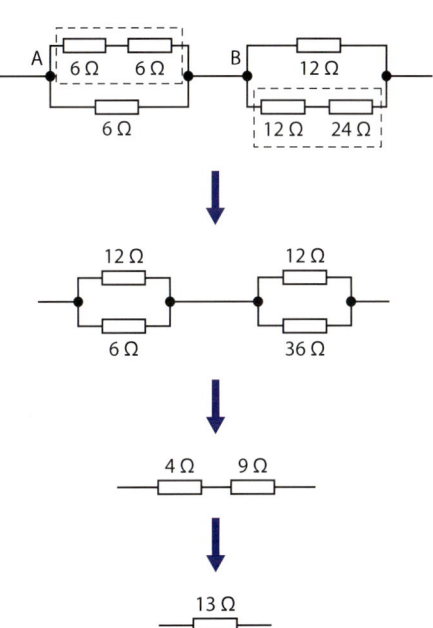

Figure 5.24 A complicated part of a circuit containing many parallel and series connections.

5 ELECTRICITY AND MAGNETISM 215

The overall resistance is thus:

$$4.0 + 9.0 = 13\,\Omega$$

Suppose now that this part of the circuit is connected to a source of emf 156 V (and negligible internal resistance). The current that leaves the source is $I = \dfrac{156}{13} = 12$ A. When it arrives at point A, it will split into two parts. Let the current in the top part be I_1 and that in the bottom part I_2. We have $I_1 + I_2 = 12$ A. We also have that $12I_1 = 6I_2$, since the top and bottom resistors of the block beginning at point A are in parallel and so have the same potential difference across them. Thus, $I_1 = 4.0$ A and $I_2 = 8.0$ A. Similarly, in the block beginning at point B the top current is 9.0 A and the bottom current is 3.0 A.

Worked examples

5.13 **a** Determine the total resistance of the circuit shown in Figure **5.25**.
 b Hence calculate the current and power dissipated in each of the resistors.

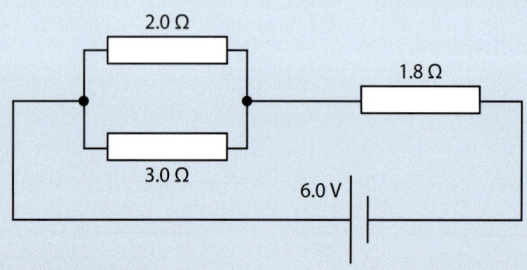

Figure 5.25

a The resistors of 2.0 Ω and 3.0 Ω are connected in parallel and are equivalent to a single resistor of resistance R that may be found from:

$$\dfrac{1}{R} = \dfrac{1}{2} + \dfrac{1}{3} = \dfrac{5}{6}$$

$$\Rightarrow R = \dfrac{6}{5} = 1.2\,\Omega$$

In turn, this is in series with the resistance of 1.8 Ω, so the total equivalent circuit resistance is $1.8 + 1.2 = 3.0\,\Omega$.

b The current that leaves the battery is thus:

$$I = \dfrac{6.0}{3.0} = 2.0\,\text{A}$$

The potential difference across the 1.8 Ω resistor is $V = 1.8 \times 2.0 = 3.6$ V, leading to a potential difference across the two parallel resistors of $V = 6.0 - 3.6 = 2.4$ V. Thus the current in the 2 Ω resistor is:

$$I = \dfrac{2.4}{2.0} = 1.2\,\text{A}$$

This leads to power dissipated of:

$$P = RI^2 = 2.0 \times 1.2^2 = 2.9 \text{ W}$$

or $P = \dfrac{V^2}{R} = \dfrac{2.4^2}{2.0} = 2.9 \text{ W}$

or $P = VI = 2.4 \times 1.2 = 2.9 \text{ W}$

For the 3 Ω resistor:

$$I = \dfrac{2.4}{3.0} = 0.80 \text{ A}$$

which leads to power dissipated of $P = RI^2 = 3.0 \times 0.80^2 = 1.9 \text{ W}$

The power in the 1.8 Ω resistor is $P = RI^2 = 1.8 \times 2.0^2 = 7.2 \text{ W}$

5.14 In the circuit of Figure **5.26** the three lamps are identical and may be assumed to have a constant resistance. Discuss what happens to the brightness of lamp A and lamp B when the switch is closed. (The cell is ideal, i.e. it has negligible internal resistance.)

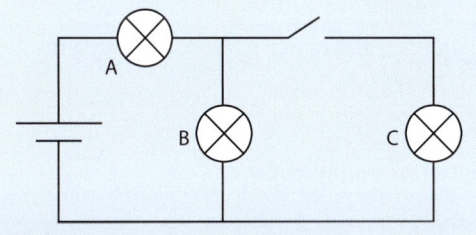

Figure 5.26

Method 1
A mathematical answer. Let the emf of the cell be ε and the resistance of each lamp be R: before the switch is closed A and B take equal current $\dfrac{\varepsilon}{(2R)}$ and so are equally bright (the total resistance is $2R$). When the switch is closed, the total resistance of the circuit changes and so the current changes as well. The new total resistance is $\dfrac{3R}{2}$ (lamps B and C in parallel and the result in series with A) so the total current is now $\dfrac{2\varepsilon}{(3R)}$, larger than before. The current in A is thus greater and so the power, i.e. the brightness, is greater than before. The current of $\dfrac{2\varepsilon}{(3R)}$ is divided equally between B and C. So B now takes a current $\dfrac{\varepsilon}{(3R)}$, which is smaller than before. So B is dimmer.

Method 2
The potential difference across A and B before the switch is closed is $\dfrac{\varepsilon}{2}$ and so A and B are equally bright. When the switch is closed the potential difference across A is double that across B since the resistance of A is double the parallel combination of resistance of B and C. This means that the potential difference across A is $2\dfrac{\varepsilon}{3}$ and across B it is $\dfrac{\varepsilon}{3}$. Hence A increases in brightness and B gets dimmer.

5 ELECTRICITY AND MAGNETISM

5.15 Look at Figure **5.27**. Determine the current in the 2.0 Ω resistor and the potential difference across the two marked points, A and B, when the switch is **a** open and **b** closed.

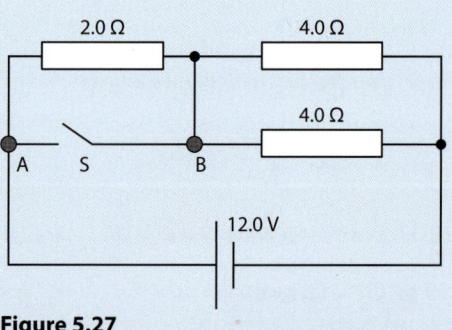

Figure 5.27

a When the switch is open, the total resistance is 4.0 Ω and thus the total current is 3.0 A.

The potential difference across the 2.0 Ω resistor is 2.0 × 3.0 = 6.0 V.

The potential difference across points A and B is thus 6.0 V.

b When the switch is closed, no current flows through the 2.0 Ω resistor, since all the current takes the path through the switch, which offers no resistance. (The 2.0 Ω resistor has been shorted out.)

The resistance of the circuit is then 2.0 Ω and the current leaving the battery is 6.0 A.

The potential difference across points A and B is now zero. (There is current flowing from A to B, but the resistance from A to B is zero, hence the potential difference is 6.0 × 0 = 0 V.)

5.16 Four lamps each of constant resistance 60 Ω are connected as shown in Figure **5.28**.
   a Determine the power in each lamp.
   b Lamp A burns out. Calculate the power in each lamp and the potential difference across the burnt-out lamp.

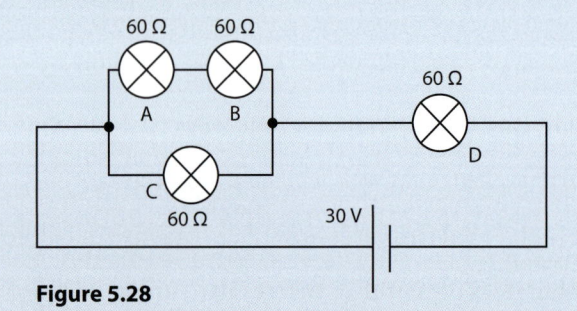

Figure 5.28

a We know the resistance of each lamp, so to find the power we need to find the current in each lamp.

Lamps A and B are connected in series so they are equivalent to one resistor of value $R_{AB} = 60 + 60 = 120\,\Omega$. This is connected in parallel to C, giving a total resistance of:

$$\frac{1}{R_{ABC}} = \frac{1}{120} + \frac{1}{60}$$

$$\frac{1}{R_{ABC}} = \frac{1}{40}$$

⇒ $R_{ABC} = 40\,\Omega$

218

Finally, this is in series with D, giving a total circuit resistance of:

$R_{total} = 40 + 60 = 100\,\Omega$

The current leaving the battery is thus:

$I = \dfrac{30}{100} = 0.30\,A$

The current through A and B is 0.10 A and that through C is 0.20 A. The current through D is 0.30 A. Hence the power in each lamp is:

$P_A = P_B$

$P_A = 60 \times (0.10)^2 = 0.6\,W$

$P_C = 60 \times (0.20)^2 = 2.4\,W$

$P_D = 60 \times (0.30)^2 = 5.4\,W$

b With lamp A burnt out, the circuit is as shown in Figure **5.29**.

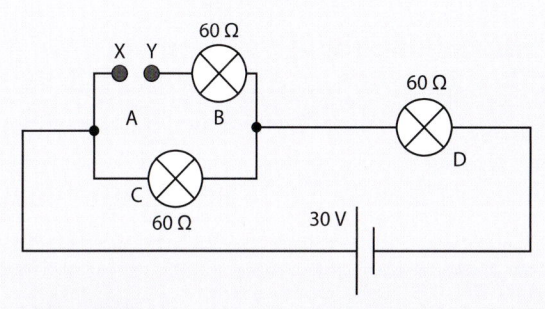

Figure 5.29

Lamp B gets no current, so we are left with only C and D connected in series, giving a total resistance of:

$R_{total} = 60 + 60 = 120\,\Omega$

The current is thus $I = \dfrac{30}{120} = 0.25\,A$. The power in C and D is thus:

$P_C = P_D = 60 \times (0.25)^2 = 3.8\,W$

We see that D becomes dimmer and C brighter. The potential difference across lamp C is:

$V = IR$

$V = 0.25 \times 60$

$V = 15\,V$

Lamp B takes no current, so the potential difference across it is zero. The potential difference across points X and Y is the same as that across lamp C, i.e. 15 V.

Multi-loop circuits

In the circuit shown earlier in Figure **5.19**, we found the current in the circuit quite easily. Let us find the current again using a different approach (Figure **5.30**). This approach will use **Kirchhoff's loop law**, which will be stated shortly. This method is best used for complicated multi-loop circuits, but once you master it, you can easily apply it in simple circuits as well, such as the circuit of Figure **5.30**.

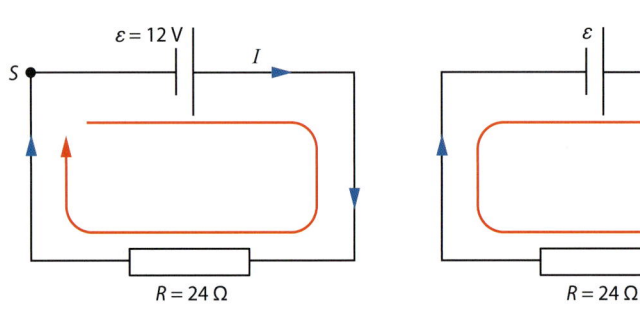

Figure 5.30 Solving a circuit using loops.

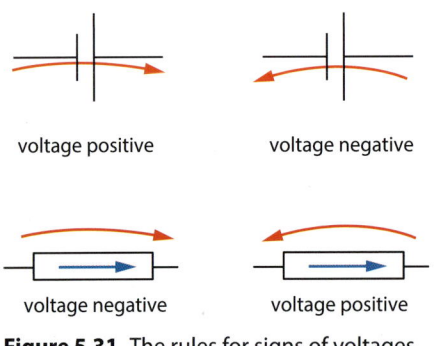

Figure 5.31 The rules for signs of voltages in Kirchhoff's loop law. The blue arrow shows the direction of the current through the resistor.

Draw a loop through the circuit and put an arrow on it (red loop). This indicates the direction in which we will go around the circuit. In the left-hand diagram we have chosen a clockwise direction. Now follow *the loop* starting anywhere; we will choose to start at point S. As we travel along the circuit we calculate the quantity $\sum V$, i.e. the sum of the voltages across each resistor or cell that the loop takes us through, according to the rules in Figure **5.31**.

Follow the clockwise loop. First we go through the cell whose emf is $\varepsilon = 12$ V. The loop takes us through the cell from the negative to the positive terminal and so we count the voltage as $+\varepsilon$, i.e. as $+12$ V.

Next we go through a resistor. The loop direction is the same as the direction of the current so we take the voltage across the resistor as negative, i.e. $-RI$, which gives $-24I$.

So the quantity $\sum V$ is $12 - 24I$.

> **Kirchhoff's loop law (Kirchhoff's second law)** states that:
> $$\sum V = 0$$

The loop law is a consequence of energy conservation: the power delivered into the circuit by the cell is εI. The power dissipated in the resistor is RI^2. Therefore $\varepsilon I = RI^2$. Cancelling one power of the current, this implies $\varepsilon = RI$ or $\varepsilon - RI = 0$ which is simply the Kirchhoff loop law for this circuit. So $12 - 24I = 0$, which allows us to solve for the current as 0.50 A.

Had we chosen a counter-clockwise loop (right-hand diagram in Figure **5.30**) we would find $\sum V = -12 + 24I = 0$, giving the same answer for the current. (This is because we go through the cell from positive to negative so we count the voltage as negative, and we go through resistors in a direction opposite to that of the current so we count the voltage as positive.)

Consider now the circuit with two cells, shown in Figure **5.32**. Again, choose a loop along which to travel through the circuit. We choose a clockwise loop. Draw the arrow for the current. With two cells it is not obvious what the correct direction for the current is. But it does not matter, as we will see. Let's calculate $\sum V$. The cells give $+12 - 9.0$ since we go through the lower cell from positive to negative. The resistors give $-4.0I - 2.0I$ and so $12 - 9.0 - 4.0I - 2.0I = 0$ which gives $I = 0.50$ A. The current has come out with a positive sign, so our original guess about its direction is correct. Had the current come out negative, the actual direction would be opposite to what we assumed.

Figure **5.33** is another example of a circuit with two sources of emf. Each of the four resistors in the circuit of Figure **5.33** is $2.0\,\Omega$. Let's determine the currents in the circuit.

First we assign directions to the currents. Again it does not matter which directions we choose. Call the currents I_1, I_2 and I_3. The loop law states that:

top loop: $\quad \sum V = +6.0 - 2I_1 - 2I_2 - 2I_1 = 0$

bottom loop: $\sum V = +6.0 - 2I_2 - 2I_3 = 0$

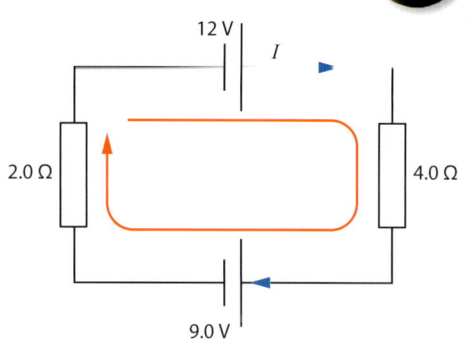

Figure 5.32 A single-loop circuit with two cells.

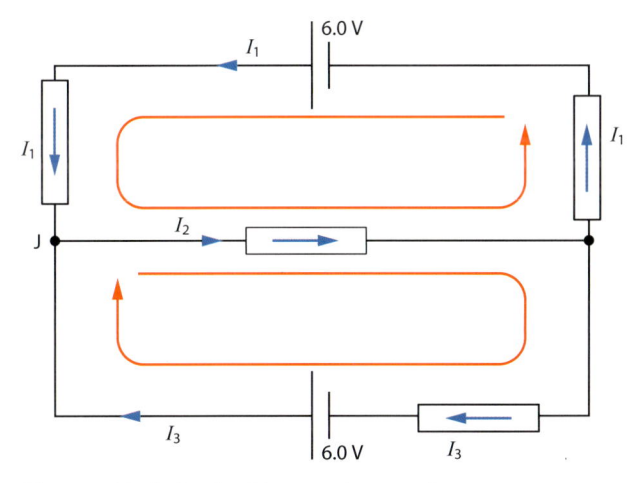

Figure 5.33 A circuit with more than one loop.

From Kirchhoff's current law at junction J (Figure **5.34**):

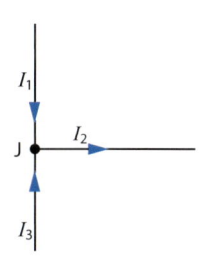

$$\underbrace{I_1 + I_3}_{\text{current in}} = \underbrace{I_2}_{\text{current out}}$$

Figure 5.34 Currents at junction J.

So the first loop equation becomes:

$+6.0 - 2I_1 - 2(I_1 + I_3) - 2I_1 = 0$

$\Rightarrow 6I_1 + 2I_3 = 6.0$

$\Rightarrow 3I_1 + I_3 = 3.0$

Exam tip
Using the current law we eliminate one of the currents (I_2), making the algebra easier.

and the second loop equation becomes:

$6.0 - 2(I_1 + I_3) - 2I_3 = 0$

$\Rightarrow 2I_1 - 4I_3 = 6.0$

5 ELECTRICITY AND MAGNETISM 221

So we need to solve the system of equations:

$$3I_1 + I_3 = 3.0$$

$$I_1 - 2I_3 = 3.0$$

Exam tip
1. For each loop in the circuit, give a name to each current in each resistor in the loop and show its direction.
2. Indicate the direction in which the loop will be travelled.
3. Calculate $\sum V$ for every cell or battery and every resistor:
   - For a cell or battery V is counted positive if the cell or battery is travelled from the negative to the positive terminal; negative otherwise.
   - For resistors the value of V is negative $(-RI)$ if the resistor is travelled in the direction of the current; positive otherwise.
4. Set $\sum V = 0$.
5. Repeat for other loops.
6. Use Kirchhoff's current law to reduce the number of currents that need to be found.

Solving, $I_1 = 0.60$ A. Substituting this into the equations gives $I_3 = 1.2$ A and $I_2 = 1.8$ A.

The IB data booklet writes the Kirchhoff current law as $\sum I = 0$. This is completely equivalent to the version $\sum I_{in} = \sum I_{out}$ used here. In using the booklet's formula you must include a plus sign for a current entering a junction and minus sign for currents leaving. So consider Figure **5.35**.

We would write $I_1 + I_2 + I_4 = I_3$. The booklet formula would write this as $I_1 + I_2 + I_4 - I_3 = 0$, two identical results.

Ammeters and voltmeters

The current through a resistor is measured by an instrument called an **ammeter**, which is connected in series to the resistor as shown in Figure **5.36**.

The ammeter itself has a small electric resistance. An **ideal ammeter**

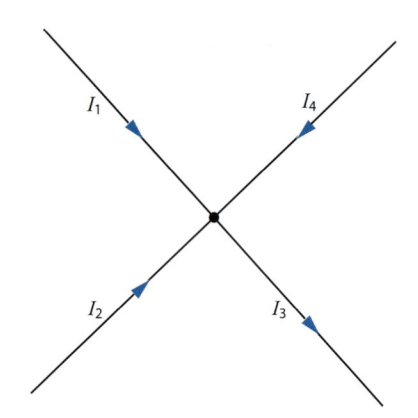

Figure 5.35 Currents entering and leaving a junction.

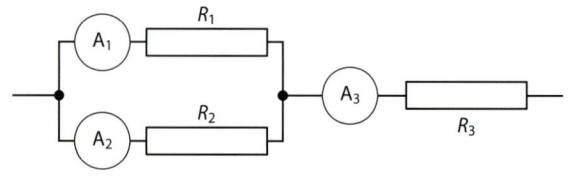

Figure 5.36 An ammeter measures the current in the resistor connected in series to it.

has zero resistance. The potential difference across a device is measured with a **voltmeter** connected in parallel to the device (Figure **5.37**).

An **ideal voltmeter** has infinite resistance, which means that it takes

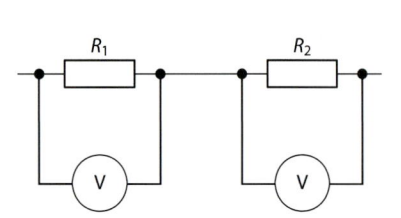

Figure 5.37 A voltmeter is connected in parallel to the device we want to measure the potential difference across.

no current when it is connected to a resistor. Real voltmeters have very high resistance. Unless otherwise stated, ammeters and voltmeters will be assumed to be ideal.

Thus, to measure the potential difference across and current through a resistor, the arrangement shown in Figure **5.38** is used.

Voltmeters and ammeters are both based on a current sensor called a galvanometer. An ammeter has a small resistance connected in parallel to the galvanometer and a voltmeter is a galvanometer connected to a large resistance in series.

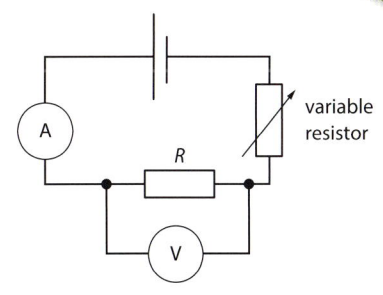

Figure 5.38 The correct arrangement for measuring the current through and potential difference across a resistor. The variable resistor allows the current in the resistor R to be varied so as to collect lots of data for current and voltage.

Worked example

5.17 In the circuit in Figure **5.39**, the emf of the cell is 9.00 V and the internal resistance is assumed negligible. A non-ideal voltmeter whose resistance is 500 kΩ is connected in parallel to a resistor of 500 kΩ.

  a Determine the reading of the (ideal) ammeter.

  b A student is shown the circuit and assumes, incorrectly, that the voltmeter is ideal. Estimate the resistance the student would calculate if he were to use the current found in **a**.

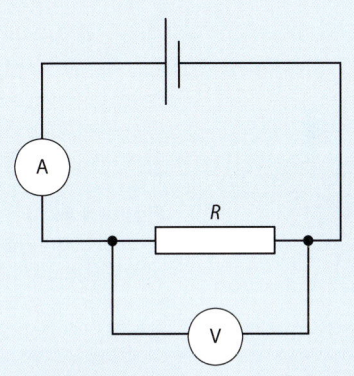

Figure 5.39

a Since the two 500 kΩ resistances are in parallel, the total resistance of the circuit is found from:

$$\frac{1}{R} = \frac{1}{500} + \frac{1}{500} = \frac{1}{250}$$

$$\Rightarrow R = 250 \, \text{k}\Omega$$

Using $I = \frac{V}{R}$, the current that leaves the battery is:

$$I = \frac{9.0}{250\,000} = 3.6 \times 10^{-5} \, \text{A}$$

$$I = 36 \, \mu\text{A}$$

This is the reading of the ammeter in the circuit.

b The reading of the voltmeter is 9.0 V. If the student assumes the voltmeter is ideal, he would conclude that the current in the resistor is 36 μA. He would then calculate that:

$$R = \frac{V}{I} = \frac{9.0 \, \text{V}}{36 \, \mu\text{A}} = 250 \, \text{k}\Omega \quad \text{and would get the wrong answer for the resistance.}$$

5 ELECTRICITY AND MAGNETISM

The potential divider

The circuit in Figure **5.40a** shows a potential divider. It can be used to investigate, for example, the current–voltage characteristic of some device denoted by resistance R. This complicated-looking circuit is simply equivalent to the circuit in Figure **5.40b**. In this circuit, the resistance R_1 is the resistance of the resistor XY from end X to the slider S, and R_2 is the resistance of the resistor from S to end Y. The current that leaves the cell splits at point M. Part of the current goes from M to N, and the rest goes into the device with resistance R. The right end of the resistance R can be connected to a point S on the resistor XY.

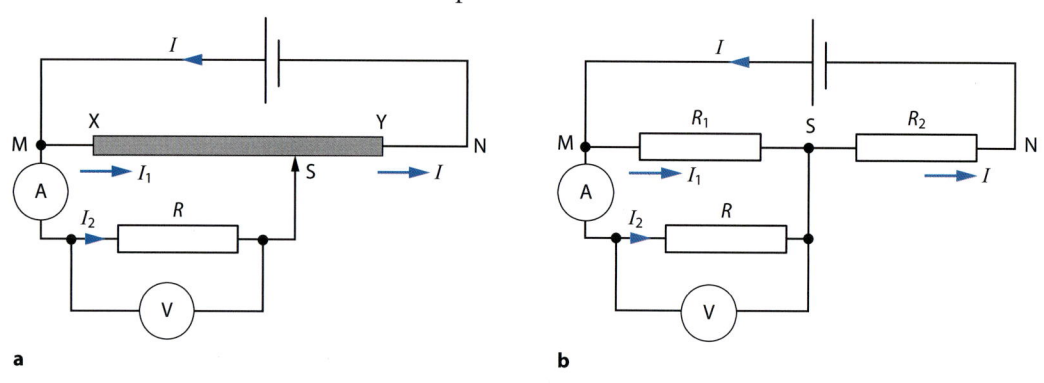

Figure 5.40 a This circuit uses a potential divider. The voltage and current in the device with resistance R can be varied by varying the point where the slider S is attached to the variable resistor. **b** The potential divider circuit is equivalent to this simpler-looking circuit.

By varying where the slider S connects to XY, different potential differences and currents are obtained for the device R. The resistor XY could also be just a wire of uniform diameter. One advantage of the potential divider over the conventional circuit arrangement (Figure **5.38**) is that now the potential difference across the resistor can be varied from a minimum of zero volts, when the slider S is placed at X, to a maximum of ε, the emf of the battery (assuming zero internal resistance), by connecting the slider S to point Y. In the conventional arrangement of Figure **5.38**, the voltage can be varied from zero volts up to some maximum value less than the emf.

Worked example

5.18 In the circuit in Figure **5.41**, the battery has emf ε and negligible internal resistance. Derive an expression for the voltage V_1 across resistor R_1 and the voltage V_2 across resistor R_2.

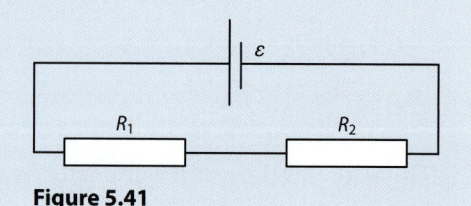

Figure 5.41

Since $I = \dfrac{\varepsilon}{R_1 + R_2}$ and $V = IR$, we have that:

$$V_1 = \left(\dfrac{R_1}{R_1 + R_2}\right)\varepsilon \quad \text{and} \quad V_2 = \left(\dfrac{R_2}{R_1 + R_2}\right)\varepsilon$$

Nature of science

In 1825 in England Peter Barlow proposed a law explaining how wires conducted electricity. His careful experiments using a constant voltage showed good agreement, and his theory was accepted. At about the same time in Germany, Georg Ohm proposed a different law backed up by experimental evidence using a range of voltages. The experimental approach to science was not popular in Germany, and Ohm's findings were rejected. It was not until 1841 that the value of his work was recognised, first in England and later in Germany. In modern science, before research findings are published they are reviewed by other scientists working in the same area (peer review). This would have shown the errors in Barlow's work and given Ohm recognition sooner.

? Test yourself

15 Outline the mechanism by which electric current heats up the material through which it flows.

16 Explain why doubling the length of a wire, at constant temperature, will double its resistance.

17 The graphs show the current as a function of voltage across the same piece of metal wire which is kept at two different temperatures.
   a Discuss whether the wire obey Ohm's law.
   b Suggest which of the two lines on the graph corresponds to the higher temperature.

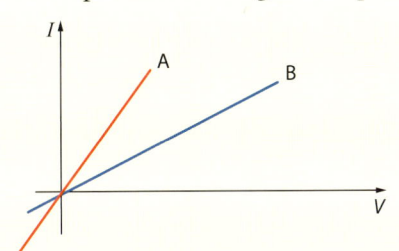

18 The current in a device obeying Ohm's law is 1.5 A when connected to a source of potential difference 6.0 V. What will the potential difference across the same device be when a current of 3.5 A flows in it?

19 A resistor obeying Ohm's law is measured to have a resistance of 12 Ω when a current of 3.0 A flows in it. Determine the resistance when the current is 4.0 A.

20 The heating element of an electric kettle has a current of 15 A when connected to a source of potential difference 220 V. Calculate the resistance of the heating element.

21 The diagram shows two resistors with a current of 2.0 A flowing in the wire.
   a Calculate the potential difference across each resistor.
   b State the potential between points B and C.

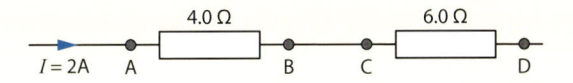

22 The filament of a lamp rated as 120 W at 220 V has resistivity 2.0×10^{-6} Ω m.
   a Calculate the resistance of the lamp when it is connected to a source of 220 V.
   b The radius of the filament is 0.030 mm. Determine its length.

23 Determine the total resistance for each of the circuit parts in the diagram.

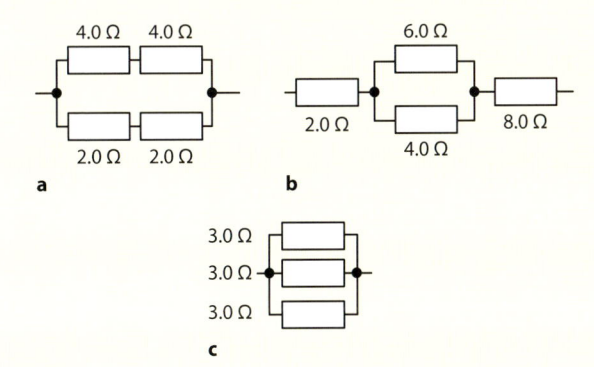

24 In the potentiometer in the diagram, wire AB is uniform and has a length of 1.00 m. When contact is made at C with BC = 54.0 cm, the galvanometer G shows zero current. Determine the emf of the second cell.

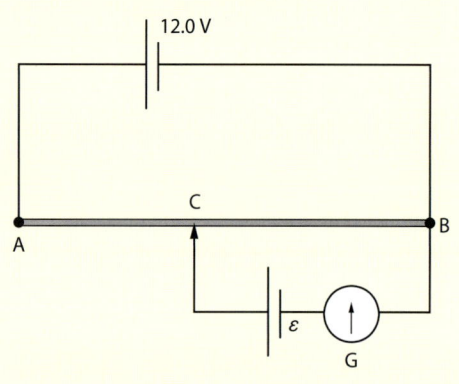

25 In the circuit shown the top cell has emf 3.0 V and the lower cell has emf 2.0 V. Both cells have negligible internal resistance.
Calculate:
a the readings of the two ammeters
b the potential difference across each resistor.

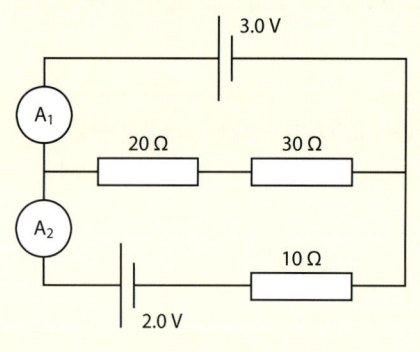

26 Calculate the current in each resistor in the circuit shown in the diagram.

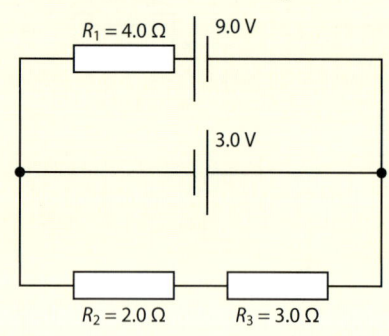

27 In the circuit the ammeter reads 1.0 A. The current leaving the unknown cell is 1.67 A. Determine the unknown emf ε.

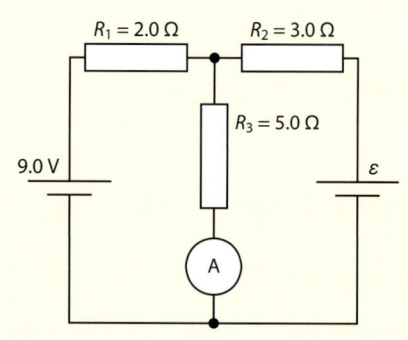

28 Two resistors, X and Y, have I–V characteristics given by the graph.

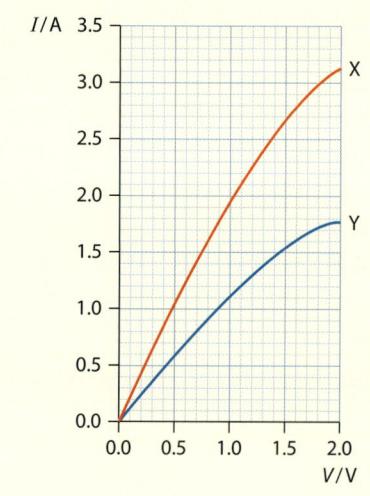

a Circuit A shows the resistors X and Y connected in parallel to a cell of emf 1.5 V and negligible internal resistance. Calculate the total current leaving the cell.

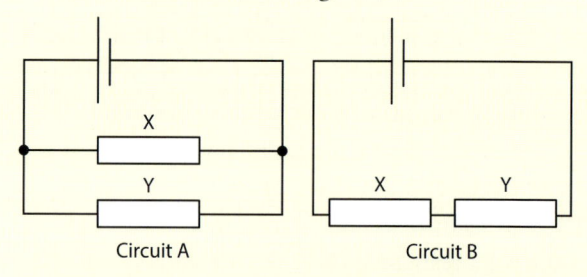

b In circuit B the resistors X and Y are connected in series to the same cell. Estimate the total current leaving the cell in this circuit.

29 The top cell in the circuit in the diagram has emf 6.0 V. The emf of the cell in the lower part of the circuit is 2.0 V. Both cells have negligible internal resistance. AB is a uniform wire of length 1.0 m and resistance 4.0 Ω. When the variable resistor is set at 3.2 Ω the galvanometer shows zero current. Determine the length AC.

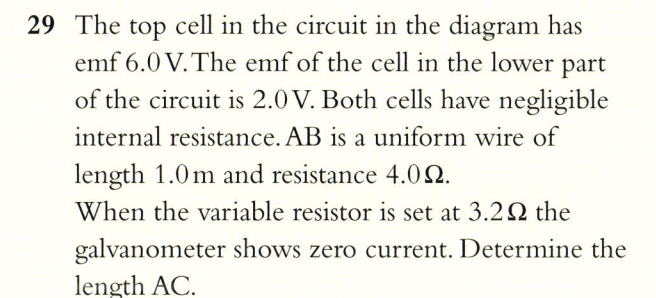

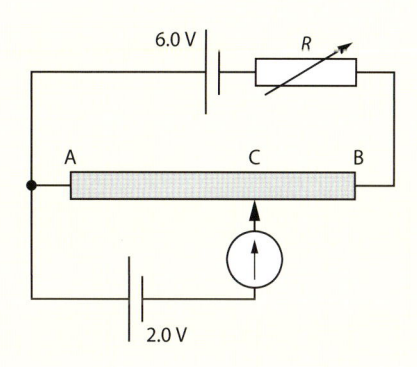

5.3 Electric cells

Batteries are now used to power watches, laptops, cars and entire submarines. Substantial advances in battery technology have resulted in batteries that store more energy, recharge faster and pose smaller environmental dangers.

Emf

We have already discussed that electric charges will not drift in the same direction inside a conductor unless a potential difference is established at the ends of the conductor. In a circuit we therefore need a source of potential difference. The most common is the connection of a **battery** in the circuit. (Others include a generator, a thermocouple or a solar cell.) What these sources do is to convert various forms of energy into **electrical energy**.

To understand the function of the battery, we can compare a battery to a pump that forces water through pipes up to a certain height and down again (Figure 5.42). The pump provides the gravitational potential energy mgh of the water that is raised. The water, descending, converts its gravitational potential energy into thermal energy (frictional losses) and mechanical work. Once the water reaches the pump, its gravitational potential energy has been exhausted and the pump must again perform work to raise the water so that the cycle repeats.

In an electric circuit a battery performs a role similar to the pump's. A battery connected to an outside circuit will force current in the circuit. Thus, the chemical energy of the battery is eventually converted into thermal energy (the current heats up the wires), into mechanical work (the circuit may contain a motor that may be used to raise a load) and into chemical energy again if it is used to charge another battery in the external circuit. Within the battery itself, negative ions are pushed from the negative to the positive terminal and positive ions in the opposite direction. This requires work that must be done on the ions (Figure 5.43). This work is provided by the **chemical energy** stored in the battery and is released by chemical reactions taking place inside the battery.

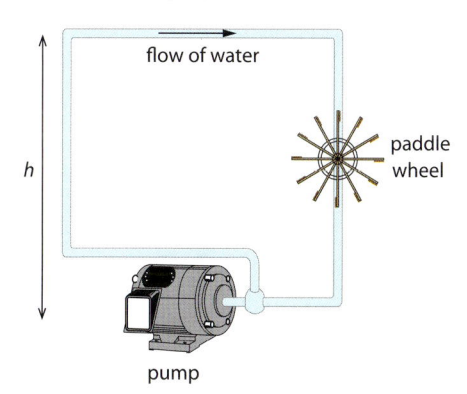

Learning objectives

- Distinguish between primary and secondary cells.
- Understand the presence of an internal resistance.
- Distinguish between emf and terminal potential difference.

Figure 5.42 In the absence of the pump, the water flow would stop. The work done by the pump equals the work done to overcome frictional forces plus work done to operate devices, such as, for example, a paddle wheel.

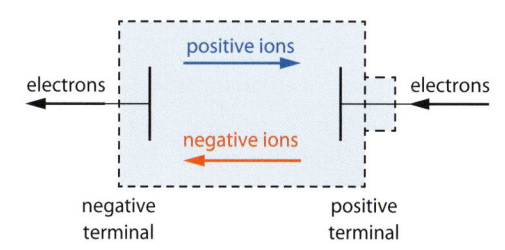

Figure 5.43 Inside the battery, negative ions move from the negative to the positive terminal of the battery. Positive ions move in the opposite direction. In the external circuit, electrons leave the negative battery terminal, travel through the circuit and return to the battery at the positive terminal.

This work is used to define emf:

> The **emf** ε (of a battery) is the work done per unit charge in moving charge from one terminal of the battery to the other. The unit of emf is the volt, V.

(In batteries, the work done is chemical work. In general, in defining emf, the work done is always non-electrical.)

By conservation of energy, this work is also equal to the work done W in moving charge q around the circuit:

$$\varepsilon = \text{emf} = \frac{W}{q}$$

If we divide both numerator and denominator by time we may also obtain the very convenient fact:

$$\varepsilon = \text{emf} = \frac{P}{I}$$

i.e. the power P provided by the battery per unit current I.

Internal resistance and terminal potential difference

A real battery (as opposed to an ideal battery) has an internal resistance, denoted by r (Figure **5.44**). We cannot isolate this resistance – it is inside the battery and it is connected in series to the battery.

The potential difference at the ends of an ideal battery (i.e. one with zero internal resistance) is the emf, ε. In the case of a non-ideal battery, the current that leaves the battery is I. Then the potential difference, across the internal resistance is Ir. The internal resistance reduces the voltage from a value of ε to the value $\varepsilon - Ir$. The potential difference across the battery is therefore:

$$V = \varepsilon - Ir$$

We see that, for a real battery, $V = \varepsilon$ only when $I = 0$. In other words, even for a real battery, the voltage across its terminals is ε when there is no current leaving the battery. So an ideal voltmeter connected across the terminals of a battery would read the emf, since in this case no current leaves the battery. But if there is a current, the voltmeter reading is less than ε.

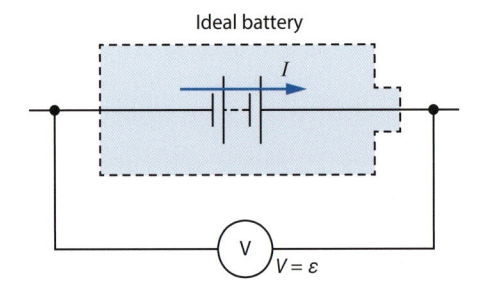

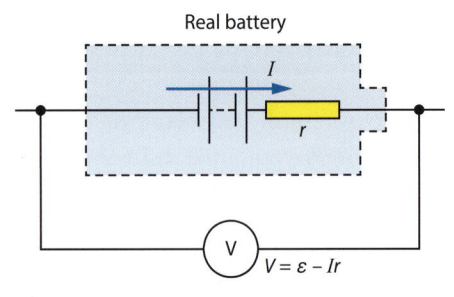

Figure 5.44 The potential difference across the terminals of a battery is equal to the emf when there is no internal resistance and is less than the emf when there is internal resistance.

Worked examples

5.19 The potential difference across the terminals of a battery is 4.8 V when the current is 1.2 A and 4.4 V when the current is 1.4 A. Determine the emf of the battery and the internal resistance.

We need to use $V = \varepsilon - Ir$ twice:

$4.8 = \varepsilon - 1.2r$

and $4.4 = \varepsilon - 1.4r$

Solving simultaneously we get $0.4 = 0.2r$ and so $r = 2.0\,\Omega$. Hence $\varepsilon = 7.2$ V.

5.20 The graph in Figure 5.45 shows how the potential difference across the terminals of a battery varies with the current leaving the battery.

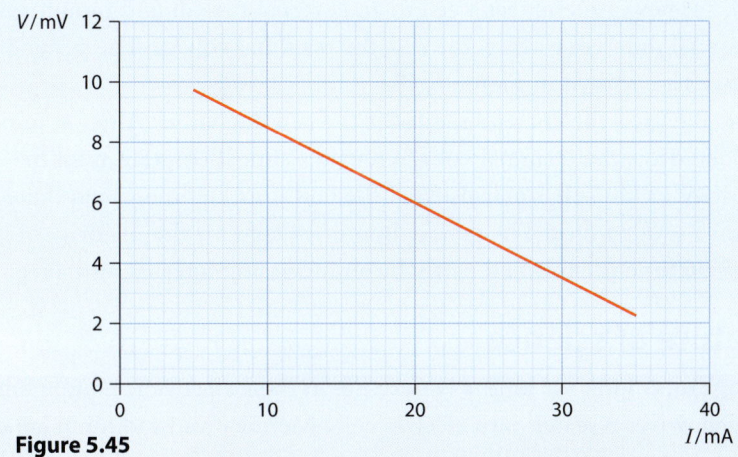

Figure 5.45

Determine the emf of the battery and its internal resistance.

We again need to use $V = \varepsilon - Ir$, from which we deduce that the emf is the vertical intercept and the internal resistance the negative of the slope of the graph. Extending the straight line we find an intercept of 11 mV, which is the emf, and a (negative) slope of $0.25\,\Omega$, which is the internal resistance.

Primary and secondary cells

The term **primary cell** applies to a cell that can only be used once (until it runs out) and is then discarded. A **secondary cell** is a cell that is rechargeable and can be used again.

Consider the circuit of Figure 5.46, which shows a battery with emf 2.0 V being charged. Applying Kirchhoff's loop law to the circuit we have that:

$\sum V = +12 - 2.0I - 6.0I - 2.0I - 2.0 - 6.0I = 0$

This gives:

$I = \dfrac{10}{16} = 0.625$ A

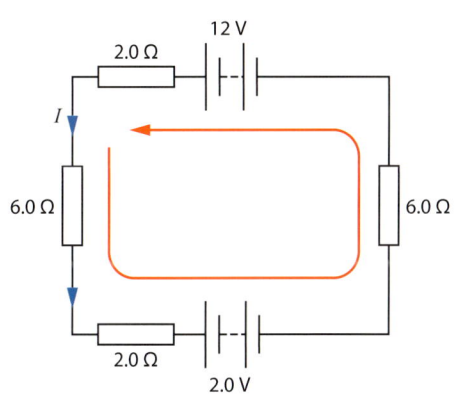

Figure 5.46 A battery that is being charged.

5 ELECTRICITY AND MAGNETISM 229

Let us now calculate the power generated by the 12 V battery:

$$P = \varepsilon I = 12 \times 0.625 = 7.5 \text{ W}$$

The total resistance of the circuit is 16 Ω and so the total power dissipated in the resistors is $16 \times 0.625^2 = 6.25$ W. The remaining 1.25 W is stored in the 2.0 V battery that is being charged. This is the same as the power 'dissipated' by the battery: $2.0 \times (-0.625) = -1.25$ W. We give the current a negative sign because it flows the 'wrong' way in the battery. The negative sign for the power means that this is power being stored, not being dissipated.

Discharging a cell

A characteristic of a cell is the amount of charge it can deliver to an external circuit in its lifetime. This is known as the **capacity** of the cell. Suppose we connect a cell to an external resistor and monitor the potential difference across the cell, the terminal voltage. The general features are shown in Figure **5.47**.

The bigger the current, the faster the cell discharges. After an initial sudden drop, the terminal voltage remains almost constant until the capacity of the cell is exhausted at the end if its lifetime, when there is again a sudden drop. The gentle drop in voltage for the majority of the cell's lifetime is explained partly by an increasing internal resistance.

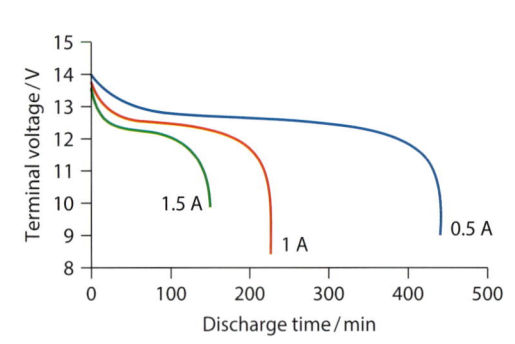

Figure 5.47 Discharge time for a cell for different currents.

Nature of science

Consumers look for longer battery life in their electronic equipment, which drives research into electric cells. Mercury and cadmium are toxic components of some cells, and other cells contain flammable or otherwise dangerous materials. Scientists working to increase the storage capacity of cells need to balance the benefits (for example electric cars, which aim to be 'greener' than cars running on gasoline) with the long-term risks associated with the disposal of the chemical components when the batteries are discarded.

? Test yourself

30 Describe the energy changes taking place in the circuit shown in the diagram.

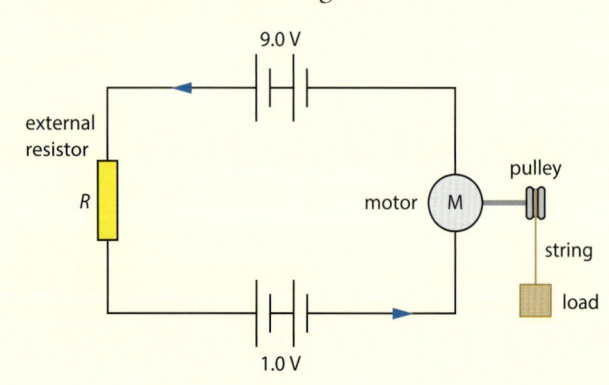

31 A battery has emf = 10.0 V and internal resistance 2.0 Ω. The battery is connected in series to a resistance R. Make a table of the power dissipated in R for various values of R and then use your table to plot the power as a function of R. For what value of R is the power dissipated maximum?

32 A battery of emf ε and internal resistance r sends a current I into a circuit.
   a Sketch the potential difference across the battery as a function of the current.
   b What is the significance of **i** the slope and **ii** the vertical intercept of the graph?

33 In an experiment, a voltmeter was connected across the terminals of a battery as shown in the diagram.

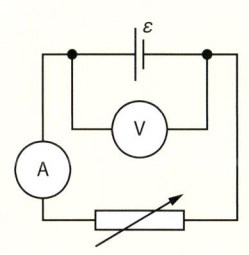

The current in the circuit is varied using the variable resistor. The graph shows the variation with current of the reading of the voltmeter.

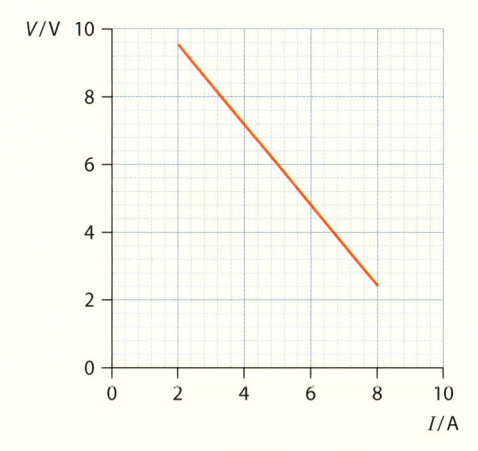

a Calculate the internal resistance of the battery.
b Calculate the emf of the battery.

34 Calculate the current in, and potential difference across, each resistor in the circuits shown in the diagram.

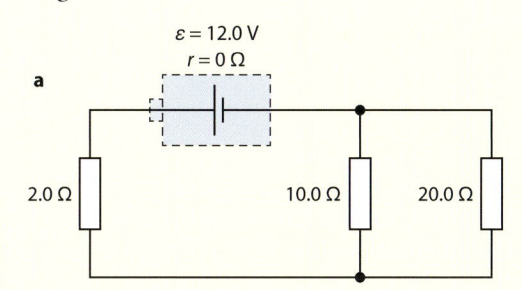

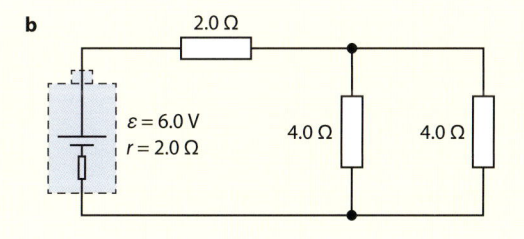

35 When two resistors, each of resistance $4.0\,\Omega$, are connected in parallel with a battery, the current leaving the battery is 3.0 A. When the same two resistors are connected in series with the battery, the total current in the circuit is 1.4 A. Calculate:
a the emf of the battery
b the internal resistance of the battery.

36 In the circuit shown in the diagram each of the cells has an internal resistance of $1.0\,\Omega$.

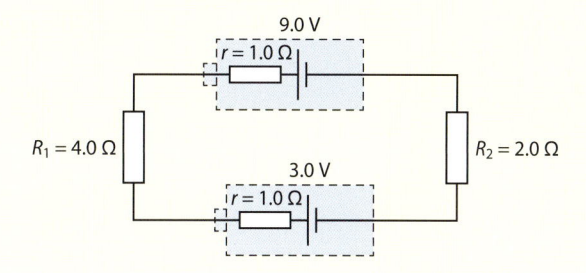

a Determine the current in the circuit.
b Calculate the power dissipated in each cell.
c Comment on your answer to **b**.

5 ELECTRICITY AND MAGNETISM

Learning objectives

- Work with magnetic fields.
- Understand how magnetic fields exert magnetic forces on moving charges and electric currents.

5.4 Magnetic fields

Effects of magnetic fields have been known since ancient times and the magnetic compass has been used in navigation since the 12th century and probably earlier. In modern times the use of magnetic fields is abundant in modern devices such as computers and mobile phones. Very powerful magnets are used to steer elementary particles in circular paths in accelerators such as the Large Hadron Collider at CERN.

How are magnetic fields produced?

Simple experiments reveal that bar magnets have two **poles**; these are called north and south. Two like poles repel and two unlike poles attract. This is very similar to positive and negative electric charges, but the poles of a magnet and electric charge are different things.

It is well known that the needle of a compass (the needle is a small bar magnet) aligns itself in an approximately north–south direction. This can be explained by assuming that the Earth is itself a large magnet. Just as an electric charge creates an electric field in the space around it, a magnet creates a similar (but distinct) field, a **magnetic field**. The magnetic needle of a compass can be used to investigate the presence of magnets. In fact, since the compass needle aligns itself with a magnetic field (Figure 5.48), it follows that we can use the direction in which a compass needle is pointing to define the direction of the magnetic field at the location of the compass. In 1819 the Danish scientist H.C. Ørsted (1777–1851) noticed a compass needle change direction when a current was turned on in a nearby wire. Although he could not explain why this happened, Ørsted had demonstrated that electric currents produce magnetic fields. (The Earth's magnetic field is also thought to be created by currents in the Earth's molten iron core.)

Like the electric field, E, the magnetic field, B, is a vector quantity – it has magnitude and direction.

Figure 5.49 shows small magnetic compasses around a long straight wire that carries current upwards. The compass needles align with the magnetic field. The direction of the needles at each point, give the direction of the magnetic field at that point. Drawing a smooth curve

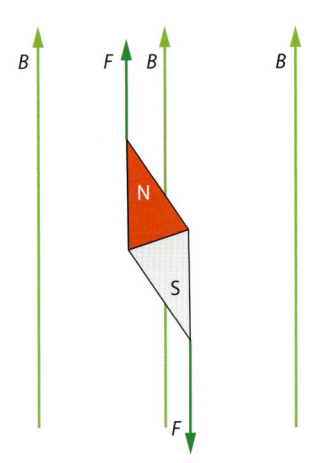

Figure 5.48 A magnetic needle in an external magnetic field experiences forces that align it with the direction of the magnetic field. The direction of the needle (from its south to the north pole) gives the direction of the external magnetic field.

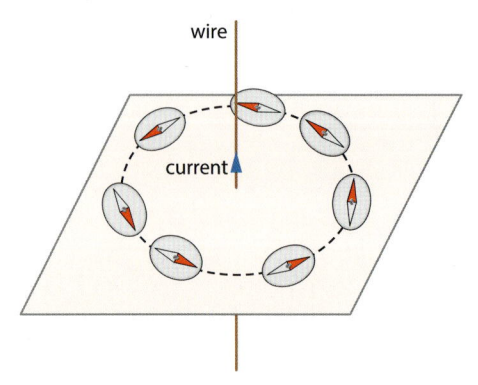

Figure 5.49 Magnetic field around a straight wire.

through the compass needles gives a circle. The magnetic field is tangent to this circle (Figure **5.50**). The imaginary curves whose tangents give the magnetic field are called **magnetic field lines**.

Figure **5.51** shows the magnetic field lines for a **solenoid** and a **bar magnet**. They are no longer circular as they were for the straight wire. The magnetic field lines within the solenoid are fairly uniform, indicating that the field is roughly constant in both magnitude and direction. Notice the similarity between the field outside the solenoid and that around the bar magnet. Notice also that magnetic field lines always exit from a north (N) pole and enter at a south (S) pole.

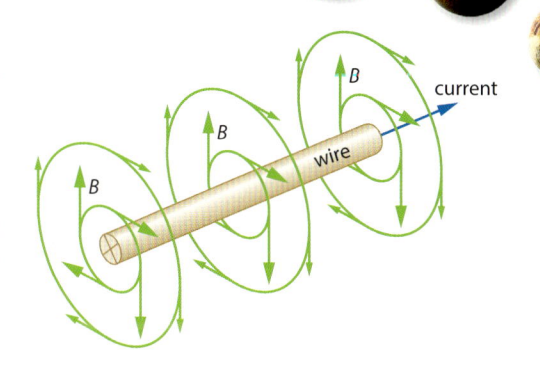

Figure 5.50 A three-dimensional view of the magnetic field pattern around a long straight wire. The magnetic field is symbolised by B. The cross in the wire indicates that the current is entering from left to right. The magnitude of the field decreases as we move away from the wire.

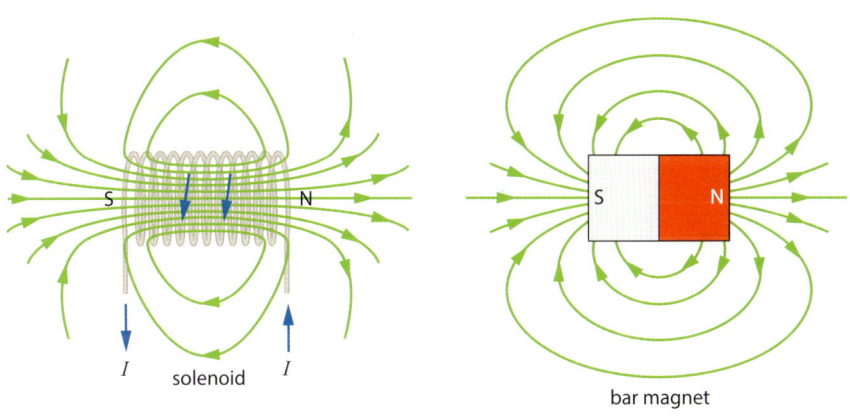

Figure 5.51 The magnetic field of a solenoid and a bar magnet.

The direction of the magnetic field around a **straight wire** carrying a current is given by the **right-hand grip rule** illustrated in Figure **5.52**.

> Grip the wire with the fingers of the right hand in such a way that the thumb points in the direction of the current. Then the direction in which the fingers curl is the direction of the 'flow' of the magnetic field vectors.

A different right-hand grip rule gives the direction of the magnetic field for a solenoid, illustrated in Figure **5.53**.

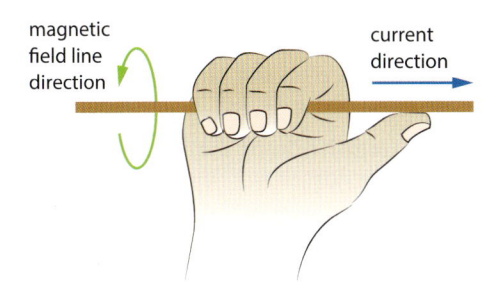

Figure 5.52 The right-hand grip rule for the magnetic field around a straight current-carrying wire. The thumb is in the direction of the current. The fingers curl in the direction of the magnetic field.

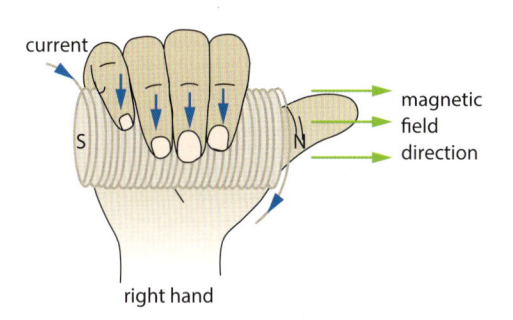

Figure 5.53 The right-hand grip rule for the magnetic field around a solenoid. The fingers curl in the direction of the current. The thumb points in the direction of the magnetic field.

5 ELECTRICITY AND MAGNETISM   233

Worked example

5.21 Figure 5.54 shows two wires carrying equal currents into the page.

State the direction of the magnetic field at point P.

Figure 5.54

Using the right-hand grip rule for each wire, the magnetic fields are as shown in Figure 5.55a. The arrows representing the field are at right angles to the line joining P to each wire. Both fields have the same magnitude, as P is equidistant from both wires and the current is the same in both wires. The resultant field points to the left (Figure 5.55b).

the magnetic field due to each current at P

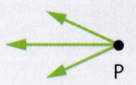

the resultant magnetic field

Figure 5.55

One of the great advances of 19th-century physics was the realisation by Maxwell that electricity and magnetism are not separate phenomena. Magnetic phenomena have their origin in electric processes.

The magnetic force on a moving charge

The direction of a magnetic feld can always be found by how a magnetic compass aligns. How is the magnitude of the magnetic field defined? Experiments show that an electric charge moving in a region of magnetic field experiences a new type of force called a **magnetic force**.

If the velocity of the charge is parallel to the direction of the field, the magnetic force is zero (Figure 5.56).

> There is no magnetic force on a moving charge if the charge moves along the field direction.

In any other direction there will be a force on the charge. If the magnetic force is F when a charge q moves with speed v making an angle θ with the direction of the field, then the **magnitude** of the field, B, also called the **magnetic flux density**, is defined to be:

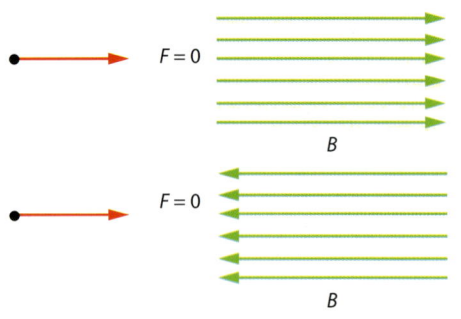

$$B = \frac{F}{qv \sin \theta}$$

Figure 5.56 There is no magnetic force if the velocity is parallel to the magnetic field.

The unit of the magnetic flux density is the tesla (T). A magnetic flux density of 1 T produces a force of 1 N on a charge of 1 C moving at $1\,\text{m}\,\text{s}^{-1}$ at right angles to the direction of the field.

A charge q moving with speed v in a region of magnetic field of magnetic flux density B will experience a magnetic force F given by:

$F = qvB \sin \theta$

We see that there is no magnetic force if the charge is *not* moving. This is different from the electric force on a charge, which is always non-zero whether the charge moves or not. The magnetic force on particles that are electrically neutral ($q = 0$) is, of course, zero.

What about the direction of the magnetic force? An example is shown in Figure 5.57. We see that the force is at right angles to both the velocity vector and the magnetic field.

There are a number of 'rules' to help us find this direction. Three of these are shown in Figure 5.58.

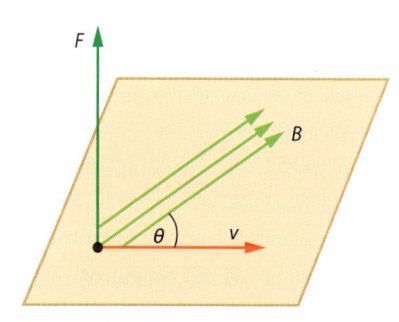

Figure 5.57 The charge shown is positive. The direction of the force is perpendicular to both the velocity vector and the magnetic field vector.

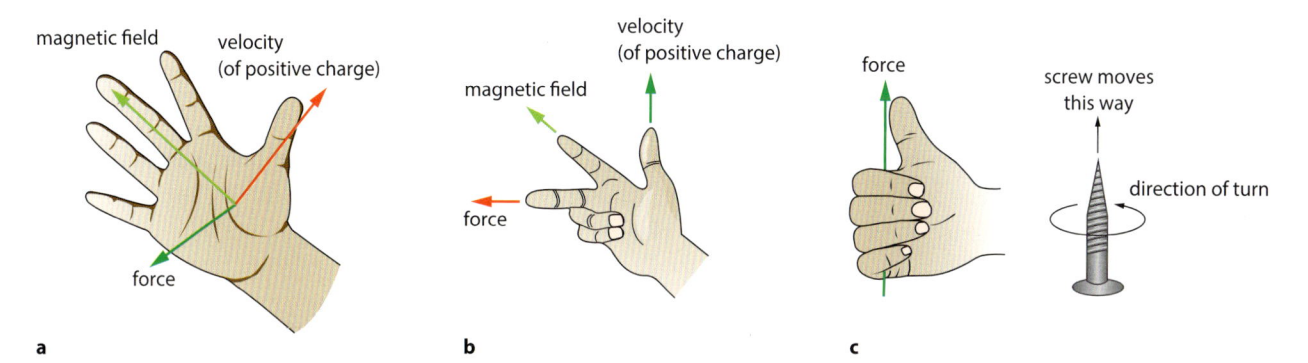

Figure 5.58 The right-hand rule gives the direction of the force on a positive charge. The force on a negative charge is in the opposite direction.

Try the different versions and choose the one that you are comfortable with.

- Version A – hold your right hand as if you are going to shake hands. Place your hand so that the four fingers point in the direction of the field and the thumb in the direction of the velocity. The direction *away* from the palm is the direction of the force.
- Variant B – hold your right hand as in version A, but then bend the middle finger at right angles to your palm. The middle finger now represents the force, the index finger the field and the thumb the velocity.
- Version C – curl the right-hand fingers so that they rotate from the vector v to the vector B (along the smallest of the two possible angles). The direction of the thumb is the direction of the force. (In this version you can also imagine you are rotating a screw in the direction from v to B. The direction the screw moves is the force direction.)

Most people find version A the simplest.

If you are familiar with the vector product of two vectors, you may recognise that $\mathbf{F} = q\mathbf{v} \times \mathbf{B}$.

5 ELECTRICITY AND MAGNETISM

Worked examples

5.22 Express the tesla in terms of fundamental units.

From the definition $B = \dfrac{F}{qv\sin\theta}$ it follows that:

$$1\,\text{T} = \dfrac{\text{N}}{\text{C} \times \text{m s}^{-1}} = \dfrac{\text{N}}{\text{A} \times \text{m}}$$

i.e. $1\,\text{T} = \dfrac{\text{kg m s}^{-2}}{\text{A} \times \text{m}} = \text{kg s}^{-2}\,\text{A}^{-1}$

5.23 An electron approaches a bar magnet, as shown in Figure **5.59**. What is the direction of the force on the electron?

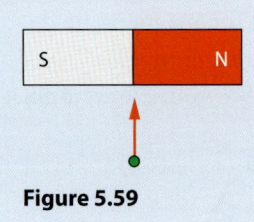

Figure 5.59

The magnetic flux density at the position of the electron is to the left. Placing the right hand so that the thumb points up the page (velocity direction) and the fingers to the left (field direction), the palm is pointing out of the page. But the charge is negative and so the force is into the page.

The magnetic force on a current-carrying wire

A current in a wire consists of moving charges. So a current-carrying wire placed in a magnetic field will experience a magnetic force because there is a force on the moving charges in the wire.

Part of the wire in Figure **5.60** is in a region of magnetic field directed out of the page. In Figure **5.60a** the current in the wire is zero and there is no force. Figures **5.60b** and Figure **5.60c** show the forces on the wire when current flows in opposite directions. The forces on the wire are also opposite.

The formula for the magnetic force on a length L (L is that length of the wire that finds itself in the region of the field) is:

$$F = BIL\sin\theta$$

where θ is the angle between the current and the direction of the magnetic field. (This formula follows from the force on moving charges, as shown in the next section.)

To find the direction of the force, use the right-hand rules for the force on a charge (Figure **5.58**) and replace the velocity by the current.

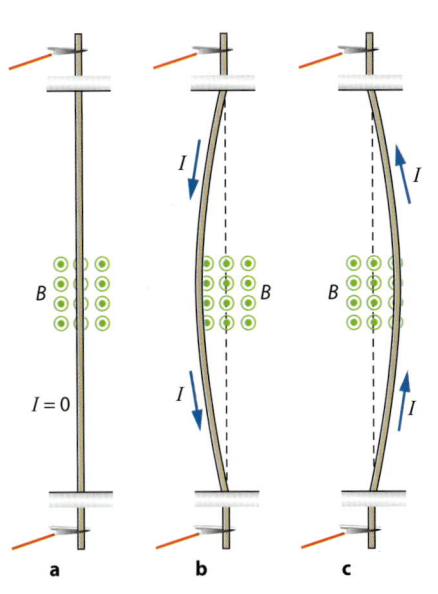

Figure 5.60 The magnetic force on a current-carrying wire.

As we will see in detail in a later section, parallel currents attract and anti-parallel currents repel. Use this information to do the next worked example.

Worked example

5.24 The diagram shows three wires, X, Y and Z, carrying currents of equal magnitude. The directions of the currents are as shown.

⊗ ⊙ ⊗
X Y Z

State the direction of the force on wire Z.

Parallel currents attract and anti-parallel repel. So X attracts Z and Y repels it. Y is closer to Z so the force it exerts is larger. Hence the force is to the right.

Exam tip
It is simpler to remember that parallel currents attract rather than having to work out the direction of the magnetic field at Z's location and then find the force.

A closer look at the magnetic force on a current-carrying wire

Consider a wire carrying a current in a region of magnetic field. Figure **5.61** shows one electron (green dot) that moves with speed v inside the wire. The electron experiences a magnetic force that pushes it downwards. The magnetic force on the moving charges makes electrons accumulate at the bottom of the wire, leaving an excess positive charge at the top of the wire.

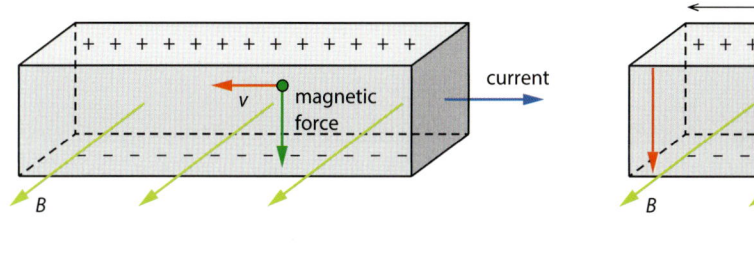

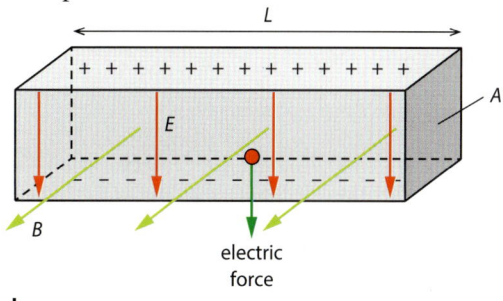

a

b

Figure 5.61 a Electrons in the wire experience a magnetic force. **b** The electric force on the fixed positive charges means there is a force on the wire itself.

The positive and negative charges at the top and bottom of the wire exert an electric force on the electrons so that no new electrons move towards the bottom of the wire: the magnetic force on the electrons is balanced by an electric force, $qE = qvB$.

So, since the magnetic force on the electrons is balanced by an electric force neither of these forces is responsible for the force on the entire wire. The electric field E between the top and bottom sides of the wire exerts an **electric** force on the fixed positive charges inside the wire (the protons in the nuclei). It is this force that acts on the wire.

Let n be the density of positive charges within the wire (number of charges per unit volume). The number of charges within a length L of cross-sectional area A is $N = nAL$ and so the force on this length of wire is:

$$F = (nAL)qE$$

But $qE = qvB$, so:

$$F = (nAL)qvB$$

$$F = (nAqv)BL$$

Using $nAqv = I$, we get:

$$F = BIL$$

as expected! (Recall that here $\sin\theta = 1$.)

Motion of charges in magnetic fields

When the velocity of a charge is at right angles to the magnetic field, the path followed by the charge is a circle, as shown in Figure **5.62**. The centripetal force is provided by the magnetic force, which is at right angles to the velocity.

(Special cases involve motion along a straight line if the velocity is parallel to the field, or helical if the velocity is at some angle to the field, Figure **5.63** – see exam-style question **15** at the end of the topic.)

Consider a charge q moving with speed v at right angles to a magnetic field B. The force on the charge is $F = qvB$ at right angles to the velocity. The charge moves in a circle of radius R, and so by Newton's second law:

$$qvB = m\frac{v^2}{R}$$

Figure 5.62 A charge in a magnetic field moves in a circle.

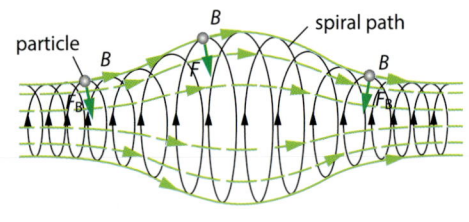

Figure 5.63 A charge enters a region of magnetic field at an angle. It follows a helical path wrapping around the field lines.

Rearranging, we get:

$$R = \frac{mv}{qB}$$

Very massive or very fast charges will move in large circles; large charges and large magnetic fields will result in small circles. The time T to make one full revolution in a magnetic field is found from:

$$T = \frac{2\pi R}{v}$$

$$T = \frac{2\pi}{v}\frac{mv}{qB}$$

$$T = \frac{2\pi m}{qB}$$

This shows that T is independent of the speed. This is an important result in experimental particle physics and forms the basis for an accelerator called the cyclotron.

Worked examples

5.25 Figure **5.64** shows a charged particle entering a region of magnetic field that is directed into the plane of the page.

The path of the particle is a quarter circle.
a Justify why the charge is positive.
b The particle is in fact a proton with mass 1.67×10^{-27} kg and charge 1.6×10^{-19} C. The magnetic flux density is 0.25 T. Calculate the radius of the proton's circular path.
c The proton enters the region of the field with a speed of 5.2×10^6 m s^{-1}. Calculate the time the proton spends in the region of magnetic field.

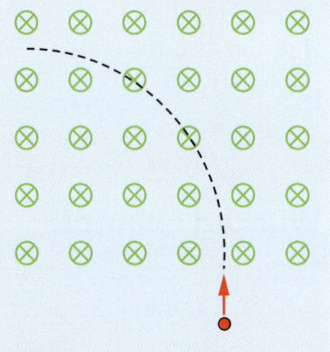

Figure 5.64

a The force must be directed towards the centre of the circle. The field is into the page so by the right-hand force rule the charge must be positive.

b From $qvB = \dfrac{mv^2}{R}$ we deduce that $R = \dfrac{mv}{qB}$. Thus:

$$R = \dfrac{1.67 \times 10^{-27} \times 5.2 \times 10^6}{1.6 \times 10^{-19} \times 0.25}$$

$R = 0.217 \approx 0.22$ m

c The path is a quarter of a circle of radius R, so the length of the path is:

$$\dfrac{2\pi R}{4} = \dfrac{2\pi \times 0.217}{4} = 0.34 \text{ m}$$

The time in the field is therefore:

$$\dfrac{0.34}{5.2 \times 10^6} = 6.6 \times 10^{-8} \text{ s}$$

5.26 Figure **5.65** shows the path of a charged particle. The particle goes through a thin metallic foil.

State and explain the direction of motion of the particle and the sign of its charge.

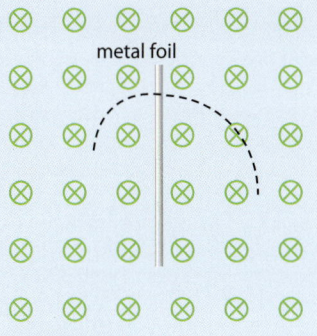

Figure 5.65

The path consists of two circular arcs of different radius. The radius gets smaller because the particle loses energy as it passes through the foil. Therefore the direction of motion is counter-clockwise. Since the field is directed into the plane of the page the charge must be positive by the right-hand force rule so that the force is directed towards the centre of the arcs.

5 ELECTRICITY AND MAGNETISM

Exam tip
$W = Fs\cos\theta$
For the magnetic force, $\theta = 90°$ giving $W = 0$.

Work done and magnetic forces

Since the magnetic force is always normal to the velocity of the charge, it follows that it cannot do any work. The big magnets in particle accelerators are used only to deflect particles, not to increase the particles' kinetic energy (that job is done by electric fields).

Worked example

5.27 Justify why the proton in Worked example **5.26** exits the region of magnetic field with the same speed as that at the entry point.

The work done on the proton by the magnetic force is zero. But the work done is the change in kinetic energy. So the kinetic energy does not change and so neither does speed.

The force between two current-carrying wires

Consider two long, straight, parallel wires carrying currents I_1 and I_2 (Figure **5.66**). The first wire (wire 1) creates a magnetic field in space. This field has magnitude B_1 at the position of the second wire (wire 2). This means wire 2 experiences a magnetic force. Similarly, wire 2 creates a magnetic field of magnitude B_2 at the position of wire 1, so that wire 1 also experiences a magnetic force. By Newton's third law, the force that wire 1 exerts on wire 2 must be accompanied by an equal and opposite force of wire 2 on wire 1. Therefore the forces experienced by the two wires are equal and opposite.

The currents are different in the two wires, so the magnetic fields are different, but the two forces are equal in magnitude.

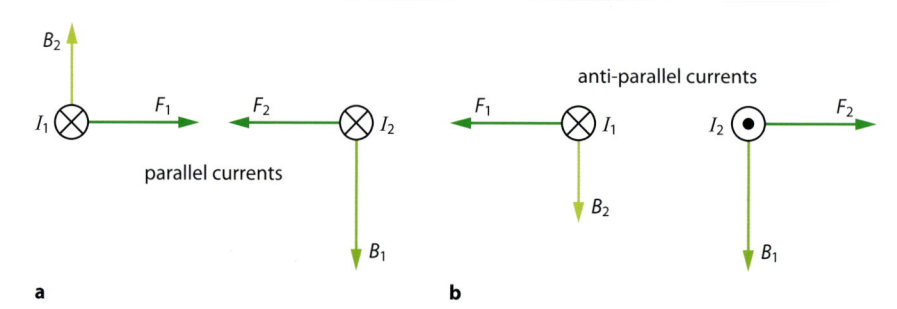

Figure 5.66 The forces on two parallel currents are equal and opposite.

We can use the right-hand rule to find the directions of these forces. Assume first that both currents are flowing into the page. Then the magnetic fields are as shown in Figure **5.66a** and the forces are attractive. If wire 1 carries current into the page and wire 2 carries current out of the page, as shown in Figure **5.66b**, the forces are repulsive. In both cases the forces are equal and opposite, consistent with Newton's third law. So we have found that if the currents are parallel, the forces are attractive, and if they are anti-parallel, the forces are repulsive.

This force between two wires is used to define the ampere, the unit of electric current.

The ampere is defined through the magnetic force between two parallel wires. If the force on a 1 m length of two wires that are 1 m apart and carrying equal currents is 2×10^{-7} N, then the current in each wire is defined to be 1 A.

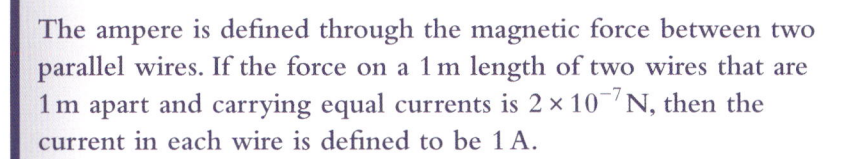

The coulomb is defined in terms of the ampere as the amount of charge that flows past a certain point in a wire when a current of 1 A flows for 1 s.

The ampere is equal to a coulomb divided by a second; but it is defined as above.

Nature of science

Introduced in the 19th century by Michael Faraday as 'lines of force', the concept of magnetic field lines allowed scientists to visualise the magnetic field around a magnet, and the magnetic field around a moving charge. A few years later, in one of the greatest unifications in physics, James Clerk Maxwell showed that all magnetic phenomena and electric phenomena are different sides of the same general phenomenon, electromagnetism, and that light is a combination of electric and magnetic fields. In the early 20th century, Albert Einstein showed that viewing electric and magnetic phenomena from different frames of reference leads naturally to the theory of relativity. At about the same time, trying to understand magnetism in different materials required the introduction of quantum theory.

? Test yourself

37 Draw the magnetic field lines for two parallel wires carrying equal currents into the page. Repeat for anti-parallel currents.

38 Determine the direction of the missing quantity from B, v and F in each of the cases shown in the diagram. The circle represents a positive charge.

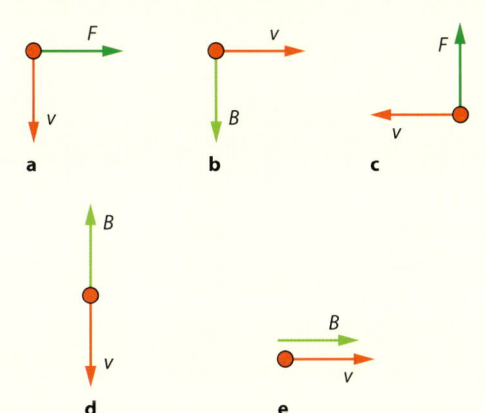

39 Draw the magnetic field lines that result when the magnetic field of a long straight wire carrying current into the page is superimposed on a uniform magnetic field pointing to the right that lies on the page.

40 A long straight wire carries current as shown in the diagram. Two electrons move with velocities that are parallel and perpendicular to the current. Determine the direction of the magnetic force experienced by each electron.

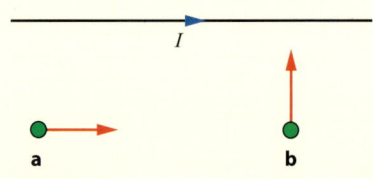

41 A proton moves past a bar magnet as shown in the diagram. Find the direction of the force it experiences in each case.

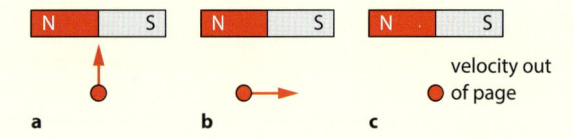

42 The diagram shows two parallel plates. The electric field is directed from top to bottom and has magnitude $2.4 \times 10^3 \, \text{N C}^{-1}$. The shaded region is a region of magnetic field normal to the page.

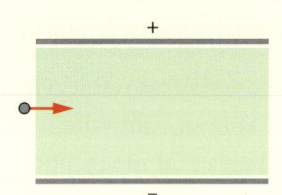

   a Deduce the magnetic field magnitude and direction so that an electron experiences zero net force when shot through the plates with a speed of $2.0 \times 10^5 \, \text{m s}^{-1}$.

   b Suggest whether a proton shot with the same speed through the plates experiences zero net force.

   c The electron's speed is doubled. Suggest whether the electron would it still be undeflected for the same magnetic field found in **a**.

43 A bar magnet is placed in a uniform magnetic field as shown in the diagram.

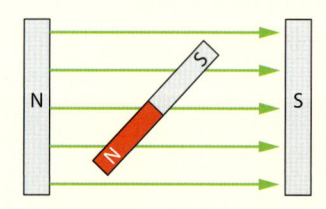

   a Suggest whether there is a net force on the bar magnet.

   b Determine how it will move.

44 A high-tension electricity wire running along a north–south line carries a current of 3000 A. The magnetic field of the Earth at the position of the wire has a magnitude of $5.00 \times 10^{-5} \, \text{T}$ and makes an angle of 30° below the horizontal. Calculate the force experienced by a length of 30.0 m of the wire.

45 a An electron of speed v enters a region of magnetic field B directed normally to its velocity and is deflected into a circular path. Deduce an expression for the number of revolutions per second the electron will make.

   b The electron is replaced by a proton. Suggest whether the answer to **a** changes.

46 A uniform magnetic field is established in the plane of the paper as shown in the diagram. Two wires carry **parallel** currents of equal magnitudes normally to the plane of the paper at P and Q. Point R is on the line joining P to Q and closer to Q. The magnetic field at position R is zero.

   a Determine whether the currents are going into the paper or out of the paper.

   b The magnitude of the current is increased slightly. Determine whether the point where the magnetic field is zero moves to the right or to the left of R.

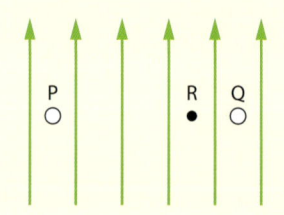

Exam-style questions

1. A small charge q is placed near a large spherical charge Q. The force experienced by both charges is F. The electric field created by Q at the position of q is:

    A $\dfrac{F}{Q}$ **B** $\dfrac{F}{q}$ **C** $\dfrac{F}{Qq}$ **D** $\dfrac{FQ}{q}$

2. Two charges are fixed as shown. The charges are $2q$ and $-q$. In which regions can the electric field strength due to the two particles be zero?

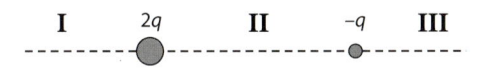

    I   2q   II   −q   III

    A I only   **B** II only   **C** III only   **D** I and III

3. The diagrams show equal lengths of wires made of the same material and various cross-sectional radii. The drift speed of electrons is indicated. In which wire is the current the greatest?

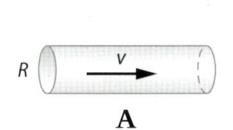

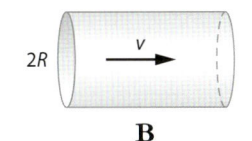

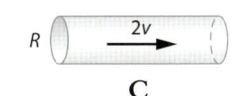

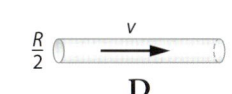

    A radius R, speed v **B** radius $2R$, speed v **C** radius R, speed $2v$ **D** radius $\dfrac{R}{2}$, speed v

4. Two charged particles X and Y are projected horizontally with the same speed from the same point in a region of uniform electric field. Gravity is not negligible.

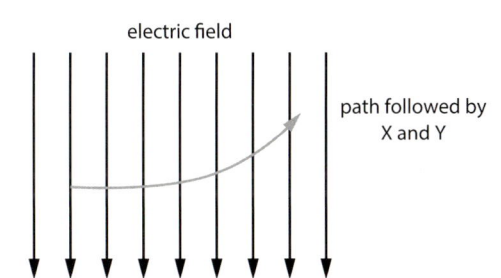

    The two particles follow identical paths. What conclusion about X and Y can one draw from this?

    A They have the same mass.
    B They have the same charge.
    C They have the same acceleration.
    D They have the same momentum.

5. A charged particle moves in a circle of radius R in a region of uniform magnetic field. The magnetic field is at right angles to the velocity of the particle and exerts a force F on the particle. After half a revolution the change in the particle's kinetic energy is:

    A 0   **B** πRF **C** $2\pi RF$ **D** RF

5 ELECTRICITY AND MAGNETISM   243

6 A negatively charged particle is at rest in a magnetic field *B*. The force on the particle is:
   - **A** parallel to *B*
   - **B** opposite to *B*
   - **C** at right angles to *B*
   - **D** zero.

7 An electron enters a region of magnetic field.

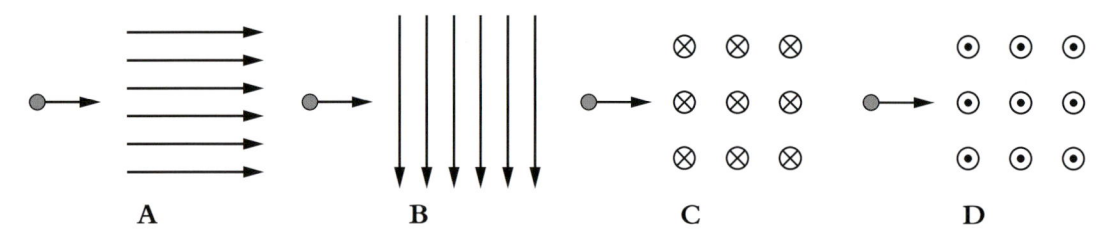

   In which case is the initial force on the electron directed towards the bottom of the page?

8 In which of the following arrangements is the total resistance 6 Ω?

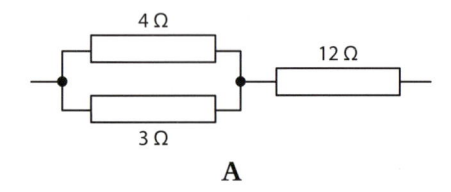

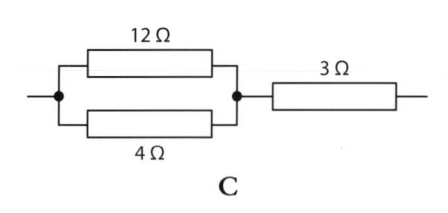

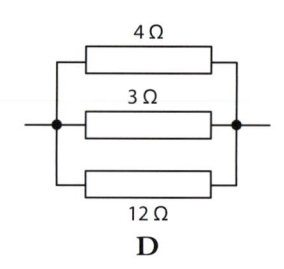

9 In which of the resistors in the circuit below is the power dissipated the least?

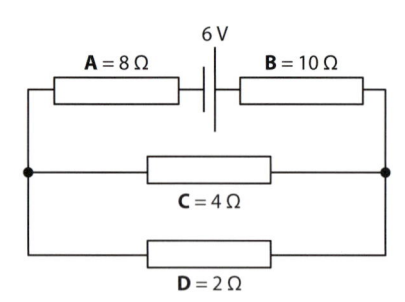

10 Two long parallel wires carry equal currents in opposite directions. What field do the two wires produce at point M, which is midway between the wires and on the plane of the paper?

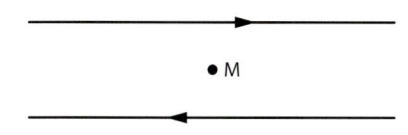

- **A** a magnetic field parallel to the wires
- **B** an electric field parallel to the wires
- **C** a magnetic field at right angles to the plane of the page
- **D** an electric field at right angles to the plane of the page

11 A student assigns currents at a junction in a circuit as shown in the diagram.

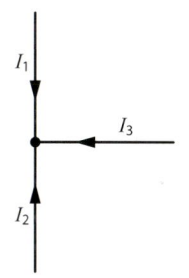

The student's calculations correctly give that $I_1 = 3$ A and $I_2 = -2$ A. The value of I_3 is:

- **A** 1 A
- **B** −1 A
- **C** 5 A
- **D** −5 A

12 The graph shows the variation with voltage V across a filament lamp with the current I though the lamp.

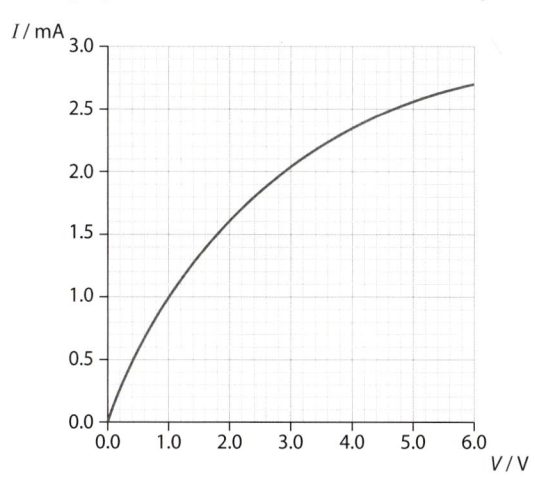

a Suggest whether the resistor obeys Ohm's law. [1]
b Calculate the resistance of the lamp when $V = 4.0$ V. [2]
c The resistivity of the filament of the lamp at a voltage of 4.0 V is 3.0×10^{-7} Ω m. The radius of the filament is 0.25 mm. Calculate the length of the filament. [2]

d Two lamps whose *I–V* characteristics are given by the graph above are connected in parallel to a battery of negligible internal resistance. The current leaving the battery is 2.0 mA. Estimate:
  i the emf of the battery [1]
  ii the power dissipated in each lamp. [1]
e Thermal energy is generated in a filament lamp when it is operating. Describe the mechanism by which this energy is generated. [3]

13 The three devices in the circuit shown are identical and may be assumed to have constant resistance. Each device is rated as 1500 W at 230 V. The emf of the source is 230 V and its internal resistance is negligible.

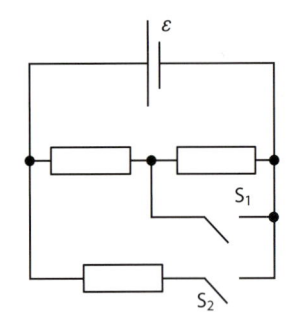

a Calculate the resistance of **one** of the devices. [2]
b Calculate the total power dissipated in the circuit when:
  i S_1 is closed and S_2 is open [1]
  ii S_1 is closed and S_2 is closed [1]
  iii S_1 is open and S_2 is open [1]
  iv S_1 is open and S_2 is closed. [1]
c In the circuit below the cell has internal resistance $0.0500\,\Omega$. When the switch in series with a motor of resistance of $25.0\,\Omega$ is open, the voltmeter reads 11.5 V and the current in the ammeter is 9.80 A.

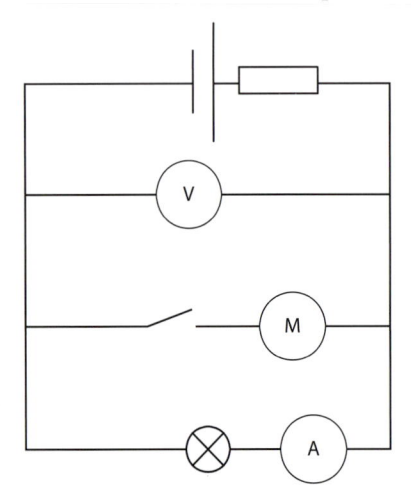

The switch is closed.
  i Determine the emf of the cell. [2]
  ii State and explain the effect, if any, of closing the switch on the brightness of the lamp. [2]
  iii Calculate the current through the motor. [2]

14 A current *I* is established in the conductor. The diagram shows one of the electrons making up the current moving with drift speed *v*. The conductor is exposed to a magnetic field *B* at right angles to the direction of motion of the electron.

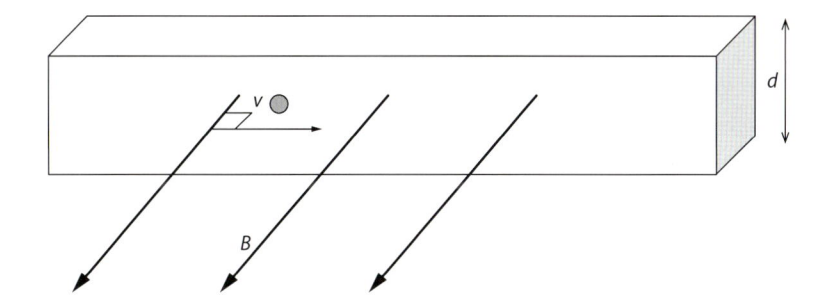

a On a copy of the diagram, draw an arrow to indicate the direction:
  i of the conventional current in the conductor [1]
  ii the magnetic force on the electron. [1]
b Show that the current in the conductor is given by $I = qnAv$, where *q* is the charge of the electron, *A* the cross-sectional area of the conductor, *v* the drift speed of the electrons and *n* is the number of free electrons per unit volume. [3]
c Explain why a potential difference will be established between the top (T) and bottom (B) faces of the conductor. [3]
d i The electric field between T and B is given by $E = \frac{V}{d}$ where *V* is the potential difference between T and B and *d* is their separation. Show that the voltage between T and B (the Hall voltage) is given by $V = vBd$. [2]
  ii The current in the conductor is 0.50 A, the number density of electrons is 3.2×10^{28} m^{-3}, the cross-sectional area of the wire is 4.2×10^{-6} m^2 and the magnetic field is 0.20 T. Calculate the Hall voltage in this conductor. [3]
e Outline how the existence of the Hall voltage can be used to verify that the charge carriers in the conductor are negatively charged. [2]

15 A proton of mass *m* and electric charge *q* enters a region of magnetic field at point X and exits at point Y. The speed of the proton at X is *v*. The path followed by the proton is a quarter of a circle.

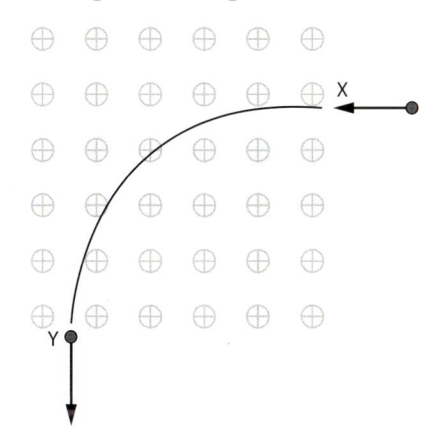

a State and explain whether the speed of the proton at Y is the same as the speed at X. [2]
b Suggest why the path of the proton is circular. [2]
c i Show that the radius of the circular path is given by $R = \frac{mv}{qB}$, where B is the magnetic flux density. [2]
  ii The speed of the proton is $3.6 \times 10^6 \, \text{m s}^{-1}$ at X and the magnetic flux density is 0.25 T. Show that the radius of the path is 15 cm. [2]
  iii Calculate the time the proton is in the region of the magnetic field. [2]
d i The proton is replaced by a beam of singly ionised atoms of neon. The ions have the same speed when they enter at X. The beam splits into two beams: B_1 of radius 38.0 cm and B_2 of radius 41.8 cm. The ions in beam B_1 have mass 3.32×10^{-26} kg. Predict the mass of the ions in beam B_2. [2]
  ii Suggest the implication of **d i** for nuclear structure. [2]

16 In the circuit shown A, B and C are three identical light bulbs of constant resistance. The battery has negligible internal resistance.

  a Determine the order of brightness of the light bulbs. [2]
  b Bulb C burns out. Predict how the brightness of A will change. [2]
  c Bulb C operates normally, but now bulb B burns out. Compare the brightness of A and of C now to the brightness they had before B burnt out. [2]

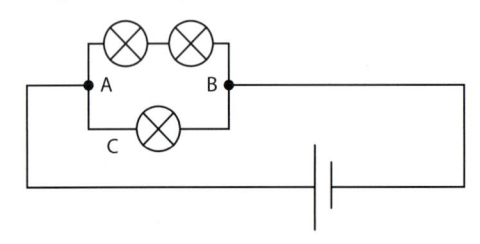

17 Consider the circuit shown in which the batteries are assumed to have negligible internal resistance.

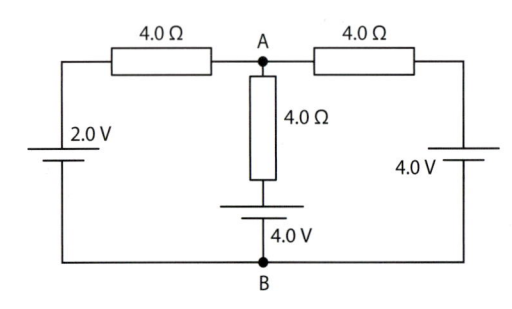

  a Calculate the current, magnitude and direction, in each battery. [4]
  b Determine the potential difference between points A and B. [2]
  c Determine the total power in each battery, commenting on your answer. [3]

Circular motion and gravitation 6

6.1 Circular motion

Circular motion is common in everyday life. Cornering in a car, the rotation of a salad spinner and most theme park rides are all examples of circular motion. A particular example is the motion of planets around the Sun in orbits that are approximately circular. As we will see, circular motion requires the presence of a force directed towards the centre of the circle. To account for the circular motion of planets around the Sun a new force was necessary: the force of gravitation.

Circular motion and angular speed

Consider the object in Figure **6.1**, which rotates in a circle of radius r in a counter-clockwise direction, with constant speed v.

Let T be the time taken to complete one full revolution. We call T the **period** of the motion. Since the speed is constant and the object covers a distance of $2\pi r$ in a time of T seconds, it follows that:

$$v = \frac{2\pi r}{T}$$

As the object moves around the circle it sweeps out an angle $\Delta\theta$ radians in a time Δt, as shown in Figure **6.2**. We can therefore define the **angular speed** of the object, denoted by ω, by:

$$\text{angular speed, } \omega = \frac{\text{angle swept}}{\text{time taken}} = \frac{\Delta\theta}{\Delta t}$$

For a complete revolution, $\Delta\theta = 2\pi$ and $\Delta t = T$, so we also have:

$$\omega = \frac{2\pi}{T}$$

Since the rotating frequency f is given by:

$$f = \frac{1}{T}$$

we have:

$$\omega = \frac{2\pi}{T} = 2\pi f$$

The units of angular speed are radians per second, rad s^{-1}.

The velocity vector is at a tangent to the circle. In a short time Δt the body travels a distance $v\Delta t$ along the circle. The angle swept in that same time is $\Delta\theta$. The distance travelled is an arc of the circle, and from trigonometry we know that the length of the arc of a circle radius r is given by $r\Delta\theta$. So we have that:

$$v\Delta t = r\Delta\theta$$

Learning objectives

- Solve problems using the concepts of period, frequency, angular displacement, angular velocity and linear velocity.
- Identify forces (such as tension, electrical, gravitational or magnetic forces) which may act as centripetal forces in circular motion.

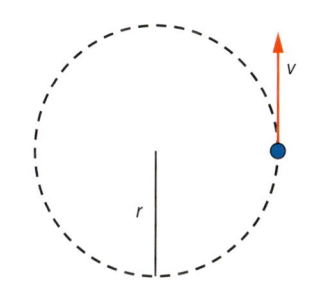

Figure 6.1 An object moving in a circle of radius r.

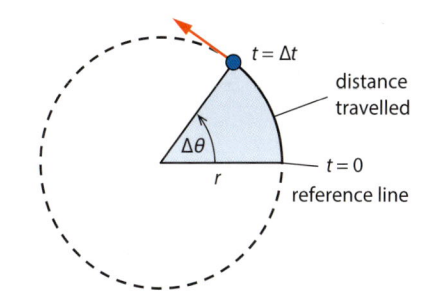

Figure 6.2 As the object rotates around the circle it sweeps out an angle measured from some arbitrary reference line.

Dividing both sides by the time Δt gives:

$$v = r\frac{\Delta \theta}{\Delta t}$$

$$v = r\omega$$

This is the relation between the **linear speed** v and the **angular speed** ω.

Worked example

6.1 The radius of the Earth's orbit is about 1.5×10^{11} m. Calculate:
   a the angular speed of the Earth as it rotates around the Sun
   b the linear speed of the Earth.

a The Earth completes one full revolution in approximately 365 days, so T is 365 days.
Using $\omega = \frac{2\pi}{T}$ for angular speed, we get:

$$\omega = \frac{2\pi}{365 \times 24 \times 60 \times 60}$$

$\omega = 1.99 \times 10^{-7} \approx 2.0 \times 10^{-7}\,\text{rad s}^{-1}$

Exam tip
Remember to convert days to seconds.

b Use the relation between angular and linear speed, $v = \omega r$:

$v = 1.99 \times 10^{-7} \times 1.5 \times 10^{11} = 29\,580 \approx 3.0 \times 10^4\,\text{m s}^{-1}$

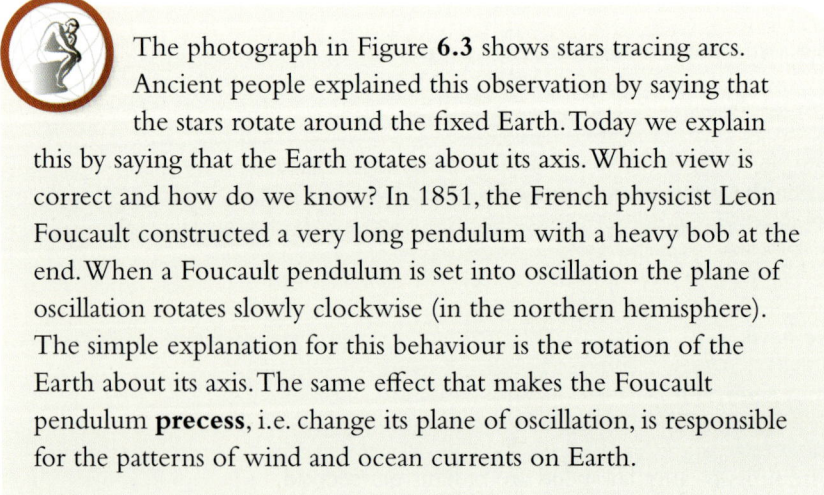

The photograph in Figure **6.3** shows stars tracing arcs. Ancient people explained this observation by saying that the stars rotate around the fixed Earth. Today we explain this by saying that the Earth rotates about its axis. Which view is correct and how do we know? In 1851, the French physicist Leon Foucault constructed a very long pendulum with a heavy bob at the end. When a Foucault pendulum is set into oscillation the plane of oscillation rotates slowly clockwise (in the northern hemisphere). The simple explanation for this behaviour is the rotation of the Earth about its axis. The same effect that makes the Foucault pendulum **precess**, i.e. change its plane of oscillation, is responsible for the patterns of wind and ocean currents on Earth.

It is quite remarkable how very simple observations reveal something deep about the world around us. In the same category we have Eratosthenes' ingeniously simple method for measuring the radius of the Earth; and Olbers' observation about the darkness of the night sky, which led to the abandonment of the Newtonian view of an infinite universe.

Figure 6.3 As the Earth rotates about its axis, stars appear to trace circles in the night sky.

Centripetal acceleration

Before going any further it is important to note that in circular motion even if the linear speed is constant the velocity is not: the velocity is changing because its direction is changing. Since the velocity changes, there is acceleration. What follows is a **derivation** of the expression for acceleration in circular motion. You may want to skip the derivation and go directly to the result just before the end of this section.

Look at Figure **6.4a**, which shows the velocity of a particle at two points P and Q as it moves in a circle. We know that the velocity vector at each point must be a tangent to the circle.

The acceleration is defined as:

$$a = \frac{\Delta v}{\Delta t}$$

where $\Delta \boldsymbol{v}$ is a vector. Thus, we have acceleration every time the velocity **vector** changes. This vector will change if:

- its magnitude changes
- the direction changes
- both magnitude and direction change.

For motion in a circle with constant **speed**, it is the direction of the velocity vector that changes. We must therefore find the difference between the velocities at P and Q:

$$\Delta \boldsymbol{v} = \boldsymbol{v}_Q - \boldsymbol{v}_P$$

This is shown in Figure **6.4b**, where we see that the angle between the vectors is $\Delta\theta$.

The magnitude of the vector $\Delta \mathbf{v}$ can be found from simple trigonometry. We know that the magnitudes of the velocity vectors at P and Q are the same – they are equal to the constant speed v of the moving particle. We use these to draw the triangle in Figure **6.4c**, which is isosceles with two sides of length v, the speed of the particle, and angle $\Delta\theta$. The third side is then the magnitude of the velocity change, Δv. If the angle $\Delta\theta$ is very small, then the distance Δv is approximately an arc of a circle of radius v and subtending an angle $\Delta\theta$ (in radians). Hence $\Delta v = v\Delta\theta$.

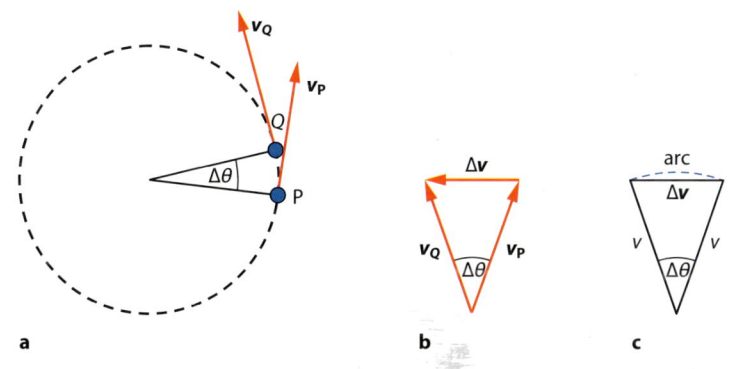

Figure 6.4 a The velocity vector changes direction as the particle moves from P to Q. **b** The change in the velocity vector from P to Q is given by Δv. **c** If the angle $\Delta\theta$ is very small, the arc length and the length of the chord are the same.

6 CIRCULAR MOTION AND GRAVITATION 251

Therefore using $a = \frac{\Delta v}{\Delta t}$ the acceleration has a magnitude given by:

$$a = v\frac{\Delta \theta}{\Delta t}$$

$$= v\omega$$

But $\omega = \frac{v}{r}$ and so the acceleration is:

$$a = v \times \frac{v}{r} = \frac{v^2}{r}$$

This gives us the magnitude of the acceleration vector for motion around a circle of radius r with constant speed v. The relationship shows that the magnitude of the acceleration vector is constant if v is constant. But what about its direction? As Δt gets smaller and smaller, the angle $\Delta \theta$ gets smaller and smaller, which means that the vector Δv, which is in the direction of acceleration, becomes perpendicular to v. This means that the acceleration vector is normal to the circle and directed towards the centre of the circle. It is a **centripetal acceleration** (Figure **6.5**).

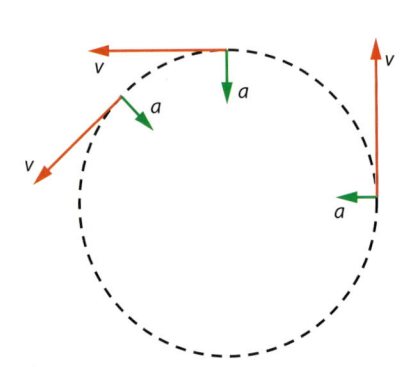

Figure 6.5 The centripetal acceleration vector is normal to the velocity vector.

A body moving along a circle of radius r with speed v experiences centripetal acceleration that has magnitude given by:

$$a = \frac{v^2}{r}$$

and is directed toward the centre of the circle.

We can find many equivalent expressions for the centripetal acceleration as follows:

Using $v = \frac{2\pi r}{T}$ we have that $a = \frac{4\pi^2 r^2}{rT^2} = \frac{4\pi^2 r}{T^2}$

Using $v = r\omega$ gives $a = \omega^2 r$

We can define a quantity called the **frequency** of the motion. This will also be useful in the context of waves. Frequency is the number of full revolutions per second. Since we make one full revolution in the course of one period T, the number of revolutions in one second is $f = \frac{1}{T}$. So we have another expression for centripetal acceleration:

$$a = 4\pi^2 r f^2$$

So we can use one of $a = \frac{v^2}{r}$ or $a = \omega^2 r$ or $a = \frac{4\pi^2 r}{T^2}$ or $a = 4\pi^2 r f^2$, depending on what is convenient.

Worked examples

6.2 A particle moves along a circle of radius 2.0 m with constant angular speed 2.1 rad s^{-1}. Determine the centripetal acceleration of the particle.

Remember that $a = \omega^2 r$ and so $a = 2.1^2 \times 2.0$

Hence $a \approx 8.8$ m s^{-2}

6.3 The radius of the Earth is $r = 6.4 \times 10^6$ m. Determine the centripetal acceleration due to the spinning Earth experienced by someone on the equator.

A mass on the equator travels a distance of $2\pi r$ in a time $T = 1$ day.

Thus: $v = \dfrac{2 \times \pi \times 6.4 \times 10^6}{24 \times 60 \times 60} = 4.65 \times 10^2$ m s^{-1}

and so: $a = \dfrac{(4.65 \times 10^2)^2}{6.4 \times 10^6} = 3.4 \times 10^{-2}$ m s^{-2}

This is quite small compared with the acceleration of free fall and we are not aware of it in daily life.

6.4 A mass moves in a circle with constant speed in a counter-clockwise direction, as in Figure **6.6a**. Determine the direction of the velocity change when the mass moves from A to B.

Draw the velocity vectors, as shown in Figure **6.6b**. The velocity at A is vertical and at B it points to the left. The change in the velocity vector is $v_B - v_A$ and this difference of vectors is directed as shown in Figure **6.6b**.

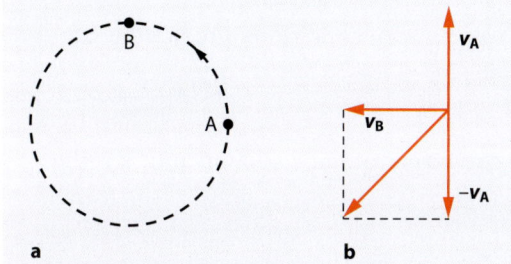

Figure 6.6 Change in velocity between two positions in circular motion.

Centripetal forces

If a body moves in a circle, there must be a net force acting on the body, since it is accelerating. If the speed is constant, the direction of the acceleration is towards the centre of the circle and therefore that is also the direction of the net force. It is a **centripetal force**. Its magnitude is given by:

$$F = \dfrac{mv^2}{r}$$

6 CIRCULAR MOTION AND GRAVITATION

which can also be written as:

$$F = m\omega^2 r$$

Consider a car moving on a circular level road of radius r with constant speed v. Friction between the wheels and the road provides the necessary force directed towards the centre of the circle that enables the car to take the turn (Figure 6.7). Note that in this example it is friction that provides the centripetal force. However, this does not mean that friction is always a centripetal force – it only applies to the case when the resulting motion is circular.

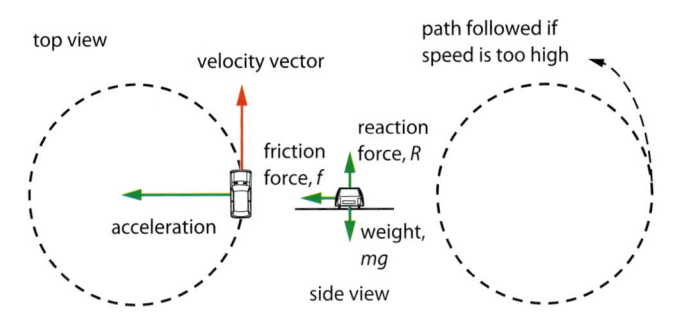

Figure 6.7 A car will skid outwards (i.e. will cover a circle of larger radius) if the friction force is not large enough.

Worked examples

6.5 a The coefficient of static friction between the tyres of a car of mass 1100 kg and dry asphalt is about 0.80. Determine the maximum speed with which a car can take a circular turn of radius 95 m.
b In wet conditions the coefficient of friction is reduced to half its value in dry conditions. Predict the safe maximum speed now.

a The *maximum* frictional force is given by $F_{max} = \mu_S N$, where μ_S is the coefficient of static friction and N is the reaction force. Hence:

$$F_{max} = 0.80 \times 1100 \times 9.81 = 8.6 \times 10^3 \, \text{N}$$

This frictional force provides the centripetal force for the car and so:

$$\frac{mv^2}{r} = F_{max}$$

$$v = \sqrt{\frac{F_{max} r}{m}}$$

$$v = \sqrt{\frac{8.6 \times 10^3 \times 95}{1100}}$$

$$v = 27 \, \text{m s}^{-1}$$

b You could repeat the calculation in part **a**, finding a new maximum force with the reduced coefficient of friction. But it would be better to find how the velocity depends on the coefficient of friction. To do this you need to go back to the original expression for F_{max}.

$$F_{max} = \mu_S N = \mu_S mg$$

Therefore:

$$\frac{mv^2}{r} = \mu_S mg \Rightarrow v = \sqrt{\mu_S gr}$$

So the mass is not relevant. In this case g and r are the same for both wet and dry conditions, so the velocity depends on the square root of the coefficient of friction.

In wet conditions the coefficient of friction is 0.40, so the new speed is:

$$v = 27\sqrt{\frac{0.40}{0.80}} \approx 19\,\mathrm{m\,s^{-1}}$$

6.6 A particle is tied to a string and moves with constant speed in a horizontal circle. The string is tied to the ceiling. Draw the forces on the particle.

Exam tip
It is very important that you understand Worked example **6.6**.

A common mistake is to put a horizontal force pointing toward the centre and call it the centripetal force. When you are asked to find forces on a body, the list of forces that are available include the weight, reaction forces (if the body touches another body), friction (if there is friction), tension (if there are strings or springs), resistance forces (if the body moves in air or a fluid), electric forces (if electric charges are involved), etc. Nowhere in this list is there an entry for a centripetal force.

Think of the word centripetal as simply an adjective that describes forces already acting on a body, not as a new force. In this example, the only forces on the particle are the weight and the tension (Figure **6.8a**). If we decompose the tension into horizontal and vertical components, we see that the weight is equal and opposite to the vertical component of the tension. This means that the only force left on the particle is the horizontal component of the tension, which points towards the centre of the circle. We may now call this force the centripetal force. But this is not a new force. It is simply the component of a force that is already acting on the particle (Figure **6.8b**).

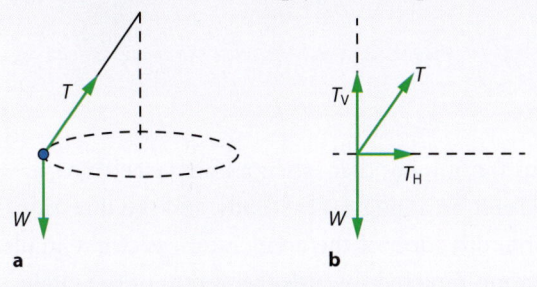

Figure 6.8 a The forces on the particle. **b** Decomposing the tension into horizontal and vertical components, T_H and T_V.

6.7 A mass m is tied to a string and made to move in a vertical circle of radius r with constant speed v.
  a Determine the tension in the string at the lowest and highest points of the circle.
  b Calculate the minimum speed so that the string never goes slack.

a The forces are as shown in Figure 6.9.

At the lowest point, the net force is $T_1 - mg$ and so:

$$T_1 - mg = \frac{mv^2}{r}$$

Rearranging, this gives:

$$T_1 = mg + \frac{mv^2}{r}$$

At the highest point, the net force is $mg + T_2$ and so:

$$T_2 = \frac{mv^2}{r} - mg$$

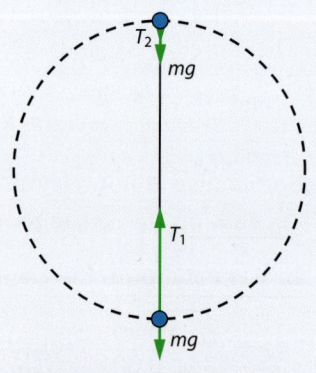

Figure 6.9 The tension in the string is different at different positions of the mass.

b The string goes slack when the tension in the string becomes zero. T_2 is less than T_1 so we need to make sure T_2 is always greater than zero,

i.e. $\dfrac{mv^2}{r} > mg$

Rearranging, we need $v^2 > gr$.

Exam tip
It is important that you understand why the centripetal force does no work. It is also important to avoid thinking about centrifugal forces, as 'centrifugal forces' do not exist.

It is important to note that, since a centripetal force is at right angles to the direction of motion, the work done by the force is zero. (Recall that $W = Fs\cos\theta$, and here the angle is a right angle.)

It is a common mistake in circular motion problems to include a force pushing the body away from the centre of the circle: a **centrifugal force**. It is important to stress that no such force exists. A body in circular motion cannot be in equilibrium and so no force pushing away from the centre is required.

Nature of science

Simple deductions

Newton's second law of motion implies that when a body accelerates a net force of magnitude ma must be acting on the body, and the direction of the force is the same as the direction of the acceleration vector. Circular motion involves an acceleration directed towards the centre of the circle. This means that the observation of the (approximate) circular motion of planets implies the existence of a force. Newton used this fact to deduce the existence of the gravitational force: the same force that causes objects to fall towards the surface of the Earth is responsible for the motion of planets around the Sun.

Test yourself

1. **a** Calculate the angular speed and linear speed of a particle that completes a 3.50 m radius circle in 1.24 s.
   b Determine the frequency of the motion.
2. Calculate the centripetal acceleration of a body that moves in a circle of radius 2.45 m making 3.5 revolutions per second.
3. The diagram shows a mass moving on a circular path of radius 2.0 m at constant speed 4.0 m s^{-1}.

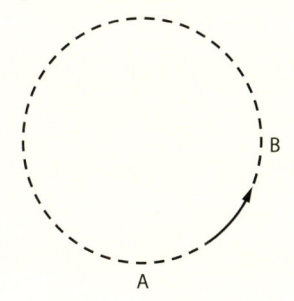

   a Calculate the magnitude and direction of the average acceleration during a quarter of a revolution (from **A** to **B**).
   b Calculate the centripetal acceleration of the mass.
4. An astronaut rotates at the end of a test machine whose arm has a length of 10.0 m, as shown in the diagram. The acceleration she experiences must not exceed 5g (take g = 10 m s^{-2}). Determine the maximum number of revolutions per minute of the arm.

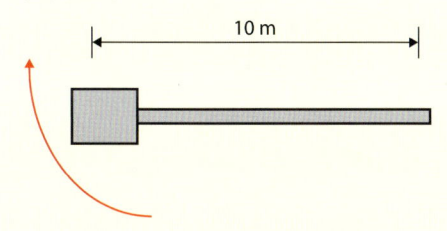

5. A body of mass 1.00 kg is tied to a string and rotates on a horizontal, frictionless table.
   a The length of the string is 40.0 cm and the speed of revolution is 2.0 m s^{-1}. Calculate the tension in the string.
   b The string breaks when the tension exceeds 20.0 N. Determine the largest speed the mass can rotate at.
   c The breaking tension of the string is 20.0 N but you want the mass to rotate at 4.00 m s^{-1}. Determine the shortest length string that can be used.

6. Estimate the length of the day if the centripetal acceleration at the equator due to the spinning Earth was equal to the acceleration of free fall (g = 9.8 m s^{-2}).
7. A neutron star has a radius of 50.0 km and completes one revolution every 25 ms.
   a Calculate the centripetal acceleration experienced at the equator of the star.
   b The acceleration of free fall at the surface of the star is 8.0×10^{10} m s^{-2}. State and explain whether a probe that landed on the star could stay on the surface or whether it would be thrown off.
8. The Earth (mass = 6.0×10^{24} kg) rotates around the Sun in an orbit that is approximately circular, with a radius of 1.5×10^{11} m.
   a Estimate the orbital speed of the Earth around the Sun.
   b Determine the centripetal acceleration experienced by the Earth.
   c Deduce the magnitude of the gravitational force exerted on the Sun by the Earth.
9. A plane travelling at a speed 180 m s^{-1} along a horizontal circle makes an angle of $\theta = 35°$ to the horizontal. The lift force L is acting in the direction shown. Calculate the radius of the circle.

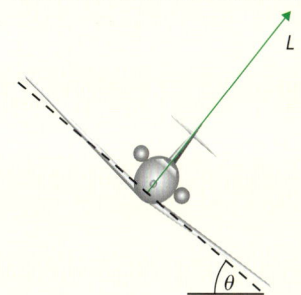

10. A cylinder of radius 5.0 m rotates about its vertical axis. A girl stands inside the cylinder with her back touching the side of the cylinder. The floor is suddenly lowered but the girl stays 'glued' to the wall. The coefficient of friction between the girl and the wall is 0.60.
    a Draw a free body diagram of the forces on the girl.
    b Determine the minimum number of revolutions per minute for which the girl does not slip down the wall.

6 CIRCULAR MOTION AND GRAVITATION

11 A loop-the-loop machine has radius r of 18 m.

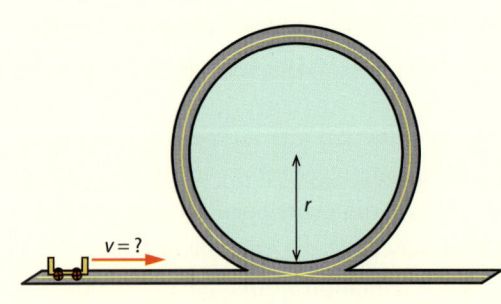

   a Calculate the minimum speed with which a cart must enter the loop so that it does not fall off at the highest point.
   b Predict the speed at the top in this case.

12 The diagram shows a horizontal disc with a hole through its centre. A string passes through the hole and connects a mass m on top of the disc to a bigger mass M that hangs below the disc. Initially the smaller mass is rotating on the disc in a circle of radius r. Determine the speed of m be such that the big mass stands still.

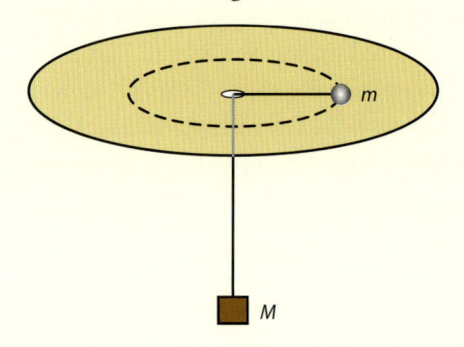

13 The ball shown in the diagram is attached to a rotating pole with two strings. The ball has a mass of 0.250 kg and rotates in a horizontal circle at a speed of $8.0 \, \text{m s}^{-1}$. Determine the tension in each string.

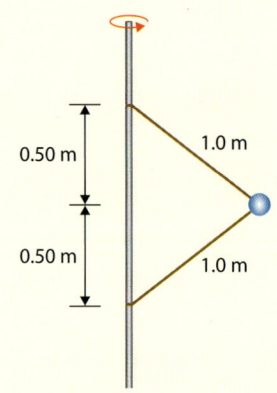

14 In an amusement park ride a cart of mass 300 kg and carrying four passengers each of mass 60 kg is dropped from a vertical height of 120 m along a frictionless path that leads into a loop-the-loop machine of radius 30 m. The cart then enters a straight stretch from **A** to **C** where friction brings it to rest after a distance of 40 m.

   a Determine the velocity of the cart at **A**.
   b Calculate the reaction force from the seat of the cart onto a passenger at **B**.
   c Determine the acceleration experienced by the cart from **A** to **C** (assumed constant).

6.2 The law of gravitation

This section will introduce us to one of the fundamental laws of physics – **Newton's law of gravitation**. The law of gravitation makes it possible to calculate the orbits of the planets around the Sun, and predicts the motion of comets, satellites and entire galaxies. Newton's law of gravitation was published in his *Philosophiae Naturalis Principia Mathematica* in 1686.

Learning objectives

- Solve problems where the gravitational force plays the role of a centripetal force, in particular orbital motion.
- Use the concepts of gravitational force, gravitational field strength, orbital speed and orbital period.
- Determine the net gravitational field strength due to two point masses.

Newton's law of gravitation

We have seen that Newton's second law implies that whenever a particle moves with acceleration, a net force must be acting on it. The proverbial apple falling freely under gravity is accelerating at $9.8\,\mathrm{m\,s^{-2}}$ and thus experiences a net force in the direction of the acceleration. This force is what we call the 'weight' of the apple. Similarly, a planet that orbits around the Sun also experiences acceleration and thus a force is acting on it. Newton hypothesised that the force responsible for the falling apple is the same as the force acting on a planet as it moves around the Sun.

Newton proposed that the attractive force of gravitation between two **point** masses is given by the formula:

$$F = G\frac{M_1 M_2}{r^2}$$

where M_1 and M_2 are the masses of the attracting bodies, r the distance between their centres of mass and G a constant called Newton's constant of universal gravitation. It has the value $G = 6.667 \times 10^{-11}\,\mathrm{N\,m^2\,kg^{-2}}$. The direction of the force is along the line joining the two masses.

This formula applies to point masses, that is to say masses that are very small (in comparison with their separation). In the case of objects such as the Sun, the Earth, and so on, the formula still applies since the separation of, say, the Sun and a planet is enormous compared with the radii of the Sun and the planet. In addition, Newton proved that for bodies that are **spherical** and of uniform density, one can assume that the entire mass of the body is concentrated at its centre – as if the body is a point mass.

The laws of mechanics, along with Newton's law of gravitation, are the basis of classical physics. They describe a perfectly **deterministic** system. This means that if we know the positions and velocities of the particles in a system at some instant of time, then the future positions and velocities of the particles can be predicted with absolute certainty. Since the beginning of the 20th century we have known that this is not true in many cases. In situations normally associated with 'chaos' the sensitivity of the system to the initial conditions is such that it is not possible to make accurate predictions of the future state.

6 CIRCULAR MOTION AND GRAVITATION 259

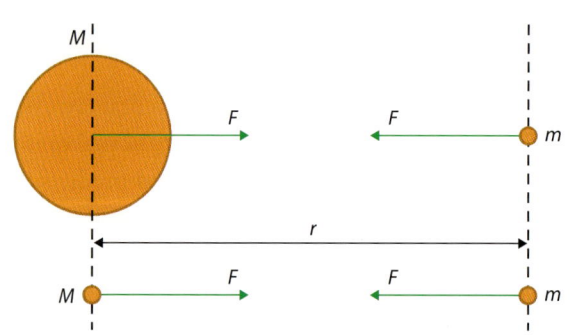

Figure 6.10 The mass of the spherical body to the left can be thought to be concentrated at its centre.

Figure **6.10** shows the gravitational force between two masses. The gravitational force is always attractive. The magnitude of the force on each mass is the same. This follows both from the formula as well as from Newton's third law.

Worked example

6.8 Estimate the force between the Sun and the Earth.

The average distance between the Earth and the Sun is $r = 1.5 \times 10^{11}$ m.
The mass of the Earth is 5.98×10^{24} kg and the mass of the Sun is 1.99×10^{30} kg.
Substituting these values into the formula $F = \dfrac{GM_1M_2}{r^2}$ gives:

$$F = \frac{6.67 \times 10^{-11} \times 5.98 \times 10^{24} \times 1.99 \times 10^{30}}{(1.5 \times 10^{11})^2}$$

So: $F = 3.5 \times 10^{22}$ N

Where did the law of gravitation come from? Not just from Newton's great intuition but also from the knowledge obtained earlier by Kepler that planets move around the Sun with a period that is proportional to the $\frac{3}{2}$ power of the average orbit radius. To get such a law, the force of gravitation had to be an inverse square law.

Gravitational field strength

Physicists (and philosophers) since the time of Newton, including Newton himself, wondered how a mass 'knows' about the presence of another mass nearby that will attract it. By the 19th century, physicists had developed the idea of a 'field', which was to provide a (partial) answer to the question. A mass M is said to create a **gravitational field** in the space around it. This means that when another mass is placed at some point near M, it 'feels' the gravitational field in the form of a gravitational force.

We define **gravitational field strength** as follows.

The gravitational field strength at a certain point is the gravitational force per unit mass experienced by a small point mass m placed at that point.

In other words, if the gravitational force exerted on m is F, then:

$$g = \frac{F}{m}$$

Turning this around, we find that the gravitational force on a point mass m is $F = mg$. But this is the expression we previously called the weight of the mass m. So we learn that the gravitational field strength is the same as the acceleration of free fall.

The force experienced by a small point mass m placed at distance r from a (spherical) mass M is:

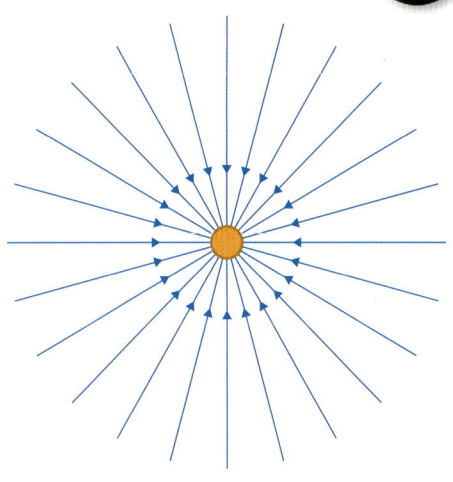

$$F = G\frac{Mm}{r^2}$$

Figure 6.11 The gravitational field around a point (or spherical) mass is radial.

So the gravitational field strength $\left(\frac{F}{m}\right)$ of the spherical mass M is:

$$g = G\frac{M}{r^2}$$

The unit of gravitational field strength is $N\,kg^{-1}$. (This unit is equivalent to $m\,s^{-2}$.)

The gravitational field strength is a vector quantity whose direction is given by the direction of the force a point mass would experience if placed at the point of interest. The gravitational field strength around a single point or spherical mass is **radial**, which means that it points towards the centre of the mass creating the field. This is illustrated in Figure 6.11. This field is not uniform – the field lines gets farther apart with increasing distance from the point mass. (You will learn more about fields in Topic 10.)

In contrast Figure 6.12 shows a field with constant gravitational field strength. Here the field lines are equally spaced and parallel. The assumption of constant acceleration of free fall (which we used for projectile motion in Topic 2) corresponds to this case.

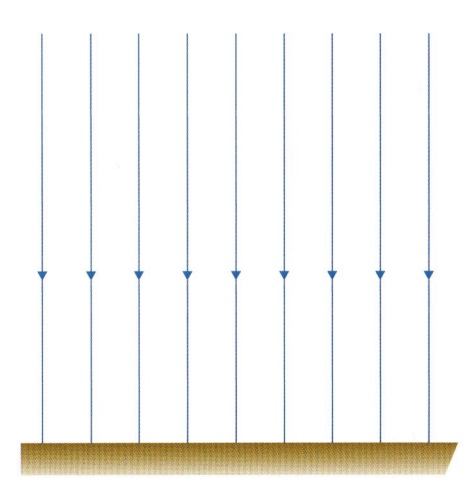

Figure 6.12 The gravitational field above a flat mass is uniform.

Worked examples

6.9 The distance between two bodies is doubled. Predict what will happen to the gravitational force between them.

Since the force is inversely proportional to the square of the separation, doubling the separation reduces the force by a factor of $2^2 = 4$.

6 CIRCULAR MOTION AND GRAVITATION

6.10 Determine the acceleration of free fall (the gravitational field strength) on a planet 10 times as massive as the Earth and with a radius 20 times as large.

From $g = \dfrac{GM}{r^2}$ we find:

$$g = \dfrac{G(10M)}{(20r_E)^2}$$

$$g = \dfrac{10GM_E}{400r_E^2}$$

$$g = \dfrac{1}{40}\dfrac{GM_E}{r_E^2}$$

$$g = \dfrac{1}{40}g_E \approx 0.25 \text{ m s}^{-2}$$

Exam tip
For this type of problem write the formula for g and then replace mass and radius in terms of those for Earth. It is a common mistake to forget to square the factor of 20 in the denominator.

6.11 Calculate the acceleration of free fall at a height of 300 km from the surface of the Earth (the Earth's radius, r_E, is 6.38×10^6 m and its mass is 6.0×10^{24} kg).

The acceleration of free fall is the same as the gravitational field strength. At height h from the surface:

$$g = \dfrac{GM_E}{(r_E + h)^2}$$

where $r_E = 6.38 \times 10^6$ m is the radius of the Earth. We can now put the numbers in:

$$g = \dfrac{6.67 \times 10^{-11} \times 6.0 \times 10^{24}}{(6.68 \times 10^6)^2}$$

$$g = 8.97 \approx 9 \text{ m s}^{-2}$$

Exam tip
Notice the addition of the height to the radius of the Earth. Watch the units.

Orbital motion

Figure 6.13 shows a particle of mass m orbiting a larger body of mass M in a circular orbit of radius r. To maintain a constant orbit there must be no frictional forces, so the only force on the particle is the force of gravitation, $F = \dfrac{GMm}{r^2}$. This force provides the centripetal force on the particle. Therefore:

$$\dfrac{mv^2}{r} = \dfrac{GMm}{r^2}$$

Cancelling the mass m and a factor of r, this leads to:

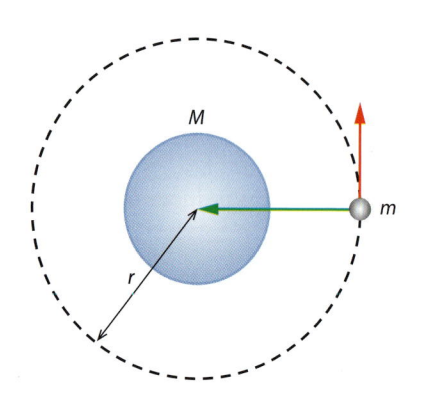

$$v = \sqrt{\dfrac{GM}{r}}$$

Figure 6.13 A particle of mass m orbiting a larger body of mass M in a circular orbit of radius r.

This gives the speed in a circular orbit of radius r. But we know that $v = \frac{2\pi r}{T}$. Squaring $v = \frac{2\pi r}{T}$ and equating the two expressions for v^2, we deduce that:

$$\frac{4\pi^2 r^2}{T^2} = \frac{GM}{r}$$

$$\Rightarrow T^2 = \frac{4\pi^2 r^3}{GM}$$

This shows that the period of planets going around the Sun is proportional to the $\frac{3}{2}$ power of the orbit radius. Newton knew this from Kepler's calculations, so he knew that his choice of distance squared in the law of gravitation was reasonable.

The same calculations apply to objects orbiting the Earth, such as communications and weather satellites or the International Space Station (Figure **6.14**).

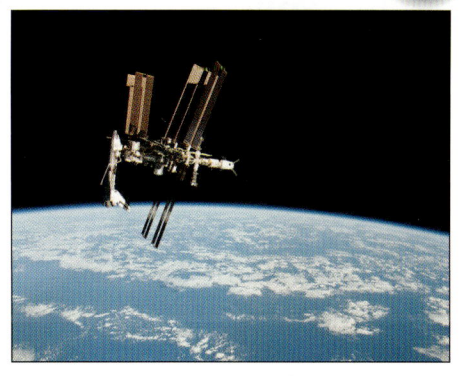

Figure 6.14 The International Space Station orbits the Earth in a circular orbit.

Nature of science

Predictions versus understanding

Combining the laws of mechanics with the law of gravitation enables scientists to predict with great accuracy the orbits of spacecraft, planets and comets. But to what degree do they enable an understanding of why planets, for example, move the way they do? In ancient times, Ptolemy was also able to predict the motion of planets with exceptional precision. In what sense is the Newtonian approach 'better'? Ptolemy's approach was specific to planets and could not be generalised to other examples of motion, whereas the Newtonian approach can. Ptolemy's method gives no explanation of the observed motions whereas Newton 'explains' the motion in terms of one single universal concept, that of a gravitational force that depends in a specific way on mass and separation. In this sense the Newtonian approach is superior and represents progress in science. But there are limits to the degree to which one demands 'understanding': the obvious question for Newton would be, 'Why is there a force between two masses?'. Newton could not answer this question – and no-one has been able to since. There is more in Option **A** on relativity about Einstein's attempt to answer this question.

6 CIRCULAR MOTION AND GRAVITATION

Test yourself

15 Calculate the gravitational force between:
   a the Earth and the Moon
   b the Sun and Jupiter
   c a proton and an electron separated by 10^{-10} m.

16 A mass m is placed at the centre of a thin, hollow, spherical shell of mass M and radius r, shown in diagram **a**.

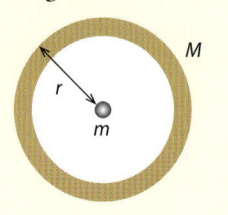

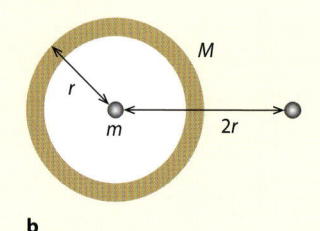

   a **b**

   a Determine the gravitational force the mass m experiences.
   b Determine the gravitational force m exerts on M.
   A second mass m is now placed a distance of $2r$ from the centre of the shell, as shown in diagram **b**.
   c Determine the gravitational force the mass inside the shell experiences.
   d Suggest what gravitational force is experienced by the mass outside the shell.

17 Stars **A** and **B** have the same mass and the radius of star **A** is nine times larger than the radius of star **B**. Calculate the ratio of the gravitational field strength on star **A** to that on star **B**.

18 Planet **A** has a mass that is twice as large as the mass of planet **B** and a radius that is twice as large as the radius of planet **B**. Calculate the ratio of the gravitational field strength on planet **A** to that on planet **B**.

19 Stars **A** and **B** have the same density and star **A** is 27 times more massive than star **B**. Calculate the ratio of the gravitational field strength on star **A** to that on star **B**.

20 A star explodes and loses half its mass. Its radius becomes half as large. Determine the new gravitational field strength on the surface of the star in terms of the original one.

21 The mass of the Moon is about 81 times less than that of the Earth. Estimate the fraction of the distance from the Earth to the Moon where the gravitational field strength is zero. (Take into account the Earth and the Moon only.)

22 The diagram shows point P is halfway between the centres of two equal spherical masses that are separated by a distance of 2×10^9 m. Calculate the gravitational field strength at point P and state the direction of the gravitational field strength at point Q.

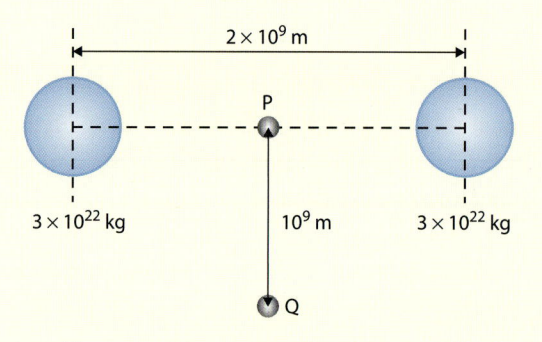

23 A satellite orbits the Earth above the equator with a period equal to 24 hours.
   a Determine the height of the satellite above the Earth's surface.
   b Suggest an advantage of such a satellite.

24 The Hubble Space Telescope is in orbit around the Earth at a height of 560 km above the Earth's surface. Take the radius and mass of the Earth to be 6.4×10^6 m and 6.0×10^{24} kg, respectively.
   a Calculate Hubble's speed.
   b In a servicing mission, a Space Shuttle spotted the Hubble telescope a distance of 10 km ahead. Estimate how long it took the Shuttle to catch up with Hubble, assuming that the Shuttle was moving in a circular orbit just 500 m below Hubble's orbit.

25 Assume that the force of gravity between two point masses is given by $F = \dfrac{Gm_1m_2}{r^n}$ where n is a constant.
   a Derive the law relating period to orbit radius for this force.
   b Deduce the value of n if this law is to be identical with Kepler's third law.

Exam-style questions

1 A child is sitting at the edge of a merry-go-round. The arrow shows the velocity of the child. At the instant shown, he releases a ball onto the ground.

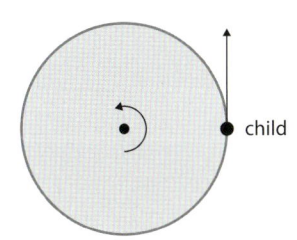

Which is the path of the ball according to a stationary observer on the ground?

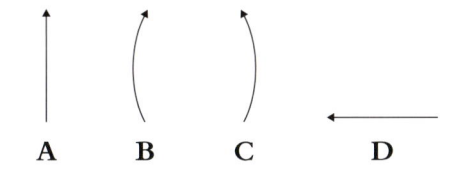

A   B   C   D

2 In which of the following examples of circular motion is the centripetal acceleration experienced by the particle the largest? In each case the arrows represent speed.

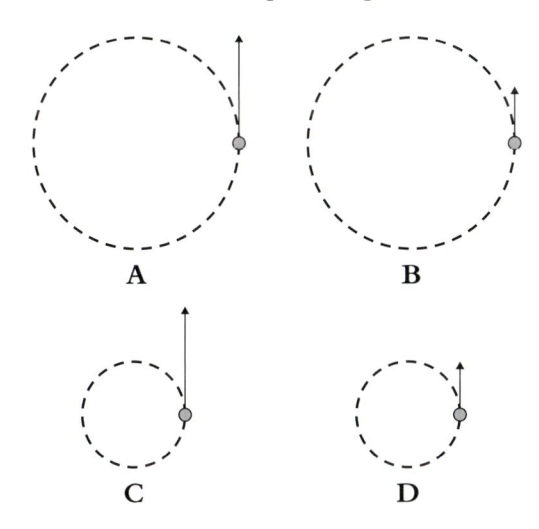

A   B   C   D

3 A horizontal disc rotates about a vertical axis through the centre of the disc. Two particles X and Y are placed on the disc.

The particles do not move relative to the disc. Which is correct about the angular speed ω and the linear speed v of X and Y?

	ω	v
A	same	same
B	same	different
C	different	same
D	different	different

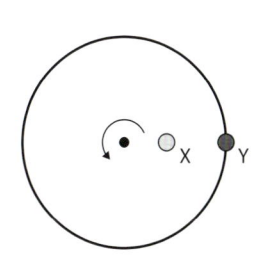

6 CIRCULAR MOTION AND GRAVITATION 265

4 In the diagram for question **3** the ratio of distances of Y to X is 2. What is the ratio of the acceleration of Y to that of X?

    A $\frac{1}{4}$ **B** $\frac{1}{2}$ **C** 2   **D** 4

5 A particle of mass m moves with speed v along a hill that may be assumed to be part of a circle of radius r.

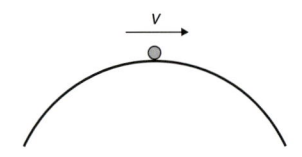

What is the reaction force on the particle at the highest point on the hill?

    A mg **B** $mg + \frac{mv^2}{r}$ **C** $mg - \frac{mv^2}{r}$ **D** $\frac{mv^2}{r} - mg$

6 A particle moves with speed v in a circular orbit of radius r around a planet. The particle is now moved to another circular orbit of radius $2r$. The new orbital speed is:

    A $\frac{v}{2}$ **B** $\frac{v}{\sqrt{2}}$ **C** $v\sqrt{2}$ **D** $2v$

7 The mass of a landing module on the Moon is 2000 kg. The gravitational field strength on the Moon is one-sixth that on Earth. What is the weight of the landing module on Earth?

    A 330 N   **B** 2000 N   **C** 12 000 N   **D** 20 000 N

8 A planet has double the mass of Earth and half its radius. What is the gravitational field strength on the surface of this planet?

    A 10 N kg^{-1} **B** 20 N kg^{-1} **C** 40 N kg^{-1} **D** 80 N kg^{-1}

9 A satellite orbits the Earth in a circular orbit. The only force on the satellite is the gravitational force from the Earth. Which of the following is correct about the acceleration of the satellite?

    A It is zero.
    B It is constant in magnitude and direction.
    C It is constant in magnitude but not in direction.
    D It is not constant in magnitude or direction.

10 The two spherical bodies in the diagram have the same radius but the left mass has twice the mass of the other. At which point could the net gravitational field of the two masses have the greatest magnitude?

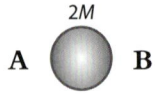

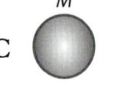

11 A horizontal disc of radius 45 cm rotates about a vertical axis through its centre. The disc makes one full revolution in 1.40 s. A particle of mass 0.054 kg is placed at a distance of 22 cm from the centre of the disc. The particle does not move relative to the disc.

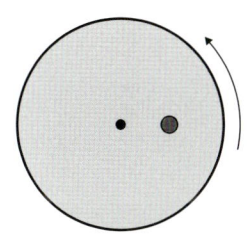

    a On a copy of the diagram draw arrows to represent the velocity and acceleration of the particle. [2]
    b Calculate the angular speed and the linear speed of the particle. [2]
    c The coefficient of static friction between the disc and the particle is 0.82. Determine the largest distance from the centre of the disc where the particle can be placed and still not move relative to the disc. [3]
    d The particle is to remain at its original distance of 22 cm from the centre of the disc.
      i Determine the maximum angular speed of the disc so that the particle does not move relative to the disc. [2]
      ii The disc now begins to rotate at an angular speed that is greater than the answer in **d i**. Describe qualitatively what happens to the particle. [2]

12 A block of mass of 5.0 kg is attached to a string of length 2.0 m which is initially horizontal. The mass is then released and swings as a pendulum. The diagram shows the mass falling to the position where the string is in the vertical position.

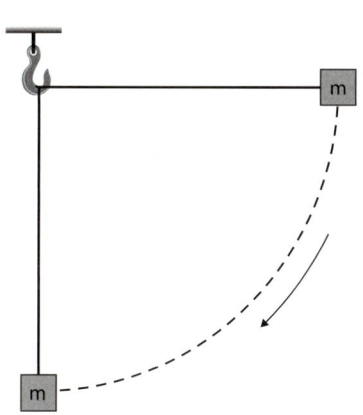

    a Calculate the speed of the block when the string is in the vertical position. [2]
    b Deduce the acceleration of the block. [1]
    c On a copy of the diagram, draw arrows to represent the forces on the block. [2]
    d For when the string is in the vertical position:
      i state and explain whether the block is in equilibrium [2]
      ii calculate the tension in the string. [2]

6 CIRCULAR MOTION AND GRAVITATION

13 A particle of mass m is attached to a string of length L whose other end is attached to the ceiling, as shown in the diagram. The particle moves in a horizontal circle making an angle of θ with the vertical. Air resistance may be neglected.

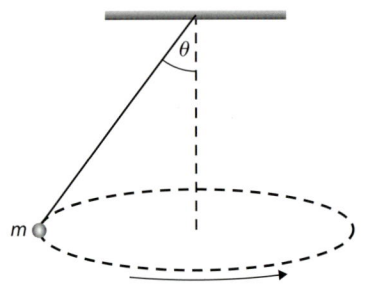

    a On a copy of the diagram draw arrows to represent the forces on the particle. [2]
    b State and explain whether the particle is in equilibrium. [2]
    c The linear speed of the particle is v and its angular speed is ω. Show that:

        i $v = \sqrt{\dfrac{gL\sin^2\theta}{\cos\theta}}$ [2]

        ii $\omega = \sqrt{\dfrac{g}{L\cos\theta}}$ [2]

    d The length of the string is 45 cm and $\theta = 60°$. Use the answer in **c** to evaluate:
        i the linear speed [1]
        ii the angular speed of the particle. [1]
Air resistance may no longer be neglected.
    e Suggest the effect of air resistance on:
        i the linear speed of the particle [1]
        ii the angle the string makes with the vertical [1]
        iii the angular speed of the particle. [1]

14 A marble rolls from the top of a big sphere, as shown in the diagram.

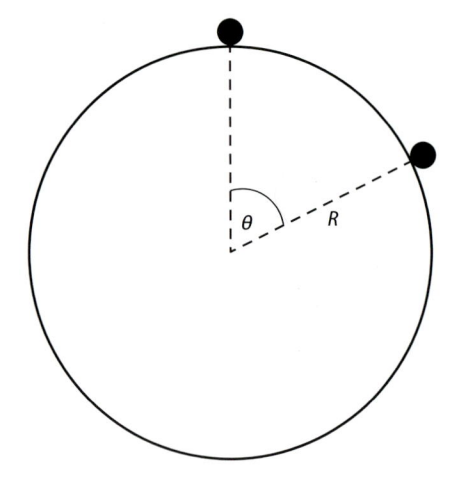

    a Show that when the marble has moved so that the line joining it to the centre of the sphere is θ, its speed is given by $v = \sqrt{2gR(1-\cos\theta)}$. (Assume a very small speed at the top.) [3]
    b Deduce that at that instant, the normal reaction force on the marble from the sphere is given by $N = mg(3\cos\theta - 2)$. [3]
    c Hence determine the angle θ at which the marble loses contact with the sphere. [1]

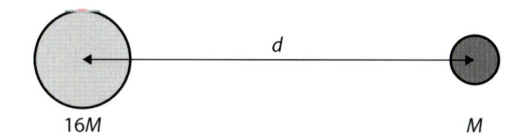

15 Consider two spherical bodies of mass 16M and M as in the diagram.

There is a point P somewhere on the line joining the masses where the gravitational field strength is zero.
  a Determine the distance of point P from the centre of the bigger mass in terms of d, the centre-to-centre distance separating the two bodies. [3]
  b Draw a graph to show the variation of the gravitational field strength g due to the two masses with the distance x from the centre of the larger mass. [2]
  c A small point mass m is placed at P.
    i State the force on m. [1]
    ii The small mass m is slightly displaced to the left of P. State and explain whether the net force on the point mass will be directed to the left or to the right. [2]
  d Describe qualitatively the motion of the point mass after it has been displaced to the left of P. [2]

16 A satellite is in a circular orbit around a planet of mass M, as shown in the diagram.

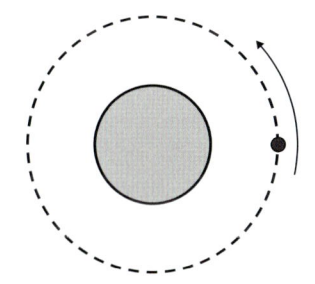

  a i On a copy of the diagram draw arrows to represent the velocity and acceleration of the satellite. [2]
    ii Explain why the satellite has acceleration even though its speed is constant. [2]
  b Show that the angular speed ω is related to the orbit radius r by $r^3\omega^2 = GM$. [3]
  c Because of friction with the upper atmosphere, the satellite slowly moves into another circular orbit with a smaller radius than the answer in **b**. Suggest the effect of this on the satellite's:
    i angular speed [1]
    ii linear speed. [1]
  d Titan and Enceladus are two of Saturn's moons. Data about these moons are given in the table.

Moon	Orbit radius / m	Angular speed / rad s^{-1}
Titan	1.22×10^9	
Enceladus	2.38×10^8	5.31×10^{-5}

    i Determine the mass of Saturn. [2]
    ii Determine the period of revolution of Titan in days. [3]

6 CIRCULAR MOTION AND GRAVITATION 269

7 Atomic, nuclear and particle physics

Learning objectives

- Describe and explain gas spectra in terms of energy levels.
- Solve problems with atomic transitions.
- Describe the fundamental forces between particles.
- Describe radioactive decay, including background radiation, and work with radioactive decay equations.
- Describe the properties of alpha, beta and gamma particles.
- Understand isotopes.

7.1 Discrete energy and radioactivity

The energy of electrons inside atoms or the energy of protons and neutrons inside nuclei is energy on a microscopic scale. The main idea of this section is that energy on this microscopic scale is discrete. Discrete energy means that the energy of a system cannot take on any arbitrary value. This is very different from macroscopic physics, where energy is a continuous property.

Discrete energy

If you expose a container of gas at low pressure to a strong electric field, light is emitted from the gas. This emitted light can be analysed by passing it through a prism or diffraction grating. The result is a series of bands of light at different wavelengths. Figure 7.1 shows the wavelengths that are present in the light emitted by hydrogen, helium and mercury vapour. The set of possible wavelengths that can be emitted is called an **emission spectrum**.

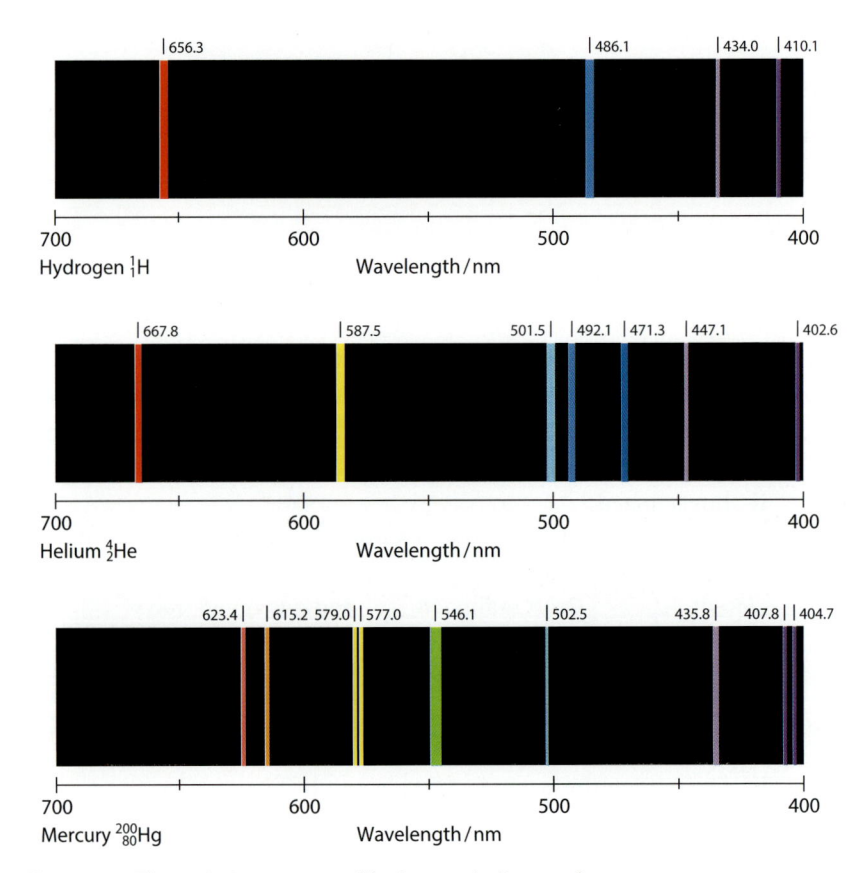

Figure 7.1 The emission spectra of hydrogen, helium and mercury vapour.

Such data have shown us that no two elements have the same wavelengths in their spectrum. The wavelengths are like fingerprints – they can be used to identify the element.

How can these spectra be understood? Niels Bohr (1885–1962) provided the first radical explanation in 1913. He argued that the energy of an atom was **discrete**, i.e. it could have one out of a specific set of values. He represented the possible energies with an **energy level diagram**. Each horizontal level represents a possible energy of the atom. By 'energy of the atom' we mean the kinetic energy of the electrons plus the electrical potential energy of the electrons and the nucleus. The diagram for hydrogen is shown in Figure **7.2** and that for mercury in Figure **7.3**.

We see that a hydrogen atom can have an energy of −13.6 eV, −3.40 eV, −1.51 eV, −0.87 eV and so on. No other value is possible. Energy in the atomic world is discrete.

How does this energy level structure help explain emission spectra? Bohr suggested that an atom can make a **transition** from a state of higher energy to a state of lower energy by emitting a **photon**, the particle of light. The energy of the emitted photon is the difference in energy between the two levels. Think of the photon as a 'tiny flash of light'. There would be one photon for each transition. With very many transitions from very many atoms the 'tiny flashes of light' in each transition add up to the observable light we see in the emission spectrum. The photon had been introduced earlier into physics by Einstein, who suggested that its energy is given by:

$$E = hf \quad \text{or} \quad E = \frac{hc}{\lambda}$$

where f and λ are the frequency and wavelength of the light (the photon), c is the speed of light and h is Planck's constant, with value 6.63×10^{-34} J s.

Let us assume that a hydrogen atom makes a transition from the level $n = 3$ (whose energy is −1.51 eV) to the level $n = 2$ (whose energy is −3.40 eV). The difference in energy between these two levels is 1.89 eV and this is the energy that will be carried by the photon emitted in this transition. Therefore:

$$\frac{hc}{\lambda} = 1.89 \, \text{eV} = 1.89 \times 1.6 \times 10^{-19} = 3.024 \times 10^{-19} \, \text{J}$$

$$\lambda = \frac{6.63 \times 10^{-34} \times 3.0 \times 10^{8}}{3.024 \times 10^{-19}}$$

$$\lambda = 6.58 \times 10^{-7} \, \text{m}$$

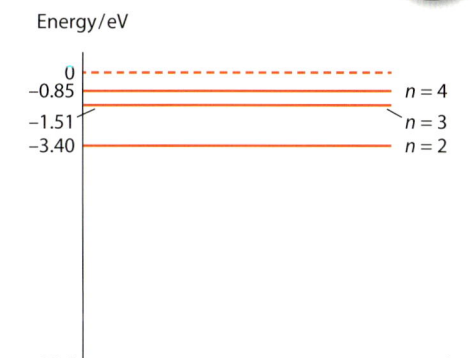

Figure 7.2 The energy level diagram for hydrogen according to Bohr's calculations.

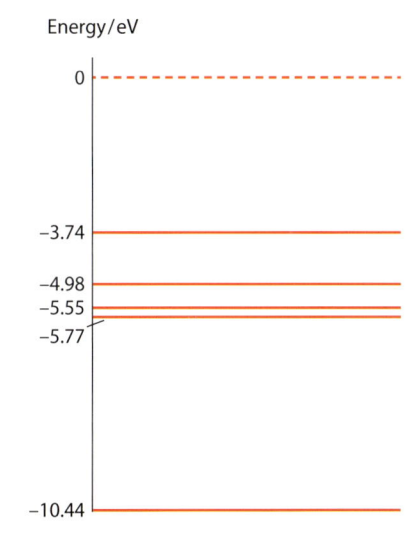

Figure 7.3 The energy level diagram for mercury.

Exam tip
Remember to convert eV into joules!

7 ATOMIC, NUCLEAR AND PARTICLE PHYSICS

Exam tip
Consider an atom that finds itself in some energy level L. If energy is supplied to this atom by incoming photons, the atom will absorb the energy only if it corresponds to the difference in energy between the energy in level L and the energy of a higher level.

However, if the energy is supplied by incoming electrons, then the atom will absorb the exact energy needed to jump to a higher energy level, leaving the electrons with the difference.

This is in excellent agreement with the wavelength of the red line in the hydrogen spectrum, shown in Figure 7.1! In hydrogen, all transitions from higher levels to the level $n=2$ emit photons of visible light.

When undisturbed, the electron in each hydrogen atom will occupy the lowest energy state, i.e. the one with $n=1$ and energy $-13.6\,\text{eV}$. The lowest energy state is called the **ground state**. If energy is supplied to the atom, the electron may move to a higher energy level (an **excited state**) by absorbing exactly the right amount of energy needed to move up. For example, to move from $n=1$ to the state with $n=3$ the energy needed is exactly $13.6 - 1.51 = 12.09\,\text{eV}$. Suppose that precisely this amount of energy is supplied to an electron in the ground state. The electron will absorb this energy and make a transition to the level $n=3$. At this point both the electron and the atom are said to be excited.

From the excited state, the electron will immediately (within nanoseconds) make a transition down to one of the available lower energy states. This process is called **relaxation**. From $n=3$ the electron can either go directly to $n=1$ (emitting a photon of energy $12.1\,\text{eV}$) or it can first make a transition to $n=2$ (emitting a photon of energy $1.89\,\text{eV}$) and then a transition from $n=2$ to $n=1$ (emitting another photon of energy $10.2\,\text{eV}$). These two possibilities are shown in Figure 7.4.

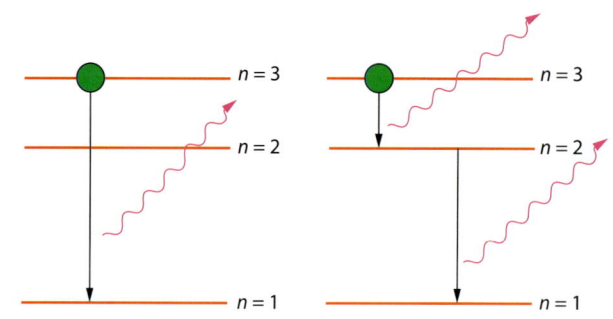

Figure 7.4 Transitions from $n=3$ in hydrogen.

Whether the electron will choose to make the direct or the indirect transition is an issue of chance: there is a probability for the one option and another probability for the other. (Theory can predict these probabilities.)

In a transition from a high to lower energy state, such that the **difference** in energy between the two states is E, the photon emitted has a wavelength given by:

$$\frac{hc}{\lambda} = E$$

That is:

$$\lambda = \frac{hc}{E}$$

So the emission spectra of elements can be understood if we accept that electrons in atoms exist in energy levels with discrete energy.

Protons and neutrons in nuclei also show an energy level structure similar to that of electrons in atoms. The protons and neutrons exist in **nuclear energy levels**. This will be discussed in Topic **12**.

Now imagine sending a beam of white light through a gas. The majority of the atoms in the gas are in their ground state. Electrons in the atoms may absorb photons in the beam and move to an excited state. This will happen only if the photon that is to be absorbed has exactly the right energy that corresponds to the difference in energy between the ground state and an excited state. This means that the light that is transmitted through the gas will be missing the photons that have been absorbed. This gives rise to **absorption spectra** (Figure **7.5**). The dark lines correspond to the wavelengths of the absorbed photons. They are at the same wavelengths as the emission spectra.

Exam tip
The electrons that absorb photons will move to an excited state, but once there, they will make a down transition, emitting the photons they absorbed. So why are the photons missing? This is because the photons are emitted in all directions and not necessarily along the direction the observer is looking. You must be able to explain this in an exam.

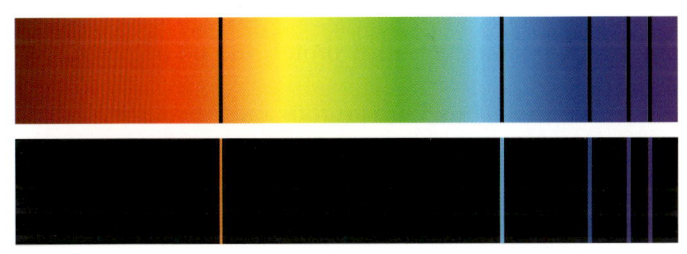

Figure 7.5 The absorption spectrum of hydrogen (top) and the emission spectrum (bottom). The emission lines and the absorption lines are at the same wavelength.

Worked example

7.1 Calculate the wavelength of the photon emitted in the transition from the first excited level to the ground state of mercury.

From Figure **7.3** the energy difference is:

$-5.77 - (-10.44) = 4.67 \, \text{eV}$

So the wavelength is found from:

$\dfrac{hc}{\lambda} = 4.67 \, \text{eV} = 4.67 \times 1.6 \times 10^{-19} \, \text{J}$

$\lambda = \dfrac{6.63 \times 10^{-34} \times 3.0 \times 10^{8}}{7.472 \times 10^{-19}}$

$\lambda = 2.7 \times 10^{-7} \, \text{m}$

This is an ultraviolet wavelength and so does not show up in the emission spectrum in Figure **7.1**.

7 ATOMIC, NUCLEAR AND PARTICLE PHYSICS

Nuclear structure

We now move deep into the atom in order to describe the structure of its nucleus. (The discovery of the nucleus will be discussed in Subtopic 7.3.) Atomic nuclei are made up of smaller particles, called protons and neutrons. The word **nucleon** is used to denote a proton or a neutron.

> The number of protons in a nucleus is denoted by Z, and is called the **atomic (or proton) number**.
>
> The total number of nucleons (protons + neutrons) is called the **mass (or nucleon) number**, and is denoted by A.
>
> The number of neutrons in a nucleus is denoted by N with $N = A - Z$.

The electric charge of the nucleus is Ze, where $e = +1.6 \times 10^{-19}$ C is the charge of a proton. We use the atomic and mass numbers to denote a nucleus in the following way: the symbol $^{A}_{Z}X$ stands for the nucleus of element X, whose atomic number is Z and mass number is A. For example:

$^{1}_{1}H$ is a hydrogen nucleus with 1 proton and no neutrons

$^{4}_{2}He$ is a helium nucleus with 2 protons and 2 neutrons

$^{40}_{20}Ca$ is a calcium nucleus with 20 protons and 20 neutrons

$^{56}_{26}Fe$ is an iron nucleus with 26 protons and 30 neutrons

$^{210}_{82}Pb$ is a lead nucleus with 82 protons and 128 neutrons

$^{238}_{92}U$ is a uranium nucleus with 92 protons and 136 neutrons.

A nucleus with a specific number of protons and neutrons is also called a **nuclide**.

We can apply this notation to the nucleons themselves. For example, the proton (symbol p) can be written as $^{1}_{1}p$ and the neutron (symbol n) as $^{1}_{0}n$. If we notice that the atomic number is not only the number of protons in the nucleus but also its electric charge in units of e, then we can extend this notation to electrons as well. The charge of the electron in units of e is -1 and so we represent the electron by $^{0}_{-1}e$. The mass number of the electron is zero – as it is neither a proton nor a neutron, and the mass number is defined as the total number of neutrons plus protons.

The photon (the particle of light) can also be represented in this way: the photon has the Greek letter gamma as its symbol. Since it has zero electric charge and is neither a proton nor a neutron, it is represented by $^{0}_{0}\gamma$. The **neutrino** (we will learn more about this in a later section) is neutral and is represented by $^{0}_{0}\nu$. Table 7.1 gives a summary of these particles and their symbols. We will meet more particles in Subtopic 7.3.

Particle	Symbol
proton	$^{1}_{1}p$
neutron	$^{1}_{0}n$
electron	$^{0}_{-1}e$
positron	$^{0}_{+1}e$
photon	$^{0}_{0}\gamma$ or just γ
alpha particle	$^{4}_{2}He$ or $^{4}_{2}\alpha$
neutrino	$^{0}_{0}\nu$ or just ν
anti-neutrino	$^{0}_{0}\bar{\nu}$ or just $\bar{\nu}$

Table 7.1 Particles and their symbols

Isotopes

Nuclei that have the same number of protons but different number of neutrons are called **isotopes** of each other. Isotopes therefore have the same atomic number Z but different neutron number N and mass number A. For example, $^{1}_{1}H$, $^{2}_{1}H$ and $^{3}_{1}H$ are three isotopes of hydrogen, and $^{235}_{92}U$, $^{236}_{92}U$ and $^{238}_{92}U$ are just three (of many) isotopes of uranium. Since isotopes have the same number of protons, their atoms have the same number of electrons as well. This means that isotopes have identical chemical properties but different physical properties. The existence of isotopes is evidence for the existence of neutrons inside atomic nuclei.

Radioactive decay

At the end of the 19th century and in the early part of the 20th century, it was discovered that most nuclides are unstable. This discovery was mainly due to the work of Henri Becquerel (1852–1908), Marie Sklodowska-Curie (1867–1934) and Pierre Curie (1859–1906). An unstable nucleus is one that **randomly** and **spontaneously** emits particles that carry energy away from the nucleus. Figure 7.6 shows that stable nuclides (points in black) have equal numbers of neutrons and protons for small values of Z but as Z increases stable nuclei have more neutrons than protons. We will understand this when we learn about the strong nuclear force. The graph also shows that most nuclides are unstable; they decay in various ways that will be discussed in the next sections.

The emission of particles and energy from a nucleus is called **radioactivity**. It was soon realised that three distinct emissions take place. The emissions are called **alpha particles**, **beta particles** and **gamma rays**. They have different **ionising** power (ability to knock electrons off atoms) and **penetrating** power (distance travelled through matter before they are stopped).

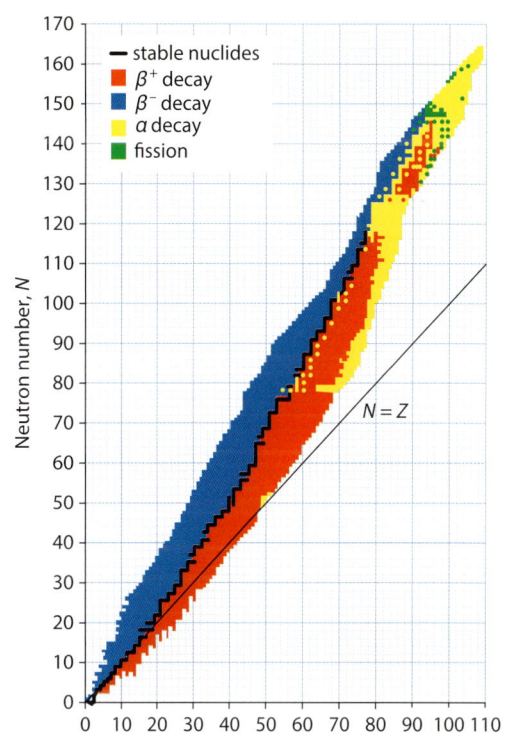

Figure 7.6 A plot of neutron number versus atomic number for nuclides. The stable nuclides are shown in black. Most nuclides are unstable.

Alpha particles and alpha decay

In **alpha decay** an alpha particle is emitted from the nucleus and the decaying nucleus turns into a different nucleus. An example is uranium decaying into thorium:

$$^{238}_{92}U \rightarrow {}^{234}_{90}Th + {}^{4}_{2}\alpha$$

The alpha particles were shown to be identical to nuclei of helium in an experiment by E. Rutherford (1871–1937) and T. Royds (1884–1955) in 1909. They collected the gas that the alpha particles produced when they came in contact with electrons and then investigated its spectrum. The spectrum was found to be identical to that of helium gas. Alpha particles have a mass that is about four times the mass of the hydrogen atom and an electric charge equal to $+2e$.

7 ATOMIC, NUCLEAR AND PARTICLE PHYSICS

Note that in the reaction equation representing this decay, the total atomic number on the right-hand side of the arrow balances the atomic number to the left of the arrow. This is because charge is a conserved quantity. The same holds also for the mass number. Two other examples of alpha decay are:

$$^{224}_{88}\text{Ra} \rightarrow ^{220}_{86}\text{Rn} + ^{4}_{2}\alpha$$

$$^{212}_{84}\text{Po} \rightarrow ^{208}_{82}\text{Pb} + ^{4}_{2}\alpha$$

Beta particles and beta decay

In **beta minus decay**, a neutron in the decaying nucleus turns into a proton, emitting an electron and an anti-neutrino. An example is the nucleus of thorium decaying into a nucleus of protactinium:

$$^{234}_{90}\text{Th} \rightarrow ^{234}_{91}\text{Pa} + ^{0}_{-1}e + ^{0}_{0}\bar{\nu}_e$$

The 'beta minus particle' is just the electron. It was called beta minus before experiments showed it was identical to the electron. Note again how the atomic and mass numbers balance in the reaction equation.

Also note that unlike alpha decay, where two particles are produced, here we have three. The third is called the 'electron anti-neutrino', $^{0}_{0}\bar{\nu}_e$, or just $\bar{\nu}_e$. The bar over the symbol indicates that this is an anti-particle. This should not concern us too much here – more on anti-particles in Subtopic **7.3**.

Two other examples of beta minus decay are:

$$^{214}_{82}\text{Pb} \rightarrow ^{214}_{83}\text{Bi} + ^{0}_{-1}e + ^{0}_{0}\bar{\nu}_e$$

$$^{40}_{19}\text{K} \rightarrow ^{40}_{20}\text{Ca} + ^{0}_{-1}e + ^{0}_{0}\bar{\nu}_e$$

Another type of beta decay is **beta plus decay**. Instead of emitting an electron the nucleus emits its anti-particle, the **positron**, which is positively charged. The third particle is the neutrino. Two examples of beta plus decay are:

$$^{22}_{11}\text{Na} \rightarrow ^{22}_{10}\text{Ne} + ^{0}_{+1}e + ^{0}_{0}\nu_e$$

$$^{13}_{7}\text{N} \rightarrow ^{13}_{6}\text{C} + ^{0}_{+1}e + ^{0}_{0}\nu_e$$

Beta decay is complicated and we will understand it a bit better in Subtopic **7.3**.

Gamma rays and gamma decay

In **gamma decay** a nucleus emits a gamma ray, in other words a photon of high-frequency electromagnetic radiation:

$$^{238}_{92}\text{U} \rightarrow ^{238}_{92}\text{U} + ^{0}_{0}\gamma$$

Unlike alpha and beta decay, in gamma decay the nucleus does not change identity. It just moves from a higher to a lower nuclear energy level. The wavelength of the photon emitted is given by:

$$\lambda = \frac{hc}{E}$$

just as with atomic transitions. Here E is the energy of the emitted photon. In contrast to the photons in atomic transitions, which can correspond to visible light, these photons have very small wavelength (smaller than 10^{-12} m) and they are called gamma rays.

Other examples of gamma decay are:

$$^{60}_{28}\text{Ni} \rightarrow {^{60}_{28}}\text{Ni} + {^{0}_{0}}\gamma$$

$$^{24}_{12}\text{Mg} \rightarrow {^{24}_{12}}\text{Mg} + {^{0}_{0}}\gamma$$

The identification of gamma rays with photons was made possible through diffraction experiments in which gamma rays from decaying nuclei were directed at crystals. The wavelengths were measured from the resulting diffraction patterns.

Properties of alpha, beta and gamma radiations

Table **7.2** summarises the properties of alpha, beta and gamma radiations. Notice that the alpha particles are the most ionising and the gamma rays the most penetrating. The beta plus particle is the positron, the antiparticle of the electron – see Subtopic **7.3**.

Characteristic	Alpha particle	Beta minus particle	Gamma ray
nature	helium nucleus	(fast) electron	photon
charge	$+2e$	$-e$	0
mass	6.64×10^{-27} kg	9.1×10^{-31} kg	0
penetrative power	a few cm of air	a few mm of metal	many cm of lead
ions per mm of air for 2 MeV particles	10 000	100	1
detection	• affects photographic film • is affected by electric and magnetic fields	• affects photographic film • is affected by electric and magnetic fields	• affects photographic film • is not affected by electric and magnetic fields

Table 7.2 Properties of alpha, beta and gamma radiations.

Decay series

The changes in the atomic and mass numbers of a nucleus when it undergoes radioactive decay can be represented in a diagram of mass number against atomic number. A radioactive nucleus such as thorium ($Z = 90$) decays first by alpha decay into the nucleus of radium ($Z = 88$). Radium, which is also radioactive, decays into actinium ($Z = 89$) by beta decay. Further decays take place until the resulting nucleus is stable. The set of decays that takes place until a given nucleus ends up as a stable

7 ATOMIC, NUCLEAR AND PARTICLE PHYSICS

nucleus is called the **decay series** of the nucleus. Figure **7.7** shows the decay series for thorium. Successive decays starting with thorium end with the stable nucleus of lead.

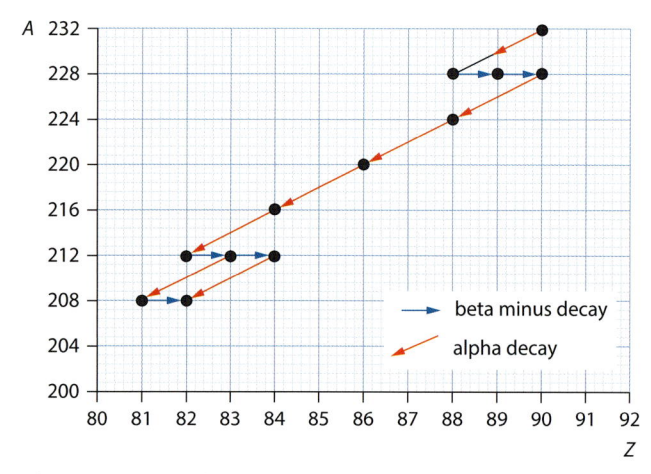

Figure 7.7 The decay series of thorium ($Z = 90$, $A = 232$). One alpha decay reduces the mass number by 4 and the atomic number by 2. One beta minus decay increases the atomic number by one and leaves the mass number unchanged. The end result is the nucleus of lead ($Z = 82$, $A = 208$).

Worked example

7.2 A nucleus $^A_Z X$ decays by alpha decay followed by two successive beta minus decays. Find the atomic and mass numbers of the resulting nucleus.

The decay equation for alpha decay is:

$$^A_Z X \rightarrow {}^{A-4}_{Z-2}Y + {}^4_2\alpha$$

Then the nucleus decays twice by beta decay. So we have:

$$^{A-4}_{Z-2}Y \rightarrow {}^{A-4}_{Z}Y + 2\,{}^{0}_{-1}e + 2\,{}^{0}_{0}\overline{\nu}_e$$

The mass number doesn't change in beta minus decay, but the proton number increases by one for each decay (since in beta minus decay a neutron turns into a proton).

So the atomic number of the resulting nucleus is Z and the mass number is $A - 4$.

The law of radioactive decay

Radioactive decay is random and spontaneous. By **random** we mean that we cannot predict which unstable nucleus in a sample will decay or when there will be a decay. It is **spontaneous** because we cannot affect the rate of decay of a given sample in any way. Although we cannot predict or influence when a particular nucleus will decay, we know that the number of nuclei that will decay per second is proportional to the number of nuclei in the sample that have not yet decayed.

278

The law of radioactive decay states that the rate of decay is proportional to the number of nuclei that have not yet decayed:

$$\frac{\Delta N}{\Delta t} \propto N$$

A consequence of this law is that the number of radioactive nuclei decreases exponentially.

Consider the beta minus decay of thallium (called the parent nucleus) into lead (the daughter nucleus):

$$^{208}_{81}\text{Tl} \rightarrow {}^{208}_{82}\text{Pb} + {}^{0}_{-1}\text{e} + {}^{0}_{0}\overline{\nu}$$

The isotope of lead is stable and does not decay. Figure **7.8a** shows how the number of thallium nuclei decreases with time. Initially (at $t=0$) there are 1.6×10^{22} nuclei of thallium. This corresponds to a mass of about 6 g of thallium. After 3 min the number of thallium nuclei left is *half* of the initial number (0.8×10^{22}). After **another** 3 min, the number is one-quarter of the initial number (0.4×10^{22}). After yet another 3 min the number of thallium nuclei is one-eighth of the initial number (0.2×10^{22}). The time of 3.0 min is called the **half-life** of thallium. It is the time after which the number of the radioactive nuclei is reduced by a factor of 2. The blue curve in Figure **7.8b** shows how the number of lead nuclei increases with time.

A concept that is useful in experimental work is that of decay rate or **activity** A: this is the number of decays per second. We cannot easily measure how many unstable nuclei are present in a sample, but we can detect the decays. The unit of activity is the becquerel (Bq): 1 Bq is equal to one decay per second.

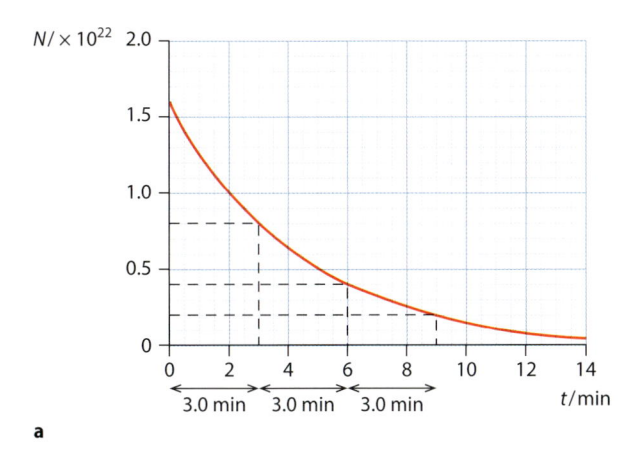

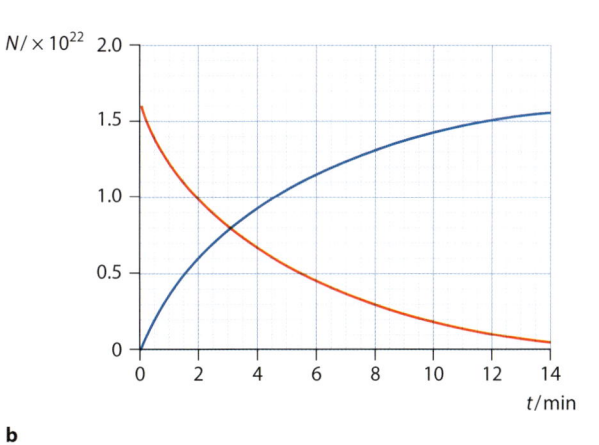

Figure 7.8 a The number of thallium nuclei decreases exponentially. **b** As thallium decays (red curve) lead is produced and so the number of lead nuclei increases (blue curve).

7 ATOMIC, NUCLEAR AND PARTICLE PHYSICS

Activity obeys the same exponential decay law as the number of nuclei. In a time equal to the half-life the activity is reduced by a factor of 2. This is shown in Figure **7.9**.

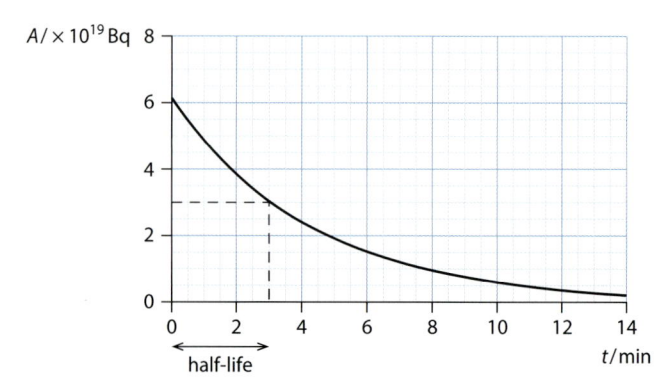

Figure 7.9 The activity of thallium decreases exponentially with time. You can also use this graph to determine half-life.

It is best to define the half-life in terms of activity:

> **Half-life** is the interval of time after which the activity of a radioactive sample is reduced by a factor of 2.

Provided the half-life is not too long, a graph of activity against time can be used to determine the half-life. In Figure **7.9** the activity approaches zero as the time increases. In practice, however, this is not the case. The detector that measures activity from the radioactive sample under study also measures the activity from natural sources. As a result, the activity does not approach zero; it approaches the activity due to all other sources of **background radiation**. These background sources include cosmic rays from the Sun, radioactive material in rocks and the ground, radiation from nuclear weapons testing grounds, and so on.

The effect of background radiation can be seen in the activity curve of Figure **7.10a**. This shows a background rate of 40 Bq. By subtracting this value from all data points we get the graph in Figure **7.10b**. Using the corrected graph we get a half-life of 6.0 min. Using Figure **7.10a** without correcting for the background gives a half-life of 6.9 min, which is inaccurate by 15%.

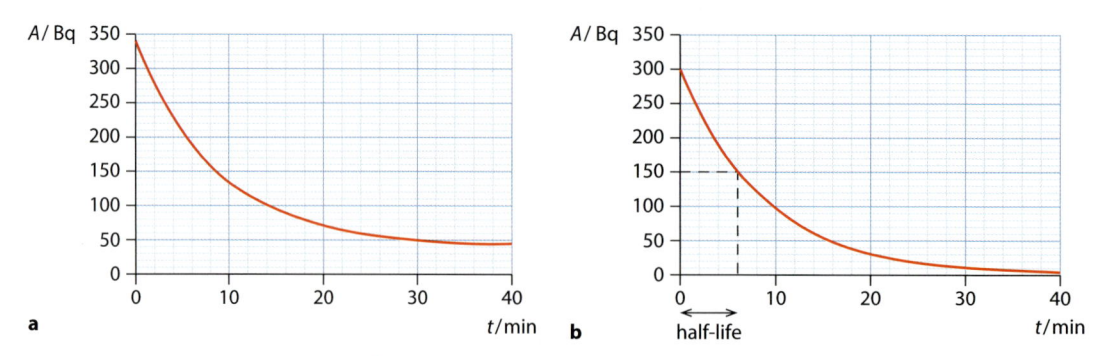

Figure 7.10 a An activity curve that includes a background rate of 40 Bq. This curve cannot be used to measure half-life as it is. The background needs to be subtracted as shown in **b**.

Worked examples

7.3 An isotope has a half-life of 20 min. Initially there are 1024 g of this isotope. Determine the time after which 128 g are left.

Find the fraction remaining: $\frac{128}{1024} = \frac{1}{8}$

This corresponds to three half-lives, as: $\frac{1}{2} \times \frac{1}{2} \times \frac{1}{2} = \frac{1}{8}$

Since the half-life is 20 min, three half-lives is:

$3 \times 20 = 60$ min

After 60 min, 128 g are left.

7.4 The activity of a sample is initially 80 decays per minute. It becomes five decays per minute after 4 h. Calculate the half-life.

$\frac{5}{80} = \frac{1}{16} = \frac{1}{2^4}$

The activity is reduced from 80 to five decays in four half-lives.

Four half-lives is 4 h, so the half-life is 1 h.

7.5 The activity of a sample is 15 decays per minute. The half-life is 30 min. Predict the time when the activity was 60 decays per minute.

One half-life before the sample was given to us the activity was 30 decays per minute, and one half-life before that it was 60 decays per minute.

So the activity was 60 decays per minute two half-lives earlier, which is 60 minutes earlier.

Half-life and probability

The meaning of a half-life can also be understood in terms of probability. Any given nucleus has a 50% chance of decaying within a time interval equal to the half-life. If a half-life goes by and the nucleus has not decayed, the chance that it will decay in the next half-life is still 50%. This is shown as a tree diagram in Figure **7.11** (overleaf).

The probability that a nucleus will have decayed by the second half-life is the sum of the probability that it decays in the first half-life and the probability that it decays during the second half-life:

$\frac{1}{2} + \left(\frac{1}{2} \times \frac{1}{2}\right) = \frac{3}{4} = 0.75$ or   75%

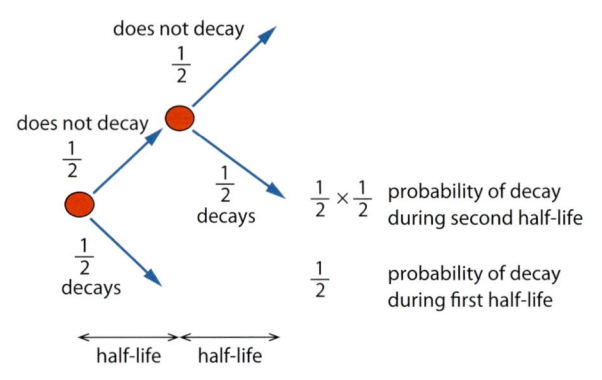

Figure 7.11 Tree diagram for nuclear decay.

Fundamental forces and their properties

According to the standard model of particles (to be discussed in some more detail in Subtopic **7.3**), there are four fundamental interactions or forces in nature. These are:

1. the **electromagnetic** interaction: this acts on any particle that has electric charge. The force is given by Coulomb's law. It has infinite range.
2. the **weak nuclear interaction**: it acts on protons, neutrons, electrons and neutrinos in order to bring about beta decay. It has very short range (10^{-18} m).
3. the **strong nuclear interaction**: this (mainly attractive) force acts on protons and neutrons to keep them bound to each other inside nuclei. It has short range (10^{-15} m).
4. the **gravitational interaction**: this is the force of attraction between masses. The small mass of atomic particles makes this force irrelevant for atomic and nuclear physics. This force has infinite range.

It is known that the electromagnetic interaction and the weak interaction are in fact two sides of one force, the **electroweak interaction**. The properties listed above are what we need for this section. They will be refined when we get to Subtopic **7.3**.

The fact that the strong force has a short range helps to explain why stable large nuclei have more neutrons than protons. As more protons are added to a nucleus the tendency for the nucleus to break apart increases because all the protons repel each other through the electromagnetic force. The electric force has infinite range. But the strong force has a short range so any one proton only attracts its very immediate neighbours. To keep the nucleus together we need more neutrons that will contribute to nuclear binding through the strong force, but which will not add to the repulsive forces.

The belief in unification

In the early 19th century there were three known forces: gravitational, electric and magnetic. Through the work of James Clerk Maxwell (1831–1879) physicists realised that electric and magnetic forces were two sides of the same force, the electromagnetic force. Thus began the notion (for some a belief, for others a prejudice) that all interactions, as more were being discovered, were part of the same 'unified' force. In the 20th century two new forces were discovered: the weak nuclear force and the strong nuclear force. In the late 1960s the electromagnetic and the weak nuclear force were unified in the standard model of particles. All efforts to unify this electroweak force with the strong nuclear force in a grand unified force have failed. All attempts to unify any of these forces with gravity have also failed. Yet, the dream of unification remains.

Nature of science

Accidental discovery

The discovery of radioactivity is an example of an accidental discovery. Henri Becquerel, working in Paris in 1896, believed that minerals made phosphorescent (emitting light) by visible light might give off X-rays. His idea was to wrap a photographic plate in black paper, and place on it a phosphorescent uranium mineral that had been exposed to bright sunlight. But the sun did not shine, and he stopped the experiment, placing the wrapped plate and the mineral in a drawer. A few days later he developed the photographic plate, expecting to see only a very weak image. To his surprise, there was a very strong image. Becquerel concluded that this image was formed by a new kind of radiation that had nothing to do with light. The radiation came from the uranium mineral. Becquerel conducted further experiments and showed that uranium minerals were the only phosphorescent minerals that had this effect.

Test yourself

1. a Discuss what is meant by the statement that the energy of atoms is discrete.
   b Outline the evidence for this discreteness.
2. Explain why the dark lines of an absorption spectrum have the same wavelengths as the bright lines of an emission spectrum for the same element.
3. Calculate the wavelength of the photon emitted in a transition from $n=4$ to $n=2$ in hydrogen. (Use Figure 7.2.)
4. Refer to Figure 7.1. Explain why the distance between the emission lines of hydrogen decreases as we move to the right.

5 A hydrogen atom is in its ground state.
   a Explain the term **ground state**.
   b Photons of energy 10.4 eV are directed at hydrogen gas in its ground state. Suggest what, if anything, will happen to the hydrogen atoms.
   c In another experiment, a beam of electrons of energy 10.4 eV are directed at hydrogen gas atoms in their ground state. Suggest what, if anything, will happen to the hydrogen atoms and the electrons in the beam.

6 State the electric charge of the nucleus $^{3}_{2}\text{He}$.

7 a State what is meant by the term **isotope**.
   b State **two** ways in which the nuclei of the isotopes $^{16}_{8}\text{O}$ and $^{18}_{8}\text{O}$ differ from each other (other than they have different neutrons).

8 Bismuth ($^{210}_{83}\text{Bi}$) decays by beta minus decay, followed by gamma emission. State the equation for the reaction and the atomic and mass number of the nucleus produced.

9 Plutonium ($^{239}_{94}\text{Pu}$) decays by alpha decay. State the equation for this reaction and name the nucleus plutonium decays into.

10 A radioactive source has a half-life of 3.0 min. At the start of an experiment 32.0 mg of the radioactive material is present. Determine how much will be left after 18.0 min.

11 The graph shows the variation with time of the activity of a radioactive sample.

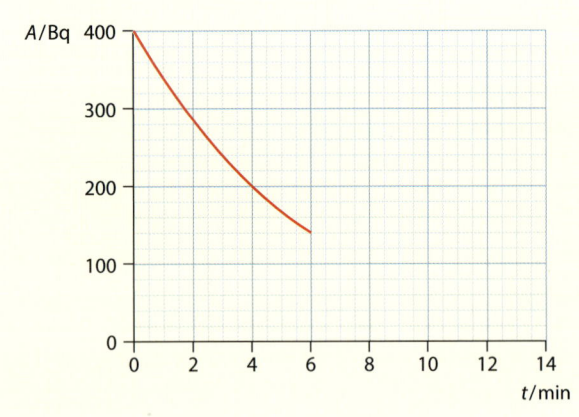

   a State what is meant by **activity**.
   b Use the graph to estimate the half-life of the sample.
   c On a copy of the graph, extend the curve to show the variation of the activity for a time up to 12 minutes.
   d The sample contains a radioactive element X that decays in to a stable element Y. At $t = 0$ no atoms of element Y are present in the sample. Determine the time after which the ratio of Y atoms to X atoms is 7.

12 In a study of the intensity of gamma rays from a radioactive source it is suspected that the counter rate C at a distance d from the source behaves as
$$C \propto \left(\frac{1}{d + d_0}\right)^2$$
where d_0 is an unknown constant. A set of data for C and d is given. Outline how the data must be plotted in order to get a straight line.

13 The intensity of gamma rays of a specific energy (monochromatic rays) decreases exponentially with the thickness x of the absorbing material according to the equation:
$$I = I_0 e^{-\mu x}$$
where I_0 is the intensity at the face of the absorber and μ a constant depending on the material.

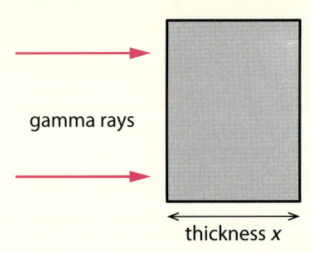

Discuss how the intensity I and thickness x should be plotted in order to allow an accurate determination of the constant μ.

14 State the name of the dominant force between two protons separated by a distance of:
   a 1.0×10^{-15} m
   b 1.0×10^{-14} m.

15 Large stable nuclei have more neutrons than protons. Explain this observation by reference to the properties of the strong nuclear force.

7.2 Nuclear reactions

This section is an introduction to the physics of atomic nuclei. We will see that the sum of the masses of the constituents of a nucleus is not the same as the mass of the nucleus itself, which implies that mass and energy are converted into each other. Methods used to calculate energy released in nuclear reactions are presented.

The unified atomic mass unit

In atomic and nuclear physics, it is convenient to use a smaller unit of mass than the kilogram. We already defined the **atomic mass unit** in Topic 3 to be $\frac{1}{12}$ of the mass of an atom of carbon-12, $^{12}_{6}C$. The symbol for the unified atomic mass unit is u.

$$1\,u = 1.660\,5402 \times 10^{-27}\,kg$$

Learning objectives

- Solve problems with mass defect and binding energy.
- Calculate the energy released in nuclear reactions.
- Describe the variation with nucleon number of the average binding energy per nucleon.

Worked example

7.6 Determine to six decimal places, in units of u, the masses of the proton, neutron and electron. Use $m_p = 1.6726231 \times 10^{-27}\,kg$, $m_n = 1.6749286 \times 10^{-27}\,kg$, and $m_e = 9.1093897 \times 10^{-31}\,kg$.

Using the relationship between u and kg, we find:

$$m_p = \frac{1.6726231 \times 10^{-27}}{1.660\,5402 \times 10^{-27}} = 1.007276\,u$$

Similarly:

$m_n = 1.008665\,u$

$m_e = 0.0005486\,u$

(This shows that, very approximately, $m_p \approx m_n \approx 1\,u$.)

The mass defect and binding energy

Protons and neutrons are very tightly bound to each other in a nucleus. To separate them, energy must be supplied to the nucleus. Conversely, energy is released when a nucleus is assembled from its constituent nucleons.

From Einstein's theory of relativity, energy E is equivalent to mass m according to the equation:

$$E = mc^2$$

where c is the speed of light. Since energy is released when nucleons are brought together to form a nucleus, this is equivalent to a loss of mass. So the mass of the constituent nucleons when far part is greater than the mass of the nucleus.

7 ATOMIC, NUCLEAR AND PARTICLE PHYSICS

Take the nucleus of helium, $^4_2$He, as an example. The mass of an **atom** of helium is 4.0026 u. This includes the mass of two electrons. So the nuclear mass is:

$$M_{\text{nucleus}} = 4.0026 - 2 \times 0.0005486$$

$$M_{\text{nucleus}} = 4.0015 \, \text{u}$$

The helium nucleus is made up of two protons and two neutrons. Adding these masses we find:

$$2m_p + 2m_n = 4.0319 \, \text{u}$$

This is larger than the mass of the nucleus by 0.0304 u, which is as expected. This leads to the concept of **mass defect**.

> The mass of the protons plus the mass of the neutrons is larger than the mass of the nucleus. The difference is known as the **mass defect** δ:
>
> δ = total mass of nucleons − mass of nucleus

This can also be written as:

$$\delta = Zm_p + (A - Z)m_n - M_{\text{nucleus}}$$

Remember that $A - Z$ is the number of neutrons in the nucleus.

Worked example

7.7 Find the mass defect of the nucleus of gold, $^{197}_{79}$Au. The **nuclear** mass is 196.924 u.

We have been given the nuclear mass directly so we do not have to subtract any electron masses.

The nucleus has 79 protons and 118 neutrons, so:

$$\delta = (79 \times 1.007276 \, \text{u}) + (118 \times 1.008665 \, \text{u}) - 196.924 \, \text{u} = 1.67 \, \text{u}$$

The energy equivalent to the mass defect is called **binding energy**.

> The binding energy of a nucleus is the work (energy) required to completely separate the nucleons of that nucleus.
>
> binding energy = δc^2

The work required to remove one nucleon from the nucleus is very roughly the binding energy divided by the total number of nucleons.

At a more practical level, the binding energy per nucleon is a measure of how stable the nucleus is – the higher the binding energy per nucleon, the more stable the nucleus.

It is convenient to find out how much energy corresponds to a mass of 1 u. Then, given a nuclear mass in u, we can easily find the energy that corresponds to it. The energy corresponding to 1 u is:

$$1\,u \times c^2 = 1.6605402 \times 10^{-27} \times (2.9979 \times 10^8)^2\,J$$
$$= 1.4923946316 \times 10^{-10}\,J$$

Changing this to eV, using $1\,eV = 1.602177 \times 10^{-19}\,J$, gives an energy equivalent to a mass of 1 u of:

$$\frac{1.4923946316 \times 10^{-10}\,J}{1.602177 \times 10^{-19}\,J\,eV^{-1}} = 931.5 \times 10^6\,eV = 931.5\,MeV$$

So:

$$1\,u \times c^2 = 931.5\,MeV \quad \text{or} \quad 1\,u = 931.5\,MeV\,c^{-2}$$

This last version is convenient for converting mass to energy, as shown in Worked example **7.8**.

Worked examples

7.8 Determine the energy equivalent to the mass of the proton, the neutron and the electron.

The masses in terms of u are $m_p = 1.0073\,u$, $m_n = 1.0087\,u$ and $m_e = 0.0005486\,u$.
For the proton, the energy is $m_p c^2$:

$$1.0073\,u \times c^2 = 1.0073 \times 931.55\,MeV\,c^{-2} \times c^2 = 938.3\,MeV$$

In other words, we multiply the mass in u by 931.5 to get the energy in MeV.
For the neutron, the energy equivalent is:

$$1.0087 \times 931.55 = 939.6\,MeV$$

For the electron, the energy equivalent is:

$$0.0005486 \times 931.55 = 0.511\,MeV$$

7.9 Determine the binding energy per nucleon of the nucleus of carbon-12.

The **nuclear** mass is the mass of the atom minus the mass of the six electrons:

$$12.00000\,u - (6 \times 0.0005486\,u) = 11.99671\,u$$

The nucleus has 6 protons and 6 neutrons, so the mass defect is:

$$(6 \times 1.007276\,u) + (6 \times 1.008665\,u) - 11.99671\,u = 0.09894\,u$$

Hence the binding energy is:

$$0.09894 \times 931.5\,MeV = 92.2\,MeV$$

The binding energy per nucleon is then:

$$\frac{92.2}{12} = 7.68\,MeV$$

7 ATOMIC, NUCLEAR AND PARTICLE PHYSICS

The binding energy curve

Figure **7.12** shows the variation with nucleon (mass) number A of the binding energy (B.E.) per nucleon, $\frac{B.E.}{A}$.

The main features of the graph are:
- The binding energy per nucleon for hydrogen, ^1_1H, is zero because there is only one particle in the nucleus.
- The curve rises sharply for low values of A.
- The curve has a maximum for $A = 62$ corresponding to nickel, which makes this nucleus particularly stable.
- There are peaks at the position of the nuclei ^4_2He, $^{12}_6C$ and $^{16}_8O$, which makes these nuclei unusually stable compared to their immediate neighbours.
- The curve drops gently from the peak at $A = 62$ and onwards.
- Most nuclei have a binding energy per nucleon between 7 and 9 MeV.

The short range of the force implies that a given nucleon can interact with its immediate neighbours only and not with all of the nucleons in the nucleus. So for large nuclei (i.e. roughly $A > 20$) any one nucleon is surrounded by the same number of immediate neighbours and so the energy needed to remove that nucleon from the nucleus is the same. Thus, the short range nature of the nuclear force explains why the binding energy per nucleon is roughly constant above a certain value of A.

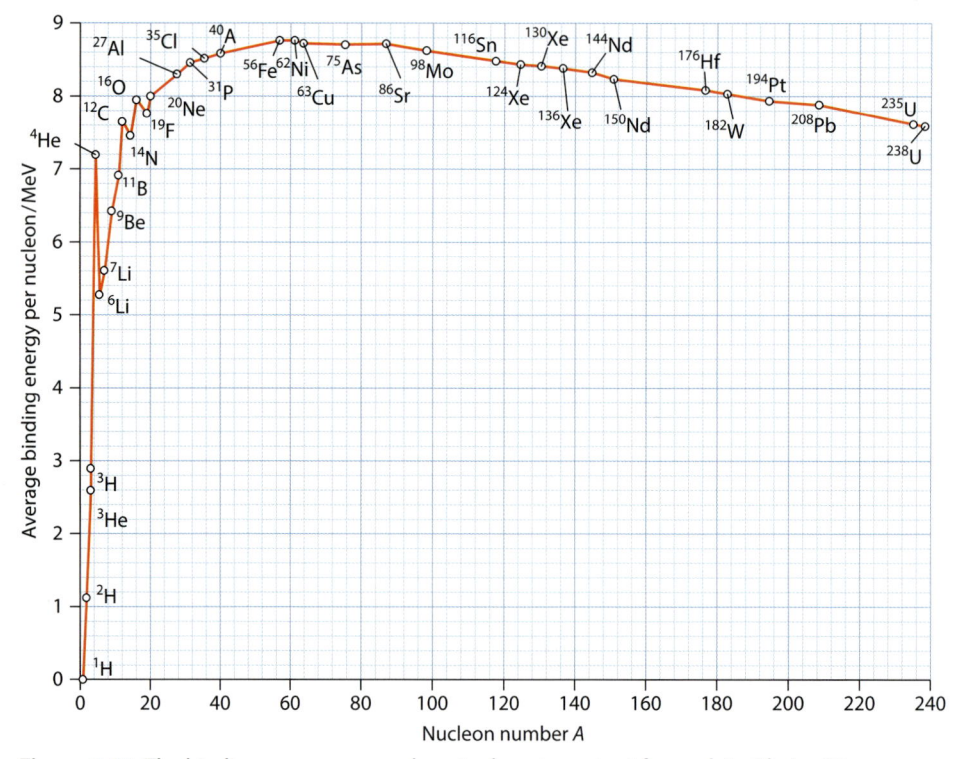

Figure 7.12 The binding energy per nucleon is almost constant for nuclei with $A > 20$.

Energy released in a decay

To decide whether energy is released in a decay, or any other reaction, we have to calculate the mass difference Δm:

Δm = total mass of reactants − total mass of products

If Δm is positive then energy will be released and the decay will occur. If Δm is negative the reactants will not react and the reaction can only take place if energy is supplied to the reactants.

We can see how this works by looking at the alpha decay of radium:

$$^{226}_{88}\text{Ra} \rightarrow {}^{222}_{86}\text{Rn} + {}^{4}_{2}\alpha$$

The mass difference is:

$\Delta m = 226.0254 − (222.0176 + 4.0026)$

$\Delta m = 226.0254 − 226.0202$

$\Delta m = 0.0052\,\text{u}$

This is positive, so energy will be released. The quantity of energy Q released is given by:

$Q = 0.0052 \times 931.5\,\text{MeV} = 4.84\,\text{MeV}$

This energy is released in the form of kinetic energy, which is shared by the alpha particle and the radon nucleus. The alpha, being much lighter than radon, has greater speed and so greater kinetic energy.

Worked example

7.10 Calculate the ratio of the kinetic energies of the alpha particle to that of the radon nucleus in the decay of radium ($^{226}_{88}$Ra) to radon ($^{222}_{86}$Rn). Assume that the radium nucleus decays at rest. Determine how much energy the alpha particle carries.

The radium nucleus is at rest, so the initial momentum is zero. By conservation of momentum, after the decay the momenta of the products are opposite in direction and equal in magnitude. Thus $p_\alpha = p_{\text{Rn}}$.

From Topic 2, kinetic energy is related to momentum by $E_K = \dfrac{p^2}{2m}$, so:

$\dfrac{E_\alpha}{E_{\text{Rn}}} = \dfrac{p_\alpha^2/2M_\alpha}{p_{\text{Rn}}^2/2M_{\text{Rn}}}$

$\dfrac{E_\alpha}{E_{\text{Rn}}} = \dfrac{M_{\text{Rn}}}{M_\alpha}$

$\dfrac{E_\alpha}{E_{\text{Rn}}} \approx \dfrac{222}{4} \approx 55$

Exam tip
Momentum conservation applies to nuclear physics as well, so use it!

This means that the energy carried by the alpha particle is $\dfrac{55}{56} \times 4.84 \approx 4.75\,\text{MeV}$.

Consider the reaction in which an alpha particle collides with a nucleus of nitrogen:

$$^{14}_{7}\text{N} + ^{4}_{2}\alpha \rightarrow ^{17}_{8}\text{O} + ^{1}_{1}\text{p}$$

$m_N = 14.003074$ u; $m_O = 16.999131$ u

Notice how the sum of the atomic and mass numbers on both sides of the reaction are equal. This is a famous reaction called the **transmutation** of nitrogen; it was studied by Rutherford in 1909. In this reaction the mass difference is negative:

$\Delta m = 18.005677 - 18.006956$

$\Delta m = -0.00128$ u

This reaction will only take place if the alpha particle has enough kinetic energy to make up for the difference. The minimum kinetic energy needed is $0.00128 \times 931.5 = 1.2$ MeV.

Nuclear fission

Nuclear fission is the process in which a heavy nucleus splits up into lighter nuclei. When a neutron is absorbed by a nucleus of uranium-235, uranium momentarily turns into uranium-236. It then splits into lighter nuclei plus neutrons. One possibility is:

$$^{1}_{0}\text{n} + ^{235}_{92}\text{U} \rightarrow ^{236}_{92}\text{U} \rightarrow ^{144}_{56}\text{Ba} + ^{89}_{36}\text{Kr} + 3^{1}_{0}\text{n}$$

This is a fission reaction.

The production of neutrons is a feature of fission reactions. In a reactor, the neutrons released can be used to collide with other nuclei of uranium-235, producing more fission, energy and neutrons. The reaction is thus self-sustaining – it is called a **chain reaction**. For the chain reaction to get going a certain minimum mass of uranium-235 must be present, otherwise the neutrons escape without causing further reactions – this is called the **critical mass**.

The energy released can be calculated as follows:

$\Delta m = 236.0526\,\text{u} - (143.92292 + 88.91781 + 3 \times 1.008665)\,\text{u}$

$\quad\quad = 0.185875\,\text{u}$

Thus for this reaction:

$Q = \Delta m c^2 = 0.185875 \times 931.5 \approx 173$ MeV

This energy appears as kinetic energy of the products. The energy can be released in a controlled way, as in a fission reactor (to be discussed in Topic **8**), or in a very short time, as in a nuclear explosion (Figure **7.13**).

Note that the fission process is an **induced** process and begins when a neutron collides with a nucleus of uranium-235. Spontaneous fission, i.e. a nucleus splitting into two roughly equal nuclei without neutron absorption, is possible for some heavy elements but is rare.

Figure 7.13 a Vast amounts of energy are released in the detonation of a nuclear weapon.
b The results are catastrophic, as this photograph of Hiroshima shows.

Worked example

7.11 One fission reaction of uranium-235 releases 173 MeV for each decay. Estimate the energy released by 1 kg of uranium-235.

A quantity of 1 kg of uranium-235 is $\frac{1000}{235}$ mol of uranium.

The number of nuclei is therefore:

$$\text{number of nuclei} = \frac{1000}{235} \times 6 \times 10^{23}$$

Each nucleus produces about 173 MeV of energy, so:

$$\text{total energy} = \frac{1000}{235} \times 6 \times 10^{23} \times 173 \text{ MeV}$$

This is 4.4×10^{26} MeV or about 7×10^{13} J.

Nuclear fusion

Nuclear fusion is the joining of two light nuclei into a heavier one with the associated production of energy. An example of a fusion reaction is:

$$^{2}_{1}\text{H} + ^{2}_{1}\text{H} \rightarrow ^{3}_{2}\text{He} + ^{1}_{0}\text{n}$$

In this reaction two deuterium nuclei (isotopes of hydrogen) produce helium-3 (an isotope of helium) and a neutron. From the mass difference for the reaction, we can work out the energy released:

$\Delta m = 2 \times 2.014102 - (3.016029 + 1.008665)$ u

$\Delta m = 0.0035$ u

Therefore:

$Q = \Delta m c^2 = 0.0035 \times 931.5 = 3.26$ MeV

Exam tip
The two deuterium nuclei will fuse when their distance apart is of order 10^{-15} m. The electrostatic potential energy at this separation is of order 10^{-13} J. To overcome the electrostatic repulsion, kinetic energy of this order of magnitude is required. Using $E = \frac{3}{2}kT$, the temperature at which the average kinetic energy is sufficient is of order 10^9 K. In stars deuterium fusion reactions take place at temperatures of order 10^6 K, which shows that at this much lower temperature, some deuterium nuclei must have energies way above average.

A kilogram of deuterium would release energy of about 10^{13} J, which is comparable to the energy produced by a kilogram of uranium in the fission process. This fusion reaction is a possible source of energy for electricity generation, which is being explored (Figure **7.14**). But there are still serious obstacles in the commercial production of energy by nuclear fusion.

Figure 7.14 The hot plasma in nuclear fusion can be confined in a tokamak. Here the hot plasma moves around magnetic field lines, never touching the container walls.

Worked example

7.12 This fusion reaction takes place in the interior of stars:

$$4\,_1^1\text{H} \rightarrow \,_2^4\text{He} + 2\,_1^0\text{e} + 2\nu_e + \,_0^0\gamma$$

Four hydrogen nuclei fuse into a helium nucleus plus two positrons, two electron neutrinos and a photon.

Calculate the energy released in this reaction. Use $M_{\text{He}} = 4.002600$ u.

We must find the masses before and after the reaction.

mass of four protons (hydrogen nuclei) = 4×1.007276 u = 4.029104 u

mass on right-hand side = $(4.0026 - 2 \times 0.0005486)$ u + 2×0.0005486 u = 4.002600 u

mass difference = 4.029104 u − 4.002600 u = 0.026504 u

This gives an energy of:

$$931.5 \times 0.026504 = 24.7 \text{ MeV}$$

(Actually, the two positrons annihilate into energy by colliding with two electrons giving an additional 2 MeV (= 4×0.511 MeV), for a total of 26.7 MeV.)

Fission or fusion?

We have already seen that fission occurs when heavy nuclei split up and fusion when light nuclei fuse together. This becomes easier to understand when we look at the curve of binding energy per nucleon against nucleon number. The dashed vertical line at nickel-62 in Figure **7.15** is at the peak of the curve – this is the most energetically stable nucleus. To the left, nuclei can become more stable by fusion, while to the right they become more stable by fission.

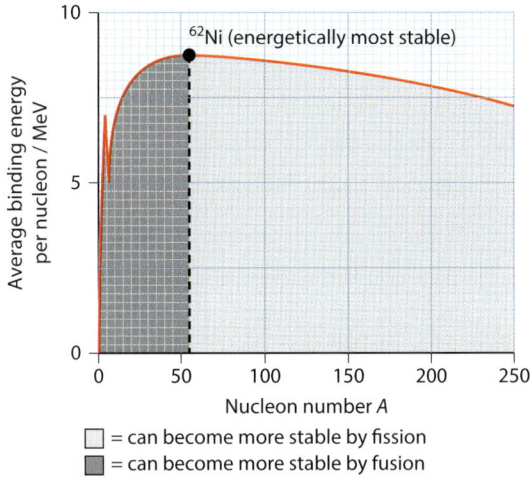

Figure 7.15 When a heavy nucleus splits up, energy is released because the produced nuclei have a higher binding energy than the original nucleus. When two light nuclei fuse, energy is produced because the products again have a higher binding energy.

Ethics and morals

This section has shown how Einstein's famous formula $E = mc^2$ applies to nuclear reactions. This formula describes the conversion of mass into energy – something that violates the law of conservation of mass as described by chemists. At the same time this formula made possible nuclear weapons that exploit the fission and fusion processes. Is this dangerous knowledge? J.R. Oppenheimer (Figure **7.16**), who led the American effort to make the atomic bomb during World War II, said, quoting from the Hindu holy book *The Bhagavad Gita*: 'I am become Death, the Destroyer of Worlds'. If some knowledge is dangerous can it ever be prevented from becoming widely available? If so, by whom?

Figure 7.16 J.R. Oppenheimer (1904–1967).

Nature of science

The graphs of proton number against neutron number (Figure **7.6**) and binding energy per nucleon (Figure **7.12**) show very clear trends and patterns. Scientists can use these graphs to make predictions of the characteristics of the different isotopes, such as whether an isotope will decay by beta plus or beta minus decay.

Test yourself

16 Find the binding energy and binding energy per nucleon of the nucleus $^{62}_{28}$Ni. The atomic mass of nickel is 61.928348 u.

17 How much energy is required to remove one proton from the nucleus of $^{16}_{8}$O? A rough answer to this question is obtained by giving the binding energy per nucleon. A better answer is obtained when we write a reaction that removes a proton from the nucleus. In this case $^{16}_{8}$O → $^{1}_{1}$p + $^{15}_{7}$N. Calculate the energy required for this reaction to take place, known as the proton separation energy. Compare the two energy values. (The atomic mass of oxygen is 15.994 u; that of nitrogen is 15.000 u.)

18 The first excited state of the nucleus of uranium−235 is 0.051 MeV above the ground state.
   a What is the wavelength of the photon emitted when the nucleus makes a transition to the ground state?
   b What part of the spectrum does this photon belong to?

19 Assume uranium-236 splits into two nuclei of palladium-117 (Pd). (The atomic mass of uranium is 236.0455561 u; that of palladium is 116.9178 u.)
   a Write down the reaction.
   b What other particles must be produced?
   c What is the energy released?

20 A fission reaction involving uranium is:

$$^{235}_{92}U + ^{1}_{0}n \rightarrow ^{98}_{40}Zr + ^{135}_{52}Te + 3^{1}_{0}n$$

Calculate the energy released. (Atomic masses: U = 235.043922 u; Zr = 97.91276 u; Te = 134.9165 u.)

21 Calculate the energy released in the fusion reaction:

$$^{2}_{1}H + ^{3}_{1}H \rightarrow ^{4}_{2}He + ^{1}_{0}n$$

(Atomic masses: $^{2}_{1}$H = 2.014102 u; $^{3}_{1}$H = 3.016049 u; $^{4}_{2}$He = 4.002603 u.)

22 In the first nuclear reaction in a particle accelerator, hydrogen nuclei were accelerated and then allowed to hit nuclei of lithium according to the reaction:

$$^{1}_{1}H + ^{7}_{3}Li \rightarrow ^{4}_{2}He + ^{4}_{2}He$$

Calculate the energy released. (The atomic mass of lithium is 7.016 u.)

23 Show that an alternative formula for the mass defect is $\delta = ZM_H + (A - Z)m_n - M_{atom}$ where M_H is the mass of a hydrogen atom and m_n is the mass of a neutron.

24 Consider the nuclear fusion reaction involving the deuterium ($^{2}_{1}$D) and tritium ($^{3}_{1}$T) isotopes of hydrogen:

$$^{2}_{1}D + ^{3}_{1}T \rightarrow ^{4}_{2}He + ^{1}_{0}n$$

The energy released, Q_1, may be calculated in the usual way, using the masses of the particles involved, from the expression:

$$Q_1 = (M_D + M_T - M_{He} - m_n)c^2$$

Similarly, in the fission reaction of uranium:

$$^{235}_{92}U + ^{1}_{0}n \rightarrow ^{98}_{40}Zr + ^{135}_{52}Te + 3^{1}_{0}n$$

the energy released, Q_2, may be calculated from:

$$Q_2 = (M_U - M_{Zr} - M_{Te} - 2m_n)c^2$$

   a Show that the expression for Q_1 can be rewritten as:

$$Q_1 = E_{He} - (E_D + E_T)$$

   where E_{He}, E_D and E_T are the binding energies of helium, deuterium and tritium, respectively.
   b Show that the expression for Q_2 can be rewritten as:

$$Q_2 = (E_{Zr} + E_{Te}) - E_U$$

   where E_{Zr}, E_{Te} and E_U are the binding energies of zirconium, tellurium and uranium, respectively.
   c Results similar to the results obtained in **a** and **b** apply to all energy-releasing fusion and fission reactions. Use this fact and the binding energy curve in Figure **7.12** to explain carefully why energy is released in fusion and fission reactions.

7.3 The structure of matter

Particle physics is the branch of physics that tries to answer two basic questions: What are the fundamental building blocks of matter? What are the interactions between these building blocks? The history of physics has shown that, as we probe matter at increasingly smaller scales, we find structures within structures: molecules contain atoms; atoms are made of nuclei and electrons; nuclei are made of nucleons (protons and neutrons); and the nucleons are made out of quarks. Will this pattern continue forever, or are there final, elementary building blocks? And if there are elementary building blocks, are these particles or are they 'strings' as many recent theories claim? These are the central questions of the part of physics called particle physics.

Learning objectives

- Describe the Rutherford, Geiger and Marsden experiment and how it led to the discovery of the nucleus.
- Describe matter in terms of quarks and leptons.
- Describe the fundamental interactions in terms of exchange particles and Feynman diagrams.
- Apply conservation laws to particle reactions.

Probing matter

In 1911, Ernest Rutherford (1871–1937) and his assistants Hans Geiger (1882–1945) and Ernest Marsden (1889–1970) performed a series of experiments that marked the beginning of modern particle physics, the quest to unravel the mysteries of the structure of matter. At that time it was believed that an atom was a sphere of positive charge of diameter about 10^{-10} m with the electrons moving inside the sphere. This picture is the **Thomson model** of the atom. This is the picture of the atom that the Rutherford experiment challenged.

In the Rutherford experiment, alpha particles were directed at a thin gold foil in an evacuated chamber. The numbers of particles deflected by different angles were recorded.

- The great majority of the alpha particles went straight through the foil with little or very small deviation. Most were detected at very small scattering angles, such as at positions A, B and C in Figure **7.17**.
- To their great surprise, Rutherford, Geiger and Marsden found that, very occasionally, alpha particles were detected at very large scattering angles.

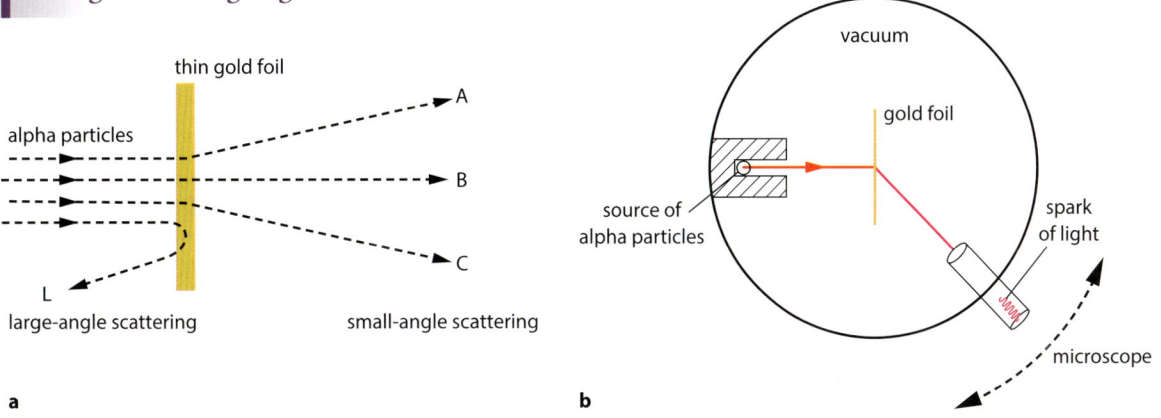

Figure 7.17 a The majority of alpha particles are slightly deflected by the gold foil. Very occasionally, large-angle scatterings take place. **b** The alpha particles are detected by the sparks of light they create when they hit a zinc sulfide screen in the microscope.

7 ATOMIC, NUCLEAR AND PARTICLE PHYSICS 295

The small deflections could be understood within the Thomson model: it was due to the electric force of repulsion between the positive charge of the gold atoms and the positive charge of the alpha particles. Note that an alpha particle is about 8000 times more massive than the electron, so the effect of the electrons of the gold atoms on the path of the alpha particles is negligible.

The large-angle scattering events could not be understood in terms of the prevailing model of the time that held that atoms were spheres of radius of the order of 10^{-10} m. Rutherford later said that 'it was as if you fired a 15-inch shell at tissue paper and it came back and hit you'.

Consequences of the Rutherford experiment

The very large deflection showed there was an enormous force of repulsion between the alpha particle and the positive charge of the atom. Since the electric force is given by $F = \dfrac{kq_1 q_2}{r^2}$ to get a large force implies that the separation r must be very small. Such a large force could not be produced if the positive charge was distributed over the entire atomic volume.

How can we get a large force in the Thomson model? Figure **7.18** shows two possible ideas for the interaction of the alpha particle with the gold atom in the Thomson model. Suppose the alpha particle approaches along the top path. The closest distance to the positive charge is r and r is of order 10^{-10} m. But the resulting force is 10^{10} times too small, so this does not work. What if the alpha **penetrates** the atom, as in the second diagram? Then, the distance r can become as small as we like. But this does not work either. In this case, only the charge within the smaller sphere would produce a force on the alpha particle and the result is again a very small force. The only way out is to imagine that the positive charge on the atom is within a sphere that is much smaller than the sphere that Thomson had imagined.

Rutherford calculated theoretically the number of alpha particles expected at particular scattering angles based on Coulomb's force law. He found agreement with his experiments if the positive atomic charge was confined to a region of linear size approximately equal to 10^{-15} m. This and subsequent experiments confirmed the existence of a nucleus inside the atom – a small, massive object carrying the positive charge of the atom and most of its mass.

Exam tip
You must be prepared to explain why the old model can account for the small deflections but not the large deflections, and why the proposed new model by Rutherford explains both the small as well as the large deflections.

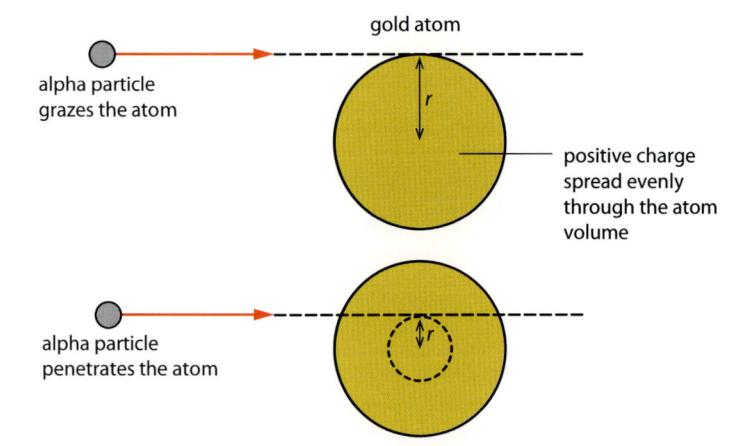

Figure 7.18 All attempts to get a large force out of the Thomson model fail.

Worked example

7.13 A sphere of charge Q has radius 10^{-15} m. Another sphere has the same charge and a radius of 10^{-10} m. Calculate the ratio of the electric fields at the surface of the two spheres.

Applying the formula for the electric field $E = \dfrac{kQ}{r^2}$ we find the ratio of the fields E_1 and E_2 for the two spheres as:

$$\frac{E_1}{E_2} = \frac{\dfrac{kQ}{(10^{-15})^2}}{\dfrac{kQ}{(10^{-10})^2}}$$

$$\frac{E_1}{E_2} = 10^{10}$$

This is why the deflecting forces in Rutherford's model are so large compared with what one might expect from Thomson's model.

Particles galore!

The electron was discovered in 1897, the nucleus in 1911, the proton in 1920 and the neutron in 1932. So by the 1930s we had all the ingredients of matter. Matter is the stuff that everything around us is made out of – the chair on which you sit, the air that you breathe and the molecules of your own body. All matter can be understood in terms of just these particles. In addition, the photon had been known since 1905. The neutrino, which features in beta decay, was hypothesised to exist in 1930 and was discovered in 1956.

This very simple and neat picture did not last very long because by the 1950s hundreds of other particles were discovered in cosmic ray experiments. Also, in particle accelerators around the world, collisions between high-energy electrons or protons produced hundreds of new, unknown particles. In a device known as the bubble chamber charged particles left a trace of their path that could be photographed and analysed (Figure 7.19). The reason these particles are not found in ordinary matter is that they are very unstable and decay very quickly. A few of these are the pions (π^+, π^-, π^0), the kaons (K^+, K^-, K^0), the etas (η, η'), the hyperons ($\Sigma^+, \Sigma^-, \Sigma^0$), the Ω^- and hundreds of others. These particles decay with half-lives ranging from 10^{-10} s to 10^{-24} s. Making sense out of all these particles was the main problem of particle physics in the 1960s.

Figure 7.19 Tracks of particles in a bubble chamber.

7 ATOMIC, NUCLEAR AND PARTICLE PHYSICS

Elementary particles

More than half a century of painstaking experimental and theoretical work has resulted in what is believed today to be the complete list of the **elementary particles** of nature.

> A particle is called **elementary** if it is not made out of any smaller component particles.

There are three classes of elementary particles: the **quarks**, the **leptons** and the **exchange particles**.

Quarks

Quarks were first proposed by two physicists working independently: Murray Gell-Mann (born 1929 – Figure **7.20**) and Georg Zweig (born 1937). There are six different types or **flavours** of quarks. The six flavours are the **up** (u), **charm** (c) and **top** (t) quarks with electric charge $\frac{2}{3}e$ and the **down** (d), **strange** (s) and **bottom** (b) quarks with electric charge $-\frac{1}{3}e$. Figure **7.21** shows a representation of the proton and neutron in terms of quarks.

> Top and bottom quarks are alternatively called **truth** and **beauty**.

There is solid experimental evidence for the existence of all six flavours of quarks. In addition we have the **anti-particles** of each of these. These have the same mass but all other properties are opposite, for example electric charge. Anti-particles are denoted with a bar on top of the symbol for the name. We have already met two anti-particles: the anti-neutrino in beta minus decay and the positron in beta plus decay.

Quarks combine in just **two** ways to form other particles called **hadrons**.

> A hadron is a particle made out of quarks.

- When three quarks combine they form a **baryon**. (When three anti-quarks combine they form an anti-baryon.)
- When a quark combines with an anti-quark they form a **meson**.

The proton is a baryon made out of two u quarks and one d quark, uud. The neutron is another baryon made out of two d quarks and one u quark, ddu.

The electric charge of the proton is thus predicted to be:

$$Q_p = +\tfrac{2}{3}e + \tfrac{2}{3}e - \tfrac{1}{3}e = e$$

and that of the neutron is predicted to be:

$$Q_n = -\tfrac{1}{3}e - \tfrac{1}{3}e + \tfrac{2}{3}e = 0$$

These are, of course, the correct values.

Figure 7.20 Murray Gell-Mann (born 1929).

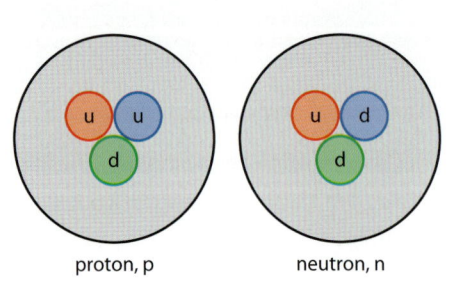

Figure 7.21 The quark structures of the proton and the neutron.

Pions are examples of mesons. The positively charged pion (π^+ meson) is made up as follows:

$$\pi^+ = (u\bar{d})$$

The bar over the 'd' shows this is an anti-particle. Thus, the positive pion is made out of a u quark and the anti-particle of the d quark (the d anti-quark).

Apart from electric charge, quarks have another property called **baryon number**, B. Each quark is assigned a baryon number of $+\frac{1}{3}$ and each anti-quark a baryon number of $-\frac{1}{3}$. To find the baryon number of the hadron that is formed by quarks, just add the baryon numbers of the quarks in the hadron. For example:

uct   baryon number $= +\frac{1}{3} + \frac{1}{3} + \frac{1}{3} = +1$ (a baryon)

u$\bar{d}$ baryon number $= +\frac{1}{3} - \frac{1}{3} = 0$ (a meson)

Since all baryons are made from three quarks, all baryons have baryon number $+1$. All anti-baryons have baryon number -1 and all mesons have baryon number 0. (Note that all other particles **not** made from quarks also have a baryon number of 0.)

Quarks interact with the strong nuclear interaction, the weak nuclear interaction and the electromagnetic interaction.

> In all reactions electric charge and baryon number are conserved, i.e. they have the same value before and after the reaction.

Consider the decays:

$$\Delta^0 \rightarrow p + \pi^-$$

$$\Lambda^0 \rightarrow p + \pi^-$$

where Δ^0 (udd) and $\Lambda^0 =$ (uds) are two different baryons. They both decay to form a proton and a pion.

In both decays the electric charge on the left is zero. On the right-hand side of the equation, the charge is also zero since the proton has charge $+e$ and the pion has charge $-e$. Similarly, the baryon number before each decay is $B = +1$ (one baryon); after the decay it is $B = +1$ for the proton (a baryon) and $B = 0$ for the pion (a meson), giving a total of $+1$.

The decays look very similar, but there is a huge difference in the time it takes for the decays to take place. The first takes about 10^{-25} s and the second 10^{-10} s.

Different lifetimes in decays is indicative of a different interaction being responsible. Short lifetimes (10^{-25} s) imply the strong interaction. Long lifetimes (10^{-10} s) imply the weak interaction. The second decay is different in that the left-hand side contains a strange quark but the right-hand side does not. It was thought to assign a new property to strange quarks only, a property called strangeness, S. For every strange quark

Exam tip
The anti-particle of some particle P has the same mass as particle P but is opposite in all other properties. Some particles have anti-particles that are identical to the particle itself. This implies that these particles are neutral. The photon is one such example. But the neutron, while neutral, is not identical to its anti-particle. The neutron has baryon number +1 while the anti-neutron has baryon number −1 and so is different.

the hadron would get −1 unit of strangeness (and so $S = +1$ for every anti-strange quark). Strangeness would then be conserved in strong and electromagnetic interactions but could be violated in weak interactions. This would explain the vast differences in lifetimes.

The properties of the different quarks are listed in Table **7.3**.

Quark flavour	Charge, Q	Baryon number, B	Strangeness, S
u	$+\frac{2e}{3}$	$+\frac{1}{3}$	0
d	$-\frac{e}{3}$	$+\frac{1}{3}$	0
s	$-\frac{e}{3}$	$+\frac{1}{3}$	−1
c	$+\frac{2e}{3}$	$+\frac{1}{3}$	0
b	$-\frac{e}{3}$	$+\frac{1}{3}$	0
t	$+\frac{2e}{3}$	$+\frac{1}{3}$	0

Table 7.3 Properties of quarks.

Worked examples

7.14 Determine the charge of the hyperon (Σ), whose quark content is dds. State whether this hadron is a baryon or a meson.

From the data booklet the charge is simply $Q_\Sigma = -\frac{1}{3}e - \frac{1}{3}e - \frac{1}{3}e = -e$ or just −1. It is made of three quarks so it is a baryon.

7.15 State the quark content of the anti-particle of the π^+ meson.

The anti-particle of the π^+ meson (positive pion) is found by replacing every particle in π^+ by its anti-particle. The anti-particle is therefore the π^- meson (negative pion), made up as $\pi^- = (\bar{u}d)$.

7.16 State the baryon number, strangeness and electric charge of the hadron $\bar{s}\bar{s}\bar{s}$.

The hadron consists of three anti-quarks so its baryon number is $B = -\frac{1}{3} - \frac{1}{3} - \frac{1}{3} = -1$

Its strangeness is $S = +1 + 1 + 1 = +3$

The electric charge is $Q = +\frac{1}{3}e + \frac{1}{3}e + \frac{1}{3}e = +e$

7.17 The reactions below do not occur; if they did, a conservation law would be violated. Identify the law in each case.
  a $p + \bar{p} \to \pi^0 + \pi^0 + n$
  b $K^0 \to \pi^+ + \pi^- + e^-$

a For this reaction the baryon number on the left side is 0 and on the right it is +1. So baryon number is not conserved.

b For this reaction electric charge is not conserved. On the left-hand side the charge is zero because the K^0 is neutral. On the right-hand side the total charge is $+e + (-e) + (-e)$, which is not zero.

7.18 State and explain whether the decay $\Sigma^- \to n + \pi^-$ takes place though the electromagnetic, the weak or the strong interaction. ($\Sigma^- = (dds)$; $\pi^- = \bar{u}d$.)

Strangeness is violated (the strangeness of Σ^- is -1, and the strangeness of $n + \pi^-$ is 0), so the decay takes place through the weak interaction.

Leptons

There are six types of lepton. These are the electron and its neutrino, the muon and its neutrino, and the tau and its neutrino. They are denoted by $e^-, \nu_e, \mu^-, \nu_\mu$, and τ^-, ν_τ. The muon is heavier than the electron, and the tau is heavier than the muon. There is now conclusive evidence that neutrinos have a very small non-zero mass. There is solid experimental evidence for the existence of all six leptons. In addition we have the anti-particles of these. The properties of leptons are given in Table 7.4.

All leptons interact with the weak nuclear interaction. Those that have electric charge (e^-, μ^- and τ^-) also interact with the electromagnetic interaction.

Leptons (and only leptons) are assigned a new quantum number called **family lepton number**. There is an electron, muon and tau lepton number. The various lepton numbers are given in Table 7.4. The family lepton number is conserved in all interactions.

Exam tip
Leptons are a different class of particle from quarks. Leptons do not consist of quarks. Note that since leptons are **not** baryons, they have a baryon number of 0. Particles that are **not** leptons have a lepton number of 0.

Lepton	Charge, Q	L_e	L_μ	L_τ
e^-	$-e$	+1	0	0
ν_e	0	+1	0	0
μ^-	$-e$	0	+1	0
ν_μ	0	0	+1	0
τ^-	$-e$	0	0	+1
ν_τ	0	0	0	+1

Table 7.4 Properties of leptons.

Exam tip
Table 7.4 assigns three types of lepton number: electron, muon and tau lepton number. In a simpler picture, we may think of just one type of lepton number: $L = +1$ to all leptons and $L = -1$ to all anti-leptons.

7 ATOMIC, NUCLEAR AND PARTICLE PHYSICS

Worked example

7.19 Investigate the reaction $\mu^+ \to e^+ + \nu_e + \bar{\nu}_\mu$ from the point of view of lepton number conservation.

The lepton number on the left-hand side is -1 because it involves the anti-muon. On the right-hand side it is similarly $-1 + 1 - 1 = -1$ so lepton number is conserved.

Investigating the individual lepton numbers we see that the left-hand side has muon lepton number equal to -1. The right-hand side has muon lepton number similarly -1. The electron muon number on the left-hand side is 0 and on the right-hand side it is $-1 + 1 = 0$.

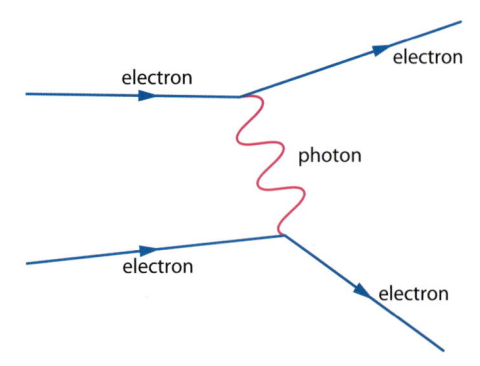

Figure 7.22 Two electrons interacting by exchanging a photon. Both electrons change direction.

Exchange particles

Why does an electron exert an electric force of repulsion on another electron? The classical answer we gave in Topic **6** is that the one electron creates an electric field to which the other electron responds by experiencing a force. Particle physics gives a very different answer to this question. Particle physics interprets an interaction between two particles as the exchange of a particle between them. In the case of the electromagnetic interaction the particle exchanged is a photon. One electron **emits** the photon and the other **absorbs** it. The emitted photon carries momentum and so the electron that emits it changes its momentum, i.e. experiences a force. Similarly, the particle that absorbs the photon changes its momentum thus also experiencing a force. This is shown schematically in Figure **7.22**.

As we will see later, the other interactions are also described in terms of exchange particles.

What is a force?

Why should two positive charged particles repel each other? And why should they do so with Coulomb's force which is an inverse square law? Why do quarks attract each other with a force that binds them tightly, for example within a proton, and why do protons and neutrons attract each other strongly when they are close to each other within a nucleus?

These 'why' questions are difficult questions. The answers to 'why' questions often lead to other 'why' questions, and so the question is always whether one has made any progress.

Feynman diagrams

In the 1950s the American physicist Richard P. Feynman (Figure **7.23**) introduced a pictorial representation of particle interactions. These representations are now called **Feynman diagrams**. The diagrams clearly express the idea that interactions between particles involve the exchange of particles.

Let us concentrate on the electromagnetic interaction. Feynman realised that every process involving electromagnetic interactions can be built up from just one basic **interaction vertex**. It has five different parts but all five consist of just one wavy line and two lines with arrows on them. All five diagrams are essentially the same if you look at them from the 'right' angle. Think of time increasing as we move to the right. A wavy line will represent a photon. A line with an arrow in the direction of time represents a particle (an electron). A line with an arrow against the direction of time represents an anti-particle (a positron), as shown in Figure **7.24**. In this way the five diagrams of Figure **7.25** represent five different physical processes:

a shows a photon coming in, which is absorbed by an electron. So this represents photon absorption by an electron.
b shows a photon coming in, which is absorbed by a positron.
c shows an electron emitting a photon.
d shows a photon that materialises into an electron and a positron, pair production.
e shows electron–positron annihilation into a photon.

Figure 7.23 Richard P. Feynman (1918–1988).

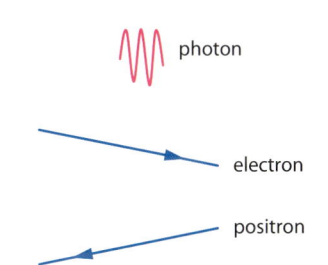

Figure 7.24 The ingredients of the interaction vertex. Electrons have arrows in the direction of time. Positrons have arrows against the direction of time.

a An electron absorbs a photon
b A positron absorbs a photon
c An electron emits a photon
d A photon materializes into an electron–positron pair
e An electron and a positron collide, annihilate each other and produce a photon

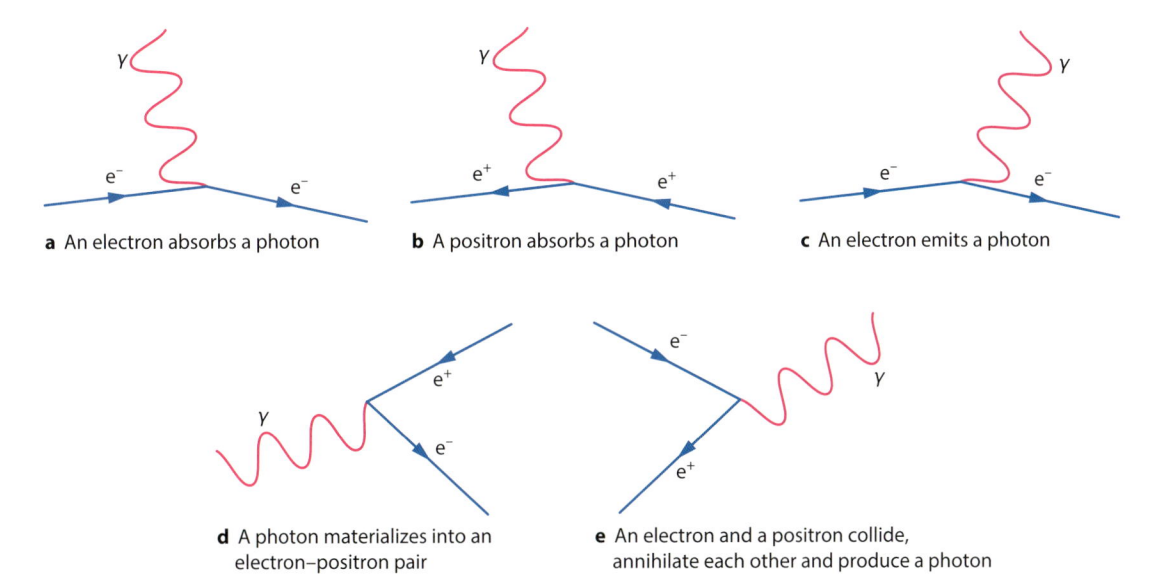

Figure 7.25 Some examples of interaction vertices. Here γ is a photon, e⁻ is an electron and e⁺ is a positron.

Exam tip
There is one process missing in Figure **7.25**, namely a photon scattering off a positron. Can you supply the diagram for this?

7 ATOMIC, NUCLEAR AND PARTICLE PHYSICS

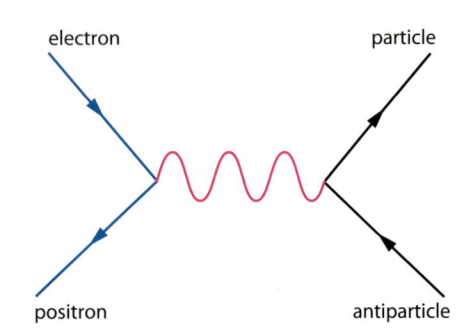

Figure 7.26 An electron and a positron annihilate into a photon and the photon in turn materialises into a new particle–antiparticle pair!

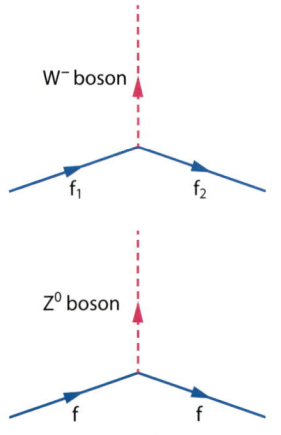

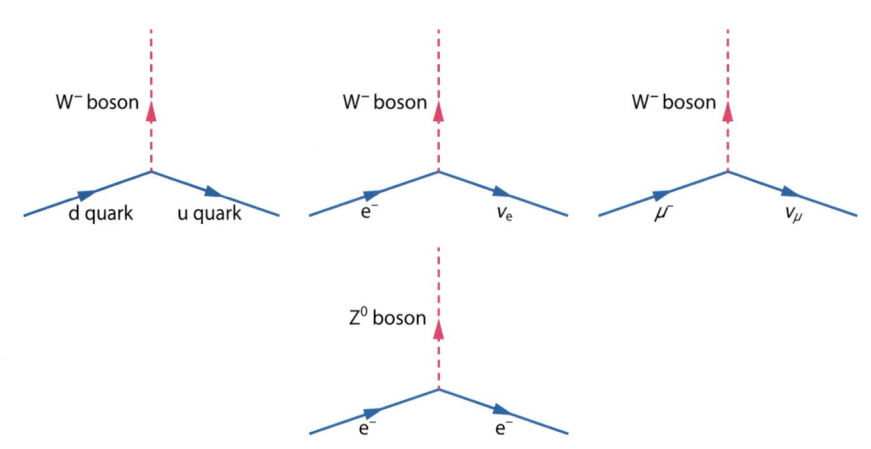

Figure 7.27 Two weak interaction vertices. In the first, f_1 and f_2 stand for quarks or leptons. This vertex allows quark flavour to change. In the second the incoming and outgoing particles are the same, and f stands for a quark or a lepton.

The power of a diagram

The diagrams Feynman introduced to represent physical processes and are now called 'Feynman diagrams' are not just pictorial representations of processes. Each diagram corresponds to a precise mathematical expression that contributes to the probability of the process occurring. Precise rules allow for the calculation of this probability from each diagram. This has revolutionised calculations in particle physics. A famous example is the Klein–Nishina formula, which gives the details of the scattering of a photon off an electron. It took Klein and Nishina 6 months to do the calculation. With Feynman diagrams it can be done in under 2 hours. Julian Schwinger, who shared the 1965 Nobel Prize in Physics with Feynman and Sin-Itiro Tomonoga, said that Feynman diagrams 'gave calculating power to the masses.'

It is quite extraordinary how so many different processes can be described by a single interaction vertex!

The idea is then to put together interaction vertices to represent interesting processes. For example, let us see how one electron can scatter off another electron. Go back to Figure 7.22. It is made up of two interaction vertices. Another possibility of great use in particle accelerators is the process represented by the Feynman diagram in Figure 7.26.

The idea can be extended to other interactions as well. There are three exchange particles for the weak interaction. These are called $W^{\pm}$ and Z^0. Unlike the photon, they have mass. This implies that there are very many interaction vertices for the weak interaction. Figure 7.27 shows two common vertices involving the W^- and the Z^0. Figure 7.28 shows specific examples of these two vertices.

Figure 7.28 Weak interaction vertices.

The interaction vertices can help explain beta decay. This is shown in Figure 7.29.

The strong interaction also has very many interaction vertices. The most common is similar to the electromagnetic interaction vertex, but now we have quarks in place of electrons and gluons in place of photons. Gluons are the exchange particles of the strong interaction. (The exchange of gluons can sometimes appear as an exchange of mesons.)

Table 7.5 is a summary of the properties of the fundamental interactions.

Interaction	Interaction acts on	Exchange particle(s)	Relative strength*	Range**
electromagnetic	particles with electric charge	photon	$\frac{1}{137}$	∞
weak	quarks and leptons only responsible for beta decay	W^+, W^- and Z^0	10^{-6}	10^{-18} m
strong	quarks and by extension particles made out of quarks, i.e. hadrons	gluons/mesons	1	10^{-15} m
gravitational	particles with mass	graviton	10^{-41}	∞

Figure 7.29 In beta minus decay a d quark turns into a u quark by emitting a W^-. The W^- then materialises into an electron and an anti-neutrino. The end result is that a neutron has turned into a proton.

Table 7.5 The fundamental interactions and the exchange particles that participate in them.

*Relative strength depends on energy so the values given here are approximate.
**The range of the strong interaction is finite even though the gluon is massless.

Worked example

7.20 In Worked example **7.18** we saw that the decay the decay $\Sigma^- \to n + \pi^-$ takes place though the weak interaction. ($\Sigma^- =$ dds, $\pi^- = \bar{u}d$.) Draw a Feynman diagram for this decay.

The diagram must use a weak interaction vertex; the s quark changes into a u quark and the W^- turns into a d and u anti-quark to create the pion.

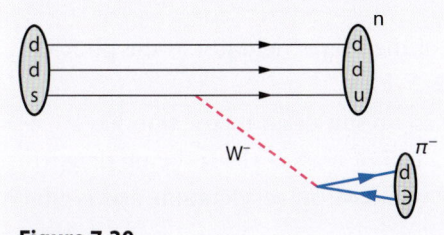

Figure 7.30

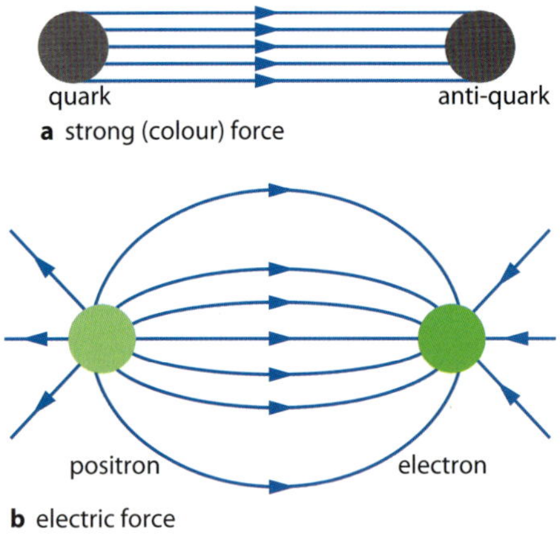

Confinement

Quarks only exist within hadrons. This has led to an important principle, that of **quark confinement**:

> It is not possible to observe isolated quarks.

Suppose that one attempts to remove a quark from inside a meson. The force between the quark and the anti-quark is constant no matter what their separation is (Figure 7.31). Therefore, the total energy needed to separate the quark from the anti-quark gets larger and larger as the separation increases. To free the quark completely would require an infinite amount of energy, and so is impossible. If one insisted on providing more and more energy in the hope of isolating the quark, all that would happen would be the production of a meson–anti-meson pair and not free quarks.

The Higgs particle

The theory of quarks, leptons and exchange particles defines what is now called the **Standard Model** of particles and interactions. All aspects of this model except one have been verified experimentally long ago. The missing link was the existence of the **Higgs particle**: a neutral particle required to exist by the theory of the standard model. The Higgs particle is closely linked to the mystery of mass. What exactly is mass and how do elementary particles acquire mass? In particular, why do the elementary particles have the mass that they have? The mathematical theory describing the electroweak interaction is one of symmetry. Among many other things, this symmetry forbids the photon and the W and Z particles from having mass. The photon is indeed massless, so this is fine. But the W and the Z are massive. For years physicists searched for a way both to preserve the mathematical symmetry of the theory and at the same time to allow the W and the Z to have mass. This is what the Higgs particle achieves.

a strong (colour) force

b electric force

Figure 7.31 The lines of force between a quark and an anti-quark are very different from those between a positive and a negative electric charge, leading to quark confinement.

> The Higgs particle is responsible, through its interactions, for the mass of the particles of the standard model, in particular the masses of the W and the Z.

The Higgs particle is the quantum of the Higgs field just as the photon is the quantum of the electromagnetic field.

The idea of mass being acquired as a result of an interaction has a counterpart in classical mechanics: a ball of mass m that is being dragged through a fluid by a pulling force F will have an acceleration that is a bit less than $\frac{F}{m}$. This is because turbulence is created in the fluid and results in a small force opposing the motion and hence a smaller acceleration than expected. This has the same effect as saying that, as a result of the interaction of the body with the fluid, the body increased its mass a bit. This is very roughly how the Higgs works.

The Higgs went undetected for about 40 years since its existence was proposed on theoretical grounds. In July 2012 physicists at CERN's Large Hadron Collider announced evidence that finally the Higgs had been discovered. Its mass is about 125 GeV c^{-2}.

Nature of science

At the time Gell-Mann proposed quarks, many hundreds of hadrons were known. Gell-Mann managed to explain the existence of each and every one of these by postulating the existence of just the three lightest quarks (the u, the d and the s). This was a purely mathematical explanation, as no quarks had been observed. Gell-Mann predicted the existence of a 'strangeness −3' baryon and used his quark model to predict its mass as well. In 1964 researchers at Brookhaven discovered the Ω− with properties exactly as predicted. The bubble chamber photograph in Figure 7.32a shows the creation and subsequent decay of the Ω−. Analysing these complex photographs and extracting relevant information is an enormously complicated task. Large-scale international collaboration later showed the existence of the other quarks and led to the Standard Model used today. Work on particles continues at CERN in Geneva (Figures 7.32b and 7.32c) and many other laboratories.

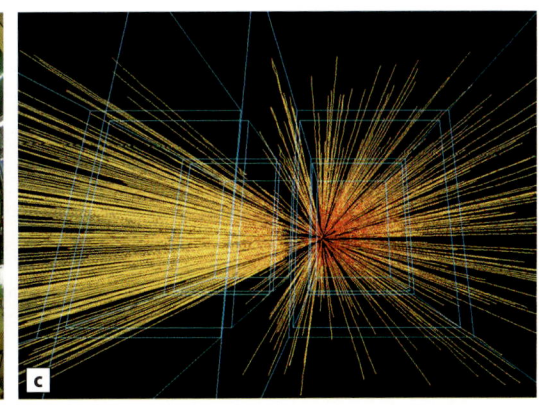

Figure 7.32 a A bubble chamber photograph of the creation and decay of the Ω−. **b** The huge CMS detector at the Large Hadron Collider at CERN illustrates the complexity of the electronics required in particle physics. **c** Computer images of particle tracks after a collision illustrate the complexity of the analysis required.

Test yourself

25 In the gold foil experiment explain why:
   a the foil was very thin
   b the experiment was done in an evacuated container.

26 Write down the quark structure of **a** the anti-neutron and **b** the anti-proton. Verify that the charges come out correctly.

27 Write down the quark structure of the anti-particle of the meson $K^+ = (u\bar{s})$.

28 State the baryon number of the hadron with quark content $\bar{c}\bar{c}\bar{c}$.

29 Determine whether the following reactions conserve or violate baryon number:
   a $p^+ \rightarrow e^+ + \gamma$
   b $p^+ + p^- \rightarrow \pi^+ + \pi^-$
   c $p^+ + p^- \rightarrow \pi^+ + \pi^- + n + \bar{n}$
   d $\Lambda^0 \rightarrow \pi^+ + \pi^-$ (The Λ particle has quark content uds.)

30 Suggest the reason that led to the introduction of the quantum number called strangeness.

31 The quark content of a certain meson is (d$\bar{s}$).
  a Write down its charge and its strangeness.
  b Determine whether it can be its own anti-particle.

32 A charmed D meson is made out of D = c$\bar{d}$.
  a Write down its charge.
  b Write down its strangeness.

33 Determine whether the following reactions conserve or violate strangeness: (use π^0 = d$\bar{d}$, K^+ = u$\bar{s}$, Λ^0 = uds, K^0 = d$\bar{s}$, Σ^- = dds)
  a $\pi^- + p^+ \to K^0 + \Lambda^0$
  b $\pi^0 + n \to K^+ + \Sigma^-$
  c $K^0 \to \pi^- + \pi^+$
  d $\pi^- + p^+ \to \pi^- + \Sigma^+$

34 In the reactions listed below, various neutrinos appear (denoted ν). In each case, identify the correct neutrino (ν_e, ν_μ, ν_τ or the anti-particles of these).
  a $\pi^+ \to \pi^0 + e^+ + \nu$
  b $\pi^+ \to \pi^0 + \mu^+ + \nu$
  c $\tau^+ \to \pi^- + \pi^+ + \nu$
  d $p^+ + \nu \to n + e^+$
  e $\tau^- \to e^- + \nu + \nu$

35 The reactions listed below are all impossible because they violate one or more conservation laws. In each case, identify the law that is violated.
  a $K^+ \to \mu^- + \bar{\nu}_\mu + e^+ + e^+$
  b $\mu^- \to e^+ + \gamma$
  c $\tau^+ \to \gamma + \bar{\nu}_\tau$
  d $p + n \to p + \pi^0$
  e $e^+ \to \mu^+ + \bar{\nu}_\mu + \bar{\nu}_e$
  f $p \to \pi^+ + \pi^-$

36 Explain whether the electric force acts:
  a on quarks
  b on neutrinos.

37 The neutron is electrically neutral. Could it possibly have electromagnetic interactions?

38 The neutral meson η_c = (c$\bar{c}$) is its own anti-particle, but the neutral K^0 = (d$\bar{s}$) is not. Explain why.

39 a Outline what is meant by the term **confinement** in the context of quarks.
  b The Feynman diagram shows the decay of a quark–anti-quark pair in a meson into two gluons. With reference to your answer in **a**, suggest what might happen to the gluons produced in this decay.

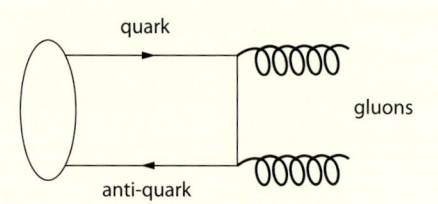

40 a The rest mass of the proton is 938 MeV c^{-2} and that of the neutron is 940 MeV c^{-2}. Using the known quark contents of the proton and the neutron, calculate the masses of the u and d quarks.
  b Using the values you calculated in **a**, predict the mass of the meson π^+ (which is made out of a u quark and an d anti-quark).
  c The actual value of the rest mass of the π^+ is about 140 MeV c^{-2}. Suggest how this enormous disagreement is resolved.

41 Describe the significance of the Higgs particle in the standard model of quarks and leptons.

42 Use the electromagnetic vertex to draw a Feynman diagram for the scattering of a photon off a positron.

43 Beta-minus decay involves the decay of a neutron into a proton according to the reaction n $\to p^+ + e^- + \bar{\nu}_e$.
  a Describe this decay in terms of quarks.
  b Draw a Feynman diagram for the process.

44 Using the basic weak interaction vertex involving a W boson and two quarks or leptons given in Figure **7.28**, draw Feynman diagrams to represent the following processes:
  a $\mu^- \to e^- + \bar{\nu}_e + \nu_\mu$
  b $e^- + \bar{\nu}_e \to \mu^- + \bar{\nu}_\mu$
  c $\pi^+ \to \mu^+ + \nu_\mu$ (quark structure of positive pion is u$\bar{d}$)
  d $K^- \to \mu^- + \bar{\nu}_\mu$ (quark structure of negative kaon is s$\bar{u}$).

45 Using the basic weak interaction vertex involving a W boson and two quarks and leptons given in Figure **7.30**, state **three** possible ways in which the W boson can decay.

46 Using the basic weak interaction vertex involving a Z boson and two quarks and leptons given in Figure **7.30**, draw Feynman diagrams to represent the following processes:
a $e^- + e^+ \rightarrow \bar{v}_\mu + v_\mu$
b $e^- + v_\mu \rightarrow e^- + v_\mu$
c $e^- + e^+ \rightarrow e^- + e^+$

Exam-style questions

1 How would the decay of a nucleus of $^{60}_{27}$Co into a nucleus of $^{60}_{28}$Ni be described?

    A alpha decay   **B** beta minus decay   **C** beta plus decay   **D** gamma decay

2 What are the number of neutrons and the number of electrons in the neutral atom of $^{195}_{78}$Pt?

	Number of neutrons	Number of electrons
A	117	195
B	117	78
C	195	78
D	195	117

3 The activity of a sample containing a radioactive element is 6400 Bq. After 36 minutes the activity is 800 Bq. What is the half-life of the sample?

    A 4.0 minutes   **B** 8.0 minutes   **C** 12 minutes   **D** 18 minutes

4 A sample contains a small quantity of a radioactive element with a very long half-life. The activity is constant and equal to A. The temperature of the sample is increased. What are the effects if any, on the half-life and activity of the sample?

	Effect on half-life	Effect on activity
A	none	none
B	none	increase
C	increase	none
D	increase	increase

5 What is the common characteristic of most nuclei with mass number greater than about 20?

    A binding energy per nucleon
    B binding energy
    C decay pattern
    D half-life

6 The binding energy per nucleon for $^{11}_{5}B$ is about 7 MeV. What is the minimum energy needed to separate the nucleons of $^{11}_{5}B$?

       A 7 MeV   **B** 35 MeV   **C** 42 MeV   **D** 77 MeV

7 The reaction $p + n \rightarrow p + \pi^0$ is impossible. Which conservation law would be violated if the reaction occurred?

       A charge   **B** lepton number   **C** baryon number   **D** strangeness

8 Which is the neutral exchange particle of the weak interaction?

       A photon   **B** gluon   **C** W   **D** Z

9 What are the charge Q and strangeness S of the baryon Λ = (uds)?

	Q	S
A	0	+1
B	+1	+1
C	0	−1
D	+1	−1

10 What process does this Feynman diagram represent?

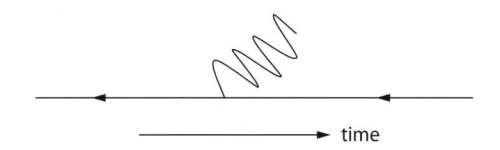

    A electron emitting photon
    B electron absorbing photon
    C positron emitting photon
    D positron absorbing photon

11 **a** Explain how the emission lines in the spectrum of a gas are evidence for discrete energy levels within atoms. [3]

The diagram shows three energy levels of a vapour.

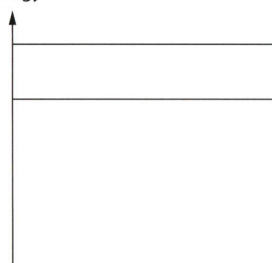

Transitions between these three levels give rise to photons of three different wavelengths. Two of these wavelengths are 486 nm and 656 nm.

b On a copy of the diagram draw arrows to identify the transitions that give rise to the wavelengths of 656 nm and 486 nm. [2]

c Calculate the wavelength of the photon that corresponds to the third transition. [3]

d White light containing wavelengths that vary from 400 nm to 700 nm is transmitted through the vapour. On a copy of the diagram below, draw lines to show the absorption lines in the transmitted light. [2]

increasing wavelength

12 a Explain why in their experiment Geiger and Marsden used:
  i an evacuated enclosure [1]
  ii a gold foil that was very thin [1]
  iii a beam of alpha particles that was very narrow. [1]

b State the name of the force responsible for the deflection of the alpha particles. [1]

c **i** Describe the deflections of the alpha particles by the gold foil. [2]
  ii Outline how the results of this experiment led to the Rutherford model of the atom. [3]

d The diagram shows a partially completed path of an alpha particle that left point P as it scatters past a nucleus of gold.

On a copy of the diagram:
  i complete the path [1]
  ii draw lines to clearly show the angle of deflection of this alpha particle [2]
  iii draw an arrow to indicate the direction of the force on the alpha particle at the point of closest approach. [1]

e **i** A second alpha particle is shot at the nucleus from position Q with identical kinetic energy, in a direction parallel to that of the alpha particle at P. On your diagram, draw the path of this particle. [2]
  ii Discuss how, if at all, the answer to **e i** would change if the nucleus of gold were replaced by a nucleus of another, heavier, isotope of gold. [2]

13 a Radioactive decay is random and spontaneous. State what you understand by this statement. **[4]**

b The graph shows how activity of a sample containing a radioactive isotope of thorium $^{225}_{90}$Th varies with time.

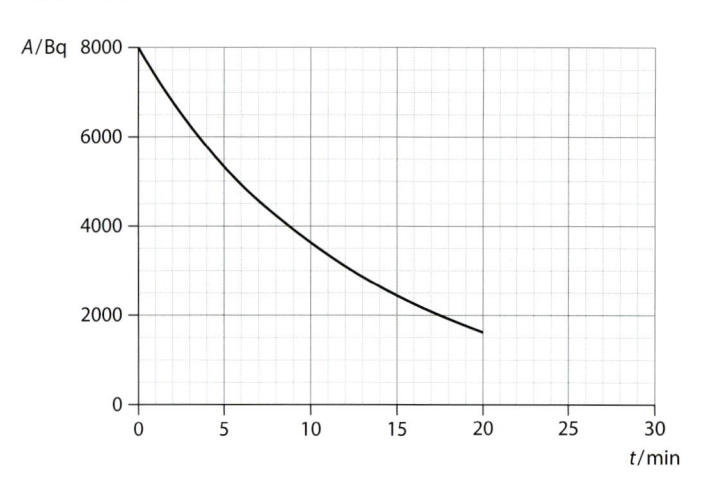

   i   State what is meant by an **isotope**. **[1]**
   ii Determine the half-life of thorium. **[2]**
   iii State **one** assumption made in obtaining the answer to **ii**. **[1]**
   iv Draw on a copy of the graph to show the variation of the activity with time to 30 minutes. **[2]**

c i Thorium undergoes alpha decay. Complete the reaction equation:

   $$^{225}_{90}\text{Th} \rightarrow {}^{?}_{?}\text{Ra} + {}^{?}_{?}a$$ **[2]**

   ii Calculate the energy released, in MeV. (Atomic masses: thorium 226.024903 u, radium 221.013917 u, helium 4.0026603 u.) **[2]**

d The nuclei of thorium are at rest when they decay. Determine the fraction of the energy released that is carried by the alpha particle. **[3]**

14 A possible fission reaction is given by the equation:

$$^{1}_{0}\text{n} + {}^{235}_{92}\text{U} \rightarrow {}^{90}_{38}\text{Sr} + {}^{143}_{54}\text{Xe} + x{}^{1}_{0}\text{n}$$

a i Calculate the number x of neutrons produced. **[1]**
   ii Use the binding energy per nucleon curve in Figure **7.12** to estimate the energy released in this reaction. **[3]**

b Suggest why most nuclei with $A > 20$ have roughly the same binding energy per nucleon. **[3]**

c Use the diagram in Figure **7.12** to explain why energy is released in nuclear fusion. **[2]**

15 a Explain, in terms of quarks, the difference between a baryon and a meson. [2]

   b In a copy of the table below, put a check mark (✓) to identify the interaction(s) that apply to hadrons and to leptons. [2]

	strong	weak
hadrons		
leptons		

   c Copy and complete the Feynman diagram to represent the beta minus decay of a neutron, making sure that you label all particles involved. [5]

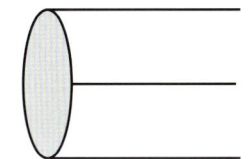

   d For this part of the question it is given that $K^- = s\bar{u}$, $\pi^+ = u\bar{d}$ and that Σ^- has strangeness -1.
      i   Using the fact that the reaction $K^- + p \rightarrow \pi^+ + \Sigma^-$ occurs, determine whether Σ^- would be classified as a baryon or as a meson. [2]
      ii Using the fact that the reaction $K^- \rightarrow \mu^- + \bar{\nu}$ occurs, determine whether the reaction takes place through the strong, the weak or the electromagnetic interaction. [2]
      iii State and explain whether the anti-neutrino in **d ii** is an electron, muon or tau anti-neutrino. [2]

16 A student suggest that the muon decays according to the reaction equation $\mu^- \rightarrow e^- + \gamma$.

    a i   State **one** similarity and **one** difference between the electron and the muon. [2]
       ii Explain why the reaction equation proposed by the student is incorrect. [2]

    b In fact, the muon decays according to $\mu^- \rightarrow e^- + \bar{\nu}_e + \nu_\mu$. A Feynman diagram for this decay is shown.

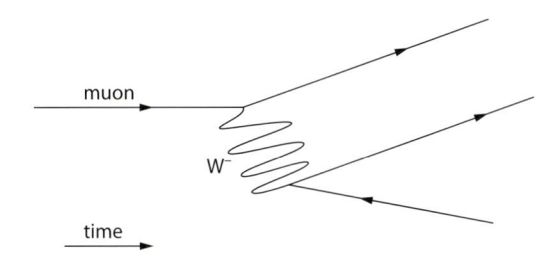

       i   Identify the **three** unlabelled particles in this diagram. [3]
       ii Using the diagram above to construct a new Feynman diagram representing the scattering of an electron anti-neutrino off a muon. [2]
       iii Write down the reaction equation representing the decay μ^+, which is the anti-particle of the μ^-. [2]

    c The interaction responsible for the decay of the muon has very short range. State the property of the exchange particle that is responsible for the short range. [1]

7 ATOMIC, NUCLEAR AND PARTICLE PHYSICS   313

8 Energy production

Learning objectives

- Solve problems with specific energy and energy density.
- Distinguish between primary and secondary energy sources and renewable and non-renewable energy sources.
- Describe fossil fuel power stations, nuclear power stations, wind generators, pumped storage hydroelectric systems, solar power cells and solar panels.
- Solve problems involving energy transformations in the systems above.

8.1 Energy sources

This section discusses energy sources and ways to produce power.

Primary and secondary energy

Primary energy is energy found in nature that has not yet been subject to processing of any kind. Examples include the energy stored in **fuels** such as crude oil, coal and natural gas, as well as solar energy, wind energy and so on. When primary energy is processed or exploited, **secondary energy** is produced. Secondary energy must be suitable for use in machines which perform mechanical work; it could also be a very versatile form of energy such as electricity. To give one example, the kinetic energy of particles of air in wind is primary energy. A simple windmill can extract some of this kinetic energy and perform mechanical work as it raises water from a well; or, the kinetic energy of the wind can be used to turn a generator producing electricity. In both cases we have primary energy being transformed to secondary energy.

How much energy can be extracted from a fuel defines the fuel's specific energy and energy density. **Specific energy**, E_S, is the amount of energy that can be extracted from a unit mass of fuel; it is measured in $J\,kg^{-1}$. **Energy density**, E_D, is the amount of energy that be extracted from a unit volume of fuel; it is measured in $J\,m^{-3}$. Table **8.1** gives the values for E_S and E_D for some common fuels.

Worked example

8.1 a Show that $E_D = \rho E_S$ where ρ is the density of the fuel.
   b Use Table **8.1** to estimate the density of uranium-235.

a E_D is the amount of energy that be extracted from a unit volume of fuel, so:

$$E_D = \frac{Q}{V}$$

where Q is the energy released from volume V.

Using the definition of density ρ as mass per unit volume, a volume V has mass m given by:

$$m = V\rho$$

$$\Rightarrow V = \frac{m}{\rho}$$

Then, $E_D = \dfrac{Q}{m/\rho} = \dfrac{Q}{m} \times \rho = \rho E_S$

314

b Table **8.1** gives values for E_D and E_S for uranium-235. Hence:

$$\rho = \frac{E_D}{E_S} = \frac{1.3 \times 10^{18}}{70 \times 10^{12}} \approx 2 \times 10^4 \, \text{kg m}^{-3}.$$

Fuel	Specific energy E_S / J kg^{-1}	Energy density E_D / J m^{-3}
uranium-235	7.0×10^{13}	1.3×10^{18}
hydrogen	1.4×10^{8}	1.0×10^{7}
natural gas	5.4×10^{7}	3.6×10^{7}
gasoline	4.6×10^{7}	3.4×10^{10}
kerosene	4.3×10^{7}	3.3×10^{10}
diesel	4.6×10^{7}	3.7×10^{10}
coal	3.2×10^{7}	7.2×10^{10}

Table 8.1 Specific energy or energy density of fossil fuels.

Specific energy or energy density are major considerations in the choice of a fuel. Obviously, all other factors being equal, the higher the specific energy or energy density, the more desirable the fuel.

We may classify energy sources into two large classes, **non-renewable** and **renewable**.

Non-renewable sources of energy are finite sources, which are being depleted much faster than they can be produced and so will run out. They include fossil fuels (e.g. oil, natural gas and coal) and nuclear fuels (e.g. uranium).

Renewable sources include solar energy (and the other forms indirectly dependent on solar energy, such as wind energy and wave energy) and tidal energy. In principle, they will be available as long as the Sun shines and that means billions of years.

The main sources of energy, and the percentage of the total energy produced of each, is given in Table **8.2**. The figures are world averages for 2011 and are approximate.

Fuel	Percentage of total energy production / %	Carbon dioxide emission / g MJ^{-1}
oil	32	70
natural gas	21	50
coal	27	90
nuclear	6	–
hydroelectric	2	–
biofuels	10	–
others	<2	–

Table 8.2 Energy sources and the percentage of the total energy production for each. The third column gives the mass of carbon dioxide emitted per unit of energy produced from a particular fuel. Fossil fuels account for about 80% of the total energy production.

8 ENERGY PRODUCTION

Fossil fuels

Fossil fuels (oil, coal and natural gas) have been created over millions of years. They are produced by the decomposition of buried animal and plant matter under the combined action of the high pressure of the material on top and bacteria.

Burning coal and oil have been the traditional ways of producing electricity. A typical fossil fuel power plant is shown in Figure **8.1**.

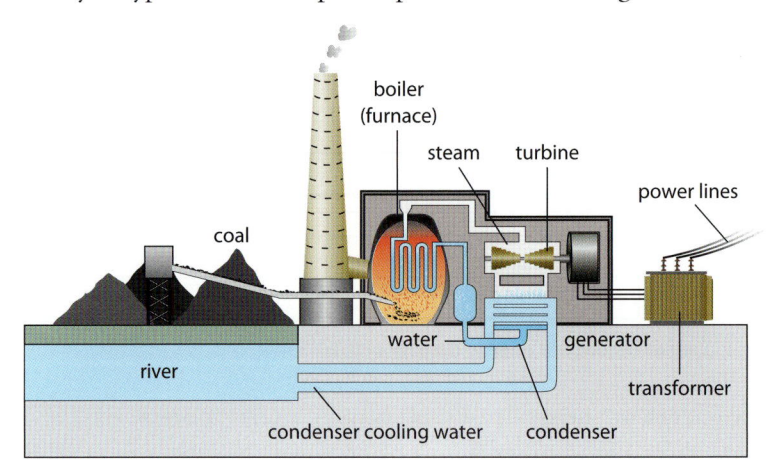

Figure 8.1 A coal-burning power plant.

Burning coal produces energy that turns water into steam in boilers. The pressurised steam forces a turbine to turn. The turbine makes the coils of a generator rotate in a magnetic field, creating electricity by electromagnetic induction (see Subtopic **11.2**). Cold water (usually from a nearby river) condenses the steam into liquid water that can again be heated in the boilers. Figure **8.2** shows a Sankey diagram for this plant.

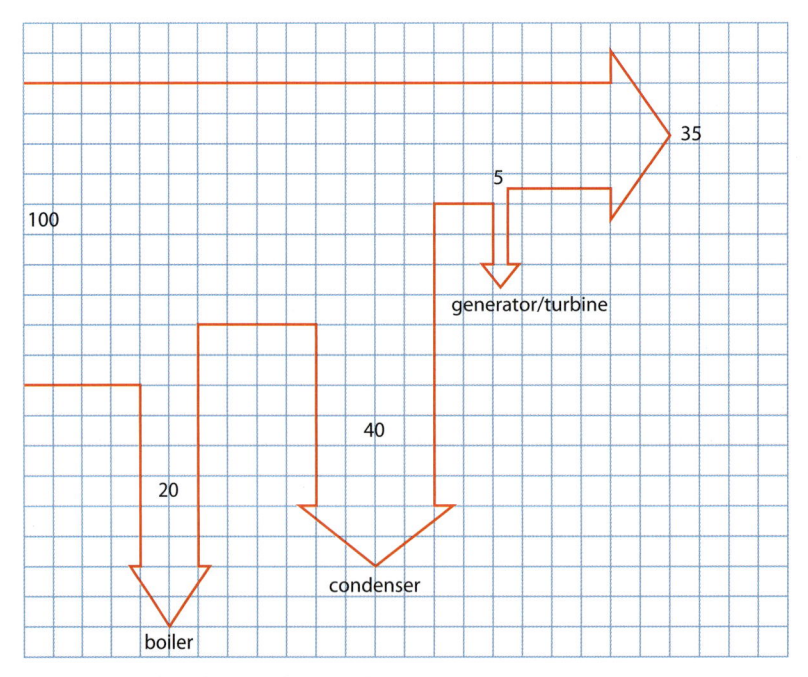

Figure 8.2 A Sankey diagram for a coal-burning power plant.

A **Sankey diagram** is an arrow block diagram representing energy flows. The width of the arrow is proportional to the amount of energy being transferred. Here, 100 units of energy created by the burning of coal enter the system. Twenty units are lost though the boilers, and an additional 40 units are lost as steam condenses into water. Of the remaining 40 units, about five are lost because of friction in the turning turbine and generator. In the end, only 35 units of energy have been produced as electricity. The efficiency, e, is defined by:

$$e = \frac{\text{useful power}}{\text{input power}}$$

The efficiency of this power plant is:

$$e = \frac{35}{100} = 0.35 \quad \text{or} \quad 35\%$$

Although reasonably efficient, fossil fuel power plants are primarily responsible for atmospheric pollution and contribute greenhouse gases to the atmosphere (Figure **8.3**). (Greenhouse gases and the greenhouse effect are discussed in Subtopic **8.2**.)

Natural gas power plants have higher efficiencies, reaching almost 60%, and have much smaller greenhouse gas emissions.

> **Power** is energy per unit time, i.e.
> $$\text{power} = \frac{\text{energy}}{\text{time}}$$

Figure 8.3 Fossil fuels produce pollution and greenhouse gases.

Worked example

8.2 A power plant produces electricity by burning coal. The thermal energy produced is used as input to a steam engine, which makes a turbine turn, producing electricity. The plant has a power output of 400 MW and operates at an overall efficiency of 35%.
   a Calculate the rate at which thermal energy is provided by the burning coal.
   b Calculate the rate at which coal is burned (use a coal specific energy of 30 MJ kg^{-1}).
   c The thermal energy discarded by the power plant is removed by water (Figure **8.4**). The temperature of the water must not increase by more than 5 °C. Calculate the rate at which the water must flow.

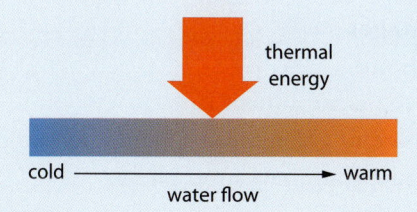

Figure 8.4

a The efficiency is the ratio of useful power output to power input. So:

$$0.35 = \frac{\text{power output}}{\text{power input}} = \frac{400\,\text{MW}}{P_{\text{input}}}$$

$$\Rightarrow P_{\text{input}} = \frac{400}{0.35} = 1.14 \times 10^3 \approx 1.1 \times 10^3 \,\text{MW}$$

8 ENERGY PRODUCTION

b Each kilogram of coal provides 30 MJ, which is 30×10^6 J. The power input is 1.14×10^3 MW, which is 1.14×10^9 J s^{-1}.

So the mass of coal that must be burned per second, $\frac{\Delta m}{\Delta t}$, is found from:

$$\frac{\Delta m}{\Delta t} \times 30 \times 10^6 = 1.14 \times 10^9$$

$$\Rightarrow \frac{\Delta m}{\Delta t} = 38 \text{ kg s}^{-1}$$

This is equivalent to:

$$38 \times 60 \times 60 \times 24 \times 365 = 1.2 \times 10^9 \text{ kg yr}^{-1}$$

c The thermal energy discarded is the difference between the energy produced by burning the coal and the useful energy output. So:

rate at which thermal energy is discarded = rate at which energy enters the water $\left(\frac{\Delta Q}{\Delta t}\right)$

$$= 1140 - 400 = 740 \text{ MW}$$

This thermal energy warms up the water according to:

$$Q = (\Delta m)c\Delta T$$

where m is the mass of water into which the thermal energy goes, c is the specific heat capacity of water (4200 J kg^{-1} K^{-1}) and ΔT is the temperature increase of the water (5 °C).

Rearranging, the rate at which thermal energy enters the water is then:

$$\frac{\Delta Q}{\Delta t} = \frac{\Delta m}{\Delta t} \times c\Delta T = 740 \text{ MW}$$

Therefore:

$$\frac{\Delta m}{\Delta t} = \frac{740 \times 10^6}{c\Delta T} = \frac{740 \times 10^6}{4200 \times 5}$$

$$\frac{\Delta m}{\Delta t} = 35 \times 10^3 \text{ kg s}^{-1}$$

The water must flow at a rate of 35×10^3 kg s^{-1}.

> **Exam tip: Fossil fuels**
> **Advantages**
> - Relatively cheap (while they last)
> - High power output (high energy density)
> - Variety of engines and devices use them directly and easily
> - Extensive distribution network is in place
>
> **Disadvantages**
> - Will run out
> - Pollute the environment
> - Contribute to greenhouse effect by releasing greenhouse gases into atmosphere

In the overall considerations over choice of fuel, it is necessary to take into account the cost of transporting the fuel from its place of production to the place of distribution. Fossil fuels have generally high costs because the mass and volume of the fuel tend to be large. Similarly, extensive storage facilities are needed. Fossil fuels, especially oil, pose serious environmental problems due to leakages at various points along the production–distribution line.

Nuclear power

A nuclear reactor is a machine in which nuclear fission reactions take place, producing energy. Fission reactions were discussed in Subtopic **7.2**.

Schematic diagrams of the cores of two types of nuclear reactor are shown in Figure **8.5**.

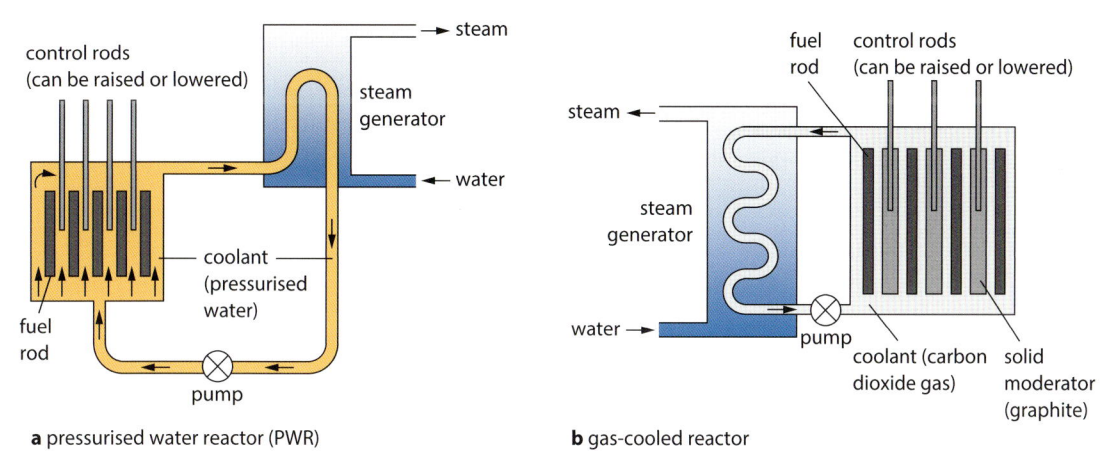

a pressurised water reactor (PWR) **b** gas-cooled reactor

Figure 8.5 Schematic diagrams of two types of fission reactor.

The **fuel** of a nuclear reactor is typically uranium-235. In **induced** fission neutrons initiate the reaction. One possible fission reaction is:

$$^{1}_{0}n + ^{235}_{92}U \rightarrow ^{140}_{54}Xe + ^{94}_{38}Sr + 2^{1}_{0}n$$

The neutrons produced can be used to collide with other nuclei of uranium-235 in the reactor, producing more fission, more energy and more neutrons. The reaction is thus self-sustaining; it is called a **chain reaction**. For the chain reaction to get going, a certain minimum mass of uranium-235 must be present, otherwise the neutrons escape without causing further reactions. This minimum mass is called the **critical mass** (for pure uranium-235, this is about 15 kg and rises to 130 kg for fuels containing 10% uranium-235). Uranium-235 will only capture neutrons if the neutrons are not too fast. The neutrons produced in the fission reactions are much too fast, and so must be slowed down before they can initiate further reactions.

The slowing down of neutrons is achieved through collisions of the neutrons with atoms of the **moderator**, the material surrounding the **fuel rods** (the tubes containing uranium). The moderator material can be graphite or water, for example. As the neutrons collide with moderator atoms, they transfer energy to the moderator, increasing its temperature. A **heat exchanger** is therefore needed to extract the heat from the moderator. This can be done using cold water that circulates in pipes throughout the moderator. The water is turned into steam at high temperature and pressure. The steam is then used to turn the turbines of a generator, finally producing electricity.

The rate of the reactions is determined by the number of neutrons available to be captured by uranium-235. Too few neutrons would result

8 ENERGY PRODUCTION

in the reaction stopping, while too many neutrons would lead to an uncontrollably large release of energy. Thus **control rods** are introduced into the moderator. These absorb neutrons when too many neutrons are present thus decreasing the rate of reactions. If the rate of reactions needs to be increased, the control rods are removed.

Worked example

8.3 As discussed in Subtopic **7.2**, one kilogram of uranium-235 releases a quantity of energy equal to 70×10^{12} J. Natural uranium (mainly uranium-238) contains about 0.7% of uranium-235 (by mass). Calculate the specific energy of natural uranium.

One kilogram of natural uranium contains 0.7% of uranium-235 and so the specific energy E_S of natural uranium as a nuclear fuel is:

$$E_S = \frac{0.7}{100} \times 70 \times 10^{12} = 4.9 \times 10^{11} \,\text{J kg}^{-1}$$

$$E_S = 490 \,\text{GJ kg}^{-1}$$

This value is substantially higher than for fossil fuels.

Risks with nuclear power

The fast neutrons produced in a fission reaction may be used to bombard uranium-238 and produce plutonium-239. The reactions leading to plutonium production are:

$$^{1}_{0}\text{n} + ^{238}_{92}\text{U} \rightarrow ^{239}_{92}\text{U}$$

$$^{239}_{92}\text{U} \rightarrow ^{239}_{93}\text{Np} + ^{0}_{-1}\text{e} + \bar{\nu}$$

$$^{239}_{93}\text{Np} \rightarrow ^{239}_{94}\text{Pu} + ^{0}_{-1}\text{e} + \bar{\nu}$$

The importance of these reactions is that non-fissionable material (uranium-238) is being converted to fissionable material (plutonium-239) as the reactor operates. The plutonium-239 produced can then be used as the nuclear fuel in other reactors. It can also be used in the production of nuclear weapons, which therefore raises serious concerns.

The spent fuel in a nuclear reactor, together with the products of the reactions, are all highly radioactive with long half-lives. Properly disposing of this material is a serious problem of the fission process. At present, this material is buried deep underground in containers that are supposed to avoid leakage to the outside. In addition, there is always the possibility of an accident due to uncontrolled heating of the moderator, which might start a fire or explosion. This would be a conventional explosion – the reactor cannot explode in the way a nuclear weapon does. In the event of an explosion, radioactive material would leak from the sealed core of

Figure 8.6 The effects of two of the world's worst nuclear accidents. **a** The nearby devastation after the explosion at the Fukushima nuclear plant in Japan on 11 March 2011. **b** Reactor number 4 in the Chernobyl nuclear power plant after the explosion on 26 April 1986.

a reactor, dispersing radioactive material into the environment. Both the explosions shown in Figure 8.6 resulted in widespread contamination. Even worse, we may have the meltdown of the entire core, as in the 1986 accident at Chernobyl.

These are serious concerns with nuclear fission as a source of commercial power. On the positive side, nuclear power does not produce greenhouse gases.

Exam tip: Nuclear power
Advantages
- High power output
- Large reserves of nuclear fuels
- Nuclear power stations do not produce greenhouse gases

Disadvantages
- Radioactive waste products difficult to dispose of
- Major public health hazard should 'something go wrong'
- Problems associated with uranium mining
- Possibility of producing materials for nuclear weapons

Worked example

8.4 A nuclear power plant produces 800 MW of electrical power with an overall efficiency of 35%. The energy released in the fission of one nucleus of uranium-235 is 170 MeV. Estimate the mass of uranium used per year.

Let P be the power produced from nuclear fission. Since the efficiency is 35%, then:

$$0.35 = \frac{800}{P}$$

$\Rightarrow P = 2286$ MW

The energy produced in one year is:

$2286 \times 10^6 \times 365 \times 24 \times 3600 = 7.21 \times 10^{16}$ J

The energy produced in the fission of one nucleus is:

$170 \times 10^6 \times 1.6 \times 10^{-19} = 2.72 \times 10^{-11}$ J

and so the number of fission reactions in a year is:

$$\frac{7.21 \times 10^{16}}{2.72 \times 10^{-11}} = 2.65 \times 10^{27}$$

The mass of uranium-235 used up in a year is therefore $2.65 \times 10^{27} \times 235 \times 1.66 \times 10^{-27}$, which is about 1000 kg.

8 ENERGY PRODUCTION

Solar power

The nuclear fusion reactions in the Sun send out an incredible, and practically inexhaustible, amount of energy, at a rate of about 3.9×10^{26} W. The Earth receives about 1400 W m^{-2} at the outer atmosphere. About 1000 W m^{-2} (1 kW m^{-2}) reaches the surface of the Earth. This amount assumes direct sunlight on a clear day and thus is the maximum that can be received at any one time. This is high-quality, free and inexhaustible energy that can be put to various uses.

Solar panels

An early application of solar energy has been in what are called 'active solar devices'. In these, sunlight is used directly to heat water or air for heating in a house, for example. The collecting surface is usually flat and covered by glass for protection; the glass should be coated to reduce reflection. A blackened surface below the glass collects sunlight, and water circulating in pipes underneath is heated. This hot water can then be used to heat water for use in the house (the heated water is kept in well-insulated containers). The general setup is shown in Figure **8.7a**. An additional boiler is available to heat the water in days with little sunlight.

These simple collectors are cheap and are usually put on the roof of a house (Figure **8.7b**). Their disadvantage is that they tend to be bulky and cover too much space.

Photovoltaic cells

A promising method for producing electricity from sunlight is that provided by **photovoltaic cells** (Figure **8.8**). The photovoltaic cell was developed in 1954 at Bell Laboratories and was used extensively in the space programme. A photovoltaic cell converts sunlight directly into direct current (dc) at an efficiency approaching 30%. Sunlight incident on the cell releases electrons and establishes a potential difference across the cell.

These systems can usefully be used to power small remote villages, pump water in agriculture, power warning lights, etc. Their environmental ill-effects are practically zero, with the exception of chemical pollution at the place of their manufacture.

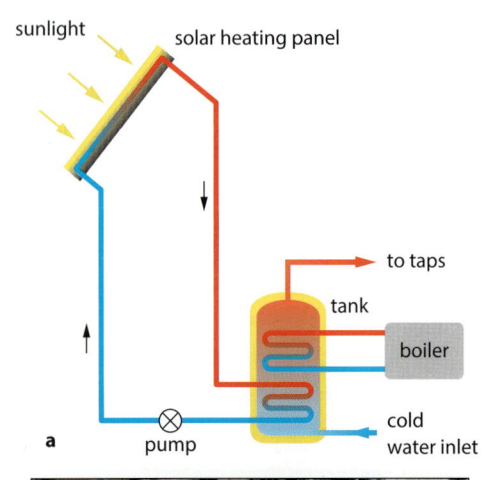

Figure 8.7 a A solar heating panel to provide warm water to a house. **b** Solar heating panels on roofs of apartment buildings.

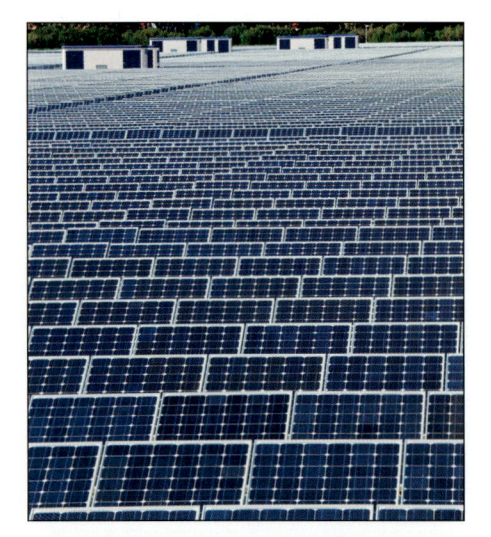

Figure 8.8 To produce appreciable amounts of electrical power very many photovoltaic cells are needed.

> **Exam tip: Solar power**
> **Advantages**
> - 'Free'
> - Inexhaustible
> - Clean
>
> **Disadvantages**
> - Works during the day only
> - Affected by cloudy weather
> - Low power output
> - Requires large areas
> - Initial costs high

Worked example

8.5 The average intensity of solar radiation incident on the Earth surface is 245 W m^{-2}. In an array of photovoltaic cells, solar energy is converted into electrical energy with an efficiency of 20%. Estimate the area of photovoltaic cells needed to provide 2.5 kW of electrical power.

The power incident on an area A m^2 is $245 \times A$.

As the cells are 20% efficient, the electrical power P provided by area A of cells is:

$P = 0.20 \times 245 \times A$

The power required is 2500 W.

$2500 = 0.20 \times 245 \times A$

$\Rightarrow A = 51 \text{ m}^2$

The area of photovoltaic cells needed to provide 2.5 kW of electrical power is 51 m^2.

Hydroelectric power

Hydroelectric power, the power derived from moving water masses, is one of the oldest and most established of all renewable energy sources (Figure **8.9**).

Hydroelectric power stations are associated with massive changes in the ecology of the area surrounding the plants. To create a reservoir behind a newly constructed dam, a vast area of land must be flooded.

The principle behind hydropower is simple. Consider a mass m of water that falls down a vertical height h (Figure **8.10**). The potential energy of

Figure 8.9 The Three Gorges Dam spanning the Yangtze River in Hubei province in China.

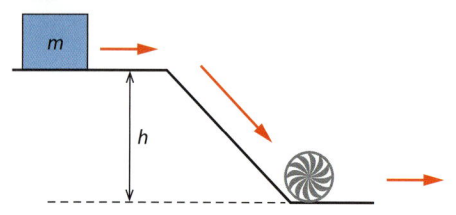

Figure 8.10 Water falling from a vertical height h has its potential energy converted into kinetic energy, which can be used to drive turbines.

Exam tip: Hydroelectric power
Advantages
- 'Free'
- Inexhaustible
- Clean

Disadvantages
- Very dependent on location
- Requires drastic changes to environment
- Initial costs high

the mass is mgh, and this is converted into kinetic energy when the mass descends the vertical distance h. The mass of the water is given by $\rho \Delta V$, where ρ is the density of water (1000 kg m^{-3}) and ΔV is the volume it occupies.

The rate of change of this potential energy, i.e. the power P, is given by the change in potential energy divided by the time taken for that change. So:

$$P = \frac{mgh}{\Delta t} = \frac{(\rho \Delta V)gh}{\Delta t} = \rho \frac{\Delta V}{\Delta t} gh$$

The quantity $Q = \frac{\Delta V}{\Delta t}$ is known as the volume flow rate (volume per second) and so:

$$P = \rho Q g h$$

This is the power available for generating electricity (or to convert into some other mechanical form) and it is thus clear that hydropower requires large volume flow rates, Q, and large heights, h.

Worked example

8.6 Find the power developed when water in a stream with a flow rate 50×10^{-3} m^3 s^{-1} falls from a height of 15 m.

Applying the power formula, we find:

$P = \rho Q g h$

$P = 1000 \times (50 \times 10^{-3}) \times 9.8 \times 15$

$P = 7.4$ kW

In a **pumped storage system**, the water that flows to lower heights is pumped back to its original height by using the generators of the plant as motors to pump the water (Figure 8.11).

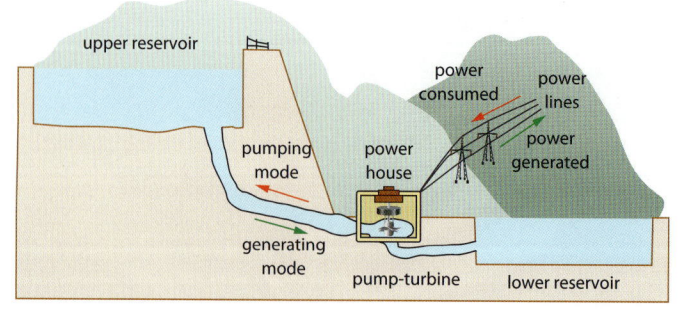

Figure 8.11 During off-peak hours water is pumped up to the higher reservoir. To do this the plant consumes electricity instead of producing it.

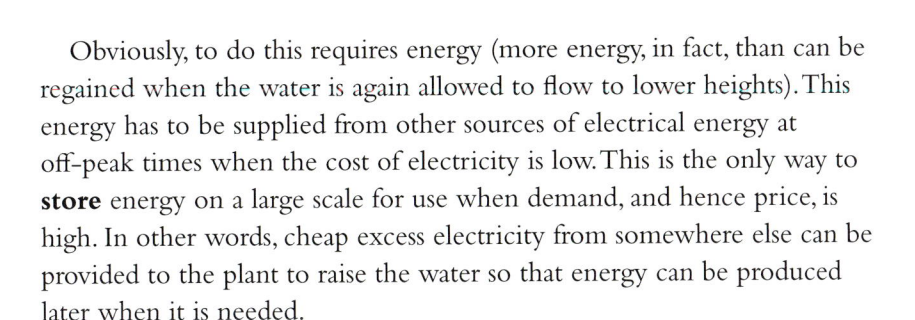

Obviously, to do this requires energy (more energy, in fact, than can be regained when the water is again allowed to flow to lower heights). This energy has to be supplied from other sources of electrical energy at off-peak times when the cost of electricity is low. This is the only way to **store** energy on a large scale for use when demand, and hence price, is high. In other words, cheap excess electricity from somewhere else can be provided to the plant to raise the water so that energy can be produced later when it is needed.

Wind power

This ancient method for exploiting the kinetic energy of wind is particularly useful for isolated small houses and agricultural use. Small wind turbines have vanes no larger than about 1 m long. Modern large wind turbines, with vanes larger than 30 m, are capable of producing up to a few megawatts of power (Figure **8.12**).

Wind generators produce low-frequency sound that affects some people's sleeping habits and many people find the sight of very many of them in wind parks unattractive. The blades are susceptible to stresses in high winds and damage due to metal fatigue frequently occurs. Serious power production from wind occurs at wind speeds from 6 to 14 m s^{-1}. But the design must also take into account gale-force winds, which may be very rare for a particular site, but would result in damage to an inadequately designed system. About 30% of the power carried by the wind can be converted into electricity (Figure **8.13**).

Let us consider the mass of air that can pass through a tube of cross-sectional area A with velocity v in time Δt (Figure **8.14**). Let ρ be the

Figure 8.12 An array of sea-based horizontal axis wind turbines.

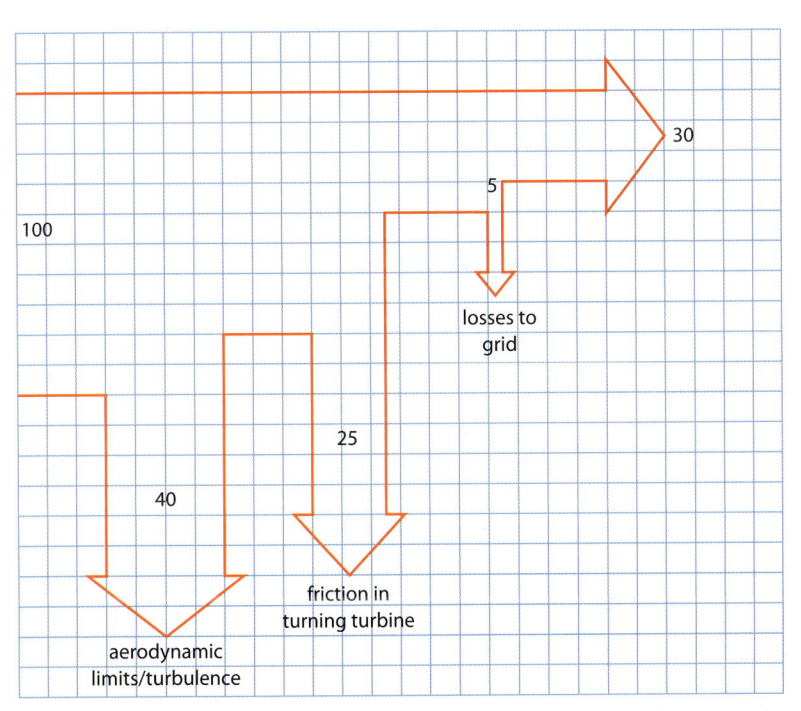

Figure 8.13 A Sankey diagram for wind energy extraction. The main loss comes from the fact the wind cannot just stop past the generator.

8 ENERGY PRODUCTION 325

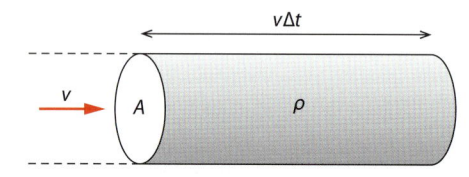

Figure 8.14 The mass of air within this cylinder will exit the right end within a time of Δt.

Exam tip: Wind power
Advantages
- 'Free'
- Inexhaustible
- Clean

Disadvantages
- Dependent on local wind conditions
- Aesthetic problems
- Noise problems

density of air. Then the mass enclosed in a tube of length $v\Delta t$ is $\rho A v \Delta t$. This is the mass that will exit the right end of the tube **within** a time interval equal to Δt. The kinetic energy of this mass of air is thus:

$$\tfrac{1}{2}(\rho A v \Delta t)v^2 = \tfrac{1}{2}\rho A \Delta t v^3$$

The kinetic energy per unit time is the power, and so dividing by Δt we find:

$$P = \tfrac{1}{2}\rho A v^3$$

This shows that the power carried by the wind is proportional to the cube of the wind speed and proportional to the area spanned by the blades.

Assuming a wind speed of $8.0\,\mathrm{m\,s^{-1}}$, an air density of $1.2\,\mathrm{kg\,m^{-3}}$ and a blade radius of $1.5\,\mathrm{m}$ (so area $7.1\,\mathrm{m^2}$) we find a theoretical maximum power of:

$$P = \tfrac{1}{2}\rho A v^3$$

$$P = \tfrac{1}{2} \times 1.2 \times 7.1 \times 8.0^3$$

$$P \approx 2.2\,\mathrm{kW}$$

Doubling the wind turbine area doubles the power extracted, but doubling the wind speed increases the power (in theory) by a factor of eight. In practice, frictional and other losses (mainly turbulence) result in a smaller power increase. The calculations above also assume that all the wind is actually **stopped** by the wind turbine, extracting all of the wind's kinetic energy. In practice this is not the case (Figure 8.15).

Figure 8.15 The 'wake' effect created by wind as it goes past one generator affects other generators down the line, decreasing the expected power output of the windmill 'farm'.

Nature of science

Society demands action

Society's demand for ever-increasing amounts of energy raises ethical debates. How can present and future energy needs be best met, without compromising the future of the planet? There are many aspects to the energy debate, and all energy sources have associated risks, benefits and costs. Although not all governments and people support the development of renewable energy sources, scientists across the globe continue to collaborate to develop new technologies that can reduce our dependence on non-renewable energy sources.

? Test yourself

1. **a** Distinguish between specific energy and energy density of a fuel.
   b Estimate the energy density of water that falls from a waterfall of height 75 m and is used to drive a turbine.

2. A power plant produces 500 MW of power.
   a Determine the energy produced in one second. Express your answer in joules.
   b Determine the energy (in joules) produced in one year.

3. A power plant operates in four stages. The efficiency in each stage is 80%, 40%, 12% and 65%.
   a Find the overall efficiency of the plant.
   b Sketch a Sankey diagram for the energy flow in this plant.

4. A coal power plant with 30% efficiency burns 10 million kilograms of coal a day. (Take the specific energy of coal to be 30 MJ kg^{-1}.)
   a Calculate the power output of the plant.
   b Estimate the rate at which thermal energy is being discarded by this plant.
   c The discarded thermal energy is carried away by water whose temperature is not allowed to increase by more than 5 °C. Calculate the rate at which water must flow away from the plant.

5. One litre of gasoline releases 34 MJ of energy when burned. The efficiency of a car operating on this gasoline is 40%. The speed of the car is 9.0 m s^{-1} when the power developed by the engine is 20 kW. Calculate how many kilometres the car can go with one litre of gasoline when driven at this speed.

6. A coal-burning power plant produces 1.0 GW of electricity. The overall efficiency of the power plant is 40%. Taking the specific energy of coal to be 30 MJ kg^{-1}, calculate the amount of coal that must be burned in one day.

7. In the context of nuclear fission reactors, state what is meant by:
   a uranium enrichment
   b moderator
   c critical mass.

8. **a** Calculate the energy released in the fission reaction:
   $$^{1}_{0}n + ^{235}_{92}U \rightarrow ^{236}_{92}U \rightarrow ^{140}_{54}Xe + ^{94}_{38}Sr + 2^{1}_{0}n$$
   (Mass data: uranium-235, $^{235}_{92}U$ = 235.043 923 u; xenon-140, $^{140}_{54}Xe$ = 139.921 636 u; strontium-94, $^{94}_{38}Sr$ = 93.915 360 u; neutron, $^{1}_{0}n$ = 1.008 665 u.)
   b The power output is 200 MW. Estimate the number of fission reactions per second.

9. The energy released in a typical fission reaction involving uranium-235 is 200 MeV.
   a Calculate the specific energy of uranium-235.
   b Estimate how much coal (specific energy 30 MJ kg^{-1}) must be burned in order to give the same energy as that released in nuclear fission with 1 kg of uranium-235.

10. **a** A 500 MW nuclear power plant converts the energy released in nuclear reactions into electrical energy with an efficiency of 40%. Calculate how many fissions of uranium-235 are required per second. Take the energy released per reaction to be 200 MeV.
    b What mass of uranium-235 is required to fission per second?

11. **a** Draw a diagram of a fission reactor, explaining the role of **i** fuel rods, **ii** control rods and **iii** moderator.
    b In what form is the energy released in a fission reactor?

12. Distinguish between a solar panel and a photovoltaic cell.

13. Sunlight of intensity 700 W m^{-2} is captured with 70% efficiency by a solar panel, which then sends the captured energy into a house with 50% efficiency.
    a The house loses thermal energy through bad insulation at a rate of 3.0 kW. Find the area of the solar panel needed in order to keep the temperature of the house constant.
    b Draw a Sankey diagram for the energy flow from the panel to the house.

8 ENERGY PRODUCTION

14 A solar heater is to heat 300 kg of water initially at 15 °C to a temperature of 50 °C in a time of 12 hours. The amount of solar radiation falling on the collecting surface of the solar panel is 240 W m^{-2} and is collected at an efficiency of 65%. Calculate the area of the collecting panel that is required.

15 A solar heater is to warm 150 kg of water by 30 K. The intensity of solar radiation is 600 W m^{-2} and the area of the panels is 4.0 m^{-2}. The specific heat capacity of water is 4.2×10^3 J kg^{-1} K^{-1}. Estimate the time this will take, assuming a solar panel efficiency of 60%.

16 The graph shows the variation with incident solar intensity I of the temperature of a solar panel used to heat water. Thermal energy is extracted from the water at a rate of 320 W. The area of the panel is 2.0 m^2. Calculate, for a solar intensity of 400 W m^{-2}:

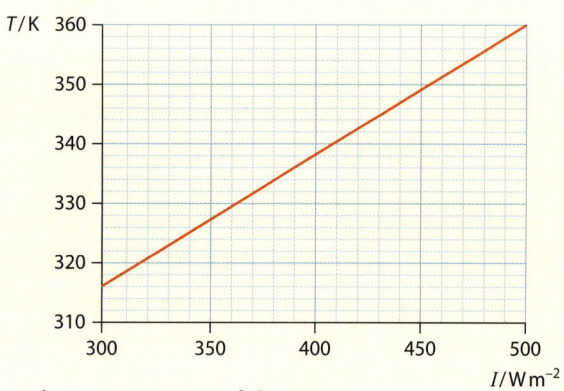

   a the temperature of the water
   b the power incident on the panel
   c the efficiency of the panel.

17 The graph shows the power curve of a wind turbine as a function of the wind speed. For a wind speed of 10 m s^{-1}, calculate the energy produced in the course of one year, assuming that the wind blows at this speed for 1000 hours in the year.

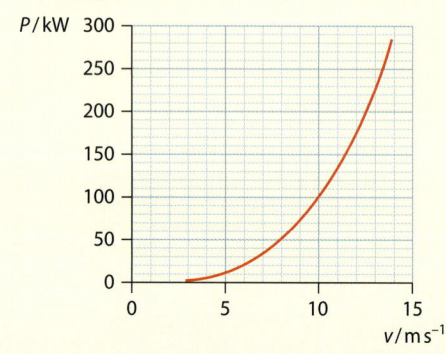

18 a State the expected increase in the power extracted from a wind turbine when:
   i the length of the blades is doubled
   ii the wind speed is doubled
   iii both the length of the blades and the wind speed are doubled.
   b Outline reasons why the actual increase in the extracted power will be less than your answers.

19 Wind of speed v is incident on the blades of a wind turbine. The blades present the wind with an area A. The maximum theoretical power that can be extracted is given by:

$$P = \tfrac{1}{2}\rho A v^3$$

State the assumptions made in deriving this equation.

20 Air of density 1.2 kg m^{-3} and speed 8.0 m s^{-1} is incident on the blades of a wind turbine. The radius of the blades is 1.5 m. Immediately after passing through the blades, the wind speed is reduced to 3.0 m s^{-1} and the density of air is 1.8 kg m^{-3}. Estimate the power extracted from the wind.

21 Calculate the blade radius of a wind turbine that must extract 25 kW of power out of wind of speed 9.0 s^{-1}. The density of air is 1.2 kg m^{-3}. State any assumptions made in this calculation.

22 Find the power developed when water in a waterfall with a flow rate of 500 kg s^{-1} falls from a height of 40 m.

23 Water falls from a vertical height h at a flow rate (volume per second) Q. Deduce that the maximum theoretical power that can be extracted is given by $P = \rho Q g h$.

24 A student explaining pumped storage systems says that the water that is stored at a high elevation is allowed to move lower, thus producing electricity. Some of this electricity is used to raise the water back to its original height, and the process is then repeated. What is wrong with this statement?

25 Make an annotated energy flow diagram showing the energy changes that are taking place in each of the following:
   a a conventional electricity-producing power station using coal
   b a hydroelectric power plant
   c an electricity-producing wind turbine
   d an electricity-producing nuclear power station.

8.2 Thermal energy transfer

This section deals with the methods of heat transfer and the role of the greenhouse effect in the physical mechanisms that control the energy balance of the Earth. The important phenomenon of black-body radiation is introduced along with the associated Stefan–Boltzmann and Wien laws.

Conduction, convection and thermal radiation

Heat can be transferred from place to place by three distinct methods: conduction, convection and radiation.

Imagine a solid with one end kept at a high temperature, as shown in Figure 8.16. The electrons at the hot end of the solid have a high average kinetic energy. This means they move a lot. The moving electrons collide with neighbouring molecules, transferring energy to them and so increasing their average kinetic energy. This means that energy is being transferred from the hot to the cold side of the solid; this is **conduction**.

Collisions between electrons and molecules is the dominant way in which heat is transferred by conduction, but if there are strong bonds between molecules there is another way. Molecules on the hot side of the solid vibrate about their equilibrium positions, stretching the bonds with neighbouring molecules. This stretching forces the neighbours to also begin to vibrate, and so the average kinetic energy of the neighbours increases. Energy is again transferred.

For a solid of cross-sectional area A, length L and temperature difference between its ends ΔT, experiments show that the rate at which energy is being transferred is:

$$\frac{\Delta Q}{\Delta t} = kA \frac{\Delta T}{L}$$

where k is called the conductivity and depends on the nature of the substance.

Convection is a method of energy transfer that applies mainly to fluids, i.e. gases and liquids. If you put a pan of water on a stove, the water at the bottom of the pan is heated. As it gets hotter the water expands, it gets less dense and so rises to the top. In this way heat from the bottom of the pan is transferred to the top. Similarly, air over a hot radiator in a room is heated, expands and rises, transferring warm air to the rest of the room. Colder air takes the place of the air that rose and the process repeats, creating **convection currents**.

Both conduction and convection require a material medium through which heat is to be transferred. The third method of heat transfer, **radiation**, does not. Energy from the Sun has been warming the Earth for billions of years. This energy arrives at Earth as radiation having travelled through the vacuum of space at the speed of light. Radiation is such an important part of climate and the energy balance of the Earth that we treat it in a separate section.

Learning objectives

- Understand the ways in which heat may be transferred.
- Sketch and interpret black-body curves.
- Solve problems using the Stefan–Boltzmann and Wien laws.
- Describe the greenhouse effect.
- Apply the Stefan–Boltzmann law to solve energy balance problems for the Earth.

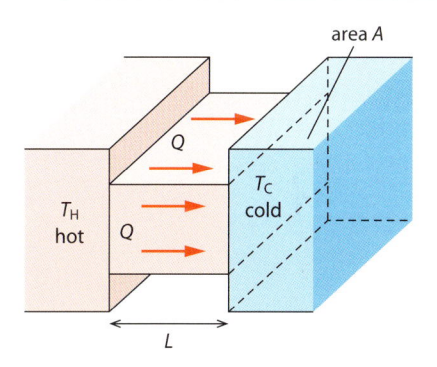

Figure 8.16 Conduction of heat through a solid as a result of a temperature difference.

Exam tip
You will not be examined on this equation.

Black-body radiation

One of the great advances in physics in the 19th century was the discovery that all bodies that are kept at some **absolute** (kelvin) temperature T radiate energy in the form of electromagnetic waves. This is radiation created by oscillating electric charges in the atoms of the body. The power radiated by a body is governed by the **Stefan–Boltzmann law**.

The amount of energy per second (i.e. the power) radiated by a body depends on its surface area A and the absolute temperature of the surface T:

$$P = e\sigma A T^4$$

This is known as the Stefan–Boltzmann law. The constant σ is known as the Stefan–Boltzmann constant and equals $\sigma = 5.67 \times 10^{-8}\,\text{W}\,\text{m}^{-2}\,\text{K}^{-4}$.

The constant e is known as the **emissivity** of the surface. Its value is between 0 and 1; it measures how effectively a body radiates. When $e = 1$ we call the body a **black body**. This is a theoretical body; it is a perfect radiator as well as a perfect absorber. A black body will absorb all the radiation falling upon it, reflecting none. This does sound somewhat strange, but a black body at low temperature radiates very little and absorbs all the radiation falling on it so it looks black. At high temperature it radiates a lot and looks very bright. A very good example of this is a piece of charcoal. A real body is a good approximation to the theoretical black body if its surface is black and dull.

Consider a body of emissivity e and surface temperature T whose surroundings have a temperature T_s and may be assumed to be a black body. The body radiates at a rate $e\sigma A T^4$ and absorbs at a rate $e\sigma A T_s^4$. The *net rate* at which energy leaves the body is therefore:

$$P_{\text{net}} = e\sigma A T^4 - e\sigma A T_s^4$$

$$P_{\text{net}} = e\sigma A (T^4 - T_s^4)$$

At equilibrium no net power leaves the body and so $T = T_s$, as we might expect. Table **8.3** gives values for the emissivity of various surfaces.

The energy radiated by a body is electromagnetic radiation and is distributed over an infinite range of wavelengths. However, most of the energy is radiated at a specific wavelength λ_{max} that is determined by the temperature of the body:

$$\lambda_{\text{max}} T = 2.90 \times 10^{-3}\,\text{K}\,\text{m}$$

This is known as **Wien's displacement law**.

Surface	Emissivity
black body	1
ocean water	0.8
ice	0.1
dry land	0.7
land with vegetation	0.6

Table 8.3 Emissivity of various surfaces.

Worked example

8.7 A human body has temperature 37 °C, the average Earth surface temperature is 288 K and the temperature of the Sun is 5800 K. In each case, calculate the peak wavelength of the emitted radiation.

We just have to apply Wien's law, $\lambda_{max} T = 2.90 \times 10^{-3}$ K m, and make sure we use kelvins in each case. So:

human body: $\lambda_{max} = \dfrac{2.90 \times 10^{-3}}{273 + 37} \approx 9 \times 10^{-6}$ m, an infrared wavelength.

Earth surface: $\lambda_{max} = \dfrac{2.90 \times 10^{-3}}{288} \approx 1 \times 10^{-5}$ m, an infrared wavelength.

Sun: $\lambda_{max} = \dfrac{2.90 \times 10^{-3}}{5800} \approx 5 \times 10^{-7}$ m, visible light that determines the colour of the Sun.

Figure **8.17** shows how the intensity of radiation emitted from the same surface changes as the temperature of the surface is varied ($T = 350$ K, 300 K and 273 K). We see that, with increasing temperature, the peak of the curve occurs at lower wavelengths and the height of the peak increases.

Figure **8.18** shows the intensity distribution of radiation from various different surfaces kept at the same temperature (300 K). The difference in the curves is due to the different emissivities ($e = 1.0$, 0.8 and 0.2). The curves are identical apart from an overall factor that shrinks the height of the curve as the emissivity decreases.

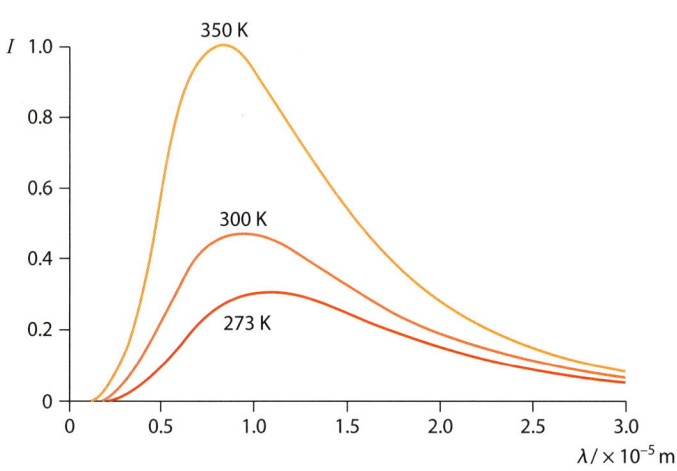

Figure 8.17 Black-body spectra for a body at the three temperatures shown. The units on the vertical axis are arbitrary. (The curves appear to start from a finite value of wavelength. This is not the case. The curves start at zero wavelength but are too small to appear on the graphs.)

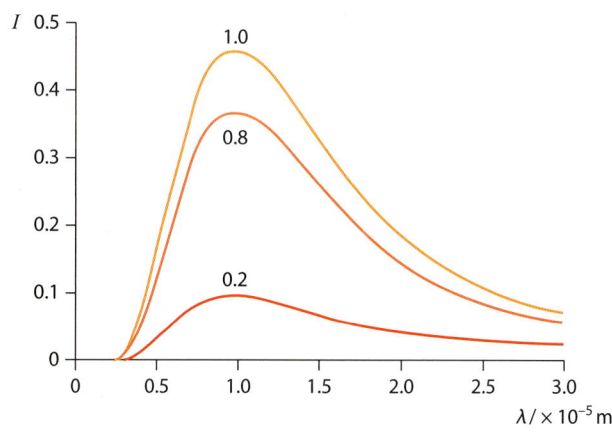

Figure 8.18 The spectra of three bodies with different emissivities at the same temperature (300 K). The units on the vertical axis are arbitrary.

Worked examples

8.8 By what factor does the power emitted by a body increase when the temperature is increased from 100 °C to 200 °C?

The temperature in kelvin increases from 373 K to 473 K. Since the emitted power is proportional to the fourth power of the temperature, power will increase by a factor:

$$\left(\frac{473}{373}\right)^4 = 2.59$$

8 ENERGY PRODUCTION

8.9 The emissivity of the naked human body may be taken to be $e = 0.90$. Assuming a body temperature of 37 °C and a body surface area of 1.60 m², calculate the total amount of energy lost by the body when exposed to a temperature of 0.0 °C for 30 minutes.

The net power lost is the difference between the power emitted by the body and the power received. Let the body temperature be T_1 and the temperature of the surroundings be T_2. Then:

$$P_{net} = e\sigma A(T_1^4 - T_2^4)$$

Substituting the values from the question:

$P_{net} = 0.90 \times 5.67 \times 10^{-8} \times 1.60 \times (310^4 - 273^4)$

$P_{net} = 301 \text{ W}$

Exam tip
Make sure the temperature is in kelvin.

So the energy lost in time t seconds is:

$E = P_{net} t$

$E = 301 \times 30 \times 60$

$E = 5.4 \times 10^5 \text{ J}$

(What does this mean for the human body? For the purposes of an estimate, assume that the body has mass 60 kg and is made out of water, with specific heat capacity $c = 4200 \text{ J kg}^{-1} \text{ K}^{-1}$. This energy loss would result in a drop in body temperature of $\Delta T = \dfrac{5.4 \times 10^5}{60 \times 4200} = 2.1 \text{ K}$. This would be serious! However, it ignores the fact that respiration provides a source of energy.)

The solar constant

The Sun may be considered to radiate as a perfect emitter (i.e. as a black body). The Sun emits a total power of about $P = 3.9 \times 10^{26}$ W. The average Earth–Sun distance is $d = 1.50 \times 10^{11}$ m. Imagine a sphere of this radius centred at the Sun. The power of the Sun is distributed over the area of this sphere and so the power per unit area, i.e. the **intensity**, received by Earth is:

$$I = \dfrac{P}{4\pi d^2}$$

Intensity is the power of radiation received per unit area.

Substituting the numerical values gives:

$$I = \dfrac{3.9 \times 10^{26}}{4\pi (1.50 \times 10^{11})^2} \approx 1400 \text{ W m}^{-2}$$

This is the intensity of the solar radiation at the top of the Earth's atmosphere. It is called the **solar constant** and is denoted by S.

If we know that radiation of intensity I is incident on a surface of area A, we can calculate the **power** delivered to that area from:

$P = IA$

Albedo

The **albedo** (from the Latin for 'white'), α, of a body is defined as the ratio of the power of radiation scattered from the body to the total power incident on the body:

$$\alpha = \frac{\text{total scattered power}}{\text{total incident power}}$$

The albedo is a dimensionless number. Snow has a high albedo (0.85), indicating that snow reflects most of the radiation incident on it, whereas charcoal has an albedo of only 0.04, meaning that it reflects very little of the light incident on it. The Earth as a whole has an average global albedo that is about 0.3. The albedo of the Earth varies. The variations depend on the time of the year (many or few clouds), latitude (a lot of snow and ice or very little), on whether one is over desert land (high albedo, 0.3–0.4), forests (low albedo, 0.1) or water (low albedo, 0.1), etc.

The calculation of the solar constant as $S = 1400\,\text{W}\,\text{m}^{-2}$ is the value at the upper atmosphere. The radiation that reaches the Earth has to go through the area of a disc of radius R. The power through this disc is therefore:

$P = S\pi R^2$

where R is the radius of the Earth (Figure **8.19**). The albedo of the Earth is α, and so a fraction $\alpha S\pi R^2$ of the incident power is reflected, leaving $(1 - \alpha)S\pi R^2$ to reach Earth. Clearly, the Earth's surface receives radiation during the day, when it faces the Sun. But if we want to define a night and day average of the incident intensity I_{av} we must divide the power through the disc by the total surface area of the Earth to get:

$$I_{av} = \frac{(1-\alpha)S\pi R^2}{4\pi R^2}$$

$$I_{av} = \frac{(1-\alpha)S}{4}$$

This average intensity amounts to $\frac{0.7 \times 1400}{4} = 245\,\text{W}\,\text{m}^{-2}$.

In other words, at any moment of the day or night, anywhere on Earth, one square metre of the surface may be thought to receive 245 J of energy every second.

Exam tip
The solar constant S is intensity. Intensity is power per unit area so:

$P = SA$

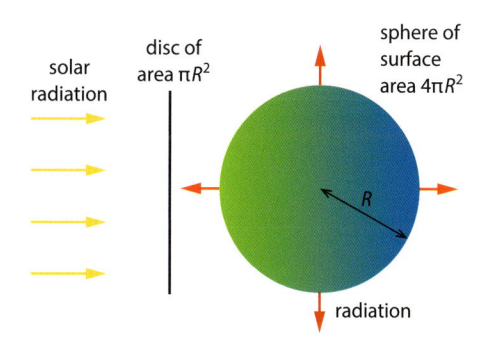

Figure 8.19 The radiation reaching the Earth must first go through a disc of area πR^2, where R is the radius of the Earth.

Energy balance

We are interested in the average temperature of the Earth. If this temperature is constant then the energy input to the Earth must equal (balance) the energy output by the Earth (Figure **8.20**).

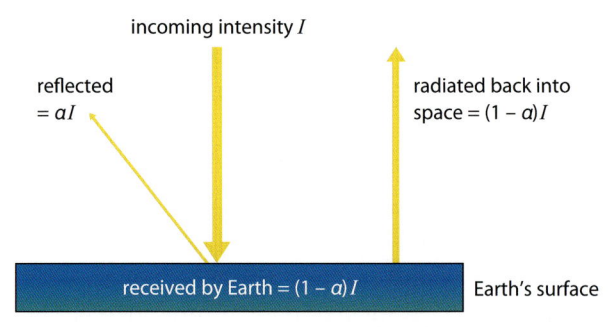

Figure 8.20 Energy diagram showing energy transfers in a model without an atmosphere. Note that the energy in equals the energy out.

The next worked example introduces a first glimpse of an **energy balance equation**.

Worked example

8.10 Assume that the Earth surface has a fixed temperature T and that it radiates as a black body. The average incoming solar radiation reaching the surface has intensity $I_{av} = \dfrac{(1-\alpha)S}{4} = 245 \text{ W m}^{-2}$. Ignore the effect of the atmosphere (other than the fact that is has reflected 30% of the incoming radiation back into space!).
  a Write down an equation expressing the fact that the power received by the Earth equals the power radiated by the Earth into space (an energy balance equation).
  b Solve the equation to calculate the constant Earth temperature.
  c Comment on your answer.

a The average intensity reaching the surface is:

$$I_{av} = \dfrac{(1-\alpha)S}{4} = 245 \text{ W m}^{-2}$$

The Earth radiates power from the entire surface area of its spherical shape, and so the power radiated, P_{out} (by the Stefan–Boltzmann law), is:

$$P_{out} = \sigma A T^4$$

(Here we are assuming that the Earth is a black body, so $e = 1$ and the surrounding space is taken to have a temperature of $0\,\text{K}$.) So the intensity radiated by the Earth, I_{out}, is:

$$I_{out} = \dfrac{P_{out}}{A} = \sigma T^4$$

Equating the incident and outgoing intensities we get:

$$\dfrac{(1-\alpha)S}{4} = \sigma T^4$$

b Solving the equation, we find:

$$T = \sqrt[4]{\frac{(1-\alpha)S}{4\sigma}}$$

This evaluates to:

$$T = \sqrt[4]{\frac{245}{5.67 \times 10^{-8}}} = 256 \text{ K}$$

This temperature is −17 °C.

c It is perhaps surprising that this extremely simple model has given an answer that is not off by orders of magnitude! But a temperature of 256 K is 32 K lower than the Earth's average temperature of 288 K, and so obviously the model is too simplistic. One reason this model is too simple is precisely because we have not taken into account the fact that not all the power radiated by the Earth actually escapes. Some of the power is absorbed by the gases in the atmosphere and is re-radiated back down to the Earth's surface, causing further warming that we have neglected to take into account. In other words, this model neglects the greenhouse effect. This simple model also points to the general fact that increasing the albedo (more energy reflected) results in lower temperatures.

Another drawback of the simple model presented above is that the model is essentially a zero-dimensional model. The Earth is treated as a point without interactions between the surface and the atmosphere. (Latent heat flows, thermal energy flow in oceans through currents, thermal energy transfer between the surface and the atmosphere due to temperature differences between the two, are all ignored.) Realistic models must take all these factors (and many others) into account, and so are very complex.

The greenhouse effect

The Earth's surface radiates as all warm bodies do. But the Earth's surface is at an average temperature of 288 K and, using Wien's law, we saw in Worked example **8.7** that the peak wavelength at which this energy is radiated is an infrared wavelength. Unlike visible light wavelengths, which pass through the atmosphere mainly unobstructed, infrared radiation is strongly absorbed by various gases in the atmosphere, the so-called **greenhouse gases**. This radiation is in turn re-radiated by these gases in all directions. This means that some of this radiation is received by the Earth's surface again, causing additional warming (Figure **8.21**).

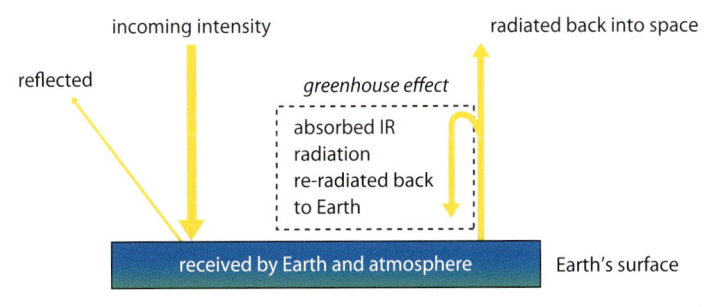

Figure 8.21 A simplified energy flow diagram to illustrate the greenhouse effect.

This is radiation that would be lost in space were it not for the greenhouse gases. Without this **greenhouse effect**, the Earth's temperature would be 32 K lower than what it is now.

> The **greenhouse effect** may be described as the warming of the Earth caused by infrared radiation, emitted by the Earth's surface, which is absorbed by various gases in the Earth's atmosphere and is then partly re-radiated towards the surface. The gases primarily responsible for this absorption (the **greenhouse gases**) are water vapour, carbon dioxide, methane and nitrous oxide.

The greenhouse effect is thus a **natural** consequence of the presence of the atmosphere. There is, however, also the **enhanced** greenhouse effect, which refers to additional warming due to **increased** quantities of the greenhouse gases in the atmosphere. The increases in the gas concentrations are due to human activity.

The main greenhouse gases are water vapour (H_2O), carbon dioxide (CO_2), methane (CH_4) and nitrous oxide (N_2O). Greenhouse gases in the atmosphere have natural as well as man-made (anthropogenic) origins (Table 8.4). Along with these sources of the greenhouse gases, we have 'sinks' as well, that is to say, mechanisms that reduce these concentrations. For example, carbon dioxide is absorbed by plants during photosynthesis and is dissolved in oceans.

Greenhouse gas	Natural sources	Anthropogenic sources
H_2O	evaporation of water from oceans, rivers and lakes	irrigation
CO_2	forest fires, volcanic eruptions, evaporation of water from oceans	burning fossil fuels in power plants and cars, burning forests
CH_4	wetlands, oceans, lakes and rivers, termites	flooded rice fields, farm animals, processing of coal, natural gas and oil, burning biomass
N_2O	forests, oceans, soil and grasslands	burning fossil fuels, manufacture of cement, fertilisers, deforestation (reduction of nitrogen fixation in plants)

Table 8.4 Sources of greenhouse gases.

Mechanism of photon absorption

As for atoms, the energy of molecules is discrete. There are energy levels corresponding to the energy of molecules due to their vibrational and rotational motion. The difference in energy between molecular energy levels is approximately the energy of an infrared photon. This means that infrared photons travelling through greenhouse gases will be absorbed. The gas molecules that have absorbed the photons will now be excited to higher energy levels. But the molecules prefer to be in low-energy states, and so they immediately make a transition to a lower-energy state by emitting the photons they absorbed. But these photons are not all emitted outwards into space. Some are emitted back towards the Earth, thereby warming the Earth's surface (Figure 8.22).

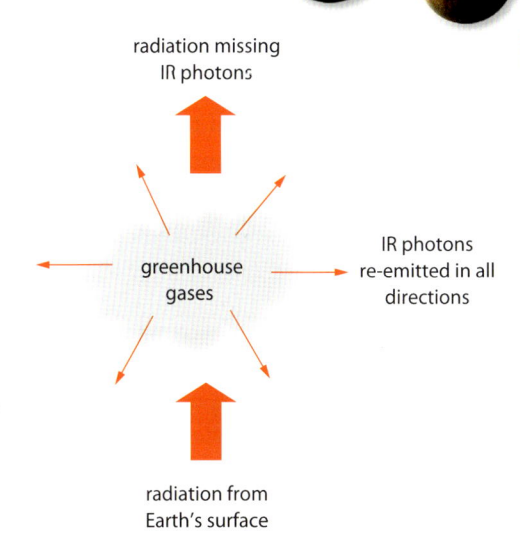

Figure 8.22 Greenhouse gases absorb infrared (IR) photons and re-radiate them in all directions.

Worked example

8.11 One consequence of warming of the Earth is that more water will evaporate from the oceans. Predict whether this fact alone will tend to increase the temperature of the Earth further or whether it will tend to reduce it.

Evaporating means that energy must be supplied to water to turn it into vapour and so this energy will have to come from the atmosphere, reducing its temperature. Further, there will be more cloud cover, so more solar radiation will be reflected back into space, further reducing temperatures. This is an example of negative feedback: the temperature increases for some reason but the effect of this increase is a tendency of the temperature to decrease and not increase further. (There is, however, another factor of **positive feedback** that will tend to increase temperatures: evaporating water means that the carbon dioxide that was dissolved in the water will now return to the atmosphere!) To decide the overall effect, detailed calculations are necessary. (Negative feedback wins in this case.)

Nature of science

Simple and complex modelling

In Topic 3 we met the kinetic theory of gases. This simple mathematical model can predict the behaviour of real gases to a good approximation. By contrast, to reach reliable predictions about climate change and its consequences, very complex and time-consuming modelling is required. Models for climate behaviour are complex because of the very large number of parameters involved, the interdependence of these parameters on various kinds of feedback effects and the sensitivity of the equations on the initial values of the parameters. This makes predictions somewhat less certain than we would like. Advances in computing power, the availability of more data and further testing and debate on the various models will improve our ability to predict climate change more accurately in the future.

Test yourself

26 A cylindrical solid tube is made out of two smaller tubes, X and Y, of different material. X and Y have the same length and cross-sectional area. The tube is used to conduct energy from a hot to a cold reservoir.

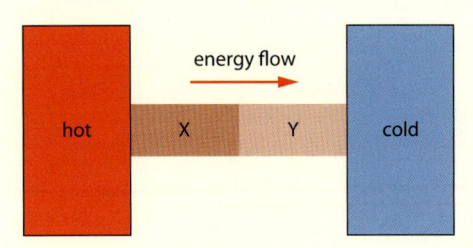

State and explain whether the following are equal or not:
- **a** the rates of flow of energy through X and Y
- **b** the temperature differences across X and Y.

27 Suggest whether there is any point in using a ceiling fan in winter.

28 Calculate the ratio of the power radiated per unit area from two black bodies at temperature 900 K and 300 K.

29
- **a** State what you understand by the term **black body**.
- **b** Give an example of a body that is a good approximation to a black body.
- **c** By what factor does the rate of radiation from a body increase when the temperature is increased from 50 °C to 100 °C?

30 The graph shows the variation with wavelength of the intensity of radiation emitted by two bodies of identical shape.

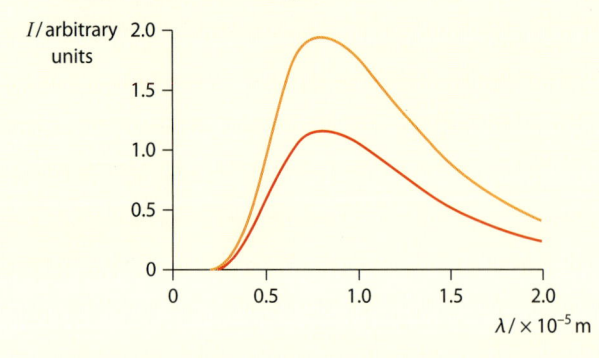

- **a** Explain why the temperature of the two bodies is the same.
- **b** The upper line corresponds to a black body. Calculate the emissivity of the other body.

31 The total power radiated by a body of area 5.00 km² and emissivity 0.800 is 1.35×10^9 W. Assume that the body radiates into a vacuum at temperature 0 K. Calculate the temperature of the body.

32 Assume that the distance d between the Sun and the Earth decreases. Then the Earth's average temperature T will go up. The fraction of the power radiated by the Sun that is received on Earth is proportional to $\frac{1}{d^2}$; the power radiated by the Earth is proportional to T^4.
- **a** Deduce the dependence of the temperature T of the Earth on the distance d.
- **b** Hence estimate the expected rise in temperature if the distance decreases by 1.0%. Take the average temperature of the Earth to be 288 K.

33
- **a** Define the term **intensity** in the context of radiation.
- **b** **Estimate** the intensity of radiation emitted by a naked human body of surface area 1.60 m², temperature 37 °C and emissivity 0.90, a distance of 5.0 m from the body.

34 A body radiates energy at a rate (power) P.
- **a** Deduce that the intensity of this radiation at distance d from the body is given by:
$$I = \frac{P}{4\pi d^2}$$
- **b** State **one** assumption made in deriving this result.

35 The graph shows the variation with wavelength of the intensity of the radiation emitted by a black body.

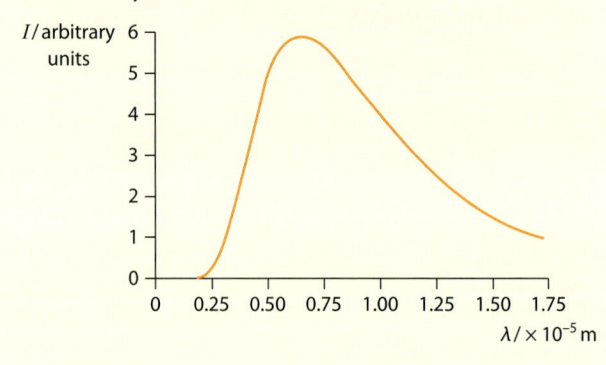

a Determine the temperature of the black body.
b Copy the diagram and, on the same axes, draw a graph to show the variation with wavelength of the intensity of radiation emitted by a black body of temperature 600 K.

36 a Define the term **albedo**.
b State **three** factors that the albedo of a surface depends on.

37 a State what is meant by the **greenhouse effect**.
b State the main greenhouse gases in the Earth's atmosphere, and for each give **three** natural and **three** man-made sources.

38 A researcher uses the following data for a simple climatic model of an Earth without an atmosphere (see Worked example 8.10): incident solar radiation = 350 W m^{-2}, absorbed solar radiation = 250 W m^{-2}.
a Make an energy flow diagram for these data.
b Determine the average albedo for the Earth that is to be used in the modelling.
c Determine the intensity of the outgoing long-wave radiation.
d Estimate the temperature of the Earth according to this model, assuming a constant Earth temperature.

39 The diagram shows a more involved model of the greenhouse effect.

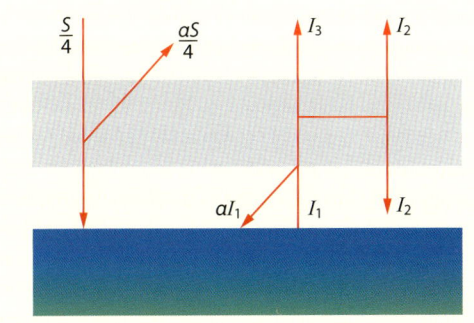

Exam tip
You will not get anything as complicated as this in the exam, but this is excellent practice in understanding energy balance equations.

The average incoming radiation intensity is $\frac{S}{4} = 350$ W m^{-2}. The albedo of the atmosphere is 0.300. Assume that only a fraction t of the energy radiated by the Earth actually escapes the Earth and that the surface behaves as a black body. The model assumes that part of the radiation from the Earth is reflected back down from the atmosphere.

a The intensity radiated by the Earth is I_1, the intensity radiated by the atmosphere is I_2 and the fraction of the intensity escaping the Earth is I_3. By examining the energy balance of the atmosphere and the surface separately, show that:

$$I_1 = \frac{2}{1-\alpha+t} \times \frac{(1-\alpha)S}{4},$$

$$I_2 = \frac{1-\alpha-t}{1-\alpha+t} \times \frac{(1-\alpha)S}{4} \text{ and}$$

$$I_3 = \frac{2t}{1-\alpha+t} \times \frac{(1-\alpha)S}{4}$$

b Show that as much energy enters the Earth–atmosphere system as leaves it.
c Show that a surface temperature of $T \approx 288$ K implies that $t = 0.556$.
d i Explain why the emissivity of the atmosphere is $1 - t - \alpha$.
   ii Calculate the temperature of the atmosphere.

40 Outline the main ways in which the surface of the Earth loses thermal energy to the atmosphere and to space.

41 a Compare the albedo of a subtropical, warm, dry land with that of a tropical ocean.
b Suggest mechanisms through which the subtropical land and the tropical ocean lose thermal energy to the atmosphere.
c If the sea level were to increase, sea water would cover dry land. Suggest **one** change in the regional climate that might come about as a result.

42 Evaporation is a method of thermal energy loss. Explain whether you would expect this method to be more significant for a tropical ocean or an arctic ocean.

43 The diagram shows two energy flow diagrams for thermal energy transfer to and from specific areas of the surface of the Earth. R represents the net energy incident on the surface in the form of radiation, E is the thermal energy lost from the Earth due to evaporation, and C is the thermal energy conducted to the atmosphere because of the temperature difference between the surface and the atmosphere.
Suggest whether the Earth area in each diagram is most likely to be dry and cool or moist and warm.

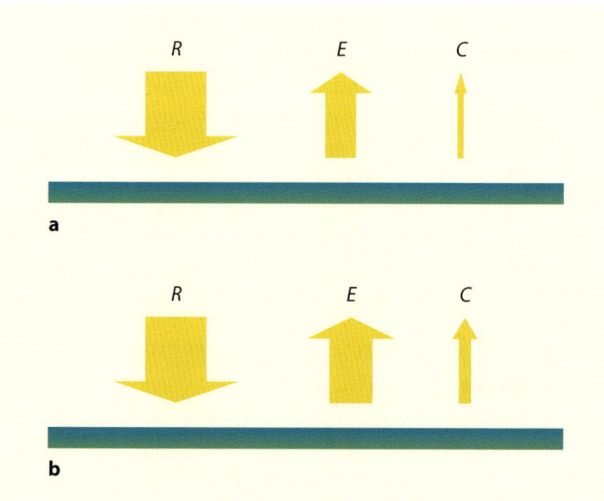

44 It is estimated that a change of albedo by 0.01 will result in a 1 °C temperature change. A large area of the Earth consists of 60% water and 40% land. Calculate the expected change in temperature if melting ice causes a change in the proportion of the area covered by water from 60% to 70%. Take the albedo of dry land to be 0.30 and that of water to be 0.10.

Exam-style questions

1 A power plant produces 500 MW of electrical power with an overall efficiency of 20%. What is the input power to the plant?

    A 100 MW   **B** 400 MW   **C** 625 MW   **D** 2500 MW

2 The specific energy of a fuel is the:

    A energy that can be extracted from a unit volume of the fuel
    B energy that can be extracted from a unit mass of the fuel
    C energy contained in a unit volume of the fuel
    D energy contained in a unit mass of the fuel.

3 What is the efficiency of a system whose Sankey diagram is shown below?

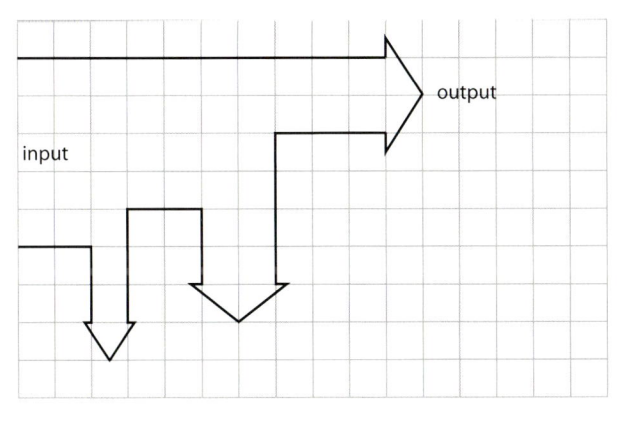

    A 10%   **B** 20%   **C** 30%   **D** 40%

4 Which of the following lists contains one renewable and one non-renewable source of power?

    A uranium, coal
    B natural gas, biomass
    C wind power, wave power
    D hydropower, solar power

5 A plastic ruler and a metallic ruler are in the same room. The metallic ruler 'feels' colder when touched. What is the reason for this?

    A Plastic has a lower specific heat capacity than metal.
    B Plastic has a higher specific heat capacity than metal.
    C Plastic is a better conductor of heat than metal
    D Plastic is a worse conductor of heat than metal.

6 A fireplace warms a room by:

    A conduction
    B convection
    C radiation
    D conduction, convection and radiation

7 A star explodes in the vacuum of space. The thermal energy transferred by the star takes place through:

    A radiation   **B** conduction   **C** convection   **D** evaporation

8 Four different rooms are losing energy to the outside through a wall. The temperature difference between the inside and the outside of the rooms is the same. Which combination of wall area and wall thickness results in the smallest rate of heat loss?

	Area	Thickness
A	S	d
B	$2S$	$\frac{d}{2}$
C	S	$2d$
D	$2S$	$2d$

9 The graph shows the variation with wavelength of the intensity from a unit area of a black body. The scale on the vertical axis on all graphs in this question is the same.

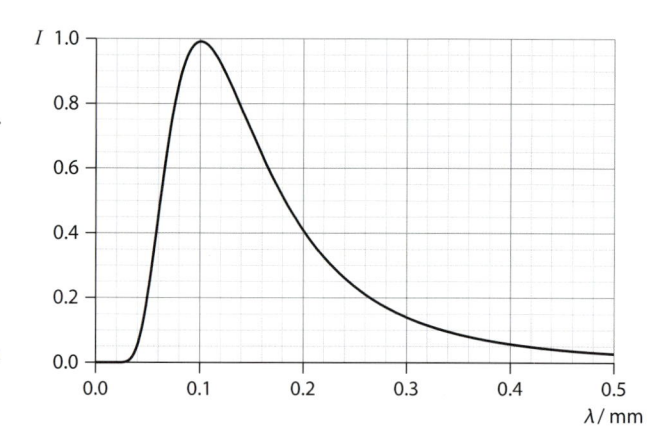

The area and the temperature of the black body are both halved. Which graph now shows the correct variation with wavelength of the intensity from a unit area of the body?

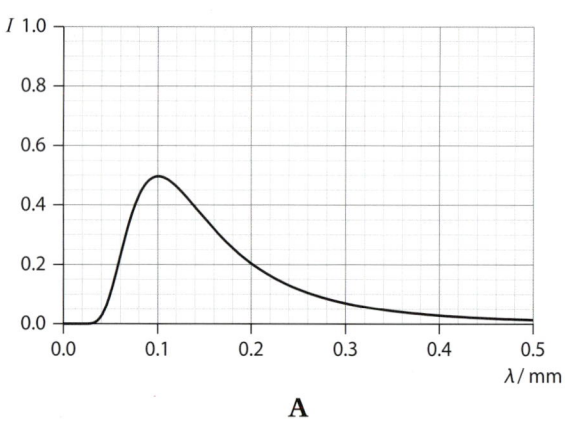

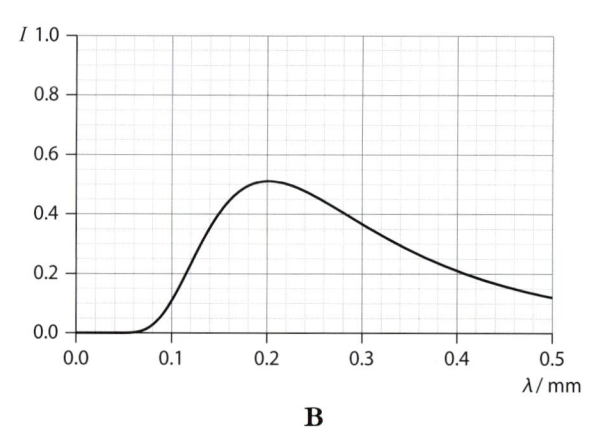

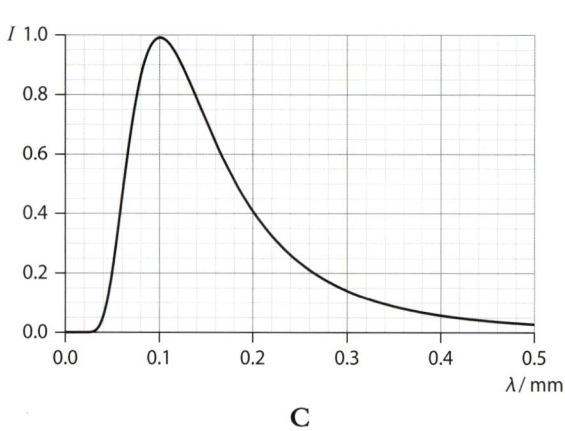

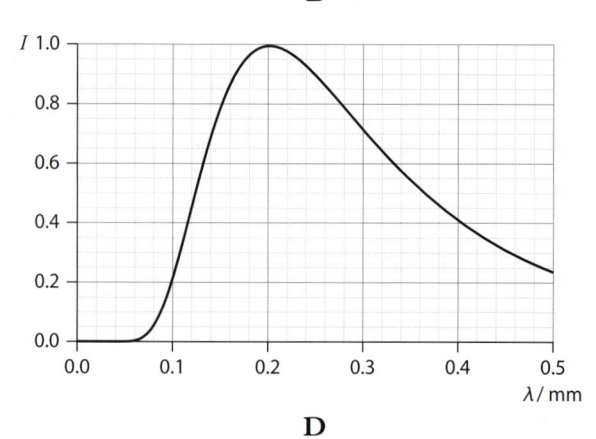

10 The intensity of solar radiation incident on a planet is S. The diagram represents the energy balance of the planet. The atmosphere reflects an intensity 0.20S and radiates 0.35S. The surface reflects 0.05S and radiates 0.40S.

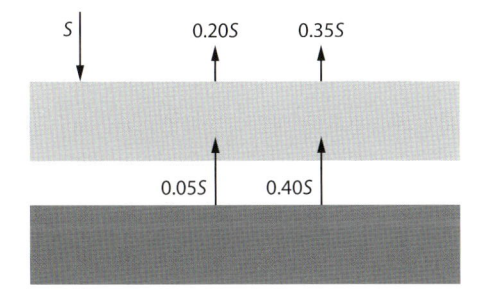

What is the albedo of the planet?

    A 0.05   **B** 0.20   **C** 0.25   **D** 0.60

11 A nuclear power plant produces 800 MW of electricity with an overall efficiency of 0.32. The fission reaction taking place in the core of the reactor is:

$$^{1}_{0}n + ^{235}_{92}U \rightarrow ^{140}_{54}Xe + ^{94}_{38}Sr + 2^{1}_{0}n$$

  a **i** Using the masses provided below show that the energy released in one fission reaction is about 180 MeV. [2]

$$^{1}_{0}n = 1.009\,u,\ ^{235}_{92}U = 235.044\,u,\ ^{140}_{54}Xe = 139.922\,u,\ ^{94}_{38}Sr = 93.915\,u.$$

      ii Estimate the specific energy of uranium-235. [2]
      iii Show that the mass of uranium-235 undergoing fission in one year is about 1100 kg. [3]
  b In a nuclear fission reactor, describe the role of:
      i the moderator [2]
      ii the control rods [2]
      iii the heat exchanger. [2]
  c Suggest what might happen to a nuclear fission reactor that does not have a moderator. [2]
  d State **one** advantage and **one** disadvantage of nuclear power. [2]

12 In a pumped storage system, the high reservoir of water has area $4.8 \times 10^4\,m^2$ and an average depth of 38 m. When water from this reservoir falls to the lower reservoir the centre of mass of the water is lowered by a vertical distance of 225 m. The water flows through a turbine connected to a generator at a rate of $350\,m^3\,s^{-1}$.

  a Calculate the mass of the water in the upper reservoir. [1]
  b Determine the loss of gravitational potential energy when the upper reservoir has been completely emptied. [2]
  c Estimate the power supplied by the falling water. [2]
      The efficiency of the plant in converting this energy into electricity is 0.60. The price of electricity sold by this power station at peak times is $0.12 per kWh. The plant can buy off-peak electrical power at $0.07 per kWh. The efficiency at which water can be pumped back up to the high reservoir is 0.64.
  d Estimate the profit made by the power plant for a single emptying and refilling of the high reservoir. [3]

13 a Outline, in the context of a wind turbine, the meaning of **primary** and **secondary** energy. [2]

b The power that can be theoretically extracted by a wind turbine of blade radius R in wind of speed v is
$P_{max} = \frac{1}{2}\pi\rho R^2 v^3$

 i State **one** assumption that has been made in deriving this expression. [1]

 ii Explain **one** other reason why the actual power derived from the wind turbine will be less than P_{max}. [2]

c A wind turbine has an overall efficiency of 0.30. The following data are available:
Density of air entering turbine = $1.2\,\text{kg m}^{-3}$
Density of air leaving turbine = $1.9\,\text{kg m}^{-3}$
Speed of air entering turbine = $8.2\,\text{m s}^{-1}$
Speed of air leaving turbine = $5.3\,\text{m s}^{-1}$
Blade radius = $12\,\text{m}$
Estimate the power extracted by this wind turbine. [3]

14 a On a hot summer day there is usually a breeze from the sea to the shore. Explain this observation. [3]

b Explain why walking on a day when the temperature is 22 °C would be described as very comfortable but swimming in water of the same temperature would be described as cool. [2]

A black body has temperature T. The graph shows the variation with wavelength of the intensity of radiation emitted by a unit area of the body. The units on the vertical axis are arbitrary.

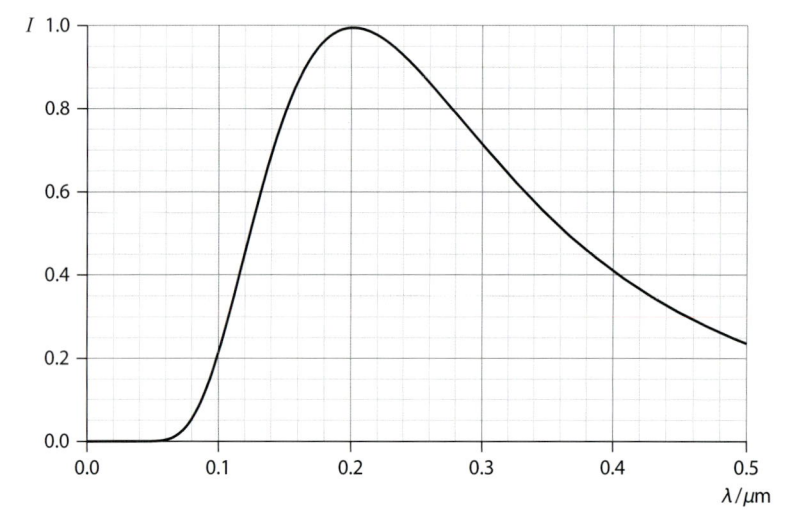

c i Describe what is meant by a **black body**. [2]

 ii Estimate T. [2]

d On a copy of the axes above sketch a graph to show the variation with wavelength of the intensity of radiation emitted by a unit area of:

 i a grey body of emissivity 0.5 and temperature T (label this graph G) [2]

 ii a black body of temperature $\frac{2T}{3}$ (label this graph B). [2]

15 The diagram shows a black body of temperature T_1 emitting radiation towards a grey body of lower temperature T_2 and emissivity e. No radiation is transmitted through the grey body.

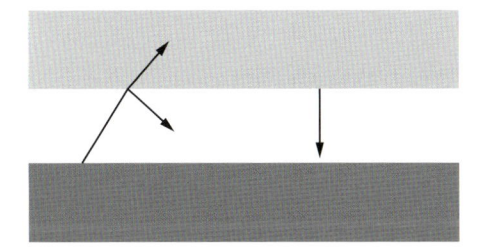

a Using all or some of the symbols T_1, T_2, e and σ, state expressions for the intensity:
  i radiated by the black body [1]
  ii radiated by the grey body [1]
  iii absorbed by the grey body [1]
  iv reflected by the grey body. [1]
b The black and the grey bodies in **a** gain as much energy as they lose. Deduce that their temperatures must be the same. [2]

16 The power radiated by the Sun is P and the Earth–Sun distance is d. The albedo of the Earth is α.

a i Deduce that the solar constant (i.e. the intensity of the solar radiation) at the position of the Earth is
$$S = \frac{P}{4\pi d^2}$$ [2]
  ii State what is meant by **albedo**. [1]
b i Explain why the average intensity absorbed by the Earth surface is $\frac{S(1-\alpha)}{4}$ [3]
  ii $P = 3.9 \times 10^{26}$ W, $d = 1.5 \times 10^{11}$ m and $\alpha = 0.30$. Assuming the Earth surface behaves as a black body, estimate the average equilibrium temperature of the Earth. [2]
c The average Earth temperature is much higher than the answer to **b ii**. Suggest why this is so. [3]

8 ENERGY PRODUCTION

9 Wave phenomena (HL)

Learning objectives

- Solve problems with SHM algebraically and graphically.
- Solve problems involving energy changes in SHM algebraically and graphically.

9.1 Simple harmonic motion

This section is a quantitative continuation of the discussion of simple harmonic motion (SHM) in Topic **4**.

The mass–spring system and the simple pendulum

We saw in Topic **4** that simple harmonic oscillations take place whenever we have a system that is displaced from its fixed equilibrium position and:
1 the acceleration is in the opposite direction to the displacement
2 the acceleration is proportional to the displacement.
We can express these **two** conditions into one equation:

$$a = -\omega^2 x$$

The minus sign shows that the acceleration is in the opposite direction to the displacement, so that the force tends to bring the system back towards its equilibrium position. The constant ω is known as the **angular frequency** of the motion. Its unit is rad per second. This equation is the defining equation for SHM.

The **period** of the motion T is related to the angular frequency by:

$$T = \frac{2\pi}{\omega}$$

From this equation, if we know ω we can work out the period of the oscillation. To show how we can use this, we look at two standard examples of simple harmonic oscillations. We start by looking again at the mass at the end of a spring that we examined in Topic **4**.

Figure **9.1** shows a block at the end of a spring. In the first diagram the block is in equilibrium. The block is then moved a distance A to the right and released. Oscillations take place because the mass is pulled back towards the equilibrium position by a **restoring force**, the tension in the spring.

Why is the motion SHM? Consider the block when it is in an arbitrary position, as in the third diagram in Figure **9.1**. At that position, the extension of the spring is x. The tension F in the spring is the only force acting horizontally on the mass, so by Hooke's law the total force has magnitude $F = kx$, where k is the spring constant. The tension force is directed to the left. Then Newton's second law states that:

$$ma = -kx$$

since the tension force is directed to the left and so is taken as negative. This equation can be rewritten as:

$$a = -\frac{k}{m}x$$

> This relationship is looked at in more detail in the section 'Consequences of the defining equation' on page 349.

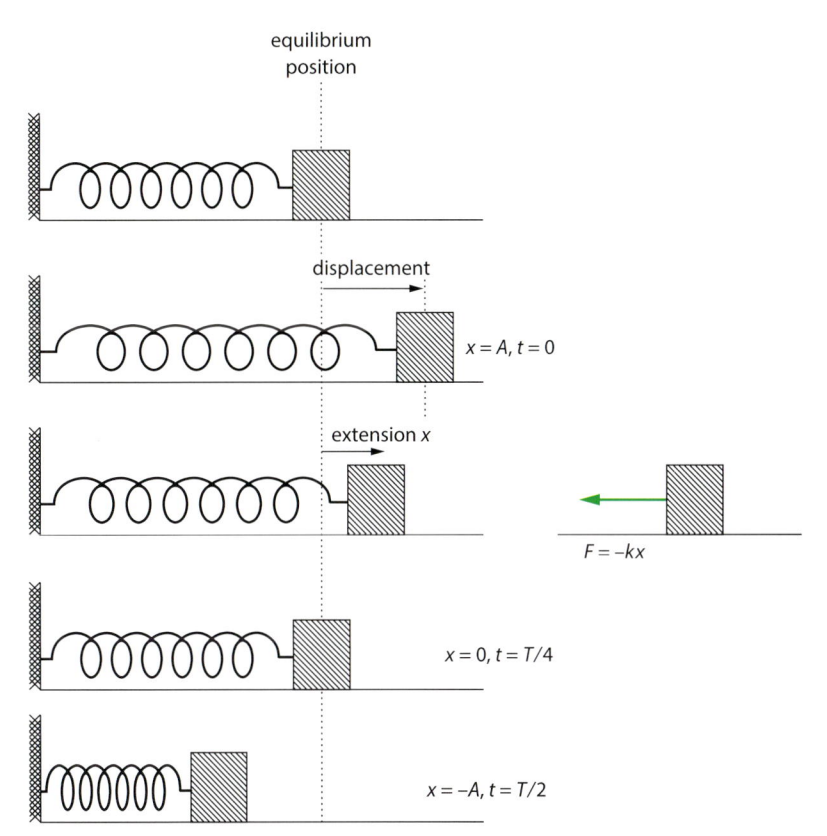

Figure 9.1 The mass–spring system. The net force on the body is proportional to the displacement and opposite to it.

Comparing with the defining equation for SHM, we see that in this example:

$$\omega^2 = \frac{k}{m} \quad \text{or} \quad \omega = \sqrt{\frac{k}{m}}$$

So we deduce that the period of a block of mass m oscillating at the end of a spring with spring constant k is:

$$T = \frac{2\pi}{\omega} = \frac{2\pi}{\sqrt{\frac{k}{m}}}$$

$$T = 2\pi\sqrt{\frac{m}{k}}$$

Let us now consider another system that shows SHM. This is the **simple pendulum**, shown in Figure 9.2.

A particle (the bob) of mass m is attached to a vertical string of length L that hangs from the ceiling. The first diagram in Figure 9.2 shows the equilibrium position of the bob. In the second diagram, the bob is displaced away from the vertical by an angle θ and then released.

The force pushing the particle back towards the equilibrium position is $mg\sin\theta$ and so we have:

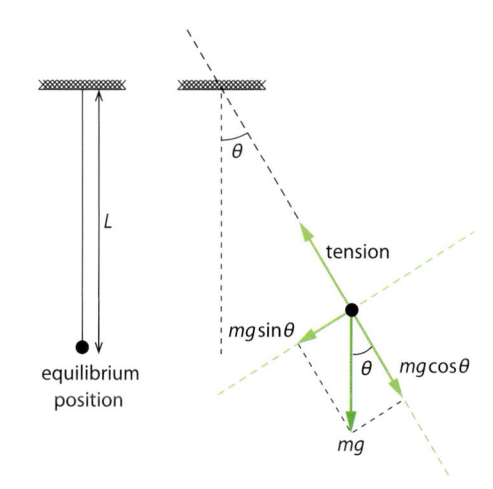

$$ma = -mg\sin\theta \quad \Rightarrow \quad a = -g\sin\theta$$

Figure 9.2 The equilibrium position of the pendulum, and the forces on the bob when the pendulum is displaced.

9 WAVE PHENOMENA (HL)

The displacement is the length of the arc, $x = L\theta$, where L and θ are as shown in Figure **9.2**, and so:

$$a = -g\sin\left(\frac{x}{L}\right)$$

The acceleration is *not proportional* to the displacement, x. But if x is small compared to L, then $\sin\left(\frac{x}{L}\right) \approx \frac{x}{L}$.

This is called the small angle approximation. You can see that this works by using some values. For example, in radians:

$$\sin(0.00357) = 0.00356999 \approx 0.00357$$

But if the angle is not small:

$$\sin(1.357) = 0.97723$$

So, for very small angles, the acceleration of the pendulum is given by:

$$a \approx -\frac{g}{L}x$$

The simple pendulum obeys the defining equation of SHM **approximately** and:

$$a = -\omega^2 x \quad \text{with} \quad \omega^2 = \frac{g}{L}$$

The approximation means that the amplitude of oscillations must be small, i.e. the bob must not be pulled to the side by a large amount.

So for *small* oscillations the period of the pendulum is then:

$$T = \frac{2\pi}{\omega} = \frac{2\pi}{\sqrt{\frac{g}{L}}}$$

$$T = 2\pi\sqrt{\frac{L}{g}}$$

So we have studied two examples where SHM takes place. In the case of the mass and the spring the oscillations are precisely SHM and in the case of the simple pendulum the oscillations are approximately SHM. The approximation gets better and better with decreasing amplitude.

Notice that the mass affects the period for the spring–mass system but does not affect the period for the simple pendulum.

> **Exam tip**
> The simple pendulum oscillations are approximately SHM. The amplitude has to be very small. In an experiment the angle the pendulum is displaced from the vertical should not exceed 10°.

Worked examples

9.1 a Calculate the length of a pendulum that has a period equal to 1.00 s.
  b Calculate the percentage increase in the period of a pendulum when the length is increased by 4.00%. Determine the new period.

a The period of the pendulum is given by: $T = 2\pi \sqrt{\dfrac{L}{g}}$

Rearranging: $L = \dfrac{T^2 g}{4\pi^2}$

Substituting the values given: $L = \dfrac{1.00^2 \times 9.81}{4\pi^2}$

$L = 0.248 \, \text{m}$

b Using the propagation of errors as in Topic 1, we have: $\dfrac{\Delta T}{T} \approx \dfrac{1}{2} \dfrac{\Delta L}{L}$

> **Exam tip**
> Be prepared to use what you have learned in one topic outside that topic!

From this we find: $\dfrac{\Delta T}{T} = \dfrac{1}{2} \times 4.00\% = 2.00\%$

Hence: $\Delta T = \dfrac{2.00}{100} \times T = \dfrac{2.00}{100} \times 1.00 = 0.02 \, \text{s}$

The new period is then $T = 1.02 \, \text{s}$.

Alternatively, you could calculate the new length L'.

$L' = 0.248 \times 1.04 = 0.2579 \, \text{m}$

Using this new length, the new period T' is:

$T' = 2\pi \sqrt{\dfrac{0.2579}{9.81}}$

$T' = 1.0188 \approx 1.02 \, \text{s}$

9.2 Explain how you would use a spring of known spring constant to measure the mass of a body in a spacecraft in orbit, for example in the International Space Station.

Objects in a spacecraft in orbit appear weightless and so ordinary scales cannot be used to measure the mass. However, if the object is attached to a spring and the spring is stretched and released the object will oscillate with period $T = 2\pi \sqrt{\dfrac{m}{k}}$. So measuring the period and knowing k can give the mass.

Consequences of the defining equation

This section is for those who have studied calculus. These mathematical details are not required for examination purposes but the reader is strongly encouraged to go through this section. (Almost all of this mathematics is included in the syllabus for higher or standard level IB mathematics.)

SHM is defined by the equation $a = -\omega^2 x$. In calculus, acceleration is written as $a = \dfrac{d^2 x}{dt^2}$ and so the defining equation becomes:

$$\dfrac{d^2 x}{dt^2} = -\omega^2 x \quad \Rightarrow \quad \dfrac{d^2 x}{dt^2} + \omega^2 x = 0$$

9 WAVE PHENOMENA (HL)

This is a differential equation whose solution is:

$$x = x_0 \cos(\omega t) \quad \text{or} \quad x = x_0 \sin(\omega t)$$

where x_0 is a constant.

To check that $x = x_0 \cos(\omega t)$ is a solution, we calculate:

$$\frac{dx}{dt} = -x_0 \omega \sin(\omega t)$$

and differentiate again to get:

$$\frac{d^2x}{dt^2} = -x_0 \omega^2 \cos(\omega t)$$

Substituting back into the second version of the defining equation:

$$\frac{d^2x}{dt^2} + \omega^2 x = -x_0 \omega^2 \cos(\omega t) + \omega^2 x_0 \cos(\omega t)$$
$$= 0$$

The working for the other solution, $x = x_0 \sin(\omega t)$, is very similar.

What is the meaning of the constant x_0? The maximum value of the cosine function or the sine function is 1, so the maximum value of x is x_0. Thus x_0 is the **amplitude** of the motion, which is the maximum displacement.

Look again at Figure 9.1. If we start the clock at the instant of the second diagram, where the displacement is greatest, the solution is:

$$x = x_0 \cos(\omega t)$$

So we use the cosine version when at $t = 0$ the displacement is the amplitude.

If the clock is started when the block is at the equilibrium position *and* moving to the right, the solution is:

$$x = x_0 \sin(\omega t)$$

So we use the sine version of the solution if at $t = 0$ the displacement is zero and the particle moves towards positive displacements.

From calculus, we know that velocity is given by $v = \frac{dx}{dt}$. So for SHM with $x = x_0 \cos(\omega t)$
we have that:

$$v = \frac{dx}{dt} = -\omega x_0 \sin(\omega t)$$

and if $x = x_0 \sin(\omega t)$, then $v = \frac{dx}{dt} = \omega x_0 \cos(\omega t)$.

Given that $x = x_0 \cos(\omega t)$, we know from mathematics that this is a periodic function with period T given by:

$$T = \frac{2\pi}{\omega}$$

The **period** is the time to complete one full oscillation.

There are other solutions for other initial situations, but we do not need these here, for example the particle having zero displacement at $t = 0$, but moving to the left.

Exam tip
The use of cosine of sine functions for displacement depends on what the situation is at $t = 0$.
- Use the cosine version when at $t = 0$ the displacement is the amplitude.
- Use the sine version when at $t = 0$ the displacement is zero and the particle moves towards positive displacements.

> In SHM the period depends only on ω and not on the amplitude or the phase.

Using mathematics, we have found that the defining equation $a = -\omega^2 x$ implies that the displacement x, velocity v and period T of the SHM that takes place are given by the following sets of equations, where x_0 is the amplitude (the maximum displacement):

> $x = x_0 \cos(\omega t)$
> $v = -\omega x_0 \sin(\omega t)$
> $a = -\omega^2 x_0 \cos(\omega t) = -\omega^2 x$
> $T = \dfrac{2\pi}{\omega}$

> $x = x_0 \sin(\omega t)$
> $v = \omega x_0 \cos(\omega t)$
> $a = -\omega^2 x_0 \sin(\omega t) = -\omega^2 x$
> $T = \dfrac{2\pi}{\omega}$

It follows that:

> - the maximum speed is ωx_0.
> - the maximum acceleration is $\omega^2 x_0$.

Recall our definition in Topic 4 of frequency f: this is defined as the number of oscillations per second. Frequency is related to period, T, through the equation $f = \dfrac{1}{T}$. It follows from $T = \dfrac{2\pi}{\omega}$ that:

$$\omega = \dfrac{2\pi}{T}$$

$$\omega = 2\pi f$$

Worked examples

9.3 The graph shows the variation with displacement x, of the acceleration a of a particle.
  a Explain why the oscillations are simple harmonic.
  b Determine the period of oscillation.
  c Determine the maximum speed in this motion.

Exam tip
Watch the unit conversion. The amplitude is read from the graph as 0.06 m.

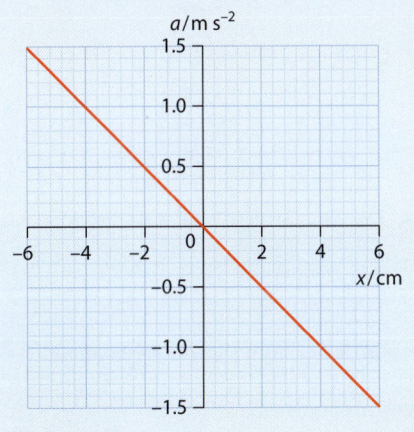

Figure 9.3

a The oscillations are simple harmonic because the acceleration is proportional to displacement (straight-line graph through the origin) and opposite to it (negative gradient). So it fits the defining equation $a = -\omega^2 x$.

b The gradient of the line in the graph is $-\omega^2$. From the graph the gradient is:

$$-\omega^2 = \frac{-3.0\,\text{m s}^{-2}}{0.12\,\text{m}}$$

$$\omega^2 = 25\,\text{s}^{-2}$$

$$\omega = 5.0\,\text{rad s}^{-1}$$

Hence the period is $T = \frac{2\pi}{\omega} = \frac{2\pi}{5.0} \approx 1.3\,\text{s}$

c The maximum speed is ωx_0, i.e. $5.0 \times 0.06 = 0.30\,\text{m s}^{-1}$.

9.4 A particle undergoes SHM with an amplitude of 4.0 mm and frequency of 0.32 Hz. At $t = 0$, the displacement is 4.0 mm.
  a Write down the equation giving the displacement and velocity for this motion.
  b State the maximum value of the speed and acceleration in this motion.

a We need to use $x = x_0 \cos(\omega t)$. We have been given frequency f so the angular frequency ω is:

$$\omega = 2\pi f = 2\pi \times 0.32 = 2.01 \approx 2.0\,\text{rad s}^{-1}$$

We also have $x_0 = 4.0$ mm. So the equation for the displacement is:

$$x = 4.0 \cos(2.0 t)$$

where t is in seconds and x is in millimetres.

The equation for the velocity is:

$$v = -x_0 \omega \sin(\omega t) = -8.0 \sin(2.0 t)$$

b From $v = -8.0 \sin(2.0 t)$ the maximum speed is $8.0\,\text{mm s}^{-1}$.

The maximum acceleration is $\omega^2 x_0$, i.e. $2.0^2 \times 4.0 = 16\,\text{mm s}^{-2}$.

9.5 The graph in Figure 9.4 shows the displacement of a particle from a fixed equilibrium position.
  a Use the graph to determine:
    i the period of the motion
    ii the maximum velocity of the particle during an oscillation
    iii the maximum acceleration experienced by the particle.
  b On a copy of the diagram, mark:
    i a point where the velocity is zero (label this with the letter Z)
    ii a point where the velocity is positive and has the largest magnitude (label this with the letter V)
    iii a point where the acceleration is positive and has the largest magnitude (label this with the letter A).

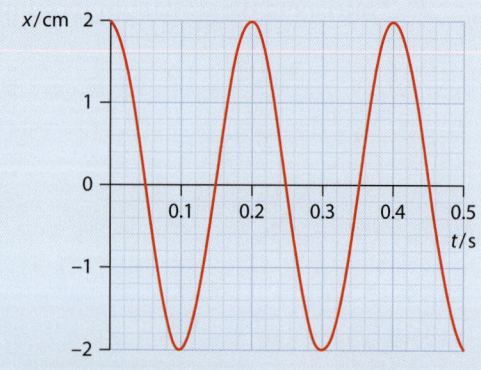

Figure 9.4 Graph showing the variation with time of the displacement of a particle performing SHM.

a **i** The period is read off the graph as $T = 0.20$ s. Since $T = \frac{2\pi}{\omega}$ we have that:

$$\omega = \frac{2\pi}{T} = 31.4 \approx 31 \text{ rad s}^{-1}$$

ii The maximum velocity is then:

$$v_{max} = \omega x_0 = 31.4 \times 0.020 = 0.63 \text{ m s}^{-1}$$

iii The maximum acceleration is found from:

$$a_{max} = \omega^2 x_0 = 31.4^2 \times 0.020 = 20 \text{ m s}^{-2}$$

b **i** The velocity is zero at any point where the displacement is at a maximum or a minimum.
ii For example at $t = 0.15$ s.
iii For example at $t = 0.10$ s or $t = 0.30$ s.

9.6 A body of mass m is placed on a horizontal plate that undergoes vertical SHM (Figure 9.5). The amplitude of the motion is A and the frequency is f.
a Derive an expression for the reaction force on the particle from the plate when the particle is at its highest point.
b Using the expression in **a**, deduce that the particle will lose contact with the plate if the frequency is higher than

$$\sqrt{\frac{g}{4\pi^2 A}}$$

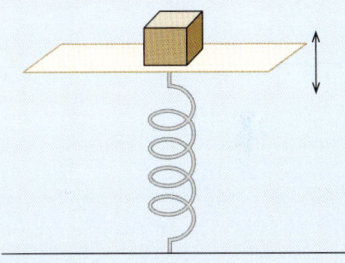

Figure 9.5 A particle on a horizontal plate executing SHM.

---

a At the highest point $x = A$ we have $a = -\omega^2 A$, so:

$R - mg = ma = -m\omega^2 A$

Substituting $\omega = 2\pi f$ gives:

$R - mg = -m(2\pi f)^2 A$

$R - mg = -4\pi^2 f^2 m A$

$\Rightarrow R = mg - 4\pi^2 f^2 m A$

b The particle will lose contact with the plate when $R \to 0$, i.e. when the frequency is such that:

$0 = mg - 4\pi^2 f^2 m A$

Rearranging:

$4\pi^2 f^2 m A = mg$

$f^2 = \frac{g}{4\pi^2 A}$

$f = \sqrt{\frac{g}{4\pi^2 A}}$

The particle will lose contact with the plate if the frequency is higher than $\sqrt{\frac{g}{4\pi^2 A}}$.

9 WAVE PHENOMENA (HL)

Energy in simple harmonic motion

As we saw in Topic 4, in simple harmonic oscillations we have transformations of energy from kinetic to potential and vice versa. When the kinetic energy is a maximum (at the equilibrium point) the potential energy is zero and when the potential energy is a maximum (at the end points) the kinetic energy is zero. The kinetic energy of a particle is given by:

$$E_K = \tfrac{1}{2}mv^2$$

In what follows we assume that $x = x_0 \cos(\omega t)$ so that $v = -\omega x_0 \sin(\omega t)$. This means:

$$E_K = \tfrac{1}{2}m\omega^2 x_0^2 \sin^2(\omega t)$$

The maximum kinetic energy is therefore $E_{K\max} = \tfrac{1}{2}m\omega^2 x_0^2$.

When the kinetic energy is a maximum the potential energy is zero and so the quantity $\tfrac{1}{2}m\omega^2 x_0^2$ is also the total energy of the system E_T. Therefore:

$$E_T = \tfrac{1}{2}m\omega^2 x_0^2$$

The total energy is the sum of the potential and kinetic energies at any time:

$$E_T = E_K + E_P$$

Therefore:

$$E_P = \tfrac{1}{2}m\omega^2 x_0^2 - E_K$$
$$E_P = \tfrac{1}{2}m\omega^2 x_0^2 - \tfrac{1}{2}mv^2$$

We can use this to find an expression for the potential energy in SHM in terms of the displacement. Since $v = -\omega x_0 \sin(\omega t)$:

$$E_P = \tfrac{1}{2}m\omega^2 x_0^2 - \tfrac{1}{2}m\omega^2 x_0^2 \sin^2(\omega t)$$
$$E_P = \tfrac{1}{2}m\omega^2 x_0^2 (1 - \sin^2(\omega t))$$
$$E_P = \tfrac{1}{2}m\omega^2 x_0^2 (\cos^2(\omega t))$$
$$E_P = \tfrac{1}{2}m\omega^2 x^2$$

We can also use $v = -\omega x_0 \sin(\omega t)$ to find an expression for the velocity in terms of displacement:

$$v^2 = \omega^2 x_0^2 \sin^2(\omega t)$$
$$v^2 = \omega^2 x_0^2 (1 - \cos^2(\omega t))$$
$$v^2 = \omega^2 x_0^2 - \omega^2 x^2$$
$$v = \pm \omega \sqrt{x_0^2 - x^2}$$

The plus or minus sign is needed because for any given displacement x, the particle may be going one way or the opposite way.

> **Exam tip**
> Choosing $x = x_0 \sin(\omega t)$ so that $v = \omega x_0 \cos(\omega t)$ gives similar results.

> **Exam tip**
> The trick used repeatedly here is that $\sin^2(\omega t) + \cos^2(\omega t) = 1$.

Using this equation, another formula for kinetic energy (this time in terms of displacement rather than time) is:

$E_K = \frac{1}{2}m\omega^2(x_0^2 - x^2)$

The kinetic and potential energies for SHM are shown on the same axes in Figure **9.6**.

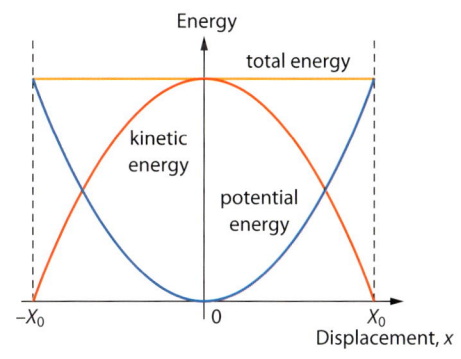

Figure 9.6 The variation with displacement of the potential energy and kinetic energy of a mass on a spring. The total energy is a horizontal straight line.

Exam tip
You must be comfortable working with energies as functions of time as well as of displacement. For $x = x_0 \cos(\omega t)$ the energies are as follows:
- functions of time
  $E_K = \frac{1}{2}m\omega^2 x_0^2 \sin^2(\omega t)$ and
  $E_P = \frac{1}{2}m\omega^2 x_0^2 \cos^2(\omega t)$
- functions of displacement
  $E_K = \frac{1}{2}m\omega^2(x_0^2 - x^2)$ and
  $E_P = \frac{1}{2}m\omega^2 x^2$

The equation $v = \pm\omega\sqrt{x_0^2 - x^2}$ allows us to see that at the extremes of the motion, $x = \pm x_0$, and so $v = 0$ as we expect. At $x = \pm x_0$ the system has potential energy only, and at $x = 0$ it has kinetic energy only. At intermediate points the system has both forms of energy: potential energy and kinetic energy. During an oscillation, we therefore have transformations from one form of energy to another.

Worked examples

9.7 The graph in Figure **9.7** shows the variation with the square of the displacement (x^2) of the potential energy E_P of a particle of mass 40 g that is executing SHM. Using the graph, determine:
  a the period of oscillation
  b the maximum speed of the particle during an oscillation.

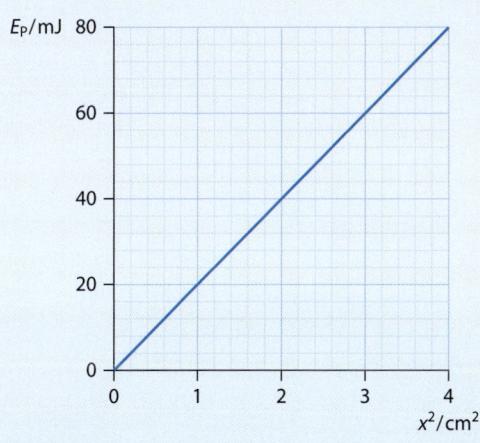

Figure 9.7 Graph showing the variation with the square of the displacement of the potential energy of a particle in SHM.

a The maximum potential energy is $E_P = \frac{1}{2}m\omega^2 x_0^2$. From the graph the maximum potential energy is 80.0 mJ (80×10^{-3} J) and the amplitude is $\sqrt{4.0 \text{ cm}^2} = 2.00$ cm (2.00×10^{-2} m). The mass of the particle is 0.040 kg. Thus:

$$80 \times 10^{-3} = \frac{1}{2} \times 0.040 \times \omega^2 \times x_0^2$$

Rearranging:

$$\omega^2 = \frac{2 \times 80 \times 10^{-3}}{0.040 \times (2.00 \times 10^{-2})^2}$$

$$\omega^2 = 10^4 \text{ s}^{-2}$$

$$\omega = 10^2 \text{ rad s}^{-1}$$

The period is $T = \frac{2\pi}{\omega}$, so:

$$T = \frac{2\pi}{10^2} = 0.063 \text{ s}$$

b The maximum speed is found from:

$$v_{\max} = \omega x_0 = 100 \times 2.00 \times 10^{-2} = 2.00 \text{ m s}^{-1}$$

9.8 The graph in Figure 9.8 shows the variation with displacement x of the kinetic energy of a particle of mass 0.40 kg performing SHM. Use the graph to determine:
  a the total energy of the particle
  b the maximum speed of the particle
  c the amplitude of the motion
  d the potential energy when the displacement is 2.0 cm
  e the period of the motion.

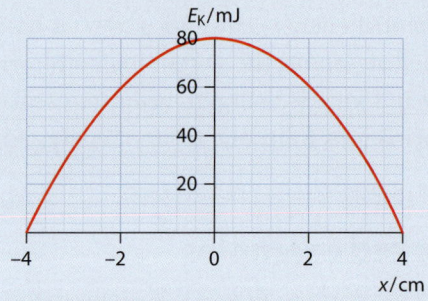

Figure 9.8 The variation with displacement of the kinetic energy of a particle.

---

a The total energy is equal to the maximum kinetic energy, i.e. 80 mJ.

b The maximum speed is found from:

$$\tfrac{1}{2}mv_{\max}^2 = E_{K\max}$$

$$v_{\max}^2 = \frac{2E_{K\max}}{m}$$

$$v_{\max} = \sqrt{\frac{2 \times 80 \times 10^{-3}}{0.40}}$$

$$v_{\max} = 0.63 \text{ m s}^{-1}$$

c The amplitude is 4.0 cm.

d When $x = 2.0$ cm, the kinetic energy is 60 mJ and so the potential energy is 20 mJ.

e The maximum potential energy is 80 mJ and equals $\frac{1}{2}m\omega^2 x_0^2$. Hence:

$$\frac{1}{2}m\omega^2 x_0^2 = E_{Pmax}$$

$$\omega = \sqrt{\frac{2E_{Pmax}}{mx_0^2}}$$

$$\omega = \sqrt{\frac{2 \times 80 \times 10^{-3}}{0.40 \times (4.0 \times 10^{-2})^2}}$$

$$\omega = 15.8 \text{ rad s}^{-1}$$

The period is $T = \frac{2\pi}{\omega}$

$$T = \frac{2\pi}{15.8} = 0.397 \approx 0.40 \text{ s}$$

9.9 The graph in Figure 9.9 shows the variation with time t of the kinetic energy E_K of a particle of mass 0.25 kg that is undergoing SHM.

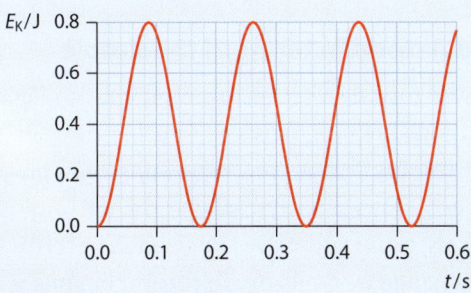

Figure 9.9

Exam tip
It is important to understand how to find the period from this graph.

For this motion, determine:
a the period
b the amplitude
c the kinetic energy when the displacement is 0.080 m.

a At $t = 0$ the kinetic energy is zero, meaning that the particle is at one extreme of the oscillation. It is zero again at about 0.17 s when it is at the other end. To find the period the particle has to return to its original position and that happens at 0.35 s, so $T = 0.35$ s.

b The angular frequency is found from $\omega = \frac{2\pi}{T}$:

$$\omega = \frac{2\pi}{0.35} = 17.95 \text{ rad s}^{-1}$$

The maximum kinetic energy is given by $E_{K\text{max}} = \frac{1}{2}m\omega^2 x_0^2$ and so:

$$0.80 = \frac{1}{2} \times 0.25 \times 17.95^2 \times x_0^2$$

Rearranging:

$$x_0^2 = \sqrt{\frac{2 \times 0.80}{0.25 \times 17.95^2}}$$

$$x_0 \approx 0.14 \text{ m}$$

> **Exam tip**
> More significant figures are being used here. This is all right – this is an intermediate calculation.

c We know the displacement so use a formula that gives kinetic energy in terms of displacement, i.e. $E_K = \frac{1}{2}m\omega^2(x_0^2 - x^2)$. This gives:

$$E_K = \frac{1}{2} \times 0.25 \times 17.95^2(0.14^2 - 0.080^2)$$

$$E_K = 0.53 \text{ J}.$$

Nature of science

The complex can be understood in terms of the simple

The equation for SHM can be solved in terms of simple sine and cosine functions. These simple solutions help physicists to visualise how an oscillator behaves. Although real oscillations are very complex, a powerful mathematical machinery called Fourier analysis allows the decomposition of complex oscillations, sounds, noise and waves in general, in terms of sines and cosines. Energy exchange in oscillating electrical circuits is modelled using this type of analysis. Therefore the simple descriptions used in this topic can also be used in more complex problems as well.

? Test yourself

1 Explain why the oscillations of a pendulum are, in general, not simple harmonic. State the condition that must be satisfied for the oscillations to become approximately simple harmonic.

2 It can be shown that the two solutions for simple harmonic oscillations, $x = x_0 \cos(\omega t)$ or $x = x_0 \sin(\omega t)$ are special cases of the more general $x = x_0 \cos(\omega t + \varphi)$ where the angle φ is known as the phase of the motion.
   a State the phase of the motion when $x = x_0 \sin(\omega t)$.
   b Show explicitly that, if $x = x_0 \cos(\omega t + \varphi)$, the period of the motion is given by $T = \frac{2\pi}{\omega}$ independently of x_0 and φ.

3 The displacement of a particle executing SHM is given by $y = 5.0 \cos(2t)$, where y is in millimetres and t is in seconds. Calculate:
   a the initial displacement of the particle
   b the displacement at $t = 1.2$ s
   c the time at which the displacement first becomes -2.0 mm
   d the displacement when the velocity of the particle is 6.0 mm s^{-1}.

4 a Write down an equation for the displacement of a particle undergoing SHM with an amplitude equal to 8.0 cm and a frequency of 14 Hz, assuming that at $t = 0$ the displacement is 8.0 cm and the particle is at rest.
   b Find the displacement, velocity and acceleration of this particle at a time of 0.025 s.

5 A point on a guitar string oscillates in SHM with an amplitude of 5.0 mm and a frequency of 460 Hz. Determine the maximum velocity and acceleration of this point.

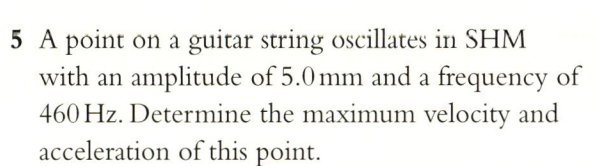

6 A guitar string, whose two ends are fixed oscillates as shown in the diagram.

The vertical displacement of a point on the string a distance x from the left end is given by $y = 6.0 \cos(1040\pi t) \sin(\pi x)$, where y is in millimetres, x is in metres and t is in seconds. Use this expression to:
  a deduce that all points on the string execute SHM with a common frequency and common phase, and determine the common frequency
  b deduce that different points on the string have different amplitudes
  c determine the maximum amplitude of oscillation
  d calculate the length L of the string
  e calculate the amplitude of oscillation of the point on the string where $x = \frac{3}{4}L$.

7 The graph shows the variation with time t of the velocity v of a particle executing SHM.

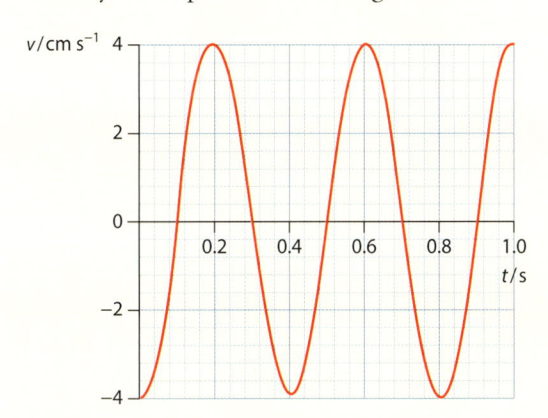

  a Using the graph, estimate the area between the curve and the time axis from 0.10 s to 0.30 s.
  b State what this area represents.
  c Hence write down an equation giving the displacement of the particle as a function of time.

8 The graph shows the variation with time t of the displacement x of a particle executing SHM.

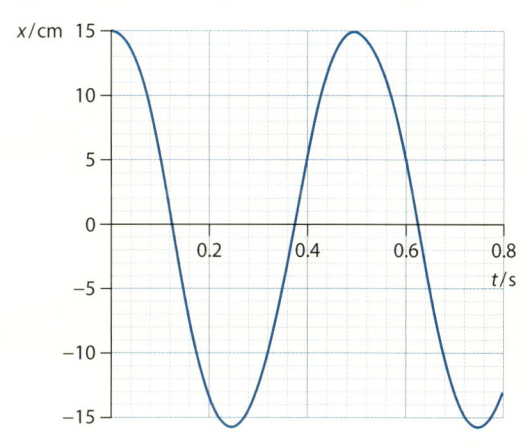

Draw a graph to show the variation with displacement x of the acceleration a of the particle (put numbers on the axes).

9 The graph shows the variation with displacement x of the acceleration a of a body of mass 0.150 kg.

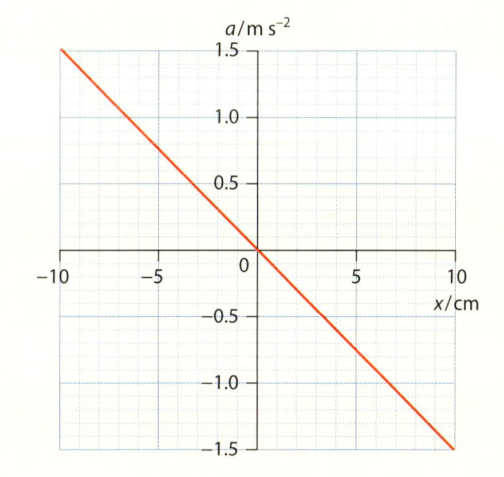

  a Use the graph to explain why the motion of the body is SHM.
     Determine the following:
  b the period of the motion
  c the maximum velocity of the body during an oscillation
  d the maximum net force exerted on the body
  e the total energy of the body.

10 A body of mass 0.120 kg is placed on a horizontal plate. The plate oscillates vertically in SHM making five oscillations per second.
  a Determine the largest possible amplitude of oscillations such that the body never loses contact with the plate.
  b Calculate the normal reaction force on the body at the lowest point of the oscillations when the amplitude has the value found in a.

11 This is a very unrealistic but interesting 'thought experiment' involving SHM.
  Imagine boring a straight tunnel from one place (A) on the surface of the Earth to another place (B) diametrically opposite, and then releasing a ball of mass m at point A. The ball then moves under the influence of gravity.
  To answer the following questions, you need to know that when the ball is at the position shown in the diagram, the gravitational force it experiences is the force of gravitation from the mass inside the dotted circle *only*. In addition, this mass inside the dotted circle may be considered to be concentrated at the centre of the Earth. Assume that the density of the Earth is uniform.

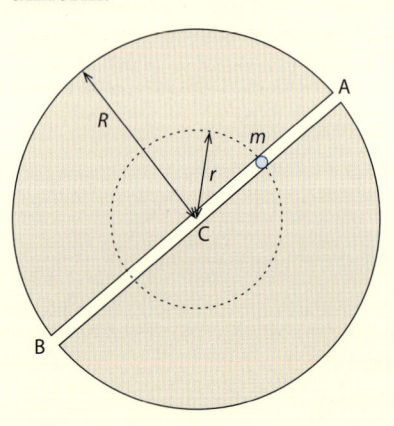

  a Denoting the mass of the Earth by M and its radius by R, derive an expression for the mass inside the dotted circle (of radius x).
  b Derive an expression for the gravitational force on the ball when at the position shown in the diagram, a distance x from the centre of the Earth.
  c Hence deduce that the motion of the ball is simple harmonic.
  d Determine the period of the motion.
  e Evaluate this period using:
    $M = 6.0 \times 10^{24}$ kg $R = 6.4 \times 10^{6}$ m
    and $G = 6.67 \times 10^{-11}$ N kg^{-2} m^{2}.
  f Compare the period of this motion with the period of rotation of a satellite around the Earth in a circular orbit of radius R.

12 A body of mass 2.0 kg is connected to two springs, each of spring constant $k = 120$ N m^{-1}.
  a The springs are connected as in part a of the diagram. Calculate the period of the oscillations of this mass when it is displaced from its equilibrium position and then released.
  b The springs are now connected as in part b of the diagram. State and explain whether the period changes.

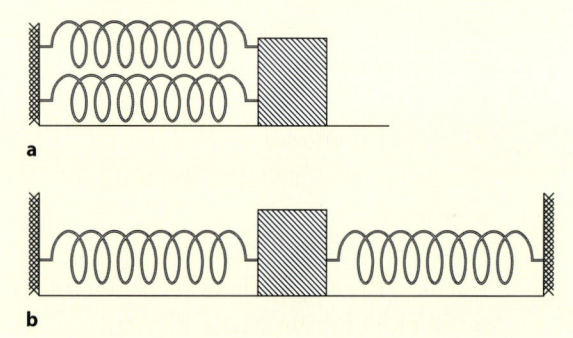

13 A woman bungee-jumper of mass 60 kg is attached to an elastic rope of natural length 15 m. The rope behaves like a spring of spring constant $k = 220$ N m^{-1}. The other end of the spring is attached to a high bridge. The woman jumps from the bridge.
  a Determine how far below the bridge she falls, before she instantaneously comes to rest.
  b Calculate her acceleration at the position you found in a.
  c Explain why she will perform SHM, and find the period of oscillations.
  d The woman will eventually come to rest at a specific distance below the bridge. Calculate this distance.
  e The mechanical energy of the woman after she comes to rest is less than the woman's total mechanical energy just before she jumped. Explain what happened to the 'lost' mechanical energy.

9.2 Single-slit diffraction

This section deals in detail with the problem of single-slit diffraction and the effect of slit width on the interference pattern produced. An interference pattern is produced because light originating from one part of the slit interferes with light from different parts of the slit.

Diffraction by a single rectangular slit

As we saw in Topic 4 when a wave of wavelength λ is incident on an aperture whose opening size is b, an important wave phenomenon called **diffraction** takes place where the wave spreads out past the aperture. The amount of diffraction is appreciable if the wavelength is of the same order of magnitude as the opening or bigger, $\lambda \geq b$. However, diffraction is negligible if the wavelength is much smaller than the opening size, $\lambda \ll b$.

Figure 9.10 shows a slit of width b through which light passes. Imagine the light as a set of plane wavefronts parallel to the slit. When a wavefront reaches the slit, the points labelled A_1 to A_5 and B_1 to B_5 are all on the same wavefront, so they are in phase. Each point on the wavefront acts as a source of waves. These waves are also in phase, so they can interfere. We see the result of the interference on a screen placed a large distance away.

In Figure 9.10 we see rays from A_1 and B_1 travelling at an angle θ to the slit. The interference between the waves is seen at point P on the screen. The wave from A_1 travels a slightly different distance to reach the screen than the wave from B_1. The interference seen at P depends on this path difference. From the diagram, the path difference for the waves from A_1 and B_1 equals the distance B_1C_1. Since P is far away, lines A_1P and B_1P are approximately parallel, so triangle $A_1B_1C_1$ is approximately right angled and angle $B_1A_1C_1$ equals θ. We see that the distance A_1B_1 is equal to $\dfrac{b}{2}$, so:

$$\text{path difference} = B_1C_1 = \frac{b}{2}\sin\theta$$

As we learnt in Topic 4, if the path difference is half a wavelength, the two waves will destructively interfere when they get to P. But we have only considered waves from A_1 and B_1. What about waves from A_2 and B_2? Figure 9.11 shows that for P a long way from the slit, the rays from A_1, A_2, B_1 and B_2 are all parallel. The points are all equally spaced along the slit so $A_1B_1 = A_2B_2$. Triangles $A_1B_1C_1$ and $A_2B_2C_2$ are both right-angled and angle $B_1A_1C_1$ = angle $B_2A_2C_2$. The triangles are therefore congruent, so the path difference B_1C_1 is equal to the path difference B_2C_2.

Since the path difference is the same, whatever phase difference exists at P from A_1 and B_1 will be the same from A_2 and B_2. Thus, if we get zero wave at P from the first pair of points, we will get the same from the second as well. For every point on the upper half of the slit there is a corresponding point on the lower half, so we see that all the points on the wavefront will result in complete destructive interference if the first pair results in destructive interference.

Learning objectives

- Discuss the effect of the slit width on the diffraction pattern.
- Derive the angle of the first diffraction minimum.
- Discuss the effect of wavelength on the diffraction pattern.

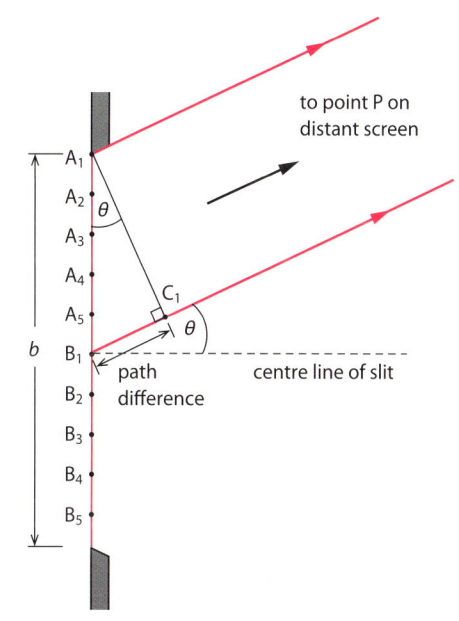

Figure 9.10 For a narrow slit each point on the wavefront entering the slit acts as a source of waves. The result of interference between waves depends on the path difference.

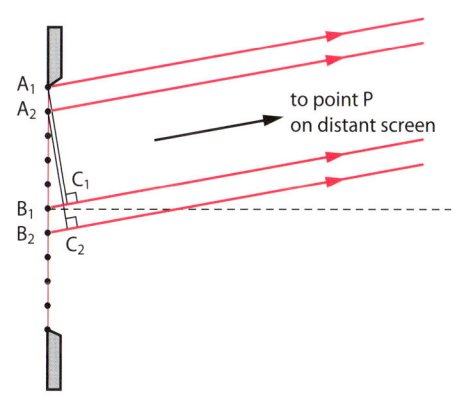

Figure 9.11 Triangles $A_1C_1B_1$ and $A_2C_2B_2$ are congruent.

Exam tip
If there is just one thing to know from this Topic it is the single-slit intensity graph.

We learnt in Topic 4 that to get destructive interference, the path difference must be a half-integral multiple of the wavelength. The path difference between waves arriving at P from A_1 and B_1 is $\frac{b}{2}\sin\theta$, so this means that we get a minimum at P if:

$$\frac{b}{2}\sin\theta = \frac{\lambda}{2}$$

$$\Rightarrow b\sin\theta = \lambda$$

By similar arguments we can show that we get **additional minima** whenever:

$$b\sin\theta = n\lambda \quad n = 1, 2, 3, \ldots$$

This equation gives the angle θ at which minima are observed on a screen behind the aperture of size b on which light of wavelength λ falls. Since the angle θ is typically small, we may approximate $\sin\theta \approx \theta$ (if the angle is in radians) and so the first minimum is observed at an angle (in radians) given by:

$$\theta = \frac{\lambda}{b}$$

The maxima of the pattern are approximately half-way between minima. The equation for the minima is very important in understanding the phenomenon of diffraction, so let us take a closer look.

The first minimum ($n = 1$) occurs at $b\sin\theta = \lambda$. If the wavelength is comparable to or bigger than b, appreciable diffraction will take place, as we said earlier. How do we see this from this formula? If $\lambda > b$, then $\sin\theta > 1$ (i.e. θ does not exist). The wave has spread so much around the aperture, the central maximum is so wide, that the first minimum does not exist. (Remember that diffraction is the spreading of the wave around the aperture, not necessarily the existence of interference maxima and minima.)

In the other extreme, if the wavelength is very small compared to b, then from $\theta \approx \frac{\lambda}{b}$ it follows that θ is approximately zero. So the wave goes through the aperture along a straight line represented by $\theta = 0$. There is no wave at any point P on the screen for which θ is not zero. There is no spreading of the wave and hence no diffraction, as we expected. For all other intermediate cases we have diffraction with secondary maxima and minima.

The intensity of light observed on a screen some distance from the slit is shown in Figure **9.12** for the red light with two different slit openings: $b = 1.4 \times 10^{-5}$ m and $b = 2.8 \times 10^{-5}$ m.

We see that as the slit width decreases the pattern becomes wider: the angular width of the central maximum becomes larger. The angular width for the graph in Figure **9.12a** is about 0.010 rad: in general it is given by $2\frac{\lambda}{b}$.

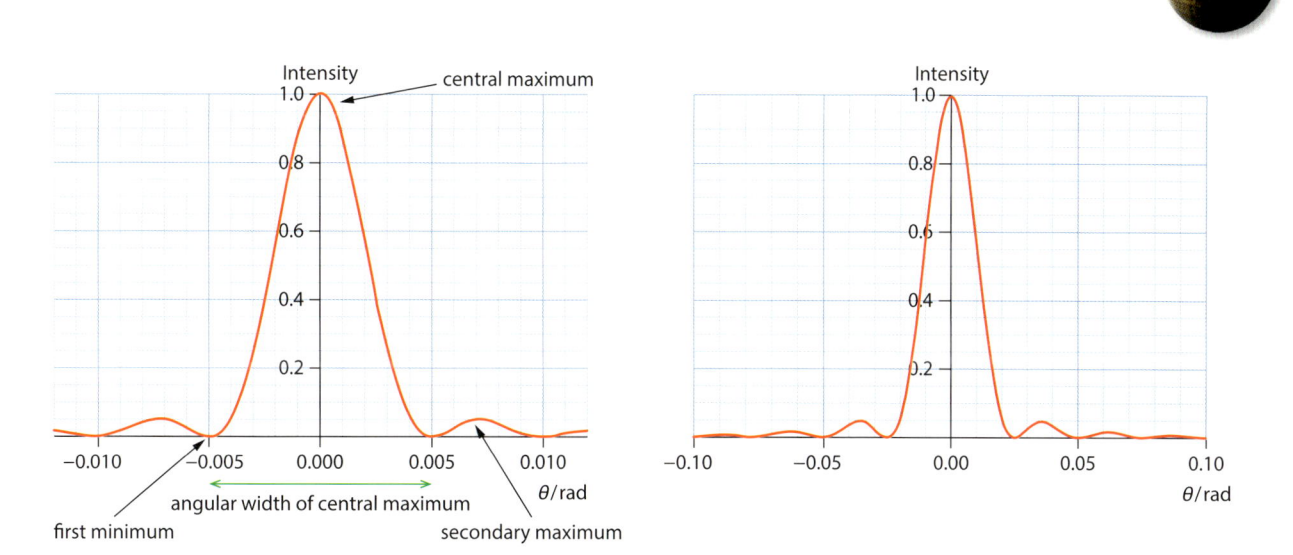

Figure 9.12 The single-slit intensity pattern for red light and slit width **a** 1.4×10^{-5} m and **b** 2.8×10^{-5} m.

The graph in Figure 9.13 shows the intensity pattern for a slit width of 1.4×10^{-5} m but with blue light. The shorter blue wavelength results in a narrower pattern compared to red light with the same slit width. Notice that the intensity of the first secondary maximum is only about 4.5% of the intensity at the central maximum. The units on the vertical axis are arbitrary.

Figure 9.14 shows the pattern as seen on a screen for a thin rectangular slit and a circular slit.

The discussion above applies to monochromatic light, i.e. light of one specific wavelength. When white light is incident on a slit there will be a separate diffraction pattern observed for each wavelength making up the white light. Figure 9.15 shows the combined patterns due to just four wavelengths. The central maximum is white since all the colours produce maxima there. But as we move away from the centre the fringes appear coloured.

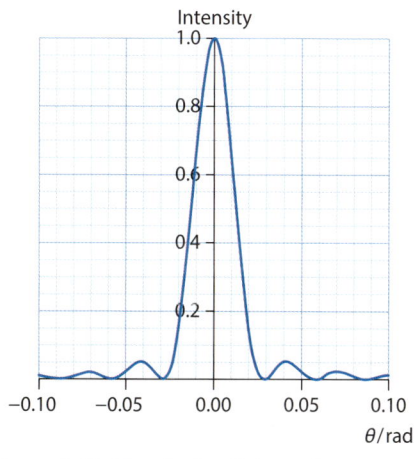

Figure 9.13 The single-slit intensity pattern for blue light and slit width 1.4×10^{-5} m.

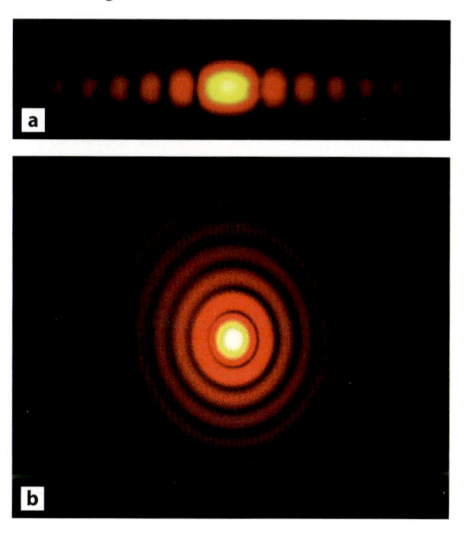

Figure 9.14 a Single-slit intensity pattern showing the central maximum for thin rectangular slit. **b** Intensity pattern for a circular slit.

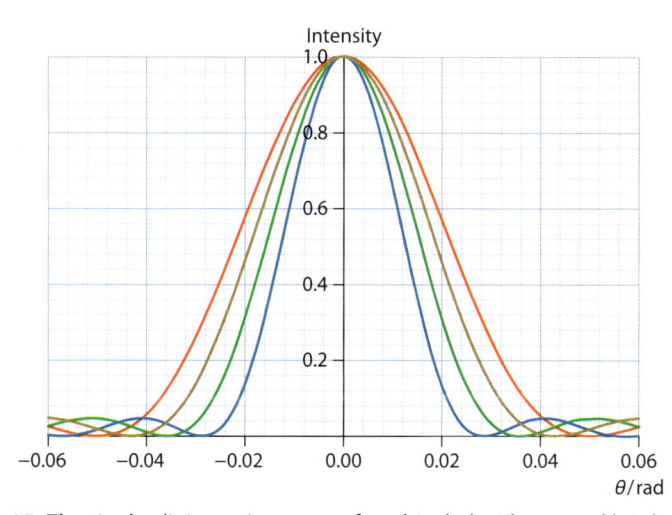

Figure 9.15 The single-slit intensity pattern for white light. The central bright spot is white but the rest of the pattern is coloured.

9 WAVE PHENOMENA (HL)

Nature of science

The interference patterns seen in diffraction through a single slit provide evidence of the wave nature of light. The pattern we see is very different from the simple geometrical shadow expected if light consisted of particles. In this section, you have seen how summing the different waves leads to the pattern observed, and how the width of the slit affects the intensity pattern. In a similar way, the waves diffracted around objects can be summed. Figure 9.16 shows the result of diffraction of light around a small circular object. There is a bright spot at the centre of the disc, where a particle model of light would predict darkness! It was this spot, predicted by Fresnel's wave theory and observed by François Arago, that led to the acceptance of the wave theory in the 19th century (the debate between Fresnel and Poisson was described in the NOS for Subtopic **4.4**). This is an example of how theory can be used to predict what should be observed. This can then be tested by experiment, to give a result supporting the theory. The bright spot in the centre is now called Fresnel's spot or Arago's spot.

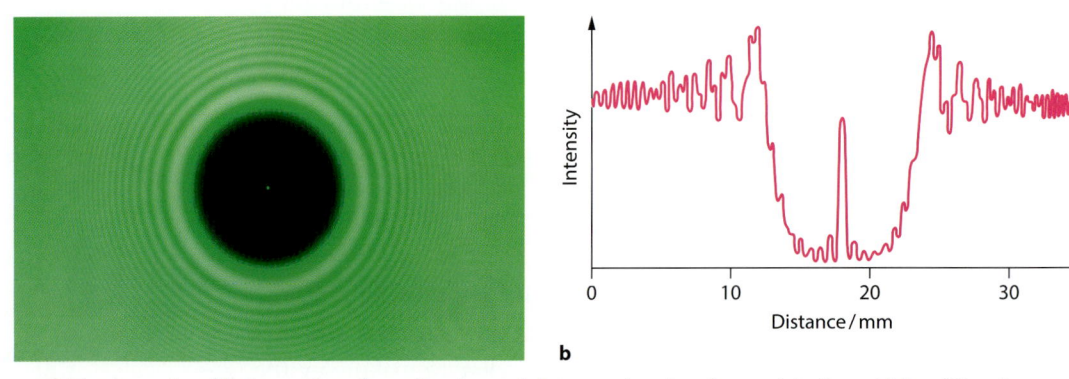

Figure 9.16 a The Fresnel spot. **b** The intensity of light as a function of horizontal distance showing the peak in the middle of the disc.

Test yourself

14 A single slit of width 1.50 μm is illuminated with light of wavelength 500.0 nm. Determine the angular width of the central maximum. (Use the approximate formula.)

15 In a single-slit diffraction experiment the slit width is 0.12 mm and the wavelength of the light used is 6.00×10^{-7} m. Calculate the width of the central maximum on a screen 2.00 m from the slit.

16 The intensity pattern for single-slit diffraction is shown in the diagram. (The vertical units are arbitrary.) The wavelength of the light used is λ.
   a Find the width of the slit b in terms of λ.
   b On a copy of the axes draw a graph to show how intensity varies with diffraction angle for a slit with:

   i width $\frac{b}{2}$ and wavelength λ

   ii width $\frac{b}{2}$ and wavelength $\frac{\lambda}{2}$.

   (You do not need numbers on the intensity axis.)

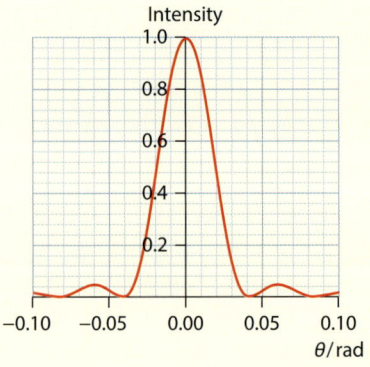

9.3 Interference

This section gives a detailed account of the phenomenon of interference from two sources. It also deals with multiple-slit diffraction and the diffraction grating.

Young's double-slit experiment

In Topic 4 we saw that when identical waves are emitted from two sources and observed at the same point in space, interference will take place. The experiment with light was first performed in 1801 by Thomas Young (1773–1829). In Young's original experiment the source of light was a candle; light from the candle was incident on a single slit, where it diffracted and then, by passing through a lens, the light turned into plane wavefronts.

In the modern version of the experiment the light incident on the two slits is laser light. Light diffracts at each slit and spreads out. The diffracted light arrives at the screen and light from one slit interferes with that from the other. The result is a pattern of bright and dark bands, as shown in Figure 9.17. The bright bands appear where there is constructive interference and the dark bands where there is destructive interference.

In Topic 4 we used the principle of superposition to deduce the following:

If the path difference is an integral multiple of the wavelength, **constructive** interference takes place:

path difference = $n\lambda$, $n = 0, \pm1, \pm2, \pm3$ ...

If the path difference is a half-integral multiple of the wavelength, **destructive** interference takes place:

path difference = $(n + \frac{1}{2})\lambda$, $n = 0, \pm1, \pm2, \pm3$ ...

Learning objectives

- Understand how the single-slit diffraction pattern modulates the two-slit intensity pattern.
- Describe the changes to the interference pattern as the number of slits increases.
- Solve problems with the diffraction grating equation.
- Describe interference in thin films qualitatively and quantitatively.

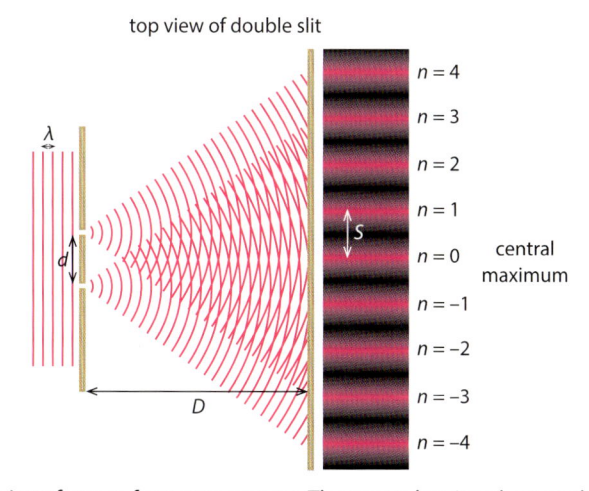

Figure 9.17 Interference from two sources. The waves leaving the two slits and arriving at a point on the screen travel different distances in getting there and so arrive with a path difference.

Figure **9.18a** shows slits S_1 and S_2 separated by a distance d. Monochromatic (i.e. light of one wavelength) laser light falls on the two slits, which then act as two sources of coherent light – the waves are exactly in phase. We shall see why this is important later. The coherent waves travel to point P on a screen, which is displaced from the centre line of the slits by an angle θ. It is clear that the wave from S_2 has further to travel than the wave from S_1. Point Z is such that the distance S_1P equals the distance ZP. The path difference is therefore S_2Z.

We want to calculate this path difference in order to derive the conditions for constructive interference at P. Note that, in practice, the distance between the slits, d, is only 0.1 mm and the distance to the screen is a few metres. This means that, approximately, the lines S_1P and ZP are parallel and the angles PS_1Z and PZS_1 are right angles. Thus, the angle S_2S_1Z equals θ, the angle defining point P (since these two angles have their sides mutually perpendicular).

Using trigonometry, the distance S_2Z, which is the path difference, is equal to $d\sin\theta$. This gives the condition necessary for constructive interference at P.

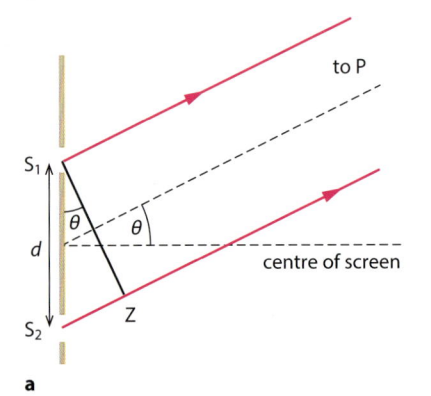

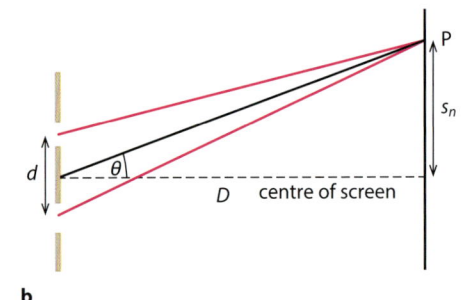

Figure 9.18 The geometry of Young's double-slit experiment. **a** Using geometry to find the path difference. **b** The nth maximum at P is a distance s_n from the centre of the screen.

> For **constructive interference**: $d\sin\theta = n\lambda$, $n = 0, \pm1, \pm2, \pm3 \ldots$

Here, d is the separation of the two slits. Because the d is very small in comparison to the distance to the screen, the angle θ is quite small, so $\sin\theta$ is small. This means we can approximate $\sin\theta$ by $\tan\theta$. You can check on your calculator that, for small angles θ in radians, it is an excellent approximation that $\sin\theta \approx \tan\theta \approx \theta$.

The angle θ is zero for the position directly opposite the slits, where we find the central maximum. Here $n = 0$ (Figure **9.17**). The angle θ increases for each successive maximum moving out from the central maximum. Figure **9.18b** shows the geometry for the nth maximum in the interference pattern. Here $\tan\theta = \dfrac{s_n}{D}$, where D is the distance of the slits from the screen and s_n is the distance of the point P from the middle point of the screen. Using the small angle approximation, we have:

$$\tan\theta \approx \sin\theta = \frac{s_n}{D}$$

$$\Rightarrow s_n = D\sin\theta$$

The condition for constructive interference is $d\sin\theta = n\lambda$, so $\sin\theta = \dfrac{n\lambda}{d}$. Substituting in the equation for s_n:

$$s_n = \frac{n\lambda D}{d}$$

The linear separation, s, on a screen of *two consecutive maxima* is thus:

$$s = s_{n+1} - s_n = (n+1)\frac{\lambda D}{d} - \frac{n\lambda D}{d} = \frac{\lambda D}{d}$$

> $s = \dfrac{\lambda D}{d}$

This is the formula for the separation of consecutive bright fringes that we used without proof in Topic 4. Using this equation, a value for the wavelength λ of the wave can be found from an interference experiment by measuring the separation s between two successive maxima and the distances D and d.

This last formula shows that the maxima of the interference pattern are equally separated. Additional work shows that these maxima are also equally bright.

Worked example

9.10 In a Young's two-slit experiment, a source of light of unknown wavelength is used to illuminate two very narrow slits a distance of 0.15 mm apart. On a screen at a distance of 1.30 m from the slits, bright spots are observed separated by a distance of 4.95 mm. What is the wavelength of light being used?

Use the equation $s = \frac{\lambda D}{d}$. Rearranging to make λ the subject, and substituting the values from the question, we get:

$\lambda = \frac{sd}{D}$

$\lambda = 4.95 \times 10^{-3} \times \frac{1.5 \times 10^{-4}}{1.30}$

$\lambda = 5.71 \times 10^{-7}$ m

The wavelength of the light is 571 nm.

Phase difference and path difference

We have derived the conditions for constructive and destructive interference based on there being a zero phase difference between the two sources. If a phase difference exists then the conditions are modified to:

Constructive interference: $d_1 - d_2 = n\lambda + \frac{\varphi}{2\pi}\lambda$, $n = 0, \pm 1, \pm 2, \pm 3 \ldots$

Destructive interference: $d_1 - d_2 = (n+\frac{1}{2})\lambda + \frac{\varphi}{2\pi}\lambda$, $n = 0, \pm 1, \pm 2, \pm 3 \ldots$

For $\phi = 0$, these conditions give the familiar ones.

The conditions for arbitrary phase difference explain, finally, why the two sources must be coherent. Two sources are **coherent** if the phase difference between the sources stays constant as time goes on. If the phase φ keeps changing, then at the point where the two waves meet and interfere the pattern will be changing from maximum to minimum very quickly. The observer only sees an average of the maximum and the minimum – there is no interference pattern at all.

9 WAVE PHENOMENA (HL)

Intensity in two-slit interference patterns

We have already seen in Topic **4** that the bright fringes in a Young-type two-slit experiment are equally bright if we have slit widths of negligible size. In Topic **4** we gave the graph of intensity as a function of the distance from the middle of the screen (Figure **4.57**). An alternative is to plot the intensity as a function of the angle θ as defined in Figure **9.18** (on page 366). Figure **9.19** shows the variation of intensity with angle θ in degrees for two slits of negligible width. This shows that the fringes are equally bright if the slit width is negligible.

For smaller slit separations the maxima are further apart. Figure **9.20** shows the intensity for a slit separation that is half that of Figure **9.19**. This shows that, for accurate measurement of the fringe separation, as small a slit separation as possible should be used.

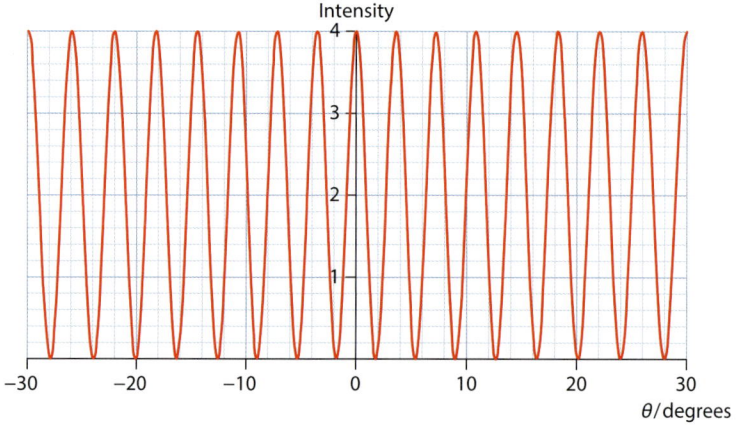

Figure 9.19 The intensity pattern for two slits of negligible width.

The effect of slit width on intensity

The slit width cannot be neglected – real slits have a width. What is the effect of the slit width on intensity? The interference pattern one sees on a screen is the result of two separate phenomena; one is the interference of light leaving one slit with light leaving the other slit and the other is the interference pattern due to one slit alone, as discussed in Subtopic **9.2**.

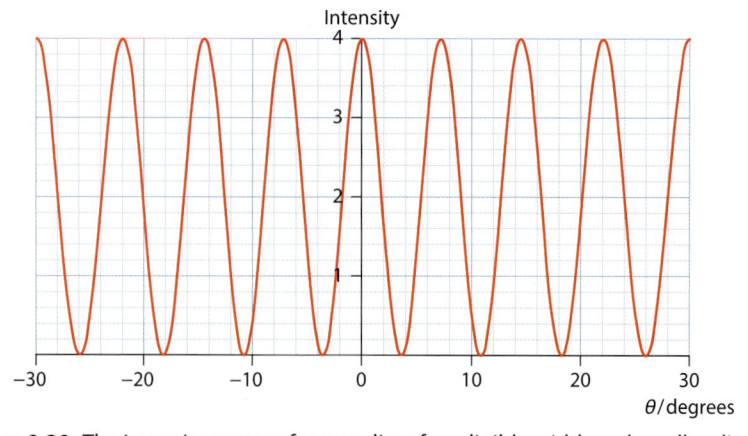

Figure 9.20 The intensity pattern for two slits of negligible width and smaller slit separation. The slit separation is eight times the wavelength.

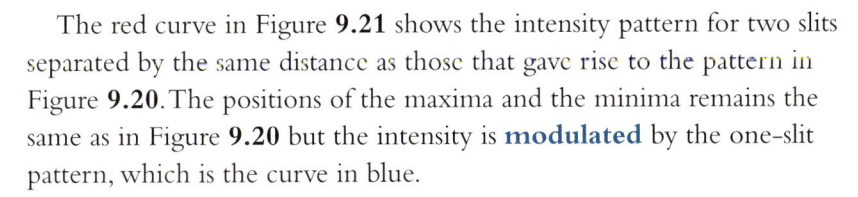

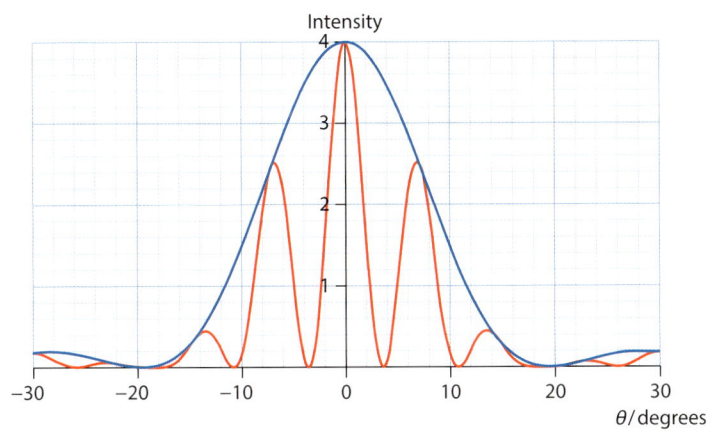

The red curve in Figure **9.21** shows the intensity pattern for two slits separated by the same distance as those that gave rise to the pattern in Figure **9.20**. The positions of the maxima and the minima remains the same as in Figure **9.20** but the intensity is **modulated** by the one-slit pattern, which is the curve in blue.

Figure 9.21 The two-slit interference intensity pattern for slits of width equal to three times the wavelength. The slit separation is eight times the wavelength.

Multiple-slit diffraction

As the number of slits increases, the interference pattern increases in complexity. Consider the case of four slits. The intensity pattern is shown in Figure **9.22**. We see that there are now two secondary maxima in-between the primary maxima.

Figure **9.23** shows the case of six slits. There are now four secondary maxima between primary maxima. As the number of slits increases the secondary maxima become unimportant. With N slits, there $N-2$ secondary maxima. The intensity of the central maximum is N^2 times the intensity of just one slit by itself.

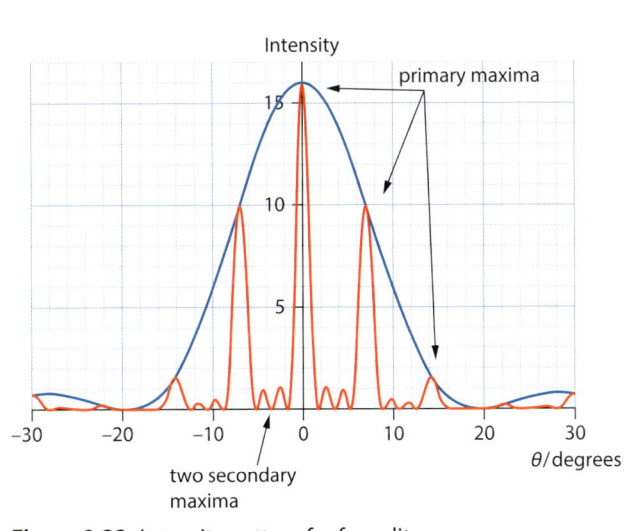

Figure 9.22 Intensity pattern for four slits.

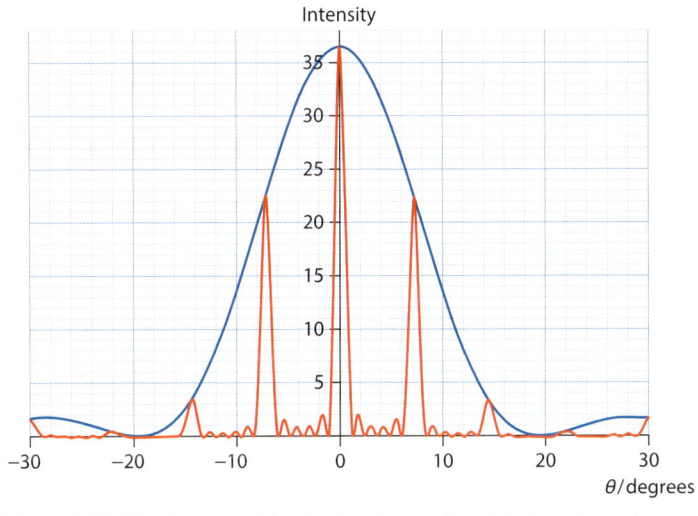

Figure 9.23 The intensity distribution for six slits. Note how the width of the maxima decreases but their position stays the same. Note also how the relative importance of the secondary maxima decreases with increasing slit number.

9 WAVE PHENOMENA (HL)

Figure **9.24** shows the case with 20 slits. The secondary maxima have all but disappeared. We also observe that as the number of slits increases, the **width** of the primary maxima decreases; the bright fringes become very sharp and easily identifiable.

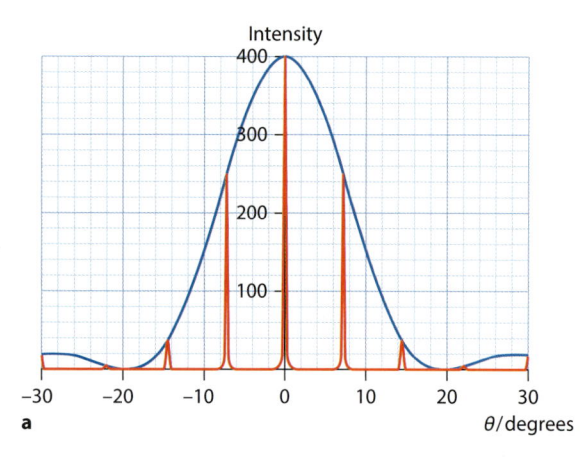

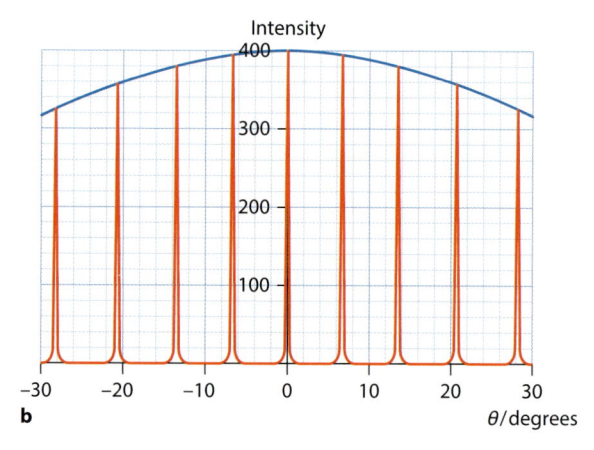

Figure 9.24 a The intensity distribution for 20 slits. The secondary maxima are completely unimportant and the primary maxima are very thin. In **b** the slit width is much smaller so that the single-slit diffraction pattern is very wide. The primary maxima now have roughly the same intensity.

> It can be proven (see next section) that for multiple slits the primary maxima are observed at angles given by:
>
> $d \sin \theta = n\lambda$, $n = 0, \pm 1, \pm 2, \pm 3, \ldots$
>
> This is the same condition as in the two-slit case. Here d is the separation of two successive slits.
> The primary maxima of the multiple-slit interference pattern are observed at the same angles as the corresponding two-slit pattern with the same slit separation.

Notice that in all diagrams we are assuming a non-zero slit width (equal to three wavelengths in fact). If the width can be ignored then the primary maxima have roughly the same intensity as the central maximum.

> In summary, if we increase the number of slits to N:
> - The primary maxima will become thinner and sharper (the width is proportional to $\frac{1}{N}$)
> - The $N - 2$ secondary maxima will become unimportant
> - The intensity of the central maximum is proportional to N^2.

Worked example

9.11 Look at Figure **9.23** (on page 369) which shows the intensity pattern for six slits. Verify that the slit width is three times the wavelength and determine the separation of two consecutive slits in terms of the wavelength.

The minimum of the single-slit diffraction pattern (the blue curve) is at about $19° \approx 0.33$ rad.

Using the approximate single-slit diffraction formula $\theta \approx \frac{\lambda}{b}$ we deduce that:

$$b \approx \frac{\lambda}{\theta} = \frac{\lambda}{0.33} \approx 3\lambda$$

So the slit separation is three times the wavelength, as claimed above.

The first primary maximum away from the central is at $\theta = 7°$. Since:

$$d \sin \theta = 1 \times \lambda$$

$$\Rightarrow d = \frac{\lambda}{\sin 7°} \approx 8\lambda$$

The diffraction grating

The **diffraction grating** is an important device in spectroscopy (the analysis of light). It is mainly used to measure the wavelength of light. A diffraction grating consists of a large number of parallel slits whose width we take to be negligible. Instead of actual slits, modern gratings consist of a transparent slide on which rulings or grooves have been precisely cut. The advantage of a large number of slits is that the maxima in the interference pattern are sharp and bright and can easily be distinguished from their neighbours (Figure **9.25**). These bright fringes are called 'lines'. Because the fringes are well separated the measurement of their separation is easier.

The maxima of the pattern are observed at angles that can be found by an argument similar to that for just two slits: Figure **9.26** shows the path difference (in light blue) between rays leaving the slits. The smallest path difference is δ: that between the top two rays. By similar triangles, any other path difference is an integral multiple of δ. So if δ is an integral multiple of λ, all other path differences will also be an integral multiple of λ. But $\delta = d \sin \theta$. Hence the condition for constructive interference is:

$$d \sin \theta = n\lambda, \quad n = 0, 1, 2, \ldots.$$

In practice, a diffraction grating is stated by its manufacturer to have 'x lines per millimetre'. This means that the separation of the slits is $d = \frac{1}{x}$ mm. It is quite common to find diffraction gratings with 600 lines per mm corresponding to a slit separation of $d = 1.67 \times 10^{-6}$ m.

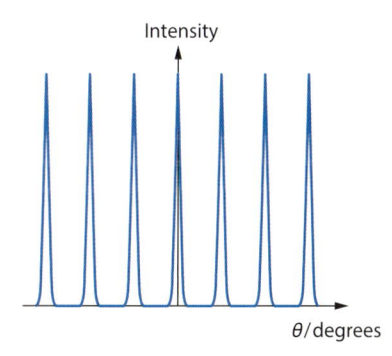

Figure 9.25 The intensity distribution for a diffraction grating. The maxima have roughly the same intensity and are very thin.

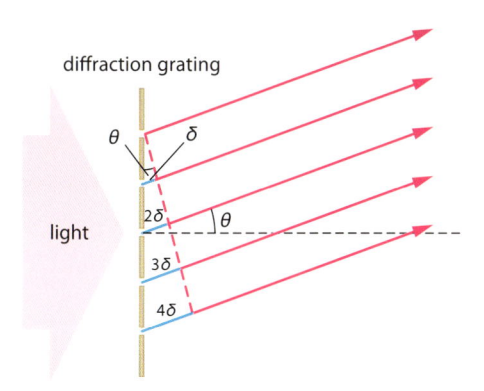

Figure 9.26 The path difference between any two rays is an integral multiple of the smallest path difference Δ between the top two rays. The dashed line is normal to the rays, which makes the angle between this line and the grating θ.

Worked example

9.12 Light of wavelength 680 nm falls normally on a diffraction grating that has 600 rulings per mm. What is the angle separating the central maximum ($n=0$) from the next ($n=1$)? How many maxima can be seen?

The separation between slits is:

$$d = \frac{1}{600} \times 10^{-3} \, \text{m}$$

With $n=1$ we find:

$$\sin\theta = 1 \times 680 \times 10^{-9} \times 600 \times 10^{3}$$

$$\sin\theta = 0.408$$

Hence $\theta = 24.1°$

The angle separating the two is therefore 24.1°.

For $n=2$ we find $\theta = 54.7°$. No solution can be found for $n=3$; the sine of the angle becomes larger than 1. Thus, we can see the central maximum and two orders on either side.

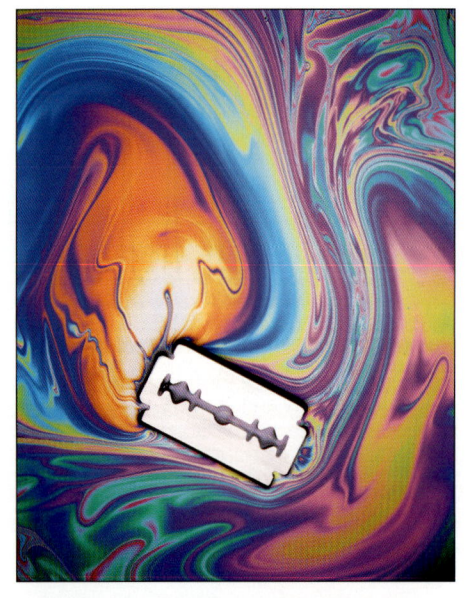

Figure 9.27 Interference pattern in a thin film of oil floating on water.

Thin film interference

The colours that are seen in a soap bubble or on a thin film of oil floating on water on the street are examples of a general effect called **thin film interference** (Figure 9.27).

To understand this phenomenon we must first realise that, upon reflection, a ray of light will undergo a **phase change** of π if it reflects off a medium of **higher** refractive index. This means that if the incident wave arrives at the boundary as a crest it will reflect as a trough. This is similar to a pulse on a rope reflecting off a fixed end.

Consider light of wavelength λ in air, incident on a thin transparent film of oil with parallel sides. The film is surrounded by air (Figure 9.28).

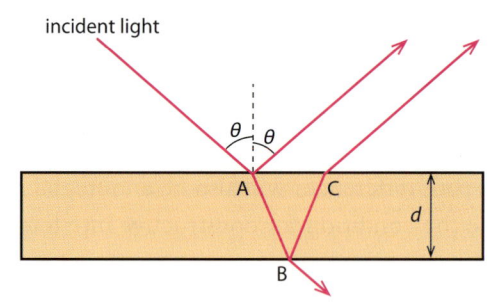

Figure 9.28 Thin film interference in oil is explained by the phase difference due to the extra distance covered by one of the rays and by the phase change upon reflection at the top surface.

Let d be the thickness of the film. A ray is incident on the film from air. At point A the ray refracts into the film and reflects. There will be a phase change of π at A since oil has a higher refractive index than air. The reflected ray enters an observer's eye. The refracted ray continues in oil and refracts and reflects at B. There is no phase change at B. The reflected

Exam tip
You must be very careful with the conditions for constructive or destructive interference with thin films. You must first check what phase changes (if any) take place.

ray continues to C, where it refracts out into air and into the observer's eye. The two rays from A and C will interfere.

Assume that the angle of incidence θ is very small so we are essentially looking normally down on the film. This means the path difference is $2d$. Normally, the condition for constructive interference is that the path difference is an integral multiple of the wavelength. But remember that here we have a phase change that turns crests into troughs. This means that the condition for constructive interference changes to:

$$\text{path difference} = (m + \tfrac{1}{2})\lambda_o$$

where λ_o is the wavelength in oil. Here m is any integer but in practice we only use $m = 0$.

The wavelength of light in oil λ_o is found from $\lambda_o = \dfrac{\lambda}{n}$, where n is the refractive index of oil and λ the wavelength of light in air. So this gives the following conditions:

	one phase change	no or two phase changes
Constructive interference:	$2dn = (m + \tfrac{1}{2})\lambda$	$2dn = m\lambda$
Destructive interference	$2dn = m\lambda$	$2dn = (m + \tfrac{1}{2})\lambda$

The colours are explained as follows: the thin film is illuminated with white light. The wavelength that suffers destructive interference will have the corresponding colour absent in the reflected light. Similarly the wavelength that suffers constructive interference will have its corresponding colour dominantly in the reflected light. These two factors determine the colour of the film.

Worked example

9.13 A solar cell must be coated to ensure as little as possible of the light falling on it is reflected. A solar cell has a very high index of refraction (about 3.50). A coating of index of refraction 1.50 is placed on the cell. Estimate the minimum thickness needed in order to **minimise** reflection of light of wavelength 524 nm.

We will have phase changes of π at **both** reflections (from the top of the coating and the solar cell surface) and we want to have destructive interference. The condition is therefore:

$$2dn = (m + \tfrac{1}{2})\lambda$$

We want the minimum thickness so $m = 0$. Therefore:

$$2dn = \tfrac{1}{2}\lambda$$

Hence the thickness is:

$$d = \dfrac{\lambda}{4n}$$

$$d = \dfrac{524 \times 10^{-9}}{4 \times 1.50}$$

$$d = 87.3 \text{ nm}$$

9 WAVE PHENOMENA (HL)

Nature of science

Curiosity and serendipity

The shimmering colours of a peacock's tail feathers, the colours inside the paua shell, and the glistening surface of a golden stag beetle's coat are all examples of iridescence in nature. Similar colours are seen in soap bubbles and oil films. Curious as to what caused these beautiful colours and effects in nature, scientists speculated on different mechanisms. One suggestion was that the surface pigments of iridescent feathers appeared to reflect different colours when viewed from different angles. Another suggestion was that the colours were formed as a result of the structure of the surface, not anything to do with the pigments. With the acceptance of the wave theory of light, scientists in the late 19th century developed a theory of interference in thin films that could explain these colours. Developments in microscopy meant that finer and finer structure could be seen, and using an electron microscope in the 20th century it was possible to see complex thin-film structures in iridescent bird feathers.

In 1817 Joseph Fraunhofer accidentally produced a thin film coating when he left nitric acid on a polished glass surface. Experimenting with different glasses, he was able to produce a surface with the same vivid colours seen in a soap bubbles. When he observed the same colours appearing as a coating of alcohol evaporated from a polished metal surface, he concluded that such colours would appear in any transparent thin film. This was the start of the technology of thin films, developed in the 20th century to make optical coatings for glass.

Figure 9.29 The iridescent 'eye' of a peacock's tail feather.

? Test yourself

17 In a Young's two-slit experiment, a coherent source of light of wavelength 680 nm is used to illuminate two very narrow slits a distance of 0.12 mm apart. A screen is placed at a distance of 1.50 m from the slits. Calculate the separation of two successive bright spots.

18 Explain why two identical flashlights pointing light to the same spot on a screen will never produce an interference pattern.

19 In a Young's two-slit experiment it is found that an nth-order maximum for a wavelength of 680.0 nm coincides with the $(n+1)$th maximum of light of wavelength 510.0 nm. Determine n.

20 Light is incident normally on two narrow parallel slits a distance of 1.00 mm apart. A screen is placed a distance of 1.2 m from the slits. The distance on the screen between the central maximum and the centre of the $n = 4$ bright spot is measured to be 3.1 mm.
   a Determine the wavelength of light.
   b This experiment is repeated in water (of refractive index 1.33). Suggest how the distance of 3.1 mm would change, if at all.

21 The graph shows the intensity pattern from a two-slit interference experiment.

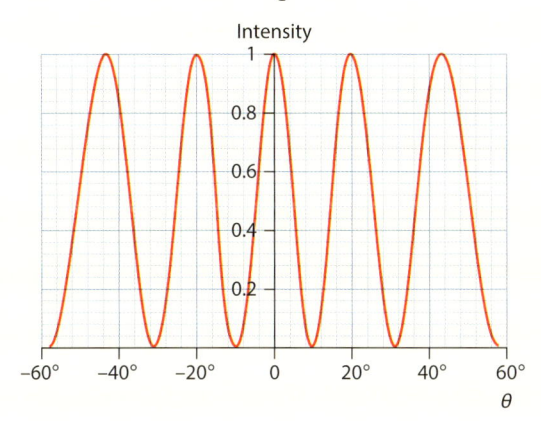

Intensity graph with peaks at approximately −40°, −20°, 0°, 20°, 40°, with intensity values on the y-axis from 0 to 1 (marked 0.2, 0.4, 0.6, 0.8), and θ on the x-axis from −60° to 60°.

   a Determine the separation of the slits in terms of the wavelength of light used.
   b Suggest how the pattern in **a** changes if the slit separation is halved.

22 A grating with 400 lines per mm is illuminated with light of wavelength 600.0 nm.
   a Determine the angles at which maxima are observed.
   b Determine the largest order that can be seen with this grating and this wavelength.

23 A piece of glass of index of refraction 1.50 is coated with a thin layer of magnesium fluoride of index of refraction 1.38. It is illuminated with light of wavelength 680 nm. Determine the minimum thickness of the coating that will result in no reflection.

24 A thin soap bubble of index of refraction 1.33 is viewed with light of wavelength 550.0 nm and appears very bright. Predict a possible value of the thickness of the soap bubble.

25 Two very narrow, parallel slits separated by a distance of 1.4×10^{-5} m are illuminated by coherent, monochromatic light of wavelength 7.0×10^{-7} m.
   a Describe what is meant by coherent and monochromatic light.
   b Draw a graph to show the intensity of light observed on a screen far from the slits.
   c By drawing another graph on the same axes, illustrate the effect on the intensity distribution of increasing the width of the slits to 2.8×10^{-5} m.

26 a Draw a graph to show the variation with angle of the intensity of light observed on a screen some distance from two very narrow, parallel slits when coherent monochromatic light falls on the slits.
   b Describe how the graph you drew in **a** changes when:
      i the number of slits increases but their separation stays the same
      ii the number of slits stays at two but their separation decreases.

9 WAVE PHENOMENA (HL)

Learning objectives

- Understand the limits on resolution placed by diffraction.
- Solve problems related to the Rayleigh criterion and resolving power (resolvance) in diffraction gratings.

9.4 Resolution

This short section deals in detail with the limits to resolution imposed by diffraction.

The Rayleigh criterion

In Section 9.2 we discussed in some detail the diffraction of a wave through a slit of linear size b. One application of diffraction is in the problem of the **resolution** of the images of two objects that are close to each other. Resolution of two objects means the ability to *see* as distinct two objects that are distinct. Light from each of the objects will diffract as it goes though the opening of the eye of the observer. The light from each source will create its own diffraction pattern on the retina of the eye of the observer. If these patterns are far apart the observer has no problem distinguishing the two sources as distinct (Figure 9.30).

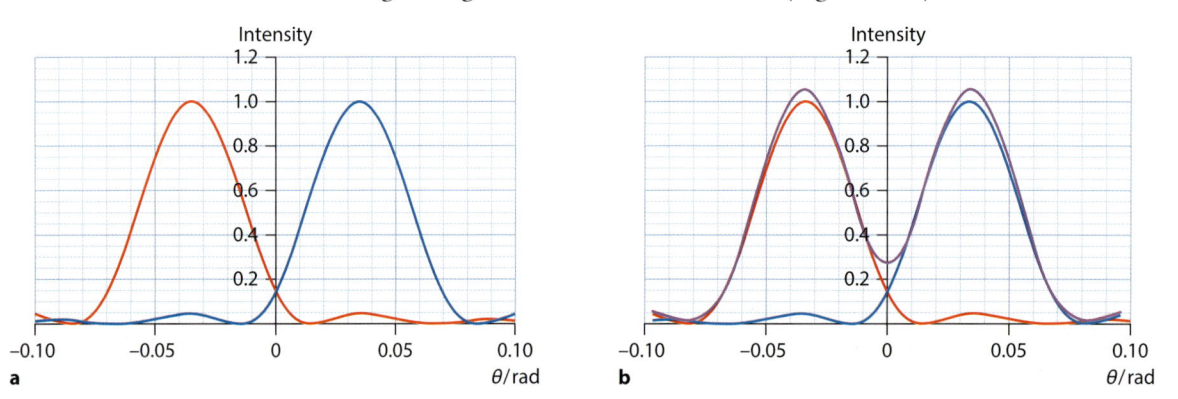

Figure 9.30 a The individual diffraction patterns for two sources that are far apart from each other (drawn in red and blue). **b** The combined pattern for the two sources. The observer clearly sees two distinct objects. There is a very clear drop in intensity in the middle of the pattern.

If on the other hand, the two sources are too close to each other then their diffraction patterns will overlap on the retina of the eye of the observer, as shown in Figure 9.31. The observer cannot distinguish the two objects.

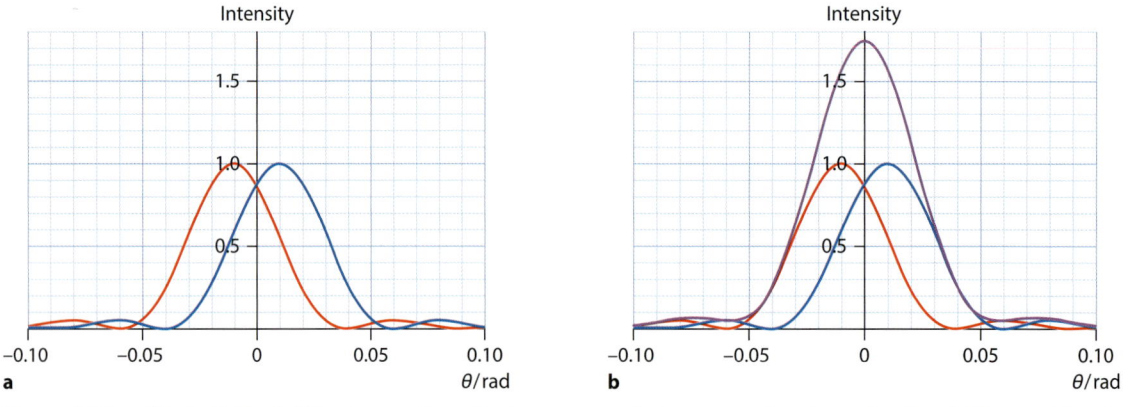

Figure 9.31 a The individual diffraction patterns for two sources that are very close to each other. **b** The combined pattern for the two sources. The observer cannot distinguish two distinct objects. The combined pattern looks very much like that from a single source.

The limiting case, i.e. when the two objects can just be resolved, is when the first minimum of the diffraction pattern of one source coincides with the central maximum of the diffraction pattern of the other source, as shown in Figure 9.32. This is known as the **Rayleigh criterion**. The photograph in Figure 9.33 illustrates what is meant by 'just resolved'.

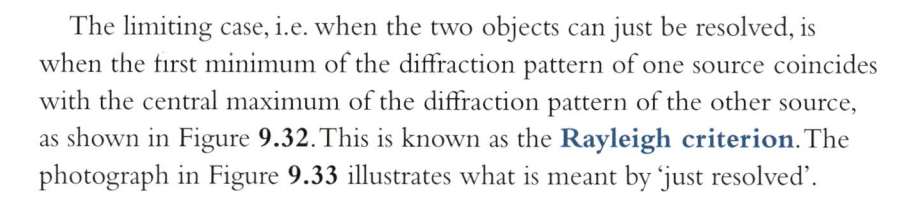

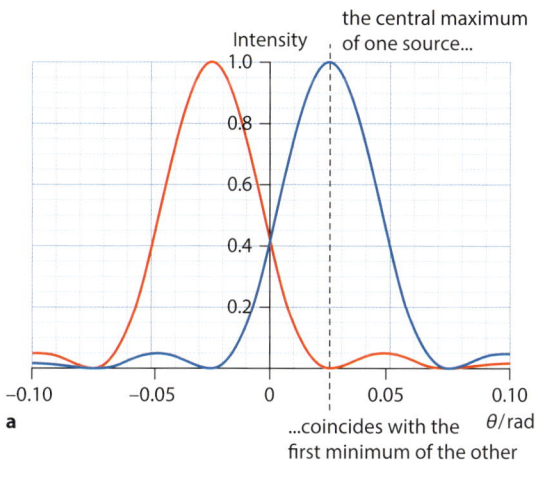

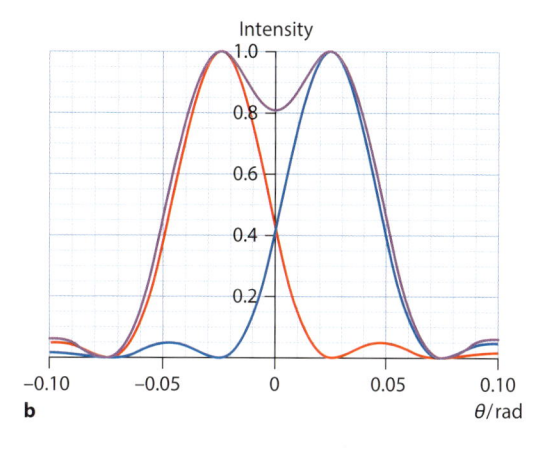

Figure 9.32 a The limiting case where resolution is thought to be just barely possible. The first minimum of one source coincides with the central maximum of the other. **b** The combined pattern for the two sources shows a small dip in the middle.

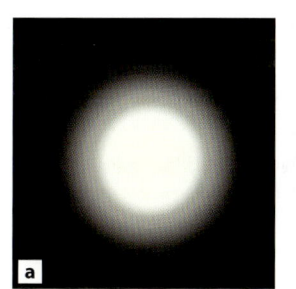

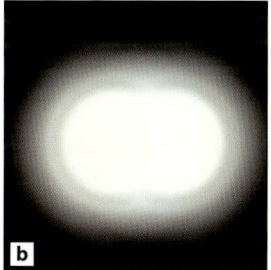

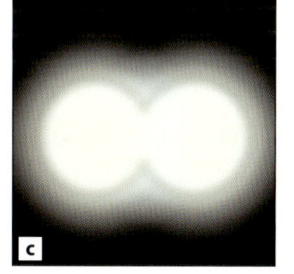

Figure 9.33 Two images that are **a** not resolvable, **b** barely resolvable and **c** clearly resolvable.

Figure 9.34 shows two objects separated by distance s. The two objects are a distance d from the observer. The angle that the separation of the objects subtends at the eye is called the **angular separation** θ_A of the two objects and is equal in radians to $\frac{s}{d}$.

Notice that the angle θ_A is also the angular separation of the central maxima of the diffraction patterns of the two sources. According to the Rayleigh criterion, resolution is just possible when this angular separation is equal to the angle of the first diffraction minimum: $\theta_D = \frac{\lambda}{b}$ (as we saw in Subtopic 9.2).

Exam tip
Solving resolution problems involves the comparison of two angles: the angular separation and the angle of diffraction. We have resolution if the angular separation is greater than or equal to the diffraction angle.

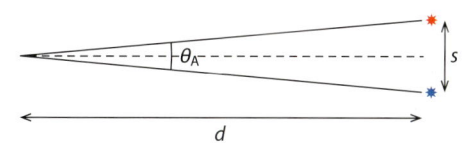

Figure 9.34 Two objects that are separated by a distance s are viewed by an observer a distance d away. The separation s subtends an angle θ_A at the eye of the observer.

9 WAVE PHENOMENA (HL)

The IB data booklet does not include the subscript D in θ_D. We have included it to stress that this refers to the diffraction angle.

For a **circular slit** things have to be modified somewhat and it can be shown that the angle of diffraction for a circular slit of diameter b is given by:

$$\theta_D = 1.22 \frac{\lambda}{b}$$

So, for a circular slit, resolution is possible when:

$$\theta_A \geq \theta_D$$

$$\frac{s}{d} \geq 1.22 \frac{\lambda}{b}$$

Worked examples

9.14 The camera of a spy satellite orbiting at 400 km has a diameter of 35 cm. Estimate the smallest distance this camera can resolve on the surface of the Earth. (Assume a wavelength of 500 nm.)

Using Rayleigh's criterion, at the limit of resolution we have that $\frac{s}{d} = 1.22 \frac{\lambda}{b}$. Therefore substituting the known values we find:

$$s = 1.22 \times \frac{\lambda}{b} \times d$$

$$s = \frac{1.22 \times 5.0 \times 10^{-7} \times 4.0 \times 10^5}{0.35}$$

$$s = 0.70 \text{ m}$$

9.15 The headlights of a car are 2 m apart. The pupil of the human eye has a diameter of about 2 mm. Suppose that light of wavelength 500 nm is being used. Estimate the maximum distance at which the two headlights are seen as distinct.

Using Rayleigh's criterion, at the limit of resolution $\frac{s}{d} = 1.22 \frac{\lambda}{b}$. Therefore solving for the distance d:

$$d = \frac{sb}{1.22\lambda}$$

$$d = \frac{2.0 \times 2.0 \times 10^{-3}}{1.22 \times 5.0 \times 10^{-7}}$$

$$d = 7000 \text{ m}$$

The car should be no more than this distance away.

9.16 The pupil of the human eye has a diameter of about 2 mm and the distance between the pupil and the back of the eye (the retina) where the image is formed is about 20 mm. Using light of wavelength 500 nm, the eye can resolve objects that have an angular separation of 3×10^{-4} rad. Use this information to estimate the distance between the receptors in the eye.

Since the angular separation θ of two objects that can be resolved is 3×10^{-4} rad, this must also be the angular separation between two receptors on the retina. Thus, the linear separation l of two adjacent receptors must be smaller than about:

$l = r\theta$

Here $r = 20$ mm, so:

$l = 20 \times 10^{-3} \times 3 \times 10^{4}$

$l = 6 \times 10^{-6}$ m

Diffraction grating resolution

An important characteristic of a diffraction grating is its ability to resolve, i.e. see as distinct, two lines in a spectrum that correspond to wavelengths λ_1 and λ_2 that are very close to each other. Because the wavelengths are close to each other the angles at which the lines are observed will also be close to each other and so difficult to resolve.

In Figure 9.35 if the angular separation of the two lines is too small the two lines will not be seen as distinct.

The **resolving power** R (or resolvance) of a diffraction grating is defined as:

$$R = \frac{\lambda_{avg}}{\Delta \lambda}$$

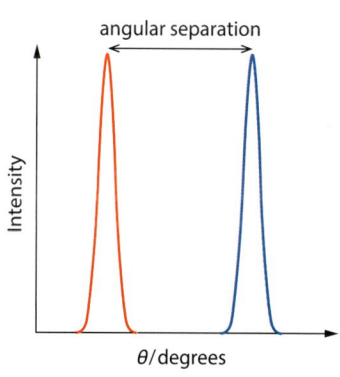

Figure 9.35 Two lines that are close to each may not be resolvable.

where λ_{avg} is the average of λ_1 and λ_2 and $\Delta \lambda$ is their difference. The higher the resolving power, the smaller the differences in wavelength that can be resolved. It can be shown that $R = mN$ where m is the order at which the lines are observed and N is the total number of slits or rulings on the diffraction grating. So we have that:

$$\frac{\lambda_{avg}}{\Delta \lambda} = mN$$

$$\Rightarrow \Delta \lambda = \frac{\lambda_{avg}}{mN}$$

This gives the smallest difference in wavelengths that can be resolved. If $\Delta \lambda$ is very small it is necessary to use a grating with a very large number of rulings.

Worked example

9.17 A beam of light containing different wavelengths is incident on a diffraction grating. The grating has 600 lines per mm and is 2.0 cm wide. The average wavelength in the beam is 620 nm. Calculate the least difference in wavelength that can be resolved by this grating in the second order.

From the formula for resolving power we have:

$$\Delta\lambda = \frac{\lambda_{avg}}{mN}$$

Since the grating is 20 mm wide we find:

$N = 600 \times 20 = 12\,000$

We are using the second order so $m = 2$ and therefore:

$$\Delta\lambda = \frac{\lambda_{avg}}{mN} = \frac{620}{2 \times 12\,000} = 0.0258 \approx 0.026 \text{ nm}$$

Nature of science

Pushing the limits of resolution

The Rayleigh criterion determines the detail that can be resolved for a given wavelength. Advances in technology have pushed the limits of what can be resolved using both large and small wavelengths. Larger diameter receiving dishes give greater resolution to radio telescopes, which use very long wavelengths. Even greater resolution is obtained using vast arrays of radio telescopes connected together, made possible through advances in signal processing. At the other extreme, small objects need small wavelengths. All other things being equal, blue light is better than red light for distinguishing detail. A huge technological advance was made when it was realised that the wave used to 'see' a small object does not even have to be an electromagnetic wave. In Topic **12** we will find out that all particles, and in particular electrons, show wave-like behaviour, and this is the basis of the images obtained by the electron microscope. The reason particle physicists need particle accelerators is because the high energies obtained give particles very short wavelengths, which can then be used to probe the structure of other tiny particles.

? Test yourself

27 Determine whether a telescope with an objective lens of diameter 20 cm can resolve two objects a distance of 10 km away separated by 1 cm. (Assume we are using a wavelength of 600 nm.)

28 a The headlights of a car are separated by a distance of 1.4 m. Estimate the distance these would be resolved as two separate sources by a lens of diameter 5 cm with a wavelength of 500 nm.
b Discuss the effect, if any, of decreasing the wavelength on the distance in **a**.

29 Assume that the pupil of the human eye has a diameter of 4.0 mm and receives light of wavelength 5.0×10^{-7} m.
   a Calculate the smallest angular separation that can be resolved by the eye at this wavelength.
   b Estimate the least distance between features on the Moon (a distance of 3.8×10^8 m away) that can be resolved by the human eye.

30 The Jodrell Bank radio telescope in Cheshire, UK, has a diameter of 76 m. Assume that it receives electromagnetic waves of wavelength 21 cm.
   a Calculate the smallest angular separation that can be resolved by this telescope.
   b Determine whether this telescope can resolve the two stars of a binary star system that are separated by a distance of 3.6×10^{11} m and are 8.8×10^{16} m from Earth (assume a wavelength of 21 cm).

31 The Arecibo radio telescope has a diameter of 300 m. Assume that it receives electromagnetic waves of wavelength 8.0 cm. Determine if this radio telescope will see the Andromeda galaxy (a distance of 2.5×10^6 light years away) as a point source of light or an extended object. Take the diameter of Andromeda to be 2.2×10^5 light years.

32 A spacecraft is returning to Earth after a long mission far from Earth. Estimate the distance from Earth, at which an astronaut in the spacecraft will first see the Earth and the Moon as distinct objects with a naked eye. Take the separation of the Earth and the Moon to be 3.8×10^8 m, and assume a pupil diameter of 4.5 mm and light of wavelength 5.5×10^{-7} m.

33 The Hubble Space Telescope has a mirror of diameter 2.4 m.
   a Estimate the resolution of the telescope, assuming that it operates at a wavelength of 5.5×10^{-7} m.
   b Suggest why the Hubble Space Telescope has an advantage over Earth-based telescopes of similar mirror diameter.

34 The spectrum of sodium includes two lines at wavelengths 588.995 nm and 589.592 nm. A sodium lamp is viewed by a diffraction grating that just manages to resolve these two lines in the third order at 12°. Determine:
   a the slit spacing d of the grating
   b the total number of rulings on the grating.

35 a A diffraction grating is 5.0 mm wide and has 600 lines per mm. A beam of light containing a range of wavelengths is incident on the grating. The average wavelength is 550 nm. Determine the least wavelength range that can be resolved in second order.
   b You can increase the resolving power by increasing the order m or the number of lines N. Suggest whether these two ways are equivalent.

9.5 The Doppler effect

This section looks at the Doppler effect, the change in the observed frequency of a wave when there is relative motion between the source and the observer. The Doppler effect is a fundamental wave phenomenon with many applications. The phenomenon applies to all waves, but only sound and light waves are considered here.

Wavefront diagrams

If you stand by the edge of a road and a car moving at high speed approaches you will hear a high-pitched sound. The instant the car moves past you the frequency of the sound will drop abruptly and will stay low

Learning objectives

- Understand the Doppler effect through wavefront diagrams.
- Solve problems involving frequency and wavelength shifts and speeds of source or observer.

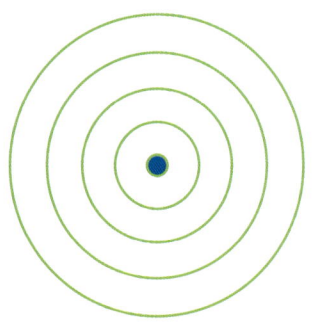

Figure 9.36 The wavefronts emitted by a stationary source are concentric. The common centre is the position of the source.

as the car moves away from you: this is the Doppler effect. It is more pronounced if the car going by is a Formula 1 racing car!

> The **Doppler effect** is the change in the observed frequency of a wave which happens whenever there is relative motion between the source and the observer.

We can explain most aspects of the Doppler effect using wavefront diagrams. Consider first a source of sound S that is stationary in still air. The source emits circular wavefronts (Figure **9.36**).

Suppose that the source emits a wave of frequency f and that the speed of the sound in still air is v. This means that f wavefronts are emitted per second. An observer who moves towards the stationary source will meet one wavefront after the other more frequently and so will measure a higher frequency of sound than f. The distance between the wavefronts does not change and so the moving observer will measure the same wavelength of sound as the source. Similarly, if the observer moves away from the source, then he or she will meet wavefronts less frequently and so will measure a frequency lower than f. The wavelength will be the same as that measured by the source.

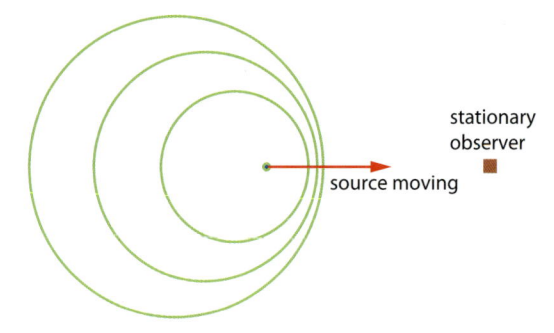

Figure 9.37 A source is approaching the stationary observer with speed u_S.

Exam tip
A very common mistake with the Doppler effect is that students confuse frequency with intensity or loudness of the sound. As a source approaches at **constant speed**, the intensity increases because the distance gets smaller. The frequency is observed to be higher than that emitted but **constant**.

If it is the source that is moving, then the wavefronts will look like those in Figure **9.37**. Because the source is moving towards the observer, the wavefronts between the source and the observer are crowding together. This means that the observer will meet them more frequently, i.e. he or she will measure a frequency higher than f. Because of the crowding of the wavefronts the wavelength measured will be less than the wavelength measured by the source. If, on the other hand, the source moves away from the observer, the frequency measured by the observer will be less than f because the wavefronts arrive at the observer less frequently. The wavelength measured is larger than that at the source because the wavefronts are further apart.

These are the main features of the Doppler effect for sound. The next two sections look at the Doppler effect quantitatively.

Moving source and stationary observer

To derive a formula relating the emitted and observed frequencies, look at the situation shown in Figure **9.38**.

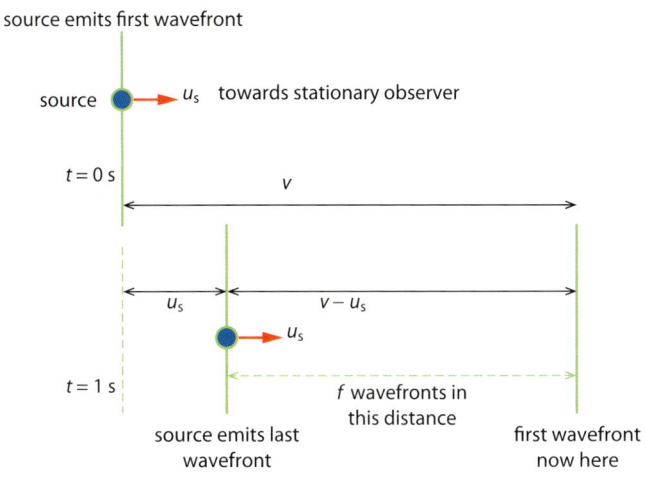

Figure 9.38 Determining the Doppler frequency.

The source emits sound of frequency f and wavelength λ. The sound has speed v in still air. So in one second, the source will emit f wavefronts. The source is moving with speed u_s towards the observer, so in one second the source will move a distance equal to u_S towards the stationary observer. The movement of the source means that these f wavefronts are all within a distance of $v - u_S$. The stationary observer will therefore measure a wavelength λ' (separation of wavefronts) equal to:

$$\lambda' = \frac{v - u_s}{f}$$

The frequency f' measured by the stationary observer is therefore:

$$f' = \frac{v}{\lambda'}$$

$$f' = \frac{v}{\frac{v - u_s}{f}}$$

$$f' = f\left(\frac{v}{v - u_s}\right) \quad \text{source moving towards observer}$$

As the source approaches, the stationary observer thus measures a higher frequency than that emitted by the source. The wavelength measured by the observer will be shorter than the wavelength measured at the source. You can see this clearly from the wavefront diagram of Figure **9.37**: the distance between the wavefronts in front of the source is smaller than that in Figure **9.36**.

Exam tip
Notice that the speed of the wave measured by the observer is still v despite the fact the source moves. The speed of a wave is determined by the properties of the medium. This is still air for both source and observer and both measure the same speed, v.

In fact:

$$\lambda' = \frac{v - u_s}{f}$$

$$\lambda' = \frac{v}{f}\left(1 - \frac{u_s}{v}\right)$$

$$\lambda' = \lambda\left(1 - \frac{u_s}{v}\right) \quad \text{source moving towards observer}$$

A similar calculation for the case of the source moving away from the stationary observer gives:

$$f' = f\left(\frac{v}{v + u_s}\right) \quad \text{source moving away from observer}$$

and

$$\lambda' = \lambda\left(1 + \frac{u_s}{v}\right) \quad \text{source moving away from observer}$$

Worked example

9.18 The siren of a car moving at $28.0\,\text{m s}^{-1}$ emits sound of frequency 1250 Hz. The car is directed towards a stationary observer X and moves away from an observer Y. Calculate the frequency and wavelength of sound observed by X and Y. The speed of sound in still air is $340\,\text{m s}^{-1}$.

We need to use the formulas for a moving source, i.e. $f' = \dfrac{vf}{v \pm u_s}$

Students are often confused as to whether the sign in the denominator should be plus or minus. The easy way to figure this out is to realise that if the source is approaching observer X we expect an increase in frequency. This means we need to use the minus sign, to make denominator smaller and so get a larger frequency.

So, substituting the values for X:

$$f' = \frac{340 \times 1250}{340 - 28} \approx 1360\,\text{Hz}$$

Remember that the speed of the sound is still v. To find the wavelength measured by X we use the relationship between speed, frequency and wavelength:

$$\lambda' = \frac{340}{1360} \approx 0.25\,\text{m}$$

For Y, $f' = \dfrac{340 \times 1250}{340 + 28} \approx 1150\,\text{Hz}$ and $\lambda' = \dfrac{340}{1150} \approx 0.30\,\text{m}$

Stationary source and moving observer

In the case of a stationary source and a moving observer we may argue as follows. First, let us consider the case of the observer moving towards the source. The observer who moves with speed u_o with respect to the source may claim that he is at rest and that it is the source that approaches him with speed u_o. But the air is also coming towards the observer with speed u_o and so the observer will measure a higher wave speed, $v + u_o$.

We can now apply the same equations as for a source moving towards the observer, and so the frequency measured by the observer is:

$$f' = f \frac{v + u_o}{v + u_o - u_o}$$

$$f' = f\left(\frac{v + u_o}{v}\right) \quad \text{observer moving towards source}$$

Similarly, if the observer moves away from the source we get

$$f' = f\left(\frac{v - u_o}{v}\right) \quad \text{observer moving away from source}$$

As we expect from the analysis with wavefront diagrams, the wavelength measured by the observer will be the same as that measured by the source. Consider the case of an observer moving towards a source:

$$\lambda' = \frac{v + u_o}{f'}$$

$$\lambda' = \frac{v + u_o}{f\left(\frac{v + u_o}{v}\right)}$$

$$\lambda' = \frac{v + u_o}{v + u_o} \times \frac{v}{f}$$

$$\lambda' = \frac{v}{f}$$

$$\lambda' = \lambda$$

The wavelengths are the same.

This is why in defining the Doppler effect we refer to the change in **frequency** measured by the observer and not the change in wavelength.

The Doppler effect has many applications. One of the most common is to determine the speed of moving objects from cars on a highway (as Worked example **9.20** shows). Another application is to measure the speed of flow of blood cells in an artery or to monitor the development of a storm. The Doppler effect applied to light is responsible for one of the greatest discoveries in science, the expansion of the Universe (see 'The Doppler effect for light').

Exam tip
The speed of sound relative to the observer is no longer v. The medium has changed. For the source the medium is still air. For the observer the medium is moving air.

Exam tip
The IB data booklet has the formulas for frequency. There is no need to remember the formulas for wavelength – just use the relationship:

$$\text{wavelength} = \frac{\text{wave speed}}{\text{frequency}}$$

Worked examples

9.19 A train sounding a 500 Hz siren is moving at a constant speed of 8.0 m s^{-1} in a straight line. An observer is in front of the train and off its line of motion. What frequencies does the observer hear? (Take the speed of sound to be 340 m s^{-1}.)

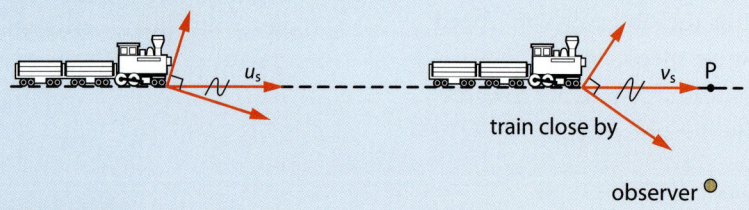

Figure 9.39

What counts is the velocity of the train along the line of sight between the train and the observer. When the train is very far away (Figure 9.39) it essentially comes straight towards the observer and so the frequency received is:

$$f' = f\left(\frac{v}{v - u_s}\right)$$

$$f' = 500 \times \frac{340}{340 - 8}$$

$$f' \approx 510 \text{ Hz}$$

When the train is again very far away to the right, the train is moving directly away from the observer and the frequency received will be:

$$f' = f\left(\frac{v}{v + u_s}\right)$$

$$f' = 500 \times \frac{340}{340 + 8}$$

$$f' \approx 490 \text{ Hz}$$

As the train approaches, we take components of the train's velocity vector in the direction along the line of sight and the direction normal to it (Figure 9.39).

From the diagram, the component along the line of sight decreases as the train gets closer to the observer. Thus, the observer will measure a decreasing frequency. The sound starts at 510 Hz and falls to 500 Hz when the train is at position P. As the train moves past P to the right, the observer will hear sound of decreasing frequency starting at 500 Hz and ending at 490 Hz.

Thus, the observer hears frequencies in the range of 510 Hz to 490 Hz, as shown in Figure 9.40.

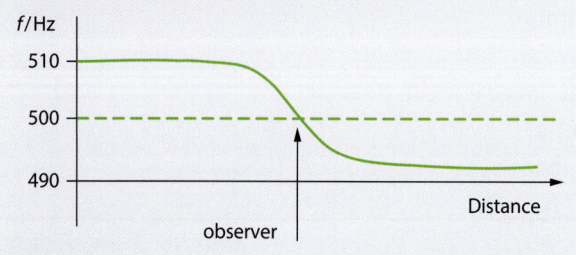

Figure 9.40

> **9.20** A sound wave of frequency 15 000 Hz is emitted towards an approaching car. The wave is reflected from the car and is then received back at the emitter at a frequency of 16 100 Hz. Calculate the velocity of the car. (Take the speed of sound to be 340 m s^{-1}.)

The car is approaching the emitter so the frequency it receives is:

$$f_1 = 15\,000 \times \frac{340 + u}{340} \text{ Hz}$$

where u is the unknown car speed.

The car now acts as an emitter of a wave of this frequency (f_1), and the original emitter will act as the new receiver. Thus, the frequency received (16 100 Hz) from the approaching car is:

$$16\,100 = \left(15\,000 \times \frac{340 + u}{340}\right) \times \frac{340}{340 - u}$$

$$\Rightarrow \frac{16\,100}{15\,000} = \frac{340 + u}{340 - u}$$

$$\frac{340 + u}{340 - u} = 1.073$$

Solving for u we find $u = 12$ m s^{-1}.

The Doppler effect for light

The Doppler effect also applies to light, but the equation giving the frequency observed is more complicated than the formula for sound. However, in the case in which the speed of the source or the observer is *small* compared to the speed of light, the equation takes a simple form:

$$\frac{\Delta f}{f} \approx \frac{v}{c}$$

In this formula v is the speed of the source or the observer, c is the speed of light and f is the emitted frequency. Then Δf gives the change in the observed frequency.

(Note that this approximate formula may also be used for sound provided the speed of the source or the observer is small compared to the speed of sound.)

Since $c = f\lambda$ it also follows that:

$$\frac{\Delta \lambda}{\lambda} \approx \frac{v}{c}$$

In this formula v is the speed of the source or the observer, c is the speed of light and λ is the emitted wavelength. Then $\Delta\lambda$ gives the change in the observed wavelength.

Remember that if the source of light **approaches** then the **frequency increases** and the **wavelength decreases**. When the wavelength decreases we say we have a **blue-shift**. If the source of light moves away then the frequency decreases and the wavelength increases. In this case we speak of a **red-shift**.

Light from distant galaxies measured on Earth shows a red-shift, i.e. it is longer than the wavelength emitted. This means that the galaxies are moving *away* from us. This great discovery in the 1920s is convincing evidence of an **expanding universe**.

Worked example

9.21 Hydrogen atoms in a distant galaxy emit light of wavelength 656 nm. The light received on Earth is measured to have a wavelength of 689 nm. State whether the galaxy is approaching the Earth or moving away, and calculate the speed of the galaxy.

The received wavelength is longer than that emitted, and so the galaxy is moving away from Earth (we have a red-shift). Using $\Delta \lambda \approx \frac{v}{c} \lambda$ we get:

$$v = \frac{c \Delta \lambda}{\lambda}$$

$$v = \frac{3.00 \times 10^8 \times (689 - 656) \times 10^{-7}}{656 \times 10^{-7}}$$

$$v = 1.5 \times 10^7 \, \text{m s}^{-1}$$

Nature of science

The Doppler effect was first proposed to explain changes in the wavelength of light from binary stars moving in relation to each other. The effect also explains the change in pitch that occurs when a fast moving source of sound passes by. Applying the theory to different types of wave in different areas of physics has led to Doppler imaging in medicine using ultrasound, hand-held radar guns to check for speeding vehicles, and improvements in weather forecasting using the Doppler shift in radio waves reflected from moving cloud systems.

The expansion of the Universe was discovered by Edwin Hubble (1889–1953) through applying the red-shift formula that is based on the Doppler effect to light from distant galaxies. Observers on Earth who measure the light emitted by galaxies find that the wavelength is longer than that emitted. The galaxies must be moving away. Yet the modern view is that space in-between galaxies is itself being stretched. This stretching makes all distances, including wavelengths, get larger. So the reason we observe red-shift is not the Doppler effect, but a much more complicated phenomenon predicted by Einstein's general theory of relativity. The Doppler effect remains as a simple, intuitive yet wrong description of what is actually going on, which gives the right answer for galaxies that are not too far away.

? Test yourself

Take the speed of sound in still air to be 340 m s^{-1}.

36 Explain, with the help of diagrams, the Doppler effect. Show clearly the cases of a source that **a** moves towards and **b** goes away from a stationary observer, as well the case of a moving observer.

37 A source approaches a stationary observer at 40 m s^{-1} emitting sound of frequency 500 Hz.
   a Determine the frequency the observer measures.
   b Calculate the wavelength of the sound as measured by **i** the source and **ii** the observer.

38 A source is moving away from a stationary observer at 32 m s^{-1} emitting sound of frequency 480 Hz.
   a Determine the frequency the observer measures.
   b Calculate the wavelength of the sound as measured by **i** the source and **ii** the observer.

39 A sound wave of frequency 512 Hz is emitted by a stationary source toward an observer who is moving away at 12 m s^{-1}.
   a Determine the frequency the observer measures.
   b Calculate the wavelength of the sound as measured by **i** the source and **ii** the observer.

40 A sound wave of frequency 628 Hz is emitted by a stationary source toward an observer who is approaching at 25 m s^{-1}.
   a Determine the frequency the observer measures.
   b Calculate the wavelength of the sound as measured by **i** the source and **ii** the observer.

41 A source of sound is directed at an approaching car. The sound is reflected by the car and is received back at the source. Carefully explain what changes in frequency the observer at the source will detect.

42 A sound wave of frequency 500 Hz is emitted by a stationary source toward a receding observer. The signal is reflected by the observer and received by the source, where the frequency is measured and found to be 480 Hz. Calculate the speed of the observer.

43 A sound wave of frequency 500 Hz is emitted by a moving source toward a stationary observer. The signal is reflected by the observer and received by the source, where the frequency is measured and found to be 512 Hz. Calculate the speed of the source.

44 Consider the general case when both the source and the observer move towards each other. Let u_s be the velocity of the source and u_o that of the observer. In the frame of reference in which the observer is at rest, the waves appear to move with velocity $v + u_o$ and the source appears to move with velocity $u_s + u_o$. Show that the frequency received by the observer is:

$$f_o = f_s \frac{c + v_o}{c - v_s}$$

45 Ultrasound of frequency 5.000 MHz reflected from red blood cells moving in an artery is found to show a frequency shift of 2.4 kHz. The speed of ultrasound in blood is $v = 1500$ m s^{-1}.
   a Explain why the appropriate formula for the frequency shift is $\frac{\Delta f}{f} = 2\frac{u}{v}$, where u is the speed of the blood cells.
   b Estimate the speed of the blood cells.
   c In practice, a range of frequency shifts is observed. Explain this observation.

46 Calculate the speed of a galaxy emitting light of wavelength 5.48×10^{-7} m which when received on Earth is measured to have a wavelength of 5.65×10^{-7} m.

47 Light from a nearby galaxy is emitted at a wavelength of 657 nm and is observed on Earth at a wavelength of 654 nm.
   a Deduce the speed of this galaxy.
   b State what, precisely, can be deduced about the direction of the velocity of this galaxy.

48 The Sun rotates about its axis with a period that may be assumed to be constant at 27 days. The radius of the Sun is 7.00×10^8 m. Discuss the shifts in frequency of light emitted from the Sun's equator and received on Earth. Assume that the Sun emits monochromatic light of wavelength 5.00×10^{-7} m.

49 In a binary star system, two stars orbit a common point and move so that they are always in diametrically opposite positions. Light from both stars reaches an observer on Earth. Assume that both stars emit light of wavelength 6.58×10^{-7} m.

   a When the stars are in the position shown in the diagram below, the observer on Earth measures a wavelength of light of 6.58×10^{-7} m from both stars. Explain why there is no Doppler shift in this case.

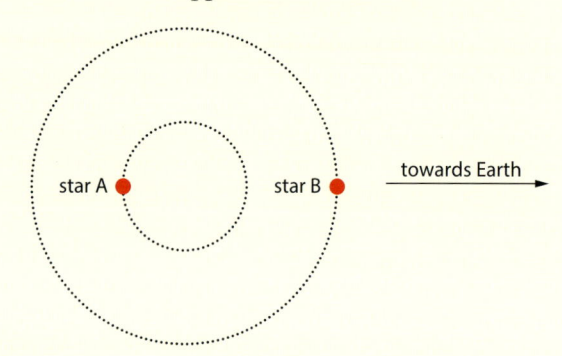

   b When the stars are in the position shown in the diagram below, the observer on Earth measures two wavelengths in the received light, 6.50×10^{-7} m and 6.76×10^{-7} m. Determine the speed of each of the stars.

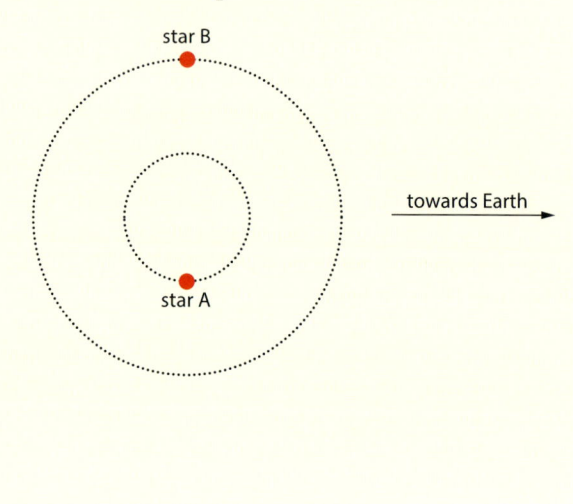

Exam-style questions

1 A ball of mass m is attached to two identical springs of spring constant k as shown. Initially the springs have their natural length. The ball is displaced a small distance to the right and is then released.

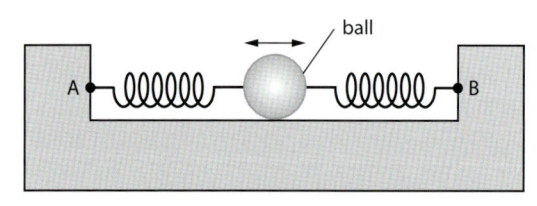

   What is the period of oscillation of the ball?

   A $2\pi\sqrt{\dfrac{m}{k}}$ **B** $2^{\frac{1}{2}}\pi\sqrt{\dfrac{m}{k}}$ **C** $2^{\frac{3}{2}}\pi\sqrt{\dfrac{m}{k}}$ **D** $2^{-\frac{1}{2}}\pi\sqrt{\dfrac{m}{k}}$

2 A particle performs simple harmonic oscillations with amplitude 1.0 mm and frequency 100 Hz. What is the maximum acceleration of this particle (in m s^{-2})?

   A 0.2π **B** 0.4π **C** $2\pi^2$ **D** $4\pi^2$

3. Which of the following graphs shows the variation with time of the potential energy of a particle undergoing simple harmonic oscillations with a period of 1.0 s?

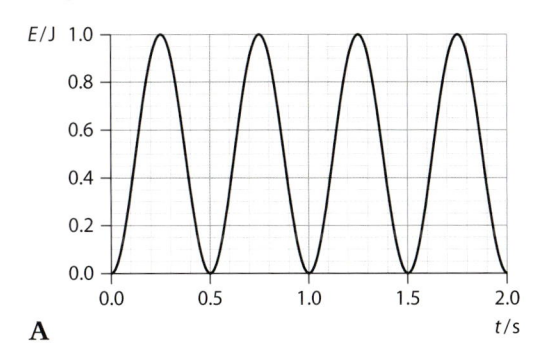

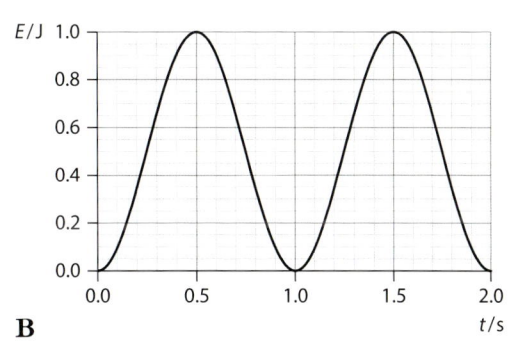

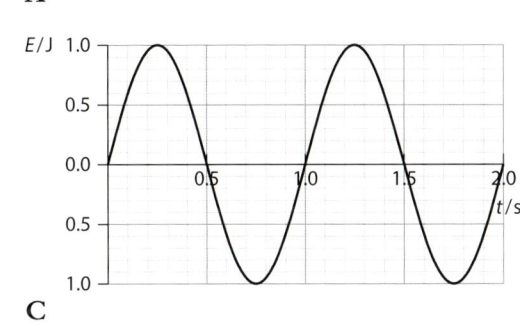

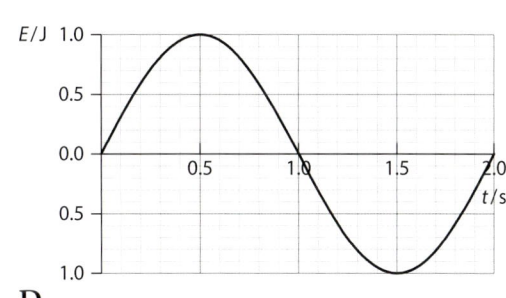

4. Light of wavelength λ is incident normally on a slit of width b. A screen is placed a distance D from the slit. What is the width of the central maximum measured along the screen?

A $\dfrac{\lambda}{b}$ B $\dfrac{2\lambda}{b}$ C $\dfrac{\lambda D}{b}$ D $\dfrac{2\lambda D}{b}$

5. Light of wavelength λ is incident on two parallel slits. An interference pattern is formed on a screen behind the slits. The separation of the slits and the width of the slits are both decreased. Which of the following is correct about the separation and the width of the bright fringes?

	separation	width
A	increases	increases
B	increases	decreases
C	decreases	increases
D	decreases	decreases

6. Two radio wave emitting stars are separated by a distance d and are both a distance r from Earth. Radio waves of wavelength λ are received by a radio telescope of diameter b on Earth. The two stars will be well resolved by the telescope if which condition is satisfied?

A $\dfrac{d}{r} < 1.22 \times \dfrac{\lambda}{b}$ B $\dfrac{d}{r} > 1.22 \times \dfrac{\lambda}{b}$ C $\dfrac{r}{d} < 1.22 \times \dfrac{\lambda}{b}$ D $\dfrac{r}{d} > 1.22 \times \dfrac{\lambda}{b}$

9 WAVE PHENOMENA (HL)

7 Coherent light of wavelength λ is incident on two parallel slits that are separated by a distance d. Angle θ is the smallest angle for which the two rays shown interfere destructively on a screen far from the slits.

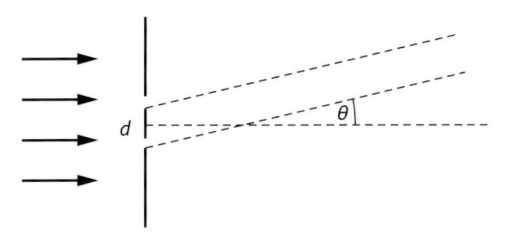

Which of the following could be correct?

A $d\sin\theta = \dfrac{\lambda}{2}$ **B** $d\sin\theta = \lambda$ **C** $d\sin\theta = \dfrac{3\lambda}{2}$ **D** $\sin\theta = 2\lambda$

8 A train sounding its horn goes past a train station without stopping. The train moves at constant speed. Which is correct about the frequency of the horn measured by the observer?

A keeps increasing then keeps decreasing
B keeps decreasing then keeps increasing
C is constant and high then constant and low
D is constant and low then constant and high

9 Light is incident essentially normally on a thin film of thickness t and refractive index 1.5. The film is on transparent glass of refractive index 2.5.

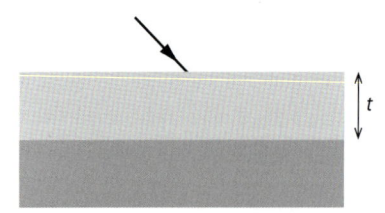

Which of the following conditions on the wavelength in air leads to destructive interference of the reflected light?

A $\lambda = 6t$
B $\lambda = 3t$
C $\lambda = t$
D $\lambda = 1.5t$

10 Light is incident on N very thin parallel slits and an interference pattern is formed on a screen a distance away. The number of slits is increased while the separation of two consecutive slits stays the same. Which is correct as N increases?

A the number of secondary maxima decreases
B the intensity of the secondary maxima increases
C the primary maxima become narrower
D the distance between the central maximum and the first primary maximum to the side increases

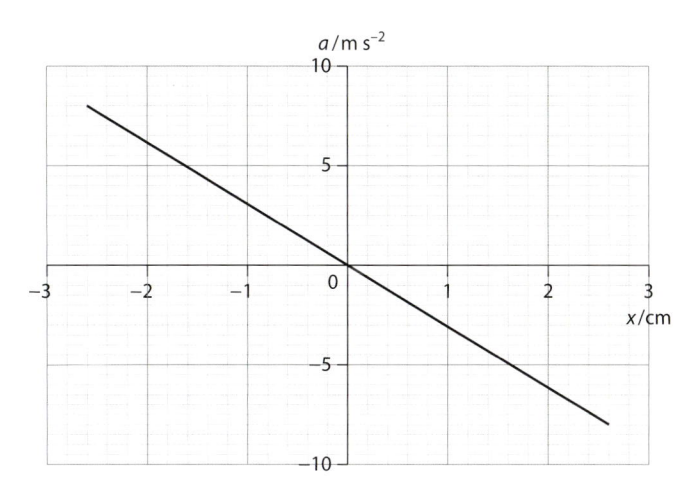

11 The graph shows how the acceleration of a particle varies with displacement from a fixed equilibrium position.

a Use the graph to explain why the particle is performing simple harmonic oscillations. [3]
b Determine:
  i the amplitude of oscillations [1]
  ii the frequency of the motion. [2]
c i The mass of the particle is 0.25 kg. Calculate the maximum potential energy of the particle. [2]
  ii Determine the speed of the particle when its kinetic energy equals its potential energy. [3]
d Sketch a graph to show how the kinetic energy varies with displacement. [2]

12 In a Young two-slit experiment, a source of light of unknown wavelength is used to illuminate two very narrow slits that are a distance 0.120 mm apart.

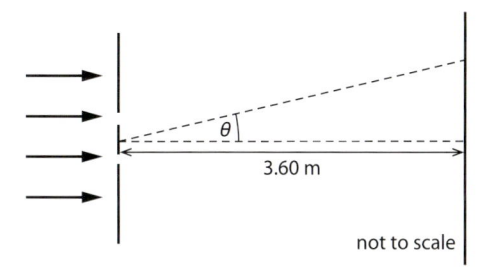

Bright fringes are observed on a screen a distance of 3.60 m from the slits. The separation between the bright fringes is 1.86 cm.

a i Explain how the bright fringes are formed. [2]
  ii Determine the wavelength of light. [3]
b Draw a graph to show how the intensity of the light observed on the screen varies with the angle θ. The intensity at the screen due to one slit alone is 20 W m^{-2}. You may neglect the slit width. [3]
c i The two slits are replaced by a diffraction grating. The light in a makes a second order maximum at an angle of 58°. Calculate the number of rulings per mm for this grating. [2]
  ii Another wavelength of visible light creates a maximum at the same angle as in c i but at a different order. Determine this wavelength and the order of its maximum. [4]

13 Monochromatic light of wavelength 5.0×10^{-7} m in air is incident on a rectangular piece of glass of refractive index 1.60 that is coated by a thin layer of magnesium fluoride of refractive index 1.38.

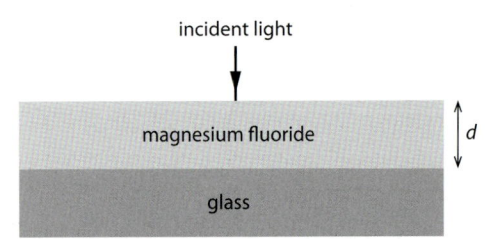

    a Copy and complete this diagram by drawing the paths of the two rays, originating with the incident ray, that will interfere in the eye of an observer looking down on the glass from above. [2]
    b Indicate on the diagram points at which reflected rays undergo phase changes. [2]
    c Calculate the least thickness d of this coating that will result in no light being reflected. Assume that the ray is incident normally. [3]

14 The graph shows the interference pattern for a number of very thin parallel slits.

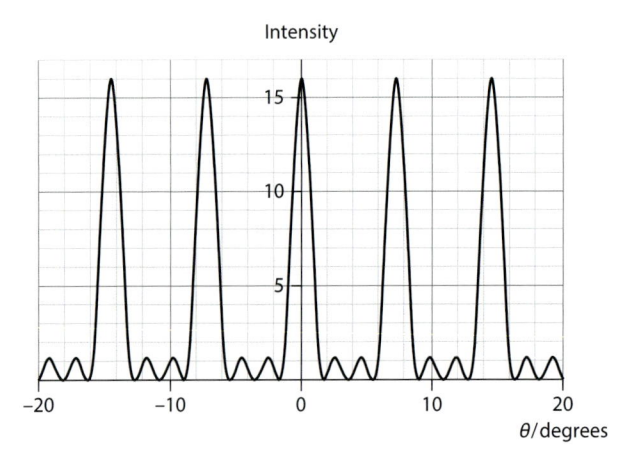

    a Justify that the number of slits is 4. [2]
    b List a total of **four** ways in which this pattern changes as:
      i the number of slits increases but their separation stays the same
      ii the number of slits stays the same but their separation decreases. [4]
    c It is required to resolve two lines in the spectrum of hydrogen: a line with wavelength 656.45 nm in $^{1}_{1}$H and a line of wavelength 656.27 nm in the isotope $^{2}_{1}$H. Calculate the least number of slits required to resolve these two lines in the second order. [3]

15 The graph shows the single-slit diffraction pattern for monochromatic light from one point source.

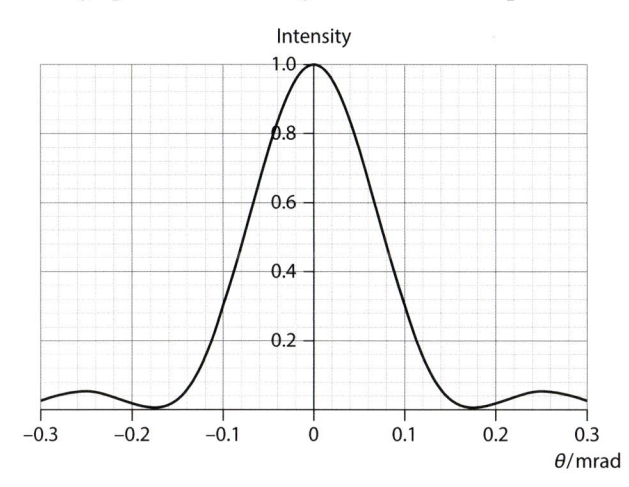

The wavelength of light is 5.0×10^{-7} m.

   a Calculate the slit diameter assuming that it is circular. [2]
   b A second source is placed at distance of 3.0 cm from the other source.
      i On a copy of the axes above draw the diffraction pattern from the second source in the case in which the two sources are just barely resolved. [2]
      ii Calculate the distance of the two sources from the slit. [2]

16 a State what is meant by the **Doppler effect**. [1]
   b Illustrate the Doppler effect for the case of a moving source using wavefront diagrams. [2]
   c Outline **one** practical application of the Doppler effect. [2]
   d A disc of radius 0.20 m rotates about its axis making eight revolutions per second. Sound of frequency 2400 Hz is emitted in all directions from a source on the circumference of the disc. The sound is received by an observer far away from the disc. Determine the range of frequencies and the range of wavelengths that the observer measures. [4]

10 Fields (HL)

Learning objectives

- Describe field patterns where sources are masses or charges.
- Understand the concept of electric and gravitational potential.
- Describe the connection between equipotential surfaces and field lines.

10.1 Describing fields

This topic deals with gravitational fields and potentials and the very closely related electric fields and potentials. We will start with gravitational quantities. Once all the gravitational material is covered, the electric quantities will be discussed.

Gravitational fields

Our starting point is that a massive spherical body of mass M will produce around it a **gravitational field**, whose magnitude is given by:

$$g = \frac{GM}{r^2}$$

We say that the mass M is the **source** of the field. A small mass m that finds itself in the presence of such a gravitational field will respond to the field by experiencing a force acting on it. The magnitude of this force will be given by $F = mg$. The direction of the force is the same as that of the gravitational field. For a point mass or a spherical mass M the gravitational field due to the mass is radial and is directed towards the centre of the mass (Figure 10.1).

However, if we look at the gravitational field of a large planet very close to its surface we see that the planet surface looks flat. The gravitational field is therefore no longer radial but approximately uniform and directed at right angles to the planet's surface (Figure 10.2).

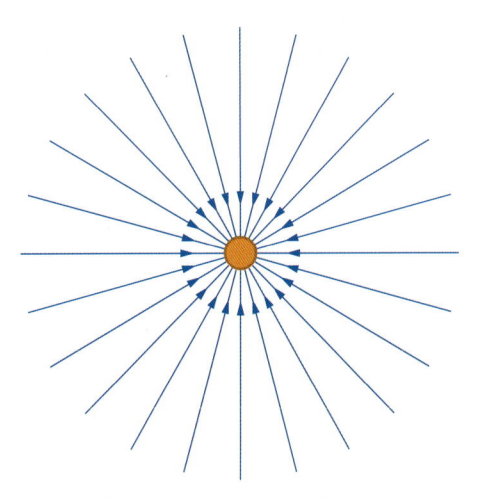

Figure 10.1 The gravitational field around a point mass is radial.

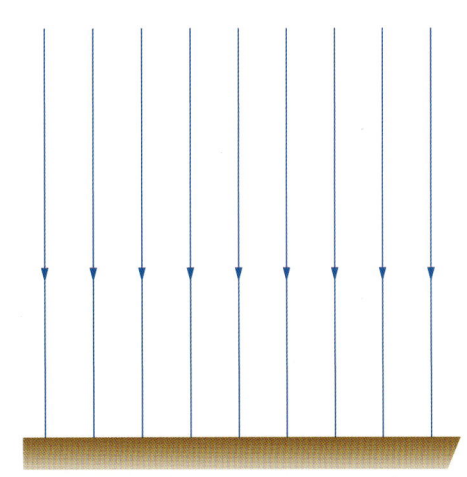

Figure 10.2 The gravitational field above a flat mass is uniform.

Gravitational potential energy

Consider a mass M placed somewhere in space, and a second mass m that is a distance r from M. The two masses share **gravitational potential energy**, which is stored in their gravitational field. This energy is the work that was done in bringing the two masses to a distance r apart from an initial separation that was infinite. For all practical purposes we consider M to be fixed in space and so it is just the small body of mass m that is moved (Figure 10.3).

> The gravitational potential energy of two bodies is the work that was done in bringing the bodies to their present position from when they were infinitely far apart.

Notice that, strictly speaking, this is energy that belongs to the pair of masses M and m and not just to one of them. So we are not quite correct when we speak of the gravitational potential energy of just one of the masses. Notice also that when we say that the masses are moved from

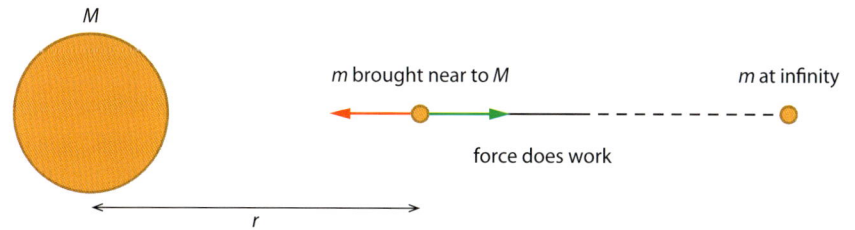

Figure 10.3 Work is done to bring the small mass from infinity to a given position away from the big mass. The red arrow is the force of attraction between the two masses. We are interested in the work done by the force represented by the green arrow, i.e. the work done by the external agent. This work is negative and is stored as potential energy. The work done is independent of the actual path followed.

infinity we are implying that they are moved at a very small constant speed, so that no kinetic energy is involved.

The gravitational force is not constant, so we cannot straightforwardly calculate the work done. We need calculus for this calculation. The total work done in moving the mass m from infinity to a distance r from the centre of a spherical mass M is:

$$W = \int_{\infty}^{r} \frac{GMm}{r^2} \, dr = -\left[\frac{GMm}{r}\right]_{\infty}^{r} = -\frac{GMm}{r}$$

Note that this is the work done by an external agent in bringing the mass m from far away to a position near M at constant speed. The force this agent exerts on m is equal and opposite to the gravitational force exerted on m by M. It is important to be very clear about who exerts forces on whom and who does work, otherwise things can get very confused.

So this work is now the gravitational potential energy of the two masses when their centres are separated by a distance r:

$$E_p = -\frac{GMm}{r}$$

This energy is negative. It implies that if we want to separate the two masses to an infinite distance apart, we must provide an amount of energy equal to $+\frac{GMm}{r}$ (Figure **10.4**). Alternatively, the negative sign indicates that the force of gravity is a force of attraction.

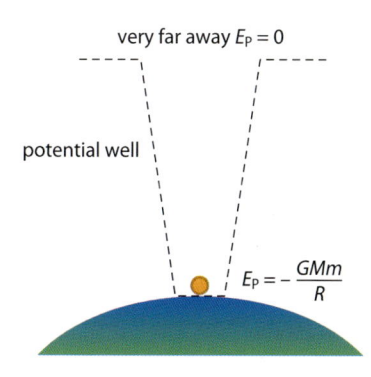

Figure 10.4 The mass m at the surface of a planet of mass M is in a **gravitational potential well**. It needs energy to get out, i.e. move away from the planet's surface.

10 FIELDS (HL)

Worked example

10.1 Calculate the difference in the potential energy of a satellite of mass 1500 kg when it is taken from the surface of the Earth (mass $M = 5.97 \times 10^{24}$ kg, radius $R = 6.38 \times 10^6$ m) to a distance of 520 km above the Earth's surface.

The potential energy of the system initially is:

$$E_P = -\frac{GMm}{R} = -\frac{6.67 \times 10^{-11} \times 5.97 \times 10^{24} \times 1500}{6.38 \times 10^6} = -9.4 \times 10^{10} \, \text{J}$$

At a distance of 520 km from the Earth's surface the separation of the masses is $r = R + 520$ km. The potential energy is therefore:

$$E_P = -\frac{GMm}{r} = -\frac{6.67 \times 10^{-11} \times 5.97 \times 10^{24} \times 1500}{6.90 \times 10^6} = -8.66 \times 10^{10} \approx -8.7 \times 10^{10} \, \text{J}$$

The difference in these potential energies is:

$$(-8.7 \times 10^{10}) - (-9.4 \times 10^{10}) = 7.0 \times 10^9 \, \text{J}$$

This difference of 7.0×10^9 J is the energy that needs to be provided to move the satellite from Earth to its new position. Notice that no kinetic energy is involved: the satellite is moved at a small constant speed so the kinetic energy is negligibly small.

Gravitational potential

Related to the concept of gravitational potential energy is that of **gravitational potential**, V_g.

Exam tip
This definition must be remembered word perfect.

> The gravitational potential at a point P in a gravitational field is the work done per unit mass in bringing a small point mass m from infinity to point P.

If the work done is W, then the gravitational potential is the ratio of the work done to the mass m, that is:

$$V_g = \frac{W}{m}$$

The gravitational potential is a **scalar** quantity. Since $W = -\frac{GMm}{r}$, the potential a distance r from a spherical mass M is:

$$V_g = -\frac{GMm/r}{m}$$

$$V_g = -\frac{GM}{r}$$

The units of gravitational potential are J kg^{-1}.

In general, if mass M produces a gravitational potential V_g at some point and we place a mass m at that point, the gravitational potential energy of the system is $E_P = mV_g$.

If a mass m is positioned at a point in a gravitational field where the gravitational potential is V_{gA} and is then moved to another point where the gravitational potential is V_{gB}, then the work that is done on the mass is the difference in gravitational potential energy:

$$W = \Delta E_P$$

$$W = mV_{gB} - mV_{gA}$$

$$W = m\Delta V_g$$

The work done depends only on the mass and the change in potential, not the actual path taken (Figure 10.5).

Exam tip
This formula is used when an external agent has to do work to move a mass m from one point in a gravitational field to another at constant small speed.

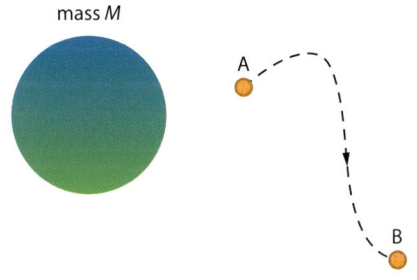

Figure 10.5 Work must be done to move a mass from one point to another in a gravitational field.

Notice that in moving the mass from one point to another, we are assuming that the mass is moved at a very small constant speed (examinations, tests and books do not always make this very clear!). In this way, the kinetic energy involved is negligible.

Worked examples

10.2 Figure 10.6 shows two spherical bodies. Calculate the gravitational potential at point P. (Masses and distances are shown on the diagram.)

4.4×10^{12} kg

6.2×10^{10} kg

3.5×10^5 m

2.0×10^5 m

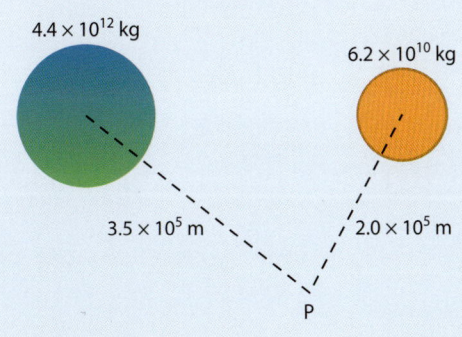

P

Figure 10.6

10 FIELDS (HL)

Gravitational potential is a scalar quantity, so we find the potential created by each mass separately and then add.

Potential from left mass:

$$V_1 = -\frac{GM}{r}$$

$$V_1 = -\frac{6.67 \times 10^{-11} \times 4.4 \times 10^{12}}{3.5 \times 10^5}$$

$$V_1 = -8.385 \times 10^{-4}\,\text{J kg}^{-1}$$

Potential from right mass:

$$V_2 = -\frac{6.67 \times 10^{-11} \times 6.2 \times 10^{10}}{2.0 \times 10^5}$$

$$V_2 = -2.068 \times 10^{-5}\,\text{J kg}^{-1}$$

The total potential is then the sum, i.e. $V = V_1 + V_2 = -8.6 \times 10^{-4}\,\text{J kg}^{-1}$.

10.3 The mass of the Moon is about 81 times smaller than that of the Earth. The distance between the Earth and the Moon is about $d = 3.8 \times 10^8$ m. The mass of the Earth is 5.97×10^{24} kg.
   a Determine the distance from the centre of the Earth of the point on the line joining the Earth to the Moon where the combined gravitational field strength of the Earth and the Moon is zero.
   b Calculate the combined gravitational potential at that point.
   c Calculate the potential energy when a 2500 kg probe is placed at that point.

a Let the point we are looking for be point P, and the distance we are looking for be x. Let the mass of the Earth be M, so the mass of the Moon is $\frac{M}{81}$.

Use the information to draw a diagram to show the situation, as in Figure **10.7**.

$d = 3.8 \times 10^8$ m

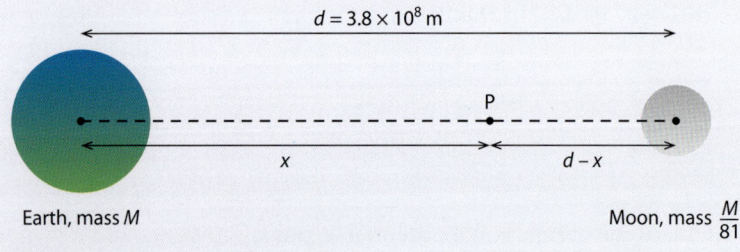

x $d - x$

Earth, mass M Moon, mass $\frac{M}{81}$

Figure 10.7 The Earth–Moon system.

The field due to the Earth at point x is then: $g_{\text{Earth}} = \frac{GM}{x^2}$

The field due to the Moon at point x is then: $g_{\text{Moon}} = \frac{GM/81}{(d-x)^2}$

The combined field is zero. The two fields are opposite in direction and must be equal in magnitude. Therefore:

$g_{Earth} = g_{Moon}$

$$\frac{GM}{x^2} = \frac{GM/81}{(d-x)^2}$$

$$\frac{1}{x^2} = \frac{1}{81(d-x)^2} \Rightarrow x^2 = 81(d-x)^2$$

$x = 9(d-x)$

$\Rightarrow x = \frac{9d}{10} = \frac{9}{10} \times 3.8 \times 10^8 = 3.4 \times 10^8 \, m$

b The combined potential at this point (we add the individual potentials for the Earth and the Moon since potential is a scalar quantity) is:

$$V_g = -\frac{GM}{x} - \frac{GM/81}{d-x}$$

$$V_g = -\frac{6.67 \times 10^{-11} \times 5.97 \times 10^{24}}{3.4 \times 10^8} - \frac{6.67 \times 10^{-11} \times 5.97 \times 10^{24}}{0.4 \times 10^8 \times 81}$$

$V_g = -1.17 \times 10^6 - 0.123 \times 10^6$

$V_g = -1.3 \times 10^6 \, J\,kg^{-1}$

c Use the equation $E_P = mV_g$.

Substituting the mass of the probe for the mass m and using the value for V_g from part **b**:

$E_P = 2500 \times (-1.3 \times 10^6)$

$E_P = -3.2 \times 10^9 \, J$

10.4 The graph in Figure **10.8** shows the variation of the gravitational potential V with distance r away from the centre of a dense compact planet of radius $2 \times 10^9 \, m$.

Use the graph to calculate the work required to move a probe of mass 3400 kg from the surface to a distance of $7.5 \times 10^6 \, m$ from the centre of the planet.

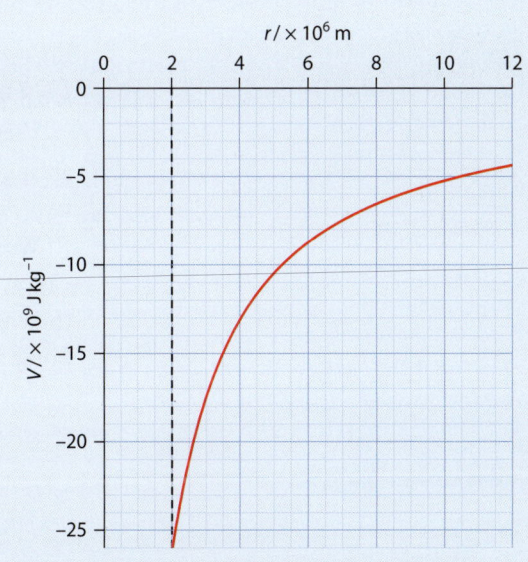

Figure 10.8 The variation with distance r of the gravitational potential V due to a spherical mass.

10 FIELDS (HL)

The work required can be found from $W = m\Delta V_g$ or from the completely equivalent $W = \Delta E_P$.

The change in gravitational potential ΔV_g is given by:

$\Delta V_g = V_{final} - V_{initial}$

$\Delta V_g = -7.0 \times 10^9 - (-26 \times 10^9)$

$\Delta V_g = 19 \times 10^9 \, \text{J kg}^{-1}$

So the work done is:

$W = m\Delta V_g$

$W = 3400 \times 19 \times 10^9$

$W = 6.5 \times 10^{13} \, \text{J}$

Electric fields

The idea of an **electric field** was introduced in Topic **5.1**. To summarise: if a positive test charge q experiences an electric force F, the electric field at the position of the test charge is defined as the ratio of the force to the charge:

$$E = \frac{F}{q}$$

The direction of the electric field is the same as the direction of the force (on the **positive** test charge q). At a point a distance r away from a point or spherical charge Q, the magnitude of the electric field is:

$$E = \frac{kQ}{r^2}$$

where k is known as the Coulomb constant and equals $k = 8.99 \times 10^9 \, \text{N m}^2 \, \text{C}^{-2}$.

Vector methods can then be used to find the electric field due to an arrangement of point charges. An example is that of the **dipole**, which has two equal and opposite charges separated by a distance a (Figure **10.9**).

We would like to find the electric field created by this dipole. It is easiest to find this field on the perpendicular bisector of the line joining the charges. At other points, the answer is more involved. Let us consider a point a distance d from the midpoint of the line joining the charges.

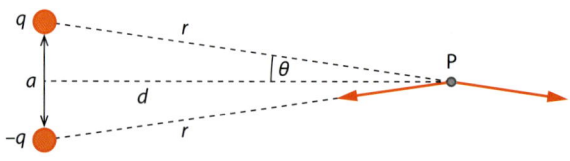

Figure 10.9 Two equal and opposite charges separated by a given distance form an electric dipole. The diagram shows the electric fields that must be added as vectors to get the net electric field at P.

402

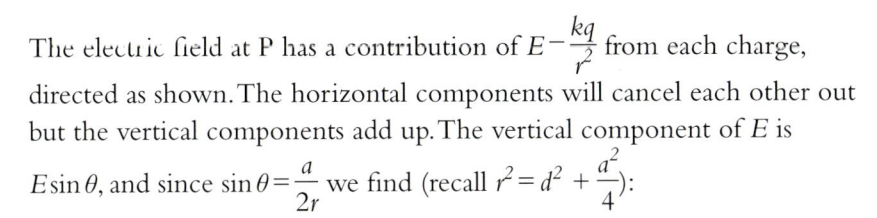

The electric field at P has a contribution of $E = \frac{kq}{r^2}$ from each charge, directed as shown. The horizontal components will cancel each other out but the vertical components add up. The vertical component of E is $E\sin\theta$, and since $\sin\theta = \frac{a}{2r}$ we find (recall $r^2 = d^2 + \frac{a^2}{4}$):

$$E = k\frac{qa}{(d^2 + \frac{a^2}{4})^{\frac{3}{2}}}$$

This is directed vertically downwards, in the direction of the vector from q to $-q$.

It is left as an exercise to show that when both charges are positive, the corresponding electric field is given by:

$$E = k\frac{2qd}{(d^2 + \frac{a^2}{4})^{\frac{3}{2}}}$$

and is horizontal (along the perpendicular bisector to the line joining the charges).

Electric potential and energy

Most of what we learned about gravitational potential energy and gravitational potential applies also to electricity. Just as a mass creates a gravitational potential around it, an electric charge creates **electric potential**. And just as two masses have gravitational potential energy between them, two electric charges also share **electric potential energy**. The formulas we derived for gravitation carry over to electricity essentially by replacing mass everywhere by charge, as we will see. The ideas are the same as those for gravitation so the derivations for electricity will be brief.

Suppose that at some point in space we place a large positive charge Q. If we place another positive charge q at infinity and try to move it closer to the large charge Q, we will have to exert a force on q, since it is being repelled by Q (Figure **10.10**). That is, we have to do work in order to change the position of q and bring it closer to Q.

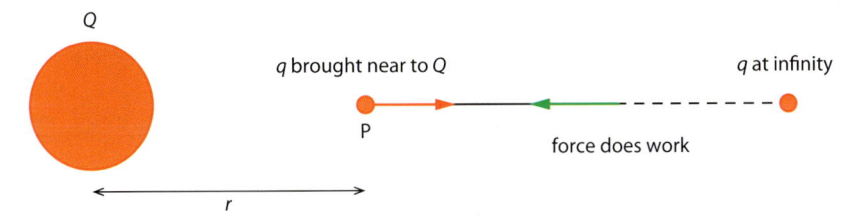

Figure 10.10 Work is done to bring the positive charge q from infinity to a given position away from positive charge Q. The red arrow is the force of repulsion between the two charges. The green arrow represents the force that moves charge q towards Q.

The electric potential at a point P is the amount of work done per unit charge as a small positive test charge q is moved from infinity to the point P:

$$V_e = \frac{W}{q}$$

The unit of potential is the volt (V), and $1\,\text{V} = 1\,\text{J}\,\text{C}^{-1}$.

The work done in moving a charge q from infinity to point P goes into **electric potential energy**, E_P.

If the electric potential at some point P is V_e, and we place a charge q at P, the electric potential energy E_P of the system is given by:

$$E_P = qV_e$$

Using calculus to calculate the work done in moving the charge q from infinity to a separation r, as we did for gravitation, results in:

$$W = \frac{kQq}{r}$$

Therefore:

$$V_e = \frac{kQ}{r}$$

and

$$E_P = \frac{kQq}{r}$$

Electric potential and electric potential energy are scalar quantities, just like gravitational potential and gravitational potential energy. For gravitational and electric fields, the work done is independent of the path followed. As with gravity, moving a charge q from one point in an electric field to another requires work (Figure **10.11**).

The work done W in moving charge q from A to B is:

$$W = q\Delta V_e = q(V_{eB} - V_{eA})$$

The quantity $V_{eB} - V_{eA}$ is the potential difference between A and B. In all these formulas, the charges must be entered with their correct sign.

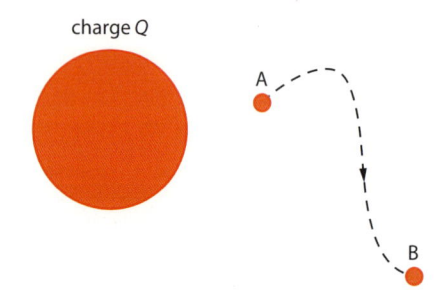

Figure 10.11 Work must be done in order to move a charge from one point to another where the potential is different.

Worked example

10.5 The hydrogen atom has a single proton and a single electron (Figure **10.12**).
   a Find the electric potential a distance of 0.50×10^{-10} m from the proton of the hydrogen atom. The proton has a charge 1.6×10^{-19} C, equal and opposite to that of the electron.
   b Use your answer to **a** to calculate the electric potential energy between the proton in a hydrogen atom and an electron orbiting the proton at a radius 0.50×10^{-10} m.

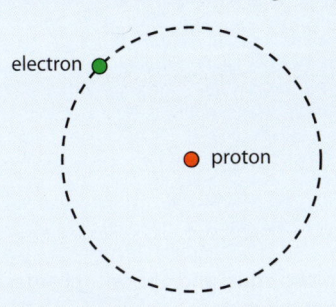

Figure 10.12

a $V_e = \dfrac{kQ}{r}$

Substituting the values from the question:

$$V_e = \dfrac{8.99 \times 10^9 \times 1.60 \times 10^{-19}}{0.50 \times 10^{-10}}$$

$V_e = 28.77 \approx 29$ V

b The electric potential energy is given by:

$$E_P = \dfrac{kQq}{r} = qV_e$$

Substituting the value for V_e from part **a**:

$E_P = 28.77 \times (1.6 \times 10^{-19})$

$E_P = 4.6 \times 10^{-18}$ J

Electric potential is a scalar quantity. So if we have two charges q_1 and q_2, the electric potential at a point P that is a distance r_1 from q_1 and a distance r_2 from q_2 is just the sum of the individual electric potentials:

$$V_e = \dfrac{kq_1}{r_1} + \dfrac{kq_2}{r_2}$$

That is, we first find the potential at P from q_1 alone, then from q_2 alone, and then add up the two (Figure 10.13). We find the electric potential for more than two charges in the same way – by adding the individual potentials.

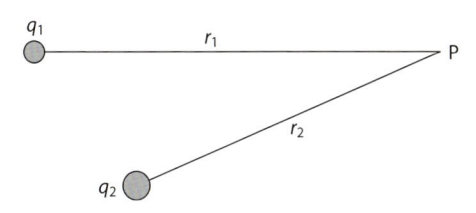

Figure 10.13 The potential at P is found by finding the potential there from the first charge, then finding the potential from the second charge, and finally adding the two.

10 FIELDS (HL) 405

One way of visualising electric potential is shown in Figure **10.14**. It shows the electric potential from one positive and one negative charge. With no charges, the surface would be flat. The potential is represented by the height from the flat surface.

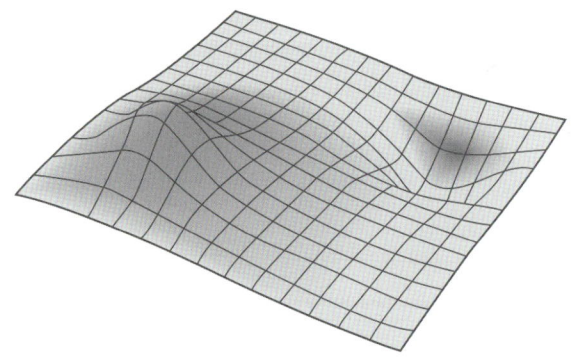

Figure 10.14 The electric potential due to two equal and opposite charges. The potential is proportional to the height of the surface.

The simple formula for electric potential works for point charges. (By point charges we mean that the objects on which the charges q_i are placed are mathematical points, or close to it.) The formula also works in another special case – when the object on which the charge q is placed is a sphere. But the result depends on where we measure the potential.

For a point P outside the sphere and at a distance r from the centre of the sphere, the potential at P is indeed:

$$V_e = \frac{kQ}{r}$$

On the surface of the sphere the potential is:

$$V_e = \frac{kQ}{R}$$

where R is the radius of the sphere.

But at any point inside the sphere, the electric potential is constant and has the same value as the potential at the surface (Figure **10.15**).

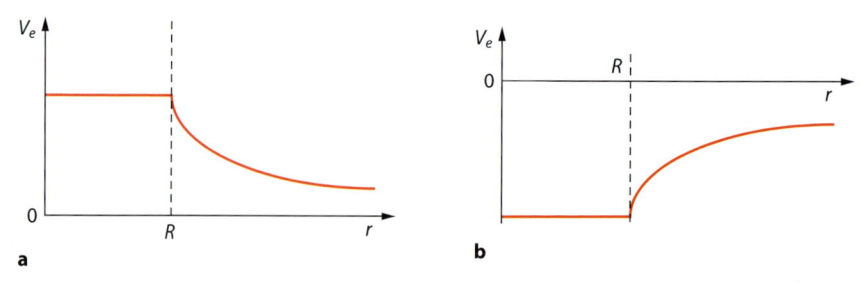

Figure 10.15 The electric potential is constant inside the sphere and falls off as $\frac{1}{r}$ outside. Shown here are **a** a positively charged sphere and **b** a negatively charged sphere.

Worked example

10.6 Figure **10.16** shows two unequal positive charges $+Q$ and $+q$. Which one of the graphs in Figure **10.17** shows the variation with distance x from the larger charge of the electric potential V_e along the line joining the centres of the charges?

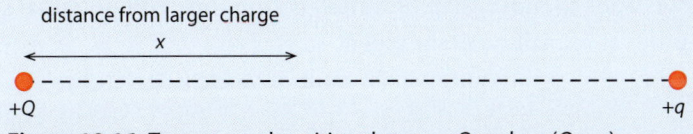

Figure 10.16 Two unequal positive charges $+Q$ and $+q$ ($Q > q$).

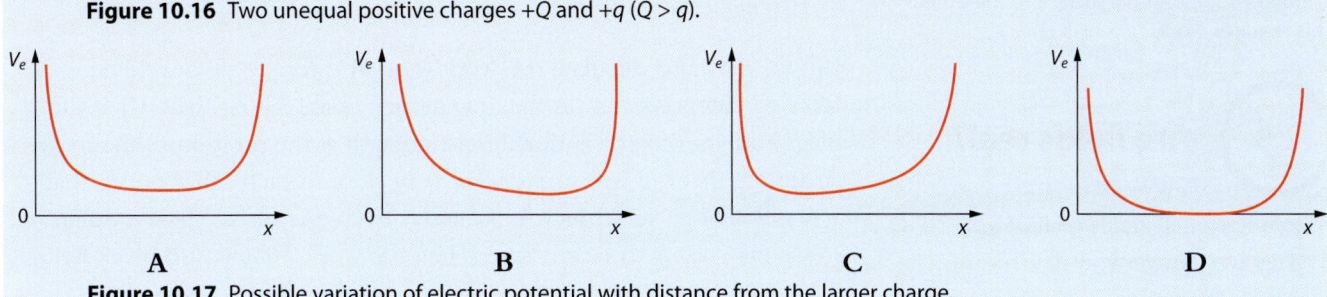

Figure 10.17 Possible variation of electric potential with distance from the larger charge.

The smaller charge will disturb the larger charge's potential only at distances close to the small charge and so the answer has to be **B**.

Equipotential surfaces

As we have seen, a spherical uniform mass M is the source of gravitational potential that, at a distance r from the centre of the source, is given by:

$$V_g = -\frac{GM}{r}$$

Similarly, a spherical charge Q is the source of electric potential that, at a distance r from the centre of the source, is given by:

$$V_e = \frac{kQ}{r}$$

In either case, those points that are at the same distance from the source (the mass or the charge) have the same potential. Points that are the same distance from the source lie on spheres. A two-dimensional representation of these spheres of constant potential is given in Figure **10.18**. They are called **equipotential surfaces**. For a point mass, they are spherical surfaces (shown here as circles on this two-dimensional graph).

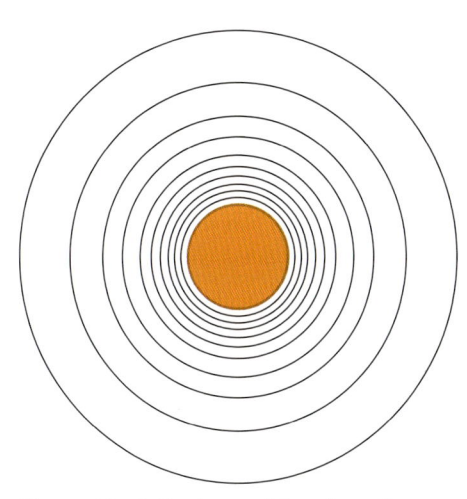

Figure 10.18 Equipotential surfaces due to one spherical mass or charge. These surfaces are usually drawn so that the difference in potential between any two adjacent surfaces is the same.

> An **equipotential surface** consists of those points that have the same potential.

10 FIELDS (HL) 407

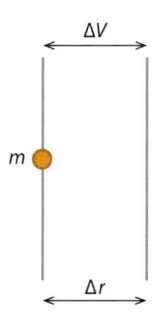

Figure 10.19 A point mass *m* is to be moved from one equipotential surface to the other. This requires work.

Are fields real?

Are electric (and gravitational) fields real, or are they just convenient devices for doing calculations? We have seen that an electric dipole creates an electric field. Suppose that the dipole is created by an electron (negative charge) and a positron (positive charge). The positron is the antiparticle of the electron (we will learn more about particles in Topic 12).

An electron and a positron can undergo pair annihilation, i.e. they can move into each other and destroy each other (there is more about this in Topic 12). In the process their mass is converted into pure energy (gamma-ray photons) according to $e^- + e^+ \rightarrow 2\gamma$. What happens to the electric field after the electron and positron have annihilated each other? Interestingly, the electric field will still exist, and be measurable, for a time $\frac{d}{c}$ after annihilation, where *d* is the distance between the charges of the dipole and *c* is the speed of light. The field exists even though its source has disappeared!

The connection between potential and field

There is a deep connection between potential and field for both gravitation and electricity. To see this connection for gravitation, consider two equipotential surfaces a distance Δr apart. Let ΔV_g be the potential difference between the two surfaces. The situation is shown in Figure 10.19. We want to move the point mass *m* from one equipotential surface to the other at a small constant speed.

We know that this requires an amount of work *W* given by:

$$W = m\Delta V_g$$

But we may also calculate the work from W = force × distance. The force on the point mass is the gravitational force $F = mg$, where *g* is the magnitude of the gravitational field strength at the position of the mass *m*. Assuming that the two surfaces are very close to each other means that *g* will not change very much as we move from one surface to the other, and so we may take *g* to be constant. Then the work done is also given by:

$$W = mg\Delta r$$

Equating the two expressions for work done gives:

$$g = \frac{\Delta V_g}{\Delta r}$$

(Can you now give a better answer to Worked example 10.6?)

A more careful treatment using calculus gives $g = -\frac{dV_g}{dr}$, the derivative of the potential with respect to distance. Since we are not using calculus and we only calculate magnitudes of the fields, the minus sign will not be of any use to us and we will ignore it. This gives the **magnitude** of the gravitational field as the rate of change with distance of the gravitational potential. In the same way, the electric field is the rate of change with distance of the electric potential:

$$E = \frac{\Delta V_e}{\Delta r}$$

(Again, calculus requires $E = -\frac{dV_e}{dr}$)

In a graph showing the variation with distance of the potential, the slope (gradient) of the graph is the magnitude of the field strength. This applies to both gravitational and electric fields.

The graph shown in Figure **10.20** is a copy of the curve in Worked example 10.4 and shows the tangent drawn at the point with $r = 4.0 \times 10^6$ m.

The slope of this tangent line is given by:

$$\frac{\Delta V_g}{\Delta r} = \frac{26 \times 10^9}{8 \times 10^6}$$

$$\frac{\Delta V_g}{\Delta r} = 3.2 \times 10^3 \approx 3 \times 10^3 \, \text{N kg}^{-1}$$

This is the magnitude of the gravitational field strength at a distance of 4.0×10^6 m from the centre of the planet.

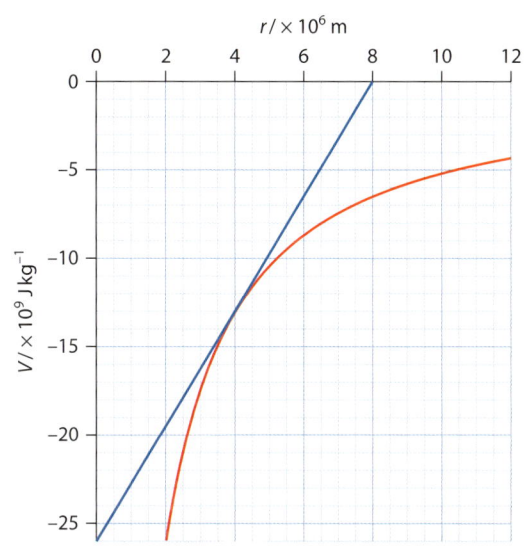

Figure 10.20 The slope of the tangent to the graph gives the gravitational field strength.

The connection between field lines and equipotential surfaces

Equipotential surfaces and field lines are normal (perpendicular) to each other. We already know this for the case of a single mass or a single charge: the field lines are radial lines and the equipotential surfaces are spheres centred at the mass or charge. Figure **10.21** shows this for the case of a mass. (Can you see why the diagram also applies to a negative charge?)

The explanation of why the field lines are at right angles to the equipotential surfaces is as follows: to move a mass from one point on an equipotential surface to another requires zero work because $W = m\Delta V$ and $\Delta V = 0$. If the field lines were not normal to the equipotential surfaces, there would be a component of the field along the equipotential and so a force on the mass. As the mass moved this force would do work, which contradicts our derivation that the work should be zero.

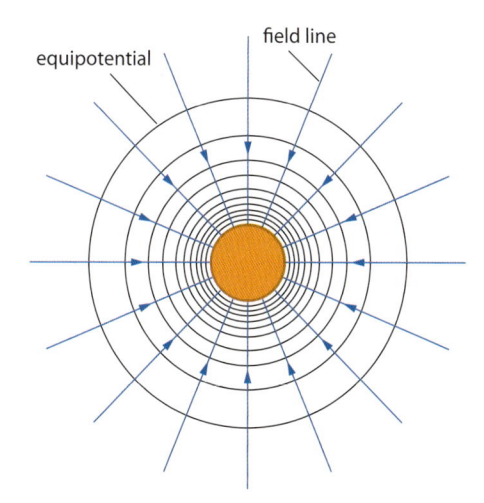

Figure 10.21 Equipotential surfaces and field lines are at right angles to each other.

10 FIELDS (HL)

Figure **10.22** shows the equipotential surfaces (in black) and field lines (in red) for two charges. In Figure **10.22a** $q_2 = q_1$ (both positive) and in Figure **10.22b** $q_2 = -q_1$. The field is zero halfway between the charges along the line joining the charges in Figure **10.22a**.

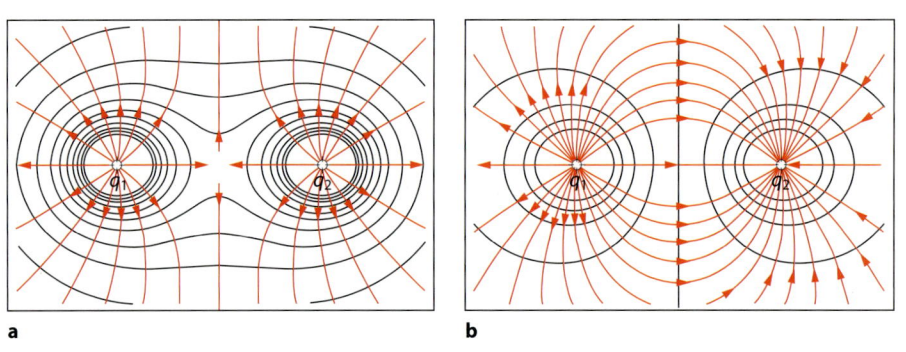

Figure 10.22 Field lines and equipotential surfaces for **a** two equal charges of the same sign and **b** two equal and opposite charges.

Figure **10.23** shows the equipotential surfaces (in black) and field lines (in red) for two charges. The field is zero closer to the smaller charge along the line joining the charges in Figure **10.23a**. In Figure **10.23a** $q_2 = 4q_1$ and in Figure **10.23b** $q_2 = -4q_1$.

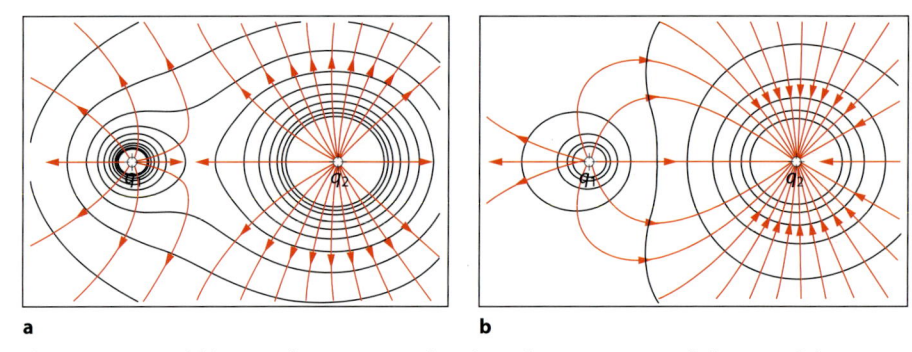

Figure 10.23 Field lines and equipotential surfaces for **a** two unequal charges of the same sign and **b** two unequal and opposite charges.

Exam tip
The field inside parallel plates is a common theme in examinations.

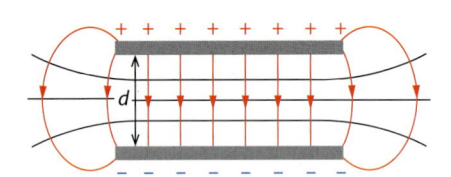

Figure 10.24 The electric field between two oppositely charged parallel plates is uniform, i.e. it is the same everywhere except near the edges of the plates. The potential increases uniformly as we move from the negative to the positive plate.

Parallel plates

There is one more case where we can find a simple expression for the electric field. This the case of two long **parallel plates** separated by a distance d (Figure **10.24**). The plates are oppositely charged. Red lines are field lines and black lines are equipotential surfaces.

Using $E = \dfrac{\Delta V_e}{\Delta r}$ we find that the electric field for parallel plates is given by:

$$E = \dfrac{V}{d}$$

where the potential difference between two parallel plates is V and the separation between the plates is d.

When the electric field between a charged cloud and the Earth exceeds $3 \times 10^6 \, \text{V m}^{-1}$, a discharge known as lightning occurs, Figure **10.25**.

Figure 10.25 A spectacular lightning display over a city.

Worked examples

10.7 A wire of length L has a potential difference V across its ends.
    a Find the electric field inside the wire.
    b Hence find the work done when a charge q is moved from one end of the wire to the other.

a From $E = \dfrac{\Delta V}{\Delta r}$ it follows that $E = \dfrac{V}{L}$

b The work done can be found in two ways.
    1 Use $W = q\Delta V = qV$
    2 Use $W = Fd = qEL = q\dfrac{V}{L}L = qV$

The answer is $W = qV$ in both cases.

10.8 The electric potential a distance r from a charge Q is $V_e = \dfrac{kQ}{r}$. Use this expression to find the electric field at the same point.

Here we must use the calculus expression (and so include the minus sign!):

$$E = -\frac{dV_e}{dr}$$

$$E = -\frac{d}{dr}\left(\frac{kQ}{r}\right)$$

$$E = \frac{kQ}{r^2}$$

This gives the result we expect.

10 FIELDS (HL)

Similarities between electricity and gravitation

As is clear from a comparison between Newton's law of gravitation and Coulomb's law, there are many similarities between electricity and gravitation (both force laws are inverse square laws). The biggest difference is, of course, the existence of positive as well as negative electric charge, which implies that the electric force can be attractive or repulsive. The one sign of the mass leads to attractive forces only. The constant G is very small compared to k. This implies that the force of gravitation is significant only when one or both of the bodies have enormous mass.

Nature of science

The Sun influences the motion of the Earth a distance of 1.5×10^{11} m away. How is the 'influence' of the Sun 'transmitted' to the position of the Earth? If the Sun were to suddenly disappear, how long would it take the Earth to leave its orbit and plunge into darkness? To answer such questions required a huge shift in scientific thinking, known as a paradigm shift. Fields were introduced, which replaced the idea of direct, observable action with a mechanism for 'action at a distance'. Fields were further refined with the concept of waves. If a charge were to suddenly appear, an electric field would be established in space at the speed of light. The 'information' about the existence of the charge is carried by electromagnetic waves travelling through vacuum at the speed of light. It is similarly believed that gravitational waves carry the 'information' about the existence of mass. But unlike electromagnetic waves, gravity waves have not yet been observed, even though no one doubts their existence.

? Test yourself

1 Consider two particles of mass m and $16m$ separated by a distance d.
   a Deduce that at point P, a distance $\frac{d}{5}$ from the particle with mass m, the gravitational field strength is zero.
   b Determine the value of the gravitational potential at P.

2 a What is the gravitational potential at a distance from the Earth's centre equal to 5 Earth radii?
   b What is the gravitational potential energy of a 500 kg satellite placed at a distance from the Earth's centre equal to 5 Earth radii?

3 a What is the gravitational potential energy stored in the gravitational field between the Earth and the Moon?
   b What is the Earth's gravitational potential at the position of the Moon?
   c Find the speed with which the Moon orbits the Earth. (The Earth–Moon distance is 3.8×10^8 m. Take the mass of the Earth to be 5.97×10^{24} kg.)

4 A spacecraft of mass 30 000 kg leaves the Earth on its way to the Moon and lands on the Moon. Plot the spacecraft's potential energy as a function of its distance from the Earth's centre. (The Earth–Moon distance is 3.8×10^8 m. Take the mass of the Earth to be 5.97×10^{24} kg and the mass of the Moon to be 7.35×10^{22} kg.)

5 The diagram shows the variation with distance from the centre of the planet of the gravitational potential due to the planet and its moon. The planet's centre is at $r=0$ and the centre of the moon is at $r=1$. The units of separation are arbitrary. At the point where $r=0.75$ the gravitational field is zero.

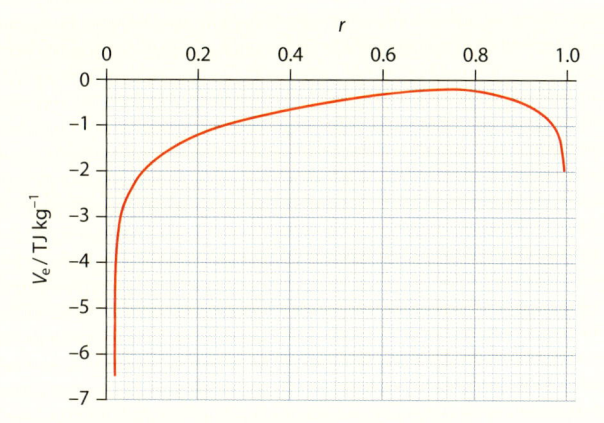

   a Determine the ratio of the mass of the planet to that of the moon.
   b With what speed must a probe be launched from the surface of the planet in order to arrive on the surface of the moon?

6 The diagram shows a planet orbiting the Sun counter-clockwise, at two positions – A and B. Also shown is the gravitational force acting on the planet at each position. By decomposing the force into components normal and tangential to the path (dotted lines), explain why it is only the tangential component that does work. Hence explain why the planet will accelerate from A to P but will slow down from P to B.

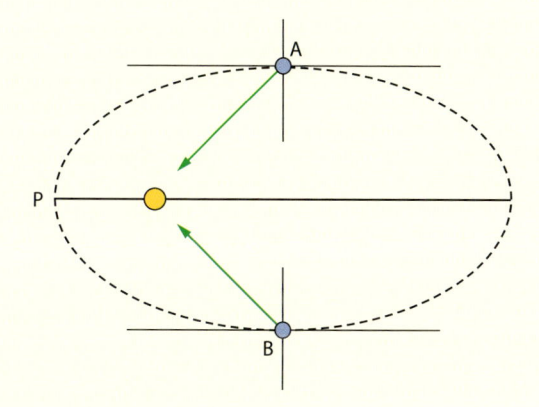

7 The diagram shows the variation of the gravitational force with distance between two masses. What does the shaded area represent?

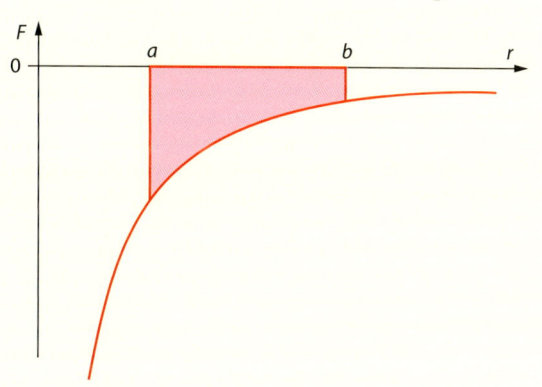

8 The diagram shows equipotential surfaces due to two spherical masses.

   a Using the diagram, explain how it can be deduced that the masses are unequal.
   b Copy the diagram and draw in the gravitational field lines due to the two masses.
   c Explain why the equipotential surfaces are spherical very far from the two masses.

9 a Determine the electric potential at the mid-point of the line joining two equal positive charges q in terms of q, the Coulomb constant and the charge separation d.
   b Repeat a for two equal but opposite charges.

10 Two charges, $q_1 = 2.0\,\mu C$ and $q_2 = -4.0\,\mu C$, are 0.30 m apart. Find the electric potential at a point P, which is 0.40 m from q_1 and 0.60 m from q_2.

10 FIELDS (HL)

11 Four equal charges of $5.0\,\mu C$ are placed at the vertices of a square of side $10\,cm$.
   a Calculate the value of the electric potential at the centre of the square.
   b Determine the electric field at the centre of the square.
   c How do you reconcile your answers to **a** and **b** with the fact that the electric field is the derivative of the potential?

12 A charge q of $10.0\,C$ is placed somewhere in space. What is the work required to bring a charge of $1.0\,mC$ from a point X, $10.0\,m$ from q, to a point Y, $2.0\,m$ from q? Does the answer depend on which path the charge follows?

13 An electron is brought from infinity to a distance of $10.0\,cm$ from a charge of $-10.0\,C$. How much work was done on the electron?

14 An electron moves from point A where the potential is $100.0\,V$ to point B where the potential is $200.0\,V$. The electron started from rest. Calculate the speed of the electron as it passes the point B.

15 Four charges are placed at the vertices of a square of side $5.00\,cm$, as shown in the diagram.

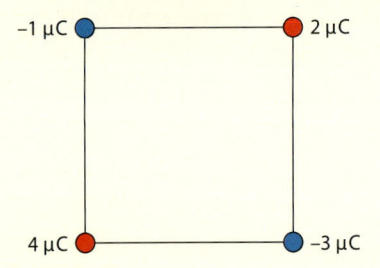

$-1\,\mu C$ $\quad\quad\quad$ $2\,\mu C$

$4\,\mu C$ $\quad\quad\quad$ $-3\,\mu C$

   a On a copy of the diagram, show the forces acting on the $2.0\,\mu C$ charge. Find the magnitude and direction of the net force on the $2.0\,\mu C$ charge.
   b Calculate the value of the electric potential at the centre of the square.
   c Determine the work that must be done in order to move a charge of $1\,nC$ initially at infinity to the centre of the square.

16 Two conducting spheres are separated by a distance that is large compared with their radii. The first sphere has a radius of $10.0\,cm$ and has a charge of $2.00\,\mu C$ on its surface. The second sphere has a radius of $15.0\,cm$ and is neutral. The spheres are then connected by a long conducting wire.
   a Find the charge on each sphere.
   b Calculate the charge density on each sphere (charge density is the total charge on the sphere divided by the surface area of the sphere).
   c Calculate the electric field on the surface of each sphere.
   d Comment on your result in the light of your answer to part **b**. Why is it stated that the wire is long?

17 The diagram shows the equipotential lines for two equal and opposite charges. Draw the electric field lines for these two charges.

18 Two long parallel plates are separated by a distance of $15.0\,cm$. The bottom plate is kept at a potential of $-250\,V$ and the top at $+250\,V$. A charge of $-2.00\,\mu C$ is placed at a point $3.00\,cm$ from the bottom plate.
   a Find the electric potential energy of the charge.
   The charge is then moved vertically up to a point $3.00\,cm$ from the top plate.
   b What is the electrical potential energy of the charge now?
   c How much work was done on the charge?

19 An electron is shot with a speed equal to $1.59 \times 10^6 \, \text{m s}^{-1}$ from a point where the electric potential is zero toward an immovable negative charge q (see the diagram).

a Determine the potential at P be so that the electron stops momentarily at P and then turns back.
b Calculate the magnitude of q.

20 Two equal and opposite charges are placed at points with coordinates $x=0$, $y=a$ and $x=0$, $y=-a$, as shown in the diagram.

a Find the electric field at the point with coordinates $x=d$, $y=0$.
b Repeat for two equal negative charges $-q$ on the y-axis.
c Sketch graphs to show the variation of these fields with the distance d.

21 Three protons are initially very far apart. Calculate the work that must be done in order to bring these protons to the vertices of an equilateral triangle of side 5.0×10^{-16} m.

10.2 Fields at work

This section deals with the application of Newton's law of gravitation to the motion of the planets around the Sun and satellites around the Earth.

Orbital motion

A satellite of mass m orbits a planet of mass M with speed v. The radius of the orbit is r (Figure 10.26). The total energy E_T of this system is the sum of the kinetic energy E_K and the gravitational potential energy E_P.

$$E_K = \tfrac{1}{2}mv^2 \quad \text{and} \quad E_P = -\frac{GMm}{r}$$

So:

$$E_T = \tfrac{1}{2}mv^2 - \frac{GMm}{r}$$

Note that we do not include any kinetic energy for the planet, as we assume it does not move.

Since the satellite is orbiting in a circle, it must have an acceleration towards the centre of the circle of magnitude $\dfrac{v^2}{r}$. From Newton's second law of motion, to provide this acceleration there must be a force F on the satellite directed towards the centre of the circle:

$$F = \frac{mv^2}{r}$$

Learning objectives

- Derive an expression for the orbital speed.
- Solve problems on orbital motion, including total energy.
- Use the concept of escape speed.
- Explain weightlessness.
- Understand the inverse square law behaviour of the electric and gravitational force.

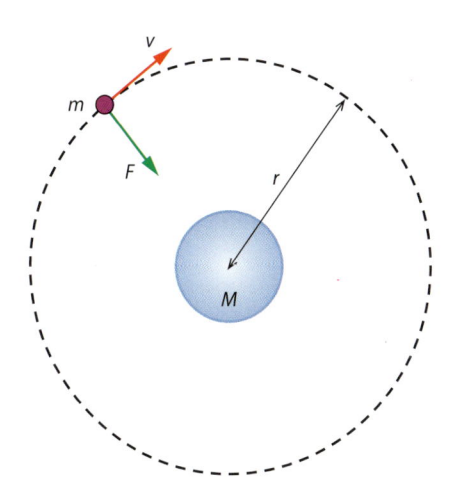

Figure 10.26 A system of a satellite orbiting a planet.

10 FIELDS (HL)

This force is the gravitational attraction between the planet and the satellite. From Newton's law of gravitation, this force is:

$$F = \frac{GMm}{r^2}$$

Exam tip
It is very important that you know how to derive the formula for orbital speed.

Equating the expressions for the force:

$$\frac{GMm}{r^2} = \frac{mv^2}{r}$$

Rearranging and simplifying, we obtain:

$$v^2 = \frac{GM}{r}$$

Finding the square root gives us a formula for the orbital speed, v_{orbit}:

$$v_{orbit} = \sqrt{\frac{GM}{r}}$$

Multiplying by $\frac{m}{2}$, the kinetic energy E_K is:

$$E_K = \frac{GMm}{2r}$$

The total energy of the system becomes:

$$E_T = \frac{GMm}{2r} - \frac{GMm}{r}$$

$$E_T = -\frac{GMm}{2r}$$

From above, $E_K = \frac{1}{2}mv^2 = \frac{GMm}{2r}$ so the equation for E_T can also be expressed as:

$$E_T = -\frac{1}{2}mv^2$$

Figure 10.27 shows the kinetic energy E_K, potential energy E_P and total energy E_T of a mass of 1 kg in orbit around the Earth, as a function of distance from the Earth's centre. This distance is measured in terms of the Earth's radius R.

The law of gravitation combined with Newton's second law of motion allows an understanding of the motion of planets around the Sun, as well as the motion of satellites around the Earth. Suppose you launched an

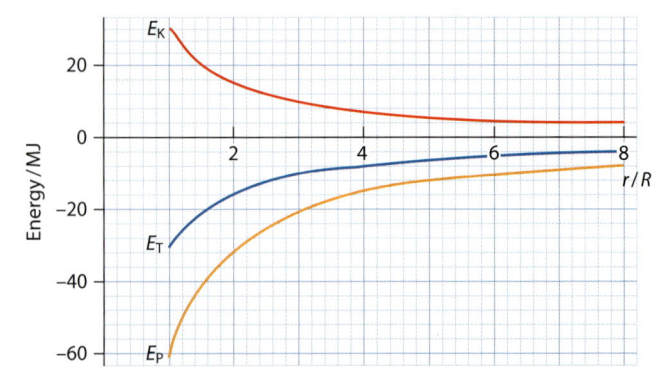

Figure 10.27 Graphs of the kinetic, potential and total energy of a mass of 1 kg in circular orbit around the Earth.

object from the surface of a planet with some speed. What would be the path followed by this object? Newton's laws give several possibilities.
- If the total energy is positive, the object will follow a hyperbolic path and never return.
- If the total energy is zero, the object will follow parabolic path to infinity, where it will just about stop. It will never return.
- If the total energy is negative, the object will go into a circular or elliptical orbit (or crash into the planet if the launching speed is too low).

Figure 10.28 illustrates these possible paths.

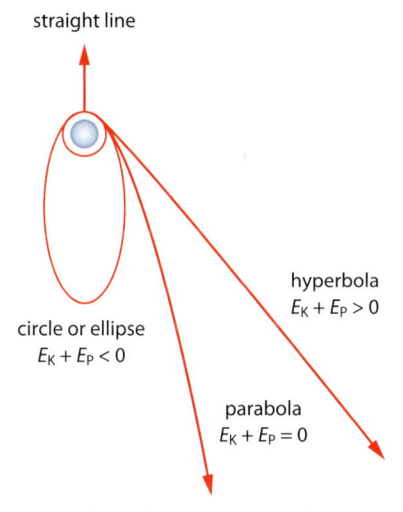

Figure 10.28 Launching a body from the surface of a planet results in various orbits, depending on the total energy E_T of the body.

Worked examples

10.9 Evaluate the speed of a satellite in orbit at a height of 500 km above the Earth's surface and a satellite that just grazes the surface of the Earth. (Take the radius of the Earth to be 6.38×10^6 m.)

The speed is given by:

$$v^2 = \frac{GM}{r}$$

The radius of orbit r of the satellite at a height of 500 km above the Earth's surface is:

$r = (6.38 \times 10^6) + (0.5 \times 10^6) = 6.88 \times 10^6$ m

Substituting for r and using the values from the question:

$$v = \sqrt{\frac{6.67 \times 10^{-11} \times 5.97 \times 10^{24}}{6.88 \times 10^6}}$$

$\Rightarrow v = 7.6 \times 10^3 \,\mathrm{m\,s^{-1}}$

For a grazing orbit, $r = 6.38 \times 10^6$ m.

Using this value and following the same method, $v = 7.9 \times 10^3 \,\mathrm{m\,s^{-1}}$.

10 FIELDS (HL)

10.10 A satellite in a low orbit will experience a small frictional force (due to the atmosphere) in a direction opposite to the satellite's velocity.
   a Explain why the satellite will move into an orbit closer to the Earth's surface.
   b Deduce that the speed of the satellite will increase.

a Since there is a frictional force acting, the satellite's total energy will be reduced.

The total energy of a satellite of mass m in a circular orbit of radius r around the Earth of mass M is:

$$E_T = -\frac{GMm}{2r}$$

The masses do not change and G is a constant. The energy E_T is negative, so reducing the energy means it becomes *more* negative. This means there must be a smaller radius, i.e. the satellite comes closer to the Earth by spiralling inwards.

b The speed of the satellite in a circular orbit is given by:

$$v = \sqrt{\frac{GM}{r}}$$

So we see that, as the satellite comes closer to Earth, its speed increases.

10.11 A probe of mass m is launched from the surface of a planet of mass M and radius R with kinetic energy $E_K = \frac{4GM}{5R}$.
   a Explain why this probe will not escape the gravitational field of the planet.
   b The probe eventually settles into a circular orbit around the planet. Calculate the radius of its orbit in terms of R.

a The total energy at launch is the sum of the kinetic and potential energies:

$$E_T = \frac{4GMm}{5R} - \frac{GMm}{R}$$

$$E_T = -\frac{GMm}{5R}$$

This is negative and so the probe cannot escape.

b The total energy in orbit is:

$$E_T = -\frac{GMm}{2r}$$

By energy conservation, the total energy once the probe is in orbit must equal the total energy at launch. So:

$$-\frac{GMm}{2r} = -\frac{GMm}{5R}$$

$$\frac{1}{2r} = \frac{1}{5R}$$

$$2r = 5R$$

So $r = \dfrac{5R}{2}$

10.12 Figure **10.29** shows the variation of the gravitational potential due to a planet and its moon with distance r from the centre of the planet. The centre-to-centre distance between the planet and the moon is d. The planet's centre is at $r = 0$ and the centre of the moon is at $r = d$.

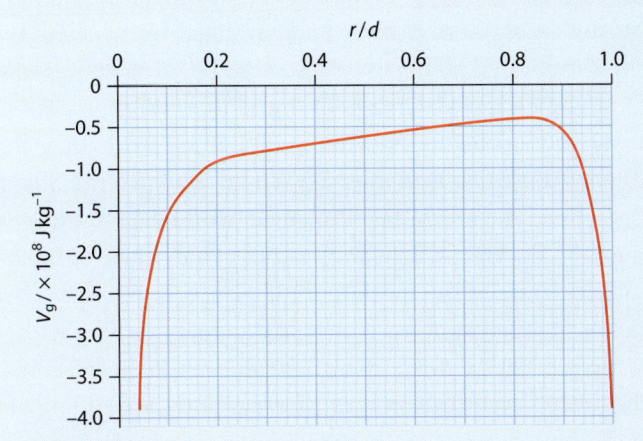

Figure 10.29

State and explain the minimum energy required so that a 850 kg probe at rest on the planet's surface will arrive on the moon.

The probe will arrive at the moon provided it has enough energy to get to the peak of the curve. Once there, the moon will pull it in.

On the surface of the planet $V_g = -3.9 \times 10^8 \, \text{J} \, \text{kg}^{-1}$. At the peak the potential is $V_g = -0.4 \times 10^8 \, \text{J} \, \text{kg}^{-1}$. The minimum energy required is equal to the work done to move through this potential difference.

$W = m \Delta V_g$

$W = 850 \times (-0.4 \times 10^8 + 3.9 \times 10^8)$

$W = 3.0 \times 10^{11} \, \text{J}$

So the minimum energy required is $3.0 \times 10^{11} \, \text{J}$.

Escape velocity

Suppose that a body of mass m is launched from the surface of a planet of mass M and radius R with speed v (Figure **10.30**). The total energy of the system is the sum of the kinetic and gravitational potential energies:

$$E_T = \tfrac{1}{2}mv^2 - \frac{GMm}{R}$$

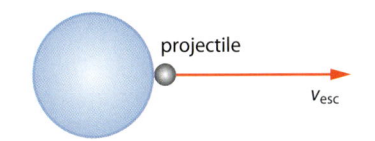

Figure 10.30 The escape speed will take the projectile from the surface of the planet to infinity, where it will come to rest.

The factor R is used in the expression for the gravitational potential energy because the centre-to-centre distance of M and m is R.

We would like to give to the mass m sufficient energy at launch so that it moves very far away from M (essentially to infinity). What should the launch speed be?

10 FIELDS (HL)

Changing ideas

The motion of the planets is the perfect application of the theory of gravitation. The understanding of the motion of the planets has undergone very many 'paradigm shifts' since ancient times. Newton was motivated by the 'laws' discovered by Kepler. Kepler's laws were published in 1619 in a book called the *Harmony of the World*, nearly 70 years before Newton published his work. In ancient times, Ptolemy constructed an involved system in which the Sun and the planets orbited the Earth. The Ptolemaic world view prevailed for centuries until Copernicus, early in the 16th century, asserted that the Sun was at the centre of the motion of the planets in the solar system. Newton's law of gravitation has had great success in dealing with planetary motion but cannot account for some small irregularities, such as the precession of the orbit of Mercury and the bending of light near very massive bodies. In 1915, Einstein introduced the general theory of relativity, which replaced Newton's theory of gravity and resolved the difficulties of the Newtonian theory.

If m gets very far away, then the potential energy will be zero. If we give the minimum energy at launch, then when the mass m reaches infinity, it will just about stop there and so will have negligible kinetic energy. The total energy will then be zero. By energy conservation, this means that the total energy at launch is also zero. Using v_{esc} as the minimum velocity needed to escape from the planet, this means:

$$\tfrac{1}{2}mv_{esc}^2 - \frac{GMm}{R} = 0$$

This implies that:

$$v_{esc} = \sqrt{\frac{2GM}{R}}$$

This minimum velocity v_{esc} that a mass must have in order to reach infinity and stop there is called the **escape velocity**. Note that the escape velocity is independent of the mass of the body escaping.

For the Earth, the escape velocity is therefore:

$$v_{esc} = \sqrt{\frac{2GM_{Earth}}{R_{Earth}}}$$

Using the fact that on Earth the gravitational field strength g is given by:

$$g = \frac{GM_{Earth}}{R_{Earth}^2}$$

we see that the escape velocity for the Earth can also be rewritten as:

$$v_{esc} = \sqrt{2gR_{Earth}}$$

The numerical value of this escape velocity is about $11.2\,\text{km}\,\text{s}^{-1}$.

> We met the expression for gravitational field strength g in Subtopic **6.2**.

25 The diagram shows cross-sections of two satellite orbits around the Earth. (To be in orbit means that only gravity is acting on the satellite.) Discuss whether either of these orbits is possible.

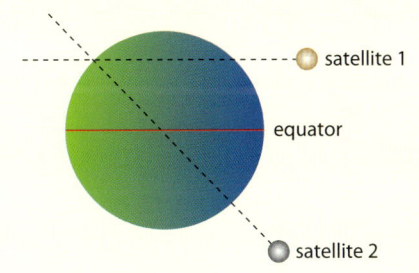

26 In the text it was calculated that the acceleration due to gravity at a height of 300 km above the Earth's surface is far from negligible, yet astronauts orbiting in a space shuttle at such a height feel weightless. Explain why.

27 A rocket is launched from the surface of a planet. At the position shown in the diagram, the rocket is a distance of $2R$ from the planet (where R is the radius of the planet) and its speed is $v = \sqrt{\dfrac{GM}{2R}}$. At that point the fuel runs out.

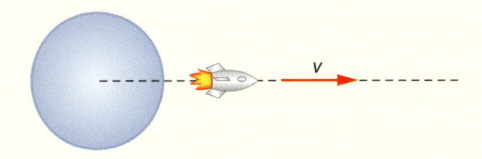

  a Explain why the probe will eventually crash onto the surface of the planet.
  b Calculate, in terms of R, the maximum distance from the centre of the planet the rocket travels to.
  c Determine the speed with which the rocket crashes onto the planet surface.
  d Draw a graph to show how the speed of the rocket varies with distance r from the centre of the planet as the rocket begins to fall back towards the planet.

28 Prove that the total energy of the Earth (mass m) as it orbits the Sun (mass M) can be expressed as either $E = -\tfrac{1}{2}mv^2$ or $E = -\dfrac{GMm}{2r}$ where r is the radius of the Earth's circular orbit. Calculate this energy numerically.

29 The diagram shows two identical satellites in circular orbits. Which satellite has the larger:
  a kinetic energy
  b potential energy
  c total energy?

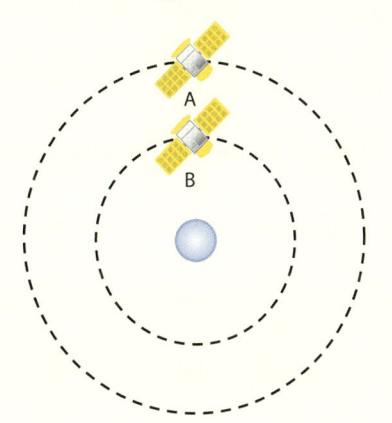

30 The total energy of a satellite during launch from the Earth's surface is $E = -\dfrac{GMm}{5r}$, where R is the radius of the Earth.
  a Explain why this satellite will not escape the Earth.
  b The satellite eventually settles into a circular orbit. Calculate the radius of the orbit in terms of R.

31 A satellite is in a circular orbit around the Earth. The satellite turns on its engines and the satellite now finds itself in a new circular orbit of larger radius. State and explain whether the work done by the engines is positive, zero or negative.

10 FIELDS (HL)

32 The diagram shows a planet orbiting the Sun. Explain why at points A and P of the orbit the potential energy of the planet assumes its minimum and maximum values, and determine which is which. Hence determine at what point in the orbit the planet has the greatest speed.

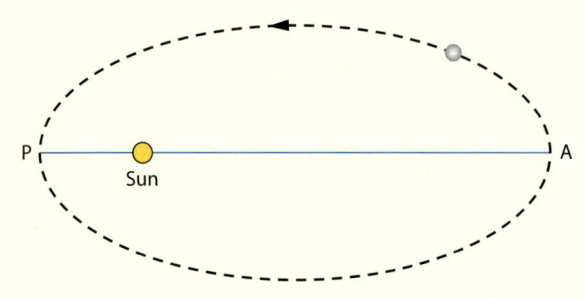

33 Show that the escape speed from the surface of a planet of radius R can be written as $v_{esc} = \sqrt{2gR}$ where g is the gravitational field strength on the planet's surface.

34 a Deduce that a satellite orbiting a planet of mass M in a circular orbit of radius r has a period of revolution given by $T = \sqrt{\dfrac{4\pi^2 r^3}{GM}}$

  b A grazing orbit is one in which the orbit radius is approximately equal to the radius R of the planet. Deduce that the period of revolution in a grazing orbit is given by $T = \sqrt{\dfrac{3\pi}{G\rho}}$ where ρ is the density of the planet.

  c The period of a grazing orbit around the Earth is 85 minutes and around the planet Jupiter it is 169 minutes. Deduce the ratio $\dfrac{\rho_{Earth}}{\rho_{Jupiter}}$.

35 a The acceleration of free fall at the surface of a planet is g and the radius of the planet is R. Deduce that the period of a satellite in a very low orbit is given by $T = 2\pi = \sqrt{\dfrac{R}{g}}$

  b Given that $g = 4.5 \, m\,s^{-2}$ and $R = 3.4 \times 10^6 \, m$, deduce that the orbital period of the low orbit is about 91 minutes.

  c A spacecraft in orbit around this planet has a period of 140 minutes. Deduce the height of the spacecraft from the surface of the planet.

36 Two stars of equal mass M orbit a common centre as shown in the diagram. The radius of the orbit of each star is R. Assume that each of the stars has a mass equal to 1.5 solar masses (solar mass = 2.0×10^{30} kg) and that the initial separation of the stars is 2.0×10^9 m.

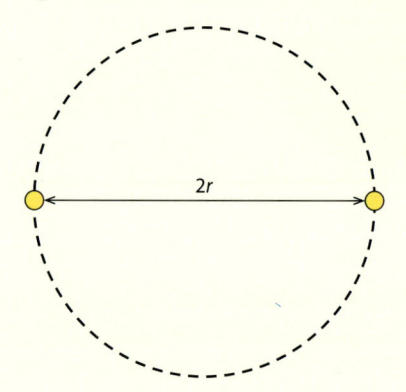

  a State the magnitude of the force on each star in terms of M, R and G.

  b Deduce that the period of revolution of each star is given by the expression:
  $$T^2 = \dfrac{16\pi^2 r^3}{GM}$$

  c Evaluate the period numerically.

  d Show that the total energy of the two stars is given by:
  $$E = -\dfrac{GM^2}{4R}$$

  e The two-star system loses energy as a result of emitting gravitational radiation. Deduce that the stars will move closer to each other.

  f i Explain why the fractional loss of energy per unit time may be calculated from the expression:
  $$\dfrac{\Delta E/E}{\Delta t} = \dfrac{3}{2}\dfrac{\Delta T/T}{\Delta t}$$
  where $\dfrac{\Delta T/T}{\Delta t}$ is the fractional decrease in period per unit time. (Hint: Use ideas of error propagation.)

  ii The orbital period decreases at a rate of $\dfrac{\Delta T/T}{\Delta t} = 72 \, \mu s \, yr^{-1}$. Estimate the fractional energy loss per year.

  g The two stars will collapse into each other when $\Delta E \approx E$. Estimate the lifetime, in years, of this binary star system.

37 A charge $-q$ whose mass is m moves in a circle of radius r around another positive stationary charge q located at the centre of the circle, as shown in the diagram.

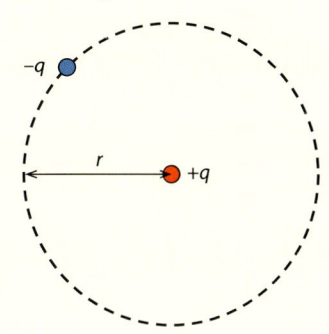

a Draw the force on the moving charge.
b Show that the velocity of the charge is given by:
$$v^2 = \frac{1}{4\pi\varepsilon_0}\frac{q^2}{mr}$$
c Show that the total energy of the charge is given by:
$$E = -\frac{1}{8\pi\varepsilon_0}\frac{q^2}{r}$$
d Hence determine how much energy must be supplied to the charge if it is to orbit around the stationary charge at a radius equal to $2r$.

38 An electron of charge $-e$ and mass m orbits the proton in a hydrogen atom as in the previous problem.
a Show that the period of revolution of the electron is given by $T^2 = \frac{4\pi^2 m}{ke^2}r^3$ where k is the Coulomb constant and r the radius of the orbit.
b Calculate this period for an orbit radius of 0.5×10^{-10} m.
c Using the results of the previous problem calculate the energy that must be supplied to the electron so it orbits the proton in an orbit of radius 2.0×10^{-10} m.

Exam-style questions

1. Two identical solid steel spheres touch. The gravitational force between them is F. The spheres are now replaced by two touching solid steel spheres of double the radius. What is the force between the spheres now?

   A $\dfrac{F}{4}$　　　　**B** $\dfrac{F}{16}$　　　　**C** $4F$　　　　**D** $16F$

2. A planet has double the mass of the Earth and double the radius. The gravitational potential at the surface of the Earth is V and the magnitude of the gravitational field strength is g. The gravitational potential and gravitational field strength on the surface of the planet are:

	Potential	Field
A	V	$\dfrac{g}{4}$
B	$2V$	$\dfrac{g}{2}$
C	V	$\dfrac{g}{2}$
D	$2V$	$\dfrac{g}{4}$

3. Four charges that are equal in magnitude are put at the vertices of a square, as shown in the diagram.

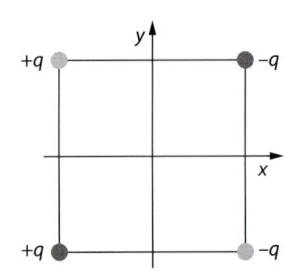

   Where is the electric potential zero?

   A At the origin only.
   B Along the x-axis.
   C Along the y-axis.
   D Along both axes.

4 Consider two spherical masses, each of mass M, whose centres are a distance d apart. Which of the following is true at the point midway on the line joining the two centres?

	Potential	Gravitational field strength
A	zero	zero
B	zero	non-zero
C	non-zero	zero
D	non-zero	non-zero

5 A probe of mass m is in a circular orbit of radius r around a planet of mass M. The probe is moved to a higher circular orbit of orbit radius $2r$. What is the work done on the probe?

A $-\dfrac{GMm}{2r}$ B $\dfrac{GMm}{2r}$ C $\dfrac{GMm}{4r}$ D $-\dfrac{GMm}{4r}$

6 A positive charge q is placed half way between two long parallel plates that are separated by a distance $2d$. The charge on one of the plates is Q and the charge on the other plate is $-Q$. The potential difference between the plates is V. What is the magnitude of the force on the charge q?

A $k\dfrac{Qq}{d^2}$ B $k\dfrac{2Qq}{d^2}$ C $\dfrac{qV}{2d}$ D $\dfrac{qV}{d}$

7 Shown are four arrangements of two unequal positive point charges separated by various distances. Which **two** arrangements result in the same electric potential energy?

I q ←— d —→ q

II q ←— d —→ $2q$

III $2q$ ←——— $2d$ ———→ q

IV $2q$ ←——— $2d$ ———→ $4q$

A I and II   B II and IV   C III and IV   D I and III

8 The figure shows two oppositely charged parallel plates a distance d apart.

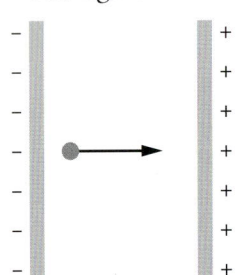

A proton is launched from the negative plate with initial speed u. The proton just reaches the positive plate. Which graph represents the variation of the speed v of the proton with distance x from the negative plate?

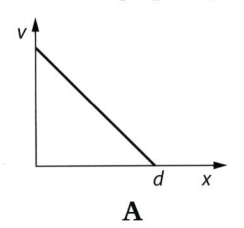

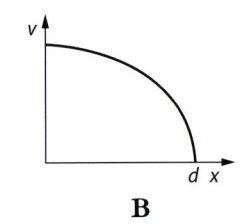

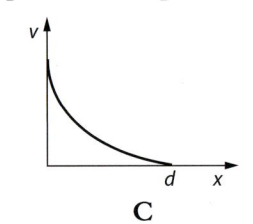

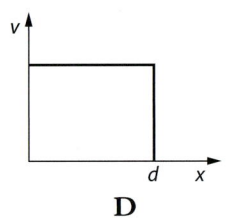

9 An amount of positive charge Q is placed uniformly on a large plane surface. A small positive point charge q placed a perpendicular distance r from the surface experiences a force F.

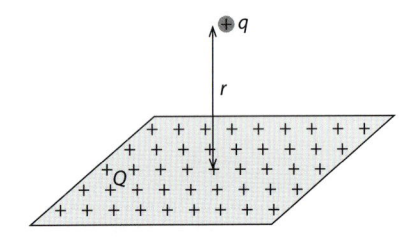

What is the magnitude of the electric field at the position of the small charge q?

A $\dfrac{kQ}{r^2}$ B $\dfrac{F}{Q}$ C $\dfrac{F}{q}$ D $\dfrac{kQ}{r}$

10 Two charges M and N are separated by a certain distance, as shown in the diagram.

Graphs I, II and III show the variation of electric potential V_e with distance x from the centre of charge M.

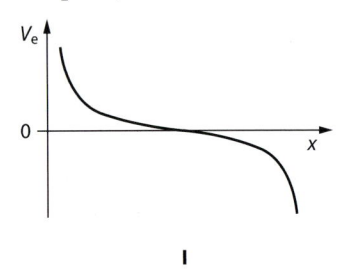

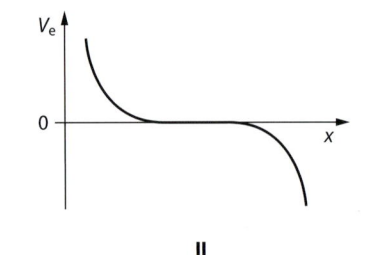

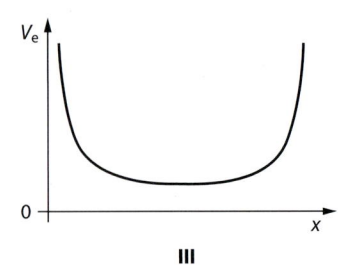

Which of the possibilities below applies to the case of two equal and opposite charges?

A I only   B II only   C III only   D I, II or III

11 The graph shows the variation with distance r of the gravitational potential V_g (in terajoules per kilogram) due to a planet of radius 2.0×10^5 m.

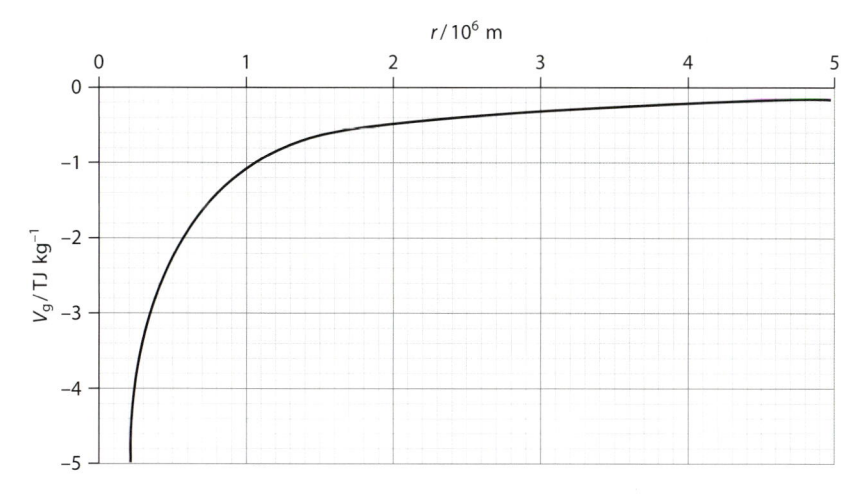

a Calculate the mass of the planet. [2]
b Show that the escape speed from the surface of the planet may be written as $v_{esc} = \sqrt{-2V}$, where V is the gravitational potential on the planet's surface. [3]
c Use the graph to determine the escape speed from this planet. [2]
d Calculate how much energy is required to move a rocket of mass 1500 kg from the surface of the planet to a distance of 1.0×10^6 m from the centre. [2]
e Determine the additional energy required to put the rocket in orbit at the distance in part **d**. [2]
f A probe is released from rest at a distance from the planet's centre of 0.50×10^6 m and allowed to crash onto the planet's surface. Determine the speed with which the probe hits the surface. [2]

12 The graph shows the variation with distance r from the centre of a planet of the combined gravitational potential V_g due to the planet (of mass M) and its moon (of mass m) along the line joining the planet and the moon. The horizontal axis is labelled $\frac{r}{d}$, where d is the centre-to-centre separation of the planet and the moon.

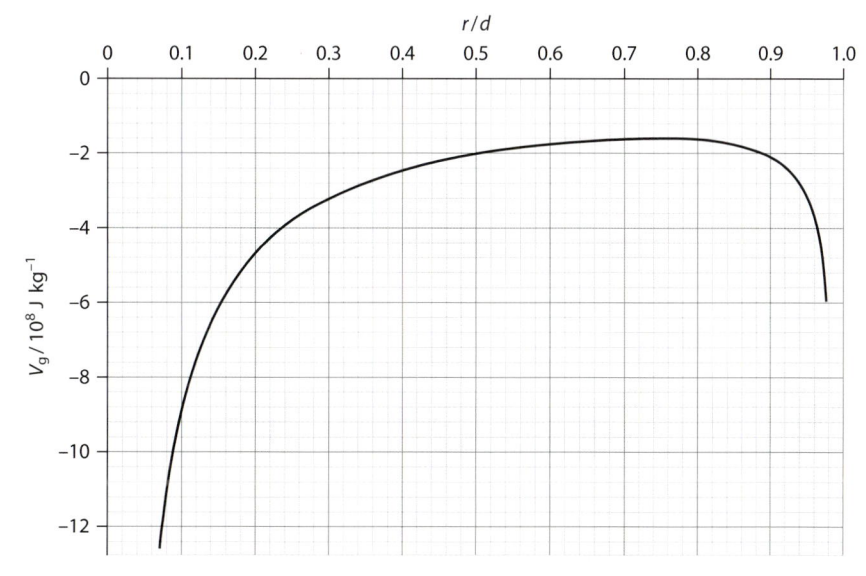

10 FIELDS (HL)   431

a The distance d is equal to 4.8×10^8 m. Use the graph to calculate the magnitude of the gravitational field strength at the point where $\frac{r}{d} = 0.20$. [3]

b Explain the physical significance of the point where $\frac{r}{d} = 0.75$. [2]

c Using the graph, calculate the ratio M/m. [3]

13 A sphere of radius 0.25 m has positive charge $+8.8\,\mu$C uniformly distributed on its surface. A small pellet of mass 0.075 kg and charge $+2.4\,\mu$C is directed radially at the sphere. When the pellet is at a distance of 0.75 m from the centre of the sphere its speed is $3.2\,\text{m s}^{-1}$.

    a Determine the distance from the centre of the sphere at which the pellet will stop. [3]
    b Describe qualitatively the subsequent motion of the pellet. [2]
    c Determine the speed of the pellet after it moves very far from the sphere. [2]

14 An electron is accelerated from rest by a potential difference of 29.1 V.

    a Show that the electron acquires a speed of $3.2 \times 10^6\,\text{m s}^{-1}$. [2]

    The accelerated electron enters the region between two parallel oppositely charged plates at point A. The electron exits the plates at point B after having moved a vertical distance of 0.25 cm. The length of the plates is 2.0 cm.

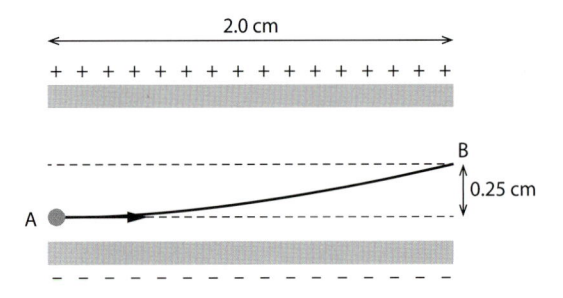

    b Calculate the time the electron spends within the plates. [2]
    c Determine the magnitude of the electric field within the plates. [2]
    d Calculate the angle that the velocity of the electron makes with the horizontal at point B. [2]
    e Calculate the work done on the electron from A to B. [2]
    f Using your answer to **e**, state the potential difference between points A and B. [1]

15 The diagram shows electric field lines for two point charges X and Y.

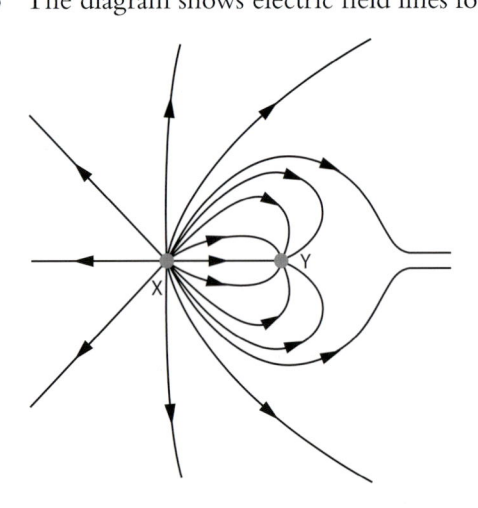

a State what is meant by field lines. [2]
b State **three** properties of electric field lines. [3]
c Determine the signs of X and Y. [1]
d i Copy the diagram. On your copy, indicate where the electric field is zero. [1]
  ii By making appropriate measurements on the diagram estimate the ratio charge X : charge Y. [2]

16 a State what is meant by an equipotential surface. [1]

b The diagram shows five equipotential lines around two spherical masses.

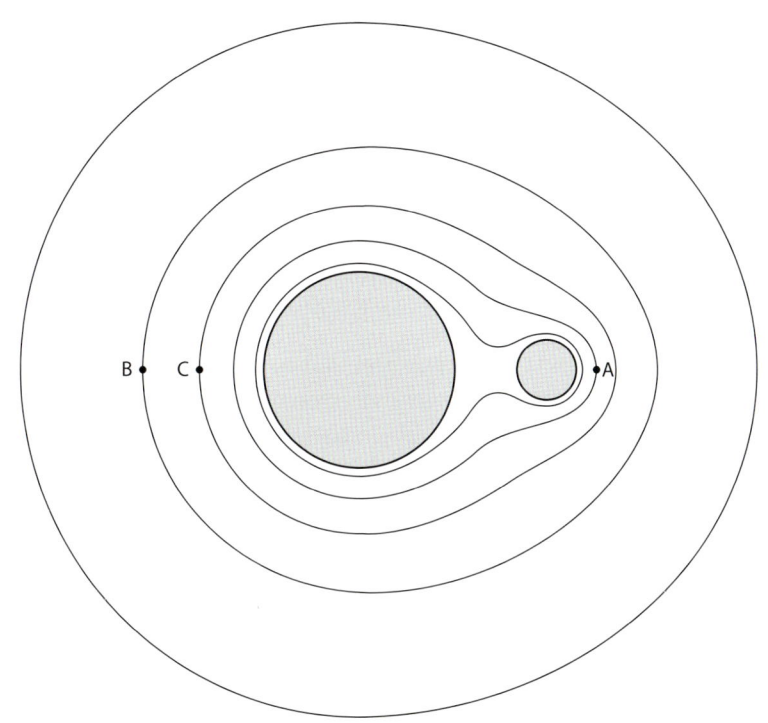

  i On a copy of the diagram, draw lines to represent field lines for this arrangement of masses. You must draw **six** field lines. [2]
  ii Two consecutive lines are separated by a potential difference of $10^6 \, J\,kg^{-1}$ and the innermost line has potential $-15.0 \times 10^6 \, J\,kg^{-1}$. Calculate the work done to move a mass of 1500 kg from point A to point B. [2]
  iii The distance between points B and C is 4.0×10^6 m. Estimate the average gravitational field strength between B and C. [2]
  iv The equipotential lines tend to become circular as the distance from the sources increases. Explain this observation. [2]
c State and explain whether the pattern for equipotential lines shown above could also apply to electric charges. [3]

11 Electromagnetic induction (HL)

Learning objectives

- Understand the concept of induced emf.
- Understand the difference between magnetic flux and magnetic flux linkage.
- Solve problems using Faraday's law of electromagnetic induction.
- Apply Lenz's law in different situations.

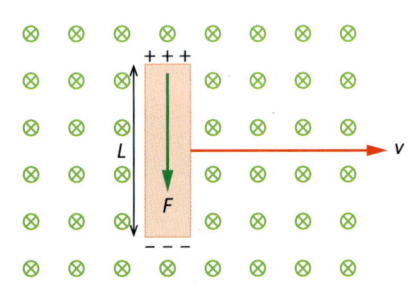

Figure 11.1 The rod is made to move normally to the magnetic field at constant speed. An emf develops between the ends of the rod.

In Topic 5 we saw that the electric force on a charge q in an electric field E is qE and the magnetic force in a magnetic field B is qvB. The expressions here are applied to an electron, whose charge is e.

11.1 Electromagnetic induction

This section deals with Faraday's law, which dictates how a changing magnetic flux through a loop induces an emf in the loop. A related law, Lenz's law, determines the direction of this emf. The principles of electromagnetic induction are the result of ingenious experimenting by the English physicist Michael Faraday (1791–1867).

Motional emf

Imagine a rod of length L that is moved with velocity v in a region of a magnetic field of constant magnitude B. Assume for convenience that the magnetic field is going into the plane of the page and that the rod moves from left to right (Figure **11.1**).

The rod is conducting – that is, it has many 'free' electrons. As it moves, the electrons within it also move from left to right. The magnetic field will exert a force on these moving electrons. The force on the electrons is directed downward (green arrow) and therefore the electrons are pushed downward. This means that the bottom end of the rod has a net negative charge and the top end has an equal net positive charge. (The net charge of the rod is zero.) The flow of electrons towards the bottom end of the rod will stop when the electrons already there are numerous enough to push any new electrons back by electrostatic repulsion. There is, in other words, an electric field established in the rod whose direction is from top to bottom.

The value of this electric field E is given by:

$$E = \frac{\varepsilon}{L}$$

where ε is the potential difference between the ends of the rod, known as the **induced emf**. The flow of electrons will stop when the electric force eE pushing the electrons back equals the magnetic force evB. Thus:

$$eE = evB$$

Dividing both sides by e and substituting for the electric field, this becomes:

$$\varepsilon = BvL$$

We have found the extraordinary result that a conducting rod of length L moving with speed v normally to a magnetic field B will have a potential difference BvL across its ends. This is called a **motional emf**, as it has been induced as a result of the motion of the conductor in the magnetic field.

It is instructive to check that the quantity BvL really has the units of potential difference, namely volts:

$$[BvL] = T\,(m\,s^{-1})\,m = \left(\frac{N}{A\,m}\right)(m\,s^{-1})\,m = \frac{J}{C\,s^{-1}}s^{-1} = \frac{J}{C} = V$$

It is important to note that, except for a very short interval of time initially, no current exists in the rod. But this example opens the way for generating an electric current out of magnetic fields.

Suppose we modify things by letting the rod slide on two wires that are joined by resistor of resistance R, as shown in Figure **11.2**. Now the moving rod behaves as a battery. There is a potential difference between the top and the bottom equal to BvL (this is the emf of the 'battery') and a current equal to $I = \dfrac{BvL}{R}$ is established in the resistor and the moving rod, i.e. in the circuit on the left side of the diagram. This is because electrons in the bottom part of the circuit now have the opportunity to move up through the resistor, thus momentarily reducing the number of electrons in the bottom. The electric field in the rod is reduced and so the downward magnetic force on the electrons pushes more electrons down, and so on.

Notice also that now that we have a current, the rod needs to be pushed if it is to continue to move at constant speed. This is because the rod carries current I and is in a magnetic field, so it experiences a magnetic force F directed to the left given by:

$$F = BIL = B\frac{BvL}{R}L = \frac{vB^2L^2}{R}$$

For speed to remain constant a force of equal magnitude needs to act on the rod, directed to the right. The power P generated by this force is:

$$P = Fv = \frac{v^2B^2L^2}{R}$$

The power dissipated in the circuit as heat in the resistor is:

$$P = \frac{\varepsilon^2}{R} = \frac{v^2B^2L^2}{R}$$

This is in perfect agreement with conservation of energy: the work done by the agent pushing the rod is dissipated in the resistor. Here, mechanical work (pushing the rod) is transformed into electrical energy and then heat.

Magnetic flux and magnetic flux linkage

In 1831, Faraday experimented with coils of wire wrapped around an iron ring (Figure **11.3**). He was hoping that, somehow, the current in the left circuit might induce a current in the right circuit. No such current was observed in the right circuit, but Faraday did notice that a small current was induced only during the opening and closing of the switch.

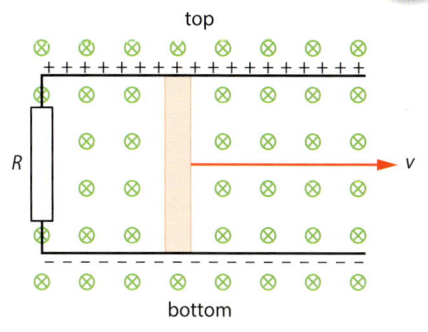

Figure 11.2 As the rod is pushed along, a current is established in the circuit.

Exam tip
The work done to move an electron from top to bottom in the wire is $W = FL$. The force is evB and so the work done is $W = evBL$. The work done per unit charge is the emf, i.e. $\varepsilon = BvL$, as expected.

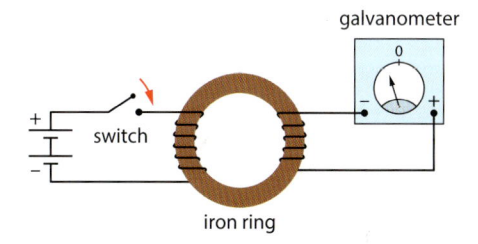

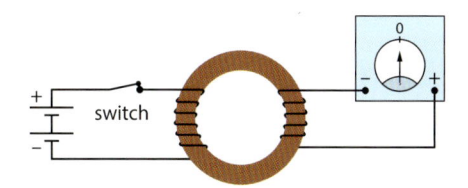

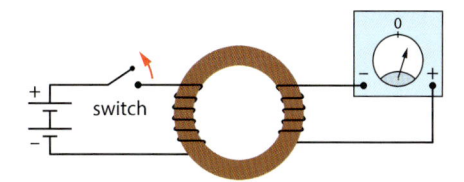

Figure 11.3 As the switch is closed a small current is registered by the galvanometer. While the switch remains closed a current exists in the circuit to the left but the current in the right circuit is zero. As the switch is opened another small current is established in the right circuit.

11 ELECTROMAGNETIC INDUCTION (HL) 435

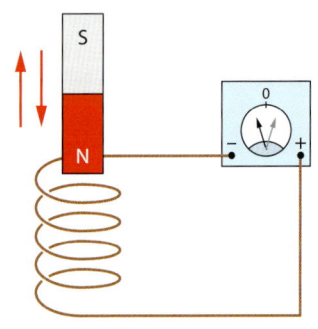

Figure 11.4 As the magnet is allowed to enter the coil a current is induced in the coil and is registered by the galvanometer. If the magnet is then pulled out of the coil the induced current is opposite.

Similar results are obtained when a magnet is moved in or out of a coil of wire that is connected to a sensitive galvanometer (Figure **11.4**). A current is induced.

If the magnet is simply placed near the coil but does not move relative to it, nothing happens. The current is created as a result of the **motion** of the magnet relative to the coil. If we move the coil toward the magnet, we again find a reading. This indicates that it is the relative motion of the coil and magnet that is responsible for the effect. If the magnet moves toward the coil faster, the reading on the galvanometer is greater. If a magnet of greater strength is used, the current produced is greater. If we try a coil with more turns of wire, we again find a greater current. We also observe that if the area of the loop is increased, the current also increases. But if the magnet is moved at an angle to the plane of the loop other than a right angle, the current decreases. To summarise, the observations are that the current registered by the galvanometer **increases** when:

- the relative speed of the magnet and the coil increases
- the strength of the magnet increases
- the number of turns increases
- the area of the loop increases
- the magnet moves at right angles to the plane of the loop.

Faraday found that the common thread behind these observations is the concept of **magnetic flux**. Imagine a loop of wire, which for simplicity we take to be planar (i.e. the entire loop lies on one plane). If this loop is in a region of magnetic field whose magnitude and direction is constant, then we define magnetic flux as follows.

> The magnetic flux Φ through the loop is:
>
> $\Phi = BA \cos \theta$
>
> where B is magnetic field strength, A is the area of the loop and θ is the angle between the magnetic field direction and the direction **normal to the loop area** (Figure **11.5**). If the loop has N turns of wire around it, the flux is given by:
>
> $\Phi = NBA \cos \theta$
>
> in which case we speak of **flux linkage**. The unit of magnetic flux is the weber (Wb): $1 \, \text{Wb} = 1 \, \text{T m}^2$.

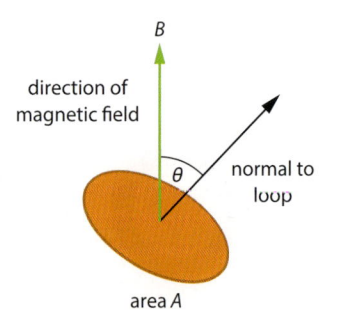

Figure 11.5 The definition of magnetic flux, $\Phi = BA \cos \theta$.

This means that if the magnetic field is along the plane of the loop, then $\theta = 90°$ and hence $\Phi = 0$ (Figure **11.6a**). The maximum flux through the loop occurs when $\theta = 0°$, when the magnetic field is normal to the loop area and its value is then BA (Figure **11.6b**).

The intuitive picture of magnetic flux is the number of magnetic field lines that cross or pierce the loop area. Note that if the magnetic field went through only half the loop area, the other half being in a region of no magnetic field, then the flux would be $\Phi = \dfrac{BA}{2}$. In other words, what counts is the part of the loop area that is pierced by magnetic field lines.

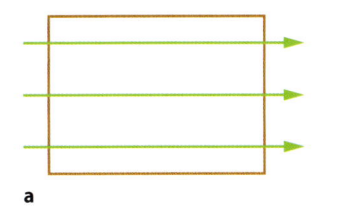

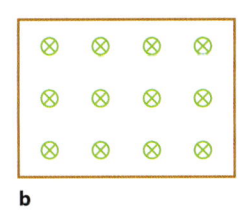

Figure 11.6 a The loop is not pierced by any magnetic field lines, so the flux through it is zero. **b** The magnetic field is normal to the loop, so the flux through it is the largest possible.

Worked example

11.1 A loop of area 8.0 cm² is in a constant magnetic field of $B = 0.15$ T. What is the magnetic flux through the loop when:
   a the loop is perpendicular to the field
   b the loop is parallel to the field
   c the normal to the loop and the field have an angle of 60° between them?

a In this case $\theta = 0°$ and $\cos 0° = 1$. The area of the loop is 8.0×10^{-4} m². Substituting in $\Phi = BA \cos\theta$, the flux Φ is given by:

$\Phi = 0.15 \times 8.0 \times 10^{-4}$

$\Phi = 1.2 \times 10^{-4}$ Wb

b In this case $\theta = 90°$ and $\cos 90° = 0$, so $\Phi = 0$.

c In this case $\theta = 60°$, so:

$\Phi = 0.15 \times 8.0 \times 10^{-4} \times 0.5$

$\Phi = 6.0 \times 10^{-5}$ Wb

Faraday's law

So what does magnetic flux have to do with the problem of how a magnetic field can create an electric current? The answer lies in a **changing magnetic flux linkage**. In Figure 11.4 we had a magnetic flux linkage through the coil, which was changing with time. As a magnet is brought closer to the loop area, the value of the magnetic field at the loop position is increasing and so is flux. If the magnet is held stationary near the loop, there is flux through the loop but it is not changing – so nothing happens. If the number of turns is increased, so is the flux linkage. Thus, there seems to be a connection between the amount of current induced and the rate of change of magnetic flux linkage through the loop.

A changing flux creates an induced emf, not necessarily a current. There will be a current only if the loop is conducting, i.e. if the resistance of the circuit is not infinite. For example, a loop containing an ideal voltmeter cannot let current through, but there will be an emf if the flux is changing.

Faraday found that the induced emf is equal to the (negative) rate of change of magnetic flux linkage, that is:

$\varepsilon = -\dfrac{N\Delta\Phi}{\Delta t}$

11 ELECTROMAGNETIC INDUCTION (HL)

So, it is an emf that is induced. If this emf is induced in a conductor then there will be current as well.

The minus sign need not concern us, as we will be finding the **magnitude** of the induced emf. However, if we use calculus, we need the minus sign:

$$\varepsilon = -\frac{N\,d\Phi}{dt}$$

This is known as **Faraday's law** (of electromagnetic induction).

Worked examples

11.2 The magnetic field through a single loop of area $0.20\,\text{m}^2$ is changing at a rate of $4.0\,\text{T s}^{-1}$. What is the induced emf?

The magnetic flux through the loop is changing because of the changing magnetic field, hence:

$\Phi = BA$

$\varepsilon = \dfrac{\Delta\Phi}{\Delta t}$

$\varepsilon = \dfrac{\Delta BA}{\Delta t}$

$\varepsilon = 4.0 \times 0.20$

$\varepsilon = 0.80\,\text{V}$

11.3 A pair of conducting rails is placed in a uniform magnetic field directed downward, as shown in Figure **11.7**. The rails are a distance $L = 0.20\,\text{m}$ apart. A rod is placed on the rails and pushed to the right at constant speed $v = 0.60\,\text{m s}^{-1}$. What is the induced emf in the loop formed by the rod and the rails?

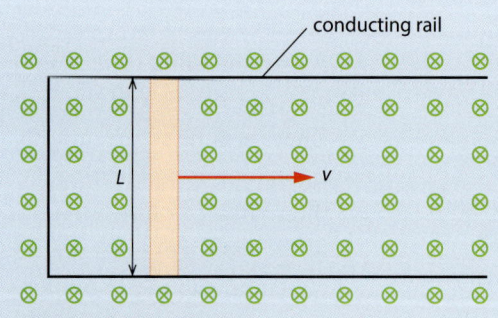

Figure 11.7 A rod on a pair of conducting rails.

438

We looked at this problem at the beginning of this section, but now we will solve it the 'easy' way using the concept of a changing flux and Faraday's law.

The flux in the loop is changing since the area of the loop is increasing. Therefore there will be an emf induced.

In a time interval Δt the rod will move to the right a distance $v\Delta t$ and so the area will increase by $\Delta A = Lv\Delta t$ (Figure 11.8).

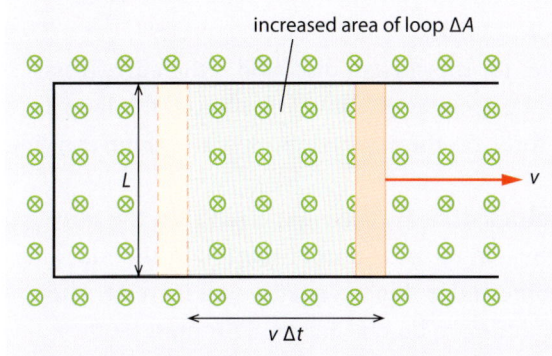

Figure 11.8 As the rod moves along the rails, the area of the loop increases.

Using $\varepsilon = \dfrac{\Delta \Phi}{\Delta t}$ and $\Phi = BA$, we see that $\varepsilon = B\dfrac{\Delta A}{\Delta t}$ and so:

$\varepsilon = B \times \dfrac{Lv\Delta t}{\Delta t}$

$\varepsilon = BLv$

$\varepsilon = 0.40 \times 0.20 \times 0.60$

$\varepsilon = 48\,\text{mV}$

Using Faraday's law

We began this section by describing a rod being dragged in a region of magnetic field. We saw, by considering the forces acting on the electrons contained in the wire, that a potential difference was induced at its ends given by:

$\varepsilon = BvL$

We can re-derive this result by making use of the concept of changing flux and Faraday's law. The rod cuts magnetic field lines as it moves in the magnetic field. In time Δt it will move a distance of $v\Delta t$ (Figure 11.9) and so the flux through the area swept by the rod is:

$\Delta \Phi = BLv\Delta t$

$\Rightarrow \varepsilon = \dfrac{\Delta \Phi}{\Delta t}$

$\varepsilon = BvL$

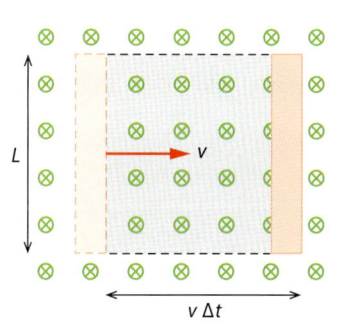

Figure 11.9 The rod sweeps out an area pierced by magnetic field lines.

11 ELECTROMAGNETIC INDUCTION (HL)

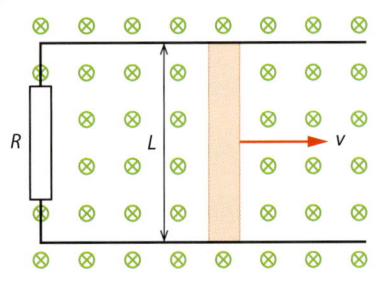

Figure 11.10 The rod is made to move to the right. The magnetic flux through the loop is increasing and a current will be established in the rod.

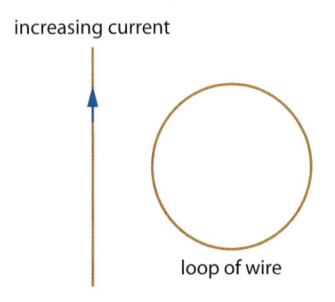

Figure 11.11 A loop of wire near a straight wire in which the current is increasing.

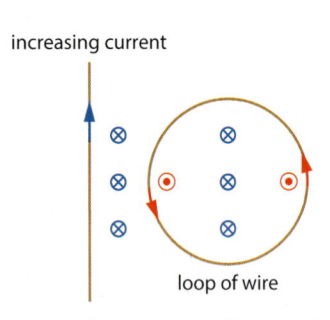

Figure 11.12 The current in the straight wire creates a magnetic field into the page at the position of the loop. The induced current in the loop produces a magnetic field in the opposite direction as to oppose the change in flux.

Lenz's law

Having seen that a changing magnetic flux will produce an emf and therefore a current in a conducting loop of wire, we now move to the interesting problem of determining the direction of this induced current. We already know the answer. In Figure 11.2 we said that the electrons move from top to bottom in the rod, i.e. the current is from bottom to top, counter-clockwise. But is there another way of getting the same answer? Let us look at Figure 11.10.

There are two possibilities for the current direction – the current will either flow in a clockwise or a counter-clockwise fashion in the loop. In either case, there will be a force on the rod because it is a current-carrying wire in a magnetic field.

- **Choice A, current is clockwise.** By the right-hand rule, the force is directed towards the right – in the direction of motion of the rod. The rod will therefore accelerate and its kinetic energy will increase. There is no obvious source for this extra kinetic energy. This must be the wrong choice for current: energy conservation would be violated.
- **Choice B, current is counter-clockwise.** By the right-hand rule, the force is directed towards the left – in the direction opposite to the motion of the rod. The rod will slow down and stop unless someone pushes it. This makes sense. This choice of current is the correct choice.

So, in Figure 11.2 we could guess the direction of the current by seeing what happens to the electrons in the rod. In Figure 11.10 we got the answer by analysing forces and energy.

It is not always easy to apply either of these methods. For example, consider the situation in which the current in a straight wire is increasing. A loop of conducting wire is next to the wire, as shown in Figure 11.11.

There will be an emf induced in the loop because the flux is changing; it is changing because the current is increasing and so the magnetic field it produces increases. What is the direction of the induced current? We cannot easily refer to forces any more. We need a more general method.

Such a general statement has been given by the Russian physicist Heinrich Lenz (1804–1865), and is called Lenz's law.

> **Lenz's law** states that the induced emf will be in such a direction as to oppose the change in the magnetic flux that created the current. It is equivalent to energy conservation.

This is a subtle and tricky formulation. Let us apply it to example of the loop of wire, as shown in Figure 11.12. The change in the magnetic flux has been an increase in magnetic flux (the blue field created by the blue current in the wire is increasing). We must oppose this increase, i.e. we must decrease the flux. We can do so by creating a magnetic field in a direction opposite to the blue field, i.e. out of the page. So the question now is: what is the direction of the current in the loop such that the field it produces is out of the page? From the right-hand rule, the current must be counter-clockwise.

Let us make sure that we understand what is going on by looking at another example.

Worked example

11.4 A loop of wire has its plane horizontal and a bar magnet is dropped from above so that it falls through the loop with the north pole first, as shown in Figure 11.13. Find the direction of the current induced in the loop.

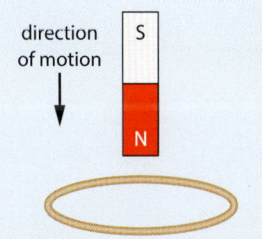

Figure 11.13 A magnet is dropped into a loop of wire.

The flux in the loop is increasing because the magnetic field at the loop is getting larger as the magnet approaches. (We are taking the normal to the loop to be in the vertically down direction.) The induced current must then oppose the increase in the flux. This can be done if the induced current produces a magnetic field in the opposite direction to that of the bar magnet, as shown by the blue arrow in Figure 11.14a. Thus, the current will flow in a counter-clockwise direction when looked at from above.

As the magnet leaves the loop from the other side, the flux is decreasing. So the current induced must produce a magnetic field in the same direction, i.e. down. This means the current is clockwise looked at from above, as shown in Figure 11.14b. (It follows that since the current changes from counter-clockwise to clockwise, at some point it must be zero.)

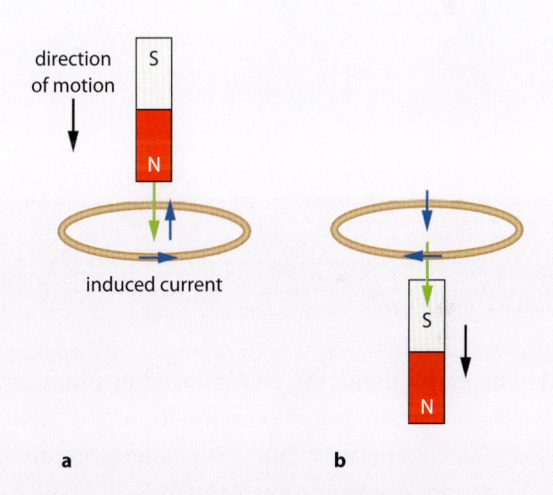

Figure 11.14 Current induced by magnet.

Nature of science

Much of the electro-mechanical technology we use today is due to the discoveries made by Michael Faraday. In 1831, using very simple equipment, Faraday observed a tiny pulse of current in one coil of wire when the current in a second coil was switched on or off, but nothing while a constant current was flowing. In further experiments he found these transient currents when he slid a magnet quickly in and out of a coil of wire. Faraday explained this electromagnetic induction using the idea of lines of force, but did not provide a mathematical relationship. The mathematical description of these phenomena was given much later by the Scottish physicist James Clerk Maxwell (1831–1879).

11 ELECTROMAGNETIC INDUCTION (HL)   441

? Test yourself

1 The flux through a loop as a function of time is given by the graph in the diagram. Sketch a graph of the emf induced in the loop as a function of time.

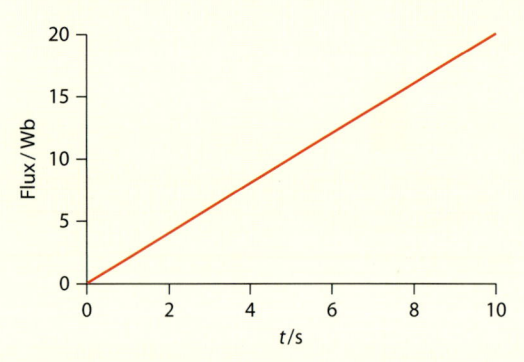

2 The flux through a loop as a function of time is given by the graph. Sketch a graph of the emf induced in the loop as a function of time.

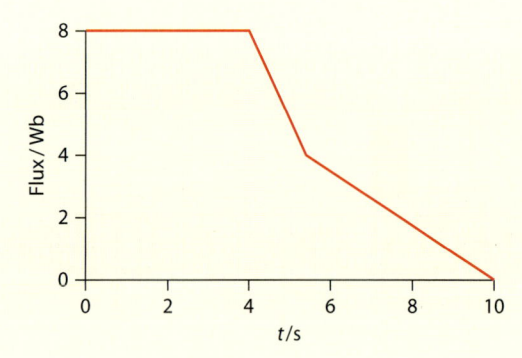

3 The graph shows the emf induced in a loop as a result of a changing flux in the loop.
   a Sketch a possible flux versus time graph that would give rise to such an emf.
   b Explain why there isn't a unique answer.

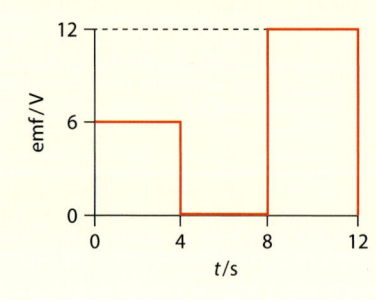

4 The diagram shows a top view of two solenoids with their axes parallel, one with a smaller diameter so that it fits inside the other. The bigger solenoid has a current flowing in the clockwise direction (looked at from above) and the current is increasing in magnitude; find the direction of the induced current in the smaller solenoid.

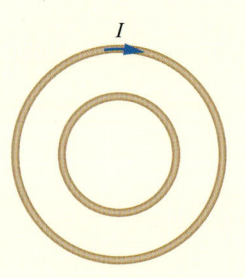

5 A metallic ring is dropped from a height above a bar magnet as shown in the diagram. Determine the direction of the induced current in the ring as the ring falls over the magnet in each case, giving full explanations for your choices.

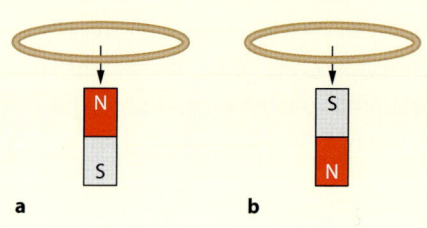

6 A magnet is dropped from above into a metallic ring as shown in the diagram. Determine the direction of the current induced in the ring in each case.

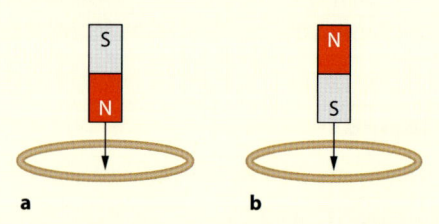

7 For the diagram in question **5a**, determine the direction of the magnetic force on the ring as it **a** enters and **b** leaves the magnetic field.

8 A metallic rod of length L is dragged with constant velocity v in a region of magnetic field directed into the page (shaded region), as shown in the diagram. By considering the force on electrons inside the rod, show that the ends of the rod will become oppositely charged. Determine the end that is positively charged.

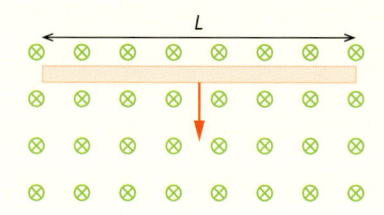

9 Find the direction of the current in the loop shown in the diagram as the current in the straight wire:
   a increases
   b decreases.

10 A large coil has a smaller coil inserted inside it so that their axes are parallel. The smaller coil has 200 turns and a diameter of 2.0 cm. A changing current in the large coil causes the magnetic field to be increasing at a rate of $0.45\,\text{T}\,\text{s}^{-1}$. Calculate the emf induced in the smaller coil.

11 Look at the diagram. The rod AB is free to move. The magnetic field is increasing. Determine what will happen to the rod AB.

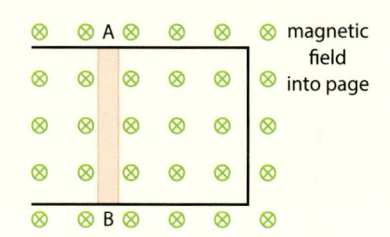

12 A magnet is attached to a spring. The magnet oscillates in and out of a coil, as shown in the diagram.
   a Draw a sketch graph to show the variation with time of the displacement of the magnet when i the switch is open and ii the switch is closed.
   b Explain your sketches in part a.

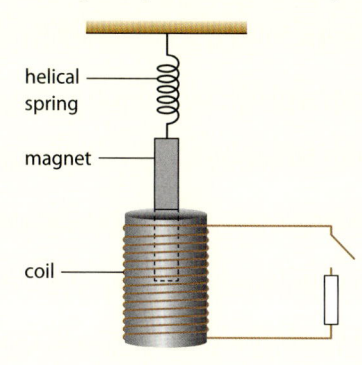

13 Two identical rings made out of conducting material are released from rest, from the same height above the ground. One ring will fall through a region of a horizontal magnetic field. State and explain which ring will reach the ground first, given that they are released at the same time.

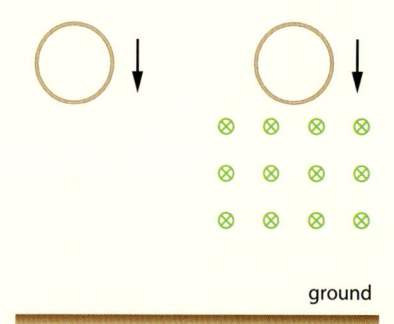

11 ELECTROMAGNETIC INDUCTION (HL) 443

Learning objectives

- Explain how alternating current is produced.
- Solve problems involving peak and rms values of current and voltage, and peak and average power.
- Understand how transformers are used.
- Understand the use of diode bridges in half-wave and full-wave rectification.

11.2 Transmission of power

Alternating current

This section discusses the production of alternating current by the ac generator and the properties of alternating current. We discuss the transformer equation and examine the use of transformers in power transmission.

The ac generator

One very important application of electromagnetic induction is the **ac generator** – the method used universally to produce electricity (Figure **11.15**). A coil is made to rotate in a region of magnetic field. This can be accomplished in a variety of ways: by a diesel engine burning oil, by falling water in a hydroelectric power station, by wind power, etc. The ends of the coil are firmly attached to two **slip rings** that rotate along with the coil. The slip rings touch **carbon brushes** that transfer the current into an external circuit.

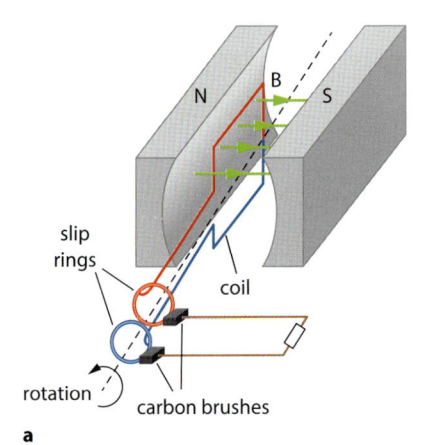

Figure 11.15 a A coil that is forced to turn in a region of magnetic field will produce an emf. **b** Generators at the Hoover hydroelectric power plant in the USA.

The flux in the coil changes as the coil rotates and so an emf is produced in it. We assume that the coil has $N = 10$ turns of wire around it, the magnetic field is $B = 0.21$ T, the coil has an area of 0.50 m^2 and the coil rotates with frequency f of 50 revolutions per second. The flux linkage in the coil changes as time goes on according to a cosine function as shown in Figure **11.16**.

The red, white and blue bar that is superposed on the graph indicates the position of the coil as we look at it along the axis of rotation: at $t = 0$ for example the coil is vertical with the part painted red on top. The equation of the flux (linkage) is, in general:

$$\Phi = NBA \cos \theta$$

where θ is the angle between the magnetic field and the normal to the coil and N is the number of turns in the coil. Assuming that the coil

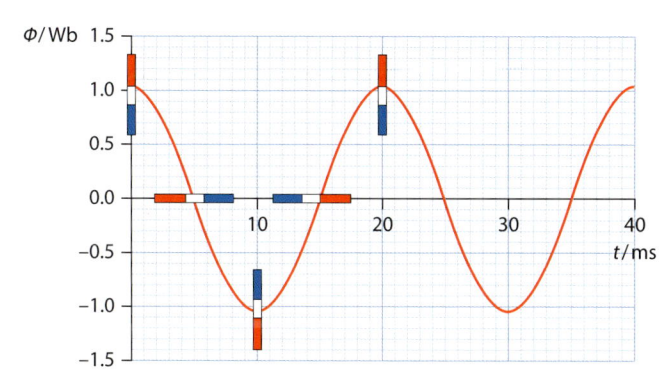

Figure 11.16 The flux linkage in the coil is changing with time.

rotates at a frequency f, then $\theta = 2\pi f t$. Alternatively, we may make use of the angular speed of rotation ω; since $\omega = 2\pi f$ it follows that $\theta = \omega t$ and so the flux becomes:

$$\Phi = NBA \cos(\omega t)$$

> By Faraday's law, the emf induced in the coil is (minus) the rate of change of the flux linkage and is given by:
>
> $$V = -\frac{d\Phi}{dt}$$
>
> $$V = \omega NBA \sin(\omega t)$$

In Subtopic **11.2** the induced emf will be denoted by the symbol V.

The quantity $V_0 = \omega NBA$ is the peak voltage produced by the generator. The variation of the induced emf with time is given by the graph in Figure **11.17**. The peak voltage in this example is 325 V.

Note that the emf induced is zero whenever the flux assumes its maximum or minimum values and, conversely, it is a maximum or minimum whenever the flux is zero. The noteworthy thing here is that the voltage can be negative as well as positive. This is what is called **alternating voltage** and the current that flows in the coil is **alternating current (ac)**. This means that, unlike the ordinary **direct current (dc)**

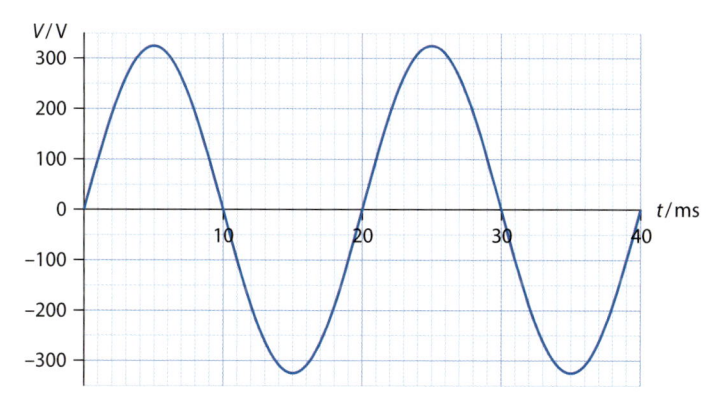

Figure 11.17 The emf induced in the loop as a function of time. The peak voltage is 325 V.

11 ELECTROMAGNETIC INDUCTION (HL) 445

that flows in a circuit connected to a battery, the electrons do not drift in the same direction but oscillate back and forth with the same frequency as that of the voltage. The flux and the emf are out of phase by $\frac{\pi}{2}$ or 90°.

The current in a circuit of resistance R can be found from:

$$I = \frac{V}{R}$$

$$I = \frac{V_0 \sin(\omega t)}{R}$$

$$I = I_0 \sin(\omega t)$$

where $I_0 = \frac{V_0}{R}$ is the peak current. For the emf of Figure 11.17 and a resistance of 16 Ω, the current is shown in Figure 11.18.

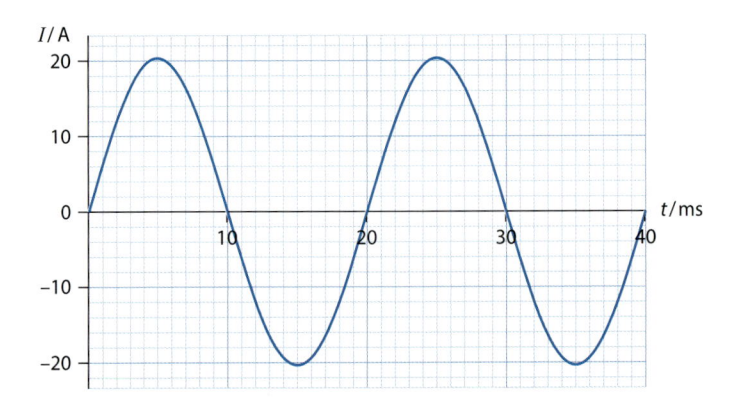

Figure 11.18 The induced current in the rotating loop. Note that the current is in phase with the emf. The peak current is found from peak voltage divided by resistance, i.e. $\frac{325}{16}$, which is about 20 A.

Power in ac circuits

The power P generated in an ac circuit is given by:

$$P = VI$$

Because both the current I and voltage V vary with time, the expression for power becomes:

$$P = V_0 I_0 \sin^2(\omega t)$$

This means that, just like the current and the voltage, power is not constant in time. It has a peak value P_{max} given by the product of the peak voltage and peak current:

$$P_{max} = V_0 I_0$$

The power as a function of time is shown in Figure 11.19. The **average power** dissipated is half the peak value.

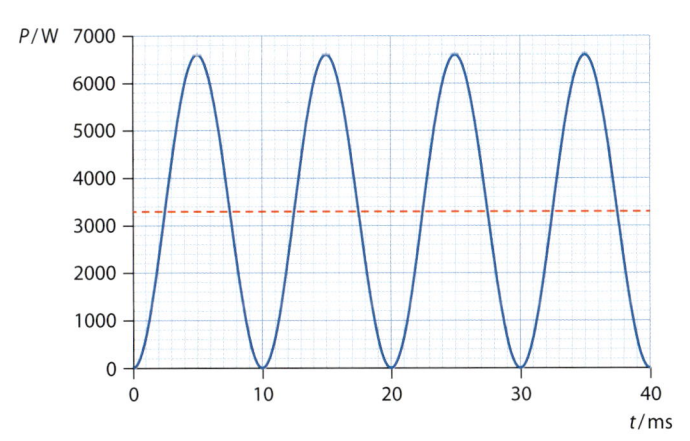

Figure 11.19 The power dissipated in a resistor as a function of time. Note that the period of one rotation of the coil is 20 ms. The power becomes zero with every half rotation of the coil. The horizontal dotted line indicates the average power, which is half the peak value.

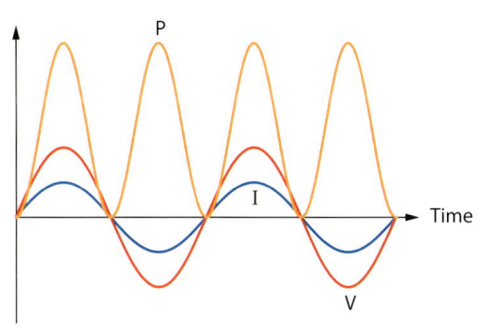

Figure 11.20 Power (orange), voltage (red) and current (blue) in an ac circuit resistor.

The relationship between voltage, current and power in an ac circuit is shown in Figure **11.20**.

It is instructive to write the expression for power in terms of the parameters of the rotating coil:

$$P = VI$$

$$P = \omega NBA \sin(\omega t) \times \frac{\omega NBA \sin(\omega t)}{R}$$

$$P = \frac{(\omega NBA)^2}{R} \sin^2(\omega t)$$

Worked example

11.5 The graph of Figure **11.21** shows the variation with time of the power delivered by an ac generator.
  a State the frequency of rotation of the generator.
  b On a copy of the graph, sketch the graph of the power delivered when the frequency of rotation is halved.

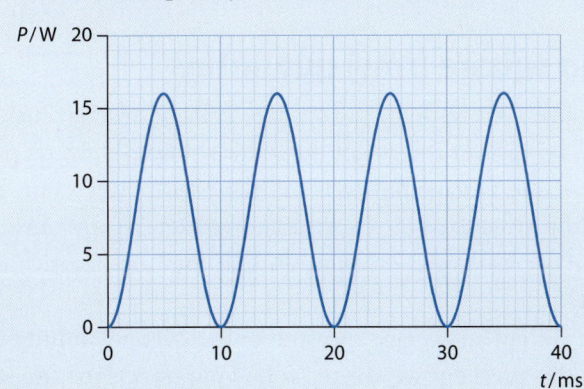

> **Exam tip**
> This is a very common examination question.

Figure 11.21 The variation with time of the power delivered by an ac generator.

11 ELECTROMAGNETIC INDUCTION (HL) 447

a The period T is found by looking at **two** loops, i.e. it is 20 ms.

So the frequency is found from $f = \dfrac{1}{T}$

$f = \dfrac{1}{0.020}$

$f = 50\,\text{Hz}$

> **Exam tip**
> It is important to understand how to get the period from a graph of power against time.

b You need to find how the power depends on frequency. To do this, you must be able to recall or derive the formula:

$$P = \dfrac{(\omega NBA)^2}{R}\sin^2(\omega t)$$

This shows that power is proportional to the square of the angular frequency, so power is also proportional to f^2 (since $\omega = 2\pi f$):

$P \propto f^2$

If you halve the frequency, then the power is reduced by a factor of 4. So the peak of the graph will be at 4 W.

Changing the frequency also changes the period. If the frequency is halved, then the period is doubled to 40 ms.

So we get the graph shown in Figure 11.22.

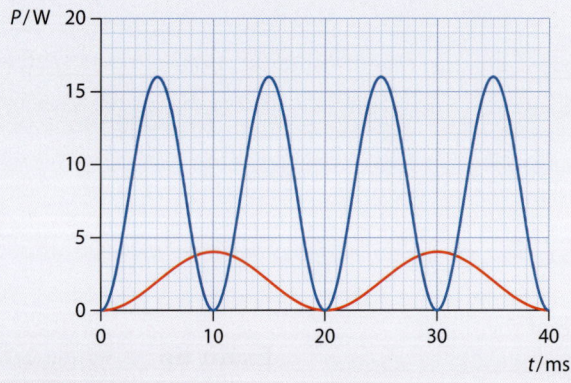

Figure 11.22 The power delivered when the frequency of rotation is halved.

Root mean square (rms) quantities

It would be convenient to define an average voltage, average current and average power. For power this is not difficult, as power is always positive. As we have seen, the average power is half the peak power value. But we can't just find the average of the current and voltage. In any one cycle, the voltage and current are as much positive as they are negative, and so average to zero.

So how can we get an average measure of the current and the voltage? To get around this problem we use the following trick. First, we square the current, getting a quantity that is always positive during the entire cycle. Then we find the average of this positive quantity. Finally, we take its square root. The result is called the **root mean square (rms)** value of the current.

How do we evaluate an rms quantity? Squaring the current gives:

$$I^2 = I_0^2 \sin^2(\omega t)$$

We can rewrite $\sin^2(\omega t)$ as $\frac{1}{2}[1 - \cos(2\omega t)]$, by making use of the double angle identity, $\cos 2\theta = (1 - 2\sin^2 \theta)$.

So:

$$I^2 = \frac{I_0^2}{2}[1 - \cos(2\omega t)]$$

Over one cycle, the cosine term averages to zero and so the average of the square of the current is:

$$\overline{I^2} = \frac{I_0^2}{2}$$

(the bar denotes an average). Thus:

$$I_{rms} = \sqrt{\overline{I^2}}$$

$$I_{rms} = \frac{I_0}{\sqrt{2}}$$

Doing exactly the same thing for the voltage results in an rms voltage of:

$$V_{rms} = \frac{V_0}{\sqrt{2}}$$

The power in an ac circuit is given by:

$$P = V_0 I_0 \sin^2(\omega t)$$

Using the double angle identity as before, this becomes:

$$P = \frac{V_0 I_0}{2}[1 - \cos(2\omega t)]$$

On averaging, the cosine term goes to zero, so the average power is:

$$\overline{P} = \frac{V_0 I_0}{2}$$

We can also write this as:

$$\overline{P} = \frac{V_0}{\sqrt{2}} \frac{I_0}{\sqrt{2}}$$

$$\overline{P} = V_{rms} I_{rms}$$

Exam tip
You will not be expected to know the proofs for the expressions of rms quantities. Dividing by $\sqrt{2}$ applies to sinusoidal currents and voltages only.

11 ELECTROMAGNETIC INDUCTION (HL)

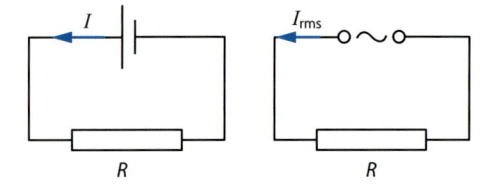

Figure 11.23 If the two currents are the same, the average power in the ac circuit is the same as that in the dc circuit.

We may also use the alternative formula for average power:

$$\overline{P} = RI_{rms}^2 = \frac{V_{rms}^2}{R}$$

The circuits in Figure **11.23** illustrate the meaning of rms quantities. If the dc current I is equal to the ac rms current I_{rms}, then the average power dissipated in the resistor in the ac circuit is the same as the power dissipated in the same resistor in the dc circuit.

So, dealing with rms quantities and average power, in effect, turns ac circuits into dc circuits.

Worked example

11.6 Find the rms quantities corresponding to the current and voltage of Figures **11.17** and **11.18**.

From Figure **11.17**, the peak voltage is 325 V giving:

$$V_{rms} = \frac{325}{\sqrt{2}}$$

$$V_{rms} \approx 230 \text{ V}$$

Similarly, the peak current is $\frac{325}{16} = 20.3$ A, as shown in Figure **11.18**, giving:

$$I_{rms} = \frac{20.3}{\sqrt{2}}$$

$$I_{rms} \approx 14.4 \text{ A}$$

The peak power is the product of peak voltage and peak current:

$$P_{max} = 325 \times \frac{325}{16} = 6600 \text{ W}$$

The average power is half the maximum value, so the average power is 3300 W.

This should equal the product of the rms current times the rms voltage; indeed this product is:

$$230 \times 14.4 = 3312 \approx 3300 \text{ W}$$

The transformer

The **transformer** is a device that takes a certain ac voltage as input and delivers a different ac voltage as output. It consists of two coils wrapped around a common iron core (Figure **11.24**). The primary coil is the one connected to the input ac source.

The primary coil has N_p turns of wire and the secondary coil has N_s turns. When the primary coil is connected to an ac source of voltage, an alternating current passes through this coil. Since this current is changing, it creates a changing magnetic field (in both magnitude and direction). The magnetic field of the primary coil enters the secondary coil, so there is magnetic flux in the secondary coil. Since the magnetic field in both

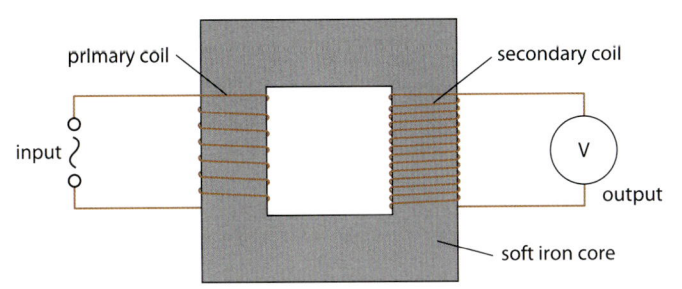

Figure 11.24 The transformer consists of two coils wrapped around a common iron core. The changing flux in the secondary coil produces an emf in that coil.

coils is changing, the flux is also changing, By Faraday's law, there will be an **induced** emf in the secondary coil.

The purpose of the iron core is to ensure that as much of the flux produced in the primary coil as possible enters the secondary coil. Iron has the property that it confines magnetic flux and so magnetic field lines do not spread out into the region outside the core.

Let the flux be changing at a rate $\frac{\Delta \Phi}{\Delta t}$ through one turn of wire. Since there are N_p turns in the secondary coil, the rate of change of flux linkage in the secondary coil is $N_s \frac{\Delta \Phi}{\Delta t}$ (assuming no flux leakage outside the iron core). The emf induced in the secondary coil, ε_s, is therefore:

$$\varepsilon_s = N_s \frac{\Delta \Phi}{\Delta t}$$

Similarly, the emf, ε_p, in the primary coil is:

$$\varepsilon_p = N_p \frac{\Delta \Phi}{\Delta t}$$

Dividing the second equation by the first, the factor $\frac{\Delta \Phi}{\Delta t}$ cancels and we get:

$$\frac{\varepsilon_p}{\varepsilon_s} = \frac{N_p}{N_s}$$

If the secondary coil has more turns than the primary, the secondary voltage is bigger than the primary voltage and we have a step-up transformer. If the secondary coil has fewer turns, the secondary voltage is smaller and we have a step-down transformer. Note that the transformer works only when the voltage in the primary coil is changing. Direct (i.e. constant) voltage fed into the primary coil would result in zero voltage in the secondary (except for the short interval of time it takes the current in the primary coil to reach its final steady value). For standard ac, the voltage varies with time as a sine function with a frequency of 50 or 60 Hz. The frequency of the voltage in the secondary coil stays the same – the transformer cannot change the frequency of the voltage.

If the primary coil has a current I_p in it, then the power dissipated in the primary coil is $\varepsilon_p I_p$. Assuming no power losses, the power dissipated in the secondary coil is the same as that in the primary and thus:

$$\varepsilon_p I_p = \varepsilon_s I_s$$

You may also see these equations using V rather than ε.

Exam tip
It is important to know that the transformer changes the voltage and the current, but not the frequency.
It is also important to know why the transformer will not work with a dc voltage in the primary coil.

11 ELECTROMAGNETIC INDUCTION (HL)

Therefore, using $\dfrac{\varepsilon_p}{\varepsilon_s} = \dfrac{N_p}{N_s}$ the relationship between the currents is:

$$\dfrac{I_p}{I_s} = \dfrac{N_s}{N_p}$$

We may put both equations together:

$$\dfrac{\varepsilon_p}{\varepsilon_s} = \dfrac{N_p}{N_s} = \dfrac{I_s}{I_p}$$

One source of power loss in a transformer is from eddy currents. **Eddy currents** are tiny currents created in the core because the free electrons of the core move in the presence of a magnetic field. These currents heat up the core, dissipating energy. Having a laminated core rather than a single block reduces power losses by eliminating eddy currents.

Further losses of energy occur due to heating of the coils themselves. Yet another source of power loss is the complex phenomenon of **magnetic hysteresis**. As a result of magnetic hysteresis, the magnetic energy stored in the magnetic field as the magnitude of the field increases is not all given back as the field magnitude decreases, resulting in power lost.

Worked example

11.7 A transformer with 3000 turns in the primary coil is to be used to step down an ac voltage of rms value 230 V to an ac voltage of peak value 9.0 V.
  a Calculate the number of turns in the secondary coil.
  b The transformer is 80% efficient. The rms current in the primary coil is 0.25 mA. Calculate the rms value of the current in the secondary coil.

a The rms value of the secondary voltage is $\dfrac{9.0}{\sqrt{2}} = 6.36$ V.

We need to use the transformer equation for voltages:

$$\dfrac{\varepsilon_p}{\varepsilon_s} = \dfrac{N_p}{N_s}$$

Substituting values, we get:

$$\dfrac{230}{6.36} = \dfrac{3000}{N_s}$$

$\Rightarrow N_s = 83$

b The average power is $P_{av} = V_{rms} \times I_{rms}$. For the primary coil this is:

$P_p = 230 \times 0.25 \times 10^{-3} = 57.5 \times 10^{-3}$ W

Since the transformer is 80% efficient, the average power in the secondary coil is:

$P_s = 0.80 \times 57.5 \times 10^{-3} = 46 \times 10^{-3}$ W

But the power in the secondary coil is the product of the rms voltage and current in the secondary. So:

$46 \times 10^{-3} = 6.36 \times I_{rms}$

$\Rightarrow \quad I_{rms} = 7.2 \times 10^{-3}$

The rms current in the secondary coil is 7.2 mA.

Transformers and power transmission

Transformers are used in the transport of electricity from power stations, where electricity is produced, to the consumer. At any given time, a city will have a power demand, P, which is quite large (many megawatts for a large city). If the power station sends out electricity at a voltage V and a current I flows in the cables from the power station to the city and back, then:

$P = VI$

The cables have resistance, however, and thus there is power loss, $P_{loss} = RI^2$, where R stands for the total resistance of the cables. To minimise this loss it is necessary to minimise the current (there is not much that can be done about minimising R). However, small I (I is still a few thousand amperes) means large V (recall, $P = VI$), which is why power companies supply electricity at large voltages. Transformers are then used to reduce the high voltage down to that required for normal household appliances (240 V or 120 V) (Figure **11.25**).

A schematic of Figure **11.25** is shown in Figure **11.26.**

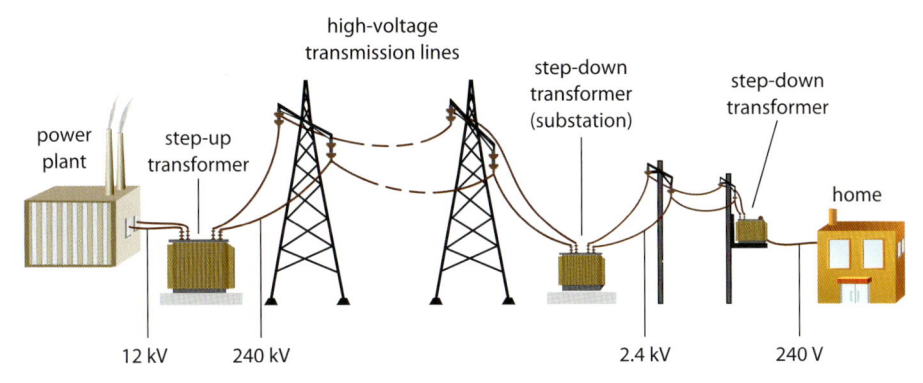

Figure 11.25 The voltage produced in the power station is stepped up to high values in order to reduce losses during transmission. Transformers are again used to step down the voltage to the standard 120 V or 240 V that consumers need.

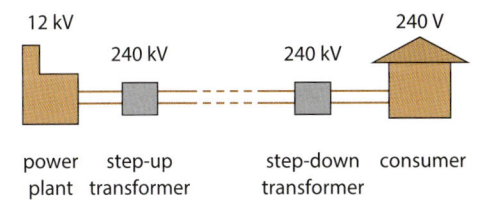

Figure 11.26 A schematic version of Figure **11.25**.

Worked example

11.8 A power plant produces 480 kW of power at a voltage of 2400 V.
   a Estimate the power lost in the transmission lines whose resistance 4.0 Ω, assuming no transformers are used in the transmission.
   b Repeat the calculation where now the power plant steps up the voltage from 2400 V to 240 kV.

a Without a transformer: from $P = VI$ the current leaving the power plant is:

$$I = \frac{480 \times 10^3}{2400}$$

$$I = 200 \text{ A}$$

The power lost is then:

$$P = RI^2 = 4.0 \times 200^2 = 160 \text{ kW}$$

This means that 33% of the power produced is lost.

b With a transformer: the transformer at the power plant steps up the voltage from 2.4 kV to 24 kV. Using:

$$\frac{\varepsilon_p}{\varepsilon_s} = \frac{N_p}{N_s} = \frac{I_s}{I_p}$$

the current in the transmission lines is:

$$\frac{2.4}{24} = \frac{I_s}{200}$$

$$\Rightarrow I_s = 20 \text{ A}$$

The power lost is then $P = RI^2 = 4.0 \times 20^2 = 1.6$ kW, or only 0.33% of the produced power.

Diode bridges and rectification

For many applications it is necessary to convert an ac current into a dc current, i.e. a current where the electrons all flow in the same direction. This can be partially achieved with a single diode. A diode allows current to pass through it in only one direction and only when the potential at A is higher then that at B, Figure **11.27**. When the current is positive (red) it is allowed to pass through the diode. When it is negative (blue) it does not. The output shown is direct current, in the sense that it is always positive, but it is not constant in magnitude. This is **half-wave rectification**. A big disadvantage of half-wave rectification is that half the power is lost in the process.

A better way to rectify current uses a **diode bridge rectifier**, shown in Figure **11.28**. This achieves **full-wave rectification**. During the first half cycle the current moves clockwise and enters the bridge through diode A. It then moves through the load from top to bottom and exits though diode C. During this half cycle diodes B and D do not conduct any current. In the next half cycle, the current is counter-clockwise. It enters the bridge through diode B and moves through the load from

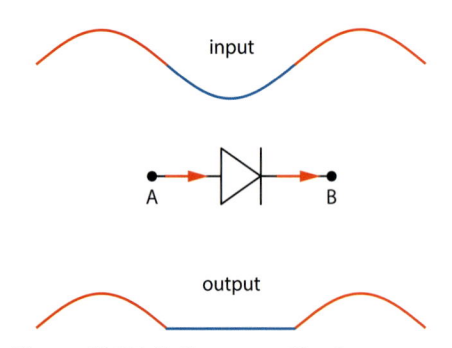

Figure 11.27 Half-wave rectification.

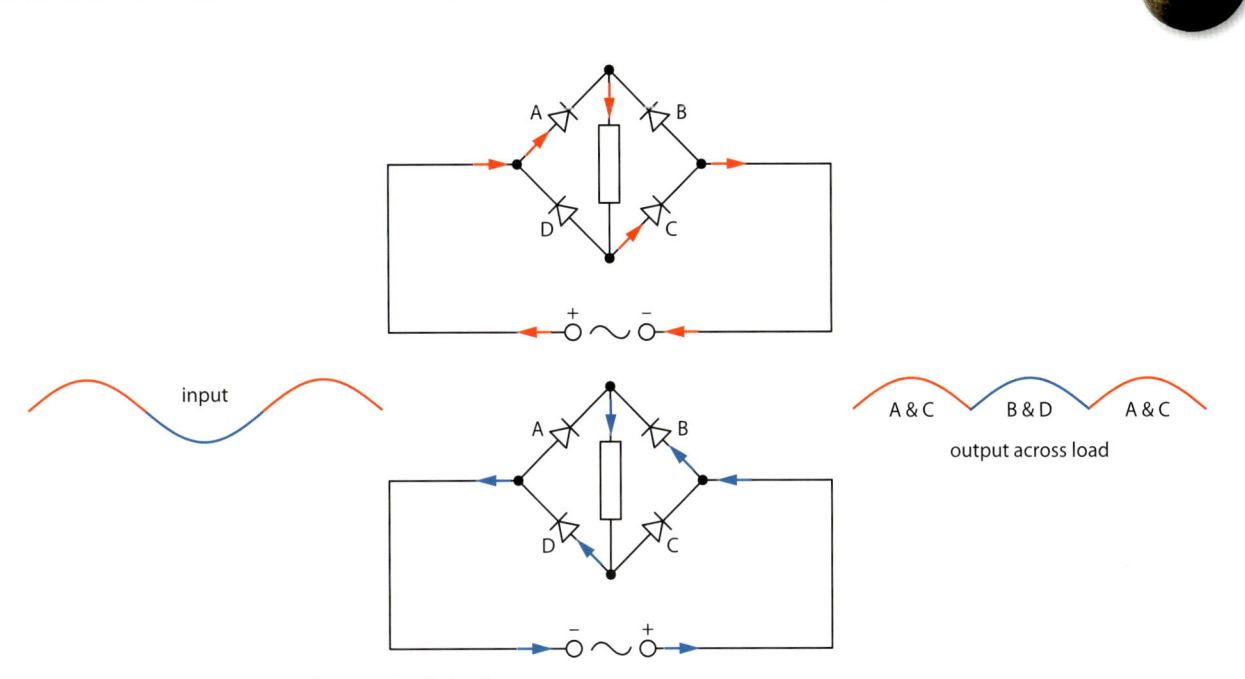

Figure 11.28 Full-wave rectification diode bridge.

top to bottom again, i.e. in the same direction as the first half cycle. The current exits the bridge through diode D. During this half cycle, diodes A and C do not conduct.

You must be aware that this diagram can be drawn in equivalent ways. For example, the bridge in Figure **11.28** may be redrawn as in Figure **11.29**. In this way all diodes point the same way, here to the 'left'.

Exam tip
Obviously it takes some practice to be able to reproduce this sort of diagram in an exam.

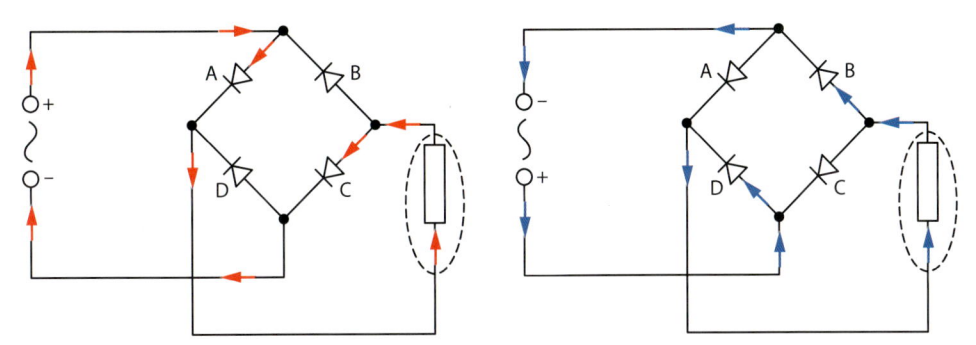

Figure 11.29 Full-wave rectification diode bridge drawn in a different way. In both cases the current in the load (shown in dotted oval) has the same direction.

Nature of science

Technology follows science

Alternating current is the current universally produced. There are many reasons for this. It can be produced quite easily in generators. It can be turned on and off much more safely than dc currents: switching off large dc currents can create dangerous induction currents, but with ac the switching can be timed to when the currents are small. Finally, the use of ac current makes the use of transformers possible and this leads to a more economical transmission of power. For these reasons the use of ac is widespread. Solid scientific reasons dictate its use.

11 ELECTROMAGNETIC INDUCTION (HL)

Test yourself

14 The graph shows the variation of the flux in a coil as it rotates in a magnetic field with the angle between the magnetic field and the normal to the coil.

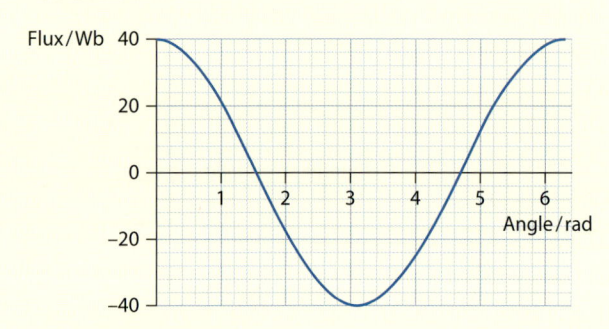

a Draw a graph to show the variation of the induced emf with angle.
The same coil is now rotated at double the speed in the same magnetic field. Draw graphs to show:
b the variation of the flux with angle
c the variation of the induced emf with angle.

15 The graph shows the variation with time of the power dissipated in a resistor when an alternating voltage from a generator is established at its ends. Assume that the resistance is constant at 2.5 Ω.
a Find the rms value of the current.
b Find the rms value of the voltage.
c Find the period of rotation of the coil.
d The coil is now rotated at double the speed. Draw a graph to show the variation with time of the power dissipated in the resistor.

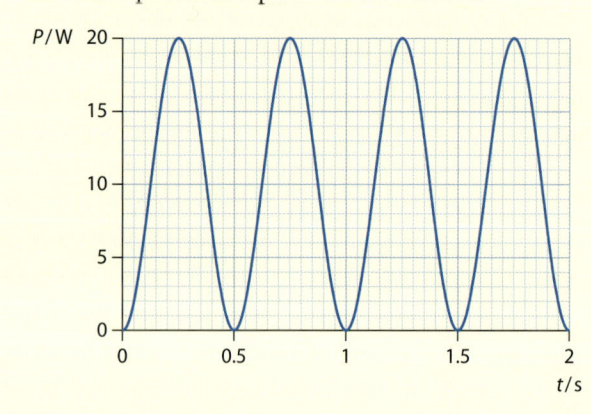

16 A transformer has 500 turns in its primary coil and 200 in the secondary coil.
a If an ac voltage of 220 V and frequency 50 Hz is established in the primary coil, find the voltage and frequency induced in the secondary coil.
b If the primary current is 6.0 A, find the current in the secondary coil, assuming an efficiency of 70%.

17 A 300 MW power station produces electricity at 80 kV, which is then supplied to consumers along cables of total resistance 5.0 Ω.
a What percentage of the produced power is lost in the cables?
b What does the percentage become if the electricity is produced at 100 kV?

18 The rms voltage output of a generator is 220 V. The coil is a square of side 20.0 cm, has 300 turns of wire and rotates at 50 revolutions per second. What is the magnetic field?

19 The graph shows the variation, with time, of the magnetic flux linkage through a loop. What is the rms value of the emf produced in the loop?

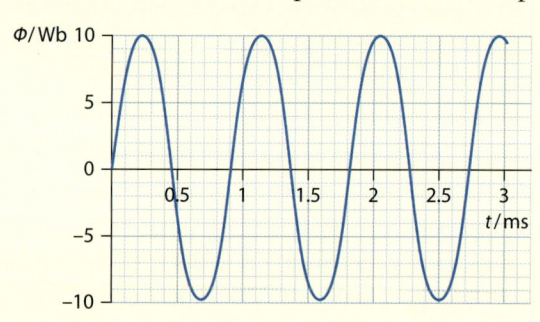

20 A power station produces 150 kW of power, which is transmitted along cables of total resistance 2.0 Ω. What percentage of the power is lost if it is transmitted at:
a 1000 V
b 5000 V?

21 Calculate the average power dissipated in a 24 Ω resistor that is connected in series to a source of a.c voltage of peak value 140 V.

11.3 Capacitance

Any arrangement of two conductors separated from each other by insulating material (or a vacuum) is called a **capacitor**. The capacitor is capable of storing electric charge and, as we will see, electrical energy. Many appliances still keep a light on for some time after they have been switched off. The component responsible for this is a capacitor. Capacitors come in various forms, but in this course we will study the parallel plate capacitor, which consists of two identical parallel plates, each of area A, separated by a distance d, as shown in Figure **11.30**. In a circuit, a capacitor is denoted by two parallel lines, also shown in Figure **11.30**.

When the wires are connected to a battery, charge will accumulate on the plates: positive charge q on one plate and an equal and opposite charge $-q$ on the other. As we already know, there will be an electric field between the parallel plates when they are charged. We will assume a uniform field everywhere with no edge effects. Suppose that the plates are connected to a battery of emf 12 V. How much charge accumulates on one of the plates? This is determined by a property of the capacitor called **capacitance**, C.

> Capacitance is defined as the charge per unit voltage that can be stored on the capacitor. In other words:
>
> $$C = \frac{q}{V}$$
>
> where q is the charge on one of the plates and V is the **potential difference** between the plates. Its unit is the farad, F (in honour of Michael Faraday), and $1\,\text{F} = 1\,\text{CV}^{-1}$.

Capacitance depends on the geometry of the capacitor. For the parallel plate capacitor:

$$C = \varepsilon \frac{A}{d}$$

where A is the area of one of the plates, d the separation of the plates and ε the permittivity of the medium between the plates. If the plates are in a vacuum, then $\varepsilon = \varepsilon_0 = 8.85 \times 10^{-12}\,\text{F m}^{-1}$.

Learning objectives

- Understand capacitance and the role of capacitors in circuits.
- Understand the effect of dielectric materials on capacitance.
- Solve problems involving series and parallel connections of capacitors in circuits.
- Solve problems involving circuits containing resistors and capacitors.

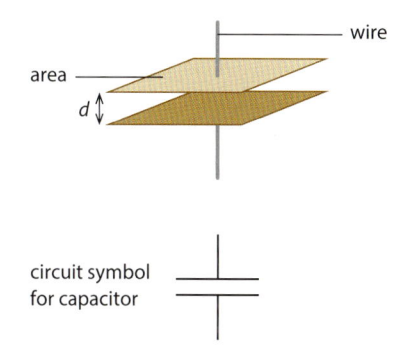

Figure 11.30 Geometry of a parallel plate capacitor and the circuit symbol.

Worked example

11.9 A parallel plate capacitor has plates of area $0.880\,\text{m}^2$, separated by a distance of 4.00 mm in a vacuum. It is connected to a dc source of potential difference 6.00 kV. Calculate:
   a the capacitance of the capacitor
   b the charge on one of the plates
   c the electric field between the plates
   d the charge per unit area on one of the plates.

11 ELECTROMAGNETIC INDUCTION (HL)

a From $C = \varepsilon \frac{A}{d}$ we find:

$$C = 8.85 \times 10^{-12} \times \frac{0.880}{4.00 \times 10^{-3}} = 1.95 \times 10^{-9} \, \text{F}$$

This shows that the farad is a big unit.

b From the definition of capacitance $C = \frac{q}{V}$, we deduce that $q = CV$ and so:

$$q = 1.95 \times 10^{-9} \times 6.00 \times 10^{3} = 1.17 \times 10^{-5} \, \text{C}$$

c The electric field is given by $E = \frac{V}{d}$ and so:

$$E = \frac{6.00 \times 10^{3}}{4.00 \times 10^{-3}} = 1.50 \times 10^{6} \, \text{N C}^{-1}$$

d The charge per unit area σ is the charge divided by the area of the plate.

$$\sigma = \frac{q}{A} = \frac{1.17 \times 10^{-5}}{0.880} = 1.33 \times 10^{-5} \, \text{C m}^{-2}$$

The effect of dielectric on capacitance

Figure **11.31a** shows an isolated parallel plate capacitor in a vacuum and Figure **11.31b** shows the same capacitor with an insulator between the plates. Insulators are also known as **dielectric** materials. If we look up tables of values of the permittivity we find that $\varepsilon > \varepsilon_0$. Since $C = \varepsilon \frac{A}{d}$, the capacitance with a diclectric is greater than that in a vacuum.

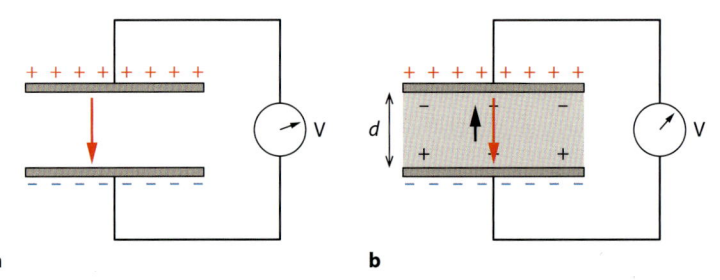

Figure 11.31 A capacitor **a** in a vacuum and **b** the same capacitor with a dielectric. The capacitors cannot discharge so the charge in **a** and **b** is the same.

Why does this happen? In Figure **11.31** the capacitor does not discharge because of the infinite resistance voltmeter that does not allow the flow of any charge: the charge on the plates cannot change. There is an electric field between the plates directed from top to bottom (red arrow). This electric field acts on the electrons of the dielectric, pulling them somewhat against the field, i.e. upwards. So there is separation of charge in the dielectric, known as **charge polarisation** (no relation to light polarisation!). This creates a small electric field within the dielectric that is directed upward (black arrow). This means that the net electric field between the parallel plates is reduced compared to that in a vacuum.

Now, the work done to move charge q from one plate to the other is given by $W = Fd = qEd$ and since E is reduced, so is the work done. But the work done is also equal to $W = qV$. This therefore implies that the potential difference across the plates has been reduced. From the definition $C = \frac{q}{V}$, it follows that the capacitance increases.

A similar effect takes place when the capacitor is connected to a battery that establishes a **constant** potential difference between the plates, as shown in Figure **11.32**.

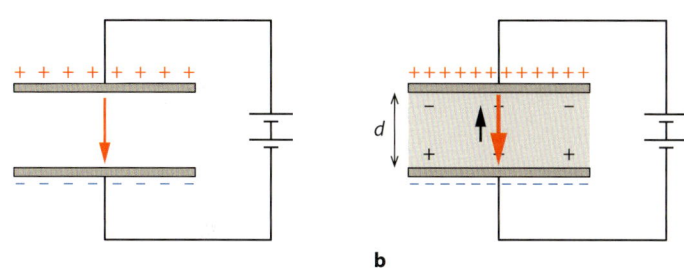

Figure 11.32 A capacitor **a** in a vacuum and **b** with a dielectric. The capacitors are connected to a battery so the potential difference across **a** and **b** is the same.

From $W = qV$ we see that the work is now constant. From $W = qEd$ we deduce that the electric fields with and without the dielectric have to be the same. So the net field in Figure **11.32a** and that in **11.32b** have to be the same. This can only happen if the red electric field in Figure **11.32a** is larger than that in **11.32b**. This implies that the charge q on the plates has increased due to the presence of the dielectric. Having established that the charge increases and the voltage stays the same, it follows from $C = \frac{q}{V}$ that the capacitance increases.

Capacitors in parallel

Figure **11.33** shows two capacitors of capacitance C_1 and C_2 connected in parallel. Both are connected to a source of potential difference V and this is the common potential difference across both capacitors.

The charge on the first capacitor is q_1 and that on the other is q_2.
We have that:

$q_1 = C_1 V$ and $q_2 = C_2 V$

The total charge on the two capacitors is:

$q = q_1 + q_2 = (C_1 + C_2) V$

We may define the total capacitance of the parallel combination as $q = C_{\text{parallel}} V$ so that:

$C_{\text{parallell}} = C_1 + C_2$

Extending this for additional capacitors in parallel, we get:

$C_{\text{parallell}} = C_1 + C_2 + \ldots$

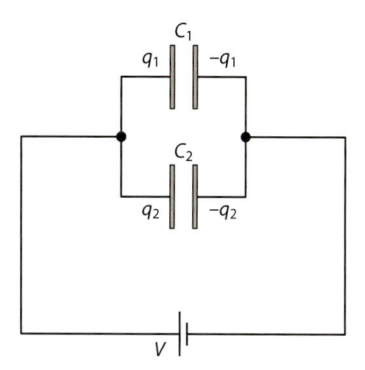

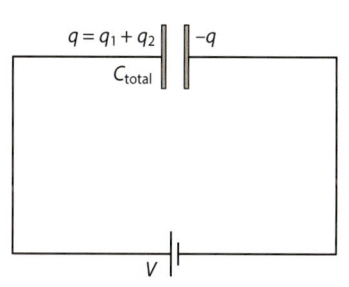

Figure 11.33 Two capacitors connected in parallel. They have the same potential difference across but different charges.

11 ELECTROMAGNETIC INDUCTION (HL)

Worked example

11.10 Two capacitors of capacitance 12 pF and 4.0 pF are connected in parallel to a source of potential difference 9.0 V. Calculate the charge on each capacitor.

With just two parallel capacitors the problem is very easy because we know the potential difference across each capacitor, 9.0 V. In other words, we do not need to use the formula for the total capacitance. We can use straight away:

$q_1 = C_1 V = 12 \times 10^{-12} \times 9.0 = 108 \, \text{pC}$

and

$q_2 = C_2 V = 4.0 \times 10^{-12} \times 9.0 = 36 \, \text{pC}$

Capacitors in series

Figure 11.34 shows two capacitors of capacitance C_1 and C_2 connected in series. In this case the charge on each capacitor is the same.

We know that $V_2 = \dfrac{q}{C_2}$, and also that the source of potential difference V is equal to $V_1 + V_2$. The total capacitance of the series combination, C_{series}, is then given by:

$$V = \frac{q}{C_{series}} = \frac{q}{C_1} + \frac{q}{C_2}$$

Dividing by q gives:

$$\frac{1}{C_{series}} = \frac{1}{C_1} + \frac{1}{C_2}$$

Extending this for additional capacitors in series, we get:

$$\frac{1}{C_{series}} = \frac{1}{C_1} + \frac{1}{C_2} + \ldots$$

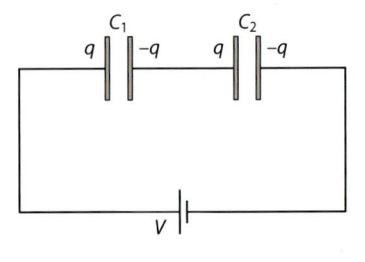

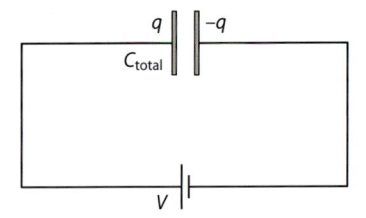

Figure 11.34 Two capacitors connected in series. They have the same charge but different potential difference across.

Worked examples

11.11 Two capacitors of capacitance 12 pF and 4.0 pF are connected in series to a source of potential difference 6.0 V. Calculate the charge on each capacitor.

We know the charge on each capacitor will be the same and equal to that on the total capacitor. The total capacitance is found from:

$$\frac{1}{C_{series}} = \frac{1}{C_1} + \frac{1}{C_2}$$

So:

$$\frac{1}{C_{series}} = \frac{1}{12} + \frac{1}{4.0} = \frac{4.0}{12}$$

$\Rightarrow C_{series} = 3.0\,\text{pF}$

The charge is then $q = CV = 3.0 \times 10^{-12} \times 6.0 = 18\,\text{pC}$.

The potential difference across each capacitor is:

$$V_1 = \frac{q}{C_1} = \frac{18 \times 10^{-12}}{12 \times 10^{-12}} = 1.5\,\text{V} \quad \text{and} \quad V_2 = \frac{q}{C_2} = \frac{18 \times 10^{-12}}{4.0 \times 10^{-12}} = 4.5\,\text{V}$$

Notice that $1.5 + 4.5 = 6.0\,\text{V}$, as we expect.

11.12 Find the charge on and potential difference across each capacitor in Figure 11.35 when points A and B are connected to a battery of emf 12 V. The capacitors all have a capacitance of 12 pF.

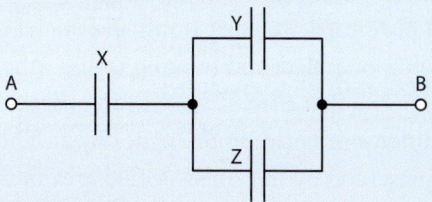

Figure 11.35

To find the charge, we need to find the combined capacitance of all three capacitors, C_{total}.

Y and Z are in parallel, so together they are equivalent to a capacitor of capacitance $2 \times 12 = 24\,\text{pF}$.

Now combine this with capacitor X. The 24 pF capacitor and X are in series, which gives a total capacitance, C_{total}, of:

$$\frac{1}{C_{total}} = \frac{1}{24} + \frac{1}{12}$$

$$\frac{1}{C_{total}} = \frac{3.0}{24}$$

$\Rightarrow C_{total} = 8.0\,\text{pF}$.

When the 8.0 pF capacitor is connected to an emf of 12 V it will acquire a charge q:

$q = C_{total} \times V = 8.0 \times 10^{-12} \times 12$

$q = 96\,\text{pC}$

This is also the charge on capacitor X, q_X. So $q_X = 96\,\text{pC}$.

Using $V = \frac{q}{C}$, the potential difference across X, V_X, is therefore:

$$V_X = \frac{96 \times 10^{-12}}{12 \times 10^{-12}} = 8.0\,\text{V}$$

The emf of the battery is 12 V, so the potential difference across Y and Z is 12 − 8.0 = 4.0 V.

The charge on Y, q_Y, is then:

$q_Y = C_Y V_Y = 12 \times 10^{-12} \times 4.0$

$q_Y = 48 \text{ pC}$

Similarly, $q_Z = 48 \text{ pC}$.

So, we have: $V_X = 8.0 \text{ V}$ $V_Y = 4.0 \text{ V}$ $V_Z = 4.0 \text{ V}$
$q_X = 96 \text{ pC}$ $q_Y = 48 \text{ pC}$ $q_Z = 48 \text{ pC}$

Exam tip
This derivation uses calculus so it cannot be examined.

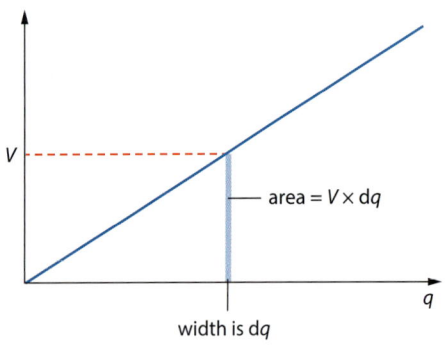

Figure 11.36 The graph of potential difference versus charge is a straight line. The area under the graph is the energy stored.

Energy stored in a capacitor

We can use calculus to derive an expression for the energy stored in a capacitor. Think of a parallel plate capacitor that is initially uncharged. We may think of charge leaving one plate and moving to the other. This requires work to be done. Suppose that a small amount of charge dq is moved when the potential difference between the plates by V. Then the work is d$W = V$dq and is represented by the small shaded area in the graph of voltage versus charge, Figure 11.36. So the total work to charge the capacitor up to charge q is the total area under the curve, i.e. the integral:

$$W = \int_0^q V \, dq$$

$$W = \int_0^q \frac{q}{C} \, dq$$

$$W = \frac{q^2}{2C}$$

This is the energy stored in the capacitor, or more precisely, in the electric field in between the capacitor plates. Using $C = \frac{q}{V}$ equivalent expressions of this energy are:

$$E = \frac{q^2}{2C} = \frac{C^2 V^2}{2C}$$

$$E = \tfrac{1}{2} C V^2$$

and

$$E = \tfrac{1}{2} q V$$

In these expressions, q is the final charge on the capacitor and V the final potential difference across its plates.

Worked examples

11.13 Figure **11.37** shows two capacitors connected in a circuit. The first capacitor has capacitance 3.20 µF and has been charged by connecting it to a source of emf 12.0 V. The other capacitor has capacitance 9.25 µF and is initially uncharged. When the switch is closed charge will move from one capacitor to the other.
  a Calculate the charge and potential difference for each capacitor after the switch is closed and charge no longer moves.
  b Compare the energy stored before the switch is closed with that stored after the switch is closed.
  c Comment on the answer to **b**.

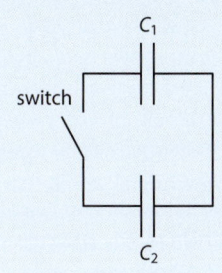

Figure 11.37 Two capacitors connected in a circuit.

a The potential difference initially across the first capacitor is 12 V and the charge is:

$$q_1 = C_1 V = 3.20 \times 10^{-6} \times 12.0 = 3.84 \times 10^{-5} \text{ C}$$

Charge will move from the first to the second capacitor. This will decrease the potential difference of the first and increase the potential difference on the second.

Charge will keep moving until the potential difference across each capacitor is the same. The charge on the capacitors will be q_1 and q_2 such that $q_1 + q_2 = q$, by charge conservation. So we have the relationships:

$$q_1 + q_2 = q$$

$$\frac{q_1}{C_1} = \frac{q_2}{C_2}$$

From the second equation, $q_2 = \frac{q_1 C_2}{C_1}$. Substituting in the first equation we get:

$$q_1 + \frac{q_1 C_2}{C_1} = q$$

$$\Rightarrow q_1 = \frac{C_1}{C_1 + C_2} q$$

This gives:

$$q_1 = \frac{3.20}{3.20 + 9.25} \times 3.84 \times 10^{-5} = 9.87 \text{ µC}$$

Hence $q_2 = 28.5$ µC.

These numbers imply that $V_1 = \frac{q_1}{C_1} = \frac{9.87 \times 10^{-6}}{3.20 \times 10^{-6}} = 3.08$ V and of course $V_2 = 3.08$ V as well.

11 ELECTROMAGNETIC INDUCTION (HL) 463

b The energy stored before the switch is closed is:

$E_{initial} = \frac{1}{2}CV^2 = \frac{1}{2} \times 3.20 \times 10^{-6} \times 12.0^2 = 2.30 \times 10^{-4}$ J

After the switch is closed it is:

$E_{final} = \frac{1}{2}C_1V_1^2 + \frac{1}{2}C_2V_2^2 = \frac{1}{2} \times 3.20 \times 10^{-6} \times 3.08^2 + \frac{1}{2} \times 9.25 \times 10^{-6} \times 3.08^2$

$E_{final} = 5.91 \times 10^{-5}$ J

c The stored energies are not the same. Energy has been dissipated as heat in the connecting wires when charge moved.

11.14 A capacitor in a vacuum has capacitance 6.00 pF and has been charged by a battery of emf 12.0 V.
  a For the capacitor in vacuum, calculate the energy stored in the electric field.
  The battery is removed. A dielectric with $\varepsilon = 6\varepsilon_0$ is now inserted in between the plates of the capacitor.
  b Calculate the energy stored now.
  c Compare the energies in **a** and **b**.

a $E = \frac{1}{2}CV^2 = \frac{1}{2} \times 6.00 \times 10^{-12} \times 12.0^2 = 432$ pJ

b The new capacitance is:

$C' = \varepsilon \frac{A}{d} = 6\varepsilon_0 \frac{A}{d} = 6C$

The charge on the capacitor remains the same. Using the expression for the energy in terms of charge and capacitance:

$E = \frac{q^2}{2C}$ (without the dielectric)

$E' = \frac{q^2}{2C'} = \frac{q^2}{12C}$ (with the dielectric)

Therefore:

$E' = \frac{E}{6} = \frac{432}{6} = 72.0$ pJ

c The energies are different. The capacitor would actually attract the dielectric and pull it in. The person inserting the dielectric would therefore have to pull back on the slab, performing negative work equal to the difference of the two energies.

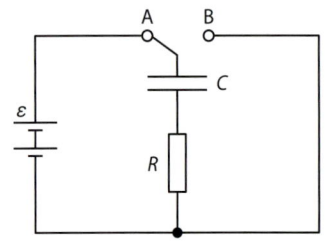

Figure 11.38 Circuit for charging and discharging a capacitor. When the switch is at A the capacitor charges. When at B it discharges.

Charging a capacitor

The circuit in Figure **11.38** may be used to investigate both the charging and the discharging of a capacitor. If the switch is moved to position A, the capacitor will charge. After the capacitor has charged, moving the switch to B the capacitor will discharge through the resistor R.

Initially the capacitor is uncharged. As soon as the switch is moved to A, a current will be established and the charge on the capacitor plates will increase. In Figure **11.38** the current is clockwise, which means electrons move in a counter-clockwise direction, making the bottom plate negative. Eventually, the potential difference across the capacitor plates will become equal to the emf ε of the battery.

Figure **11.39** shows how the potential difference V across the capacitor varies with time t. As time increases the potential approaches 6.0 V, which must be the emf of the charging battery. The graph assumes a resistance of 1.0 kΩ and a capacitance of 2.0 μF.

Since $q = CV$ the graph showing the variation of charge with time has the same shape as that of potential difference. This is shown in Figure **11.40**. The final charge is $q = C\varepsilon$.

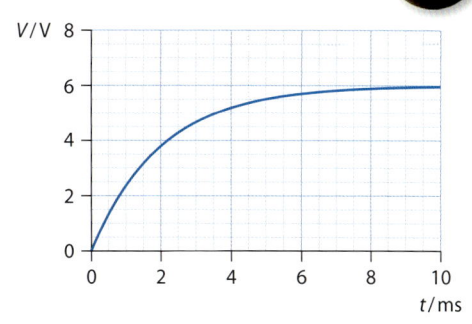

Figure 11.39 The variation of potential difference with time for a charging capacitor.

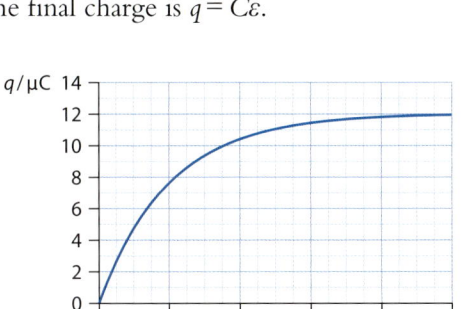

Figure 11.40 The variation of charge with time for a charging capacitor.

Figure **11.41** shows how the current in the circuit varies with time. The current starts out large but decreases, eventually reaching zero. This is because electrons on the negatively charged plate push back any new electrons trying to get there, stopping the current. Notice that the initial current is equal to $I_0 = \dfrac{\varepsilon}{R}$. This means that, initially, it is as if the capacitor is not there at all. But after a long time the current stops, so now the capacitor behaves as if the circuit had been broken at the position of the capacitor.

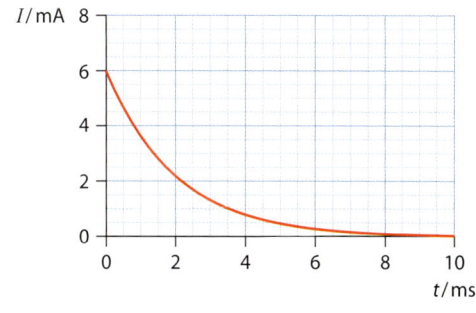

Figure 11.41 The variation of current with time for a charging capacitor.

Worked example

11.15 The graph in Figure **11.42** shows the variation with time t of the charge q on a capacitor plate as the capacitor is being charged in a circuit like that in Figure **11.38**.

The capacitance is 4.0 μF and the resistance of the resistor R is 2.0 kΩ.
a Use the graph to estimate the emf of the charging battery.
b Sketch a graph to show the variation with time of the current in the circuit while the capacitor is being charged, putting numbers on the vertical axis.

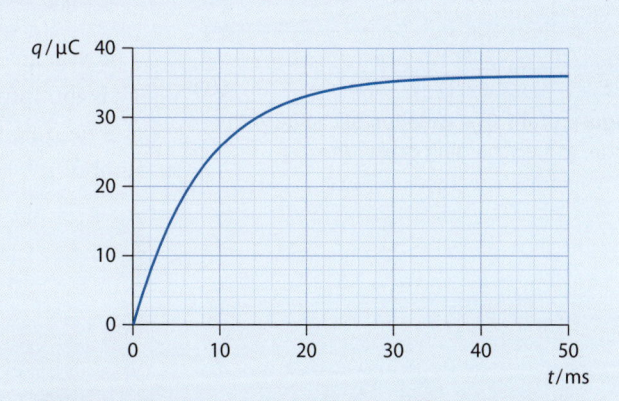

Figure 11.42 The variation with time t of the charge q on a capacitor plate.

11 ELECTROMAGNETIC INDUCTION (HL) 465

a From the graph, the final charge q is $36\,\mu C$. Since $q = C\varepsilon$, we get:

$$\varepsilon = \frac{36 \times 10^{-6}}{4.0 \times 10^{-6}} = 9.0\,\text{V}$$

b The question asks for values of current, so we need to work out the initial current:

$$I_0 = \frac{\varepsilon}{R} = \frac{9.0}{2.0 \times 10^3} = 4.5\,\text{mA}$$

The current drops exponentially, and so we have a graph like Figure **11.43**.

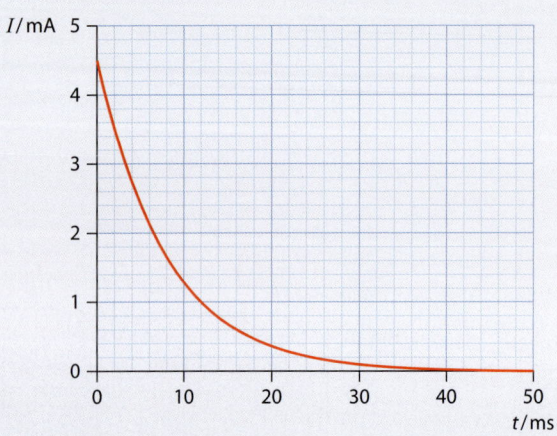

Figure 11.43 The variation with time of the current in the circuit.

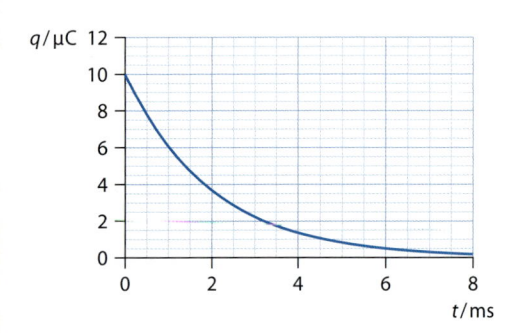

Figure 11.44 The variation of charge with time for a discharging capacitor.

Discharging a capacitor

Suppose that we now let a capacitor, with an initial charge q_0 on its plates, discharge through a resistor of resistance R. The charge will eventually reach zero – the capacitor discharges (Figure **11.44**). After a time t seconds the charge left on the capacitor plate is given by:

$$q = q_0 e^{-\frac{t}{RC}}$$

The voltage across the capacitor is similarly given by $V = V_0 e^{-\frac{t}{RC}}$ where V_0 is the initial voltage.

The quantity RC is called the **time constant** and is denoted by the symbol τ:

$$\tau = RC$$

So:

$$q = q_0 e^{-\frac{t}{\tau}} \quad \text{and} \quad V = V_0 e^{-\frac{t}{\tau}}$$

The time constant determines the time scale for the discharge of the capacitor: a large time constant means that it will take a long time for the charge on the plates to decrease appreciably. More precisely, after a time $t = \tau$ the charge will be:

$$q = q_0 e^{-\frac{t}{\tau}} = \frac{q_0}{e} \approx 0.37 q_0$$

> In other words, the time constant is the time after which the charge decreases to about 37% of its initial value.

Looking at Figure 11.44, we see that the charge decreases to 37% of its initial value after a time of about 2.0 ms, which is therefore the time constant for this circuit.

The electric current can be obtained from $I = \frac{dq}{dt}$:

$$I = \frac{d}{dt}\left(q e^{-\frac{t}{\tau}}\right) = -\frac{q_0}{\tau} e^{-\frac{t}{\tau}}$$

The minus current is of no use to us here. It just says that the capacitor is discharging and so the charge is decreasing. We will ignore it from now on.

The initial current is given by $I_0 = \frac{q_0}{\tau}$. So we may also write:

$$I = I_0 e^{-\frac{t}{\tau}}$$

This relationship is shown in Figure 11.45.

The initial charge is given by $q_0 = C\varepsilon$, where ε is the emf of the battery that charged the capacitor. In this case then:

$$I_0 = \frac{q_0}{\tau} = \frac{C\varepsilon}{RC} = \frac{\varepsilon}{R}$$

as might be expected.

The discharge curves are exponential, like those for radioactive decay we saw in Topic 7. We may ask for the time it takes for the charge to decrease to half its initial value. This would be the 'half-life' $T_{1/2}$ of the capacitor: we substitute $q = \frac{1}{2} q_0$ to get:

$$\frac{1}{2} q_0 = q_0 e^{-\frac{T_{1/2}}{\tau}}$$

Dividing both sides by the initial charge q_0 and taking reciprocals:

$$2 = e^{\frac{T_{1/2}}{\tau}}$$

Taking logarithms to base e gives:

$$\ln 2 = \frac{T_{1/2}}{\tau}$$

i.e.

$$\tau = \frac{T_{1/2}}{\ln 2}$$

> **Exam tip**
> The formulas in the IB data booklet refer to a capacitor that is discharging. They cannot be used for charging the capacitor.

> **Exam tip**
> It is useful to know that $I_0 = \frac{q_0}{\tau}$. This equation is **not** in the IB data booklet.

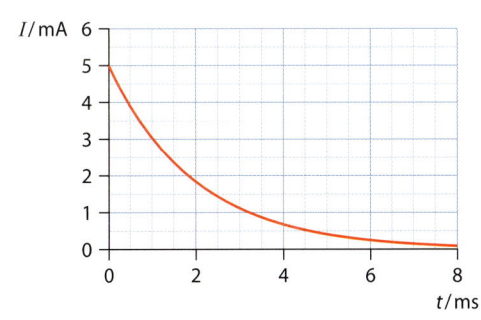

Figure 11.45 The variation of current with time for a discharging capacitor.

> So the time constant is the time needed for the charge to decrease to half its initial value, divided by ln 2.

11 ELECTROMAGNETIC INDUCTION (HL)

Worked examples

11.16 Show that the unit of $\tau = RC$ is that of time.

First write the units:

$[\tau] = \Omega \times F$

Now simplify the units by finding appropriate formulas.

For resistance: $R = \dfrac{V}{I}$ and so $\Omega = \dfrac{V}{A}$

From the definition of capacitance: $C = \dfrac{q}{V}$ and so $F = \dfrac{C}{V}$.

Hence:

$[\tau] = \dfrac{V}{A} \times \dfrac{C}{V} = \dfrac{C}{A}$

But $q = It$, so $C = A \times s$. Therefore:

$[\tau] = \dfrac{A \times s}{A} = s$

11.17 A charged capacitor discharges through a resistor. After 5.00 s the voltage across the capacitor plates drops to 10% of the initial voltage. Calculate:
  a the time constant of the circuit
  b the time after which the voltage is reduced to 5% of its initial value.

a The voltage across the capacitor is given by $V = V_0 e^{-\frac{t}{\tau}}$

So we have that:

$0.10 V_0 = V_0 e^{-\frac{t}{\tau}}$

Dividing both sides by V_0, substituting values from the questions, and taking logarithms gives:

$\ln 0.10 = -\dfrac{5.00}{\tau}$ and so $\tau = \dfrac{5.00}{\ln 0.10} = 2.17\,\text{s}$

b Using again the equation $V = V_0 e^{-\frac{t}{\tau}}$:

$0.05 V_0 = V_0 e^{-\frac{t}{\tau}}$

Again, dividing both sides by V_0 and taking logarithms:

$\ln 0.05 = -\dfrac{t}{2.17}$

This gives:

$t = -2.17 \times \ln 0.05 = 6.50\,\text{s}$

11.18 Consider the circuit in Figure 11.46. The switch is closed for a long time so that the capacitor is charged. The switch is then opened. Find the current in resistor R_2 after 5.00 ms. Use the data: $R_1 = 12.0\,\text{k}\Omega$, $R_2 = 18.0\,\text{k}\Omega$, emf = 12.0 V, $C = 2.00\,\mu\text{F}$.

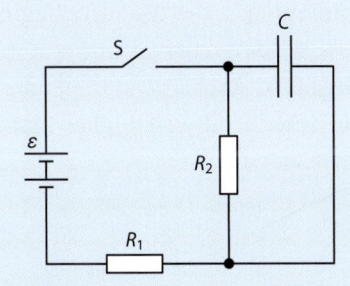

Figure 11.46 Circuit containing a capacitor and resistors.

After a long time the capacitor will be fully charged and there will be no current in the loop containing the capacitor. In the other loop, the total resistance is 30.0 kΩ and so the current in that loop will be:

$$I = \frac{12.0}{30.0 \times 10^3} = 0.400 \times 10^{-3}\,\text{A}$$

The potential difference across resistor R_2 will be:

$$V_2 = IR_2 = 0.400 \times 10^{-3} \times 18.0 \times 10^3 = 7.20\,\text{V}$$

This is also the steady potential difference across the capacitor. The charge on the capacitor plates is then given by:

$$q_0 = CV = 2.00 \times 10^{-6} \times 7.20 = 14.4\,\mu\text{C}$$

When the switch is opened, current will flow only in the loop of the capacitor. The time constant for the circuit is then $R_2 C$:

$$\tau = 18.0 \times 10^3 \times 2.00 \times 10^{-6} = 3.6 \times 10^{-2}\,\text{s}$$

The current is found using the equation:

$$I = I_0 e^{-\frac{t}{\tau}}$$

Remember that $I_0 = \frac{q_0}{\tau}$. Then we have:

$$I = \frac{q_0}{\tau} e^{-\frac{t}{\tau}}$$

$$I = \frac{14.4 \times 10^{-6}}{3.6 \times 10^{-2}} \times \exp\left(-\frac{5.00 \times 10^{-3}}{3.6 \times 10^{-2}}\right)$$

$$I = 348\,\mu\text{A}$$

Capacitors in rectification

The output of the diode bridge rectifier may be processed further to make it smoother. This can be done by adding a capacitor in parallel to the load, as shown in Figure 11.47. The output is now smoother.

Why is the output smoother? For the first half cycle the current is clockwise. The current moves from top to bottom in the load. Now, in the first quarter cycle the capacitor charges. At the end of the first quarter cycle the potential at the top plate of the capacitor is a maximum. In the second quarter cycle (green), the potential at the top plate begins to decrease and so the capacitor discharges, sending current through the load from top to bottom. (The capacitor begins to discharge at the end of the third quarter cycle as well.) The 'ripple' is reduced with higher capacitance or load resistance.

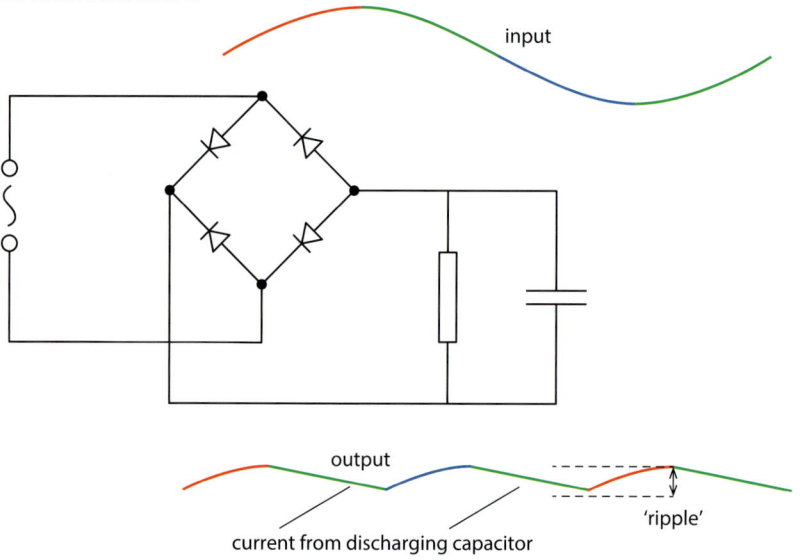

Figure 11.47 A capacitor in parallel to the load resistor smooths out the output voltage.

Worked example

11.19 Figure 11.48 shows an ac voltage that has been smoothed by a diode bridge circuit. Use the graph to answer these questions.
  a State the peak voltage in the ac signal.
  b Determine the frequency of the ac voltage.
  c The capacitance of the capacitor in the smoothing bridge circuit has a value of 12 µF. Determine the change in the charge on the capacitor plates during one discharge of the capacitor.
  d Hence estimate the average current during a discharge and the resistance through which the capacitor discharges.

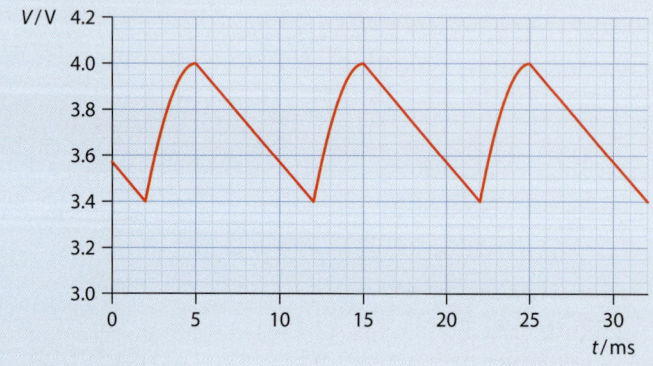

Figure 11.48

a The peak voltage is 4.0 V.

b The period is 20 ms (we look from the peak at 5 ms to that at 25 ms; the peak at 15 ms is a 'rectified trough') and so the frequency is:

$$f = \frac{1}{20 \times 10^{-3}} = 50\,\text{Hz}$$

c The voltage changes by 0.6 V due to the discharge. So:

$$\Delta q = C\Delta V = 12 \times 10^{-6} \times 0.6 = 7.2\,\mu\text{C}$$

d The discharge lasted for 7.0 ms, and so:

$$I = \frac{\Delta q}{\Delta t} = \frac{7.2 \times 10^{-6}}{7.0 \times 10^{-3}} = 1.0\,\text{mA}$$

The average voltage across the resistor is 3.7 V and so an estimate of the resistance is:

$$R = \frac{V}{I} = \frac{3.7}{1.0 \times 10^{-3}} \approx 3.7\,\text{M}\Omega$$

Nature of science

Common formalism

The mathematics of RC circuits follows closely the mathematics of radioactive decay. Therefore the same techniques of analysis that have been used in one area can also be used in the other. This happens countless times in physics – examples include oscillations in mechanics and oscillations in electrical circuits; electrostatics and gravitation; and thermodynamics and the physics of black hole event horizons.

? Test yourself

22 A parallel plate capacitor in a vacuum has a capacitance of 1.0 F. The plates are separated by a distance of 1 cm. Calculate the area of one of the capacitor plates. Comment on your answer.

23 Calculate the charge on one of the plates of a parallel plate capacitor of area 0.25 m². The plates are separated by a distance of 8.0 mm, in a vacuum. The potential difference across the plates is 24 V.

24 A 12 µF capacitor is charged to a potential difference of 220 V in 15 ms. Estimate the average current needed to charge the capacitor.

25 A 9.0 V battery is used to charge a 20 mF capacitor. Calculate:
  a the charge on the capacitor
  b the energy stored in the capacitor.
  The capacitor discharges in a time of 50 ms.
  c Estimate the power released during the discharge.

26 Two capacitors of capacitance 120 µF and 240 µF are connected in parallel. The two are then connected to a source of potential difference 6.0 V. Calculate:
  a the total capacitance of the arrangement
  b the charge stored on each capacitor
  c the energy stored in each capacitor.

11 ELECTROMAGNETIC INDUCTION (HL)

27 Repeat question **26** where now the capacitors are connected in series.

28 A capacitor of capacitance 25 pF is connected to a battery of emf 24 V for a long time. The battery is then removed and the capacitor is connected to an uncharged capacitor of capacitance 75 pF. Calculate:
  a the charge on each capacitor
  b the change in total energy stored before and after the battery was disconnected.
  c Comment on the answer to **b**.

29 A 250 mF capacitor is charged by a battery of emf 12 V.
  a Calculate the energy stored in the capacitor.
  b Estimate the time for which the lamp is lit, listing any assumptions you make.
  The capacitor discharges through a lamp rated 12 V, 6.0 W.

30 a Sketch a graph to show how the potential difference V across a parallel plate capacitor varies with charge q on one of the plates.
  b Suggest what the area under the graph represents.

31 A capacitor of capacitance 25.0 μF is charged by a battery of emf 48 V. The battery is removed and the capacitor is connected to a resistor of resistance 15 kΩ through which it discharges. Determine **a** the charge, **b** the current and **c** the voltage after a time of 0.20 s.

32 The graph shows how the voltage V on the plate of a capacitor of capacitance 50.0 μF varies with time t as the capacitor discharges through a resistor of resistance R.

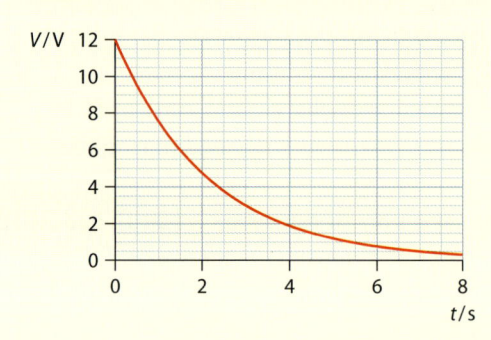

  a Use the graph to estimate the time constant of the system.
  b Calculate the resistance R.

33 A capacitor of capacitance 250 μF is charged by a battery of emf 12 V. The battery is removed and the capacitor is connected to a resistor of resistance 75 kΩ through which it discharges. Determine **a** the charge and **b** the current when the voltage across the capacitor is 6.0 V.

34 A capacitor of capacitance 2.00 μF is charged by connecting it to a battery of emf 9.00 V. The capacitor then discharges through a resistor of resistance 5.00 MΩ. Determine at a time of $t = 1.00$ s:
  a the rate at which charge is leaving the capacitor plate
  b the rate at which energy is being dissipated in the resistor
  c the rate at which energy is being lost by the capacitor.

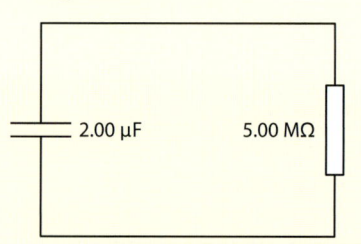

35 Refer to Figure **11.47** on page 470. The input voltage is sinusoidal.
  a sketch a graph to show how voltage varies with time across
    i diode A
    ii diode B
  b suggest how the output can be made even smoother.

Exam-style questions

1. A magnetic field of uniformly increasing magnitude is directed into the plane of the page as shown. A conducting loop of wire is on the plane of the page.

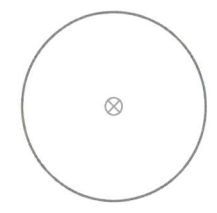

   Which is correct about the direction and magnitude of the induced current in the wire?

	Direction	Magnitude
A	clockwise	constant
B	counter-clockwise	varying
C	clockwise	varying
D	counter-clockwise	constant

2. A loop of wire contains two identical light bulbs, L_1 and L_2. The region in the loop contains a changing magnetic field whose direction is normal to the plane of the page. Both light bulbs are lit. A copper wire is placed across the loop as shown in the diagram.

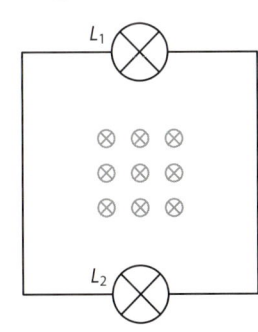

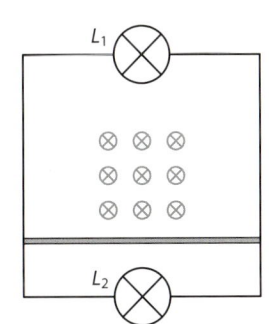

   What will be the effect of this wire on the brightness of the light bulbs?

       A L_1 will go out and L_2 will get dimmer.
       B L_1 will go out and L_2 will get brighter.
       C L_2 will go out and L_1 will get brighter.
       D L_2 will go out and L_1 will get dimmer.

3 A conducting loop of wire is in a region of magnetic field directed into the plane of the page. The loop is rotated about axes I, II and III.

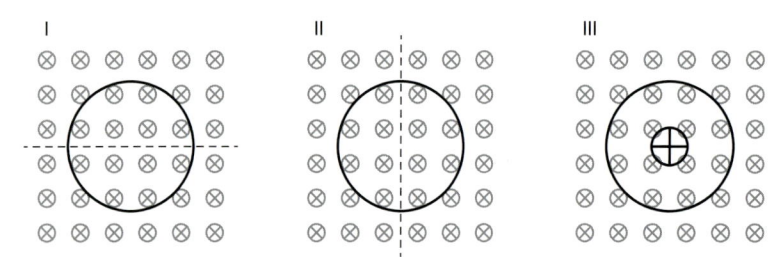

In which case or cases will there be an induced current in the loop?

    A I and II only   **B** I only   **C** II only   **D** I, II and III

4 The graph shows the variation with time of the power dissipated in a resistor of resistance $2.0\,\Omega$ in an ac circuit.

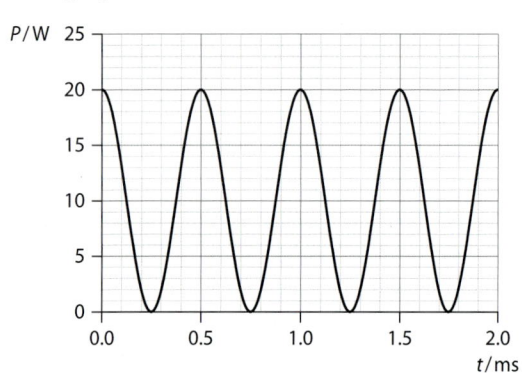

What is the rms value of the voltage across the resistor and the period of the current?

	Rms voltage	Period
A	$\sqrt{20}$ V	0.5 s
B	$\sqrt{20}$ V	1.0 s
C	$\sqrt{40}$ V	0.5 s
D	$\sqrt{40}$ V	1.0 s

5 A parallel plate capacitor is connected to a battery of fixed emf. The energy stored in the capacitor is E and the charge on one of the plates is q. A dielectric is inserted between the plates. Which row in the table gives the correct change(s), if any, in the capacitance and charge stored?

	Capacitance	Charge
A	no change	no change
B	increases	increases
C	decreases	no change
D	no change	increases

6 Capacitor X has capacitance 200 pF and potential difference 100 V. Capacitor Y has capacitance 100 pF and potential difference 200 V. Which row in the table is correct about the energy and charge stored by capacitor Y?

	Energy stored by Y	Charge stored by Y
A	same as X	same as X
B	greater than X	same as X
C	same as X	greater than X
D	greater than X	greater than X

7 In the circuit shown a capacitor that is initially uncharged is being charged by a battery.

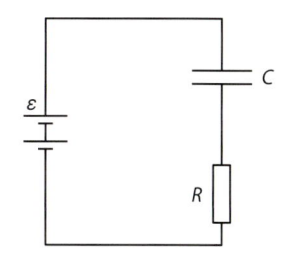

Which of the following is a correct graph of the variation of the potential difference V across the plates with charge q on one of the capacitor plates?

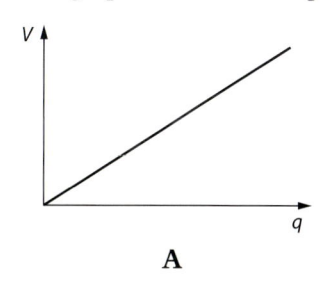

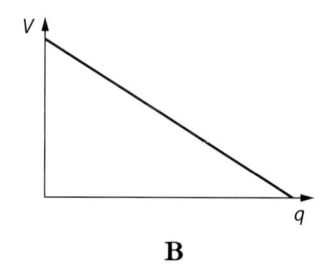

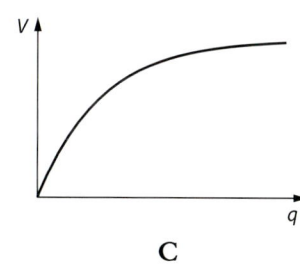

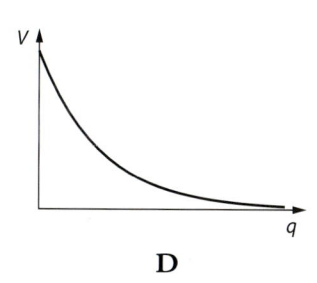

A — linear increasing
B — linear decreasing
C — exponential approach to maximum
D — exponential decay

8 What will the initial current be in the circuit below the instant the switch is closed, and what will it be eventually a long time after the switch is closed?

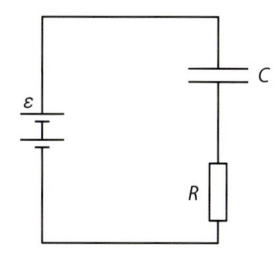

	Initial	Eventual
A	$\dfrac{\varepsilon}{R}$	0
B	$\dfrac{\varepsilon}{R}$	$\dfrac{\varepsilon}{R}$
C	0	0
D	0	$\dfrac{\varepsilon}{R}$

9 The graph shows the variation with time t of the current I for a discharging capacitor.

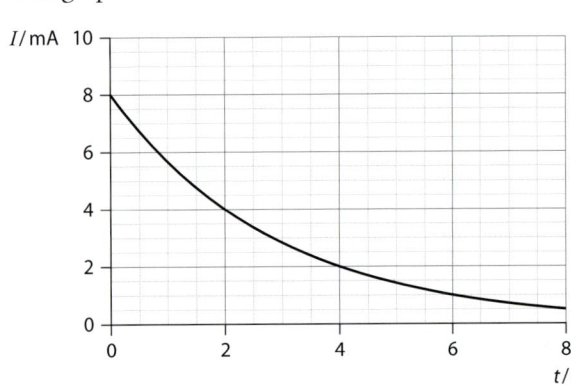

What is the time constant of this system?

A 2.0 s **B** $2.0\sqrt{2}$ s **C** $\dfrac{2.0}{\sqrt{2}}$ s **D** $\dfrac{2.0}{\ln 2}$ s

10 In which of these circuits can full-wave rectification take place?

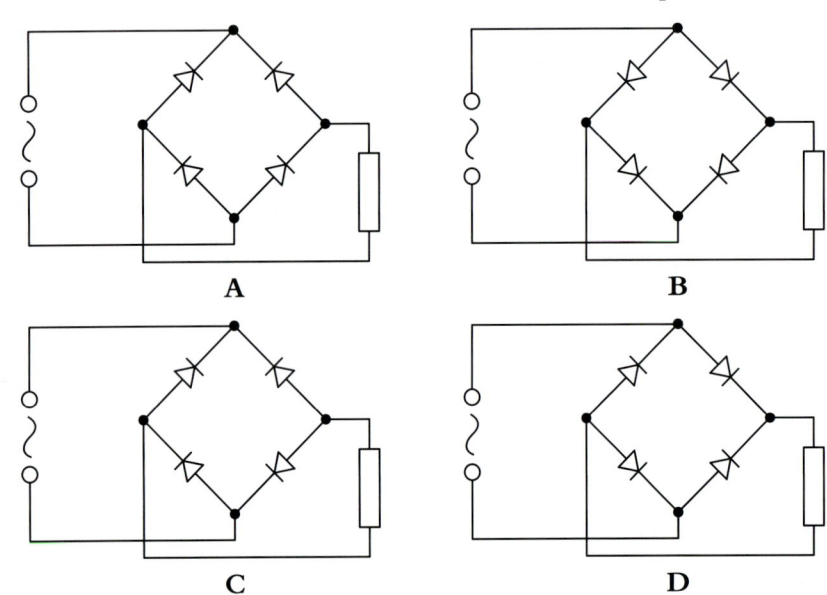

A

B

C

D

11 The diagram shows a small magnet that has been dropped from above a solenoid. As the magnet falls through the solenoid, a sensor shows how the induced emf in the solenoid varies with time.

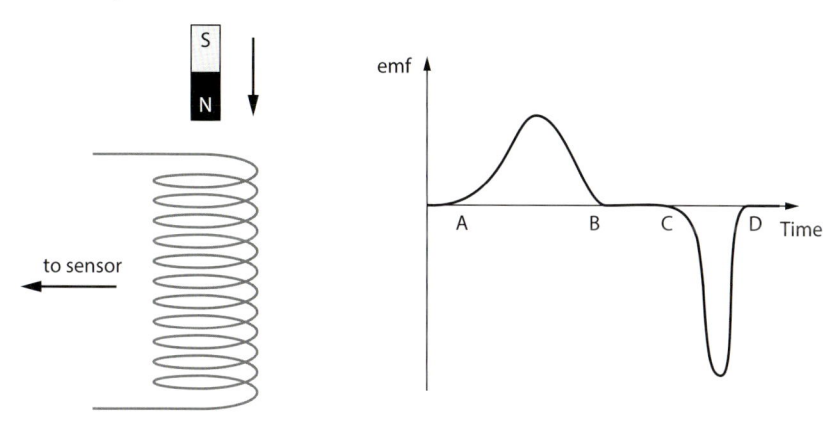

   a Explain why an emf is induced in the solenoid from **A** to **B**. [3]
   b Explain why the induced emf from **C** to **D**, when compared to that from **A** to **B**, has:
      i   a greater peak value [2]
      ii a shorter duration. [1]
   c Suggest:
      i   what the areas between the graph and the time axis from **A** to **B** and from **C** to **D** represent [2]
      ii whether these areas are equal. [2]

12 A square loop of side $0.25\,\text{m}$ is made to move at constant speed $0.050\,\text{m s}^{-1}$. The loop enters a region of uniform magnetic field of strength $0.40\,\text{T}$ directed into the plane of the page. There are 50 turns of conducting wire around the loop.

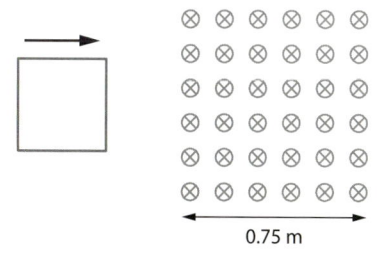

   The loop begins to enter the region of magnetic field at $t = 0$.

   a On a copy of the axes below, draw a graph to show the variation with time t of:
      i   the magnetic flux linkage Φ through the loop. [3]
      ii the induced emf in the loop. [3]
   b The total resistance of the wire around the loop is $0.75\,\Omega$.

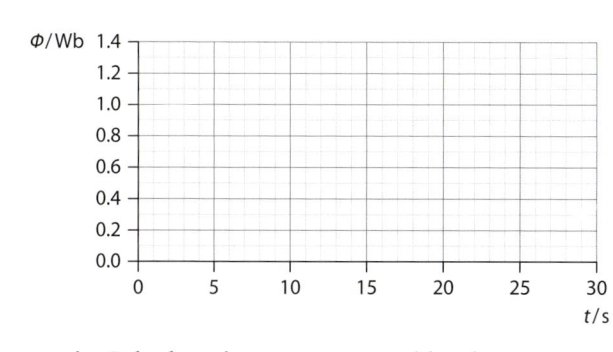

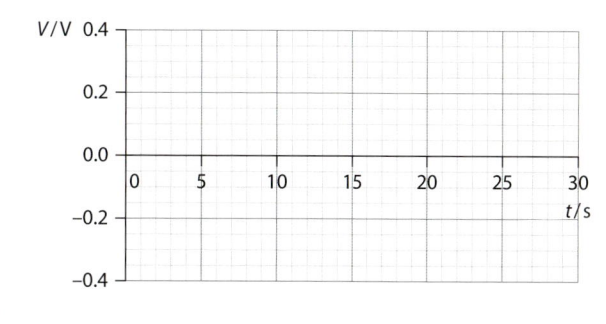

      i   Calculate the power exerted by the agent pushing the loop. [3]
      ii Explain what has become of this power. [2]

13 A wind generator provides power to a factory whose equipment operates at 120 kW and 240 V. The factory is connected to the wind generator with cables of total resistance 0.80 Ω.

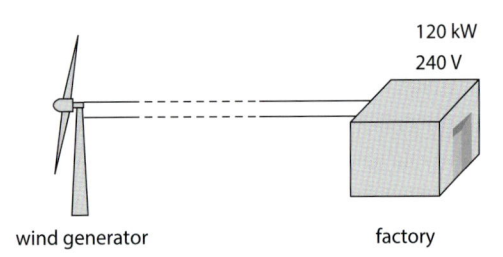

    a Calculate:
        i the power lost in the cables [2]
        ii the voltage at the wind generator [2]
        iii the efficiency of the transmission system. [1]
    b It is suggested that a transformer be used to step up the voltage of the wind generator so that the step-down transformer near the factory would bring the voltage down from 2.4 kV to 240 V.

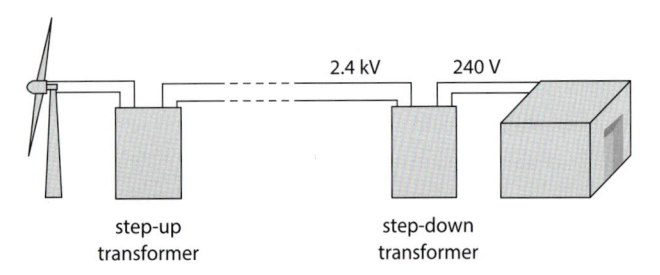

    Determine the power loss in the cables now. [2]

    c The graph shows the variation with time of the voltage in a particular piece of machinery in the factory.

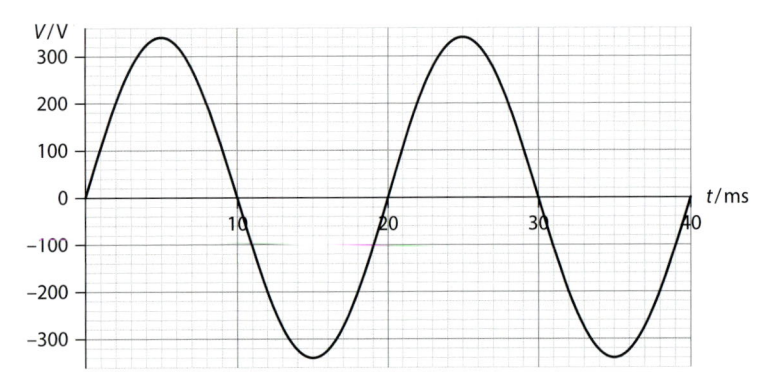

        i Show that the rms value of the voltage is 240 V. [1]
        ii The average power dissipated in this machinery is 18 kW. Calculate the peak current in the machinery. [2]

d The diagram shows a simple transformer.

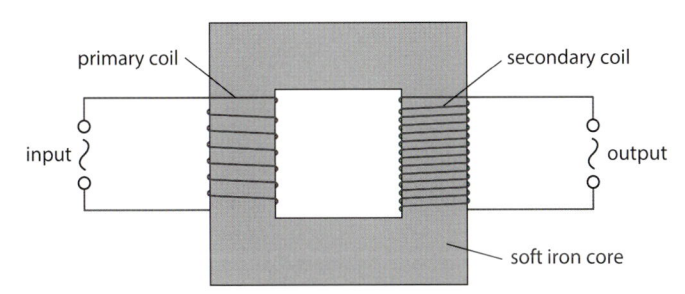

   i Explain how an ac voltage in the primary coil gives rise to an ac voltage in the secondary coil. Make sure you mention the function of the iron core in your answer. [4]
   ii Explain why the core gets warm while the transformer is operating. [2]

14 Each of the capacitors in the diagram has capacitance 180 pF.

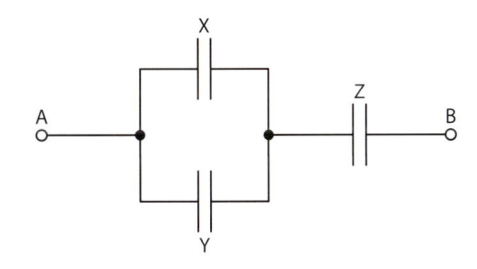

   a i State what is meant by **capacitance**. [1]
       ii Discuss whether a capacitor stores charge or energy or both. [2]
   b Calculate the total capacitance of the system. [2]
   c Points **A** and **B** are connected to a source of emf 12 V. Calculate:
       i the charge on **one** plate of capacitor **Z** [2]
       ii the potential difference across capacitor **Z** [1]
       iii the charge on **one** plate of capacitor **X**. [2]

15 The diagram shows a charged parallel plate capacitor in a vacuum connected to an ideal voltmeter. The reading on the voltmeter is 9.0 V.

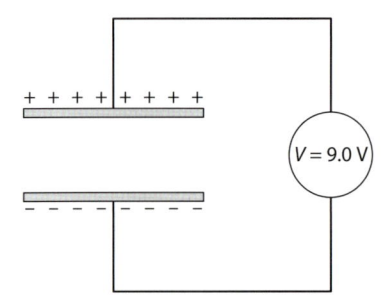

a Explain why the capacitor does not discharge. [2]
b The plates are 4.4 mm apart and have an area of 0.68 m².
   i   Calculate the capacitance of the capacitor. [2]
   ii Determine the charge on **one** of the parallel plates of the capacitor. [2]
   iii Calculate the energy stored in the electric field in between the plates. [2]
c A dielectric of electric permittivity $\varepsilon = 12\varepsilon_0$ is inserted between the parallel plates of the capacitor. State and explain the effect of this, if any, on:
   i   the charge on one of the plates [1]
   ii the potential difference between the plates [3]
   iii the capacitance. [2]

16 a Using the components below draw a circuit that will make it possible to first charge the uncharged capacitor and then let it discharge. [3]

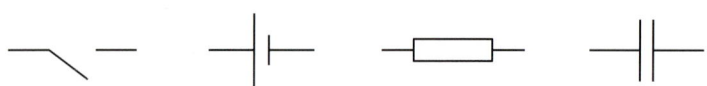

b The graph shows how the charge on the capacitor in **a** varies with time as the capacitor is being charged.

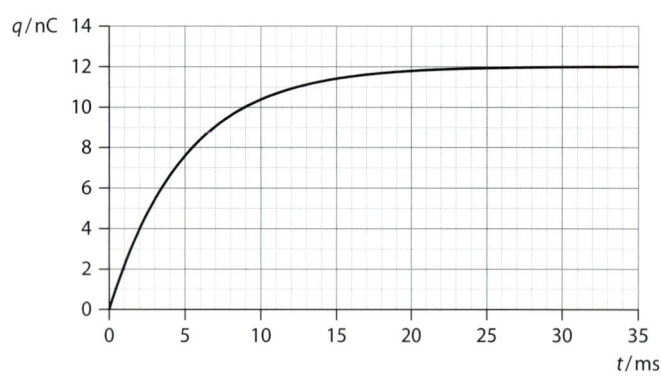

   i Estimate the charge on one of the capacitor plates after charging for a long time. [1]
c The emf of the battery that charged the capacitor was 6.0 V.
   i   Show that the capacitance of the capacitor is 2.0 nF. [2]
   ii Calculate the energy transferred by the battery during the charging of the capacitor. [2]
   iii Calculate the energy stored in the capacitor after it is fully charged. [2]
   iv Compare and contrast the answers to **ii** and **iii**. [2]
d The capacitor is now allowed to discharge through a resistor of resistance 2.5 MΩ. Calculate the current through the resistor when the charge on one of the plates has been reduced to 8.0 nC. [4]

Quantum and nuclear physics (HL) 12

12.1 The interaction of matter with radiation

This section deals with an array of new phenomena. The photoelectric effect and the spectra of atoms were unsolved problems in physics for the entire second half of the 19th century. Their solution paved the way for quantum theory, with its own array of unusual concepts and phenomena such as the wavefunction, the uncertainty principle and tunnelling.

Photons and light

Light is said to be an **electromagnetic wave** consisting of oscillating electric and magnetic fields. This was Maxwell's great discovery in the 19th century. The wave has some wavelength λ and a frequency f and, as with all waves, the wave speed c is given by:

$$c = f\lambda$$

where in this case the wave speed is the speed of light.

Through Maxwell's theory, complex phenomena such as diffraction, interference, polarisation and others could be understood. The successful application of Maxwell's theory meant that light was definitely and without any doubt a wave. It therefore came as a shock that, in a phenomenon known as the photoelectric effect, light did not behave as a wave should. (We shall look at this phenomenon in more detail in the next subsection.)

As we will see, Einstein suggested that light should be thought of as a collection of quanta, or bundles of energy. Each **quantum** or bundle of light has energy E given by $E = hf$, where f is the frequency of the light and h is Planck's constant. A beam of light of frequency f is now to be thought of as a very large number of these quanta moving at the speed of light. The total energy of the beam is then the product of hf (the energy of one quantum) times N the number of quanta in the beam. The energy of the beam is therefore an integral multiple of the basic unit hf. No amount of energy less than hf would ever be found in the beam. These quanta have definite energy and are localised in space; this means that they behave as particles. But the theory of relativity states that if a particle moves at the speed of light it has to have zero mass. So this quantum of light, which came to be known as the **photon**, is a particle with zero mass and zero electric charge.

In Topic **7** we saw that a photon can be created when an atom makes a transition from a high to a lower energy. Its energy is the energy difference of the two levels. A photon can also be absorbed by an atom. An atom in a low energy state can absorb a photon of just the right energy and make a transition to a higher energy level. When we look at the light from a light bulb we see a continuous emission of light. But if we could slow down the

Learning objectives

- Understand the nature of photons and why they were needed to explain experimental results.
- Discuss the photoelectric effect.
- Understand the concept of matter waves.
- Solve problems involving pair production and pair annihilation.
- Understand the consequences of angular momentum quantisation in the Bohr model.
- Understand the concept of the wavefunction.
- Work with the Heisenberg uncertainty principle.
- Qualitatively understand barrier tunnelling and the factors affecting the tunnelling probability.

process by a few billion times, the continuity in the emission of light would stop. We would see different spots on the filament emit tiny flashes of light (photons) at random interval of time; the spots on the filament would be on (emitting) and off (not emitting) randomly. The discreteness of energy we talked about in Topic **7** would surface again.

In Einstein's theory of special relativity the total energy E, the momentum p and the mass m of a particle are related according to:

$$E^2 = p^2c^2 + m^2c^4$$

The mass of the photon is zero, so $E = pc$. The photon therefore has momentum $p = \dfrac{E}{c}$. (This implies that the conventional Newtonian formula for momentum, $p = mv$, does not apply to particles with zero mass.) So the momentum of the photon is:

$$p = \frac{E}{c} = \frac{hf}{c} = \frac{h}{\lambda}$$

Exam tip
Remember the basic formula from waves: $c = f\lambda$.

Worked examples

12.1 Estimate how many photons of wavelength 5.0×10^{-7} m are emitted per second by a 60 W lamp, assuming that 1% of the energy of the lamp goes into photons of this wavelength.

Let there be N photons per second emitted.

Then the energy they carry is $\dfrac{Nhc}{\lambda}$ in one second.

This has to be 1% of 60 J, that is 0.60 J.

So: $\dfrac{Nhc}{\lambda} = 0.60$

$$N = \frac{0.60\lambda}{hc}$$

$$N = \frac{0.60 \times 5.0 \times 10^{-7}}{6.63 \times 10^{-34} \times 3.0 \times 10^{8}}$$

$\Rightarrow \quad N = 1.5 \times 10^{18}$ photons per second.

12.2 All the photons from Worked example **12.1** are incident normally on a mirror of area $0.5\,\text{m}^2$ and are reflected by it. Estimate the pressure these photons exert on the mirror.

Each photon has a momentum of $\dfrac{E}{c}$ or $\dfrac{h}{\lambda}$

The momentum **change** upon reflection is $2\dfrac{h}{\lambda}$ (momentum is a vector!).

Since there are N such reflections per second, the force F on the mirror is:

$$F = 2N\dfrac{h}{\lambda}$$

$$F = 2 \times 1.5 \times 10^{18} \times \dfrac{6.63 \times 10^{-34}}{5.0 \times 10^{-7}}$$

$\Rightarrow \quad F = 4.0 \times 10^{-9}\,\text{N}$

The pressure is thus:

$$\dfrac{F}{A} = 8.0 \times 10^{-9}\,\text{N}\,\text{m}^{-2}$$

(Note that if the photons were absorbed rather than reflected, the pressure would be half that obtained here.)

The photoelectric effect

The **photoelectric effect** is the phenomenon in which light (or other forms of electromagnetic radiation) incident on a metallic surface causes electrons to be emitted from the surface.

To investigate the facts about the photoelectric effect, apparatus like the one in Figure 12.1 may be used.

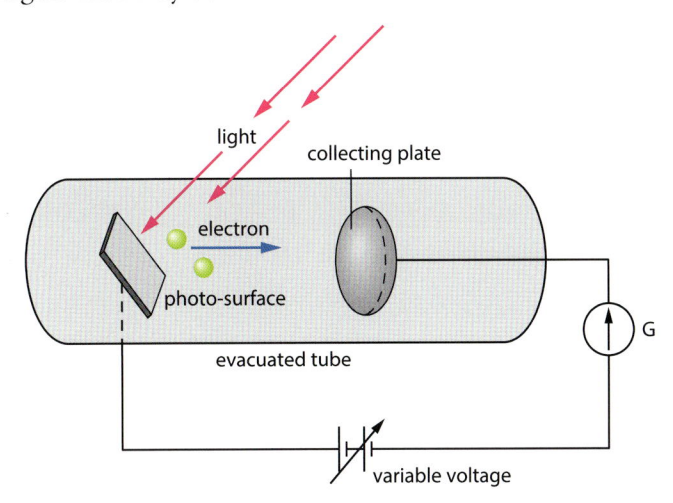

Figure 12.1 Apparatus for investigating the photoelectric effect. The variable voltage decelerates the emitted electrons and eventually stops them.

It consists of an evacuated tube, inside which is the **photo-surface** (the metallic surface that light is incident on). Light passes through an opening in the tube and falls on the photo-surface, which emits electrons. Some of the emitted electrons arrive at the collecting plate. The photo-surface and the collecting plate are part of a circuit as shown. Those electrons that

Exam tip
The stopping voltage is strictly negative but we work with its magnitude.
It is very important to understand that the stopping voltage gives the **maximum** kinetic energy of the emitted electrons.

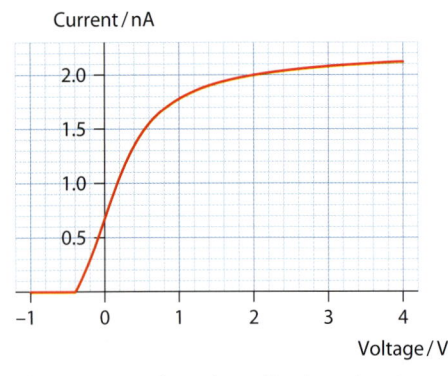

Figure 12.2 When the collecting plate is connected to the negative terminal of the power supply, there is a voltage at which the current becomes zero (V_s).

make it to the collecting plate complete the circuit and so we have an electric current that is recorded by the sensitive galvanometer.

Notice that in Figure 12.1 the negative terminal of the variable power supply is connected to the collecting plate. This means that the collecting plate actually repels the emitted electrons. Only the very energetic electrons will make it to the plate. As the magnitude of the voltage is increased (i.e. made more negative) fewer and fewer electrons make it to the plate; eventually no electron will arrive there and at that point the current becomes zero. The voltage at which the current becomes zero is called the **stopping voltage**, V_s. Its significance is that the maximum kinetic energy of the emitted electrons must be eV_s. We see this as follows: let the maximum kinetic energy of the electrons be E_{max} as they leave the photo-surface; the work done in moving an electron from the photo-surface to the collecting plate is eV_s. From mechanics we know that the work done is the change in the kinetic energy of the electron. So:

$$eV_s = E_{max}$$

We now connect the positive terminal of the power supply to the collecting plate. The electrons are now attracted to the collecting plate and the current increases. As the voltage is increased even more the current saturates, i.e. it approaches a constant value. This is because the collecting plate is so positive that it attracts every single emitted electron (even those that were not directed at the collected plate). So we have a current–voltage graph like the one in Figure 12.2.

Worked example

12.3 Using the graph of Figure 12.2 determine:
   a the stopping voltage
   b the maximum energy of the emitted electrons
   c the maximum speed of the emitted electrons.

a The current becomes zero when the voltage is -0.40 V so the stopping voltage is 0.40 V.

b The maximum kinetic energy of the emitted electrons is $0.40 \, eV = 6.4 \times 10^{-20}$ J.

c From $E_{max} = \frac{1}{2}mv^2$, we find $v = \sqrt{\frac{2E_{max}}{m}}$, giving:

$$v = \sqrt{\frac{2 \times 6.4 \times 10^{-20}}{9.1 \times 10^{-31}}} = 3.8 \times 10^5 \, m\,s^{-1}$$

The results of this experiment reveal two immediate surprises: the first is that changing the intensity of the light does not affect the stopping voltage! Light from a candle and light from an airport searchlight give the same stopping voltage. Figure 12.3 shows that the stopping voltage for weak light (thin line) and intense light (thick line) are the same.

> The stopping voltage is independent of the intensity of the light source.

The second surprise is that the stopping voltage depends on the frequency of the light. The higher the frequency, the higher the magnitude of the stopping voltage. This is shown in Figure **12.4**: the violet curve corresponds to violet light and the green curve to green light of lower frequency. The stopping voltages are 0.40 V for green and 1.0 V for violet.

If we plot the kinetic energy of the electrons (which equals eV_s) versus frequency, we find a straight line as shown in Figure **12.5a**.

The puzzling feature of this graph is that there exists a frequency, called the critical (or threshold) frequency f_c, such that no electrons at all are emitted if the frequency of the light source is less than f_c. This is true even if very intense light is allowed to fall on the photo-surface. When the experiment is repeated with a different photo-surface and the kinetic energy of the electrons is plotted versus frequency, a line parallel to the first is obtained, as shown in Figure **12.5b**.

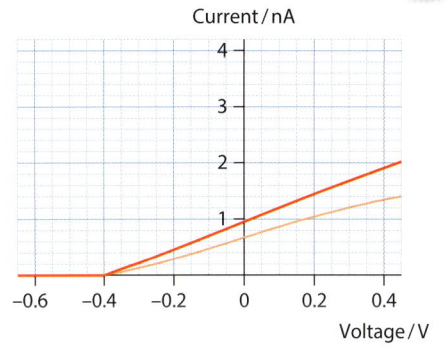

Figure 12.3 The stopping voltage for weak light (thin line) and intense light (thick line) of the same frequency.

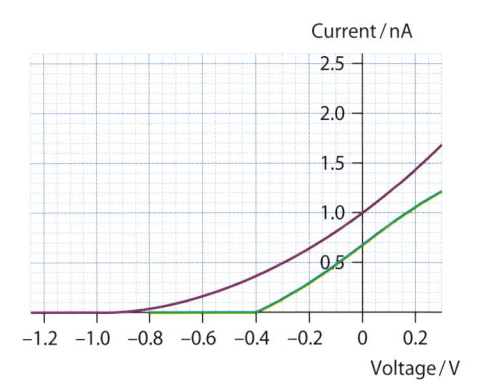

Figure 12.4 The stopping voltages for green and violet light.

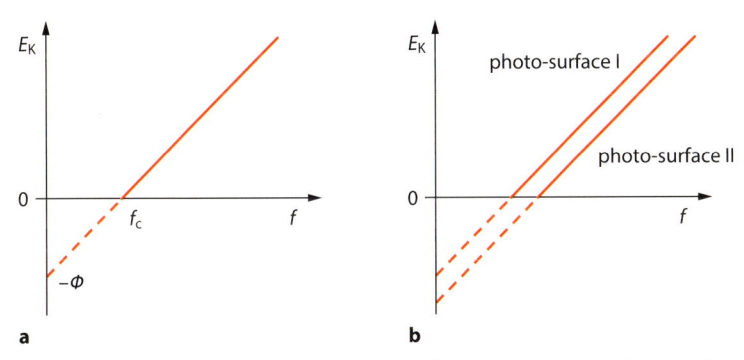

Figure 12.5 a The graph of kinetic energy versus frequency is a straight line. The horizontal intercept is the critical frequency, f_c. **b** When another photo-surface is used, a line parallel to the first is obtained.

The final puzzling observation in these experiments is that the electrons are emitted immediately after the light is incident on the photo-surface, with no apparent time delay.

We now have four surprising observations:

1. The intensity of the incident light does not affect the energy of the emitted electrons.
2. The electron energy depends on the frequency of the incident light.
3. There is a certain minimum frequency below which no electrons are emitted.
4. Electrons are emitted with no time delay.

These four observations cannot be understood in terms of light as a wave for several reasons:
- If light is a wave, then an intense beam of light carries a lot of energy and so it should cause the emission of electrons that have more energy.

12 QUANTUM AND NUCLEAR PHYSICS (HL)

Exam tip
A simple analogy to see the difference between light as a wave and light as a particle is the following: imagine winning a huge amount of money in a lottery, say 100 million euro. If this were to be given to you in the wave model of light you might have to wait a very long time to get all the money, if the money were paid to you at a rate of one million euro a year. In the photon model, all the money would be given to you at once.

- The formula for the energy of a light wave does not include the frequency, and so frequency should play no role in the energy of the emitted electrons. In the same way there can be no explanation of a critical frequency.
- Finally, a very low intensity beam of light carries little energy. An electron might have to wait for a considerable length of time before it accumulated enough energy to escape from the metal. This would cause a delay in its emission.

Einstein's explanation

The explanation of all these strange observations was provided by Albert Einstein in 1905.

> Einstein suggested that light consists of photons, which are **quanta or bundles of energy and momentum**. The energy of one such quantum is given by the formula:
>
> $E = hf$
>
> where f is the frequency of the electromagnetic radiation and $h = 6.63 \times 10^{-34}$ J s is a constant, known as Planck's constant.

Einstein's mechanism for the photoelectric effect is that a single photon of frequency f is absorbed by a single electron in the photo-surface, so the electron's energy increases by hf. The electron will have to spend a certain amount of energy, let us say Φ, to free itself from the pull of the nuclei of the atoms of the photo-surface. The electron will be emitted (become free) if hf is bigger than Φ. The difference $hf - \Phi$ will simply be the kinetic energy E_K of the (now) free electron (Figure 12.6). That is:

$E_K = hf - \Phi$

The value of Φ (called the **work function**) is read off the graph, from the intercept of the straight line with the vertical axis. Note that the work function and the critical frequency are related by:

$hf_c = \Phi$

since $E_K = 0$ in that case.

In the photoelectric apparatus, the maximum kinetic energy of the electrons is measured to be $eV_s = E_{max}$. So:

$E_{max} = hf - \Phi$

It follows that:

$eV_s = hf - \Phi$

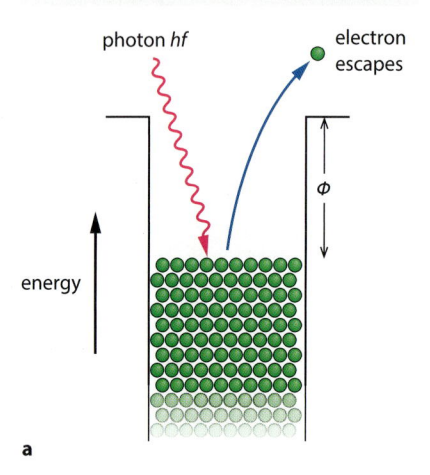

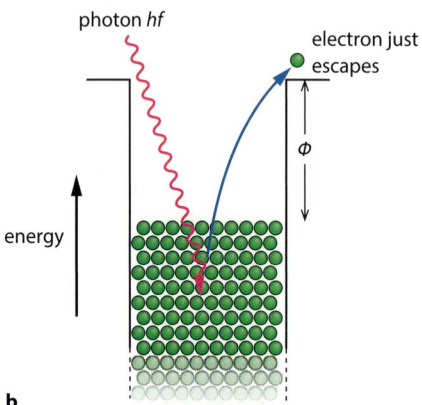

$V_s = \dfrac{h}{e}f - \dfrac{\Phi}{e}$

Figure 12.6 a A single photon of light may release a single electron from a metal. **b** A more tightly bound electron needs more energy to release it from the metal.

That is, in a graph of stopping voltage versus frequency, the graph is a straight line with slope h/e.

Worked examples

12.4 A photo-surface has a work function of 1.50 eV.
  a Determine the critical frequency.
  b Light of frequency 6.10×10^{14} Hz falls on this surface. Calculate the energy and speed of the emitted electrons.

Exam tip
Remember to use energy in joules to calculate the critical frequency.

a The critical frequency f_c is given in terms of the work function by $hf_c = \Phi$ and thus:

$$f_c = \frac{\Phi}{h} = \frac{1.50 \times 1.6 \times 10^{-19}}{6.63 \times 10^{-34}}$$

$$f_c = 3.62 \times 10^{14} \text{ Hz}$$

b The maximum kinetic energy of the electron is $E_{max} = hf - \Phi$, i.e.
$E_{max} = hf - hf_c = h(f - f_c)$
$E_{max} = 6.63 \times 10^{-34} \times (6.10 - 3.62) \times 10^{14} = 1.64 \times 10^{-19}$ J ($= 1.03$ eV)

From $E = \frac{1}{2}mv^2$ we find:

$$v = \sqrt{\frac{2E_{max}}{m}}$$

$$v = \sqrt{\frac{22 \times 1.64 \times 10^{-19}}{9.1 \times 10^{-31}}} \quad \text{(Use joules for } E_{max} \text{ to find } v.)$$

$\Rightarrow v = 6.0 \times 10^5$ m s^{-1}

12.5 Monochromatic light of power P and wavelength 4.0×10^{-7} m falling on a photo-surface whose critical frequency is 6.0×10^{14} Hz releases 2.0×10^{10} electrons per second.
  a Determine the current collected in the anode.
  b The power of the light is increased to $2P$. Predict the value of the new current.
  c Light of power $2P$ and wavelength 6.0×10^{-7} m falls on this photo-surface. Determine the current in this case.

a The definition of electric current is $I = \frac{\Delta q}{\Delta t}$.

In a time of 1 second, the number of electrons emitted is 2.0×10^{10} and so the charge they carry is $e \times 2.0 \times 10^{10}$.

The current is thus $I = e \times 2.0 \times 10^{10}$, i.e.

$I = 3.2 \times 10^{-9}$ A.

b If the power doubles, the number of photons will double and so the number of electrons emitted will double. Thus, so will the current, giving $I = 6.4 \times 10^{-9}$ A.

c The critical frequency f_c is 6.0×10^{14} Hz. From the wave equation, $c = f_c \times$ critical wavelength.

So the critical wavelength is:

$$\lambda_c = \frac{c}{f_c} = \frac{3 \times 10^8}{6.0 \times 10^{14}} = 5.0 \times 10^{-7} \text{ m}$$

So if the wavelength becomes 6.0×10^{-7} m, no electrons will be emitted at all, hence $I = 0$.

12.6 The green light in Figure **12.4** has a wavelength of 496 nm.
   a Determine the work function of the photo-surface.
   b Estimate the wavelength of the violet light in that experiment.

a The stopping voltage is 0.40 V and so, using $eV_s = hf - \Phi$ we deduce that:

$$\Phi = \frac{hc}{\lambda} - eV_s$$

$$\Phi = \frac{1.24 \times 10^{-6}}{4.96 \times 10^{-7}} - 0.40$$

$$\Phi = 2.10 \text{ eV}$$

b We again use $eV_s = hf - \Phi$ to get that $\frac{hc}{\lambda} = eV_s + \Phi$.

The stopping voltage is 1.0 eV and so:

$$\frac{hc}{\lambda} = 1.0 + 2.1$$

$$\frac{hc}{\lambda} = 3.1 \text{ eV}$$

Hence:

$$\lambda = \frac{hc}{3.10}$$

$$\lambda = \frac{1.24 \times 10^{-6}}{3.1}$$

Exam tip
Notice the use of $hc = 1.24 \times 10^{-6}$ eV m, which makes calculations much faster. This constant is in the IB data booklet.

$$\lambda = 4.0 \times 10^{-7} \text{ m}$$

Matter waves

In 1923, Louis de Broglie suggested that to any particle of momentum p, there corresponds a wave of wavelength given by the formula (h is Planck's constant):

$$\lambda = \frac{h}{p}$$

The de Broglie hypothesis, as this is known, thus assigns wave-like properties to something that is normally thought to be a particle. This state of affairs is called the **duality of matter**. All moving particles (not just electrons) are assigned a wavelength.

What does it mean to say that the electron has wave-like properties? One thing it does not mean is to think that the electron oscillates up and down as it moves along.

Showing wave-like properties means showing the basic phenomena of waves: diffraction and interference. A wave of wavelength λ will diffract around an obstacle of size d if λ is comparable to or bigger than d. In Worked example 12.7 we calculated a typical electron wavelength to be of order 10^{-10} m. This distance is typical of the separation of atoms in crystals, and it is there that electron diffraction and interference will be seen.

Worked example

12.7 Find the de Broglie wavelength of an electron that has been accelerated from rest by a potential difference of 54 V.

The kinetic energy of the electron is given by $E_K = \dfrac{p^2}{2m}$

The work done in accelerating the electron through a potential difference V is qV, and this work goes into kinetic energy. Thus:

$$\dfrac{p^2}{2m} = qV$$

$$\Rightarrow p = \sqrt{2mqV}$$

Hence:

$$\lambda = \dfrac{h}{\sqrt{2mqV}}$$

$$\lambda = \dfrac{6.63 \times 10^{-34}}{\sqrt{2 \times 9.1 \times 10^{-31} \times 1.60 \times 10^{-19} \times 54}}$$

$$\lambda = 1.7 \times 10^{-10} \text{ m}$$

Exam tip
It is preferable to use $E_K = \dfrac{p^2}{2m}$ for kinetic energy rather than $E_K = \tfrac{1}{2}mv^2$.

Exam tip
The formula $\lambda = \dfrac{h}{\sqrt{2mqV}}$ is very useful in paper 1 questions, where it is often required to know that $\lambda \propto \dfrac{1}{\sqrt{V}}$

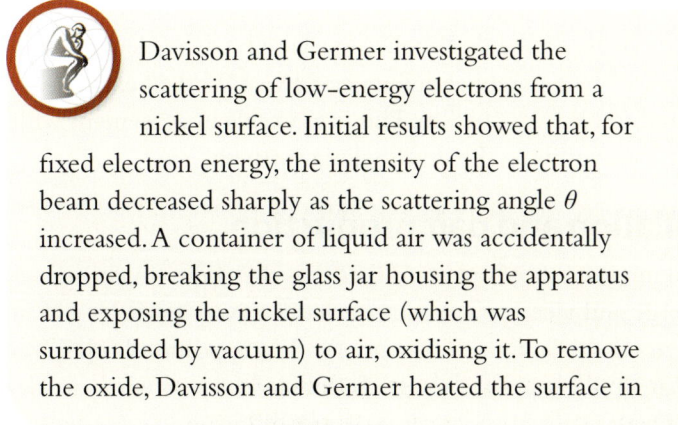

Davisson and Germer investigated the scattering of low-energy electrons from a nickel surface. Initial results showed that, for fixed electron energy, the intensity of the electron beam decreased sharply as the scattering angle θ increased. A container of liquid air was accidentally dropped, breaking the glass jar housing the apparatus and exposing the nickel surface (which was surrounded by vacuum) to air, oxidising it. To remove the oxide, Davisson and Germer heated the surface in an atmosphere of hydrogen. The scattering of electrons was continued but now the results were very different. The intensity of the scattered electron beam varied strongly with scattering angle. After much thought, Davisson and Germer realised that they were dealing with scattering from a single crystal of nickel (that had grown on the surface as a result of heating it). Using crystals of known interatomic spacing, they eventually concluded they were seeing of electron diffraction with a wavelength given by the de Broglie formula.

Experiments showing the wave nature of the electron were carried out in 1927 by Clinton J. Davisson (1881–1958) and Lester H. Germer (1896–1971), and also by George Thomson (1892–1975), son of J.J. Thomson, the discoverer of the electron. In the Davisson–Germer experiment, electrons of kinetic energy 54 eV were directed at a surface of nickel where a single crystal had been grown and were scattered by it (Figure 12.7).

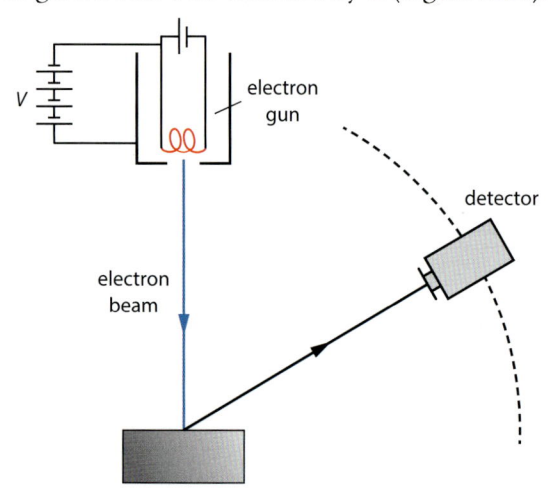

Figure 12.7 The apparatus of Davisson and Germer. Electrons emitted from the hot filament of the electron gun are accelerated through a known potential difference V and are then allowed to fall on a crystal. The positions of the scattered electrons are recorded by a detector.

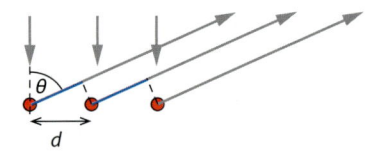

Figure 12.8 Electrons scattering off the top layer of atoms in a crystal will interfere. The path difference is shown in blue.

Because the electron energy is low, the electrons could not penetrate the crystal and were scattered by just the top layer of atoms (Figure 12.8). The path difference between successive scattered electrons is $d \sin \theta$. When this is an integer multiple of the wavelength, we have constructive interference (the argument is the same as that given in Topic 9 for the diffraction grating):

$$d \sin \theta = n\lambda$$

In the Davisson–Germer experiment the distance d was known to be 0.215 nm. The first maximum ($n = 1$) was observed at an angle $\theta = 54°$. This allows determination of the wavelength:

$$\lambda = d \sin \theta = 0.215 \times 10^{-9} \times \sin 54° = 1.7 \times 10^{-10}\,\text{m}$$

We have already calculated the de Broglie wavelength of the electron that had been accelerated by a potential difference 54 V in Worked example 12.7; it was found to be 1.7×10^{-10} m. This is in excellent agreement with the experiment, thus verifying the de Broglie hypothesis.

Pair annihilation and pair production

One of the striking features of quantum theory is the ability to convert matter into energy and vice versa. We know that for every particle there exists an anti-particle with the same mass (but opposite all other properties). What would happen if a particle collided with its anti-particle (Figure 12.9)? This process is known as **pair annihilation**.

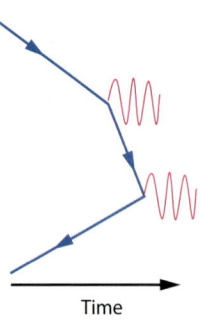

Figure 12.9 Feynman diagram for pair annihilation.

Consider for simplicity an electron of kinetic energy E_K that collides with a positron (the anti-particle of the electron) that moves in the opposite direction with the same kinetic energy. The total energy of the electron–positron system before they collide is $E_T = 2(mc^2 + E_K)$. This energy will be converted into the energy of two photons: the photons must be moving with the same energy in opposite directions and so they have the same wavelength:

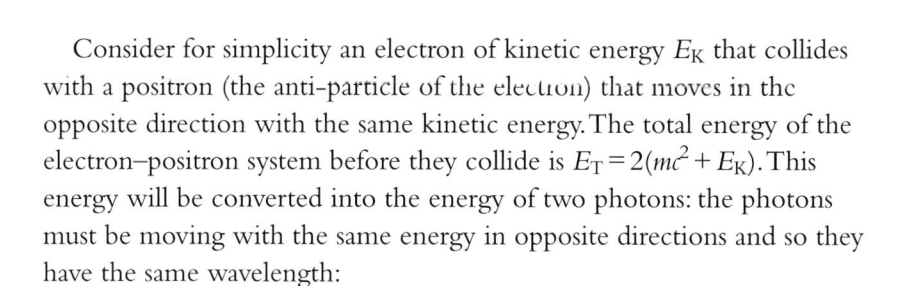

$$\lambda = \frac{hc}{mc^2 + E_K}$$

The longest wavelength will be emitted when the particles are more or less at rest, $E_K = 0$, and so in this case:

$$\lambda = \frac{hc}{mc^2}$$

$$\lambda = \frac{1.24 \times 10^{-6}}{0.511 \times 10^6} \quad \text{(recall from the IB data booklet that, for the electron, } mc^2 = 0.511 \times 10^6 \, \text{eV)}$$

$$\lambda = 2.4 \times 10^{-12} \, \text{m}$$

A **single** photon cannot materialise into a particle–anti-particle pair because such a process cannot conserve energy and momentum. But a single photon can make use of a nearby nucleus (Figure 12.10) to produce a particle–anti-particle pair. The presence of the nucleus helps conserve energy and momentum. This process of **pair creation**, in effect, is a case where energy is converted into matter.

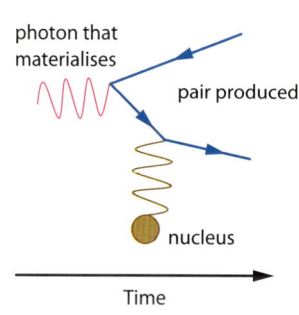

Figure 12.10 Feynman diagram for pair production. A nearby nucleus is required.

Worked example

12.8 a Estimate the wavelength of a photon that can just produce an electron–positron pair.
   b Explain why this is only an estimate and not an accurate result.

a 'Just' producing the pair means producing it at rest. Thus the energy that needs to be provided is just the rest energy of particle, i.e. $2mc^2$. This energy is therefore $2 \times 0.511 = 1.02$ MeV.
The energy of a photon is $\frac{hc}{\lambda}$ and so:

$$\frac{hc}{\lambda} = 1.02 \times 10^6$$

$$\lambda = \frac{hc}{1.02 \times 10^6}$$

$$\lambda = \frac{1.24 \times 10^{-6} \, \text{eV m}}{1.02 \times 10^6 \, \text{eV}}$$

$$\lambda = 1.2 \times 10^{-12} \, \text{m}$$

b This is only an estimate because one photon by itself cannot create the pair. It needs the presence of a nucleus that will share in energy and momentum conservation. The answer in **a** has not taken into account the nucleus.

Quantisation of angular momentum

Niels Bohr (1885–1962) was a Danish physicist who studied the hydrogen atom (Figure **12.11**). This is the simplest atom, consisting of a nucleus of a single proton and a single electron orbiting it (Figure **12.12**).

Figure 12.11 A young Niels Bohr.

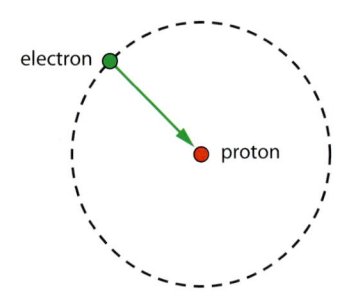

Figure 12.12 An electron orbiting a proton. The force on the electron is the electric force.

Exam tip
There is a lot of algebra in this derivation that must be learned carefully.

There are clear similarities here with the work done in Topic **10** on orbital motion in gravitation.

Exam tip
Bohr objected to the Rutherford model because an electron in orbit would emit electromagnetic radiation and so would plunge into the nucleus. Bohr assumed that the electron could only exist in orbits satisfying the angular momentum quantization condition. In these orbits the electron would not radiate.

Let us calculate the total energy E_T of the orbiting electron. It is:

$$E_T = \underbrace{\frac{1}{2}mv^2}_{\text{kinetic}} + \underbrace{\left(-\frac{ke^2}{r}\right)}_{\text{electric potential}}$$

But the electron is acted upon by the electric force, and so:

$$\frac{ke^2}{r^2} = \frac{mv^2}{r}$$

From this we deduce that $mv^2 = \frac{ke^2}{r}$, and so the total energy becomes:

$$E_T = \frac{1}{2}\frac{ke^2}{r} - \frac{ke^2}{r}$$

$$E_T = -\frac{1}{2}\frac{ke^2}{r}$$

At this point Bohr made the revolutionary assumption that the **angular momentum** of the orbiting electron, i.e. the quantity $L = mvr$, is quantised. By this he meant that L is an integral multiple of a basic unit, the unit being $\frac{h}{2\pi}$. Here h is Planck's constant. The Bohr condition is therefore:

$$mvr = \frac{nh}{2\pi}$$

If we accept this for a moment, then we have that:

$$m^2v^2r^2 = \frac{n^2h^2}{4\pi^2}$$

and so $mv^2 = \frac{n^2h^2}{4\pi^2 mr^2}$

But earlier we found that $mv^2 = \frac{ke^2}{r}$, so substituting for mv^2 we get:

$$\frac{ke^2}{r} = \frac{n^2h^2}{4\pi^2 mr^2}$$

This gives the extraordinary result that the orbital radius cannot be anything we wish: it equals

$$r = \frac{h^2}{4\pi^2 ke^2 m} \times n^2$$

Putting in the constants (using slightly more accurate values than those listed in the data booklet) gives:

$$r = \frac{(6.626 \times 10^{-34})^2}{4\pi^2 \times 8.988 \times 10^9 \times (1.602 \times 10^{-19})^2 \times 9.109 \times 10^{-31}} \times n^2$$

$$r = 0.5 \times 10^{-10} \times n^2 \, \text{m}$$

What is now even more extraordinary is that the total energy of the orbiting electron is:

$$E = -\frac{2\pi^2 me^4 k^2}{h^2} \times \frac{1}{n^2}$$

We can combine all the constants in the first term in the expression as C, to give:

$$E = -\frac{C}{n^2}$$

Here k is the constant in Coulomb's law, m is the mass of the electron, e is the charge of the electron and h is Planck's constant. Numerically (again, using slightly more accurate values) C equals:

$$C = \frac{2\pi^2 (9.109 \times 10^{-31})(1.602 \times 10^{-19})^4 (8.988 \times 10^9)^2}{(6.626 \times 10^{-34})^2} \times n^2$$

$$C = 2.170 \times 10^{-18} \, \text{J}$$

$$C = 13.6 \, \text{eV}$$

So that finally, we obtain:

$$E = -\frac{13.6}{n^2} \, \text{eV}$$

In other words, the theory predicts that the electron in the hydrogen atom has discrete or **quantised energy**. As we saw in Topic 7, this explains the emission and absorption spectra of hydrogen.

Worked examples

12.9 In gravitation the period of revolution T of a planet in a circular orbit of radius R around the Sun obeys $T^2 \propto R^3$. Deduce the corresponding relation in the Bohr hydrogen model for an electron.

We know that $v^2 = \dfrac{ke^2}{mr}$ and so $\left(\dfrac{2\pi r}{T}\right) = \dfrac{ke^2}{mr}$ leading to $T^2 \propto R^3$ as in gravitation.

12.10 Before Bohr, Johann Balmer (1825–1898) deduced experimentally that the photons emitted in transitions from a level n to the level $n = 2$ of hydrogen have wavelengths given by:

$$\lambda = \dfrac{Bn^2}{n^2 - 4}$$

where B is a constant. Justify this formula on the basis of the Bohr theory for hydrogen and find an expression for the constant B.

Balmer considered transitions from an energy level n down to the energy level 2. Let the difference in energy of the electron in level n and level $n = 2$ be ΔE. Then:

$$\Delta E = -\dfrac{C}{n^2} - \left(-\dfrac{C}{2^2}\right)$$

where $C = \dfrac{2\pi^2 m e^4 k^2}{h^2}$. This energy ΔE is equal to the energy of the emitted photon, i.e. $\dfrac{hc}{\lambda}$. Thus:

$$\dfrac{hc}{\lambda} = \dfrac{C}{n^2} - \left(-\dfrac{C}{2^2}\right)$$

$$\dfrac{1}{\lambda} = \dfrac{C}{hc}\left(\dfrac{1}{4} - \dfrac{1}{n^2}\right)$$

$$\dfrac{1}{\lambda} = \dfrac{C}{hc} \times \left(\dfrac{n^2 - 4}{4n^2}\right)$$

This implies finally that $\lambda = \dfrac{4hc}{C} \times \dfrac{n^2}{n^2 - 4}$

This is precisely Balmer's formula with $B = \dfrac{4hc}{C}$

12.11 Show that the Bohr condition for the quantisation of angular momentum is equivalent to $2\pi r = n\lambda$, where λ is the de Broglie wavelength of the electron and r the radius of its orbit.

The Bohr condition is that: $mvr = \dfrac{nh}{2\pi}$

This can be re-written as: $2\pi r = \dfrac{nh}{mv}$

But according to de Broglie, $\dfrac{h}{mv} = \lambda$, and so we have the result.

The result of Worked example **12.11** shows that the allowed orbits in the Bohr model of hydrogen are those for which an integral number of electron wavelengths fit on the circumference of the orbit. Figure **12.13** shows the electron wave for $n=6$. The circle in blue is the actual orbit. The solid red and the dotted red lines show the extremes of the electron wave. This is reminiscent of standing waves: the electron wave is a standing wave on the circumference. We know that standing waves do not transfer energy. This is a partial way to understand why the electrons do not radiate when in the allowed orbits.

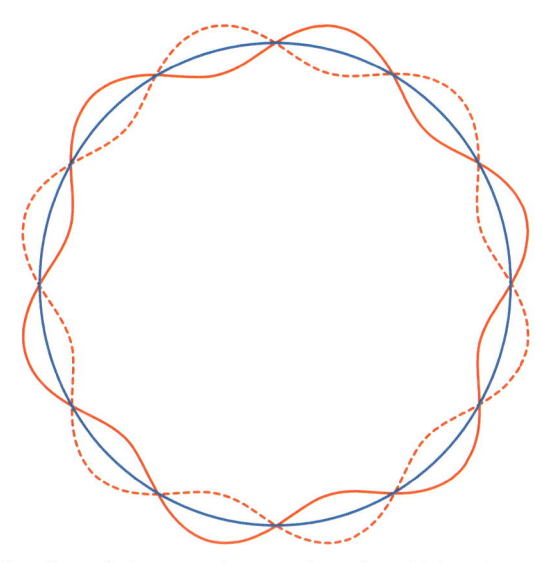

Figure 12.13 The allowed electron orbits are those for which an integral number of electron wavelengths fits on the circumference of the orbit.

The wavefunction

In the section on matter waves we said that particles exhibit wave-like behaviour; in the previous section we showed that the electron wave is a standing wave on the circumference of the orbit. But we have never specified what kind of waves we are talking about.

In 1926 the Austrian physicist Erwin Schrödinger (1887–1961) (Figure **12.14**) provided a realistic, quantum model for the behaviour of electrons in any atom – not just the hydrogen atom. The **Schrödinger theory** assumes as a basic principle that there is a wave associated with the electron (very much like de Broglie had assumed). This wave is called the **wavefunction**, $\psi(x, t)$, and is a function of position x and time t. Given the forces that act on the electron, it is possible, in principle, to solve a complicated differential equation obeyed by the wavefunction (the Schrödinger equation) and obtain $\psi(x, t)$. For example, there is one wavefunction for a free electron, another for an electron in the hydrogen atom, etc.

The interpretation of what $\psi(x, t)$ really means came from the German physicist Max Born (1882–1970). He suggested that the **probability** $P(x, t)$ that an electron will be found within a small volume ΔV near position x at time t is:

$$P(x, t) = |\psi(x, t)|^2 \Delta V$$

Figure 12.14 Erwin Schrödinger.

The theory only gives probabilities for finding an electron somewhere – it does not pinpoint an electron at a particular point in space. This is a radical change from classical physics, where objects have well-defined positions.

The Copenhagen interpretation of quantum mechanics

Through Bohr's own work and the numerous discussions of Bohr with his visitors at his institute at Blegdamsvej 17 in Copenhagen, the presently accepted interpretation of quantum mechanics is called the **Copenhagen interpretation**. It states that any physically meaningful quantity about a system can only be obtained from knowledge of its Schrödinger wavefunction, ψ. It also states that at any one time the system's wavefunction is a **superposition of all possible states** available to the system and that once a measurement is made that shows, for example, that the system has a particular momentum, then the wavefunction collapses to a wavefunction representing that particular momentum.

Not everyone has been comfortable with this interpretation. Schrödinger himself devised a situation that purports to show this interpretation is not sound. He thought of a cat in a box along with some radioactive atoms and a flask of poison. By some arrangement, if an atom decays the flask breaks releasing the poison and killing the cat. So the wavefunction of the cat is a superposition of the two states available to the cat, dead or alive. If we open the box and see that the cat is alive then the cat's wavefunction collapses to one representing a live cat. But before opening the box we don't know. This bothers many physicists. Physics Nobel prize winner Steven Weinberg says in a July 2013 interview in *Physics Today*:

> Some very good theorists seem to be happy with an interpretation of quantum mechanics in which the wavefunction only serves to allow us to calculate the results of measurements. But the measuring apparatus and the physicist are presumably also governed by quantum mechanics, so ultimately we need interpretive postulates that do not distinguish apparatus or physicists from the rest of the world, and from which the usual postulates like the Born rule can be deduced. This effort seems to lead to something like a 'many worlds' interpretation, which I find repellent. Alternatively, one can try to modify quantum mechanics so that the wavefunction does describe reality, and collapses stochastically and nonlinearly, but this seems to open up the possibility of instantaneous communication. I work on the interpretation of quantum mechanics from time to time, but have gotten nowhere.

So, finally, the kind of wave that we are referring to is a probability wave: a wave that gives the probability of finding a particle near a particular position. So when we say that the scattered electrons in the Davisson–Germer experiment interfere, what we mean is that the probability waves of the electrons interfere.

When the Schrödinger theory is applied to the electron in a hydrogen atom, it gives all the results that Bohr derived (the correct energy levels, for example). But it also predicts the probability that a particular transition will occur. This is necessary in order to understand why some spectral lines are brighter than others. Thus the Schrödinger theory explains atomic spectra for hydrogen and all other elements.

The uncertainty principle

The Heisenberg uncertainty principle is named after Werner Heisenberg (1901–1976), one of the founders of quantum mechanics (Figure **12.15**). He discovered the principle in 1927. The basic idea behind it is the wave–particle duality. Particles sometimes behave like waves and waves sometimes behave like particles, so that we cannot cleanly divide physical objects as either particles or waves.

Duality

We have seen conflicting descriptions of physical objects. In Topic **9** we saw clear evidence that light behaves as a wave. In Topic **12** we see that light behaves as particles. In Topic **5** the motion of electrons in electric and magnetic fields was seen to obey the laws of Newtonian particle mechanics. In Topic **12** de Broglie tells us that electrons diffract the way waves do. This state of affairs is called the duality of matter – it shows the inadequacy of ordinary language to provide adequate descriptions of physical objects. It is made worse when we realise that two-slit interference experiments have been performed with light that is so weak that photons go through the slits one at a time. If so, what is the one photon going through a slit at a particular instant of time interfering with? Similar arguments may be made for electrons going through slits one at a time. The way out is to insist that the correct description during the passage through the slits is the wave description. In that case we can understand interference because a wave describes the object through the slits and the wave, because of its spread-out wavefront, covers both slits.

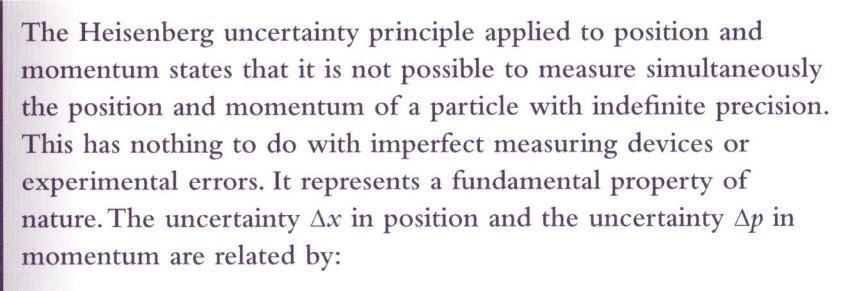

Figure 12.15 Werner Heisenberg.

The Heisenberg uncertainty principle applied to position and momentum states that it is not possible to measure simultaneously the position and momentum of a particle with indefinite precision. This has nothing to do with imperfect measuring devices or experimental errors. It represents a fundamental property of nature. The uncertainty Δx in position and the uncertainty Δp in momentum are related by:

$$\Delta x \Delta p \geq \frac{h}{4\pi}$$

where h is Planck's constant.

This says that making momentum as accurate as possible makes position inaccurate, whereas accuracy in position results in inaccuracy in momentum. In particular, if one is made zero, the other has to be infinite.

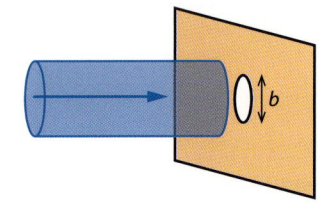

Figure 12.16 The narrower the beam, the smaller the uncertainty in the vertical position of an electron.

Where does a formula like this come from? To get a rough answer consider the following argument due to Heisenberg. Imagine a horizontal beam of electrons travelling towards a circular aperture (Figure **12.16**). We wish to make this beam as narrow as possible.

When the beam is made narrow the uncertainty in the vertical position of an electron is reduced. We can have a beam of width b if we let the beam go through a hole of diameter b. The uncertainty in position Δx is then:

$$\Delta x \approx \frac{b}{2}$$

We can make the electron beam as thin as possible by making the opening as small as possible.

However, we will run into a problem as soon as the opening becomes of the same order as the de Broglie wavelength of the electrons. A wave of wavelength λ will **diffract** when going through an aperture of about the same size as the wavelength. The electron will diffract through the opening, which means that a few electrons will emerge from the opening with a direction that is no longer horizontal.

We can describe this phenomenon by saying that there is an uncertainty in the electron's momentum in the vertical direction, of magnitude Δp. Figure **12.17** shows that there is a spreading of the electrons within an angular size 2θ.

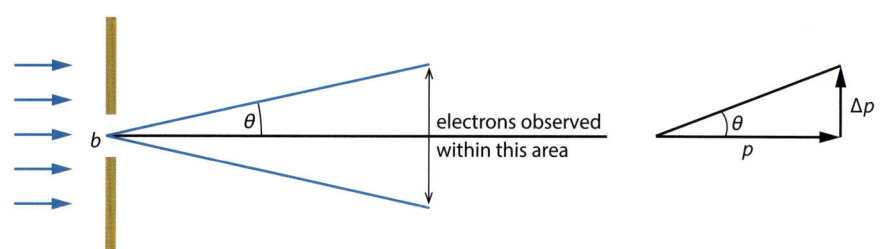

Figure 12.17 An electron passing through a slit suffers a deflection in the vertical direction.

The angle by which the electron is diffracted is given by:

$$\theta \approx \frac{\lambda}{b}$$

where b is the opening size. But from Figure **12.17**, $\theta \approx \frac{\Delta p}{p}$. Therefore:

$$\frac{\lambda}{b} \approx \frac{\Delta p}{p}$$

But $b \approx 2\Delta x$ so:

$$\frac{\lambda}{2\Delta x} \approx \frac{\Delta p}{p}$$

$$\Rightarrow \quad \Delta x \Delta p \approx \frac{\lambda p}{2}$$

The de Broglie wavelength is given by $\lambda = \frac{h}{p}$. So:

$$\Delta x \Delta p \approx \frac{h}{2}$$

This is a simple explanation of where the uncertainty formula comes from. (This is derivation is only approximate, which is why we are missing a factor of 2π.)

Worked example

12.12 A very fine beam of electrons with speed $10^6\,\text{m s}^{-1}$ are directed horizontally towards a slit whose opening is $10^{-10}\,\text{m}$. Electrons are observed on a screen at distance of 1 m from the slit. Estimate the length on the screen where appreciable numbers of electrons will be observed.

There is an uncertainty of $10^{-10}\,\text{m}$ in the vertical component of the position of the electron. Therefore there will be an uncertainty in the vertical component of momentum of:

$$\Delta p_y \approx \frac{6.63 \times 10^{-34}}{4\pi \times 10^{-10}} \approx 5 \times 10^{-25}\,\text{N s}$$

The momentum of the electrons is $p \approx 9.1 \times 10^{-31} \times 10^6 \approx 9 \times 10^{-25}\,\text{N s}$. The electrons will therefore be deviated by an angle θ given by:

$$\theta \approx \frac{\Delta p_y}{p} \approx \frac{5 \times 10^{-25}}{9 \times 10^{-25}} \approx 0.5\,\text{rad}$$

The electrons will therefore be observed in region of length $2 \times 0.5 \times 1 = 1\,\text{m}$.

'Electron in a box'

As an application of the uncertainty principle, consider an electron confined in a region of size L. The electron can only move back and forth along a straight line of length L. Then the uncertainty in position must satisfy $\Delta x \approx \frac{L}{2}$, and so the uncertainty in momentum must be:

$$\Delta p \approx \frac{h}{4\pi \Delta x} \approx \frac{h}{2\pi L}$$

The electron must then have a kinetic energy of:

$$E_K = \frac{p^2}{2m} \approx \frac{\Delta p^2}{2m} = \frac{h^2}{8\pi^2 m L^2}$$

We may apply this result to an electron in the hydrogen atom. The size of the region within which the electron is confined is about $L \approx 10^{-10}\,\text{m}$. Then:

$$E_K \approx \frac{h^2}{8\pi^2 m L^2} = \frac{(6.6 \times 10^{-34})^2}{8\pi^2 (9.1 \times 10^{-31})(10^{-10})^2}$$

$$E_K \approx 6 \times 10^{-19}\,\text{J} \approx 4\,\text{eV}$$

which is in fact just about right for the electron's kinetic energy. This shows that the uncertainty principle is an excellent tool for making approximate estimates for various quantities.

Exam tip
An uncertainty in position Δx implies an uncertainty in the momentum: $\Delta p \approx \dfrac{h}{4\pi \Delta x}$

Now the momentum will be measured to be $p_0 + \Delta p$. The least magnitude of p_0 is 0, and so the least possible magnitude of the momentum of the electron is Δp. The energy of the electron is then at least:

$$E_K \approx \frac{p^2}{2m} \approx \frac{\Delta p^2}{2m}$$

12 QUANTUM AND NUCLEAR PHYSICS (HL)

Exam tip
In the examination, the uncertainty relations will be used for rough estimates. In that case rough equalities rather than inequalities will do:

$$\Delta x \Delta p \approx \frac{h}{4\pi}$$

$$\Delta E \Delta t \approx \frac{h}{4\pi}$$

Uncertainty in energy and time

The uncertainty principle also applies to measurements of energy and time. If the energy of a state is measured with an uncertainty ΔE, then the lifetime of the state is of order Δt such that:

$$\Delta E \Delta t \geq \frac{h}{4\pi}$$

This is also applies to decaying particles, where ΔE is the uncertainty in the measured value of the energy released and Δt is the lifetime of the particle.

Worked example

12.13 In the decay $\rho^0 \to \pi^+ + \pi^-$ the uncertainty in the energy released is 153 MeV. Calculate the expected lifetime of the ρ^0 meson and hence identify the interaction through which the decay takes place.

We will apply the uncertainty relation for energy and time $\Delta t \approx \frac{h}{4\pi \Delta E}$ to get:

$$\Delta t \approx \frac{6.63 \times 10^{-34}}{4\pi \times 154 \times 10^6 \times 1.6 \times 10^{-19}}$$

$$\Delta t \approx 2 \times 10^{-24} \, \text{s}$$

Lifetimes that are this short are typical of the strong interaction.

Figure 12.18 The total energy of the ball is not enough to go over the barrier so the ball will not go over the barrier.

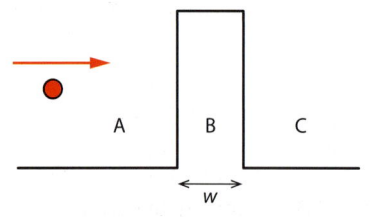

Figure 12.19 A potential barrier to a proton. The energy needed to go over is eV.

Tunnelling

Consider a ball of mass 2 kg that moves with speed 10 m s^{-1} along the path shown in Figure 12.18. The kinetic energy of the ball is 100 J. Ahead of the ball is a hill of height 6 m. If the ball was placed at the top of the hill it would have potential energy $mgh = 120$ J. The total energy of the ball is only 100 J and so we do not expect the ball to get to the top of the hill and roll down the other side.

The probability of finding the ball to the right of the hill is zero. The ball will be 'reflected' by the hill. The hill acts as a 'potential barrier' to the ball. It does not allow the ball to go over the barrier if the ball does not have enough energy to get to the top of the barrier.

In microscopic physics the corresponding situation might involve protons of total energy E that face a region of positive electric potential as shown in Figure 12.19. If the electric potential is V then the energy needed by one proton to go over the barrier is eV.

We expect that if the total energy of the proton is less than eV the proton has zero probability of moving from region A, through region B and into the 'forbidden' region C.

But one of the most impressive phenomena of quantum mechanics, **tunnelling**, makes this possible. This is intimately related to the fact that particles have wave properties and are described by wavefunctions. The Schrödinger theory must be used to determine the wavefunction of the protons in each of the three regions A, B and C in such a way that the wavefunctions in the three regions join smoothly (no jumps and no corners). This makes it necessary to have a non-zero wavefunction in region C. It is as if the wavefunction 'leaks' into region C. The probabilities are shown in Figure **12.20**.

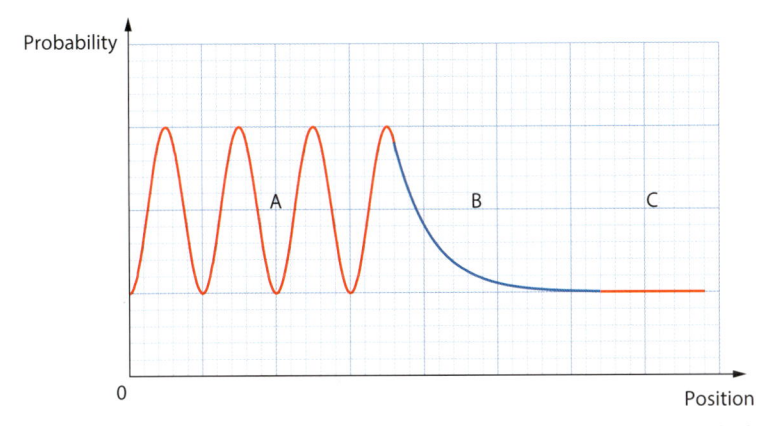

Figure 12.20 The wavefunction 'leaks' into the forbidden region C. (The graph shows the probability for finding the electron, not the wavefunction itself.)

In region A we see an oscillating probability. This is evidence for the presence of a standing wave: the wavefunction of the incoming protons gets superposed with that of the reflected protons. In region B the probability is exponentially decreasing (shown in blue). At the end of region B and the beginning of region C the probability is not zero. There is a non-zero wavefunction that describes the transmitted protons, those that tunnelled through the potential barrier. There is a small but non-zero probability of finding protons in the forbidden region C.

Three factors affect the probability of transmission:
1 the mass m of the particles
2 the width w of the barrier
3 the difference ΔE between the energy of the barrier and that of the particles.

The larger each of these quantities is, the smaller the transmission probability. In fact it is known that $p \propto \exp(-w\sqrt{m\Delta E})$. So everything else being equal, the transmission probability for electrons is greater than for protons, for example.

It is important to realise that the particles that emerge in region C have the same energy as they did in region A! Thus the de Broglie wavelength in region C is the same as in region A. Strange as it seems, the tunnelling phenomenon has very many practical applications, including the scanning tunnelling microscope (the microscope that can 'see' atoms) (Figure **12.21**) and the tunnel diode (a diode in which the current can be very quickly switched between on and off).

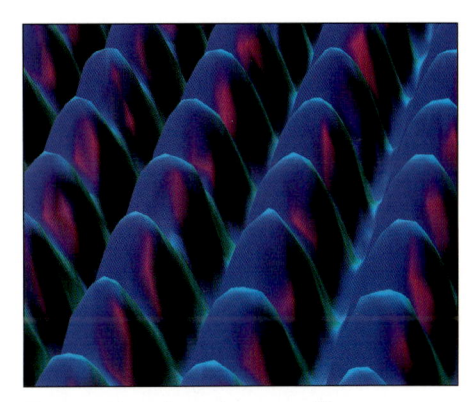

Figure 12.21 Scanning tunnelling microscope image of nickel atoms. (Image originally created by IBM Corporation.)

12 QUANTUM AND NUCLEAR PHYSICS (HL)

Nature of science

Quantum physics

The study of emission spectra from flames revealed characteristic lines that could be used to identify different elements. Observations of the spectrum of sunlight showed dark absorption lines. In the 1800s improved instruments allowed for more accurate measurements of the wavelengths of light corresponding to the bright and dark lines in spectra. But what was the reason for these lines? As we saw in Topic **7**, a quantum model was needed to explain these patterns. The first of these quantum models was the Bohr model of the hydrogen atom, which could predict the wavelengths of the lines in the spectrum of hydrogen. To explain the puzzling observations seen in the photoelectric effect, Einstein suggested that light existed as packets of energy called photons – a quantum model for light. Accepting the idea of a wave–particle duality revolutionised scientific thinking. Any moving particle could have wave-like characteristics! New ideas opened up new avenues for research, and led to the idea of the wavefunction for electrons in atoms, the uncertainty principle and probability functions. A whole new branch of physics was born – quantum physics.

Test yourself

1. **a** Explain what is meant by the **photoelectric effect**.
   b A photo-surface has a work function of 3.00 eV. Determine the critical frequency.

2. **a** What evidence is there for the existence of photons?
   b A photo-surface has a critical frequency of 2.25×10^{14} Hz. Radiation of frequency 3.87×10^{14} Hz falls on this surface. Deduce the voltage required to stop electrons from being emitted.

3. Light of wavelength 5.4×10^7 m falls on a photo-surface and causes the emission of electrons of maximum kinetic energy 2.1 eV at a rate of 10^{15} per second. The light is emitted by a 60 W light bulb.
   a Explain how light causes the emission of electrons.
   b Calculate the electric current that leaves the photo-surface.
   c Determine the work function of the surface.
   d Estimate the maximum kinetic energy of the electrons when the power of the light becomes 120 W.
   e Estimate the current from the photo-surface when the power is 120 W.

4. **a** State **three** aspects of the photoelectric effect that cannot be explained by the wave theory of light. For each, outline how the photon theory provides an explanation.
   b Light of wavelength 2.08×10^{-7} m falls on a photo-surface. The stopping voltage is 1.40 V.
   i Outline what is meant by **stopping voltage**.
   ii Calculate the largest wavelength of light that will result in emission of electrons from this photo-surface.

5. **a** The intensity of the light incident on a photo-surface is doubled while the wavelength of light stays the same. For the emitted electrons, discuss the effect of this, if any, on **i** the energy and **ii** the number of electrons emitted..
   b To determine the work function of a given photo-surface, light of wavelength 2.3×10^{-7} m is directed at the surface and the stopping voltage, V_s, recorded. When light of wavelength 1.8×10^{-7} m is used, the stopping voltage is twice as large as the previous one. Determine the work function.

6 Light falling on a metallic surface of work function 3.0 eV gives energy to the surface at a rate of 5.0×10^{-4} W per square metre of the metal's surface. Assume that an electron on the metal surface can absorb energy from an area of about 1.0×10^{-18} m².
   a Estimate how long will it will take the electron to absorb an amount of energy equal to the work function.
   b Outline the implication of this.
   c Describe how the photon theory of light explains the fact that electrons are emitted almost instantaneously with the incoming photons.

7 a From the graph of electron kinetic energy E_K versus frequency of incoming radiation, deduce:
      i the critical frequency of the photo-surface
      ii the work function.
   b What is the kinetic energy of an electron ejected when light of frequency $f = 8.0 \times 10^{14}$ Hz falls on the surface?
   c Another photo-surface has a critical frequency of 6.0×10^{14} Hz. On a copy of the graph below, sketch the variation with frequency of the emitted electrons' kinetic energy.

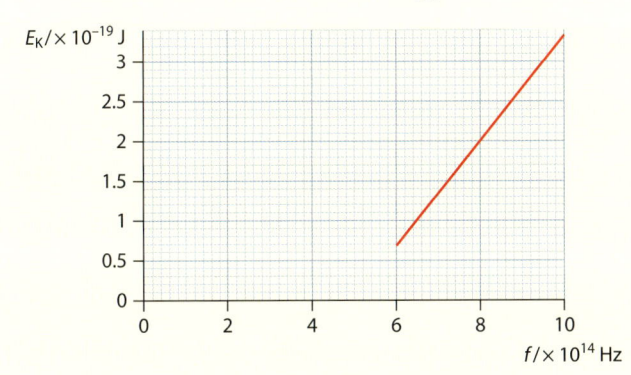

8 An electron of kinetic energy 11.5 eV collides with a hydrogen atom in its ground state. With what possible kinetic energy can this electron rebound off the atom?

9 This question will look at the intensity of radiation in a bit more detail. The intensity of light, I, incident normally on an area A is defined to be $I = \dfrac{P}{A}$, where P is the power carried by the light.
   a Show that $I = \Phi h f$, where Φ is the photon flux density, i.e. the number of photons incident on the surface per second per unit area, and f is the frequency of the light.
   b Calculate the intensity of light of wavelength $\lambda = 5.0 \times 10^{-7}$ m incident on a surface when the photon flux density is $\Phi = 3.8 \times 10^{18}$ m^{-2} s^{-1}.
   c The wavelength of the light is decreased to $\lambda = 4.0 \times 10^{-7}$ m. Calculate the new photon flux density so that the intensity of light incident on the surface is the same as that found in b.
   d Hence explain why light of wavelength $\lambda = 4.0 \times 10^{-7}$ m and of the same intensity as that of light of wavelength $\lambda = 5.0 \times 10^{-7}$ m will result in fewer electrons being emitted from the surface per second.
   e State **one** assumption made in reaching this conclusion.

10 a What is the evidence for the existence of energy levels in atoms?
   b Electrons of kinetic energy **i** 10.10 eV, **ii** 12.80 eV and **iii** 13.25 eV collide with hydrogen atoms and can excite these to higher states. In each case, find the largest n corresponding to the state the atom can be excited to. Assume that the hydrogen atoms are in their ground state initially.

11 a What do you understand by the term **ionisation energy**?
   b What is the ionisation energy for a hydrogen atom in the state $n = 3$?

12 a Find the smallest wavelength that can be emitted in a transition in atomic hydrogen.
   b What is the minimum speed an electron must have so that it can ionise an atom of hydrogen in its ground state?

13 Consider a brick of mass 0.250 kg moving at 10 m s^{-1}.
   a Estimate its de Broglie wavelength.
   b Comment on whether it makes sense to treat the brick as a wave.

14 a Describe an experiment in which the de Broglie wavelength of an electron can be measured directly.
   b Determine the speed of an electron whose de Broglie wavelength is equal to that of red light (680 nm).

15 **a** Show that the de Broglie wavelength of an electron that has been accelerated from rest through a potential difference V is given by:
$$\lambda = \frac{h}{\sqrt{2meV}}$$
   b Calculate the ratio of the de Broglie wavelength of a proton to that of an alpha particle when both have been accelerated from rest by the same potential difference.
   c Calculate the de Broglie wavelength of an electron accelerated from rest through a potential difference of 520 V.

16 **a** Find the de Broglie wavelength of a proton (mass 1.67×10^{-27} kg) whose kinetic energy is 200.0 MeV.
   b What is the de Broglie wavelength of an electron in the $n = 2$ state of hydrogen?

17 Using the uncertainty principle, show that an electron in a hydrogen atom will have a kinetic energy of a few eV.

18 **a** State the de Broglie hypothesis.
   b Calculate the de Broglie wavelength of an electron that has been accelerated by a potential difference of 5.0 V.
   c Explain why precise knowledge of the wavelength of an electron implies imprecise knowledge of its position.

19 An experimenter wishes to make a very narrow beam of electrons. To do that, she suggests the arrangement shown in the diagram. She expects that the beam can be made as narrow as possible by reducing the size b of the aperture through which the electrons will pass.

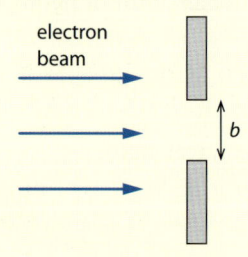

   a Explain why in principle it is not possible to make a perfectly narrow beam.
   b Are her chances of producing a narrow beam better with slow or fast electrons?

20 A tennis ball is struck so that it moves with momentum 6.0 N s straight through an open square window of side 1.0 m. Because of the uncertainty principle, the tennis ball may deviate from its original path after going through the window. Estimate the angle of deviation of the path of the tennis ball. Comment on your answer.

21 Theoretically it is possible in principle to balance a pencil on its tip so that it stands vertically on a horizontal table. Explain why in quantum theory this is impossible in principle. (You can turn this problem into a good theoretical extended essay if you try to estimate the time the pencil will stay up after it has been momentarily balanced!)

22 The graphs represent the wavefunctions of two electrons. Identify the electron with:
   a the least uncertainty in momentum
   b the least uncertainty in position.
   Explain your answers.

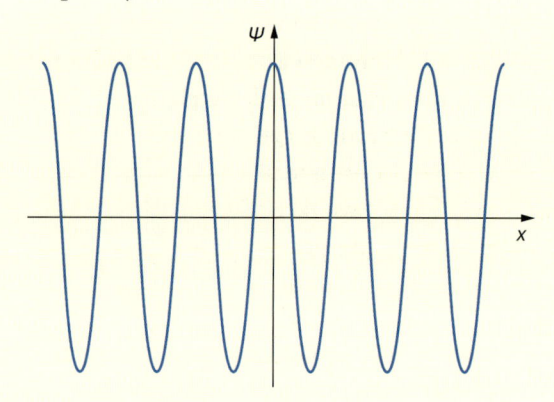

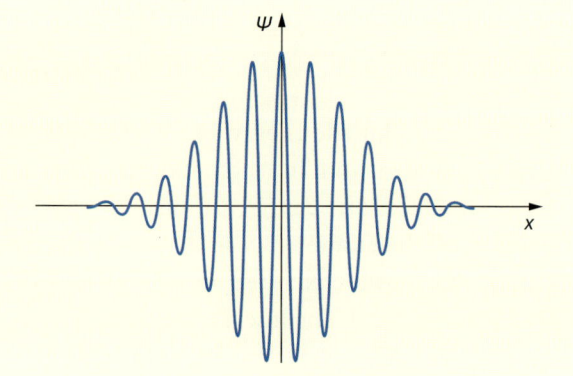

23 Assume that an electron can exist within a nucleus (size 10^{-15} m) such that its associated wave forms a first harmonic mode standing wave with nodes at the edges of the nucleus.
  a Estimate the wavelength of this electron.
  b Calculate the kinetic energy of the electron in MeV.
  c Using your answer in **b**, comment on whether the electron emitted in beta-minus decay could have existed within the nucleus before the decay.

12.2 Nuclear physics

In this section we will examine ideas we met earlier in some more detail. These include Rutherford scattering (and more importantly, deviations from it), nuclear energy levels, the neutrino and the mathematics of radioactive decay.

Rutherford scattering

In scattering experiments such as Rutherford's (see Section **7.3**), simple energy considerations can be used to calculate the **distance of closest approach** of the incoming particle to the target. Consider, as an example, an alpha particle (of charge $q = 2e$) that is projected head-on toward a stationary nucleus of charge $Q = Ze$ (Figure **12.22**).

Initially the system has a total energy consisting of the alpha particle's kinetic energy $E = E_K$. We take the separation of the alpha particle and the nucleus to be large so no potential energy exists. At the point of closest approach, a distance d from the centre of the nucleus, the alpha particle stops and is about to turn back. Thus, the total energy now is the electric potential energy of the alpha and the nucleus, given by:

$$E = k\frac{Qq}{d}$$

$$E = k\frac{(2e)(Ze)}{d}$$

$$E = k\frac{2Ze^2}{d}$$

(We are assuming that the nucleus does not recoil, so its kinetic energy is ignored.)
Then, by conservation of energy:

$$E_K = k\frac{2Ze^2}{d}$$

$$\Rightarrow \quad d = k\frac{2Ze^2}{E_K}$$

Learning objectives

- Understand how the Rutherford scattering experiment led to the idea of the nucleus.
- Discuss how scattering experiments may be used to determine nuclear radii.
- Understand the nature of nuclear energy levels.
- Understand the nature of the neutrino.
- Solve problems involving the radioactive decay law.

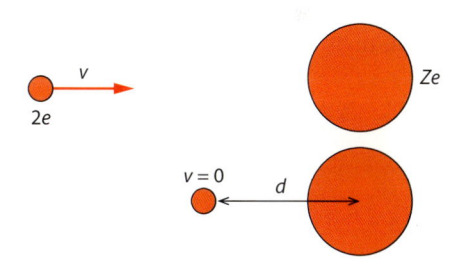

Figure 12.22 The closest approach of an alpha particle happens in a head-on collision.

Assuming a kinetic energy for the alpha particle equal to 2.0 MeV directed at a gold nucleus ($Z=79$) gives $d = 1.1 \times 10^{-13}$ m. This is outside the range of the nuclear force, so the alpha particle is simply repelled by the electrical force.

If the energy of the incoming particle is increased, the distance of closest approach decreases. The smallest it can get will be the radius of the nucleus. Experiments of this kind have been used to estimate the nuclear radii. A result of these experiments is that the nuclear radius R depends on mass number A through:

$$R = R_0 A^{\frac{1}{3}} \quad \text{where} \quad R_0 = 1.2 \times 10^{-15} \text{ m}$$

This has the unexpected consequence that all nuclei have the same density. Worked example **12.14** shows how this is derived.

Worked example

12.14 Show that all nuclei have the same density.

The volume is:

$$V = \frac{4\pi}{3} R^3$$

But $R = R_0 A^{\frac{1}{3}}$, so:

$$V = \frac{4\pi}{3} (1.2 \times 10^{-15} \times A^{\frac{1}{3}})^3$$

$$V = 7.24 \times 10^{-45} \times A \text{ m}^3$$

The mass of the nucleus is A u, i.e. $A \times 1.66 \times 10^{-27}$ kg. Using density = $\frac{\text{mass}}{\text{volume}}$, the density is:

$$\rho = \frac{\cancel{A} \times 1.66 \times 10^{-27}}{7.24 \times 10^{-45} \times \cancel{A}} \quad \text{(note how } A \text{ cancels out)}$$

$$\rho \approx 2.3 \times 10^{17} \text{ kg m}^{-3}$$

So all nuclei have the same density.

Another set of experiments aimed at determining nuclear radii involve sending beams of neutrons or electrons at nuclei. We know from diffraction that if the de Broglie wavelength λ of the electrons or neutrons is about the same as that of the nuclear diameter, the electrons and neutrons will diffract around the nuclei. A minimum will be formed at an angle θ to the original direction according to:

$$\sin \theta \approx \frac{\lambda}{b}$$

where b is the diameter of the diffracting object, i.e. the nucleus. (We met this relationship for diffraction in Topic **9**.) The advantage of using electrons is that the strong force does not act upon them and so they probe the nuclear charge distribution. Neutrons also have an advantage because, being neutral, they can penetrate deep into matter and get very close to the nucleus.

Worked example

12.15 In a neutron diffraction experiment, a beam of neutrons of energy 85 MeV are incident on a foil made out of lead and diffracted. The first diffraction minimum is observed at an angle of 13° relative to the central position where most of the neutrons are observed. From this information, estimate the radius of the lead nucleus.

The neutrons are diffracted from the lead nuclei, which act as 'obstacles' of size b. From our knowledge of diffraction, the first minimum is given by $\sin\theta \approx \frac{\lambda}{b}$, where λ is the de Broglie wavelength of the neutron.

The mass of a neutron is $m = 1.67 \times 10^{-27}$ kg and, since its kinetic energy is 85 MeV, the wavelength is $\lambda = \frac{h}{p}$ where:

$$p = \sqrt{2E_K m}$$

$$p = \sqrt{2 \times 85 \times 10^6 \times 1.6 \times 10^{-19} \times 1.67 \times 10^{-27}}$$

$$p = 2.13 \times 10^{-19} \text{ N s}$$

Using this value of p in the equation for wavelength:

$$\lambda = \frac{6.6 \times 10^{-34}}{2.13 \times 10^{-19}}$$

$$\lambda = 3.1 \times 10^{-15} \text{ m}$$

Therefore the diameter of the nucleus is given by:

$$b = \frac{\lambda}{\sin 13°} = \frac{3.1 \times 10^{-15}}{\sin 13°}$$

$$b = 14 \times 10^{-15} \text{ m}$$

This corresponds to a radius of 7×10^{-15} m.

Deviations from Rutherford scattering

Rutherford derived a theoretical formula for the scattering of alpha particles from nuclei. The Rutherford formula states that as the scattering angle θ increases, the number of alpha particles scattered at that angle decreases very sharply. This is shown in Figure **12.23a**. In fact, Rutherford's formula states that the number N of alpha particles scattering at an angle θ is proportional to $1/\sin^4\left(\frac{\theta}{2}\right)$. If this is the case, the product $N\sin^4\left(\frac{\theta}{2}\right)$ should be constant. Table **12.1** contains some of the original

Angle of scattering, $\theta/°$	N	$N\sin^4\left(\dfrac{\theta}{2}\right)$
15	132 000	38.4
30	7 800	35.0
45	1 435	30.8
60	477	29.8
75	211	29.1
105	69	27.5
120	52	29.0
150	33	28.8

Table 12.1 Data from the Geiger–Marsden experiment, reproduced in the book by E. Rutherford, J. Chadwick and C. D. Ellis *Radiations from Radioactive Substances*, Cambridge University Press, 1930.

data in the Geiger–Marsden experiment with a gold foil. The last column in the table shows that the product $N\sin^4\left(\dfrac{\theta}{2}\right)$ is indeed fairly constant, which is strong evidence in support of the Rutherford formula.

The derivation of the Rutherford formula is based on a number of assumptions. The most important is that the only force in play during the scattering process is the electric force. As the energy of the alpha particles increases, the alpha particles can get closer to the nucleus. When the distance of closest approach gets to be about 10^{-15} m or less, deviations from the Rutherford formula are observed (Figure **12.23b**). This is due to the fact that the alpha particles are so close to the nucleus that the strong nuclear force begins to act on the alpha particles.

> Therefore, the presence of these deviations from perfect Rutherford scattering is evidence for the existence of the strong nuclear force.

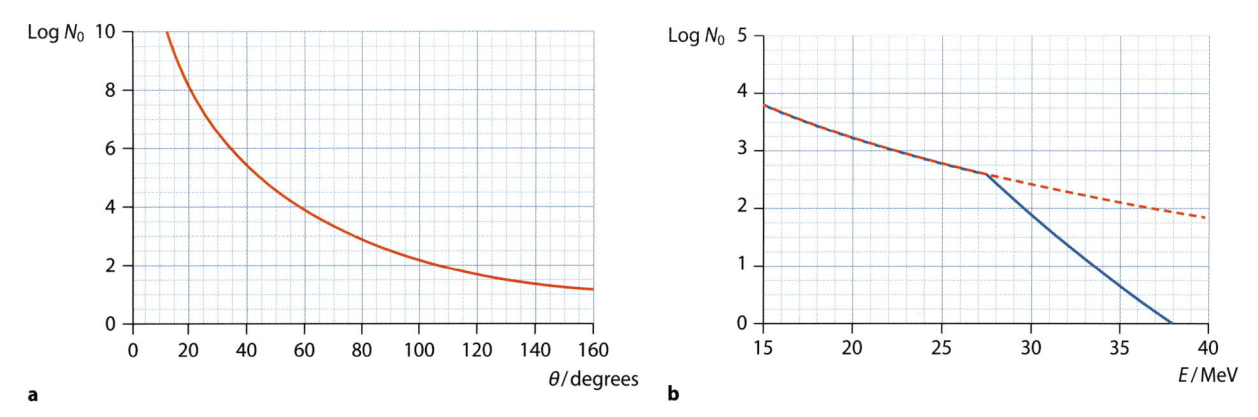

Figure 12.23 a The logarithm of the number of alpha particles scattered at some angle θ as a function of θ. **b** The logarithm of the number of alpha particles scattered at an angle of 60° as a function of the alpha particle energy. The dotted curve is based on Rutherford scattering. The blue curve is the observed curve. We see deviations when the energy exceeds about 28 MeV. The energy at which deviations start may be used to estimate the nuclear radius.

Worked example

12.16 Suggest how the results of the scattering of alpha particles would change if the gold ($^{197}_{79}$Au) foil was replaced by an aluminium ($^{30}_{13}$Al) foil of the same thickness.

Aluminium has a smaller nuclear charge and so the alpha particles would approach closer to the nucleus. This means that the alpha particles would start feeling the effects of the nuclear force and deviations from perfect Rutherford scattering would be observed.

Nuclear energy levels

The nucleus, like the atom, exists in discrete energy levels. The main evidence for the existence of nuclear energy levels comes from the fact that the energies of the alpha particles and gamma ray photons that are emitted by nuclei in alpha and gamma decays are **discrete**. (This is to be contrasted with beta decays, in which the electron has a continuous range of energies.)

Figure **12.24** shows the lowest nuclear energy levels of the magnesium nucleus $^{24}_{12}$Mg. Also shown is a gamma decay from the level with energy 5.24 MeV to the first excited state. The emitted photon has energy 5.24 − 1.37 = 3.87 MeV.

Figure **12.25** shows an energy level of plutonium ($^{242}_{94}$Pu) and a few of the energy levels of uranium ($^{238}_{92}$U). Also shown are two transitions from plutonium to uranium energy levels. These are alpha decays:

$$^{242}_{94}\text{Pu} \rightarrow {}^{238}_{92}\text{U} + {}^{4}_{2}\alpha$$

The energies of the emitted alpha particles are 4.983 − 0.148 = 4.835 MeV and 4.983 − 0.307 = 4.676 MeV.

Worked example **12.17**, overleaf applies these ideas to beta decay.

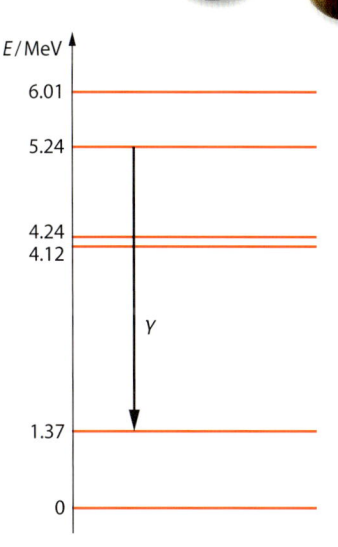

Figure 12.24 Nuclear energy levels of magnesium, $^{24}_{12}$Mg. Notice the difference in scale between these levels and atomic energy levels.

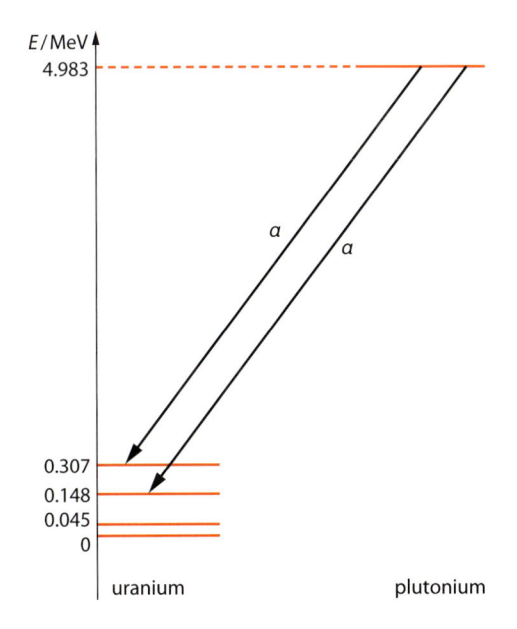

Figure 12.25 Energy levels for plutonium and uranium. Transitions from plutonium to uranium energy levels explain the discrete nature of the emitted alpha particle in the alpha decay of plutonium.

12 QUANTUM AND NUCLEAR PHYSICS (HL)

Worked example

12.17 The nucleus of bismuth ($^{211}_{83}$Bi) decays into lead ($^{207}_{82}$Pb) in a two-stage process. In the first stage, bismuth decays into polonium ($^{211}_{84}$Po). Polonium then decays into lead. The nuclear energy levels that are involved in these decays are shown in Figure **12.26**.

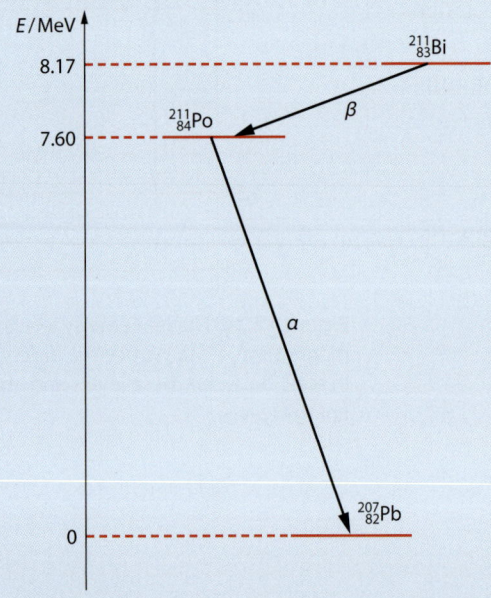

Figure 12.26 The two-stage decay of bismuth into lead.

- **a** Write down the reaction equations for each decay.
- **b** Calculate the energy released in the beta decay.
- **c** Explain why the electron does not always have this energy.

a $^{211}_{83}\text{Bi} \rightarrow {}^{211}_{84}\text{Po} + {}^{0}_{-1}e + {}^{0}_{0}\bar{\nu}$ and $^{211}_{84}\text{Po} \rightarrow {}^{207}_{82}\text{Pb} + {}^{4}_{2}\alpha$

b The energy released is the difference in the energy levels involved in the transition, i.e. 0.57 MeV.

c The energy of 0.57 MeV must be shared between the electron, the anti-neutrino and the polonium nucleus. So the electron does not always have the maximum energy of 0.57 MeV. Depending on the angles (between the electron, the anti-neutrino and the polonium nucleus), the electron energy can be anything from zero up to the maximum value found in **b**.

The neutrino

In the 1930s it was thought that beta minus decay was described by:

$$^{1}_{0}n \rightarrow {}^{1}_{1}p + {}^{0}_{-1}e$$

The mass difference for this decay is:

$$1.008665\,u - (1.007276 + 0.0005486)\,u = 0.00084\,u$$

and corresponds to an energy of:

$$Q = 0.00084 \times 931.5\,\text{MeV} = 0.783\,\text{MeV}$$

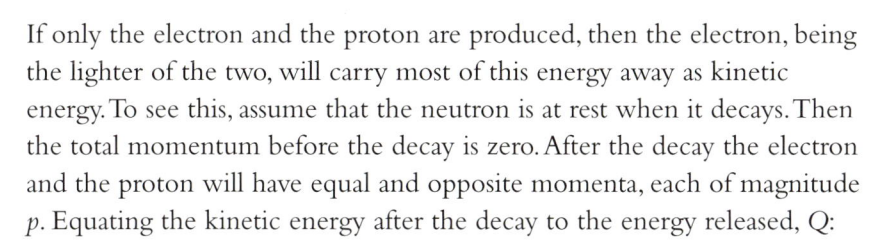

If only the electron and the proton are produced, then the electron, being the lighter of the two, will carry most of this energy away as kinetic energy. To see this, assume that the neutron is at rest when it decays. Then the total momentum before the decay is zero. After the decay the electron and the proton will have equal and opposite momenta, each of magnitude p. Equating the kinetic energy after the decay to the energy released, Q:

$$\frac{p^2}{2m_e} + \frac{p^2}{2m_p} = Q$$

$$p^2 = \frac{2Qm_e m_p}{m_e + m_p}$$

And so:

$$E_e = \frac{p^2}{2m_e} = \frac{Qm_p}{(m_e + m_p)}$$

$$E_e = \frac{0.783 \times 1.007}{5.49 \times 10^{-4} + 1.007}$$

$$E_e = 0.78257 \approx 0.783 \, \text{MeV}$$

Thus, we should observe electrons with kinetic energies of about 0.783 MeV. In experiments, however, the electron has a **range** of energies from zero up to 0.783 MeV (Figure 12.27) If the electron is not carrying 0.783 MeV of energy, where is the missing energy?

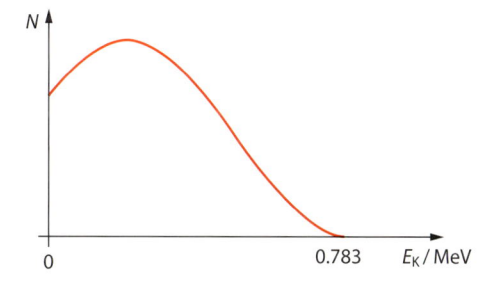

Figure 12.27 The number of electrons that carry a given energy as a function of energy.

Wolfgang Pauli hypothesised the existence of a third particle in the products of a beta decay in 1933. Since the energy of the electron in beta decay has a range of possible values, it means that a third very light particle must also be produced so that it carries the remainder of the available energy.

Enrico Fermi coined the word **neutrino** for the 'little neutral one' (Fermi is shown with Pauli and Heisenberg in Figure **12.28**).

Figure 12.28 W. Pauli (right), E. Fermi (left) either side of W. Heisenberg.

12 QUANTUM AND NUCLEAR PHYSICS (HL)

Research into neutrino physics is a great example of very large international research teams that work together and collaborate widely (by the Kamiokande and the super Kamiokande Japanese–American collaboration, the GALLEX and SAGE groups in Italy and Russia and the SNO (the Solar Neutrino Observatory) in Canada with Canadian, American and British participation).

As the neutrino is electrically neutral, it has no electromagnetic interactions. Its mass is negligibly small and so gravitational interactions are irrelevant. It is a lepton, so it does not have strong interactions. This leaves the weak interaction as the only interaction with which the neutrino can interact. This means that the neutrino can go through matter with very few interactions. In fact, about 10 billion neutrinos pass through your thumbnail every second, yet you do not feel a thing. For every 100 billion neutrinos that go through the Earth only one interacts with an atom in the Earth! Most of the neutrinos that arrive at Earth are produced in the Sun in the fusion reaction $p + p \rightarrow {}^{2}_{1}H + e^{+} + \nu_e$. Read the fascinating story of the solar neutrino problem in the Nature of science section at the end of this topic.

The radioactive decay law

As discussed in Topic 7, the law of radioactive decay states that the rate of decay is proportional to the number of nuclei present that have not yet decayed:

$$\frac{dN}{dt} = -\lambda N$$

The constant of proportionality is denoted by λ and is called the **decay constant**. To see the meaning of the decay constant we argue as follows: in a short time interval dt the number of nuclei that will decay is $dN = \lambda N \, dt$ (we ignore the minus sign). The probability that any one nucleus will decay is therefore:

$$\text{probability} = \frac{dN}{N}$$

$$\text{probability} = \frac{N\lambda \, dt}{N}$$

$$\text{probability} = \lambda \, dt$$

and finally, the probability of decay per unit time is:

$$\frac{\text{probability}}{dt} = \lambda$$

> The decay constant λ is the probability of decay per unit time.

The decay law is a differential equation, which when integrated gives:

$$N = N_0 e^{-\lambda t}$$

This is the number of nuclei present at time t given that the initial number (at $t = 0$) is N_0.

As expected, the number of nuclei of the decaying element decreases exponentially as time goes on (Figure **12.29**).

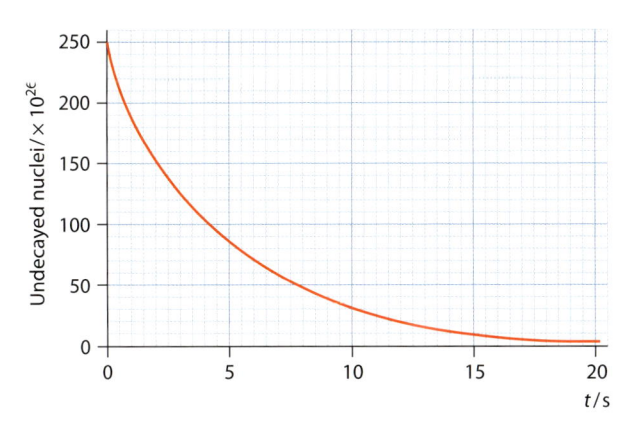

Figure 12.29 Radioactive decay follows an exponential decay law.

The (negative) rate of decay (i.e. the number of decays per second) is called **activity**, A:

$$A = -\frac{dN}{dt}$$

It follows from the exponential decay law that activity also satisfies an exponential law:

$$A = \lambda N_0 e^{-\lambda t}$$

Thus, the initial activity of a sample is given by the product of the decay constant and the number of atoms initially present, $A_0 = \lambda N_0$. Notice also that $A = \lambda N$.

After one half-life, $T_{\frac{1}{2}}$, half of the nuclei present have decayed and the activity has been reduced to half its initial value. So using either the formula for N or A (here we use the N formula):

$$\frac{N_0}{2} = N_0 e^{-\lambda t}$$

Taking logarithms we find:

$$\lambda T_{\frac{1}{2}} = \ln 2$$

$$\lambda T_{\frac{1}{2}} = 0.693$$

This is the relationship between the decay constant and the half-life.

Exam tip
It is important to know that the initial activity A_0 is λN_0.

Exam tip
A graph of A versus N gives a straight line whose slope is the decay constant.

Worked examples

12.18 Carbon-14 has a half-life of 5730 yr and in living organisms it has a decay rate of $0.25\,\text{Bq}\,\text{g}^{-1}$. A quantity of 20 g of carbon-14 was extracted from an ancient bone and its activity was found to be 1.81 Bq. What is the age of the bone?

Using the relationship between decay constant and half-life:

$$\lambda = \frac{\ln 2}{T_{\frac{1}{2}}}$$

$$\lambda = \frac{\ln 2}{5730} \text{yr}^{-1}$$

$$\lambda = 1.21 \times 10^{-4} \text{yr}^{-1}$$

When the bone was part of the living body the 20 g would have had an activity of $20 \times 0.25 = 5.0$ Bq. If the activity now is 1.81 Bq, then:

$$A = A_0 e^{-\lambda t}$$

$$1.81 = 5.0 e^{-1.21 \times 10^{-4} t}$$

$$e^{-1.21 \times 10^{-4} t} = 0.362$$

$$-1.21 \times 10^{-4} t = -1.016$$

$$t = \frac{1.016}{1.21 \times 10^{-4}}$$

$$t \approx 8400 \text{ yr}$$

12.19 A container is filled with a quantity of a pure radioactive element X whose half-life is 5.0 minutes. Element X decays into a stable element Y. At time zero no quantity of element Y is present. Determine the time at which the ratio of atoms of Y to atoms of X is 5.

After time t the number of atoms of element X is given by $N = N_0 e^{-\lambda t}$. And the number of atoms of element Y is given by $N = N_0 - N_0 e^{-\lambda t}$. The decay constant is $\lambda = \frac{\ln 2}{5.0} = 0.1386 \text{ min}^{-1}$ and so we have that:

$$\frac{N_0 - N_0 e^{-0.1386t}}{N_0 e^{-0.1386t}} = 5$$

$$1 - e^{-0.1386t} = 5 e^{-0.1386t}$$

$$e^{-0.1386t} = \frac{1}{6}$$

$$0.1386 \times t = 1.7981$$

$$t = 12.9 \text{ min}$$

Nature of science

The solar neutrino problem

In 1968, Ray Davis announced results of an experiment that tried to determine the number neutrinos arriving at Earth from the Sun. The idea was that the very rare interaction of neutrinos with ordinary chlorine would produce radioactive chlorine atoms that could then be detected, and hence the number of neutrinos determined. The results showed that the number of neutrinos was about one-third of what the theoretical calculation predicted. This created the 'solar neutrino problem'. There were three ways out: either the Davis experiment was wrong or the theory was wrong, or there was new physics involved.

Happily, it turned out that it was the last possibility that actually was in play. The number of neutrinos predicted by theory was based on the assumption that the neutrino was massless. If the neutrino had mass, then the theory would have to be modified because in that case 'neutrino oscillations' would take place. This is a rare quantum phenomenon, in which the three types of neutrinos could turn into each other. The Davis and subsequent experiments all measured electron neutrinos. Much later, when advances in instrumentation and computing power allowed experiments to detect all three types of neutrinos, the number was in agreement with the theory. But the neutrinos produced in the Sun were only electron neutrinos!

By this time, experiments in Japan and elsewhere provided convincing evidence that neutrinos had a tiny mass. So, because of neutrino oscillations, by the time the electron neutrinos reached Earth some of them had turned into muon neutrinos and some into tau neutrinos. On the average, about one-third would be electron neutrinos, in agreement with Davis's results! Ray Davis shared the 2002 Nobel prize in Physics.

Test yourself

24 An alpha particle is fired head-on at a stationary gold nucleus from far away. Calculate the initial speed of the particle so that the distance of closest approach is 8.5×10^{-15} m. (Take the mass of the alpha particle to be 6.64×10^{-27} kg.)

25 A particle of mass m and charge e is directed from very far away toward a massive ($M \gg m$) object of charge $+Ze$ with a velocity v, as shown in the diagram. The distance of closest approach is d. Sketch (on the same axes) a graph to show the variation with separation of:
 a the particle's kinetic energy
 b the particle's electric potential energy.

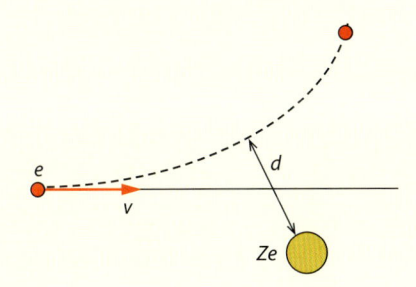

26 a Deviations from Rutherford scattering are expected when the alpha particles reach large energies. Suggest an explanation for this observation.
 b Some alpha particles are directed at a thin foil of gold ($Z=79$) and some others at a thin foil of aluminium ($Z=13$). Initially, all alpha particles have the same energy. This energy is gradually increased. Predict in which case deviations from Rutherford scattering will first be observed.

27 Show that the nuclear density is the same for all nuclei. (Take the masses of the proton and neutron to be the same.)

28 a State the evidence in support of nuclear energy levels.
 Radium's first excited nuclear level is 0.0678 MeV above the ground state.
 b Write down the reaction that takes place when radium decays from the first excited state to the ground state.
 c Find the wavelength of the photon emitted.

12 QUANTUM AND NUCLEAR PHYSICS (HL)

29 Plutonium ($^{242}_{94}$Pu) decays into uranium ($^{238}_{92}$U) by alpha decay. The energy of the alpha particles takes four distinct values: 4.90 MeV, 4.86 MeV, 4.76 MeV and 4.60 MeV. In all cases a gamma ray photon is also emitted except when the alpha energy is 4.90 MeV. Use this information to suggest a possible nuclear energy level diagram for uranium.

30 The diagram shows a few nuclear energy levels for $^{40}_{18}$Ar, $^{40}_{19}$K and $^{40}_{20}$Ca.

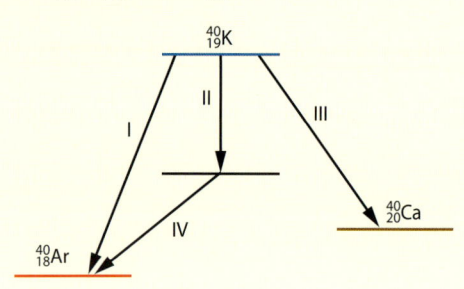

Identify the **four** indicated transitions.

31 **a** Find the decay constant for krypton-92, whose half-life is 3.00 s.
   b Suppose that you start with $\frac{1}{100}$ mol of krypton. Estimate how many undecayed atoms of krypton there are after **i** 1 s, **ii** 2 s, **iii** 3 s.

32 **a** State the probability that a radioactive nucleus will decay during a time interval equal to a half-life.
   b Calculate the probability that it will have decayed after the passage of three half-lives.
   c A nucleus has not decayed after the passage of four half-lives. State the probability it will decay during the next half-life.

33 Estimate the activity of 1.0 g of radium-226 (molar mass = 226.025 g mol^{-1}). The half-life of radium-226 is 1600 yr.

34 The half-life of an unstable element is 12 days. Find the activity of a given sample of this element after 20 days, given that the initial activity was 3.5 MBq.

35 A radioactive isotope of half-life 6.0 days used in medicine is prepared 24 h prior to being administered to a patient. The activity must be 0.50 MBq when the patient receives the isotope. Estimate the number of atoms of the isotope that should be prepared.

36 The age of very old rocks can be found from uranium dating. Uranium is suitable because of its very long half-life: 4.5×10^9 yr. The final stable product in the decay series of uranium-238 is lead-206. Find the age of rocks that are measured to have a ratio of lead to uranium atoms of 0.80. You must assume that no lead was present in the rocks other than that due to uranium decaying.

37 The isotope $^{40}_{19}$K of potassium is unstable, with a half-life of 1.37×10^9 yr. It decays into the stable isotope $^{40}_{18}$Ar. Moon rocks were found to contain a ratio of potassium to argon atoms of 1:7. Find the age of the Moon rocks.

38 Two unstable isotopes are present in equal numbers (initially). Isotope A has a half-life of 4 min and isotope B has a half-life of 3 min. Calculate the ratio of the activity of A to that of B after: **a** 0 min, **b** 4 min, **c** 12 min.

39 A sample contains two unstable isotopes. A counter placed near it is used to record the decays. Discuss how you would determine each of the half-lives of the isotopes from the data.

40 The half-life of an isotope with a very long half-life cannot be measured by observing its activity as a function of time, since the variation in activity over any reasonable time interval would be too small to be observed. Let m be the mass in grams of a given isotope of long half-life.
   a Show that the number of nuclei present in this quantity is $N_0 = \frac{m}{\mu} N_A$ where μ is the molar mass of the isotope in g mol^{-1} and N_A is the Avogadro constant.
   b From $A = -\frac{dN}{dt} = N_0 \lambda e^{-\lambda t}$, show that the initial activity is $A_0 = \frac{mN_A}{\mu}\lambda$ and hence that the half-life can be determined by measuring the initial activity (in Bq) and the mass of the sample (in grams).

Exam-style questions

1. Light of wavelength λ is incident on a surface. The stopping voltage is V_s. The wavelength of the light is halved. What is the stopping voltage now?

    A V_s **B** between V_s and $2V_s$ **C** $2V_s$ **D** greater than $2V_s$

2. Light of wavelength λ and intensity I is incident on a metallic surface and electrons are emitted. Which of the following change will, by itself, result in a greater number of electrons being emitted?

    A increase λ **B** decrease λ **C** increase I **D** decrease I

3. The absorption spectra of hydrogen atoms at a low temperature and at a high temperature are compared. What is the result of such a comparison?

    A The spectra are identical.
    B The spectra are identical but the high temperature spectrum is more prominent.
    C There are more lines in the absorption spectrum at low temperature.
    D There are more lines in the absorption spectrum at high temperature.

4. An electron orbiting a proton in the $n=2$ state of hydrogen has speed v. The electron is put in the $n=3$ state of hydrogen. What is the speed of the electron in the new orbit?

    A $\dfrac{v}{9}$ **B** $\dfrac{v}{2}$ **C** $\dfrac{3v}{2}$ **D** $\dfrac{2v}{3}$

5. A particle of mass m is confined within a region of linear size L. Which is an order of magnitude **estimate** of the particle's kinetic energy?

    A $\dfrac{mh^2}{L^2}$ **B** $\dfrac{h^2}{mL^2}$ **C** $\dfrac{mL^2}{h}$ **D** $\dfrac{L^2}{mh^2}$

6. Two beams of electrons of the same energy approach two potential barriers of the same height. One barrier has width w and the other width $2w$. Which is a correct comparison of the tunnelling probability and the de Broglie wavelength of the transmitted electrons in the two beams?

	Probability	Wavelength
A	same	same
B	same	different
C	different	same
D	different	different

7 The graph shows the wavefunction of a particle. Near which position is the particle most likely to be found?

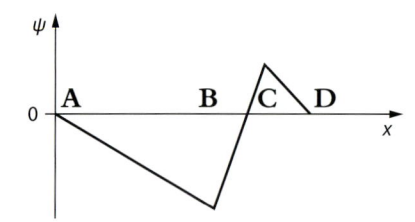

8 The activity of a pure radioactive sample is A when the number of nuclei present in the sample is N. Which graph shows the variation of A with N?

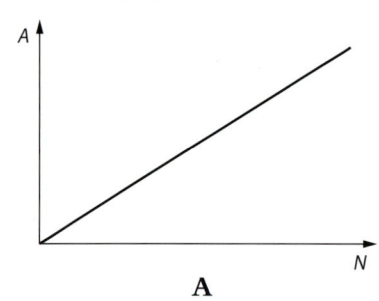

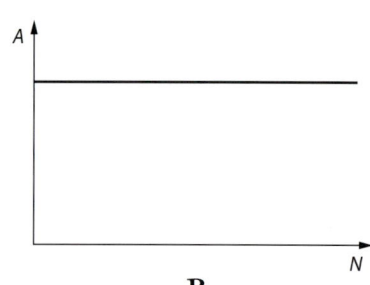

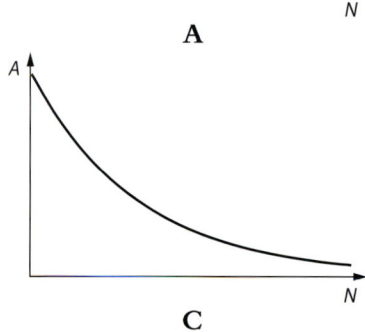

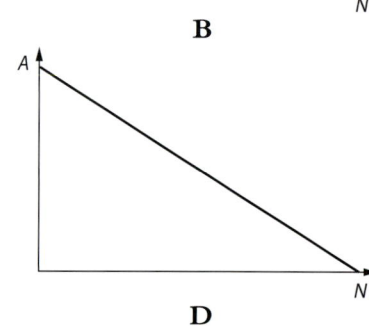

9 Alpha particles of energy E are directed at a thin metallic foil made out of atoms of atomic number Z. For what values of E and Z are deviations from Rutherford scattering likely to be observed?

	E	Z
A	low	low
B	high	low
C	low	high
D	high	high

10 Which is evidence for the existence of nuclear energy levels?

  A The short range of the nuclear force.
  B The energies of alpha and gamma particles in radioactive decay.
  C The energies of beta particles in radioactive decay.
  D The emission spectra of gases at low pressure.

11 a In a photoelectric effect experiment a constant number of photons is incident on a photo-surface.
   i Outline what is meant by **photons**. [2]
   ii On a copy of the axes below, sketch a graph to show the variation of the electric current I that leaves the photo-surface, with photon frequency f. [2]

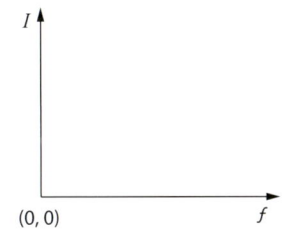

   iii Explain the features of the graph you drew in **ii**. [2]
  b i State **one** feature of the photoelectric effect that cannot be explained by the wave theory of light. [1]
    ii Describe how the feature stated in **i** is explained by the photon theory of light. [2]
  c In another experiment, a source of constant intensity and variable frequency f is incident on a metallic surface. The graph shows the variation of the stopping potential V with photon frequency f, for a particular value of intensity.

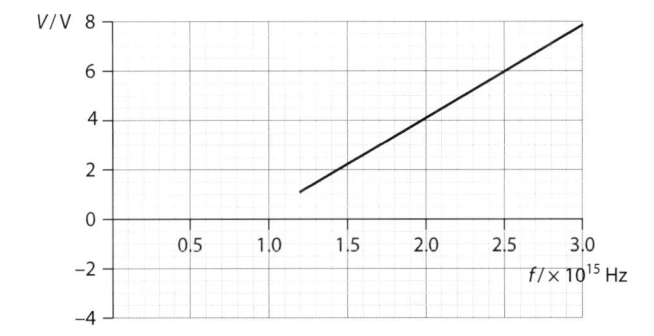

   Use the graph to estimate:
      i   the work function of the metallic surface [2]
      ii the Planck constant obtained from this experiment [3]
      iii the longest wavelength of light that will result in electron being emitted from the surface. [2]
  d The intensity of the source in **c** is doubled. Discuss how the graph in **c** will change, if at all. [2]

12 In a hydrogen atom an electron of mass m orbits the proton with speed v in a circular orbit of radius r.

  a By writing down an expression for the net force on the electron, deduce that $v^2 = \dfrac{ke^2}{mr}$, where k is the Coulomb constant. [2]

  b Using the Bohr condition show that $r = \dfrac{h^2}{4\pi ke^2 m} \times n^2$. [3]

  c Hence deduce that the total energy of the electron is given by $E = -\dfrac{1}{2}\dfrac{ke^2}{r}$ [2]

  d State the significance of the negative sign in the total energy. [1]

  e Demonstrate that the Bohr condition is equivalent to $2\pi r = n\lambda$ where λ is the de Broglie wavelength of the electron. [2]

  The diagram shows an electron wave in hydrogen.

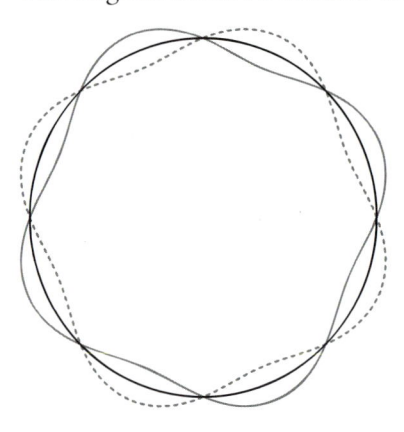

  f i State what is meant by an **electron wave**. [1]

  ii Determine the radius of the circular orbit of this electron. [3]

  iii Predict the energy that must be supplied for this electron to become free. [1]

  g According to the Bohr model, the electron in the hydrogen atom in **f** has a well-defined circular orbit radius. Discuss, by reference to the wave-like properties of the electron, why this is not quite correct in quantum theory. [3]

13 a Outline what is meant by the **de Broglie hypothesis**. [2]

  b i Show that the de Broglie wavelength of an electron that has been accelerated from rest by a potential difference V is given by $\lambda = \dfrac{h}{\sqrt{2mqV}}$. [2]

  ii Calculate the de Broglie wavelength of an electron that has been accelerated from rest by a potential difference of 120 V. [1]

  c Outline an experiment in which the de Broglie hypothesis is tested. [3]

  d A bullet of mass 0.080 kg leaves a gun with speed 420 m s^{-1}. The gun is in perfect condition and has been fired by an expert marksman. The bullet must pass through a circular hole of diameter 5.0 cm on its way to its target. A student says that the bullet will miss its mark because of de Broglie's hypothesis. By suitable calculations determine whether the student is correct. [4]

14 a State what is meant by **tunnelling**. [2]

b The graph shows the wavefunction of electrons that undergo tunnelling. (The graph does not take reflected electrons into account.)
The values on the vertical axis are arbitrary.

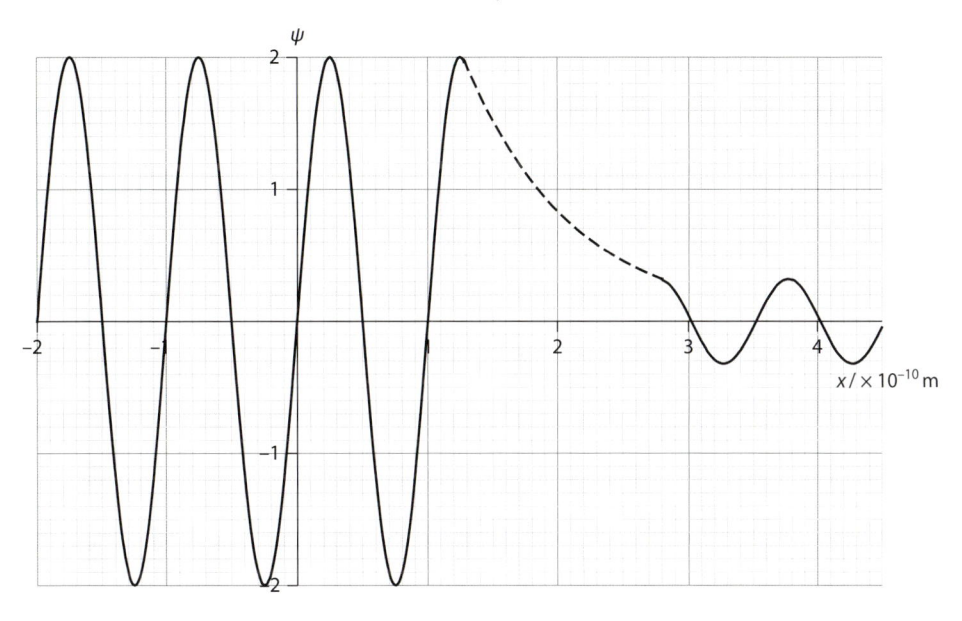

Use the graph to determine:
  i the width of the barrier [1]
  ii the ratio of the kinetic energy of the electrons after tunnelling to the kinetic energy before tunnelling [2]
  iii the fraction of the incident electrons that tunnel though the barrier. [2]

c Outline how your answer to **b iii** would change, if at all, if protons with the same energy were directed at the barrier. [1]

15 Carbon-14 is unstable and decays to nitrogen by beta minus emission according to the reaction equation:

$${}^{14}_{6}C \rightarrow {}^{14}_{7}N + {}^{0}_{-1}e + ?$$

a State, for the missing particle in the reaction equation:
  i its name [1]
  ii **two** of its properties. [2]

b Outline the evidence that made the presence of this particle in beta decay necessary. [2]

In a living tree, the ratio of carbon-14 to carbon-12 atoms is constant at 1.3×10^{-12}.

c Suggest why this ratio will decrease after the tree dies. [2]

A 15 g piece of charcoal is found in an archaeological site. The half-life of ${}^{14}_{6}C$ is 5730 years.

d Calculate the number of atoms of carbon-12 in the piece of charcoal. [2]
e The piece of charcoal has an activity of 1.40 Bq. Deduce that the ratio of carbon-14 to carbon-12 atoms in the charcoal is 4.85×10^{-13}. [3]
f Deduce the age of the charcoal. [3]

12 QUANTUM AND NUCLEAR PHYSICS (HL)

16 a Outline the evidence in support of nuclear energy levels. [2]
   b The diagram shows nuclear energy levels for $^{244}_{96}$Cm and $^{240}_{94}$Pu.
      i On a copy of the diagram, indicate the alpha decay of $^{244}_{96}$Cm into $^{240}_{94}$Pu that is followed by the emission of a photon of energy 0.043 MeV. [1]
      ii Deduce the energy of the emitted alpha particle. [1]

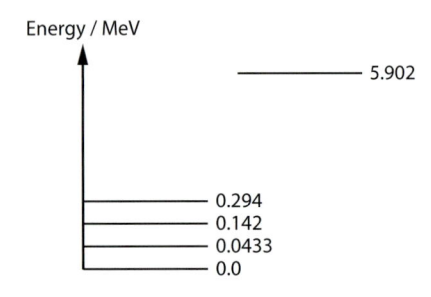

   Energy / MeV
   ——— 5.902
   ——— 0.294
   ——— 0.142
   ——— 0.0433
   ——— 0.0

   c The diagram shows the variation of the potential energy of an alpha particle with distance from the nuclear centre. The nuclear radius is R. The total energy of an alpha particle within the nucleus is 5.9 MeV.

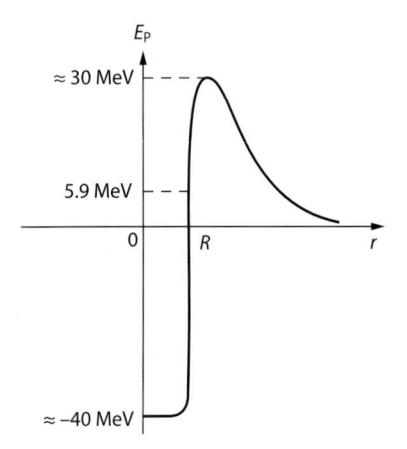

      E_P
      ≈ 30 MeV
      5.9 MeV
      0   R   r
      ≈ −40 MeV

      i   The potential energy for distances $r > R$ is entirely electric potential energy. Suggest why, for these distances, there is no contribution to the potential energy from the strong nuclear force. [2]
      ii Explain why the alpha particle cannot leave the nucleus according to the laws of classical mechanics. [2]
      iii The alpha particle does in fact leave the nucleus. By reference to the laws of quantum mechanics explain how this is possible. [2]
   d The lifetimes of nuclei decaying by alpha decay can vary from 10^{-7} s to 10^{10} years. Suggest, by reference to the diagram in c and your answer to c iii, what might cause such great variation in lifetime. [2]
   e Use the uncertainty principle to deduce that the kinetic energy of an alpha particle confined within a nucleus is of order 1 MeV. [3]

17 a i Neutrons of energy 54 MeV are directed at lead nuclei. A strong minimum in the number of scattered neutrons is observer at a scattering angle of 16°. Estimate the diameter of lead nuclei. [3]
  ii Show that the density of all nuclei is about 2×10^{17} kg m^{-3}. [3]
b In Rutherford scattering, alpha particles of energy 5.2 MeV are directed head-on at lead nuclei. Estimate the distance of closest approach between the alpha particles and the centre of a lead nucleus. [3]
c The graph shows how the number of alpha particles that are observed at a fixed scattering angle depends on alpha particle energy according to Rutherford's scattering formula.

  i State **one** assumption the Rutherford scattering formula is based on. [1]
  ii On a copy of the diagram above, indicate deviations from the Rutherford scattering. Explain your answer. [2]

Appendices

1 Physical constants

The values quoted here are those usually used in calculations and problems. Fewer significant digits are often used in the text. The constants are known with a much better precision than the number of significant digits quoted here implies.

Atomic mass unit	$1\,u = 1.661 \times 10^{-27}\,kg = 931.5\,MeV\,c^{-2}$
Avogadro constant	$N_A = 6.02 \times 10^{23}\,mol^{-1}$
Boltzmann constant	$k = 1.38 \times 10^{-23}\,J\,K^{-1}$
Coulomb's law constant	$\dfrac{1}{4\pi\varepsilon_0} = 8.99 \times 10^9\,N\,m^2\,C^{-2}$
Electric permittivity	$\varepsilon_0 = 8.85 \times 10^{-12}\,N^{-1}\,m^{-2}\,C^2$
Gravitational constant	$G = 6.67 \times 10^{-11}\,N\,kg^{-2}\,m^2$
Magnetic permeability	$\mu_0 = 4\pi \times 10^{-7}\,T\,m\,A^{-1}$
Magnitude of electronic charge	$e = 1.60 \times 10^{-19}\,C$
Mass of the electron	$m_e = 9.11 \times 10^{-31}\,kg = 5.49 \times 10^{-4}\,u = 0.511\,MeV\,c^{-2}$
Mass of the neutron	$m_n = 1.675 \times 10^{-27}\,kg = 1.008\,665\,u = 940\,MeV\,c^{-2}$
Mass of the proton	$m_p = 1.673 \times 10^{-27}\,kg = 1.007\,276\,u = 938\,MeV\,c^{-2}$
Planck constant	$h = 6.63 \times 10^{-34}\,J\,s$
Speed of light in a vacuum	$c = 3.00 \times 10^8\,m\,s^{-1}$
Stefan–Boltzmann constant	$\sigma = 5.67 \times 10^{-8}\,W\,m^{-2}\,K^{-4}$
Universal gas constant	$R = 8.31\,J\,mol^{-1}\,K^{-1}$
Solar constant	$S = 1.36 \times 10^3\,W\,m^{-2}$
Fermi radius	$R_0 = 1.2 \times 10^{-15}\,m$

A few unit conversions

astronomical unit	$1\,AU = 1.50 \times 10^{11}\,m$
atmosphere	$1\,atm = 1.01 \times 10^5\,N\,m^{-2} = 101\,kPa$
degree	$1° = \dfrac{\pi}{180°}\,rad$
electronvolt	$1\,eV = 1.60 \times 10^{-19}\,J$
kilowatt–hour	$1\,kW\,h = 3.60 \times 10^6\,J$
light year	$1\,ly = 9.46 \times 10^{15}\,m$
parsec	$1\,pc = 3.26\,ly$
radian	$1\,rad = \dfrac{180°}{\pi}$

2 Masses of elements and selected isotopes

Table A2.1 gives atomic masses, including the masses of electrons, in the neutral atom. The masses are averaged over the isotopes of each element. In the case of unstable elements, numbers in brackets indicate the approximate mass of the most abundant isotope of the element in question. The masses are expressed in atomic mass units, u. Table A2.2 gives the atomic masses of a few selected isotopes

Atomic number	Name and symbol	Atomic mass / u
1	Hydrogen, H	1.0080
2	Helium, He	4.0026
3	Lithium, Li	6.941
4	Beryllium, Be	9.012 18
5	Boron, B	10.811
6	Carbon, C	12.000 000
7	Nitrogen, N	14.007
8	Oxygen, O	15.999
9	Fluorine, F	18.998
10	Neon, Ne	20.180
11	Sodium, Na	22.999
12	Magnesium, Mg	24.31
13	Aluminium, Al	26.981
14	Silicon, Si	28.086
15	Phosphorus, P	30.974
16	Sulphur, S	32.066
17	Chlorine, Cl	35.453
18	Argon, Ar	39.948
19	Potassium, K	39.102
20	Calcium, Ca	40.078
21	Scandium, Sc	44.956
22	Titanium, Ti	47.90
23	Vanadium, V	50.942
24	Chromium, Cr	51.996
25	Manganese, Mn	54.938
26	Iron, Fe	55.847
27	Cobalt, Co	58.933
28	Nickel, Ni	58.71
29	Copper, Cu	63.54

Atomic number	Name and symbol	Atomic mass / u
30	Zinc, Zn	65.37
31	Gallium, Ga	69.723
32	Germanium, Ge	72.59
33	Arsenic, As	74.921
34	Selenium, Se	78.96
35	Bromine, Br	79.91
36	Krypton, Kr	83.80
37	Rubidium, Rb	85.467
38	Strontium, Sr	87.62
39	Yttrium, Y	88.906
40	Zirconium, Zr	91.224
41	Niobium, Nb	92.906
42	Molybdenum, Mo	95.94
43	Technetium, Tc	(99)
44	Ruthenium, Ru	101.07
45	Rhodium, Rh	102.906
46	Palladium, Pd	106.42
47	Silver, Ag	107.868
48	Cadmium, Cd	112.40
49	Indium, In	114.82
50	Tin, Sn	118.69
51	Antimony, Sb	121.75
52	Tellurium, Te	127.60
53	Iodine, I	126.904
54	Xenon, Xe	131.30
55	Caesium, Cs	132.91
56	Barium, Ba	137.34
57	Lanthanum, La	138.91
58	Cerium, Ce	140.12

Table A2.1 Atomic numbers and atomic masses of the elements.

APPENDICES 525

Atomic number	Name and symbol	Atomic mass / u
59	Praseodymium, Pr	140.907
60	Neodymium, Nd	144.24
61	Promethium, Pm	(144)
62	Samarium, Sm	150.4
63	Europium, Eu	152.0
64	Gadolinium, Gd	157.25
65	Terbium, Tb	158.92
66	Dysprosium, Dy	162.50
67	Holmium, Ho	164.93
68	Erbium, Er	167.26
69	Thulium, Tm	168.93
70	Ytterbium, Yb	173.04
71	Lutetium, Lu	174.97
72	Hafnium, Hf	178.49
73	Tantalum, Ta	180.95
74	Tungsten, W	183.85
75	Rhenium, Re	186.2
76	Osmium, Os	190.2
77	Iridium, I	192.2
78	Platinum, Pt	195.09
79	Gold, Au	196.97
80	Mercury, Hg	200.59
81	Thallium, Tl	204.37

Atomic number	Name and symbol	Atomic mass / u
82	Lead, Pb	207.2
83	Bismuth, Bi	208.980
84	Polonium, Po	(210)
85	Astatine, At	(218)
86	Radon, Rn	(222)
87	Francium, Fr	(223)
88	Radium, Ra	(226)
89	Actinium, Ac	(227)
90	Thorium, Th	(232)
91	Protactinium, Pa	(231)
92	Uranium, U	(238)
93	Neptunium, Np	(239)
94	Plutonium, Pu	(239)
95	Americium, Am	(243)
96	Curium, Cm	(245)
97	Berkelium, Bk	(247)
98	Californium, Cf	(249)
99	Einsteinium, Es	(254)
100	Fermium, Fm	(253)
101	Mendelevium, Md	(255)
102	Nobelium, No	(255)
103	Lawrencium, Lr	(257)

Table A2.1 contd.

Atomic number	Name	Atomic mass / u
1	Hydrogen, H	1.007 825
1	Deuterium, D	2.014 102
1	Tritium, T	3.016 049
2	Helium-3	3.016 029
2	Helium-4	4.002 603
3	Lithium-6	6.015 121
3	Lithium-7	7.016 003
4	Beryllium-9	9.012 182
5	Boron-10	10.012 937
5	Boron-11	11.009 305
6	Carbon-12	12.000 000
6	Carbon-13	13.003 355
6	Carbon-14	14.003 242

Atomic number	Name	Atomic mass / u
7	Nitrogen-14	14.003 074
7	Nitrogen-15	15.000 109
8	Oxygen-16	15.994 915
8	Oxygen-17	16.999 131
8	Oxygen-18	17.999 160
19	Potassium-39	38.963 708
19	Potassium-40	39.964 000
92	Uranium-232	232.037 14
92	Uranium-235	235.043 925
92	Uranium-236	236.045 563
92	Uranium-238	238.050 786
92	Uranium-239	239.054 291

Table A2.2 Atomic masses of a few selected isotopes.

3 Some important mathematical results

In physics problems, the following are useful.

$$a^{-x} = \frac{1}{a^x} \qquad a^x a^y = a^{x+y} \qquad \frac{a^x}{a^y} = a^{x-y}$$

$$\log a = x \Rightarrow 10^x = a \qquad \ln a = x \Rightarrow e^x = a$$

$$\ln(ab) = \ln a + \ln b \qquad \ln\left(\frac{a}{b}\right) = \ln a - \ln b$$

$$\ln(a^x) = x \ln a \qquad \ln(1) = 0 \qquad e^0 = 1$$

$$\sin 2x = 2 \sin x \cos x$$

$$\cos 2x = 2\cos^2 x - 1 = 1 - 2\sin^2 x = \cos^2 x - \sin^2 x$$

The quadratic equation $ax^2 + bx + c = 0$ has two roots given by

$$x = \frac{-b \pm \sqrt{b^2 - 4ac}}{2a}$$

The following approximations are useful:

$$\sin x \approx x - \frac{x^3}{6} + \ldots$$

and

$$\cos x \approx 1 - \frac{x^2}{2} + \ldots$$

valid when x in radians is small.

From geometry, we must know the following expressions for lengths, areas and volumes.

Property	Formula
Circumference of a circle of radius R	$2\pi R$
Area of a circle of radius R	πR^2
Surface area of a sphere of radius R	$4\pi R^2$
Volume of a sphere of radius R	$\frac{4\pi R^3}{3}$
Volume of a cylinder of base radius R and height h	$\pi R^2 h$

The length of an arc of a circle of radius R that subtends an angle θ at the centre of the circle is $s = R\theta$. In this formula the angle must be expressed in radians. An angle of 2π radians is equivalent to an angle of $360°$, so

$$1 \text{ radian} = \frac{360°}{2\pi} = 57.3°$$

Answers to test yourself questions

Note: Only numerical answers have been provided. Expanded answers requesting explain or discuss, show on the graph, etc, can be viewed in the online material.

Topic 1 Measurements and uncertainties

1.1 Measurement in physics

Many of the calculations in the problems of this section have been performed without a calculator and are estimates. Your answers may differ.

1. 3.3×10^{-24} s
2. 3.6×10^{51}
3. 3.3×10^{60}
4. 2.6×10^{9}
5. 2×10^{11}
6. 10^{10}
7. 1.0×10^{25}
8. 2.0×10^{27}
9. 4×10^{17} kg m^{-3}
10. 10 hr
11. a 4×10^{-19} J
    b 54 eV
12. 2.2×10^{-5} m^3
13. 8.4×10^{-3} m
14. a 0.2 kg
    b 1 kg
    c 0.2 kg
15. 5×10^{9} kg m^{-3}
16. about 0.7
17. 2×10^{28}
18. 4×10^{42}
20. 27 W
21. 391 J
22. a $\dfrac{243}{43} \approx \dfrac{250}{50} = 5$
    b $2.80 \times 1.90 \approx 3 \times 2 = 6$
    c $\dfrac{312 \times 480}{160} \approx \dfrac{300 \times 500}{150} = 1000$
    d $\dfrac{8.99 \times 10^9 \times 7 \times 10^{-16} \times 7 \times 10^{-6}}{(8 \times 10^2)^2}$
    $\approx \dfrac{10^{10} \times 50 \times 10^{-22}}{60 \times 10^4} \approx 10^{-16}$
    e $\dfrac{6.6 \times 10^{-11} \times 6 \times 10^{24}}{(6.4 \times 10^6)^2}$
    $\approx \dfrac{27 \times 10^{-11} \times 6 \times 10^{24}}{(6 \times 10^6)^2}$
    $\approx \dfrac{40 \times 10^{13}}{36 \times 10^{12}} \approx 10$

1.2 Uncertainties and errors

23. sum = 180 ± 8 N; difference = 60 ± 8 N
24. a 2.0 ± 0.3
    b 85 ± 13
    c 2 ± 3
    d 100 ± 6
    e 25 ± 8
25. $F = (7 \pm 2) \times 10$ N
26. a 18 ± 2 cm^2
    b 15 ± 1 cm
27. area = 37 ± 3 cm^2; perimeter = 26 ± 1 cm
28. 1%
29. 12%
30. The line of best fit intersects the vertical axis at about 4 mA, which is within the uncertainty in the current. A line within the error bars can certainly be made to pass through the origin.
31. The line of best fit intersects the vertical axis at about 10 mA, which is outside the uncertainty in current. No straight line within the error bars can be made to pass through the origin.
32. circle
33. a $\ln V_0 = 4 \Rightarrow V_0 = e^4 = 55$ V
    b 6.9 s
    c $R = 2$ MΩ
34. b $\alpha = 3.4$

1.3 Vectors and scalars

35

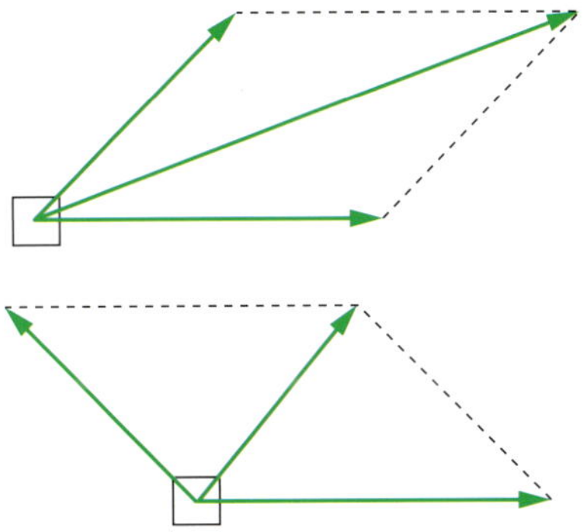

37 **a** $A + B$: magnitude = 18.2, direction = 49.7°
   b $A - B$: magnitude = 9.2, direction = −11.8°
   c $A - 2B$: magnitude = 12.4, direction = −52.0°
38 **a** 5.7 cm at 225°
   b 201 km at −52°
   c 5 m at −90°
   d 8 N at 0.0°
39 **a** A: magnitude 3.61, direction 56.3°
   b B: magnitude 5.39, direction 112°
   c $A + B$: magnitude 8.00, direction 90°
   d $A - B$: magnitude 4.47, direction −26.6°
   e $2A - B$: magnitude 6.08, direction 9.46°
40 (2, 6)
41 Magnitude 14.1 m s^{-1}, direction south-west (225°)
42 $\Delta p = \sqrt{2 - \sqrt{3}}\, p = 0.52p$
43 **a** 8 m s^{-1} at 0.0°
   b 5.66 m s^{-1} at 135°
   c 5.66 m s^{-1} at 45°; it is the sum of the answers to **a** and **b**
44 A (−7.66, 6.43)
   B (−8.19, −5.74)
   C (3.75, −9.27)
   D (7.43, −6.69)
   E (−5.00, −8.66)
45 C has magnitude $6\sqrt{3} \approx 10.4$ and direction 270° to the positive x-axis
46 **a** 25.1 N at 36.2° to the positive x-axis
   b 23.4 N at 65.2° to the positive x-axis
   c $\theta = 3.14°$

Topic 2 Mechanics

2.1 Motion

1 15 km h^{-1}
2

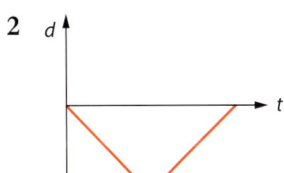

3 **a** 30 km
   b 60 km
4 **a** 4.0 m s^{-1}
   b 0 m s^{-1}
5 3.0 m s^{-2}
6 126 m
7 −1.6 m s^{-2}
8 8.0 s
9 60 m s^{-1}
10 **a** 220 m
   b 200 m
   c 20 m
   d less
11 **a** 24.5 m
12 **a** 20 m s^{-1}
13 2.0 m s^{-2}
14

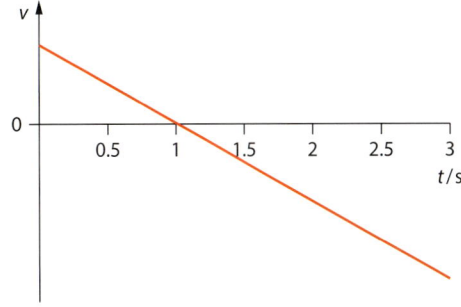

15

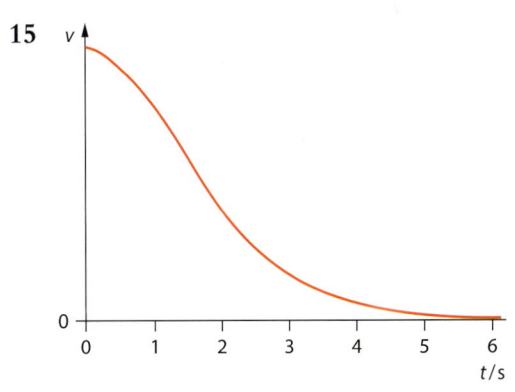

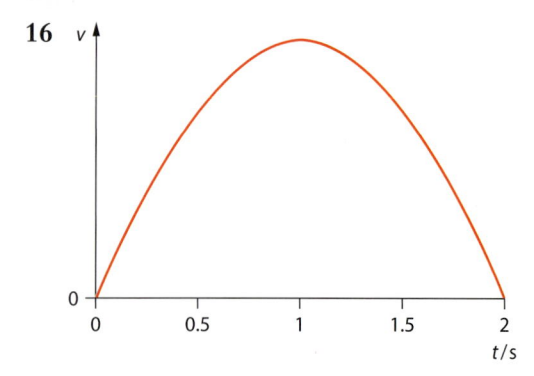

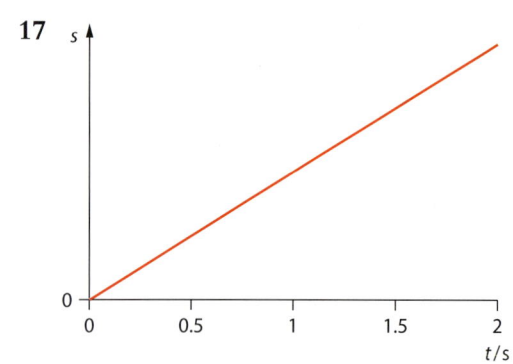

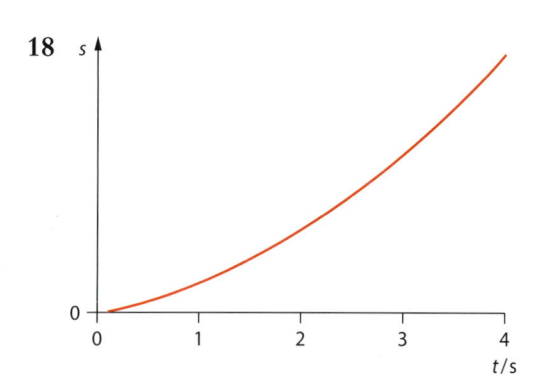

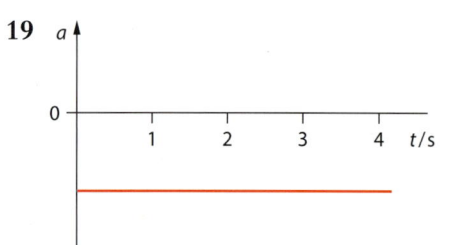

16 [graph: v vs t/s, parabolic curve from 0 at t=0 peaking near t=1 returning to 0 at t=2]

17 [graph: s vs t/s, straight line from origin]

18 [graph: s vs t/s, upward-curving line from origin, 0 to 4 s]

19 [graph: a vs t/s, constant negative horizontal line]

20 5.0 s
21 a negative
    b zero
    c positive
    d positive

23 a 3.2 m from top of cliff
    b 3.56 s
    c $-27.6\,\text{m s}^{-1}$
    d 41.4 m
    e average speed = $11.6\,\text{m s}^{-1}$; average velocity = $-9.83\,\text{m s}^{-1}$

24 a 60 m
    b $40\,\text{m s}^{-1}$

25 1.0 m

26 a 1.5 m
    b $5.7\,\text{m s}^{-1}$

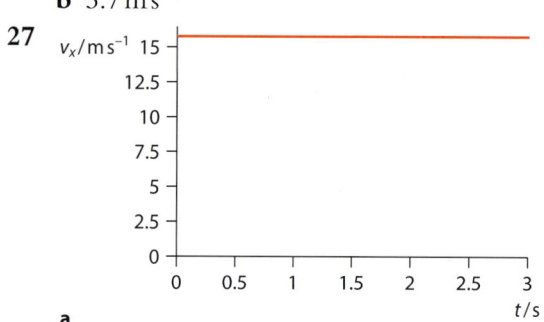

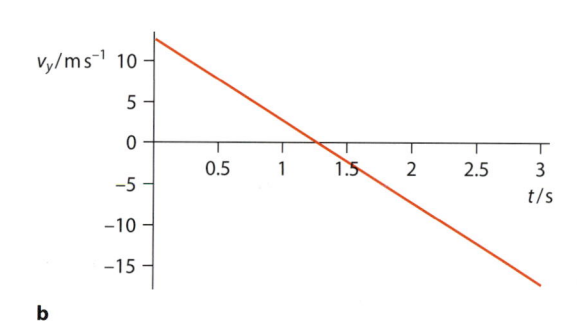

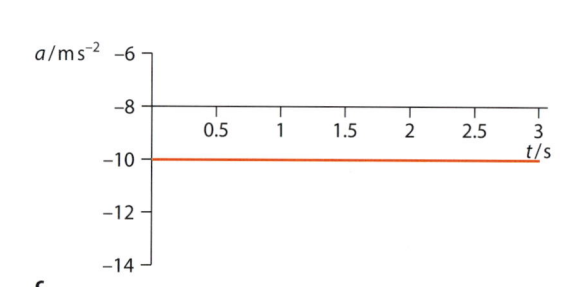

27 [graph a: $v_x/\text{m s}^{-1}$ vs t/s, constant at 15]

    [graph b: $v_y/\text{m s}^{-1}$ vs t/s, linearly decreasing from about 10 to about -17]

    [graph c: $a/\text{m s}^{-2}$ vs t/s, constant at -10]

28 12 m

530

29

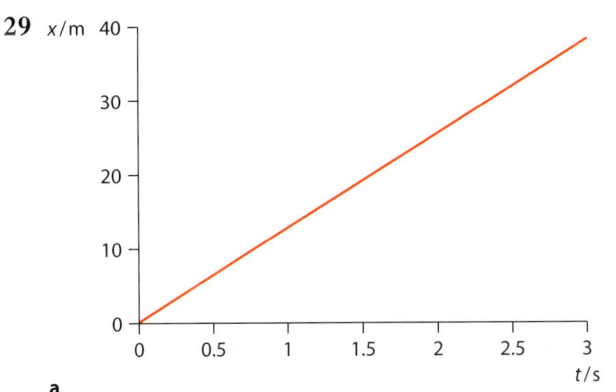

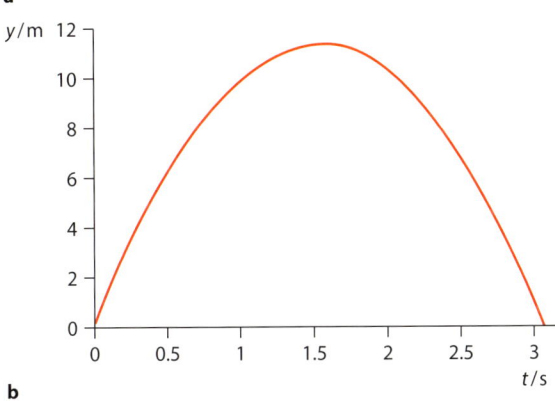

a. [graph: x/m vs t/s, linear from 0 to ~38 m at t=3 s]

b. [graph: y/m vs t/s, parabola peaking at ~11.5 m near t=1.5 s]

30 Unfortunately the chimp gets hit (assuming the bullet can get that far)

31 a i $v_x = 30\,\text{m s}^{-1}$; $v_y = 20\,\text{m s}^{-1}$
  ii 34°
  iii $g = 20\,\text{m s}^{-2}$

b horizontal arrow for velocity, vertical for acceleration

c range and maximum height half as large, as shown here

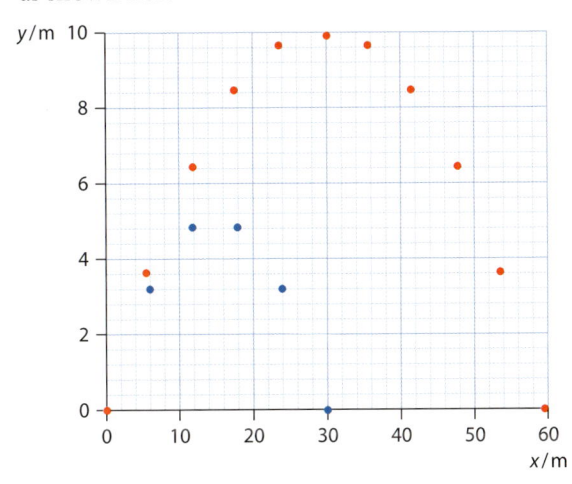

[graph: y/m vs x/m]

32 a $v = 39.7 \approx 40\,\text{m s}^{-1}$

b speed is less and angle is greater

2.2 Forces

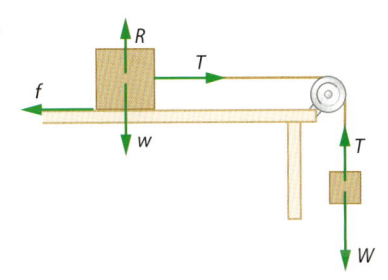

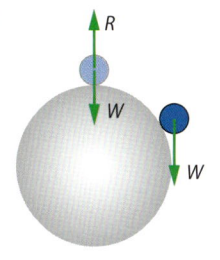

34 [free-body diagram: block on table with forces R (up), W (down), f (friction left), T (tension right), over pulley to hanging block with T (up) and W (down)]

35 [diagram: large sphere with small ball on top (R up, W down) and small ball on side (W)]

36 They are the same.

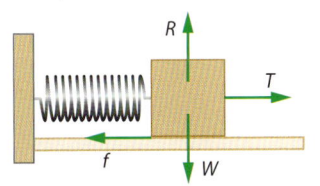

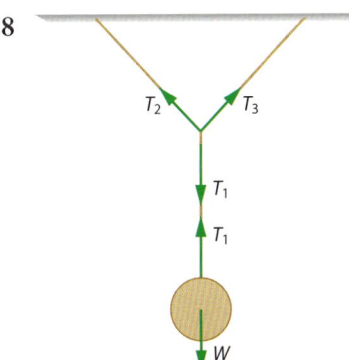

37 [diagram: block attached to spring on surface with forces R, W, T, f]

38 [diagram: mass hanging from strings with tensions T_2, T_3, T_1, T_1, W]

39 A 30 N to the right
  B 6 N to the right
  D 8 N to the left
  D 15 N to the right
  E 10 N down
  F 20 N up

40 28 N up

41 There is no vertical force to balance the weight.

42 a top
  b bottom

43 1.2 kg

44 80 N

45 200 N

46 $\sin\theta = \dfrac{m}{M}$

47 a decreasing mass
   b increasing mass
48 $0.43\,\text{m}\,\text{s}^{-2}$
49 a i mg
      ii mg
      iii $mg - ma$
      iv 0
   b The man is hit by the ceiling.
51 c $210\,\text{N}$
   d $5.0\,\text{m}\,\text{s}^{-2}$
53 a $15.0\,\text{N}$
   b yes
54 $3.0\,\text{m}\,\text{s}^{-2}$

2.3 Work, energy and power

55 $1.2 \times 10^2\,\text{J}$
56 $-7.7\,\text{J}$
57 $3.5 \times 10^2\,\text{J}$
58 $7.3\,\text{N}$
59 $0.16\,\text{J}$
60 a i $8.9\,\text{m}\,\text{s}^{-1}$ ii $6.3\,\text{m}\,\text{s}^{-1}$
   b $8.1\,\text{m}\,\text{s}^{-1}$; $10\,\text{m}\,\text{s}^{-1}$
61 $21\,\text{N}$
62 a $88\,\text{J}$
   b $9.4\,\text{m}\,\text{s}^{-1}$
63

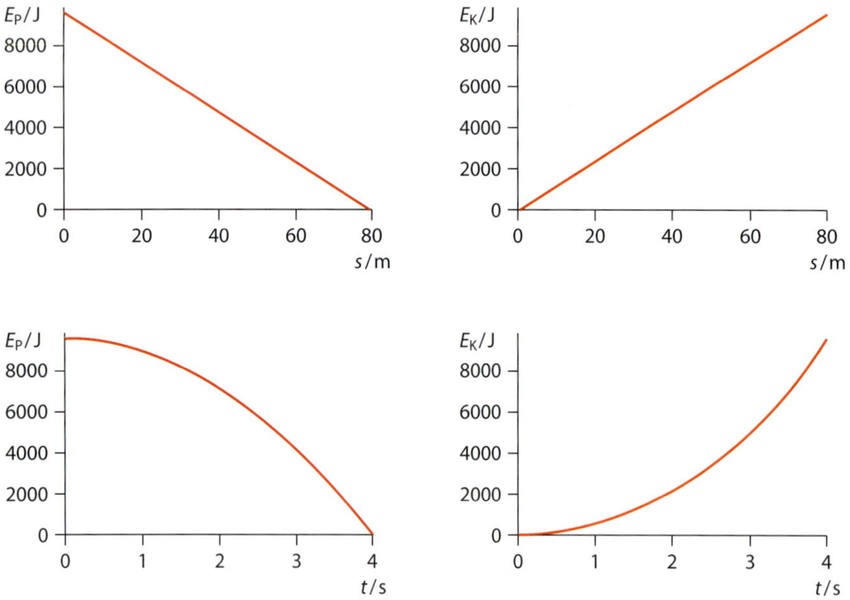

64 $3240\,\text{N}$ so estimated at $3000\,\text{N}$ to 1 s.f.
65 a $0.21\,\text{m}\,\text{s}^{-1}$
66 a $59\,\text{W}$
   b 0.74
   c $250\,\text{s}$
67 $3750\,\text{N}$
69

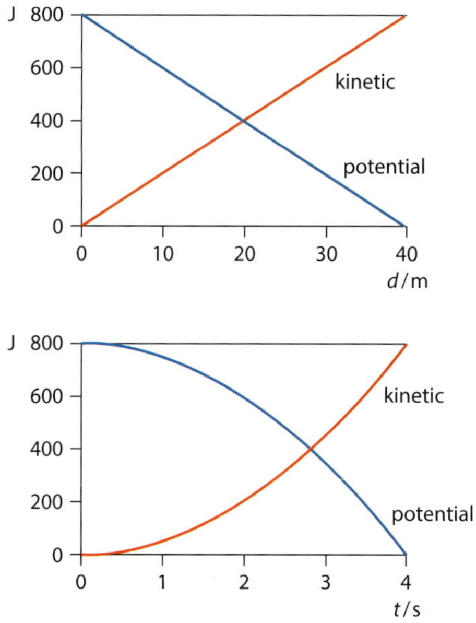

70 a $T = mg\sin\theta$
   b $W = mgd\sin\theta$
   c $W = -mgd\sin\theta$
   d zero
   e zero
71 a 50 m
   b 90 m
   c 15 s from start
   d [graph: v/m s⁻¹ vs t/s]
   e [graph: E/J vs d/m, showing E_K and E_P]
   f from 5 s on
   g 22.5 W
   h 45 W

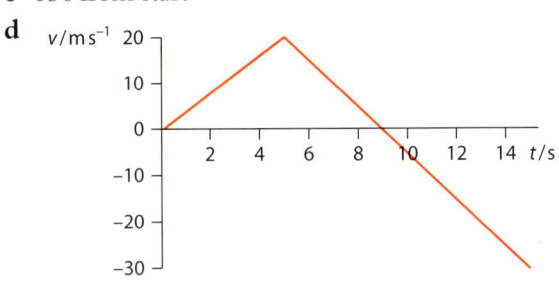

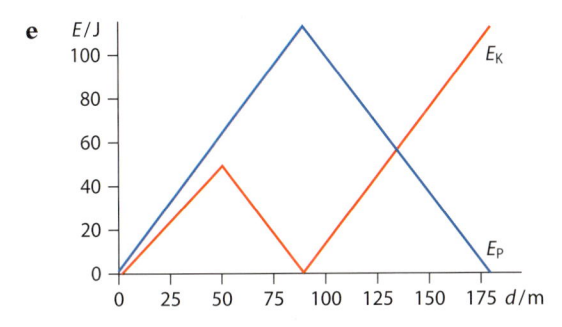

2.4 Momentum and impulse

72 6.00 N
73 a 0.900 N s
   b 7.20 N
74 zero
75 a 1.41 N s away from the wall
76 7.0 m s⁻¹ to the right
77 a 88 N s
   b 22 m s⁻¹
   c −22 m s⁻¹
78 a 2.0 m s⁻¹
79 b $R = 49.2 \approx 49$ N
81 a 1 s
   b About 50 N s
   c About 50 N
82 14 J
83 50.0 kg

Topic 3 Thermal physics

3.1 Thermal concepts

2 a, b 513 J kg⁻¹ K⁻¹
3 2800 J kg⁻¹ K⁻¹
4 4100 J kg⁻¹ K⁻¹
5 $\Delta\theta = 73$ K
6 a $C = 1.17 \times 10^5$ J K⁻¹
   b 87 min
7 35 g
8 3.73×10^8 J
9 a 84 min
10 a 2.2×10^4 J
    b 3.3×10^5 J
    c 4.2×10^4 J
11 112 g
12 95 °C

3.2 Modelling a gas

13 8×10^{24}
14 1.5
15 3.3
16 3.0 g
17 $P_2 = 16.0 \times 10^5$ Pa
18 4.2×10^{-3} m³
19 1.46×10^9 Pa
20 87.9 g
21 10.1 min
22 [p vs V diagram with points a, b, c]

23 10 atm
24 a 1.0×10^3 Pa
    b 1.2×10^{22}
    c 7.3×10^{-2} m³
25 56 g; 0.045 m³
26 1.04×10^5 Pa
27 a 0.030
    b 1.81×10^{22}
    c 0.87 g

28 a $V = 2.27 \times 10^{-2}\,\text{m}^3$
   b $p = 0.176\,\text{kg m}^{-3}$
   c $p = 1.41\,\text{kg m}^{-3}$
29 $1.35\,\text{kg m}^{-3}$
30 $2300\,\text{m s}^{-1}$
32 a $6.2 \times 10^{-21}\,\text{J}$
   b $\dfrac{c_1}{c_2} = \sqrt{8}$

Topic 4 Waves

4.1 Oscilliations

5 a ii $8.0\,\text{s}$
  b

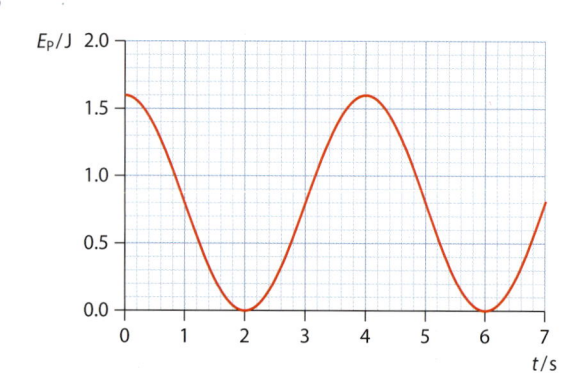

4.2 Travelling waves

10 a From left to right: down, down, up
   b From left to right: up, up, down
11 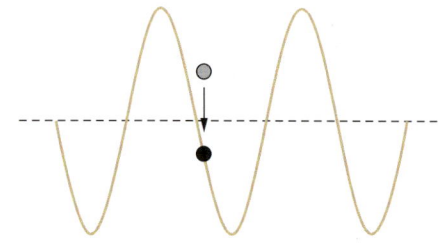
12 a $1.29\,\text{m}$
   b $1.32 \times 10^{-2}\,\text{m}$
13 b i

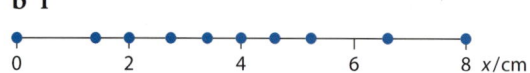

   ii compression at $x = 4\,\text{cm}$
   c ii compression at $x = 5\,\text{cm}$
14 a $850\,\text{Hz}$
   b i $0.30\,\text{m}$
     ii $0.10\,\text{m}$

4.3 Wave characteristics

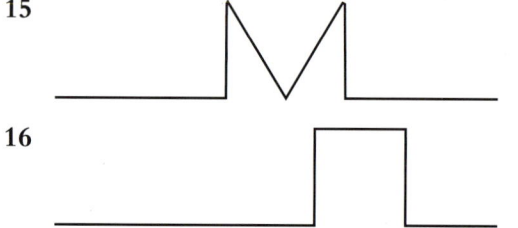

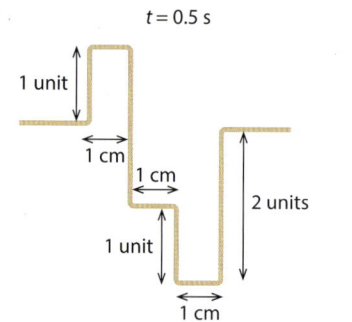

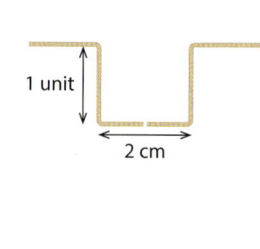

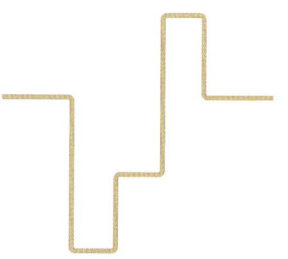

15
16
17
18 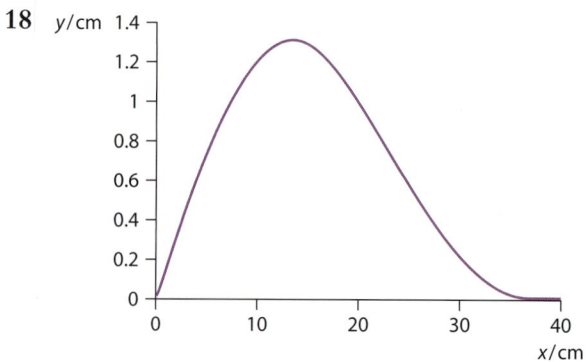
23 b 82%
24 b yes, $\dfrac{I_0}{8}$
   c no light transmitted

534

4.4 Wave behaviour

25 a 22.9°
   b $1.9 \times 10^8 \, m\,s^{-1}$
   c $1.1 \times 10^{-6} \, m$
26 a $1.0 \times 10^{-8} \, s$
   b 6×10^6
27 1.1 cm
28 13.1°
31 800 m

4.5 Standing waves

36 354 Hz
37 2
38 a 225 Hz
   b 1.51 m
40 0.83 m; 1.4 m
41 a $342 \, m\,s^{-1}$
   b $L' = 0.600 \, m$
42 a $n = 5$ and $n = 6$
   b 2.8 m
43 2
44 $16 \, cm\,s^{-1}$
45 b 8.0 m
   c π; $y = -5.0 \cos(45\pi t)$
46 b $13 \times 10^3 \, m\,s^{-1}$
   c 5.6 kHz

Topic 5 Electricity and magnetism

5.1 Electric fields

1 a 29 N
  b i $\dfrac{F}{4}$ ii $\dfrac{F}{2}$ iii F
2 90 N to the right
3 3.22 cm from the left charge
4 73 N at 225° to the horizontal
5 a $8.0 \times 10^{-9} \, C$
  b 5.0×10^{10} electronic charges
6 a 2×10^{28}
  b $10^{27} \, N$
  c One assumption is that the body consists entirely of water, but a more significant assumption is the use of Coulomb's law for bodies that are fairly close to each other and are not point charges.
  d The net charge of a person is zero because of the protons that have been neglected in this estimate. This leads to zero force.
7 $6.0 \, N\,C^{-1}$
8 $3.84 \times 10^5 \, N\,C^{-1}$ to the right
9 $6.4 \times 10^5 \, N\,C^{-1}$ vertically down
10 $12.45 \approx 12 \, A$
11 a 1.2 A
   b $5.5 \times 10^{-5} \, m\,s^{-1}$
12 $4.3 \times 10^{-5} \, m\,s^{-1}$
13 a $3.6 \times 10^4 \, C$
   b 2.2×10^{23}
14 a 0
   b 0
   c $1.6 \times 10^6 \, N\,C^{-1}$
   d $9.0 \times 10^5 \, N\,C^{-1}$

5.2 Heating effect of electric currents

17 a yes
18 14 V
19 12 Ω
20 15 Ω
21 a 8.0 V across 4 Ω resistor; 12 V across 6 Ω resistor
   b 0 V
22 a 400 Ω
   b 0.57 m
23 a 2.7 Ω
   b 12.4 Ω
   c 1.0 Ω
24 6.48 V
25 a A1 reads 0.16 A; A2 reads −0.10 A
   b 1.2 V, 1.8 V and 1.0 V (lower R)
26 3.0 A in R_1 and 0.60 A in the other two
27 10 V
28 a 4.2 A
   b 1.1 A
29 0.60 m

5.3 Electric cells

31 $2.0\,\Omega$

32 a

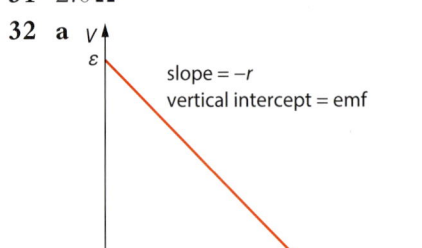

  (graph: V vs I, slope = –r, vertical intercept = emf)

  b i the negative of the internal resistance
     ii the emf of the source

33 a $1.2\,\Omega$
    b $12\,V$

34 a *(circuit diagram: 2.8 V, 1.38 A; 9.2 V, 0.92 A; 9.2 V, 0.46 A)*

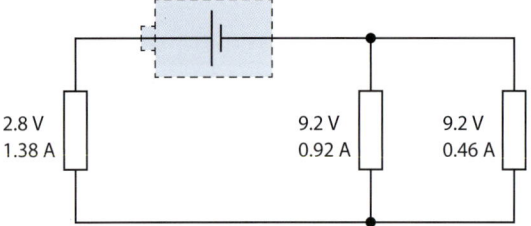

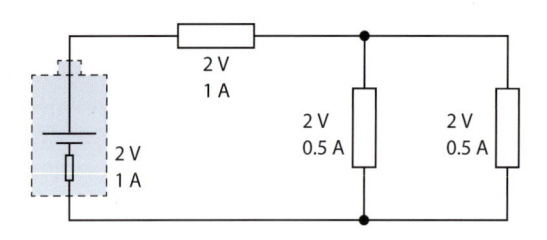

    b *(circuit diagram: 2 V, 1 A; 2 V, 1 A; 2 V, 0.5 A; 2 V, 0.5 A)*

35 a $16\,V$
    b $3.25\,\Omega$

36 a $0.75\,A$
    b $+6.8\,W$ in $9.0\,V$ cell and $-2.2\,W$ in $3.0\,V$ cell
    c The power in the $3.0\,V$ cell is negative, implying that it is being charged.

5.4 Magnetic fields

38 a B into page
    b F into page
    c B out of page
    d force zero
    e force zero

40 a force down
    b force right

41 a into page
    b zero
    c force up

42 a $0.012\,T$ into page
    b yes
    c no

43 a no
    b It will rotate counter-clockwise.

44 $2.25\,N$

45 a $\dfrac{eB}{2\pi m_e}$
    b $\dfrac{eB}{2\pi m_p}$

46 a out of the paper
    b left

Topic 6 Circular motion and gravitation

6.1 Circular motion

1 a $v = 17.7\,\mathrm{m\,s^{-1}}$
   b $f = 0.806\,\mathrm{Hz}$

2 $1.2 \times 10^3\,\mathrm{m\,s^{-2}}$

3 a $7.20\,\mathrm{m\,s^{-2}}$ north west
   b $8.0\,\mathrm{m\,s^{-2}}$

4 $21\,\mathrm{rpm}$

5 a $10\,N$
   b $2.83\,\mathrm{m\,s^{-1}}$
   c $0.80\,m$

6 $84.5\,\mathrm{min}$

7 a $3.2 \times 10^9\,\mathrm{m\,s^{-2}}$
   b The normal reaction force on the probe would not be zero so it could stay on the surface.

8 a $30\,\mathrm{km\,s^{-1}}$
   b $6.0 \times 10^{-3}\,\mathrm{m\,s^{-2}}$
   c $3.6 \times 10^{22}\,N$

9 $4.7\,\mathrm{km}$

10 a *(diagram: friction upward, reaction to the right, weight downward)*

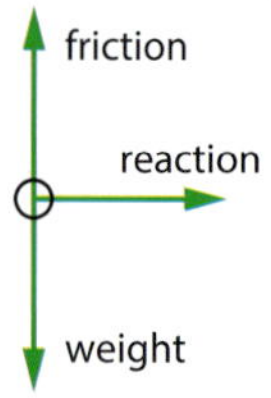

    b about 17 per minute

11 a $30\,\mathrm{m\,s^{-1}}$
    b $13\,\mathrm{m\,s^{-1}}$

12 $v = \sqrt{\dfrac{Mgr}{m}}$

13 top string tension = 13.1 N, bottom = 8.22 N

14 a $49\,\text{m s}^{-1}$
   b $1800\,\text{N}$
   c $30\,\text{m s}^{-2}$

6.2 The law of gravitation

15 a $1.99 \times 10^{20}\,\text{N}$
   b $4.17 \times 10^{23}\,\text{N}$
   c $1.0 \times 10^{-47}\,\text{N}$

16 a zero
   b zero
   c $\dfrac{Gm^2}{4R^2}$
   d $\dfrac{Gm(m+M)}{4R^2}$

17 $\dfrac{1}{81}$

18 $\dfrac{1}{2}$

19 3

20 twice as large

21 0.9

22 at P, $g = 0$; at Q, g is directed vertically upwards

23 a $4.2 \times 10^7\,\text{m}$
   b It looks down at the same point on the equator so is useful for communications.

24 a $7.6 \times 10^3\,\text{m s}^{-1}$
   b about 10 hours

25 a $T^2 \propto r^{n+1}$
   b $n = 2$

Topic 7 Atomic, nuclear and particle physics

7.1 Discrete energy and radioactivity

3 $4.9 \times 10^{-7}\,\text{m}$

6 $2\,|e|$

8 $^{210}_{83}\text{Bi} \rightarrow \, ^{0}_{-1}\text{e} + \bar{\nu}_e + \, ^{0}_{0}\gamma + \, ^{210}_{84}\text{Po}$

9 $^{239}_{94}\text{Pu} \rightarrow \, ^{4}_{2}\alpha + \, ^{235}_{92}\text{U}$

10 0.5 mg

11 b 4 min
   d 12 min

12 plot d against $\dfrac{1}{\sqrt{c}}$

13 plot $\ln I$ against x

7.2 Nuclear reactions

16 545.3 MeV; 8.79 MeV

17 8.03 MeV; 11.9 MeV

18 a $2.44 \times 10^{-11}\,\text{m}$
   b gamma ray

19 a $^{236}_{92}\text{U} \rightarrow 2 \times \, ^{117}_{46}\text{Pd} + 2 \times \, ^{0}_{0}\text{n}$
   c 179 MeV

20 184 MeV

21 18 MeV

22 17.3 MeV

7.3 The structure of matter

26 a $\bar{\text{n}} = \bar{\text{u}}\,\bar{\text{d}}\,\bar{\text{d}}$; $Q_{\bar{n}} = -\dfrac{2}{3} + \dfrac{1}{3} + \dfrac{1}{3} = 0$
   b $\bar{\text{p}} = \bar{\text{u}}\,\bar{\text{u}}\,\bar{\text{d}}$; $Q_{\bar{p}} = -\dfrac{2}{3} - \dfrac{2}{3} + \dfrac{1}{3} = -1$

27 $\bar{\text{u}}$ s

28 -1

29 a violate
   b conserve
   c conserve
   d violate

31 a $Q = 0$, $S = +1$
   b no

32 a $Q = 1$
   b $S = 0$

33 a conserve
   b conserve
   c violate
   d violate

34 a ν_e
   b ν_μ
   c $\bar{\nu}_\tau$
   d $\bar{\nu}_e$
   e $\bar{\nu}_e$ and ν_τ

35 a electron lepton number
   b electron and muon lepton number
   c electric charge
   d baryon number
   e energy and muon lepton number
   f baryon number and electric charge

40 a $m_u = 312\,\text{MeV}\,c^{-2}$, $m_d = 314\,\text{MeV}\,c^{-2}$
   b $626\,\text{MeV}\,c^{-2}$

42

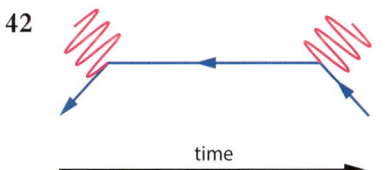

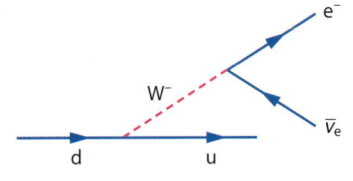

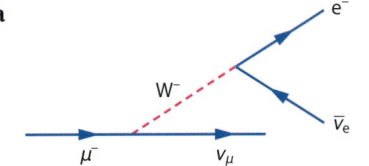

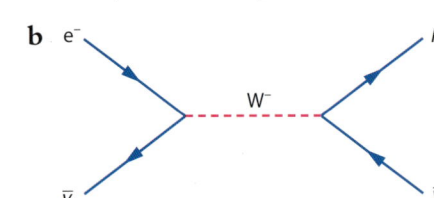

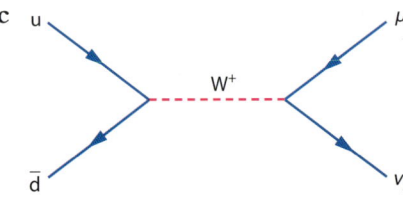

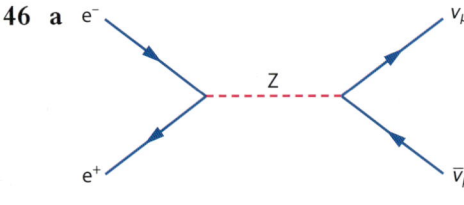

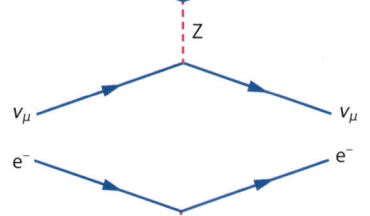

43 a $d \to u + e^- + \bar{v}_e$
b [Feynman diagram: d → u with W⁻ emitting e⁻ and $\bar{v}_e$]

44 a [Feynman diagram: μ⁻ → v_μ with W⁻ emitting e⁻ and $\bar{v}_e$]
b [Feynman diagram: e⁻ + $\bar{v}_e$ → μ⁻ + $\bar{v}_\mu$ via W⁻]
c [Feynman diagram: u + $\bar{d}$ → μ⁺ + v_μ via W⁺]
d [Feynman diagram: s + $\bar{u}$ → μ⁻ + $\bar{v}_\mu$ via W⁻]

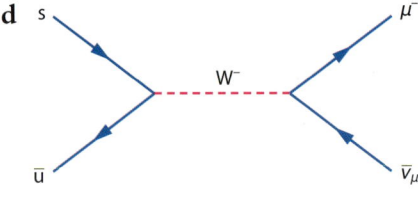

45 $W^- \to \bar{u} + d$

46 a [Feynman diagram: e⁻ + e⁺ → v_μ + $\bar{v}_\mu$ via Z]
b [Feynman diagram: e⁻ + v_μ → e⁻ + v_μ via Z]
c [Feynman diagram: e⁻ + e⁺ → e⁻ + e⁺ via Z]

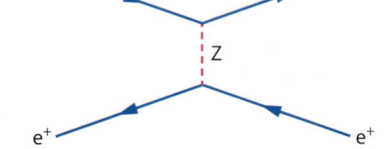

Topic 8 Energy production

8.1 Energy sources

1 b $E_D = 7.4 \times 10^5 \, \text{J m}^{-3}$
2 a $5.0 \times 10^8 \, \text{J}$
  b $1.6 \times 10^{16} \, \text{J}$
3 a 2.5%
4 a $1.0 \times 10^9 \, \text{W}$
  b $2.4 \times 10^9 \, \text{W}$
  c $1.2 \times 10^5 \, \text{kg s}^{-1}$
5 6.1 km
6 $7.2 \times 10^6 \, \text{kg day}^{-1}$
8 a 185 MeV or $2.96 \times 10^{-11} \, \text{J}$
  b $N = 6.8 \times 10^{18} \, \text{s}^{-1}$
9 a $8.20 \times 10^{13} \, \text{J kg}^{-1}$
  b $2.7 \times 10^6 \, \text{kg}$
10 a $3.9 \times 10^{19} \, \text{s}^{-1}$
   b $1.5 \times 10^{-5} \, \text{kg s}^{-1}$
13 a 12.2 (so about 12) m²
   b [Sankey diagram: 85 kW input with outputs 25 kW, 30 kW, 30 kW]

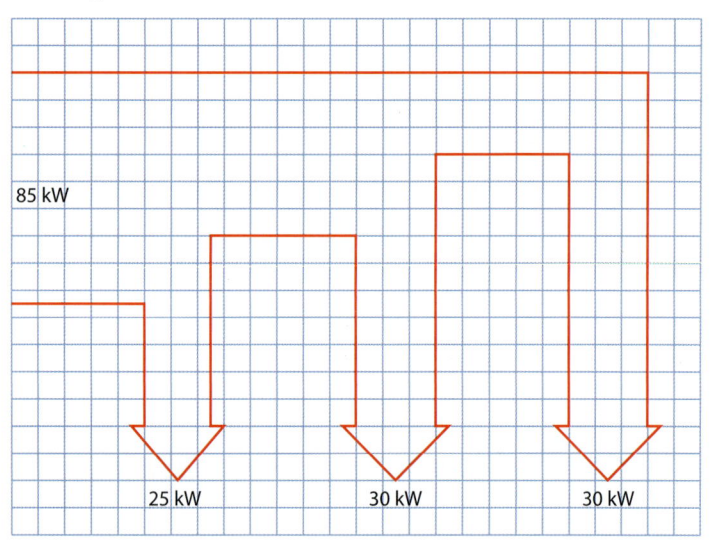

14 6.5 m²
15 3.6 h
16 a 338 K
   b 800 W
   c 0.40 (40%)
17 $3.6 \times 10^{11} \, \text{J}$
18 a i increases by a factor of 4
      ii increases by a factor of 8
      iii increases by a factor of 32
20 2.0 kW
21 4.3 m
22 $2.0 \times 10^8 \, \text{W}$

8.2 Thermal energy transfer

26 **a** yes
  b no
28 81
29 **c** 1.8
30 **b** 0.6
31 278 K
32 **a** $T \propto \dfrac{1}{\sqrt{d}}$
  b 1.4 K
33 **b** 2.4 W m^{-2}
35 **a** $(4.5 \pm 0.1) \times 10^2$ K
38 **b** 0.29
  c 250 W m^{-2}
  d 258 K
39 **d ii** 242 K
44 approximately 2 K increase in temperature

Topic 9 Wave phenomena (HL)

9.1 Simple harmonic motion

2 **a** $-\dfrac{\pi}{2}$
3 **a** 5.0 mm
  b -3.7 mm
  c 0.99 s
  d ± 4.0 mm
4 **a** $8.0\cos(28\pi t)$
  b $y = -4.7$ cm, $v = -5.7$ m s^{-1}, $a = 3.6 \times 10^2$ m s^{-2}
5 $v = 14$ m s^{-1}; $a = 4.2 \times 10^4$ m s^{-2}
6 **a** 520 Hz
  c 6.0 mm
  d 1.0 m
  e 4.2 mm
7 **a** 0.51 cm
  b twice the amplitude
  c $-0.25 \sin(5\pi t)$
8

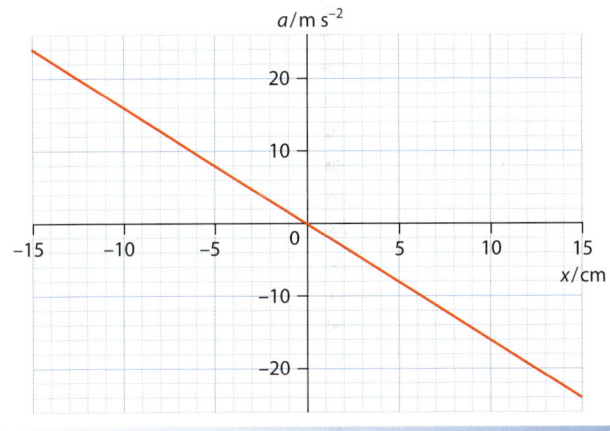

9 **b** 0.39 m s^{-1}
  c 0.40 m s^{-1}
  d $0.225 \approx 0.22$ N
  e 0.012 J
10 **a** 9.94 mm
   b 2.35 N
11 **a** mass $= M\left(\dfrac{x}{R}\right)^3$
   b force $= GMm\left(\dfrac{x_3}{R^3}\right)$
   d period $= 2\pi\sqrt{\dfrac{R^3}{GM}}$
   e 85 minutes
   f same
12 **a** 0.57 s
13 **a** $h \approx 27$ m
   b $a = 34$ m s^{-2}
   c $T = 3.28 \approx 3.3$ s
   d $17.7 \approx 18$ m

9.2 Single-slit diffraction

14 38.2°
15 0.020 cm
16 **a** $b \approx \dfrac{\lambda}{0.0041} \approx 24\lambda$
   b i New curve in blue;
     ii Same as original (shown in red)

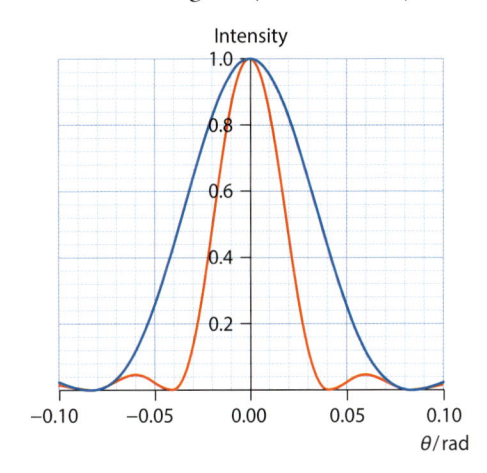

9.3 Interference

17 8.5 mm
19 $n = 3$
20 **a** 6.46×10^{-7} m
21 **a** $\lambda = 6.46 \times 10^{-7} \approx 6.5 \times 10^{-7}$ m
22 **a** 0.0°; 13.89°; 28.69°; 46.05°; 73.74°
   b $n = 4$

24 123 nm
25 b

[Intensity graph showing waveform with peaks at ~4, plotted against θ/rad from −0.10 to 0.10]

c

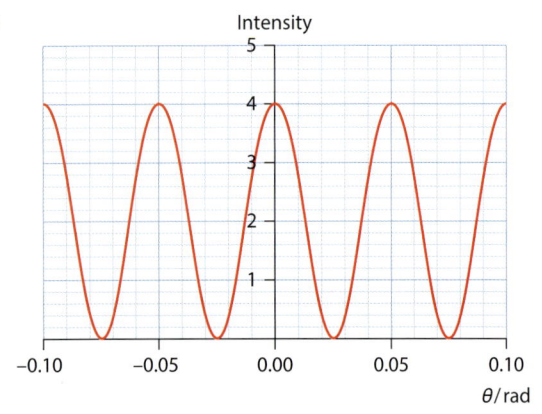

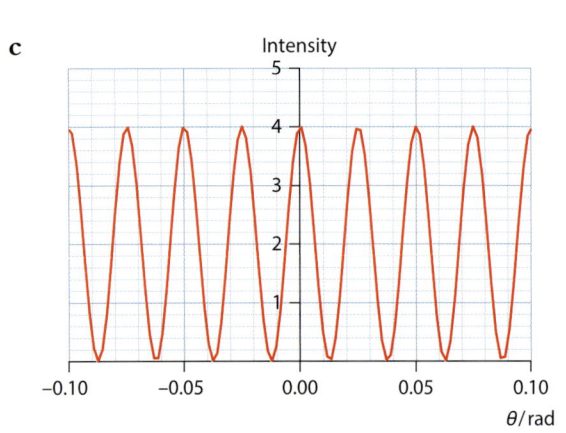

[Intensity graph showing waveform with more peaks at ~4, plotted against θ/rad from −0.10 to 0.10]

9.4 Resolution

27 no; can resolve 3.6 cm
28 a 115 km
29 a 1.5×10^{-4} rad
 b 58 km
30 a 3.4×10^{-3} rad
 b cannot resolve, as $3.4 \times 10^{-3} > 4.1 \times 10^{-6}$ rad
31 $3.3 \times 10^{-4} < 0.088$ rad, so seen as extended object
32 2.5×10^{12} m
33 a 2.8×10^{-7} rad
34 a 8.5×10^{-6} m
 b 329
35 a $\Delta\lambda = 0.092$ nm

9.5 The Doppler effect

37 a 570 Hz
 b i 0.68 m   ii 0.60 m
38 a 440 Hz
 b i 0.71 m   ii 0.78 m
39 a 490 Hz
 b i 0.66 m   ii 0.66 m
40 a 670 Hz
 b i 0.54 m   ii 0.54 m
42 $6.9 \, \text{m s}^{-1}$
43 $4.0 \, \text{m s}^{-1}$
45 b $0.36 \, \text{m s}^{-1}$
46 $9.3 \times 10^{6} \, \text{m s}^{-1}$
47 a $1.4 \times 10^{6} \, \text{m s}^{-1}$
48 ± 3.8 GHz
49 b $3.65 \times 10^{6} \, \text{m s}^{-1}$ and $8.21 \times 10^{6} \, \text{m s}^{-1}$

Topic 10 Fields (HL)

10.1 Describing fields

1 b $V = -\dfrac{25 Gm}{d}$
2 a $-1.25 \times 10^{7} \, \text{J kg}^{-1}$
 b -6.25×10^{9} J
3 a $E_p = -7.6 \times 10^{28}$ J
 b $V = -1.0 \times 10^{6} \, \text{J kg}^{-1}$
 c $v = 1.0 \times 10^{3} \, \text{m s}^{-1}$
4

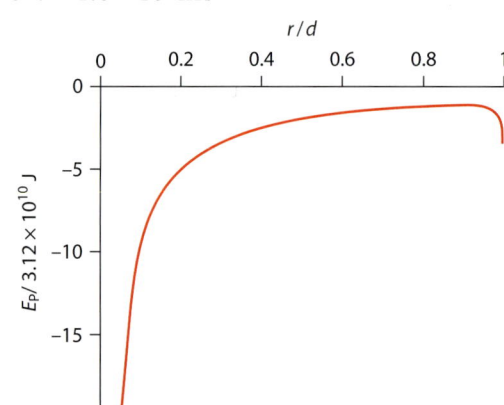

[Graph of $E_p / 3.12 \times 10^{10}$ J vs r/d, curve rising from large negative values toward 0]

5 a 9 : 1
 b $v = 3.5 \times 10^{6} \, \text{m s}^{-1}$
7 the work required to move the mass on which the force is acting from $r = a$ to $r = b$
9 a $\dfrac{Q}{\pi \varepsilon_0 d}$ or $\dfrac{4kQ}{d}$
 b zero
10 -15 kV
11 a $V = 2.5 \times 10^{6}$ V
 b $E = 0$
12 3.6×10^{7} J
13 1.44×10^{-7} J
14 $5.93 \times 10^{6} \, \text{m s}^{-1}$

15 a 11.8 N at 75.4° below the horizontal
    b 5.1×10^5 V
    c 5.1×10^{-4} J
16 a 0.8 µC (smaller sphere) and 1.2 µC
    b 6.37×10^{-6} C m^{-2} (smaller sphere) and 4.24×10^{-6} C m^{-2}
    c 7.2×10^5 N C^{-1} (smaller sphere) and 4.8×10^5 N C^{-1}
18 a 0.30×10^{-3} J
    b -0.30×10^{-3} J
    c -0.60×10^{-3} J
19 a -7.19 V
    b -1.6×10^{-19} C
20 a $\dfrac{qa}{2\pi\varepsilon_0(d^2+a^2)^{3/2}}$ or $\dfrac{2kqa}{(d^2+a^2)^{3/2}}$ vertically down
    b $\dfrac{qd}{2\pi\varepsilon_0(d^2+a^2)^{3/2}}$ or $\dfrac{2kqd}{(d^2+a^2)^{3/2}}$ horizontally to the left
21 $E_p = 1.4 \times 10^{-12}$ J ≈ 8.6 MeV

10.2 Fields at work

22 a 7.6×10^3 m s^{-1}
    b 95 minutes
24 a about 35 870 km (i.e. about 42 250 km from the Earth's centre)
25 Orbit 1 is not possible, orbit 2 is.
26 The normal reaction force from the spacecraft floor is zero.
27 a The total energy is $E = -\dfrac{GMm}{4R}$, i.e. negative.
    b $r = 4R$
    c $v = \sqrt{\dfrac{3GM}{2R}}$
28 $E_T = -2.7 \times 10^{33}$ J
29 a B
    b A
    c A
30 a Its total energy is negative.
    b $\dfrac{5R}{2}$
31 positive because the total energy increases
34 c about 4
35 c 1.1×10^6 m
36 a $F = \dfrac{GM^2}{4R^2}$
    c $T = 7.8$ h
    f ii 3.9×10^{-9} J yr^{-1}
    g 2.6×10^8 yr

37 d $\dfrac{q^2}{16\pi\varepsilon_0 r}$ or $\dfrac{kq^2}{4r}$
38 b 1.4×10^{-16} s
    c 1.7×10^{-18} J

Topic 11 Electromagnetic induction (HL)

11.1 Electromagnetic induction

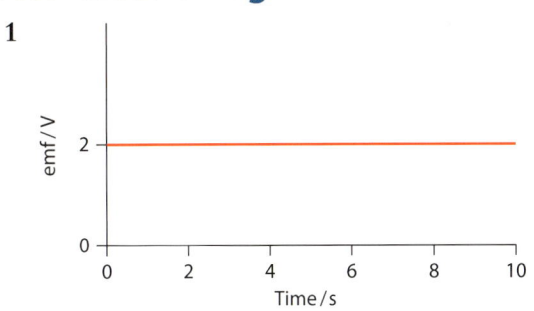

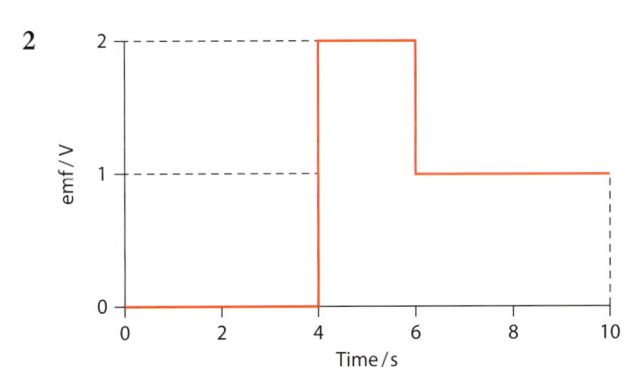

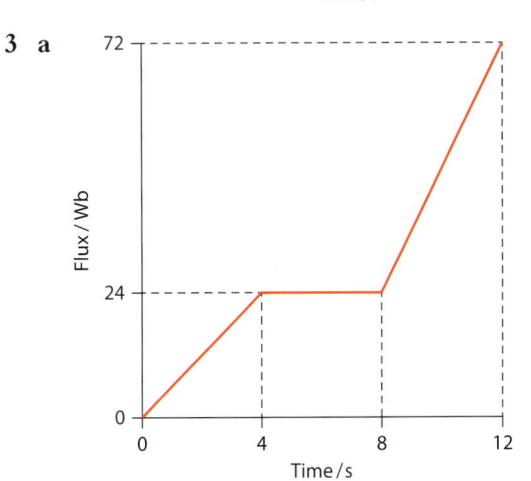

1

2

3 a

4 counter-clockwise
5 a clockwise, then zero, then counter-clockwise
  b counter-clockwise, then zero, then clockwise
6 a counter-clockwise, then zero, then clockwise
  b clockwise, then zero, then counter-clockwise
7 a force is upward
  b force is upward
8 right end is positive
9 a clockwise
  b counter-clockwise
10 28 mV

11.2 Transmission of power

14 b The graph in question 14 remains unchanged.
   a, c The emf has double the amplitude at the high speed but the dependence on angle is otherwise the same. Note that no numbers have been put on the emf axis as we do not know the rate of rotation.

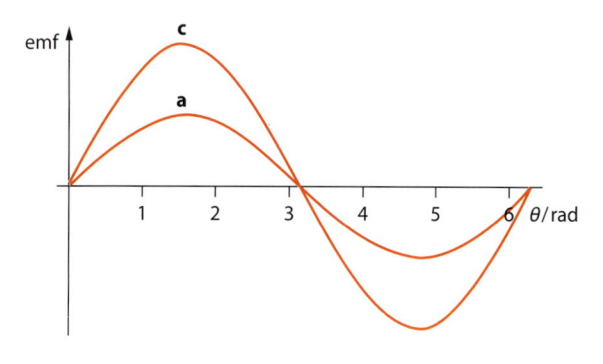

15 a $I_{rms} = 2.0$ A
   b $V_{rms} = 5.0$ V
   c 1.0 s
   d

16 a 88 V; 50 Hz
   b 10.5 A
17 a 23%
   b 15%
18 0.0825 T
19 4.9×10^4 V
20 a 30%
   b 1.2%
21 410 W

11.3 Capacitance

22 About 1100 km^2
23 6.6 nC
24 0.18 A
25 a 180 mC
   b 0.81 J
   c 16 W
26 a $V = 360$ μC
   b 7.2×10^{-4} C and 1.4×10^{-3} C
   c 2.2×10^{-3} J and 4.3×10^{-3} J
27 a 80 μF
   b 4.8×10^{-4} C each
   c 9.6×10^{-4} J and 4.8×10^{-4} J
28 a The 24 pF has charge 1.5×10^{-10} C and the other 4.5×10^{-10} C.
   b 5.4×10^{-9} J
29 a 18 J
   b 6.0 s if we assume that the lamp will be lit for a time equal to the time constant
31 a 0.70 mC
   b $I = 1.3 \times 10^{-3}$ A
   c 27 V
32 a just over 2 s (2.1 s)
   b $R = 43$ kΩ
33 a $Q = 1.5 \times 10^{-3}$ C
   b 80 μA
34 a 1.6 μA
   b 13 μW
   c 13 μW

Topic 12 Quantum and nuclear physics (HL)

12.1 The interaction of matter with radiation

1 b 7.24×10^{14} Hz
2 b 0.671 V
3 b 1.6×10^{-4} A
  c 0.20 eV
  d 2.1 eV
  e 3.2×10^{-4} A

542

4 b ii 2.7×10^{-7} m
5 b 3.90 eV
6 a 16 min
7 a i 5.0×10^{14} Hz
      ii 2.1 eV
   b 1.2 eV
   c the graph is parallel to the original graph
8 11.5 eV or 1.3 eV
9 b $i = 1.5$ W m^{-2}
   c $f = 3.0 \times 10^{18}$ m^{-2} s^{-1}
   d There are fewer photons incident on the surface per second and so fewer electrons are emitted.
   e One assumption is that, at both wavelengths, the same percentage of photons incident on the surface cause emission of electrons.
10 b i no excitation
      ii 4
      iii 6
11 b 1.51 eV
12 a $\lambda = 9.1 \times 10^{-8}$ m
    b 2.2×10^{6} m s^{-1}
13 a 2.65×10^{-34} m
14 b 1.1×10^{3} m s^{-1}
15 b $\sqrt{8} \approx 2.83$
    c 5.4×10^{-11} m
16 a 2.0×10^{-15} m
    b 6.6×10^{-10} m
18 b 5.5×10^{-10} m
20 $\theta_D \approx 1 \times 10^{-34}$ rad
22 a top diagram
    b bottom diagram
23 a 2×10^{-15} m, i.e. of order 10^{-15} m
    b $E_K \approx 10^4$ MeV

12.2 Nuclear physics

24 $v = 3.7 \times 10^{7}$ m s^{-1}
25

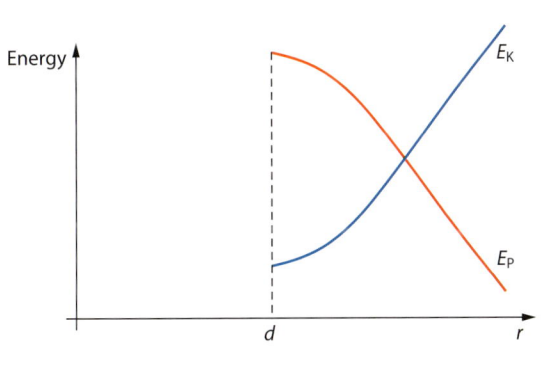

28 b $^{226}_{88}\text{Ra} \rightarrow {}^{226}_{88}\text{Ra} + {}^{0}_{0}\gamma$
   c 1.83×10^{-11} m
30 I and IV are beta plus decays, II is a gamma decay and III is beta minus decay
31 a 0.231 s^{-1}
   b i 4.78×10^{21}
      ii 3.79×10^{21}
      iii 3.01×10^{21}
32 a 0.5
   b 0.875
   c 0.5
33 3.7×10^{10} Bq
34 1.10×10^{6} Bq
35 $N_0 = 4.2 \times 10^{11}$
36 3.8×10^{9} yr
37 4.1×10^{9} yr
38 a 0.75
   b 0.95
   c 1.50

Glossary

absolute uncertainty a quantity giving the extremes a measured value falls within

absolute zero the temperature at which all random motion of molecules stops

absorption spectra the set of wavelengths of photons absorbed by a substance

ac generator a rotating coil in a magnetic field that generates ac voltage

acceleration of free fall the acceleration due to the pull of the Earth on a body

accurate a measurements where the systematic error is small and so close to the 'true' value

activity the rate of decay of a radioactive sample

albedo the ratio of scattered to incident intensity of radiation

alpha decay a decay producing an alpha particle

alpha particle the nucleus of helium-4

alternating current (ac) current in which electrons oscillate instead of moving with same drift speed in the same direction

alternating voltage voltage that takes positive as well as negative values

ammeter an instrument that measures the electric current through it

Amontons' law or Gay-Lussac's law the relation between pressure and temperature of a fixed quantity of an ideal gas when the volume is kept constant

amplitude the largest value of the displacement from equilibrium of an oscillation

angular frequency same as angular speed

angular momentum the product of mass, speed and orbit radius of a particle

angular separation the angle that the distance between two objects subtends at the observer's eye

angular speed the ratio of angle turned to time taken

antinode a point in a medium with a standing wave where the displacement is momentarily a maximum

anti-particle a particle with the same mass as its particle but with all other properties opposite, such as electric charge

atmosphere a non-SI unit of pressure

atomic (or proton) number the number of protons in a nucleus

atomic mass the mass of an atom measured in units of u

atomic mass unit a unit of mass equal to $\frac{1}{12}$ of the mass of a neutral atom of carbon-12

average another word for mean

average power for sinusoidally varying voltages and currents the average power in a conductor is half the peak value

average speed the ratio of distance travelled to total time taken

average velocity the ratio of displacement to total time taken

Avogadro constant the number of particles in one mole

background radiation radiation from natural sources

bar magnet a rectangular piece of iron that has a magnetic field

baryon a particle made up of three quarks

baryon number a conserved quantum number; it is assigned to each quark and by extension to baryons

battery a source of emf

best estimate the average value of a set of measurements of a given quantity that will serve as the quoted value for that quantity

beta particle an electron

beta minus decay a decay producing an electron and an anti-neutrino

beta plus decay a decay producing a positron and a neutrino

binding energy the minimum energy that must be supplied to completely separate the nucleons in a nucleus or the energy released when a nucleus is assembled

black body a theoretical body that reflects none of the radiation incident on it and so absorbs all of it

blue-shift an decrease in the observed wavelength

boiling the change from the liquid to the vapour state at a specific constant temperature

bottom a flavour of quark with electric charge $-\frac{1}{3}e$, but heavier than the strange quark

Boyle's law the relation between pressure and volume of a fixed quantity of an ideal gas when the temperature is kept constant

capacitance the charge that can be stored on a capacitor per unit voltage

capacitor a device that can store electric charge

carbon brushes conducting, soft material that joins the slip rings to the external circuit in an ac generator

centripetal acceleration the acceleration due to a changing direction of velocity

centripetal force a force pointing to the centre of a circular path

chain reaction a self-sustaining reaction

charge carrier charged particles that are able to move, creating an electric current

charge polarisation the separation of charge when a dielectric is exposed to an external electric field

Charles' law the relation between volume and temperature of a fixed quantity of an ideal gas when the pressure is kept constant

charm a flavour of quark with electric charge $+\frac{2}{3}e$, but heavier than the up quark

circular slit an opening in the shape of a circle through which diffraction takes place

coefficient of dynamic friction the ratio of the force of friction to the normal reaction force on a body while the body is sliding on a surface

coefficient of static friction the ratio of the maximum force of friction that can develop between two bodies to the normal reaction force on a body while the body is at rest

coherent sources whose phase difference is constant in time

compression a point in a medium through which a wave is travelling that has maximum density

condensation the change from the vapour to the liquid state

conduction the transfer of heat through electron and molecular collisions

conductor an object or material through which electric current can pass

conservation of energy the principle that energy cannot be destroyed or created but can only be changed from one form into another

conservation of momentum when the net force on a system is zero, the total momentum of the system is constant

conservative forces forces for which work done is independent of the path followed.

conserved a quantity that stays the same before and after an interaction

constructive interference the superposition of two identical waves that arrive at a point in phase

contact force another name for a reaction force

control rod a rod that regulates the rate of energy release in a nuclear fission reactor by regulating the absorption of neutrons

convection current motion of a fluid as result of differences in fluid density

convection the transfer of heat in fluids through differences in fluid density

Coulomb's law the electric force between two point charges is proportional to the product of the charges and inversely proportional to the square of their separation; $F = \frac{1}{4\pi\varepsilon_0}\frac{q_1 q_2}{r^2}$

crest a point on a wave of maximum displacement

critical angle the angle of incidence for which the angle of refraction is a right angle

critical mass the smallest mass of fissionable material that can sustain fission reactions

decay constant the probability per unit time for a nucleus to decay

decay series the sequence of decays that occurs until a radioactive element reaches a stable nuclide

destructive interference the superposition of two identical waves that arrive at a point 180° out of phase

dielectric an insulator that shows charge polarisation

diffraction the spreading of a wave past an aperture or an obstacle

diffraction grating a series of very many and very narrow slits

diode a device that lets current through it only in one direction

diode bridge rectifier a circuit that achieves full-wave rectification

dipole a pair of two equal and opposite electric charges

direct current (dc) current in which electrons move in the same direction with the same average drift speed

discrete energy that can take a set of specific values as opposed to a continuous range of values

dispersion the dependence of refractive index on wavelength

displacement the change in position; for an oscillation, the difference between the position of a particle and its equilibrium position

distance of closest approach the smallest distance between an incoming particle and the target in a scattering experiment

distance the length of the path followed by a particle or object

Doppler effect the change in measured frequency when there is relative motion between source and observer

down a flavour of quark with electric charge $-\frac{1}{3}e$

drag force a force of resistance to motion

dynamic or kinetic friction a force opposing motion when a body moves

eddy currents small induced currents in a conductor where the flux is changing that dissipate energy

efficiency the ratio of useful work or power to input work or power

elastic potential energy the energy stored in a spring when it is compressed or stretched

electric charge a conserved property of matter

electric field the field produced by electric charges

electric field strength the electric force per unit charge experienced by a small point positive charge

electric potential the work done per unit charge by an external agent in bringing a small point positive charge from infinity to a point

electric potential energy the work that needs to be done by an external agent in order to bring a set of charges from where they were separated by an infinite distance to their current position

electric resistance the ratio of the voltage across a device to the current through it

electrical energy same as electric potential energy

electromagnetic an interaction mediated by the exchange of photons

electromagnetic waves   transverse waves moving at the speed of light in vacuum consisting of oscillating electric and magnetic fields at right angles to each other

electroweak interaction   the interaction that is the unification of the electromagnetic and the weak nuclear interactions

elementary particles   particles that have no constituents

emf   the work done per unit charge in moving charge across the terminals of a battery

emission spectrum   the set of wavelengths of photons radiated by a substance

emissivity   the ratio of the intensity radiated by a body to the intensity radiated by a black body of the same temperature

energy   something that can be stored and which can be used in order to do things

energy balance equation   an equation expressing the equality of incoming and outgoing intensities of radiation

energy density   the energy that can be obtained from a unit volume of fuel

energy level diagram   a diagram showing the discrete energies a system can take

equation of state   the equation relating pressure, volume, temperature and number of moles of a gas

equilibrium   the state when the net force on a system is zero

equipotential surfaces   set of points that have the same potential

error bar   the representation of absolute uncertainty in a graph of plotted points

escape velocity   the minimum speed at launch so that a particle can move to infinity and never return

exchange particle   an elementary particle used as the intermediary of an interaction

excited state   a state of energy higher than the ground state energy

expanding universe   the distance between distant galaxies is increasing as space between them stretches

expansion   another name for rarefaction

family lepton number   a quantum number assigned to each lepton in each family

Faraday's law   the induced emf in a loop is the rate of change of magnetic flux linkage through the loop

Feynman diagram   a pictorial representation of an interaction

first harmonic   the mode of vibration of a standing wave of lowest frequency

flavour   a type of quark

fluid resistance force   a force of resistance to motion when a body moves through a fluid

flux linkage   the magnetic flux in a loop times the number of turns in the loop

force   something that accelerates a body

force of reaction   a force that develops as a result of two bodies being in contact

force pair   two forces acting on different bodies that are equal and opposite according to Newton's third law

fractional uncertainty   the ratio of the absolute uncertainty to the mean value of a quantity

free-body diagram   a diagram showing a body in isolation with all forces acting on it drawn as arrows

freezing   the change from the liquid to the solid state at a specific constant temperature

frequency   the number of full oscillations or waves in unit time

friction laws   empirical 'laws' about frictional forces

fuel   a source of energy

fuel rods   containers of nuclear fuels, e.g. oxides of uranium-235 or plutonium-239, in a nuclear fission reactor

full-wave rectification   the turning of ac current into dc current during both halves of the cycle

fundamental unit   in the SI system, the kilogram, metre, second, kelvin, mole, ampere and candela are fundamental units; all other units are combinations of these and are called derived units

gamma decay   a decay producing a gamma ray photon

gamma ray   a photon

Gay-Lussac's law or Amontons' law   the relation between pressure and temperature of a fixed quantity of an ideal gas when the volume is kept constant

gravitational field   the field produced by mass; its strength is the gravitational force per unit mass experienced by a small point mass

gravitational field strength   the gravitational force per unit mass experienced by a small point mass

gravitational interaction   an interaction mediated by the exchange of gravitons

gravitational potential   the work done per unit mass by an external agent in bringing a small point mass from infinity to a point

gravitational potential energy   the work that must be performed by an external agent to raise a mass to certain height from a position where the height is zero, or to bring a set of masses to their current position from when they were separated by an infinite distance

greenhouse effect   the phenomenon in which infrared radiation emitted by the Earth's surface is absorbed by greenhouse gases in the atmosphere and then re-radiated in many directions, including back down to Earth

greenhouse gas   a gas in the atmosphere that absorbs infrared radiation

ground state   the state of lowest energy

hadron   a particle made up of quarks

half-life   the time for the activity of a radioactive sample to be reduced to half its initial value

half-wave rectification   the turning of ac current into dc current by allowing the passage of current during one half of the cycle only

heat exchanger   system that extracts thermal energy from the moderator of a nuclear reactor

heat the energy transferred as a result of a temperature difference

Higgs particle the particle whose interactions with other particles gives mass to those particles

Hooke's law the tension in a spring is proportional to the extension or compression

hydroelectric power plant producing power by converting the potential or kinetic energy of water

ideal gas an idealised version of a gas obeying the gas laws at all pressures, volumes and temperatures

impulse the product of force and the time interval for which the force acts; it equals the change in momentum

inertia the tendency of a massive body to remain in its current state of motion

instantaneous speed the speed at an instant of time; the rate of change of distance with time

instantaneous velocity the velocity at an instant of time; the rate of change of displacement with time

insulator an object or material which electric current cannot pass through

intensity power of radiation per unit area; power per unit area carried by a wave – intensity is proportional to the square of the amplitude of the wave

interaction vertex a building block of Feynman diagrams representing a fundamental interaction process

internal energy the total random kinetic energy and intermolecular potential energy of the molecules of a substance

inverse square law a law where a physical quantity is inversely proportional to the square of the distance from the source of that quantity; intensity of light from a source obeys an inverse square law

ionising the ability to knock electrons off atoms

isolated a system whose total energy stays constant

isotopes nuclei of the same element containing the same number of protons but different numbers of neutrons

kinetic energy the energy a body has as a result of its motion

Kirchhoff's current law $\Sigma I_{in} = \Sigma I_{out}$

Kirchhoff's loop law $\Sigma V = 0$

Lenz's law the direction of the induced emf is such as to oppose the change in flux that created it

lepton an elementary particle

linear momentum the product of mass and velocity

longitudinal wave a wave where the displacement is parallel to the direction of energy transfer

magnetic field a field created by electric currents and moving charges

magnetic field lines imaginary curves whose tangents give the magnetic field

magnetic flux the product of the component of the magnetic field strength normal to an area

magnetic flux density another name for the magnetic field strength B; it is the force per unit charge on a charge moving with unit velocity at right angles to the field

magnetic force the force experienced by a magnetic field on a moving charge or an electric current

magnetic hysteresis the lagging of an effect behind its cause, as when the change in magnetism of a body lags behind changes in the magnetic field

magnitude the length of a vector; the size of a quantity

Malus's law the transmitted intensity of polarised light through a polariser is reduced by a factor of $\cos^2\theta$

mass (or nucleon) number the number of protons plus neutrons in a nucleus

mass defect the difference in mass between the mass of the nucleons making up a nucleus and the nuclear mass

mean the sum of a set of measurements divided by the number of measurements

mean value the average value of a set of measurements of a given quantity that will serve as the quoted value for that quantity

melting the change from the solid to the liquid state at a specific constant temperature

meson a particle made up of one quark and one anti-quark

method of mixtures a method to measure specific heat capacity by measuring the temperature increase when a hot body is put into a liquid in a calorimeter

moderator body whose molecules slow down the fast neutrons produced in a fission reaction through collisions with the neutrons

modulated the change in the two-slit intensity pattern when the single-slit diffraction effect is taken into account

molar mass the mass of one mole of a substance

mole a quantity of a substance containing as many particles as atoms in 12 g of carbon-12

motional emf the emf generated when a conductor moves in a region of magnetic field

net force the one force whose effect is the same as that of a number of forces combined

neutrino a neutral particle with very small mass that interacts very weakly

Newton's first law particle moves with a constant velocity (which may be zero) when no forces act on it

Newton's law of gravitation there is a force of attraction between any two point masses that is proportional to the product of the masses and inversely proportional to the square of their separation; the force is directed along the line joining the two masses

Newton's second law the net force on a body is the rate of change of the body's momentum

Newton's third law when a body A exerts a force on body B, body B will exert an equal but opposite force on body A

node a point in a medium with a standing wave where the displacement is always zero

non-renewable sources of energy that are being used at a much faster rate than that at which they are being produced and so will run out

nuclear fission the reaction in which a heavy nucleus splits into two medium-sized nuclei plus neutrons, releasing energy

nuclear fusion the reaction in which two light nuclei join to form a heavier nucleus, releasing energy

nucleon a proton or neutron

nuclide a nucleus with a specific number of neutrons and protons

Ohm's law at constant temperature the current through most metallic conductors is proportional to the voltage across the conductor

order of magnitude an estimate given as just a power of 10

pair annihilation the disappearance of a particle and its anti-particle when they collide

pair creation the production of a particle and its anti-particle from a vacuum

parallel connection resistors connected so that they have the same potential difference across them

parallel plates two parallel and equally but oppositely charged plates

path difference the difference in the distance from a point to two sources of waves

penetrating the ability to move deep into a material

period the time needed to produce one full oscillation or wave

periodic motion that repeats

permittivity of vacuum the constant ε appearing in Coulomb's law when the charges are situated in a vacuum

phase change the phase of a wave increases by π (radians) upon reflection from a medium of higher refractive index

phase difference the quantity $\frac{\text{shift}}{\text{period}} \times 360°$ or $\frac{\text{shift}}{\text{wavelength}} \times 360°$

phase the state of a substance depending on the separation of its molecules; we consider the solid, liquid and vapour phase in this course

photoelectric effect the phenomenon in which electromagnetic radiation incident on a metallic surface forces electrons to move from the surface

photon the particle of light, a quantum of energy

photo-surface a metallic surface that ejects electrons when electromagnetic radiation is incident on it

photovoltaic cell a device that converts solar energy into electrical energy

plane polarised light whose electric field oscillates on one plane

point particle a particle that is assumed to be a mathematical point

polariser a device such that light passing through it emerges polarised

position generally a vector from some origin to the place where a particle is situated

positron the anti-particle of the electron

potential difference the work done per unit charge in moving a small point positive charge between two points

potential energy the energy a system has as a result of its state

power the rate at which work is being done or energy is being dissipated

precise measurements where the random error is small

pressure the normal force on an area per unit area

primary cell a source of emf that, once discharged, has to be discarded

primary energy energy that has not being processed in any way

pulse an isolated disturbance in a medium carrying energy and momentum

pumped storage system plant in which water is pumped back up to higher elevations during off-peak hours so that it can again be released later during periods of high demand for electricity

quantised a quantity that can take on a discrete set of values

quantised energy energy that takes values from a set of values that are not continuous

quantum a unit of something, for example, energy

quark an elementary particle making up nucleons (and hadrons) appearing in six flavours

quark confinement the principle that free quarks cannot be observed

radial the direction towards or away from the centre of a spherical body

radiation energy in the form of electromagnetic waves

radioactivity the phenomenon in which nuclei emit particles and energy randomly and spontaneously

random uncertainty an error due to inexperience of the observer and the difficulty of reading instruments

rarefaction a point in a medium through which a wave is travelling that has minimum density

ray the direction of energy transfer of a wave

Rayleigh criterion the condition for resolving two objects; resolution is possible when the central maximum in the diffraction pattern of one source coincides with the first minimum of the diffraction pattern of the other

real gas a gas obeying the gas laws approximately for limited ranges of pressures, volumes and temperatures

red-shift an increase in the observed wavelength

reflection the scattering of radiation off a surface such that the angle of incidence is equal to the angle of reflection

refraction the change in speed of a wave as it enters another medium and the subsequent change of direction (except at normal incidence)

refractive index the ratio of the speed of light in vacuum to the speed of light in a material

renewable sources of energy from a source that has, for all practical purposes, an infinite lifetime

resistivity the resistance of a conductor of unit length and unit cross-sectional area

resolution the ability to see as distinct two objects that are distinct

resolving power the ability of a diffraction grating to see as distinct two wavelengths that are close to each other

restoring force a force directed towards the equilibrium position of a system

right-hand grip rules the right-hand grip rule for a current-carrying wire gives the direction of the magnetic field due to the current in a wire; the right-hand grip rule for a solenoid gives the direction of the magnetic field due to the current in a solenoid; the right-hand rule gives the direction of the magnetic force on a moving charge

root mean square (rms) value of a current or a voltage that would give the same average power dissipation in a dc circuit component as in the ac circuit

Sankey diagram a pictorial way to represent energy losses and transfers

scalar a quantity that has magnitude but no direction

Schrödinger theory the theory that determines the wavefunction of a system

Schwarzschild radius the distance from the centre of a star where the escape speed is the speed of light

secondary cell a rechargeable source of emf

secondary energy energy that has been processed in some way so as to make it useful

series connection resistances connected one after the other so they take the same current

simple harmonic motion (SHM) oscillatory motion in which the acceleration is opposite and proportional to displacement from equilibrium

simple pendulum a small mass attached to a fixed length of string that oscillates

slip rings conducting rings used to connect the rotating coil of a generator to the external circuit so that ac current is delivered to it

Snell's law the law relating the angles of incidence and refraction to the speeds of the wave in two media

solar constant the intensity of the Sun's radiation at the position of the Earth's orbit

solenoid a long, tightly wound coil

specific energy the energy that can be obtained from a unit mass of fuel

specific heat capacity the energy required to raise the temperature of a unit mass by one degree

specific latent heat of fusion the energy needed to change a unit mass from the solid to the liquid phase at constant temperature

specific latent heat of vaporisation the energy needed to change a unit mass from the liquid to the vapour phase at constant temperature

standard deviation a measure of the spread of a set of measurements around the mean

Standard Model the presently accepted model of elementary particles and interactions for quarks and leptons

standing wave a wave formed from the superposition of two identical travelling waves moving in opposite directions

state of a gas a gas with a specific value of pressure, volume, temperature and number of moles

static friction a force opposing the tendency to motion when a body is at rest

Stefan–Boltzmann law the power radiated by a black body is proportional to the body's surface area and the fourth power of its kelvin temperature; $P = \sigma A T^4$

stopping voltage the voltage in a photoelectric experiment that makes the photocurrent zero

strange a flavour of quark with electric charge $-\frac{1}{3}e$, but heavier than the down quark

strong nuclear interaction an interaction mediated by the exchange of gluons

superposition the displacement when two waves meet is the sum of the individual displacements

systematic error an error due to incorrectly calibrated instruments – it is the same for all data points and cannot be reduced by repeated measurements

temperature a measure of the 'coldness' or 'hotness'; the absolute temperature is a measure of the average random kinetic energy of the particles of a substance

tension the force developed in a string or spring as a result of stretching and compressing

terminal speed the eventual constant speed attained by a body experiencing a speed-dependent resistance force.

thermal equilibrium the state in which the temperature remains constant

thermistor a resistor whose resistance varies strongly with temperature

thin film interference a type of interference caused by reflected rays from the two boundaries of a thin film

Thomson model an early model of the atom as a positive sphere of positive charge with electrons moving about in the sphere

time constant the time after which the charge on a discharging capacitor is reduced to about 37% of its original value

top a flavour of quark with electric charge $+\frac{2}{3}e$, but heavier than the charm

total internal reflection when the angle of incidence is greater than the critical angle, the incident ray only reflects with no refracted ray

total mechanical energy the sum of the kinetic energy, gravitational potential energy and elastic potential energy of a body

transfer of thermal energy the transfer of energy from one body to another as a result of a temperature difference

transformer a device that takes a given ac voltage as input and delivers a higher or lower ac voltage

transition the change from one energy level to another with the associated release or absorption of energy

transverse wave a wave where the displacement is at right angles to the direction of energy transfer

trough a point on a wave of minimum displacement

tunnelling the ability of subatomic particles to move into regions forbidden by energy conservation

uniform motion motion with constant velocity

uniformly accelerated motion motion with constant acceleration

unpolarised light whose electric field oscillates on many planes

up a flavour of quark with electric charge $+\frac{2}{3}e$

upthrust an upward force exerted on a body immersed in a fluid

vaporisation the change from the liquid to the vapour state

vector a quantity that has magnitude and direction

voltage the potential difference between two points in a circuit

voltmeter an instrument that measures the potential difference across its ends

wave a periodic disturbance that carries energy and momentum with no large-scale motion of the medium

wavefront surfaces of constant phase (usually only drawn through crests)

wavefunction a function of time and position whose magnitude squared is related to the probability of finding a particle somewhere

wavelength the length of a full wave; the distance between two consecutive crests or troughs

weak nuclear interaction an interaction mediated by the exchange of W and Z bosons

weight the force of attraction between the mass of the Earth and a body

Wien's displacement law the wavelength at which most of the power of a black body is radiated is inversely proportional to the body's temperature; $\lambda = \dfrac{2.90 \times 10^{-3}}{T}$

work done the product of the force and the distance travelled in the direction of the force

work function the minimum amount of energy that must be supplied to an electron so it can escape a metal

work–kinetic energy relation the work done by the net force on a body equals the change in the body's kinetic energy

Index

absolute (kelvin) temperature 116, 330
absolute uncertainties 12–16
absolute zero 116, 132, 134
absorption of photons 337
absorption spectra 273, 493
acceleration 37–43
   centripetal 251–3
   Newton's second law 67–75
   in orbital motion 415
   and projectile motion 45–51
   in SHM 147–50, 346
     maximum 351, 352–3
acceleration-displacement graphs 148, 150, 351–2
acceleration of free fall 43–4
   air resistance in 51–2
   and gravitational field strength 261, 262
   and Newton's law 67–8
   and weight 58
   see also projectile motion
acceleration-time graphs 40, 52
   SHM 149
ac circuits 446–50
accuracy 10
ac generators 444–6, 447–8
activity 279–81, 513
ac voltage 445, 446, 450–3, 470–1
addition of uncertainties 13
addition of vectors 22, 23–4, 28–9
air molecules 157–8, 185
air resistance 51–2, 60
   and power 93
   see also frictional forces
albedo 333, 335
alpha decay 275–6, 277–8
   discrete energies in 509
alpha particles 275–6, 277
   energies of 289–90, 509
   scattering with 295–7, 505–8
alternating current (ac) 444–50
   rectification to dc 454–5, 469–71
   in transformers 450, 451–4
alternating voltage see ac voltage
ammeters 222–3
Amontons' law 134
ampere 1, 201, 240–1
amplitude 146
   in SHM 148, 151, 350, 351
   from energy graphs 356–8
   of waves 155, 156, 163–4
   standing waves 182, 183, 185
angle of diffraction 377–8
angle of incidence 172, 173, 175–6
angle of reflection 172
angle of refraction 173, 175–6

angular frequency in SHM 346, 351
angular momentum, quantisation of 492–5
angular separation 377, 379
angular speed 249–50
annihilation 303–4, 490–1
anti-neutrinos 276, 305, 510–12
antinodes 182
   waves in pipes 185–6, 187–8
   waves on strings 183
anti-particles 298, 299, 300
   annihilation/production 490–1
   of leptons 301
asperities 61
atmosphere (unit) 128
atomic mass 127
atomic mass unit 126, 285
atomic (proton) number 274, 275
   on decay series 277–8
atoms 116
   electron collisions with 207
   energy level diagrams of 271
   hydrogen 272–3, 494, 499
   models of 295–7
   in a mole 126
   transitions 272–3, 481, 494
average power 446–7, 450, 452–3
averages 11–12
average speed 39, 42
average velocity 35–6, 38, 39, 42
Avogadro constant 1, 126–7

background radiation 280
ballistic motion 421
bar magnets, field round 233
baryon numbers 299, 300–1
baryons 298, 299, 300
batteries 227–9
   in circuits 212, 465–6
   life of 230
   see also cells
best estimate 11, 12
best-fit lines 16–18
beta decay 276
beta minus decay 276, 510–11
   in decay series 277–8
   exchange particles in 305
beta particles 276, 277
beta plus decay 276
binding energy 285–8, 293
binding energy curve 288, 293
black-body radiation 330–2
black holes 422
blue-shift 387–8
Bohr model 492–5, 496
boiling 120

see also vaporisation
Boltzmann equation 137–9
bosons 304–5
Boyle's law 129–31

calibration of thermometers 117
candela 1
capacitance 457–62
   and dielectric 458–9
   and energy stored 462–4
   in parallel 459–60
   in series 460–2
capacitors 457–71
   charging 464–6, 470
   discharging 464, 466–9, 470–1
   energy stored in 462–4
   in parallel 459–60
   in rectification 469–71
   in series 460–2
capacity of cells 230
carbon dioxide 336, 337
cells 227–31
   in circuits 212, 213, 220–2
   discharging 230
Celsius scale 117
centrifugal force 256
centripetal acceleration 251–3
centripetal forces 81, 253–6
   charges in fields 238–9
   gravitational force as 262–3
chain reactions 290, 319
change of phase 120–3
charge 200–5
   in capacitors 457–62, 470–1
     charging capacitors 464–6, 470
     discharging capacitors 466–9
     energy stored 462–4
   conservation of 299
   in electric fields 403–11
     equipotential surfaces 407, 409–10
     force on 402–3
     inverse square law 423–4
   on elementary particles 298–9, 300, 301
   and exchange particles 305
   in magnetic fields 234–6, 238–9
   moving see moving charge
   of nuclei 274
   point 198–9, 200, 403–6
   properties 196–7
charge carriers 197, 202
   see also electrons
charge polarisation 458
charging capacitors 464–6, 470
Charles' law 132
chemical energy 78, 227–8

INDEX 551

circuits 212–19
  ac circuits 446–50
  capacitors in 459–62, 463–4
    with resistors 464–71
  meters in 222–3
  multi-loop 220–2
  potential dividers in 224
  resistors in 213–19
    with capacitors 464–71
circular motion 81, 249–56
  and angular speed 249–50
  charges in fields 238–9
  see also orbits
circular slits, resolution in 378
climate change 337
coal as fuel 316–18
coefficient of dynamic friction 61–2
coefficient of static friction 61–2
coherent light 366, 367
collisions 105–6
  of electrons with lattice atoms 207
compasses 232
components of forces 65–7
components of vectors 25–30
compression
  in springs 59
  in waves 156
    sound waves 157, 158
condensation 120
  specific latent heat of 121
conduction 329
conductors 197
  free electrons in 201–3
confinement, quark 306
conservation of charge 197
conservation of energy 78–9
  and induced current/emf 440
conservation of momentum 103–4, 105, 108
  in nuclear physics 289
conservation of total energy of systems 87
conservative forces 86
constant velocity 35–7
constructive interference 178–9, 180
  diffraction gratings 371
  of electrons 490
  thin films 373
  two sources 365, 366–7
contact forces 59–60, 61
control rods 320
convection 329
convection currents 329
Copenhagen interpretation 496
coulomb, definition of 241
Coulomb's law 198–9, 282
crest of waves 153, 182
critical angle 175–6
critical mass 290, 319
critical (threshold) frequency 485, 486, 487–8
current 201–3, 207–9, 210

in ac circuits 446–7
and battery emf 228–9
charging capacitors 464–6
in circuits 213–19
  multi-loop 220–2
  parallel resistors 214–15
  series resistors 213–14
discharging capacitors 467, 469, 470–1
eddy currents 452
induced see induced current
measuring with ammeters 222–3
peak 446, 450
in potential dividers 224
rms 448–50, 452–3
current-carrying wires
  force between two 240–1
  magnetic field around 232–4
  magnetic force on 236–8
current-voltage graphs 208
  photoelectric effect 484

de Broglie hypothesis 488–90, 494
decay
  of particles 299, 500
  radioactive 275–82, 289–90, 512–14
decay constant 512–14
decay rate 513–14
decay series 277–8
derived units 1–2
destructive interference 178–9, 367
  and path difference 365, 367
  and single-slit diffraction 361–2
  on standing waves 182
  thin films 373
deterministic systems 259
deuterium 292
dielectric materials 458–9, 464
diffraction 176–7, 361–4
  of electrons 489, 498, 506
  multiple-slit 369–71
  of neutrons 505–6
  and resolution 376–80
diffraction gratings 371–2
  and resolution 379–80
diode bridges 454–5, 469–71
diodes 208, 454
dipoles, electric field from 402–3
direct current (dc) 201, 445–6
  rectification produces 454–5
discharging capacitors 464, 466–9
  in rectification 470–1
discharging cells 230
discrete energy 270–3, 482, 493
  and nuclear transitions 509–10
dispersion of light 174, 175
displacement 36–7
  in free fall 43–4
  and longitudinal waves 157–8
  and projectile motion 45–6, 48, 49
  in SHM 147–50, 346

equation for 351, 352
of standing waves 182, 183
and transverse waves 154–6
in uniformly accelerated motion 41, 42, 43
and work done 79
see also distance travelled; position
displacement-distance graphs
  wave motion 155, 157
    longitudinal waves 158
displacement-energy graphs 151
displacement-time graphs
  SHM 148, 149, 150, 352–3
  standing waves 182, 183
  waves 155–6, 178
distance travelled 36–7, 38, 42
  and work done 79, 81–2
  see also displacement; position
division of uncertainties 14, 16
Doppler effect 381–8
double-slit interference 179–80, 365–9
double-source interference 177–9
drag forces 60
  see also air resistance
drift speed 201–3, 209
duality of matter 488–9, 497
dynamic friction 61–2

Earth
  albedo of 333, 335
  energy from the Sun 322, 329, 333
  escape velocity 420–1
  greenhouse effect 335–7
  magnetism of 232
  motion of 250
  temperature of 117–18, 334–7
    and energy balance 334–5
eddy currents 452
efficiency 93–5
  of photovoltaic cells 323
  of power plants 317–18
elastic collisions 105
elastic potential energy 86
  in simple harmonic motion 151
  of stretched springs 84
  and total mechanical energy 87, 88
electrical devices, rating of 211
electrical energy 78, 227
electric cells 227–31
electric charge see charge
electric current see current
electric fields 196–205, 402–11
  between parallel plates 410
  and capacitance 458–9
  in EM waves 158–9, 481
  equipotential surfaces 407, 409–10
  and polarisation 167–70
  and potential difference 203–5
  in the Rutherford model 296–7
electric field strength 200–1
  on potential-distance graphs 408–9

552

electric force 64, 198–9
   and electric fields 200–1, 402–3
   inverse square law for 423–4
   particle acceleration 204–5
electricity
   generation 444
      fossil fuels 316
      hydroelectric power 324
      nuclear power 319–21
      pumped storage 324–5
      solar power 322
      wind power 325
      and gravitation compared 412
   transmission of 453–4
electric potential 403–11
   between parallel plates 410
   connection with fields 408–9
   equipotential surfaces 407, 409–10
   tunnelling through 500–1
electric potential energy 403–5
electric power 210–11
   dissipation in circuits 217
   see also power
electromagnetic force 283
electromagnetic induction 434–41
   in ac generators 444–6
   Faraday's law 437–9
   Lenz's law 440–1
   magnetic flux 435–7
   in transformers 451–2
electromagnetic interaction 299, 300
   exchange particles 303–4, 305
   as fundamental force 282
   and leptons 301
electromagnetic radiation
   in the photoelectric effect 483
   wavelength emitted 330–1
   see also gamma rays; infrared; light
electromagnetic spectrum 159
electromagnetic waves 158–60
   all bodies emit 330
   light as 481
   polarisation 167–70
electromotive force *see* emf
electron in a box 499
electron microscopes 380
electrons
   in atoms
      and binding energy 286, 287
      Bohr model 492–5, 496
      transitions and spectra 271–3, 494
   in beta minus decay 276, 305
   and charge 196, 197
   collisions with lattice atoms 207
   diffraction 489, 498, 506
   discovery of 297
   electron-positron pairs 491
   Feynman diagrams 303–4, 305
   free 197, 201–3
   interference of 489, 490, 497

kinetic energy
   in conduction 329
   in the photoelectric effect 484–7
   as leptons 301
   in photoelectric effect 483–6
   symbol for 274
   uncertain location of 495–6, 497–9
   wave-like properties 489–90, 494–5
electronvolt 204–5
electroweak interaction 282, 306
elementary particles 298–302
elements, spectra of 270–3, 496
emf (electromotive force) 212
   of batteries 227–9, 465–6
   induced 434, 437–9, 444–6, 451
   motional 434–5
emission spectra 270–3, 493
emissivity 330, 331, 332
EM waves *see* electromagnetic waves
energy 78–9
   of alpha particles 289–90, 509
   of beta particles/electrons 509, 511
   binding energy 285–8, 293
   change of state 121
   conservation of 78–9
      and induced current/emf 440
   converting to mass/matter 285–8, 491
   discrete energy 270–3, 482, 493, 509–10
   and greenhouse effect 337
   internal 87, 118–19, 138–9
   kinetic *see* kinetic energy
   mechanical energy 86–92
   nuclear fission produces 290–1, 293
      in reactors 321
   nuclear fusion produces 291–2, 293
   of photons 271, 481–3
      gamma emission 277, 509
   potential *see* potential energy
   quanta of 481, 486–7
   radioactive decay releases 289–90
   resistors generate 211
   in SHM 151, 354–8
   sources of 314–26
   stored in capacitors 462–4
   Sun gives 322, 329, 333
   thermal *see* thermal energy
   transfers *see* energy transfer
   and uncertainty principle 500
   waves carry 163–4
energy balance equation 334–5
energy density 314–15
energy-displacement graphs, SHM 355, 356
energy level diagrams 271
energy levels
   molecular 337
   nuclear 273, 277, 509–10
   transitions 271–3, 481, 494
      nuclear 509–10
energy transfer
   rate and power 92–3

on Sankey diagrams 317
and temperature difference 87, 117, 118
thermal energy/heat 79, 87, 329–37
   by waves 153
      longitudinal waves 157
      standing waves 182
      transverse waves 154, 159
equation of state 129, 135–7, 138
equilibrium 64–7
equipotential surfaces 407, 409–10
   between parallel plates 410
error bars 16–18
errors 19
   propagation of 12–16
      in SHM problems 349
   reading errors 9, 11–12
   systematic 7–9
   see also uncertainty
escape velocity 419–22
estimates 2, 3–4, 9
   best estimate 11, 12
ethics 293, 326
exchange particles 302–5
excited state 272, 273
explosions
   nuclear explosions 290, 291
   in nuclear reactors 320–1

Faraday's law 437–9
Feynman diagrams 303–5
field lines 233, 409–10
fields 396–424
   applications of 415–24
   connection with potential 408–9
   describing 396–412
   electric *see* electric fields
   gravitational *see* gravitational fields
   magnetic *see* magnetic fields
field strength 408–9
   electric 200–1, 408–9
   gravitational 58, 260–2, 400–1
      on potential-distance graphs 408–9
   magnetic 436
fission *see* nuclear fission
fluid resistance 51–2
   see also frictional forces
fluids 60
   convection in 329
flux linkage 435–7
   in ac generators 444–6
   Faraday's law 437–9
force-distance graphs 81–2
force-extension graphs 83–4
force pairs 63
forces 57–62, 302
   centripetal 81, 238–9, 253–6, 262–3
   electric *see* electric force
   and equilibrium 64–7
   fluid resistance 51–2

INDEX 553

free-body diagrams 62
fundamental 282–3
in ideal and real gases 128–9
inter-particle 116, 118–19
magnetic 234–8, 240–1
and momentum 98–103
in Newton's first law of motion 63
in Newton's second law of motion 67–75
in Newton's third law of motion 63–4
in orbital motion 415–16
and pressure 127–8
restoring 147, 346
in SHM 346
work done by 79–82
on a particle 82–3
force-time graphs 101–3
fossil fuels 315, 316–18
fractional uncertainties 12–14, 15
free-body diagrams 62
free electrons 197, 201–3
free fall *see* acceleration of free fall
freezing 120
specific latent heat of fusion 121
frequency
of ac, in *RC* circuits 470–1
in circular motion 249, 252
critical 485, 486, 487–8
and Doppler effect 381–8
in the photoelectric effect 485, 486–7
of rotation of ac generators 445
power from 447–8
in SHM 149, 351, 353
angular 346, 351
and standing waves 184, 187–8
of voltage in transformers 451
of waves 154, 156, 157
frictional forces 60–2
centripetal 254–5
and efficiency 93–4
in orbital motion 418
work done by 88–9, 92
see also air resistance
friction laws 61
fringe separation 367
fringe spacing 180
fringes and slit width 368
fuel rods 319
fuels
energy density 314–15
fossil fuels 316–18
in nuclear power reactors 319–21
full-wave rectification 454–5
fundamental forces 282–3
fundamental interactions 282, 305
see also interactions
fundamental units 1, 236
fusion, nuclear *see* nuclear fusion
fusion, specific latent heat of 121

gamma decay 276–7
energies of 277, 509
gamma rays 276–7
energies of 277, 509
gas constant 135
gases
Boltzmann equation 137–9
bonds between particles in 116
change of phase 120, 121
convection in 329
equation of state 135–7, 138
gas laws 129–37
graphs of 130, 131–2, 133–4
ideal 128–9, 131, 135–7
internal energy of 138–9
modelling 126–40
pressure-temperature law 133–5
pressure-volume law 129–31
real gases 129, 131
speed of molecules in 137–9
volume-temperature law 131–3
gas power plants 317
Gay-Lussac's law 134
gluons as exchange particles 305
gradient on graphs 17
uncertainty in 18–19
graphs
best-fit lines 16–18
gradient and intercept 18–19
gravitation 259–63
and electricity compared 412
and planetary motion 420
gravitational fields 260, 396
connection with potential 408–9
gravitational field strength 260–2
between Earth and Moon 400–1
potential-distance graphs give 408–9
and weight 58
gravitational force
between point masses 259–60
and gravitational field strength 260–2
inverse square law for 423–4
and Newton's third law 64
in orbital motion 262–3, 415–16
and work done 397
gravitational interaction 282, 305
gravitational potential 398–402
connection with fields 408–9
equipotential surfaces 407
gravitational potential energy 86, 396–8
and escape velocity 419–22
in orbital motion 415–18
and total mechanical energy 87, 88, 89–91
gravitational potential well 397
gravitons 305, 424
gravity, work done by 85–6
greenhouse effect 335–6
greenhouse gases 317, 335–7
ground state 272, 273

hadrons 298–301, 306
exchange particles 305
half-life 279–82, 513–14
half-wave rectification 454
harmonics 183–6
waves on pipes 185–6, 187, 188
waves on strings 183–4, 187
heat 118–20
and change of phase 120–3
see also thermal energy
heat exchangers 319
heat transfer 79, 87, 329–37
and temperature difference 87, 117, 118
height reached of projectiles 50, 52
Heisenberg uncertainty principle 497–500
helium 275, 291–2
Higgs particle 306–7
Hooke's law 59, 83
hydroelectric power 323–5, 444
hydrogen
electrons in
Bohr model 492–5, 496
kinetic energy of 499
transitions 272–3, 494
in nuclear fusion 291, 292
spectra 270–3, 493, 496
transitions of 272–3
hysteresis, magnetic 452

ideal ammeters 222
ideal gases 128–9, 131
equation of state 135–7, 138
internal energy of 138–9
ideal voltmeters 223
images, resolution of 376–9
impulse 101–3
inclined planes 74–5, 94–5
induced current 435–6, 437–8
ac generators produce 446
and Lenz's law 440–1
induced emf 434, 437–9
ac generators produce 444–6
in transformers 451
inelastic collisions 105
inertia 63
infrared radiation (IR) 335–7
instantaneous speed 39
instantaneous velocity 38–9
insulators 197
as dielectric materials 458
intensity
and Doppler effect 382
in the photoelectric effect 484–5
of radiation 331, 332–3
transmitted through polarisers 169
in two-slit interference 368–9
of waves 163–4
in interference 180
intensity patterns 180
diffraction gratings 371–2, 379

multiple-slit diffraction 369–71
  and resolution 376–7
  single-slit diffraction 362–3
  in two-slit interference 368–9
interactions 299–300, 301
  exchange particles in 302–5
  fundamental 282, 305
  standard model of 306
intercept on graphs, uncertainty in 18–19
interference 177
  double-slit 179–80, 365–9
  and double-slit diffraction 361
  double-source 177–9
  of electrons 489, 490, 497
  and multiple-slit diffraction 369–71
  thin film 372–3
internal energy 87, 118–19
  of ideal gases 138–9
internal resistance 228–9
inter-particle forces 116, 118–19
inter-particle potential energy 118–19
inverse square law 163–4, 423–4
ionising power 275, 277
isochronous oscillations 147
isolated systems 87
isothermal curves/isotherms 130, 137
isotopes 275

joule (unit) 80

kelvin 1, 116, 117, 330
kilogram 1
kinematical quantities 35–7
kinetic energy 82
  of accelerated particles 204–5
  of electrons
    in hydrogen atoms 499
    in the photoelectric effect 484–7
  and escape velocity 419–22
  in hydroelectric power 324
  of molecules
    in phase changes 121
    and temperature 116, 137–9
  and momentum 104, 105–6
  in orbital motion 415–18
  of particles 118–19
    in conduction 329
    in decay 289–90
    in fission 290
  in SHM 151, 354–8
  and total mechanical energy 87–8, 89, 91
  of wind, in wind power 325–6
  and work done 82–3
kinetic friction 61
Kirchhoff's current law 214, 221–2
Kirchhoff's loop law 220–2

lamp filament, I-V graph 208–9
latent heat 121, 123–4
Lenz's law 440–1

lepton numbers 301–2
leptons 301–2
  exchange particles 304, 305
  neutrinos as 512
light
  diffraction 361–4
    and resolution 376–80
  and Doppler effect 387–8
  interference 179–80, 365–73
  in the photoelectric effect 483–6
  and photons 481–3
  polarisation 167–70
  reflection of 172, 173
  refraction 172–5
  stars and escape velocity 422
  total internal reflection 175–6
  wave nature of 170, 172, 181, 364
light bulbs 208–9, 211
lightning 410–11
linear momentum 98
linear speed in circular motion 249–50
lines, best-fit 16–18
liquids 116
  change of phase 120, 121–3
  convection in 329
  positive ion charge carriers in 197
longitudinal waves 156–8
loudness and Doppler effect 382

magnetic field lines 233
magnetic fields 232–41
  in EM waves 159, 481
  induced emf in 434–5, 437–9
  and Lenz's law 440–1
  and magnetic flux 435–7
  motion of charges in 238–9
  in transformers 450–1, 452
  see also electromagnetic induction
magnetic field strength 436
magnetic flux 435–7, 440–1
  in transformers 450–1
magnetic flux density 234–5
magnetic flux linkage see flux linkage
magnetic forces
  on a current-carrying wire 236–8
  on moving charges 234–6
  two current-carrying wires 240–1
magnetic hysteresis 452
magnitude of vectors 21, 25, 27–8, 29
Malus's law 168–9
mass
  converting to energy 285–7, 289–90
  and gravitation 259–62, 398–402
    equipotential surfaces 407, 409
    inverse square law for 423–4
  and Higgs particles 306–7
  and momentum 98–9, 107–8
  point masses 259–62, 396
  in second law of motion 67–75, 98–9
mass defect 285–7

mass (nucleon) number 274
  and binding energy 288
  on decay series 277–8
mass-spring system 147–8, 346–7, 348, 349
matter
  duality of 488–9
  energy conversion to 491
  interaction with radiation 481–502
  particle model of 116
  structure of 295–307
matter waves 488–90
Maxwell's equations 159
mean 11–12
measurements 1–7
  current and voltage 222–3
  heat capacity and latent heat 123–4
  temperature 117
mechanical energy 86–92
melting 120, 121–3
melting temperature 121, 122–3
mesons 298, 299, 300, 305
metals
  free electrons in 197, 201–3
  resistivity 209
methane as a greenhouse gas 336
method of mixtures 123–4
metre 1
metric multipliers 2
microscopic-macroscopic connection 205
modelling climate change 337
modelling gases 126–40
moderator 319, 320
modulated intensity 369
molar mass 127
molecular energy levels 337
molecules 116
  of air and waves 157–8, 185
  in ideal and real gases 128–9
  kinetic energy and conduction 329
  in a mole 126, 127
  motion of 121, 137–9
moles 126–7
  in the equation of state 135–7
mole (unit) 1
momentum 98–108
  angular, quantisation of 492–5
  conservation of 103–4, 105, 108
  in nuclear physics 289
  and exchange particles 302
  in Heisenberg uncertainty principle 497–9
  and impulse 101–3
  and kinetic energy 105–6
  of photons 482, 483
  quanta of 486–7
  rocket equation 107–8
  transfer by waves 153
morals and ethics 293
motion 35–53
  acceleration of free fall 43–4

INDEX 555

and air resistance 51–2
and gravitational field strength 261, 262
and Newton's law 67–8
and weight 58
circular 81, 238–9, 249–56
fluid resistance 51–2
graphs of 40
acceleration-time 40, 52
position-time *see* position-time graphs
velocity-time *see* velocity-time graphs
Newton's laws of 63–4, 67–75, 98–100
non-uniform 38–43
orbital *see* orbits
projectile motion 45–51, 52
uniformly accelerated 37–51
motional emf 434–5
moving charge
magnetic force on 234–6
work done 203–5, 209, 403–4
and emf 212
in wires 411
multiple-slit diffraction 369–71
multiplication of uncertainties 14, 15
multiplication of vectors 21
multipliers, metric 2
muons 301

negative feedback 337
net force 64, 65, 67
neutrinos 276, 301, 510–12
solar 514–15
symbol for 274
neutron number 274, 275
neutrons
anti-particle of 300
as baryons 298
in beta minus decay 276, 305
diffraction of 505–6
discovery of 297
in fission 290–1, 319–20
in nuclei 273, 282
and binding energy 285–7
Newton's constant of universal gravitation 259
Newton's first law of motion 63
Newton's law of gravitation 259–60
Newton's second law of motion 67–75, 98–100
Newton's third law of motion 63–4
nitrous oxide as a greenhouse gas 336
nodes 182
waves in pipes 185–6, 187–8
waves on strings 183
non-ohmic conductors 209
non-renewable energy 315, 326
normal reaction forces 59–60, 61
and weightlessness 423
nuclear energy levels 273, 509–10
in gamma emission 277
nuclear explosions 290, 291

nuclear fission 290–1, 293
nuclear reactors 319–20, 321
nuclear fusion 291–3, 322
nuclear power 319–21
nuclear reactions 285–93
nuclei 274–5
binding energy of 285–8
discovery of 296–7
energy level structure 273
in fission 290–1
in radioactive decay 275–82
decay series 277–8
energy released 289–90
numbers of 512–13
radius of 506–7, 508
and strong interaction 282
nucleon number *see* mass (nucleon) number
nucleons 274, 288
see also neutrons; nuclei; protons
nuclides 274, 275
see also nuclei

Ohm's law 207–10
oil as a fossil fuel 316
optical fibres, total internal reflection in 176
orbital radius, Bohr model of 493
orbital speed 415–16, 417–18
orbits 250, 262–3, 415–19
of electrons, Bohr model 492–5
of planets 259
and weightlessness 423
orders of magnitude 2–3
oscillations 146–52
simple harmonic motion 147–52, 346–58
see also waves

pair annihilation/production 490–1
parallel
capacitors in 459–60
resistors in 214–19
parallel plate capacitors 457–8
parallel plates 410
particle model of matter 116
particle nature of light 481–2
particles 126–7
atoms *see* atoms
decay of 299, 500
discovery of 297
electrons *see* electrons
elementary 298–302
exchange particles 302–5
in Heisenberg uncertainty principle 497
Higgs particle 306–7
kinetic energy of 118–19
in conduction 329
leptons 301–2, 304, 305, 512
molecules *see* molecules
motion in phase changes 121
neutrinos *see* neutrinos

neutrons *see* neutrons
pair annihilation/production 490–1
protons *see* protons
quarks 298–301
standard model 282, 283, 306, 307
tunnelling of 500–1
wave nature 488–9, 497
work done by forces on 82–3
path difference 177–9, 367
diffraction gratings 371
interference from two sources 365
single-slit diffraction 361–2
thin films 373
peak current 446, 450
peak power 446, 450
peak voltage 350, 445, 446
in *RC* circuits 470–1
pendulums 90
simple 146, 147, 347–9
penetrating power 275, 277
percentage uncertainty 12–13
period 146
of ac, in *RC* circuits 471
in circular motion 249
of orbits 263
electrons 494
in SHM 148, 346, 350–3
energy graphs 355–6, 356–7
mass-spring system 347
simple pendulum 348–9
of waves 154, 156, 157
periodic motion 146
permittivity 198
phase changes
and reflection 166, 167
in thin film interference 372–3
phase difference 367
and interference 178
thin films 372
in SHM 149
and wavefronts 163
phases of matter, change of 120–3
photoelectric effect 483–8
photons 481–3
absorption of 337
discovery of 297
emission 271, 272, 273, 277
as exchange particles 302, 305
in Feynman diagrams 303–4
inverse square law for 424
in pair annihilation/production 491
in the photoelectric effect 486, 487
symbol for 274
photovoltaic cells 322–3
pions 299
pipes, standing waves in 185–6, 187–8
Planck's constant 486, 488, 492, 497
planets 259, 263, 416, 420
escape velocity 419–22
plastic collisions 105

plutonium 320
point charges 198–9, 200, 403–6
point masses 259–62, 396
point particle 62
point sources and wavefronts 163
polarisation 167–70
polarisers 168–9
poles 232
position 35–7
   uncertainty in 497–9
   in uniformly accelerated motion 38–40, 42, 43
   see also displacement; distance travelled
position-time graphs 40
   projectiles 49, 52
   uniform acceleration 39, 40, 42
   uniform motion 35
positive feedback 337
positive ions as charge carriers 197
positrons 276, 303–4, 491
potential
   connection with field 408–9
   electric 403–11, 500–1
   equipotential surfaces 407, 409–10
   gravitational 398–402, 407, 408–9
potential barriers 500
potential difference 203, 210
   across a battery 228–9
   and capacitors 457–9
      charging capacitors 465–6
      discharging capacitors 466, 468, 469
      energy stored in 462–4
      in parallel 459–60
      in series 460–2
   in circuits 213–19
      multi-loop 220–2
   measuring, voltmeters 222–3
   and potential dividers 224
   and resistance 207–9, 210
   terminal 228–9
   see also voltage
potential-distance graphs
   electric fields 406–7
   field strength from 408–9
   gravitational fields 401, 419
potential dividers 224
potential energy 86
   elastic 84, 86, 151
      total mechanical energy 87, 88
   electric 403–5
   gravitational *see* gravitational potential energy
   in hydroelectric power 323–4
   inter-particle 118–19
   in SHM 151, 354–8
power 92–3
   in ac circuits 446–8, 449–50
   and albedo 333
   average power 446–7, 450, 452–3
   in batteries 228, 229–30

electric 210–11, 217
   and energy carried by waves 163–4
   hydroelectric power 323–5, 444
   and intensity 332–3
   radiated/emitted, and temperature 330–2
   transformer losses 451–3
   transmission losses 453–4
   wind power 325–6
powers of numbers 14, 15, 16
power stations 317–18
   ac generation in 444
   hydroelectric 323–5, 444
   nuclear power 319–21
   transmission of electricity 453–4
power transmission 453–4
precision 10
predictions 263
prefixes in the SI system 2
pressure 127–8
   in gases 129
      in gas laws 129–31, 133–7
   and sound waves 158
pressure-temperature law 133–5
pressure-volume law 129–31
primary cells 229–30
primary energy 314–15
prisms 172, 174, 175
probability
   and electron location 495–6
   in radioactive decay 281–2, 512
   in tunnelling 500–1
probability waves 496
production, pair 490–1
projectile motion 45–51, 52
protons 196, 297
   as baryons 298
   in beta minus decay 305
   in nuclei 273, 282, 285–7
pulses 153
pumped storage systems 324–5

quanta
   of angular momentum 492–5
   of energy 481, 486–7, 493
   of momentum 486–7
quantised charge 197
quantum mechanics 496, 502
   pair annihilation/production 490–1
   tunnelling 500–1
quarks 298–301
   confinement 306
   on Feynman diagrams 304, 305
   prediction of 307

radial fields 261
radiation
   black-body 330–2
   electromagnetic *see* electromagnetic radiation
   as heat transfer 329

   interaction with matter 481–502
   thermal 329
   see also radioactive decay
radioactive decay 275–82
   energy released in 289–90
   law of 278–81, 512–14
radioactivity 275
radio telescopes 380
radius of nuclei 506–7, 508
random uncertainties 7, 9–10, 12
rarefaction in waves 156
   sound waves 157, 158
Rayleigh criterion 376–9
rays 162–3
RC circuits 464–71
reaction forces 59–60, 61, 423
reading errors 9, 11–12
real gases 129, 131
reconstructing vectors 27–8
rectification 454–5, 469–71
red-shift 387–8
reflection
   of light 172, 173
   polarisation by 170
   of pulses 166–7
   in thin film interference 372–3
   total internal 175–6
refraction 172–5, 176
   in thin film interference 372–3
refractive index 173–5
relativity 481, 482
relaxation 272
renewable energy 315, 322–6
resistance 207–10
   in ac circuits 446
   in parallel 215–19
   and power generated 211
   and power losses 453, 454
   in rectification 470–1
   in series 213
resistivity 209–10
resistors 210
   in ac circuits 447
   in circuits with capacitors 464–71
   in multi-loop circuits 220–2
   in parallel 214–19
   and potential dividers 224
   power and energy generated in 210–11
   in series 213–19
resolution 376–80
resolving power 379–80
restoring force 147, 346
risk and nuclear power 320–1
rms 448–50, 452
rocket equation 107–8
root mean square (rms) 448–50, 452
roots and uncertainties 14, 15, 16
rounding 5–6
Rutherford scattering 295–7, 505–8

INDEX 557

Sankey diagrams 316–17, 325
satellites 263, 398, 415–18
scalars 21
scale diagrams 23–4
scattering experiments 295–7, 505–8
Schrödinger theory 495, 501
Schwarzschild radius 422
scientific notation 5
second 1
secondary cells 229–30
secondary energy 314–15
series
    capacitors in 460–2
    resistors in 213–14, 215–19
SHM *see* simple harmonic motion
significant figures (s.f.) 4–6, 11–12
simple harmonic motion 147–51, 346–58
    defining equation 349–53
    energy in 151, 354–8
    graphs of 150
        acceleration-displacement 148, 150, 351–2
        acceleration-time 149
        displacement-energy 151
        displacement-time 148, 149, 150, 352–3
        energy-displacement 355, 356
        velocity-time 148, 149
    and waves 154
simple harmonic oscillations 146–52
simple pendulums 146, 347–9
isochronous oscillations 147
single-slit diffraction 361–4
SI system 1–2
    see also units
slits
    circular slits, resolution in 378
    width of 180, 368–9
    see also interference
small angle approximation 348
Snell's law 173, 174, 175
society and energy 326
solar constant 332–3
solar neutrinos 514–15
solar panels 322
solar power 315, 322–3
solenoids, magnetic fields round 233
solids
    change of phase 120, 121–3
    particles in, bonds between 116
sound 157
    and Doppler effect 381–7
    speed of 187–8
source of fields 396
special relativity 482
specific energy 314–15, 320
specific heat capacity 119–20
    measuring 123–4
specific latent heat 121–2
spectra
    absorption 273, 493

    black-body 331
    electromagnetic spectrum 159
    emission 270–3, 493
    of hydrogen 270–3, 493, 496
speed
    angular speed 249–50
    average speed 39, 42
    in circular motion 249–50, 251
    drift speed 201–3, 209
    instantaneous speed 39
    of light 159, 172–4, 481
    maximum in SHM 351–2, 355–6
    of molecules 137–9
    orbital speed 415–16, 417–18
    and power 93
    of rockets, varying with mass 107–8
    of sound 187–8
    terminal speed 51–2
    of waves 154, 156, 157
spheres, charge around 406
spring constant 59
springs, stretching 59, 83–4
standard deviation 11
standard model 282, 283, 306, 307
standing waves 182–8, 495, 501
stars 292, 422
state of a gas 129
static friction 61–2
Stefan-Boltzmann law 330
step-down transformers 451, 453
step-up transformers 451, 453
stopping voltage 484–5, 486–7, 488
straight-line graphs, best fit lines 17
straight-line motion 35–7
strangeness (quarks) 299–300, 301
stretching springs 59, 83–4
strings, standing waves on 183–4, 186, 187
strong interaction 299, 300
    exchange particles 305
    as fundamental force 282
strong nuclear force 508
structure of matter 295–307
subtraction of uncertainties 13
subtraction of vectors 22, 24–5, 28
Sun 322, 329, 332–3
superposition 165–6, 177–8
    standing waves from 182
surface temperature 330
surroundings 78–9, 87, 88, 89
symbols
    for circuits 212, 457
    for nuclides and particles 274
system 78–9, 87–92
    and momentum 103, 107
systematic errors 7–9, 10, 12
systems, deterministic 259

taus 301
temperature 116–18
    of Earth 117–18, 334–7

    and energy transfer 87, 117, 118
    of gases in gas laws 131–7
    and power of emitted radiation 330–2
    and resistance of conductors 209
    and specific heat capacity 119–20
    and speed of molecules 137–9
tension 58–9
    and centripetal forces 255–6
terminal speed 51–2
tesla 234, 236
thermal energy 118–23
    fossil fuel power stations 317–18
    generated in resistors 211
    work done by frictional forces 88, 89
thermal energy transfer 79, 87, 329–37
thermal equilibrium 117
thermal radiation 329
    see also radiation
thermistors, *V-I* graph of 208
thermometers 117
thin film interference 372–3
Thomson model 295–6
time
    and oscillations 147, 152
    and uncertainty principle 500
time constant 466–9
Tolman-Stewart experiment 197
total energy 79, 87, 118–19
    and escape velocity 419–22
    mechanical energy 87–92
    in orbital motion 415–19
    in SHM 151, 354–5, 356
total internal reflection 175–6
total mechanical energy 87–92
transfer of energy *see* energy transfer
transformations of energy 151, 354–5
transformers 450–4
transitions 271–3, 481, 494
    nuclear energy levels 509–10
transmission of electricity 453–4
transmutation 290
transverse waves 154–6, 159
travelling waves 153–61, 182
trough of waves 153
tubes, standing waves in 185–6, 187–8
tunnelling 500–1

uncertainty in measurements 7–10
    on graphs 16–19
    propagation of 12–16, 349
    and standard deviation 11
    see also errors
uncertainty principle 497–500
unification 283
unified atomic mass unit 285
uniform fields, gravitational 396
uniformly accelerated motion 37–51
uniform motion 35–7
units 1–2
    ampere 1, 201, 240–1

atomic mass unit 126, 285
  of charge 197
  electronvolt 204–5
  farad 457, 458
  tesla 234, 236
Universe 117, 388
upthrust 60
uranium nuclear fuel 319–20

vacuum 159, 173–4
vaporisation 120, 121
vapours
  change of phase of 120, 121
  see also gases
vectors 21–30
  addition of 22, 23–4, 28–9
  components of 25–30
  multiplication by scalars 21
  reconstructing 27–8
  subtraction of 22, 24–5, 28
velocity
  in acceleration of free fall problems 43–4
  average velocity 35–6, 38, 39, 42
  in circular motion 249, 251–2, 253
  constant velocity 35–7
  escape velocity 419–22
  instantaneous velocity 38–9
  and momentum 98–100
  and impulse 101–3
  in Newton's first law of motion 63
  in non-uniform motion 38–43
  in projectile motion 45–51
  in SHM 148–9, 150, 151
  equations for 351, 352–3, 354
  in uniformly accelerated motion 37–51
  in uniform motion 35–7
velocity-time graphs 40
  projectiles 47, 52
  SHM 148, 149
  uniform acceleration 37, 39, 42
  uniform motion 35
voltage 210
  in ac circuits, and power 446–7
  peak 445, 446, 450
  in *RC* circuits 470–1
  and power losses 453–4
  rms 449–50
  stopping voltage 484–5, 486–7, 488
  see also potential difference
voltmeters 222–3
volume of gases 129–33, 135–7
volume-temperature law 131–3

water vapour as a greenhouse gas 336, 337
wavefronts 162–3
  in diffraction 176–7, 361
  Doppler effect 381–3
wavefunctions 495–6, 501
wavelength 153, 155
  in diffraction 176–7, 361–3

diffraction gratings 371–2
  multi-slit 370–1
  resolution 377–80
and dispersion 174
and Doppler effect 382–5, 387–8
of electrons 489–90, 494–5
in emission spectra 270–1, 272, 273
in interference 180
  thin films 373
  two-sources 365–7
of particles 488–9
of photons 272, 273, 277
of standing waves 183–4, 185–8
in Wien's displacement law 330–1
wave nature of electrons 489–90
wave nature of light 364, 485–6
wave-particle duality 497
waves 153–4
  behaviour of 172–81
  characteristics of 162–70
  diffraction of 176–7, 369–71, 376–80
  Doppler effect 381–8
  electromagnetic 158–60
  energy carried by 163–4
  graphs of
    displacement-distance 155, 157, 158
    displacement-time 155–6, 178, 182, 183
  interference 177–80, 361, 365–73
  longitudinal 156–8
  matter 488–90
  probability 496
  standing 182–8, 495, 501
  superposition 165–6, 177–8, 182
  transverse 154–6, 159
  travelling 153–61, 182
  see also oscillations
wave speed of EM waves 481
weak interaction 299, 300, 301
  exchange particles 304, 305
  as fundamental force 282
weight 58, 60
  and gravitation 259
  work done by 85–6
weightlessness 423
white light 172, 174, 175
Wien's displacement law 330–1
wind power 325–6
wires
  current-carrying 236–8, 240–1
  magnetic fields round 232–3
  resistance of 207
work done
  in a battery 227–8
  and binding energy 286
  by forces 79–83
    frictional forces 88–9, 92
    gravity/weight 85–6
    magnetic forces 240
  and gravitational potential 398–9, 401–2

and gravitational potential energy 396–7
  and heating 119
  moving charge 203–5, 209, 403–4
    and emf 212
    in wires 411
  and potential difference 203–5
  and power 92–3
  in stretching springs 83–4
work function 486, 487, 488
work-kinetic energy relation 82–3

Young's double-slit experiment 365–7

Credits

The authors and publishers acknowledge the following sources of copyright material and are grateful for the permissions granted. While every effort has been made, it has not always been possible to identify the sources of all the material used, or to trace all copyright holders. If any omissions are brought to our notice, we will be happy to include the appropriate acknowledgements on reprinting.

Artwork illustrations throughout © Cambridge University Press

The chapter on Nature of Science was prepared by Dr Peter Hoeben.

The publisher would like to thank Ben Canning of Sequoia High School, Redwood City, California for reviewing the content of this sixth edition.

Cover image: B.A.E. Inc/Alamy; p. 9 Charistoone-Stock/Alamy; p. 37t Alamy; p. 37b Sotcktrek Images, Inc/Alamy; p. 49 Design Pics Inc./Alamy; p. 63 Art Directors & Trip/Alamy; 64t Dr P. Marazzi/SPL; p. 64b Peter Chisholm/Alamy; p. 107 Worldspec/NASA/Alamy; p. 117 StudioSource/Alamy; p. 118 MonthlyMeanT.gif (Jan): PZmaps used under the Creative Commons Share-Alike 3.0. Unported license; pp. 120, 250 David Nunuk/SPL; pp. 158, 492 SPL; pp. 170t, 170b Adrian Davies/Alamy; pp. 177l, 177r, 184 Andrew Lambert Photography/SPL; pp. 180, 363t, 363b, 364 GiPhotostock/SPL; p. 211 Richard Megna/Fundamental/SPL; p. 263 NASA/SPL; p. 291l US Department of Energy/SPL; p. 291r Ria Novosti/SPL; p. 292 Monty Rakusen/SPL; p. 293 Science Source/SPL; p. 297 Lawrence Berkeley Lab/SPL; p. 298 Klaus Guldbrandensen/SPL; p. 303, 307r CERN/SPL; p. 307l Brookhaven National Laboratory/SPL; p. 307c Massimo Brega, The Lighthouse/SPL; p. 317 JLImages/Alamy; p. 321l Robert Gilhooly/Alamy; p. 321r ITAR-TASS Photo Agency/Alamy; 322t Sheila Terry/SPL; 322b Ken Welsh/Alamy; p. 323 Top Photo Corporation/Alamy; p. 325 Mike Hughes/Alamy; p. 326 Vattenfall, Horns Rev 1 © Vattenfall; p. 372 Peter Aprahamian/SPL; p. 374 Tim Gainey/Alamy; p. 377 http://cnx.org/content/m42517/1.5/; p. 411 Steve Murray/Alamy; p. 423 RGB Ventures LLC dba Superstock/Alamy; p. 444 Stephen Bay/Alamy; p. 495 Francis Simon/American Institute of Physics/SPL; p. 496 Text for Steve Weinberg, Reproduced with permission from *Physics Today*. Copyright 2013, AIP Publishing LLC; p. 497 Sergre Collection/American Institute of Physics/SPL; p. 501 IBM image archive/Image originally created by IMB Corporation; p. 508 Table 12.1 Data from the Geiger–Marsden experiment, reproduced in the book by E. Rutherford, J. Chadwick and C. D. Ellis *Radiations from Radioactive Substances*, Cambridge University Press, 1930; p. 511 American Institute of Physics/SPL

Key
l = left, r = right, t = top, b = bottom, c = centre
SPL = Science Photo Library